Organizational BEHAVIOR

Organizational BEHAVIOR

Second Edition

GREGORY MOORHEAD
Arizona State University

RICKY W. GRIFFIN
Texas A & M University

HOUGHTON MIFFLIN COMPANY   *Boston*

Dallas   Geneva, Illinois   Palo Alto   Princeton, New Jersey

Cover Photo

© Gary Greene, Woodinville, Washington.

Part Opener Photos

Part I, Jerry Howard/Positive Images; Part II, Jerry Howard/Positive Images; Part III, Barbara M. Marshall; Part IV, Jerry Howard/Positive Images; Part V, Barbara M. Marshall; Part VI, Barbara M. Marshall.

Printed in the U.S.A.

Library of Congress Catalog Card Number: 88-81348

ISBN: 0-395-43334-7

CDEFGHIJ-DOC-9543210

This is for Linda, Alex, and Lindsay.
G.M.
. . . and this one is for Ashley.
R.W.G.

CONTENTS

Contents

Contents

Contents

Contents

Contents

Contents

Contents

Contents

Contents

PREFACE

The field of organizational behavior, still in its infancy as a science, remains full of competing and conflicting models and theories. There are few laws or absolute principles that dictate proper conduct for organizational personnel. The role of human resources in the long-term viability of any business or not-for-profit enterprise is nevertheless recognized as enormously significant. Other resources—financial, informational, and material—are also essential, but only human resources are virtually boundless in their potential impact (positive or negative) on the organization.

The primary objective of the first edition of *Organizational Behavior* was to provide some of the tools and insights necessary to understand and analyze the characteristics of human beings and organizational situations in order to contribute to the long-run survival of an enterprise. Hopefully, the first edition also initiated in its readers some degree of excitement and enthusiasm for the field of organizational behavior. Responses from many instructors, students, and other readers have indicated that the first edition accomplished these objectives.

In the second edition we have tried to build on this solid foundation in several ways. First, we have updated the research on many of the topics discussed in the book. We have also utilized current examples from real organizations to illustrate how the research and new developments in the field apply to the everyday situations of typical organizations. We introduce several new theories and approaches that improve and add to the understanding of people and situations in organizations. In addition we have carefully edited and rewritten major portions of the book in an effort to augment its readability and interest level. Finally, in response to feedback from students and instructors, some topics and several chapters have been reorganized.

We hope that our enthusiasm for the field of organizational behavior is contagious and will promote motivation to learn more about the dynamic nature of the behavior of people in organizations.

ORGANIZATION OF THE BOOK

The content of *Organizational Behavior,* Second Edition is divided into five general categories that emanate from the characteristics of the field: the individual, the individual–organizational interface, organizational characteristics, organizational processes, and the change and development practices that apply to the other four areas. Chapter 1 in Part I discusses basic concepts of the field, the importance of the study of organizational behavior, and a brief history of the field. The six chapters in Part II focus on key aspects of individual behavior in organizations: learning and perception, individual differences, motivation, goal setting and rewards, and stress. Important dynamic elements of the individual–organizational interface—job design and role dynamics; group dynamics; intergroup behavior; leadership; and power, politics, and conflict— are discussed in five chapters in Part III. Characteristics of organizations are presented in four chapters in Part IV—basic organization structure, environment and technology, organization design, and organizational culture. Part V includes four chapters on the key organizational processes of decision making and creativity, communication and information processing, performance evaluation, and international aspects of organizations. Finally, organization change and development are discussed in the two chapters of Part VI.

New to the Second Edition

There are several areas in which the second edition of *Organizational Behavior* has been fine tuned. Beginning with a comprehensive list of topics in the field, both classic and new, we made an extensive review of what coverage users wanted to see in a revised text. The result is the revised organization of this edition.

The most apparent change is the addition of five new chapters which, in turn, necessitated some reorganization of the remaining chapters. New chapters include *Stress* (Chapter 7), *Environment and Technology* (Chapter 14), *Organizational Culture* (Chapter 16), *Careers in Organizations* (Chapter 20), and *International Aspects of Organizations* (Chapter 21). Other changes include the movement of material on the history of organizational behavior to Chapter 1. The balance of the content of Chapter 2 in the first edition (theory and research in the field) has been expanded and placed in an Appendix. This placement is intended to provide flexibility for professors teaching the course, some of whom want to cover the topic and some of whom do not.

Several other minor changes were made. The discussion of rewards has been coupled with goal setting in Chapter 6, Part II, allowing us to devote a full chapter to performance appraisal (Chapter 19). Similarly, the discussion of role dynamics was paired with job design (Chapter 18), and conflict was included with power and politics (Chapter 12), leaving group dynamics and intergroup behavior as separate chapters (Chapters 9 and 10, respectively).

New examples are incorporated throughout the book; a concerted effort has been made to show how theories and concepts are applied in real organizations. Finally, all cases and boxed items are new and written expressly for this edition.

FEATURES OF THE BOOK

Readability and Ease of Use

We expect that readers will find the style of the second edition to be engaging and accessible. Without sacrificing the level of sophistication with which the content is treated, the language of the text is aimed at the student. In addition to the writing style, the handsome design of this edition contributes to the ease of use—for instructors and students alike. The functional use of color in the design highlights the organization and structure of the chapters.

Contemporary Focus

The theory and research on each topic in this text represent current, state-of-the-art thinking. Examples are included to illustrate the current use of these ideas and concepts. New developments in the field have been included throughout the book, such as discussions of the 1988 revised Vroom-Yetton-Jago model of decision making, escalation of commitment in decision making, and the population ecology approach to environmental analysis. Each chapter features a specially selected topic of current research that is included in a boxed insert entitled "A Look at Research."

Applications

Throughout the book the companies cited in examples, cases, and boxed items represent a blend of large, well-known and smaller, less well-known firms, in order to show the applicability of the material in all types of organizations. Each chapter opens with a brief critical incident, which provides a concrete example of an issue in organizational behavior, and closes with two cases, one of which is from a real organization and the other of which is hypothetical. In addition, every chapter contains a boxed insert entitled "Management in Action," the subject of which has been carefully chosen to show the application of a concept discussed in the chapter.

International Emphasis

In the second edition of *Organizational Behavior* we have endeavored to show the international nature of organizational behavior. This has been accomplished in three ways. First, we include an entire chapter (Chapter 21) on international aspects of organizations. Second, each chapter includes a boxed insert entitled "International Perspective" that describes how a topic or concept is applied internationally. Finally, we have tried to include as many international examples as possible throughout the text.

Pedagogical Aids

The learning process is facilitated by several features of this book. Each chapter opens with a list of chapter objectives and closes with a section entitled "Summary of Key Points." At the end of each chapter are several discussion questions, designed to stimulate discussion among students. The end-of-chapter cases are designed to help students make the transition from textbook learning to real-world application. In addition, an experiential exercise is included at the end of each chapter to assist in this transition.

SUPPLEMENTAL MATERIALS

Two other books are available to assist students in mastering the textbook material. The first, the *Study Guide,* contains a pretest, chapter synopsis, chapter objectives, chapter outline, list of key terms, and sample test questions (including answers) for each chapter. Second, the activities manual—*Organizational Behavior: Cases, Exercises, Readings, and an Extended Simulation,* Second Edition—contains additional cases and exercises to help students bridge the gap between theory and practice. The additional readings are included to further stimulate students who seek to learn more on several important topics. A new feature of this edition of the activities manual is an extended in-class simulation that provides a context of organizational situations and will enrich the learning experience.

ACKNOWLEDGMENTS

Although this book bears the names of two authors, numerous people have contributed to it. Through the years many people have contributed to our professional development, including Jack Ivancevich, Art Jago, Bob Keller, Skip Szilagyi, Dick Montanari, Mike Hitt, Allen Slusher, Jim Wall, Tom Dougherty, Bob Kreitner, Angelo Kinicki, Dick Daft, David Van Fleet, Dick Woodman, Barbara Keats, Tom Bateman, CynD Fisher, Ken Evans, Jerry Ferris, Mike Abelson, Stuart Youngblood, Don Hellriegel, and Peter Hom.

Several reviewers were also important to the development of the second edition. Their contributions were essential to helping us identify areas in need of reworking or minor fine tuning. Any and all errors of omission, interpretation, and emphasis remain the responsibility of the authors. We would like to express a special thanks to the following reviewers for taking the time to provide us with their valuable assistance.

Mary-beth Beres
Mercer University Atlanta

Allen Bluedorn
University of Missouri

Dan R. Dalton
Indiana University

Thomas W. Dougherty
University of Missouri

Eliezer Geisler
Northeastern Illinois University

John R. Hollenbeck
Michigan State University

Robert T. Keller
Louisiana State University

Peter Lorenzi
Marquette University

Edward K. Marlow
Eastern Illinois University

Alan N. Miller
University of Nevada

Stephan J. Motowidlo
Pennsylvania State University

Richard T. Mowday
University of Oregon

Mary Lippitt Nichols
University of Minnesota

Robert J. Paul
Kansas State University

James C. Quick
University of Texas at Arlington

Carol S. Saunders
Texas Christian University

Randall S. Schuler
New York University

Herff L. Moore
University of Central Arkansas

Bruce H. Johnson
Gustavus Adolphus College

Bobby C. Vaught
Southwest Missouri State University

Joseph Foerst
Georgia State University

Richaurd R. Camp
Eastern Michigan University

Stanley W. Elsea
Kansas State University

Jack W. Waldrip
American Graduate School of International Management

Margaret A. Neale
University of Arizona

The second edition could never have been completed without the support of Arizona State University and Texas A&M University. Larry Penley, Chair of the Management Department and John Kraft, Dean of the College of Business at Arizona State University, and Mike Hitt, Head of the Management Department and A. Benton Cocanougher, Dean of the College of Business Administration at Texas A&M University facilitated our work by providing the environment that encourages scholarly activities and contributions to the field.

Several secretaries and graduate assistants were also involved in the development of the second edition. We extend our appreciation to Tracy Tipton,

Preface

Vicki Linkenhoger, Susan Leasure, Monroe White, Terry Lovell, Rick Ference, Roger Meyers, Milind Kamat, and Tammy Pilcher.

Finally, we would like to acknowledge the daily reminders that we get from our families of the importance of our work. They equip us with perspective. When we work too much they drag us away to play. When we play too much they remind us of work that we must do. Mixed in among swim team practices, baseball games, school functions, battles over who is next on the computer, monopoly games, doctor appointments, soccer games, and gymnastics practices, we devoted the time to prepare this revision! Without the support and love of our families we could not survive. It is with all of our love that we dedicate this book to them.

G.M.
R.W.G.

Organizational
BEHAVIOR

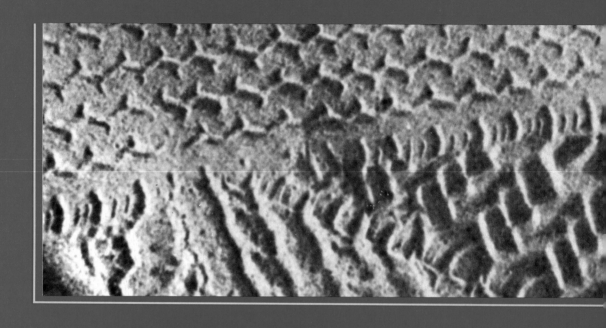

An
Overview of
Organizational
Behavior

PART 1

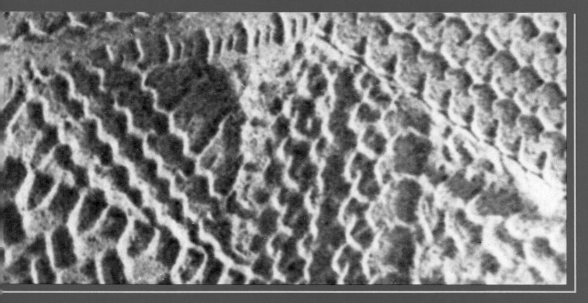

C H A P T E R

1

The Field of
Organizational Behavior

Chapter Objectives

After reading this chapter, you should be able to

► define *organizational behavior.*

► trace the historical roots of organizational behavior.

► discuss the emergence of organizational behavior, including its precursors, the Hawthorne studies and human relations.

► describe contemporary organizational behavior—its basic characteristics, concepts, and importance.

► identify and discuss emerging perspectives in organizational behavior.

any people would consider him the most successful executive in New England. The organization he manages has always represented excellence and has achieved unparalleled success in its industry. He has a reputation for always making the right decisions and is considered a master of motivation. Who is he? Red Auerbach, president of the Boston Celtics.

Auerbach has worked for the Celtics for thirty-six years, first as coach, then as general manager, and now as president. The team has won more world championships than any other team in the National Basketball Association and began selling shares as a public corporation and was recently listed on the New York Stock exchange.

Why has Auerbach been so successful? He credits six basic rules of management for his accomplishments. First, he builds loyalty among the players. Second, he emphasizes the importance of team success over individual performance. Third, he plans for the future, trading for players and draft picks to improve the team in coming years. Fourth, he works to anticipate and manage change. Fifth, Auerbach trusts other people, and in turn expects them to trust him. Finally, he tries to keep organizational practices as simple and direct as possible.[1]

What can we learn from manager Auerbach? One key point involves people. In particular, note that Auerbach does not cite financial management, marketing, or player talent as factors in his success. Instead, he focuses on building an effective team of people who are willing and able to work together toward a common goal.

While their ultimate objectives may differ, the Boston Celtics organization is not unlike General Motors, IBM, or your neighborhood 7-Eleven. Likewise, Auerbach's job is not very different from many other managerial jobs. Any manager, whether responsible for a basketball team, a large industrial firm, or a local pizza parlor, must consider the people who work in the organization.

This book is about those people. It is also about the organization itself and the managers who operate it. The study of organizations and of the collection of people within them together comprise the field of organizational behavior. In this introductory chapter we first provide a comprehensive definition of organizational behavior and a framework for its study. We then trace the field's historical roots and its emergence as an independent field. Contemporary organizational behavior, including an overview of the rest of this book, is discussed next. Finally, we conclude by discussing several emerging perspectives that are of special interest to the field.

WHAT IS ORGANIZATIONAL BEHAVIOR?

Organizational behavior (OB) is the study of human behavior in organizational settings, the interface between human behavior and the organization,

---

[1] Charles Stein, "The Lessons of Chairman Red," *Boston Globe,* April 26, 1987, pp. 64, 69.

Figure 1.1

The Nature of
Organizational Behavior

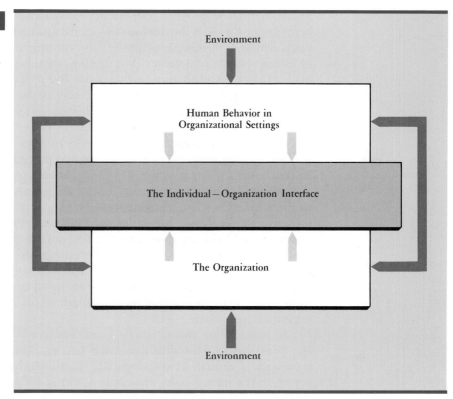

and the organization itself.[2] Although we can focus on any one of these three areas, do remember that all three are ultimately relevant to a comprehensive understanding of organizational behavior. For example, we can study individual behavior without explicitly considering the organization. But because the organization influences and is influenced by the individual, we can't understand the individual's behavior completely without learning something about the organization. Similarly, we can study organizations without focusing specifically on the people within them. But again, we are looking at only a portion of the puzzle. Eventually we must consider the other pieces, as well as the whole.

Figure 1.1 illustrates this view of organizational behavior. The figure shows the linkages among human behavior in organizational settings, the individual-organization interface, the organization, and the environment surrounding the organization. Each individual brings to an organization a unique set of personal characteristics, experiences from other organizations, and personal background.

---

[2] See Larry Cummings, "Toward Organizational Behavior," *Academy of Management Review,* January 1978, pp. 90–98, for a discussion of the meaning of organizational behavior.

In considering the people who work in organizations, therefore, organizational behavior must look at the unique perspective that each individual brings to the work setting. For example, suppose Texas Instruments hires a consultant to investigate employee turnover. As a starting point, he or she might analyze the kinds of people usually hired by the firm. The goal of this analysis would be to learn as much as possible about the nature of the company's work force as individuals—their expectations, personal goals, and so forth.

But individuals do not work in isolation. They come in contact with other individuals and the organization in a variety of ways. Points of contact include managers, coworkers, the formal policies and procedures of the organization, and various changes implemented by the organization. Over time, the individual, too, changes, as a function both of personal experiences and maturity and of work experiences and the organization. The organization is also affected by the presence and eventual absence of the individual. Clearly, then, the study of organizational behavior must consider the ways in which the individual and the organization interact. Thus, the consultant studying turnover at Texas Instruments might next look at the orientation procedures for newcomers to the organization. The goal of this phase of the study would be to understand some of the dynamics of how incoming individuals interact with the broader organizational context.

An organization characteristically exists before a particular person joins it and continues to exist after he or she has left. Thus the organization itself represents a crucial third perspective from which to view organizational behavior. For instance, the consultant studying turnover would also need to study the structure of Texas Instruments. An understanding of factors like the performance evaluation and reward systems, decision-making and communication patterns, and the design of the firm itself can provide added insight into why some people choose to leave a company and others elect to stay.

Thus the field of organizational behavior is both exciting and complex. Myriad variables and concepts go along with the interactions just described, and together these factors greatly complicate the manager's ability to understand, appreciate, and manage others in the organization. They also provide unique opportunities to enhance personal and organizational effectiveness. The key, of course, is understanding. To provide a groundwork for this understanding, we look next at the historical roots of the field.

THE HISTORICAL ROOTS OF ORGANIZATIONAL BEHAVIOR

Some fields, such as physics and chemistry, are thousands of years old. Management has also been around in one form or another for centuries, as described in *International Perspective*. But because serious interest in the study of management did not develop until around the turn of this century,

International
Perspective

Advice From the Classics

Consider the following story: A senior executive and his top assistant are working to accomplish a goal vital to their organization's success. Unfortunately, the executive is concerned more with enhancing his own image than with accomplishing the goal. He treats the assistant badly, behaves like an autocratic tyrant, and gives rewards and punishments on whims. The assistant is also not without fault. He avoids the conflict at the expense of progress toward the goal and allows his feelings of being taken for granted to get in the way of his performance. A scene from corporate America? No—the general plot of the *Iliad,* the saga of conflict between the ancient Greeks and Trojans written by the Greek poet Homer almost 3,000 years ago. The executive was the Greek king Agamemnon, the assistant his general Achilles. Little wonder that it took the vastly superior Greek army ten years to accomplish its objective of sacking Troy!

More and more, managers are recognizing the importance of intellectual history as an aid to understanding contemporary organizational behavior. In particular, classic writings provide many insights into human behavior and managerial practice. Literature's most enduring works, from the days of Homer to the present, reveal many themes studied in the field of organizational behavior.

In his *Republic,* for example, Plato sets forth numerous guidelines for effective management. The *Republic* argues that managers need to spend time interacting with their subordinates as a way of keeping informed, and it identifies several of the conditions important for enhancing and maintaining creativity. Plato saw the importance of clear goals and a strong corporate culture. He knew that employee attitudes were important, and recognized the need to change leadership styles to fit the situation. Finally, Plato was one of history's first equal rights advocates.

The *Odyssey* (also by Homer) highlights the importance of setting goals. Machiavelli's *The Prince* is a classic story of power and its abuses. Shakespearean plays such as *Othello* and *King Lear* reveal critical mistakes all managers should avoid. *The Peloponnesian Wars,* by Thucydides, is an insightful analysis of the decision-making process. Strong arguments for job enrichment can be inferred from the writings of Karl Marx. And Chaucer's *The Canterbury Tales* demonstrates the importance of individual differences. More recently, Winston Churchill, in *The Second World War,* provided dramatic insights into the management of governmental organizations and the ways successful leaders interact with their followers.

The message, then, is clear: management is not solely a modern phenomenon. By looking to the past, we can learn not only about our present, but also about our future.

Sources: John K. Clemens and Douglas F. Mayer, "The Classics: Management's New Literature," *Business Week's Careers,* Fall 1986, pp. 42–47; Marilyn Wellemeyer, "Books Bosses Read," *Fortune,* April 27, 1987, pp. 145–148; and Michael J. Gent, "Theory X in Antiquity, or the Bureaucratization of the Roman Army," *Business Horizons,* January–February 1984, pp. 52–56.

organizational behavior is only a few decades old.[3] One reason for the relatively late development of management as a scientific field is that few large business organizations existed until around a hundred years ago. Although management is just as important to a small organization as to a large one, large firms were necessary to provide both a stimulus and a laboratory for management research.

A second reason for the late emergence of management as a scientific field was the assumption that management and other business issues were part of economics. Economists in turn assumed that management practices were by nature efficient and effective, and therefore concentrated their attention on higher levels of analysis such as national economic policy and industrial structures.

Finally, in addition to being a relatively young field of study, management is a social science rather than a natural science, and so its variables and concepts are more difficult to identify, define, measure, and predict than those associated with physical phenomena. A physical scientist can formulate a hypothesis or law such as "If you apply this process to this material under these specified conditions, the result will always be of the form . . . ." Other scientists can easily verify the proposed relationship and take it as a given in subsequent research. A social scientist, in contrast, can seldom say "If you provide a person in the workplace with a certain reward, the response will always be of the form . . ." The complexities of individual understanding, perception, and motivation are too great to permit the formulation of such laws. (Social scientists try to do so sometimes, but the result is generally controversial.) Hence, the social sciences tend to progress more slowly than the natural sciences.

Scientific Management

One of the first approaches to the study of management, popularized during the first years of this century, was **scientific management**. Several individuals helped establish scientific management, including Frank and Lillian Gilbreth, Henry Gantt, and Harrington Emerson, but the name of Frederick W. Taylor is most closely identified with this approach.[4] Early in his life, Taylor developed an interest in efficiency and productivity. While working as a foreman at Midvale Steel Company in Philadelphia from 1878 to 1890, he became aware of a phenomenon he called *soldiering*, the practice of working considerably slower

---

[3] Daniel A. Wren, *The Evolution of Management Thought,* 2nd ed. (New York: Wiley, 1979), Chapter 1. See also Stephen J. Carroll and Dennis A. Gillen, "Are the Classical Management Functions Useful in Describing Managerial Work?" *Academy of Management Review,* January 1987, pp. 38–51; and Daniel A. Wren, "Management History: Issues and Ideas for Teaching and Research," *Journal of Management,* Summer 1987, pp. 339–350.

[4] Frederick W. Taylor, *Principles of Scientific Management* (New York: Harper, 1911). See also Wren, *The Evolution of Management Thought,* Chapter 6.

than one can. Because managers had never systematically studied jobs in the plant—and in fact had little idea how to gauge worker productivity—they were unaware of this practice.

To counteract the effects of soldiering, Taylor developed several innovative techniques. He studied all the jobs in the plant and developed a standardized method for performing each one. He also installed a piece-rate pay system in which each worker was paid for the amount of work he or she completed during the workday rather than for the time spent on the job. These changes boosted productivity markedly.

After leaving Midvale, Taylor spent several years working as a management consultant for industrial firms. At Bethlehem Steel Company, for instance, he developed several efficient techniques for loading and unloading rail cars. And at Simonds Rolling Machine Company, he redesigned jobs, introduced rest breaks to combat fatigue, and implemented a piece-rate pay system. In every case, Taylor claimed his ideas and methods greatly improved worker output. His book entitled *Principles of Scientific Management*, published in 1911, was greeted with enthusiasm by practicing managers and quickly became a standard reference.

The essence of scientific management is summarized in Figure 1.2. Note that the manager is supposed to play the roles of planner and coordinator. An additional aspect of Taylor's approach, not shown in the figure but reflected in his enthusiasm for piece-rate pay systems, was his belief that all employees are economically motivated. That is, he assumed that monetary rewards were the primary incentive managers could use to motivate workers to achieve higher levels of output.

Scientific management quickly became a mainstay of American business thinking. It facilitated job specialization and mass production, profoundly influencing the American business system. Taylor had his critics, however. Labor opposed scientific management because of its explicit goal of getting more output from workers. Congress investigated Taylor's methods and ideas because some argued that his incentive system would dehumanize the workplace and reduce workers to little more than robots. Later theorists recognized that Taylor's views of employee motivation were inadequate and narrow. And there have been recent allegations that Taylor falsified some of his research findings and paid someone to do his writing for him. Still, scientific management remains a cornerstone of contemporary thought.[5]

---

[5] See Charles D. Wrege and Amedeo G. Perroni, "Taylor's Pig-Tale: A Historical Analysis of Frederick W. Taylor's Pig-Iron Experiment," *Academy of Management Journal,* March 1974, pp. 6–27; and Charles D. Wrege and Ann Marie Stoka, "Cooke Creates a Classic: The Story Behind Taylor's Principles of Scientific Management," *Academy of Management Review,* October 1978, pp. 736–749, for critical analyses. See Edwin A. Locke, "The Ideas of Frederick W. Taylor: An Evaluation," *Academy of Management Review,* January 1982, pp. 14–24, for a more favorable review.

Figure 1.2

Phases of Scientific
Management

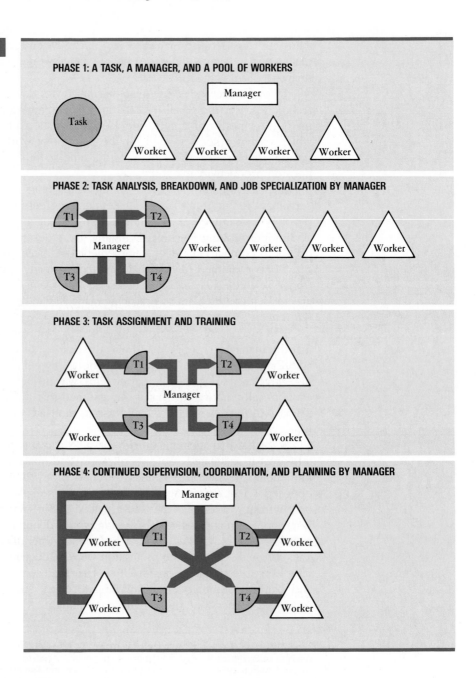

Classical Organization Theory

Scientific management dealt almost exclusively with the interaction between a person and his or her job. During the period of scientific management's popularity, another school of management thought also emerged. Generally referred to as **classical organization theory**, it was concerned with structuring organizations effectively. Whereas scientific management studied how individual workers could be made more efficient, classical organization theory studied how a large number of workers and managers could be most effectively organized into an overall structure.

Major contributors to classical organization theory included Henri Fayol, Lyndall Urwick, and Max Weber. Weber, the most prominent of the three, proposed a "bureaucratic" form of structure he thought would work for all organizations.[6] Although the term *bureaucracy* today generally connotes paperwork, red tape, and inflexibility, Weber's model bureaucracy embraced logic, rationality, and efficiency. Weber assumed that the bureaucratic structure would always be the most efficient approach. (Such a blanket prescription represents a universal approach.) The elements of Weber's ideal bureaucracy are summarized in Figure 1.3.

In contrast to Weber's views, contemporary organization theorists recognize that different organization structures may be appropriate in different situations. However, Weber's ideas and the concepts associated with his bureaucratic structure are still interesting and relevant today. (Chapters 13–16 discuss contemporary organization theory.)

THE EMERGENCE OF ORGANIZATIONAL BEHAVIOR

The central themes of both scientific management and classical organization theory were rationality, efficiency, and standardization. The roles of individuals and groups in organizations were either ignored altogether or given only minimal attention. A few writers and managers, however, recognized the importance of individual and social processes in organizations.

Precursors of Organizational Behavior

In the early nineteenth century, Robert Owen, a British industrialist, attempted to improve the condition of industrial workers. He improved working conditions, raised minimum ages for hiring children, introduced meals for employees, and shortened working hours. Early in the twentieth century, the noted German psychologist Hugo Munsterberg argued that the field of psychology could

---

[6] Max Weber, *Theory of Social and Economic Organization,* A. M. Henderson and T. Parsons, transl. (London: Oxford University Press, 1921). See also Wren, *The Evolution of Management Thought,* Chapter 10.

Figure 1.3   Elements of Weber's Ideal Bureaucracy

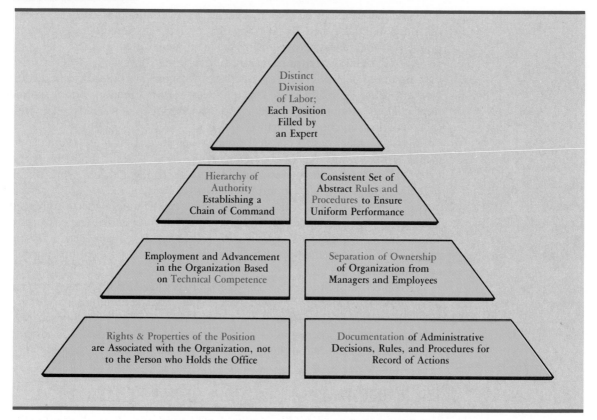

provide important insights into areas such as motivation and the hiring of new employees. Another writer in the early 1900s, Mary Parker Follett, believed that management should become more democratic in its dealings with employees. An expert in vocational guidance, Follett argued that organizations should strive harder to accommodate their employees' human needs.[7]

Owen, Munsterberg, and Follett held minority views, however, that were not widely shared by practicing managers. Not until the 1930s did much change in management's perception of the relationship between the individual and the workplace. At that time a series of research studies led to the emergence of organizational behavior as a field of study.

---

[7] Hugo Munsterberg, *Psychology and Industrial Efficiency* (Boston: Houghton Mifflin, 1913). See also Wren, *The Evolution of Management Thought,* Chapter 9.

The Hawthorne Studies

The **Hawthorne studies** were conducted between 1927 and 1932 at Western Electric's Hawthorne Plant near Chicago. General Electric initially sponsored the research but withdrew its support after the first study was finished. Several researchers were involved, the best known being Elton Mayo and Fritz Roethlisberger, Harvard faculty members and consultants, and William Dickson, chief of Hawthorne's Employee Relations Research Department.[8]

The first major experiment at Hawthorne studied the effects of different levels of lighting on productivity. The researchers systematically manipulated the lighting of the area in which a group of women worked. The group's productivity was measured and compared with that of another group (the control group) whose lighting was left unchanged. As lighting was increased for the experimental group, productivity went up—but, surprisingly, so did the productivity of the control group. Even when lighting was subsequently reduced, the productivity of both groups continued to increase. Not until the lighting had become about as dim as moonlight did productivity decline.

In another major experiment, a piecework incentive system was established for a nine-man group that assembled terminal banks for telephone exchanges. Proponents of scientific management would have expected each man to work as hard as he could to maximize his own personal income. But the Hawthorne researchers found instead that the group as a whole established an acceptable level of output for its members. Individuals who failed to meet this level were dubbed "chiselers," while those who exceeded it by too much were branded "rate busters." A worker who wanted to be accepted by the group could not produce at too high or too low a level. Thus as a worker approached the accepted level each day, he slowed down so as not to overproduce.

After a follow-up interview program with several thousand workers, the Hawthorne researchers concluded that the human element in the workplace was considerably more important than previously thought. The lighting experiment, for example, suggested that productivity might increase simply because workers were singled out for special treatment and thus perhaps felt more valued. In the incentive system experiment, being accepted as a part of the group evidently meant more to the workers than earning extra money. Several other studies supported the overall conclusion that individual and social processes are too important to ignore.

Like the work of Taylor, the Hawthorne studies have recently been called into question. Critics cite deficiencies in research methods and alternative explanations of the findings. Again, however, these studies played a major role

---

[8] Elton Mayo, *The Human Problems of Industrial Civilization* (New York: Macmillan, 1933); and Fritz J. Roethlisberger and William J. Dickson, *Management and the Worker* (Cambridge, Mass.: Harvard University Press, 1939).

in the advancement of the field and are still among its most frequently cited works.[9]

Human Relations

The Hawthorne studies created quite a stir among managers and management researchers, providing the foundation for an entirely new school of management thought, which came to be known as the **human relations movement.** The basic premises underlying the human relations movement were that people respond primarily to their social environment, that motivation depends more on social needs than economic needs, and that satisfied employees work harder than unsatisfied employees. This perspective represented a fundamental shift away from the philosophy and values of scientific management and classical organization theory.

The values of the human relationists are exemplified in the work of Douglas McGregor and Abraham Maslow.[10] McGregor is best known for his classic book *The Human Side of Enterprise*, in which he identified two opposing perspectives that he believed typified managerial views of employees. Some managers, McGregor said, subscribed to what he labeled Theory X, whose characteristics are summarized in Table 1.1. Theory X takes a generally negative and pessimistic view of human nature and employee behavior. In many ways, it is consistent with the tenets of scientific management. A much more optimistic and positive view of employees is to be found in Theory Y, also summarized in Table 1.1. Theory Y, generally representative of the human relations perspective, was the approach McGregor himself advocated.

In 1943, Abraham Maslow published a pioneering theory of employee motivation that became well known and widely accepted among managers. Maslow's theory, which we describe in detail in Chapter 4, assumes that motivation arises from a hierarchical series of needs. As the needs at each level are satisfied, the individual progresses to the next higher level.

The Hawthorne studies and the human relations movement played major roles in developing the foundations for the field of organizational behavior. Some of the early theorists' basic premises and assumptions were incorrect, though. For example, most human relationists believed that employee attitudes such as job satisfaction were the major causes of such employee behaviors as

---

[9] Alex Carey, "The Hawthorne Studies: A Radical Criticism," *American Sociological Review,* June 1967, pp. 403–416; and Lyle Yorks and David A. Whitsett, "Hawthorne, Topeka, and the Issue of Science versus Advocacy in Organizational Behavior," *Academy of Management Review,* January 1985, pp. 21–30. See also Wren, *The Evolution of Management Thought,* Chapter 13.

[10] Douglas McGregor, *The Human Side of Enterprise* (New York: McGraw-Hill, 1960); and Abraham Maslow, "A Theory of Human Motivation," *Psychological Review,* July 1943, pp. 370–396. See also Paul H. Lawrence, "Historical Development of Organizational Behavior," in Jay W. Lorsch, ed., *Handbook of Organizational Behavior* (Englewood Cliffs, N.J.: Prentice-Hall, 1987), pp. 1–9.

Table 1.1	*Theory X assumptions*
Theory X and Theory Y	1. People do not like work and try to avoid it. 2. People do not like work, so managers have to control, direct, coerce, and threaten employees to get them to work toward organizational goals. 3. People prefer to be directed, to avoid responsibility, to want security; they have little ambition. *Theory Y assumptions* 1. People do not naturally dislike work; work is a natural part of their lives. 2. People are internally motivated to reach objectives to which they are committed. 3. People are committed to goals to the degree that they receive personal rewards when they reach their objectives. 4. People will both seek and accept responsibility under favorable conditions. 5. People have the capacity to be innovative in solving organizational problems. 6. People are bright, but under most organizational conditions their potentials are underutilized.

Source: Douglas McGregor, *The Human Side of Enterprise* (New York: McGraw-Hill, 1960), pp. 33–34, 47–48. Used with permission of publisher.

job performance. As we note in Chapter 5, this is usually not the case at all. Also, many of the human relationists' views were unnecessarily limited and situation specific. There was still plenty of room for refinement and development in the emerging field of human behavior in organizations.

Toward Organizational Behavior

Most scholars would agree that organizational behavior began to emerge as a mature field of study in the late 1950s and early 1960s. That period saw the field's evolution from the simple assumptions and behavioral models of the human relationists to the concepts and methodologies of a scientific discipline. Since that time, organizational behavior as a scientific field of inquiry has made considerable strides, although there have been occasional steps backward as well. Many of the ideas discussed in this book have emerged over the past two decades. We turn now to contemporary organizational behavior.[11]

CONTEMPORARY ORGANIZATIONAL BEHAVIOR

Characteristics of the Field

Contemporary organizational behavior has an interdisciplinary focus and a descriptive nature. That is, it draws from a variety of other fields and attempts to describe behavior (as opposed to prescribing how behavior can be changed in consistent and predictable ways).

---

[11] See Lorsch, *Handbook of Organizational Behavior,* for an overview of the current state of the field.

AN INTERDISCIPLINARY FOCUS   In many ways, organizational behavior synthesizes several other fields of study. Psychology, especially industrial or organizational psychology, is perhaps the greatest contributor to the field of organizational behavior. Psychologists study behavior, and industrial or organizational psychologists deal specifically with the behavior of people in organizational settings. Many of the concepts that interest psychologists, such as learning and motivation, are also central to students of organizational behavior.

Sociology, too, has had a major impact on the field of organizational behavior. Sociologists study social systems such as a family, an occupational class, a mob, or an organization. Because a major concern of organizational behavior is the study of organizational structures, the field clearly overlaps with areas of sociology that focus on the organization as a social system.

Anthropology is concerned with the interactions between people and their environments, especially their cultural environment. Culture is a major influence on the structure of organizations as well as on the behavior of people within organizations.

Political science also interests organizational behaviorists. We usually think of political science as the study of political systems such as governments. But themes of interest to political scientists include how and why people acquire power, political behavior, decision making, conflict, the behavior of interest groups, and coalition formation. These are also major areas of interest in organizational behavior.

Economists study the production, distribution, and consumption of goods and services. Students of organizational behavior share the economist's interest in such areas as labor market dynamics, productivity, human resource planning and forecasting, and cost-benefit analysis.

Engineering has also influenced the field of organizational behavior. In particular, industrial engineering has long been concerned with work measurement, productivity measurement, work flow analysis and design, job design, and labor relations. Obviously these areas are also relevant to organizational behavior.

Most recently, medicine has come into play in connection with the study of human behavior at work, specifically in the study of stress. Increasingly, research is showing that controlling the causes and consequences of stress in and out of organizational settings is important for the well-being of the individual as well as the organization.

A DESCRIPTIVE NATURE   The primary goal of organizational behavior is to describe, rather than prescribe, relationships between two or more behavioral variables. The theories and concepts of the field cannot, for example, predict with certainty that changing variables x, y, and z will improve employee performance by a certain amount. At best, the field can suggest that certain general concepts or variables tend to be related to one another in certain settings. For instance, research might indicate that in one organization, employee satisfaction and individual perceptions of working conditions correlate positively. However, we do not know if better working conditions lead to more satisfaction, if more satisfied people see their jobs differently from dissatisfied people, or if both satisfaction and perceptions of working conditions are actually related through other variables. Also, the observed relationship between satisfaction and perceptions of working conditions may be considerably stronger, weaker, or even nonexistent in other settings.

Organizational behavior is descriptive for several reasons: the immaturity of the field; the complexities involved in studying human behavior; and the lack of valid, reliable, and accepted definitions and measures. Whether the field will ever be able to make definitive predictions and prescriptions is still an open question. But the value of studying organizational behavior is nonetheless firmly established.

Because behavioral processes pervade most managerial functions and roles, and because the work of organizations is done primarily by people, the knowledge and understanding gained from the field can help managers significantly in many different ways.[12]

Basic Concepts of the Field

The concepts of primary interest to organizational behavior can be grouped into five basic categories: **individual characteristics,** the **individual-organization interface, organizational characteristics, organizational processes,** and **organization change and development.** As shown in Figure 1.4, we use these categories as the basic framework for this book.

The six chapters of Part II cover individual characteristics. Chapter 2 explores *learning, perception,* and *attribution.* Key *individual differences* like *attitudes* and *personalities* are the topic of Chapter 3. Chapters 4 and 5 cover *employee motivation,* a critical variable in any organization. Chapter 6 discusses *goal setting* and *rewards.* Finally, employee *stress* is the subject of Chapter 7.

The individual-organization interface (that is, interactions between people and organizations) is the topic of Part III. Chapter 8 discusses *job design* and *role dynamics. Group* and *intergroup dynamics* are the subjects of Chapters 9 and 10, respectively. Chapter 11 covers *leadership,* while Chapter 12 explores *power, politics,* and *conflict.*

Part IV is devoted to important organizational characteristics. Chapter 13 describes *organization structure.* Two important contextual variables, *environment* and *technology,* are the subject of Chapter 14. Chapter 15 is an in-depth

---

[12] Joseph W. McGuire, "Retreat to the Academy," *Business Horizons,* July–August 1982, pp. 31–37; and Kenneth Thomas and Walter G. Tymon, "Necessary Properties of Relevant Research: Lessons From Recent Criticisms of the Organizational Sciences," *Academy of Management Review,* July 1982, pp. 345–353. See also Jeffrey Pfeffer, "The Theory Practice Gap: Myth or Reality?" *Academy of Management Executive,* February 1987, pp. 31–32.

Figure 1.4   The Basic Framework for Understanding Organizational Behavior

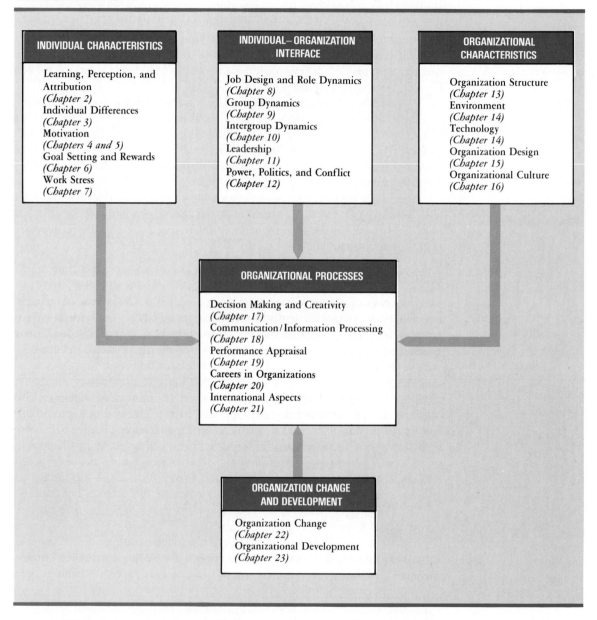

INDIVIDUAL CHARACTERISTICS

Learning, Perception, and Attribution
(Chapter 2)
Individual Differences
(Chapter 3)
Motivation
(Chapters 4 and 5)
Goal Setting and Rewards
(Chapter 6)
Work Stress
(Chapter 7)

INDIVIDUAL–ORGANIZATION INTERFACE

Job Design and Role Dynamics
(Chapter 8)
Group Dynamics
(Chapter 9)
Intergroup Dynamics
(Chapter 10)
Leadership
(Chapter 11)
Power, Politics, and Conflict
(Chapter 12)

ORGANIZATIONAL CHARACTERISTICS

Organization Structure
(Chapter 13)
Environment
(Chapter 14)
Technology
(Chapter 14)
Organization Design
(Chapter 15)
Organizational Culture
(Chapter 16)

ORGANIZATIONAL PROCESSES

Decision Making and Creativity
(Chapter 17)
Communication / Information Processing
(Chapter 18)
Performance Appraisal
(Chapter 19)
Careers in Organizations
(Chapter 20)
International Aspects
(Chapter 21)

ORGANIZATION CHANGE AND DEVELOPMENT

Organization Change
(Chapter 22)
Organizational Development
(Chapter 23)

treatment of *organization design*. Finally, *organizational culture* is the topic of Chapter 16.

These three broad sets of concepts all affect organizational processes, the subject of Part V. Chapter 17 describes *decision making* and *creativity*. *Communication* and *information processing* are the topics of Chapter 18. Chapter 19 discusses *performance appraisal*, and Chapter 20 explores *careers* in organizations. Chapter 21, on *international aspects of organizational behavior*, completes Part V.

Part VI concludes the book with a discussion of *organization change*, in Chapter 22, and *organization development*, in Chapter 23. Finally, an appendix summarizes *research methods* used in organizational behavior.

The Importance of Organizational Behavior

Most people are born and educated in organizations, acquire most of their material possessions from organizations, and die as members of organizations. Many of their activities are regulated by organizations called governments. And most adults spend the better part of their lives working in organizations. If organizations influence our lives so thoroughly, we have every reason to be concerned about how and why those organizations function.

In our relationships with organizations, we may adopt any one of several roles or identities. For example, we can be consumers or employees or adversaries (such as Ralph Nader in his crusade against General Motors). Since most readers of this book are present or future managers, we take a managerial viewpoint here. Organizational behavior can greatly clarify the factors that affect how managers manage. It is the field's job to describe the complex human context in which managers work and to define the problems associated with that realm. The value of organizational behavior is that it isolates important aspects of the manager's job and offers specific perspectives on the human side of management: people as organizations, people as resources, people as people.

The Manager's Job

The job of a manager is most often described in terms of management functions and management roles. Four managerial functions and ten managerial roles are commonly defined, as illustrated in Figure 1.5.

MANAGERIAL FUNCTIONS   The four basic managerial functions are planning and decision making, organizing, leading, and controlling. **Planning** is the process of determining the organization's desired future position and deciding how best to get there. The planning process at Sears, Roebuck, for example, includes scanning the environment, deciding on appropriate goals, outlining strategies for achieving those goals, and developing tactics to assist in executing the strategies. Behavioral processes and characteristics pervade each of these activities. Perception, for instance, plays a major role in environmental

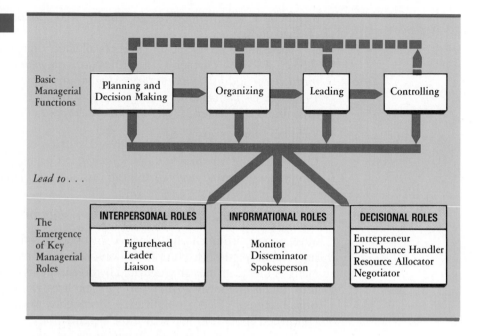

Figure 1.5

The Manager's Job

scanning, and creativity and motivation influence how managers set goals, strategies, and tactics.

Organizing is the process of designing jobs, grouping jobs into manageable units, and establishing patterns of authority among jobs and groups of jobs. This process designs the basic structure of the organization, and for large organizations like Sears, that structure can be extensive and complicated. As noted earlier, the processes and characteristics of the organization itself are a major theme of organizational behavior.

Leading is the process of getting members of the organization to work together toward the organization's goals. Major components of leading include motivating employees, managing group dynamics, and leadership per se, all of which are closely related to major areas of organizational behavior.

The fourth managerial function, **controlling**, is the process of monitoring and correcting the actions of the organization and its people so as to keep them headed toward their goals. Again, behavioral processes and characteristics are a key part of this function. Performance evaluation, reward systems, and motivation, for example, all enter into control.

MANAGERIAL ROLES   In an organization, as in a play or movie, a role is the part a person plays in a given situation. Much of our knowledge about managerial roles comes from the work of Henry Mintzberg.[13] Mintzberg

---

[13] Henry Mintzberg. "The Manager's Job: Folklore and Fact," *Harvard Business Review,* July–August 1975, pp. 49–61.

identified the ten basic managerial roles in three general categories that are shown in Figure 1.5.

Interpersonal roles are primarily social in nature; that is, they are roles in which the manager's main task is to relate to other people in certain ways. The manager may sometimes serve as a *figurehead* for the organization. Taking visitors to dinner and attending ribbon-cutting ceremonies are part of the figurehead role. In the role of *leader*, the manager works to hire, train, and motivate employees. Finally, the *liaison* role consists of relating to others outside the group or organization. For example, a manager at Intel might be responsible for handling all price negotiations with a key supplier of electronic circuit boards. Obviously, each of these interpersonal roles involves behavioral processes.

Mintzberg's three **informational roles** involve some aspect of information processing. The *monitor* actively seeks information that might be of value to the organization in general or to specific managers. The manager who transmits this information to others is carrying out the role of *disseminator*. The *spokesperson* speaks for the organization to outsiders. For example, the manager chosen by Pillsbury to appear at a press conference announcing a merger or other major deal (such as the recent decision to sell its Godfather's Pizza chain) would be serving in this role. Again, behavioral processes are part of each of these roles, since information is almost always exchanged between people.

Finally, Mintzberg's research identified four **decision-making roles**. The *entrepreneur* voluntarily initiates change (such as innovations, new strategies, etc.) in the organization. The *disturbance handler* helps settle disputes between various parties, such as other managers and their subordinates. The *resource allocator* decides who will get what—how resources in the organization will be distributed among various individuals and groups. The last role is that of the *negotiator*, who represents the organization in reaching agreements with other organizations. Contracts between management and labor unions are the result of negotiations. Again, behavioral processes are clearly crucial in each of these decisional roles.

Mintzberg's research also provided quite a lot of insight into how managers allocate their time in performing these roles, especially senior managers at the top of an organization. *A Look at Research* summarizes his findings.

The Human Context of Management

In addition to understanding the on-going behavioral processes involved in their own jobs, managers must understand the basic human element of their work. Organizational behavior offers three major ways of understanding this context: people as organizations, people as resources, and people as people.

Above all, organizations are people, and without people, there would be no organizations. A neighborhood grocery store owned and operated by a husband-and-wife team; Exxon, one of the world's largest industrial corporations;

A LOOK AT

RESEARCH

What do Managers Do?

What do managers do? This apparently simple question is actually quite difficult to answer. No two managers do the same thing. Further, no single manager ever does exactly the same thing two days in a row. There are, however, a few things we do know about managerial work. A starting point in any discussion of managerial work is the research of Henry Mintzberg.

Mintzberg studied a group of CEO's in the mid-1970s. He closely observed their day-to-day activities and learned a good deal about the nature of their jobs. He found, for example, that the CEOs spent an average of 59 percent of their time in scheduled meetings, 22 percent of their time at their desks, 10 percent in unscheduled meetings, 6 percent on the telephone, and 3 percent walking around the company.

Overall, their work was characterized by many different activities, frequent interruptions, and a frantic pace. Breaks were few and far between, and the work week grew longer and longer. You can see, too, that much of the work was interacting with other people. The only activity just noted not directly involving interaction with others is desk time, and much of that work involves reading or writing correspondence. Clearly, then, managers need to have a keen understanding of human behavior.

Managers interact with subordinates, superiors, and peers. Thus, the manager needs to be able to relate well to others in a variety of settings and contexts. By understanding the behavioral processes and interactions that permeate their jobs, managers can perform more effectively.

Sources: Henry Mintzberg, *The Nature of Managerial Work* (New York: Harper & Row, 1973); and Henry Mintzberg, "The Manager's Job: Folklore and Fact," *Harvard Business Review,* July–August 1975, pp. 49–61.

the Smithsonian Institution in Washington; a neighborhood street gang; the Mayo Clinic, one of this country's finest health care facilities; your college or university—all are organizations, and although they differ dramatically in size, purpose, and structure, they have one thing in common: people. Thus, if managers are to understand the organizations in which they work, they must first understand the people who make up the organizations.

As resources, people are one of an organization's most valuable assets. People create the organization, guide and direct its course, and vitalize and revitalize it. People make its decisions, solve its problems, and answer its questions. In recent years many Americans have been alarmed by the way productivity growth in the United States has slowed in relation to that of other industrial countries, including Japan, West Germany, and France. People are at the core of many of the factors cited as possibly causing this trend. To reverse declining productivity, many organizations have taken steps to boost the contribution from their human resources. Some companies have taken steps to encourage management and labor to cooperate better and others have increased employee participation in decision making and problem solving. At Westinghouse, for example, groups of employees meet regularly to study major problems faced by the company and to recommend solutions. As managers increasingly recognize the value of potential contributions by their employees, it will become more and more important for managers and employees to grasp the complexities of organizational behavior.

Finally, there is people as people—an argument derived from the simple notion of humanistic management. People spend a large part of their lives in organizational settings, mostly as employees. They have a right to expect something in return beyond wages and employee benefits. Employees seek satisfaction, and many want the opportunity to grow and develop and to learn new skills. An understanding of organizational behavior can help the manager better appreciate this variety of individual needs and expectations.

Of course, human life in organizations can have a negative side. People who are unhappy with their jobs are more likely to be frequently absent to look for work elsewhere than people who are happy. Recent years have seen increasing attention to the causes and consequences of employee stress at work. Knowledge of organizational behavior can help managers recognize the problems of the workplace and improve the quality of individual work experiences.

EMERGING PERSPECTIVES ON ORGANIZATIONAL BEHAVIOR

Three contemporary perspectives have increasingly influenced organizational behavior: the systems view, the contingency view, and the interactional view. Many of the concepts and theories discussed in the chapters that follow reflect these perspectives; they represent basic points of view that influence much of our contemporary thinking about behavior in organizations.

The Systems View

Systems theory, or the theory of systems, was first developed in the physical sciences, but it has been extended to other areas, such as management.[14] A **system** is an interrelated set of elements functioning as a whole. Figure 1.6 shows a general framework for viewing organizations as systems.

An organizational system receives four kinds of inputs from its environment: material, human, financial, and informational. The organization then combines and transforms the inputs, returning them to the environment in the form of products or services, profits or losses, employee behaviors, and additional

---

[14] Fremont Kast and James Rosenzweig, "General Systems Theory: Applications for Organization and Management," *Academy of Management Journal,* December 1972, pp. 447–465.

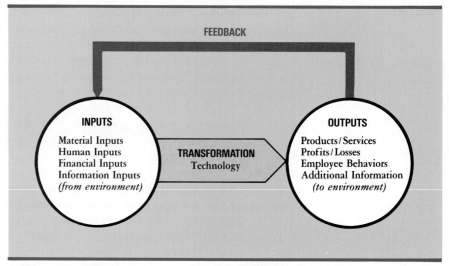

Figure 1.6

Systems Theory

FEEDBACK

INPUTS

Material Inputs
Human Inputs
Financial Inputs
Information Inputs
(from environment)

TRANSFORMATION
Technology

OUTPUTS

Products / Services
Profits / Losses
Employee Behaviors
Additional Information
(to environment)

Source: R. W. Griffin, *Management,* 2nd ed. (Boston: Houghton Mifflin, 1987),
p. 56. Used with permission.

information. Finally, the system receives feedback from the environment
regarding these outputs.

As an example, we can apply systems theory to Shell Oil Company. Material
inputs include pipelines, crude oil, and the machinery used to refine petroleum.
Financial inputs take the form of money received from oil and gas sales,
stockholder investment, and so forth. Human inputs are oil field workers,
refinery workers, office staff, and other people employed by the company.
Finally, the company receives information inputs from forecasts about future
oil supplies, geological surveys about potential drilling sites, sales projections,
and similar analyses.

Through complex refining and other processes, these inputs are combined
and transformed to create products like gasoline and motor oil. As outputs,
these products are sold to the consuming public. Profits from operations are
fed back into the environment through taxes, investments, and dividends; losses,
when they occur, hit the environment by reducing stockholders' incomes. In
addition to their on-the-job contacts with customers and suppliers, employees
live in the community and participate in a variety of activities away from the
workplace. In varying degrees, at least some part of this behavior is influenced
by their experiences as Shell workers. Finally, information about the company
and its operations is also released into the environment. The environment, in
turn, responds to these outputs and influences future inputs. For example,
consumers may buy more or less gasoline depending on the quality and price
of Shell's product, and banks may be more or less willing to lend Shell money
based on financial information released about the company.

Figure 1.7

Universal and
Contingency Perspectives

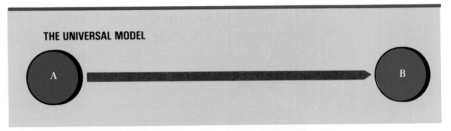

THE UNIVERSAL MODEL

A   →   B

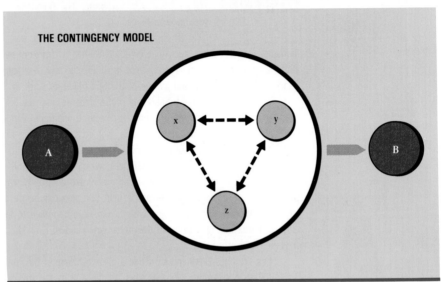

THE CONTINGENCY MODEL

The Contingency View

Another useful viewpoint for understanding behavior in organizations comes from **contingency theory**. In the earlier days of management studies, both researchers and practicing managers searched for universal answers to organizational questions. They sought prescriptions that could be applied to any organization under any conditions. For example, early leadership researchers tried to discover forms of leadership behavior that would always stimulate employees to be more satisfied and to work harder. Eventually, however, researchers realized that the complexities of human behavior and organizational settings make universal conclusions virtually impossible. They discovered that in organizations most situations and outcomes are contingent; that is, the relationship between any two variables is likely to be influenced by other variables.[15]

Figure 1.7 distinguishes universal and contingency perspectives. The universal model presumes a direct cause-and-effect linkage between variable *A*

---

[15] See Fremont Kast and James Rosenzweig, eds., *Contingency Views of Organization and Management* (Chicago: SRA, 1973), for a classic overview and introduction.

Contingency Theory in Practice: Jim Treybig and Tandem Computers Inc.

Jim Treybig and Tandem Computers were legend. Treybig left a lucrative position with Hewlett-Packard to start Tandem in the mid-1970s. The Tandem computer was especially designed for organizations like banks and airlines where a computer failure would be disastrous. The basic Tandem computer, called the Nonstop II, is actually two computers in one. If one unit fails, the other picks right up and keeps working. The system was a big success, but the company was an even bigger one.

In his management style, Treybig was more like a cheerleader than a manager. He passed out stock to everyone, installed a company swimming pool and jogging path, and was everyone's friend. Things were great for the first few years. Sales and profits soared, and Tandem enjoyed a reputation as one of the best places to work in Silicon Valley.

Then, troubles emerged. Sales and profits dropped, and the SEC accused the company of fraud. After all the dust had settled, the problem became apparent: Tandem had simply grown too large for Treybig's laid-back management style. Not everyone working for the company was as dedicated to performance as Treybig himself, and the organization lacked an effective control system.

Treybig quickly realized that changes were necessary. While keeping his basic management philosophy intact, he implemented a comprehensive control system so he could keep track of the goings on in the company. Whereas he held few meetings before, he now schedules staff meetings on a regular basis. He also dropped his laissez-faire approach to leadership and has become much more authoritarian. As a result of these changes, Tandem is on the road to regaining its earlier pace of growth and prosperity.

Thus Treybig's experiences provide a clear example of the contingency nature of management. His initial style was quite effective when matched with the small, informal organization that was once Tandem. As the company grew, however, that style bred trouble. When Treybig himself changed to fit his new situation, the company regained its lost effectiveness.

Sources: "Beyond the Better Mousetrap (Tandem Computers Personnel Management Works Wonders)," *Forbes,* June 22, 1981, p. 58; Myron Magnet, "Managing by Mystique at Tandem Computers," *Fortune,* June 28, 1982, pp. 84–91; and Brian O'Reilly, "How Jimmy Treybig Turned Tough," *Fortune,* May 25, 1987, pp. 102–103.

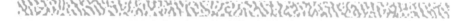

and variable *B*; for example, an increase in *A* will cause an increase in *B*; a decrease in *A* will cause a decrease in *B*. Moreover, this linkage is expected to exist in all settings. The contingency model, on the other hand, includes several other variables that alter the direct relationship. That is, the relationship between *A* and *B* is affected by variables *x*, *y*, and *z*. The effect of *A* on *B* will depend on the presence, absence, level, and pattern of *x, y,* and *z*.

The field of organizational behavior has gradually shifted from a universal approach in the 1950s and early 1960s to a contingency approach. The contingency orientation is especially strong in the areas of motivation (Chapter

Figure 1.8

The Interactional View
of Behavior

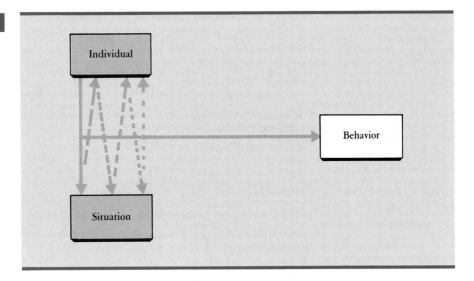

6), job design (Chapter 8), leadership (Chapter 11), and organization design (Chapter 17), but it is becoming more and more important throughout the field.

Management in Action tells a story of the contingency view's relevance to the real world. Jim Treybig found one style of management to work well when his organization was fairly small. As Tandem grew, however, he found it necessary to adapt his approach to the new circumstances.

The Interactional View

The interactional view is a relatively new approach to understanding behavior in organizational settings. First presented in terms of interactional psychology, this view assumes that individual behavior results from a continuous and multidirectional interaction between characteristics of the person and characteristics of the situation. More specifically, **interactionalism** attempts to explain how people select, interpret, and change various situations.[16] Figure 1.8 illustrates this perspective. Note that the individual and the situation are presumed to interact continuously. This interaction is what determines the individual's behavior.

The interactional view implies that simple cause-and-effect descriptions of organizational phenomena are not enough. One set of research studies, for

---

[16] James Terborg, "Interactional Psychology and Research on Human Behavior in Organizations," *Academy of Management Review,* October 1981, pp. 569–576; and Benjamin Schneider, "Interactional Psychology and Organizational Behavior," in Larry Cummings and Barry Staw, eds., *Research in Organizational Behavior,* Vol. 5 (Greenwich, Conn.: JAI Press, 1983), pp. 1–32. See also Arnon E. Reichers, "An Interactionist Perspective on Newcomer Socialization Rates," *Academy of Management Review,* April 1987, pp. 278–287.

example, may suggest that job changes will lead to improved employee attitudes. Another set of studies may suggest that attitudes influence how people perceive their jobs in the first place. Both positions are probably incomplete—employee attitudes may influence job perceptions, but these perceptions may in turn influence future attitudes.

Because the interactional view is a fairly recent contribution to the field, it is less prominent in the chapters that follow than the systems and contingency theories. Nonetheless, the interactional view appears to offer many promising ideas for future development in the field.

SUMMARY OF KEY POINTS

Organizational behavior (OB) is the study of human behavior in organizational settings, the interface between human behavior and the organization, and the organization itself.

Serious interest in the study of management did not develop until around the beginning of this century. Two of the earliest approaches were scientific management (best represented by the work of Taylor) and classical organization theory (best represented by the work of Weber).

Organizational behavior began to emerge as a scientific discipline as a result of the Hawthorne studies. McGregor and Maslow led the human relations movement that grew from those studies.

Contemporary organizational behavior attempts to describe, rather than pre-scribe, behavioral forces in organizations. Ties to psychology, sociology, anthropology, political science, economics, engineering, and medicine give organizational behavior an interdisciplinary focus.

Basic concepts of the field are divided into five categories: individual characteristics, the individual-organization interface, organizational characteristics, organizational processes, and organization change and development. Those categories form the framework for this book.

The study of organizational behavior is important for several reasons. The manager's job, including its four basic functions and ten roles, involves a number of behavioral processes. There is also a distinctly human context to managerial work.

Three important emerging perspectives on the field of organizational behavior are the systems view, the contingency view, and the interactional view.

DISCUSSION QUESTIONS

1. What elements of a manager's job are not affected by behavior or behavioral processes?

2. Is organizational behavior comparable to such functional areas as finance, marketing, and production? Why or why not?

3. Identify some managerial jobs that are highly affected by human behavior and others that are less so.

4. Can you think of reasons besides those cited in the text for the importance of organizational behavior? If so, what are they?

5. Some people argue that an organization's human resources are its most important asset. Do you agree or disagree? Why?

6. The text states that people working in an organization have a right to satisfaction and to the opportunity to grow and develop. How would you defend this position? How would you argue against it?

7. Consider each of the basic concepts of organizational behavior. How do they apply to a typical classroom setting? That is, can you think of examples from the classroom setting to illustrate each concept? What are they?

8. Do you think the field of organizational behavior has the potential to become prescriptive, as opposed to descriptive? Why or why not?

9. Are the notions of systems, contingency, and interactionalism independent? If not, describe ways in which they are related.

10. Get a recent issue of a popular business magazine like *Business Week* or *Fortune* and scan its major articles. Do some of them reflect concepts from organizational behavior? Describe.

`Case 1.1`   ## Reawakening Colgate-Palmolive

Reuben Mark is not exactly a household name. Yet Mark is rapidly gaining a reputation in corporate America as a consummate manager. Demonstrating a keen understanding of both management and people, he has transformed Colgate-Palmolive, which had become a stodgy, ineffective also-ran, back into an innovative, growing company.

Mark went to college in the Northeast and earned his MBA from Harvard in 1963. When he graduated, he received job offers from both Colgate and its archrival Procter & Gamble. He opted for Colgate, mainly because he thought the company had better opportunities for advancement.

By 1972 he was in charge of Colgate's Venezuelan division. After stints in Canada and the Far East, he was promoted to group vice president of Colgate's domestic operations. He worked quietly in the shadow of CEO Keith Crane for the next several years. Many insiders felt he would one day be in charge.

That day came in 1984. Since that time, Mark has transformed Colgate-Palmolive into a powerhouse. Colgate has two primary competitors: Procter & Gamble and Unilever (the European firm that operates in this country as Lever Brothers). Colgate was historically a distant third to its rivals and operated as a plodding, copycat bureaucracy. Mark wanted no part of that mentality and immediately went to work turning things around. From 1984 through 1987, income increased from $71 million to $177.5 million, sales have increased to $5 billion, and the company's stock price has tripled. Two basic tenets underlie Mark's success: understanding people and understanding the organization.

Mark has been particularly effective on the people side. He is equally comfortable working with top managers and operating employees, and he understands each very well. At the managerial level, he saw a need to increase freedom and create an entrepreneurial spirit. He outlined a broad set of initiatives and encouraged people to work toward achieving them. He began offering managers performance-based bonuses for the first time, and gave them much more autonomy in making decisions. He also takes a personal interest in them, sending birthday and anniversary cards to the many individual managers he knows.

Mark has not neglected the operating employee, either. One of his motivational programs has been to give stock to employees in return for innovative ideas and cost-cutting suggestions. And as noted earlier, he relates to operating employees at an interpersonal level. For example, when he recently visited a Mexico City facility, the workers there were somewhat nervous about meeting such an important executive. Mark disarmed them easily, however, by joking with them in fluent Spanish.

Mark works hard at communication and regularly visits facilities around the world to meet with company employees. When he can't go personally, he sends videotapes outlining things that the company is planning.

When Mark took over, though, he knew that the overall organization needed attention. Colgate had too many employees and several unproductive plants. He reluctantly but firmly laid off unneeded employees and closed the plants. He also removed one entire layer of management from the organizational structure.

To date, Mark has done a superb job of revitalizing the company. Most managers at Colgate see things in terms of a new corporate culture, a culture based on entrepreneurial spirit and unity of purpose. Still, things remain to be done. Procter & Gamble and Unilever are each three times the size of Colgate and so remain formidable competitors. Some of Colgate's divisions are still not as profitable as they should be. Analysts see two big challenges ahead for the company. First, it needs to become even more efficient. Second, Mark must find ways to keep alive the new culture he has created and to keep Colgate employees fired up about the company and their work.

Case Questions

1. The *Management in Action* box on page 28 outlines some problems encountered by Tandem Computers when its management style failed to keep pace with growth. Is this a possibility at Colgate? Why or why not?

2. What are some things Mark might do to meet the challenges outlined at the end of the case?

3. Identify some of the basic concepts of organizational behavior illustrated in this case.

Case Sources

H. John Steinbreder, "The Man Brushing Up Colgate's Image," *Fortune,* May 11, 1987, pp. 106–112; Rita Koselka, "Consumer Products: Some Improvements on the Scoreboard but Conditions Are Still Tough," *Forbes,* January 12, 1987, pp. 114–115; "Colgate Posts Profits Totaling $30 Million for Fourth Quarter," *Wall Street Journal,* February 13, 1987, p. 11.

Case 1.2

Difficult Transitions

Tony Stark had just finished his first week at Reece Enterprises and had decided to drive upstate to a small lake-front lodge for some fishing and relaxation. Tony had worked for the past ten years for the O'Grady Company. O'Grady had suffered through some hard times of late, though, and had recently shut down several of its operating groups, including Tony's, to cut costs. Fortunately, Tony's experience and recommendations had made finding another position fairly easy. As he drove the interstate, he reflected on the ten years past and the apparent situation at Reece.

At O'Grady (Tony's first employer), things had been great. He had been part of the team from day one. The job had met his personal goals and expectations perfectly, and Tony felt he had grown greatly as a person. His work was appreciated and recognized—and he had received three promotions and many more pay increases.

Tony had also liked the company itself. The firm was decentralized, allowing its managers considerable autonomy and freedom. The culture was relaxed and easygoing. Communication was open; it seemed that everyone knew what was going on at all times. And, if you didn't know about something, it was easy to find out.

The people had also been a plus. Tony and three other managers went to lunch often and played golf every Saturday. They got along well both personally and professionally and truly worked together as a team. Their boss had been very supportive, giving them the help they needed but also staying out of the way and letting them work.

When word came down about the shutdown, Tony had almost cried. He felt nothing could replace O'Grady. After the final closing, he spent only a few weeks looking around before he found a comparable position at Reece Enterprises.

As he drove, he reflected that *comparable* was probably not the right word. Indeed, Tony realized that Reece and O'Grady were about as different as you could get. Top managers at the new company apparently didn't worry too much about who did a good job and who didn't. They seemed to promote and reward people based on how long they had been there and how well they played the political games that went on all the time.

Maybe this stemmed from the organization itself, Tony pondered. Reece was a bigger organization than O'Grady and was structured much more bureaucratically. It seemed that no one was allowed to make a decision of any sort without getting three signatures from higher up. Those signatures, though, were hard to get. All the top managers were usually too busy to see anyone, and interoffice memos apparently had very low priority.

Tony had also had some problems fitting in. His peers treated him with polite indifference. He sensed that a couple of them resented that he, an outsider, had been brought right in at their level, after they had had to work themselves up the ladder. On Tuesday he had asked a couple of men his age about playing golf. They had politely declined, saying that they did not play very often. Later in the week, though, he had overheard the two of them making arrangements to play that very Saturday.

That was when Tony decided to go fishing. As he steered his car off the interstate to get gas, he wondered if perhaps he had made a mistake in accepting the Reece offer without finding out more about what he was getting into.

Case Questions

1. Identify several concepts and characteristics from the field of organizational behavior that are illustrated in this case.

2. What advice could you give Tony? How is this advice supported or tempered by behavioral concepts and processes?

Experiential Exercise

Purpose: This exercise will help you develop an appreciation for the importance and pervasiveness of organizational behavior concepts and processes in both contemporary organizational settings and popular culture.

Format: Your instructor will divide the class into small groups of from three to five members each. Each group will then be assigned the "task" of watching television. In particular, each group will be assigned a specific television program to watch before the next class meeting.

Arrange to watch the program as a group. Each person should have a pad of paper and pencil handy. As you watch the show, jot down examples of individual behavior, interpersonal dynamics, organizational characteristics, and other concepts and processes relevant to organizational behavior. After the show, spend a few minutes comparing notes. Compile one list for the entire group. (It is advisable to turn off the television during this discussion!)

During the next class meeting, have someone in the group summarize the plot of the show you watched and list the concepts illustrated by it.

The following television shows are especially good for illustrating behavioral concepts in organizational settings:

Current Shows	Syndicated Shows
Cheers	M*A*S*H
Miami Vice	Barney Miller
Dallas	WKRP in Cincinnati
Newhart	Star Trek
Moonlighting	Taxi
Night Court	Trapper John, M.D.

Follow-Up Questions

1. What does this exercise illustrate about the pervasiveness of organizational effects on contemporary society?
2. Can you think of recent and/or classic movies that provide similar kinds of examples?

Individual
Aspects of
Organizational
Behavior

PART II

Part Contents

CHAPTER 2

Learning, Perception, and Attribution

Chapter Objectives

After reading this chapter, you should be able to

- ▶ define *learning,* summarize classical conditioning, and discuss learning as a cognitive process.

- ▶ discuss reinforcement theory, including types of reinforcement, schedules of reinforcement, and related aspects of learning.

- ▶ identify key managerial implications of learning.

- ▶ define *perception* and describe basic perceptual processes.

- ▶ discuss the attribution process and describe internal and external attributions.

- ▶ identify key managerial implications of perception and attribution.

A lthough few people know his name, John C. Malone is rapidly becoming one of the most powerful men in the television industry. Malone runs Tele-Communications, Inc. (TCI), the largest cable television company in the country. One out of every five cable subscribers in the United States is a TCI customer.

Since the early 1980s, TCI has spent over $3 billion to acquire 150 cable networks. If they are to make a profit, cable networks like MTV and ESPN almost have to have access to TCI's eight million subscribers. Because of his clout, some networks, like HBO, charge Malone 30 percent less than they charge other cable companies.

Over the years, Malone has developed a reputation as a shrewd manager. He is decisive, often making major deals in a matter of hours, and treats his employees well. He also controls costs and makes sure that all of his cable companies are run as efficiently as possible.

Interestingly, Malone's peers in the industry are quite divided in their assessment of his approach. Some of them, it is true, credit him with making the cable industry more profitable for everyone. His friends note that he loves to make deals and has a unique ability to assess potential investments and make effective decisions. They also see him as being fair and aboveboard in all his business dealings.

Other associates, though, cast Malone in a quite different light. They describe him as a ruthless bully intent only on adding to his own wealth. Some resent his assuming the role of spokesman for the whole cable industry. A few describe him as Darth Vader, a powerful empire builder who will destroy all opposition to get his way.[1]

W hat explains these different opinions? How can two sets of informed people look at the same man and see such different things? Part of the answer lies in the nature of perception, the process by which we interpret our environment. Differing perceptions like those of Malone are actually quite common. Consider, for example, stories of two eyewitnesses to an accident who report having "seen" completely different chains of events.

Perception is one of two important dimensions of organizational behavior we explore in this chapter. First we examine the role of learning in organizations and then describe an important model of learning called reinforcement theory. We then discuss perception and the attribution processes that often follow perception.

THE ROLE OF LEARNING

Learning Defined

Learning can be defined as a relatively permanent change in behavior or potential behavior that results from direct or indirect experience.[2] Each part of

---

[1] "The King of Cable TV," *Business Week,* October 26, 1987, pp. 88–96.

[2] S. H. Hulse, J. Deese, and H. Egeth, *The Psychology of Learning,* 5th ed. (New York:

this definition deserves attention. First, learning involves change. After we have learned, we are somehow different from what we were before—for better or worse. We learn new job skills and new ideas; we may also learn to steal and to avoid work.

Second, the change brought about by learning tends to be long lasting. Thus, a student who memorizes material for an exam and then promptly forgets it has not really learned anything. Likewise, workers who get less done at the end of the day than in the morning have not learned to work more slowly. They are simply tired.

Third, learning affects behavior or potential behavior. Because we cannot read minds, we must depend on observation to see how much learning has occurred. If a secretary who typed seventy words a minute before a new training course can now type eighty-five words a minute, we can infer that learning has occurred. Other kinds of learning are harder to discern. Suppose a new fellow who has been arriving at work on time sees the boss scold some workers who come in late. The punctual worker now has an added incentive to be on time every day. Even though actual behavior has not been altered, learning has taken place because pontential behavior—the likelihood of being tardy—has been reduced.

Finally, the changes brought about by learning result from direct or indirect experience. The secretary probably sat and practiced at an actual keyboard during the training session (an example of direct experience). But the punctual employee learned about punishment for tardiness only by observing what the boss said to coworkers; nothing was done or said to him directly. This is learning through indirect experience (also called vicarious learning). We should also distinguish between experience and simple physical maturation. A grownup can lift a 20-pound sack of potatoes that a five-year-old cannot handle—not because of experience and resultant learning, but because physical maturation has made the adult stronger.

Classical Conditioning

To understand contemporary thinking on learning, we need to be aware of its historical roots. By far the most influential historical approach to learning is **classical conditioning**, as described by Ivan Pavlov.[3] The concept of classical conditioning is illustrated in Figure 2.1.

Pavlov's theory was based on a series of famous experiments with dogs. Pavlov knew that if he gave meat to the dogs, they would salivate. The meat was an unconditioned, or natural, stimulus and the salivation an unconditioned, or reflexive, response. This link is shown as step 1 in Figure 2.1. Pavlov next began to ring a bell at the same time that he presented the meat. Prior to that

---

McGraw-Hill, 1980). See also Gib Akins, "Varieties of Organizational Learning," *Organizational Dynamics,* Autumn 1987, pp. 36—48.

[3] Ivan P. Pavlov, *Conditional Reflexes* (New York: Oxford University Press, 1927).

Figure 2.1

Classical Conditioning

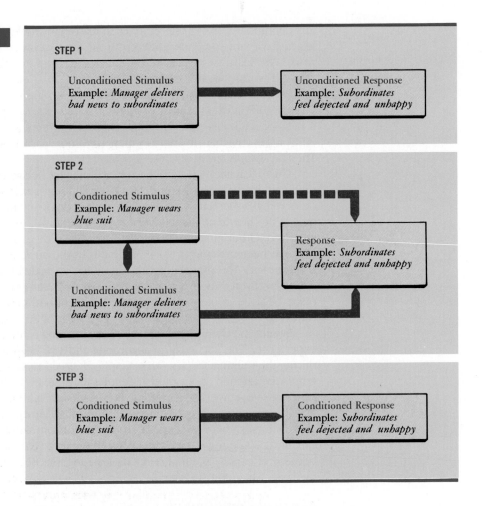

the dogs did not associate the ringing of the bell with eating, so the bell alone brought no response. But by ringing the bell while presenting the meat, Pavlov established a relationship between the two stimuli in the minds of the dogs. In the figure, this linkage is step 2. Eventually, the dogs associated eating with the sound of the bell so completely that they would salivate when the bell was rung, even if no meat was forthcoming (step 3). The bell had become a conditioned stimulus able to call up the newly conditioned, or learned, response.

Even though Figure 2.1 includes an organizational example of classical conditioning, simple forms of this conditioning seldom occur among human beings. Learning theorists soon recognized that although classical conditioning offered some interesting insights into the learning process, it inadequately explained human learning. For one thing, classical conditioning relies on simple cause-and-effect relationships between one stimulus and one response; it cannot

Figure 2.2

Learning As a Cognitive Process

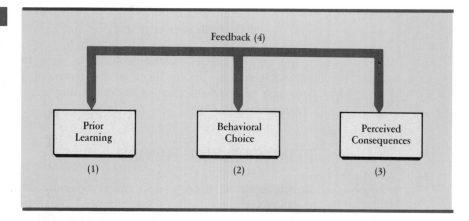

deal with more complex forms of learned behavior that typify human beings. For another, classical conditioning ignores the concept of choice. Classical conditioning assumes that behavior is reflexive, or involuntary. Therefore, this perspective cannot explain situations in which people consciously and rationally choose one course of action among many. Because of these shortcomings of classical conditioning, theorists eventually moved on to other approaches that seemed more useful in explaining the processes associated with complex learning.

Learning as a Cognitive Process

Although it is not tied to a single theory or model, contemporary learning theory generally views learning as a **cognitive process**. People, it is assumed, are conscious, active participants in how they learn.[4] Figure 2.2 illustrates some of the underpinnings of the cognitive view of learning.

First, in the cognitive view, people draw on their experiences and use past learning as a basis for present behavior. These experiences represent presumed knowledge, or cognitions. For example, an employee faced with a choice of job assignments will use previous experiences in making a decision about which one to accept. Second, people make choices about their behavior. The employee recognizes her two alternatives and chooses one. Third, people recognize the consequences of their choices. Thus, when the employee finds the job assignment rewarding and fulfilling, she will recognize that the choice was a good one and will understand why. Finally, people evaluate those

[4] Hulse, Deese, and Egeth, *The Psychology of Learning.* See also Douglas F. Cellar and Gerald V. Barrett, "Script Processing and Intrinsic Motivation: The Cognitive Sets Underlying Cognitive Labels," *Organizational Behavior and Human Decision Processes,* August 1987, pp. 115–135; and Max H. Bazerman and John S. Carroll, "Negotiator Cognition," in L. L. Cummings and Barry M. Staw, Eds., *Research in Organizational Behavior,* Vol. 9 (Greenwich, Conn.: JAI Press, 1987), pp. 247–288 for recent perspectives.

consequences and add them to prior learning, affecting future choices. Faced with the same job choices next year, the employee will very likely choose the same one.

As implied earlier, several perspectives on learning take a cognitive view. Perhaps foremost among them is reinforcement theory. In any event, this approach is most relevant to understanding human learning processes in organizational settings.

REINFORCEMENT THEORY

Reinforcement theory, also called **operant conditioning**, is generally associated with the work of B. F. Skinner.[5] In its simplest form, reinforcement theory suggests that behavior is a function of its consequences.[6] Thus, behavior that results in pleasant consequences is more likely to be repeated, and behavior that results in unpleasant consequences is less likely to be repeated.

Reinforcement theory further suggests that in any given situation, people will explore a variety of possible behaviors. Future behavioral choices are affected by the consequences of earlier behaviors. Cognitions, as already described, also play an important role. So rather than assume a mechanical stimulus-response linkage suggested by early research, contemporary theorists believe that people consciously explore different behaviors and systematically choose those that result in the most desirable outcomes.

Suppose, for example, that a new employee at General Dynamics in St. Louis wants to learn the best way to get along with his boss. At first, the employee is very friendly and informal, but the boss responds by acting aloof and, at times, annoyed. Because the boss does not react positively, the employee is not likely to continue this behavior. In fact, the employee starts acting more formal and professional and finds the boss much more receptive to this posture. In all likelihood, the employee will continue this new set of behaviors because they result in positive consequences.

Types of Reinforcement

The consequences of behavior are called **reinforcement**. Managers may be able to use various kinds of reinforcement to affect employee behavior; that is, we do not mean our discussion of reinforcement to be prescriptive. We simply describe four kinds of reinforcement; how to use them depends on the situation. Figure 2.3 summarizes the concepts underlying the four basic kinds of reinforcement.

---

[5] B. F. Skinner, *Science and Human Behavior* (New York: Macmillan, 1953), and *Beyond Freedom and Dignity* (New York: Knopf, 1972).

[6] Fred Luthans and Robert Kreitner, *Organizational Behavior Modification and Beyond* (Glenview, Ill.: Scott, Foresman, 1985).

Figure 2.3

Kinds of Reinforcement

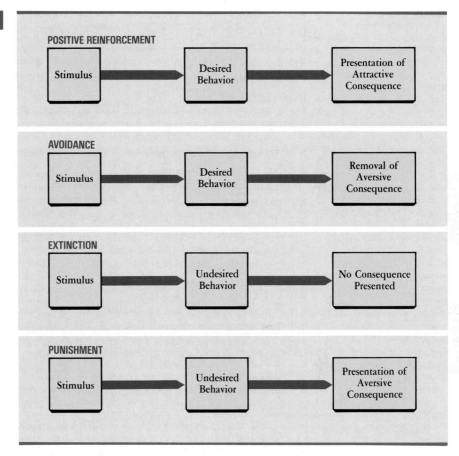

POSITIVE REINFORCEMENT   **Positive reinforcement** is the concept of reinforcement theory that is perhaps most familiar to people outside the fields of psychology and organizational behavior. Positive reinforcement is a reward that follows desirable behavior. A compliment from the boss after completing a difficult job and a salary increase following a period of high performance are both examples of positive reinforcement. Its effect is to maintain or increase the frequency of a desired behavior.[7] Managers might define desirable employee behavior as hard work, punctuality, conscientiousness, and loyalty and commitment to the organization. When employees exhibit these behaviors, the manager may reward them with pay increases, praise, some kind of formal recognition, promotions, and the like. In terms of reinforcement theory, the rewards are intended to ensure the same type of behavior in the future. Of

---

[7] Luthans and Kreitner, *Organizational Behavior Modification and Beyond.*

course, different people work for different reasons. Therefore, to be useful as positive reinforcement, rewards should be tailored to the needs of the individual. In addition, a reward should be directly linked with the desired behavior, and the individual should have ample opportunity to achieve the reinforcement. For example, a person who gets a raise in salary following a period of high performance should be made aware explicitly that the raise was given *because* of the performance. Likewise, the level of performance needed to get the raise should not be set so high as to be impossible to reach.

AVOIDANCE   **Avoidance**, also known as **negative reinforcement**, is another means of increasing the frequency of desired behavior. Rather than receiving a reward following a desired behavior, however, the person is given the opportunity to avoid an unpleasant consequence. For example, an employee's boss may habitually criticize individuals who dress casually. To avoid criticism, the employee may routinely dress to suit the supervisor's tastes. The employee is engaging in desired behavior (at least from the supervisor's viewpoint) to avoid an unpleasant, or aversive, consequence.

EXTINCTION   Whereas positive reinforcement and avoidance increase the frequency of desired behavior, **extinction** decreases the frequency of undesired behavior, especially behavior that was previously rewarded. That is, if rewards are withdrawn for behaviors that were previously reinforced, the behaviors will probably become less frequent and eventually die out. For example, a manager with a small staff may encourage frequent visits from subordinates as a way of keeping in touch with what is going on. Positive reinforcement might include cordial conversation, attention to subordinate's concerns, and encouragement to come in again soon. As the staff grows, however, the manager might find that such unstructured conversations now make it difficult to get her own job done. She might then brush off casual conversation and reward only to-the-point business conversations. Withdrawing the rewards for casual chatting will probably extinguish that behavior. Be sure to note, too, that if managers, accidentally or otherwise, cease to reward valuable behaviors such as good performance and punctuality, those behaviors also may become extinct.[8]

PUNISHMENT   Punishment, like extinction, also tends to decrease the frequency of undesired behaviors. **Punishment** is presented as an unpleasant, or aversive, consequence of undesirable behavior. In the workplace, undesired behavior might include slacking off, being late, stealing, or arguing unnecessarily with the boss. Examples of punishment are verbal or written reprimands, pay cuts, loss of privileges, layoffs, and termination. Punishment is by nature controversial, and we therefore discuss arguments for and against it in a separate section later in the chapter.

---

[8] Luthans and Kreitner, *Organizational Behavior Modification and Beyond.*

Table 2.1	
Schedules of Reinforcement	**Continuous Reinforcement**—Behavior is reinforced every time it occurs.
	Fixed Interval Reinforcement—Behavior is reinforced according to some predetermined, constant schedule based on time.
	Variable Interval Reinforcement—Behavior is reinforced after periods of time, but the time span varies from one time to the next.
	Fixed Ratio Reinforcement—Behavior is reinforced according to the number of behaviors exhibited, with the number of behaviors needed to gain reinforcement held constant.
	Variable Ratio Reinforcement—Behavior is reinforced according to the number of behaviors exhibited, but the number of behaviors needed to gain reinforcement varies from one time to the next.

Schedules of Reinforcement

Should the manager try to reinforce every instance of desired behavior, or is it better to apply reinforcement according to some plan or schedule? Generally, that depends on the situation. Five **schedules of reinforcement** used effectively by psychologists and managers are summarized in Table 2.1.[9]

CONTINUOUS REINFORCEMENT   Continuous reinforcement rewards behavior every time it occurs. Continuous reinforcement is very effective in increasing the frequency of a desired behavior. When reinforcement is withdrawn, however, extinction sets in very quickly. The schedule poses serious practical difficulties as well: the manager must monitor every behavior of an employee and provide effective reinforcement. This schedule, then, is seldom worth much to managers. Offering partial reinforcement according to one of the other four schedules is much more typical.

FIXED INTERVAL REINFORCEMENT   Fixed interval reinforcement means providing reinforcement on a predetermined, constant schedule. The Friday afternoon paycheck is a good example of a fixed interval reinforcement. Unfortunately, in many situations, the fixed interval schedule is not necessarily going to maintain high levels of performance. If employees know that the boss will drop by to check on them every day at 1:00 P.M., they are likely to be working hard at that time, hoping to gain praise and recognition or to avoid the boss's wrath. But at other times of the day, the employees probably will not work as hard because they have learned that reinforcement is unlikely except during the daily visit.

VARIABLE INTERVAL REINFORCEMENT   This schedule also uses time as the basis for applying reinforcement but varies the interval between reinforcements. Although this schedule is inappropriate for paying wages, it can work well for other types of positive reinforcement, such as praise and recognition,

---

[9] Luthans and Kreitner, *Organizational Behavior Modification and Beyond.*

and for avoidance. Consider again the group of employees just described. Suppose that instead of coming by at exactly 1:00 every day, the boss visits at a different time each day. Thus, he comes by at 9:30 on Monday, 2:00 on Tuesday, 11:00 on Wednesday, and so on. The following week, the times change. Since the employees do not know just when to expect the boss, they will probably work fairly hard until his visit. Afterward, they may drop back to lower levels, because they have learned that he will not be back until the next day.

FIXED RATIO REINFORCEMENT   The fixed and variable ratio schedules gear reinforcement to the number of desired or undesired behaviors rather than to blocks of time. Under the fixed ratio schedule, the number of behaviors needed to obtain reinforcement is constant. Assume, for example, that a work group enters its cumulative performance totals into the office computer every hour. The manager of the group uses the computer to monitor its activities. She might adopt a practice of dropping by to praise the group every time it reaches a performance level of 500 units. Thus, if the group does this three times on Monday, she stops by each time; if it reaches the mark only once on Tuesday, she stops by only once. The fixed ratio schedule can be fairly effective in maintaining desired behavior. Employees tend to develop a feel for what it takes to be reinforced and work hard to keep up their performance.

VARIABLE RATIO REINFORCEMENT   Under the variable ratio schedule, the number of behaviors required for reinforcement varies over time. An employee performing under a variable ratio schedule is motivated to work hard because each successful behavior increases the probability that the next one will result in reinforcement. With this schedule, the exact number of behaviors needed to obtain reinforcement is not crucial; what is important is that the intervals between reinforcement not be so long that the worker gets discouraged and stops trying. The supervisor in the fixed ratio example could reinforce her work group after it reaches performance levels of 450, 525, 325, 600, and so on. A variable ratio schedule can be quite effective but is difficult and cumbersome to use when formal organizational rewards, such as pay increases and promotions, are the reinforcers. A fixed interval system is the most common way to administer these rewards.

   To sum up, relying on any given schedule for all rewards is difficult or impractical. Instead, the manager should use the schedule best suited to the kind of reinforcement being used and try to link outcomes with behaviors according to the needs of the organization and its employees.

RELATED ASPECTS OF LEARNING

Several additional aspects of learning bear on individual behavior in organizations. Among them are stimulus generalization, stimulus discrimination, vicarious learning, and the arguments for and against punishment.

Stimulus Generalization

Stimulus generalization is how people recognize the same or similar stimuli in different settings.[10] That is, it is the process by which they can generalize a contingent reinforcement from one setting to another. Figure 2.4 illustrates a simple example of the process. Following an initial stimulus-response-consequence sequence, a person learns the behaviors likely to produce some kind of reinforcement. Later, when presented with a similar stimulus in different surroundings, he or she knows that the same response is likely to elicit a similar consequence.

Consider, for example, the case of a plant manager with a history of effective troubleshooting. Over the years, he has been assigned to several different plants, each with a serious operating problem. After successfully dealing with the difficulties, he has always received an extended vacation, a bonus, and a boost in his base salary. He has learned the basic contingencies, or requirements, of reinforcement for his job: the stimulus is the assignment, the response is correcting problems, and the consequences are several positive reinforcers. When the manager gets his next assignment, he will probably generalize from his past experiences. Even though he will be in a different plant with different problems and employees, he will understand what it takes to be rewarded.

Stimulus Discrimination

Stimulus discrimination is the ability to recognize differences between stimuli.[11] This process is also shown in Figure 2.4. As in stimulus generalization, the person learns the basic stimulus-response-consequence sequence for one stimulus. When confronted with a new stimulus, however, he or she can discriminate between the two different stimuli and respond differently.

Suppose the troubleshooting plant manager is assigned to a plant that is running smoothly. His routine response to new situations has always been to identify and solve problems, but he must now discriminate between his new situation and his earlier ones. He will then also recognize that a different set of behaviors, or responses, is needed for him to receive positive reinforcement.

Vicarious Learning

Vicarious learning, or **modeling**, is learning through the experiences of others.[12] A person can learn to do a new job by observing others, for example,

---

[10] W. R. Nord, "Beyond the Teaching Machine: The Neglected Area of Operant Conditioning in the Theory and Practice of Management," *Organizational Behavior and Human Performance,* Vol. 4, 1969, pp. 375–401.

[11] Nord, "Beyond the Teaching Machine."

[12] H. M. Weiss, "Subordinate Imitation of Supervisory Behavior: The Role of Modeling in Organizational Socialization," *Organizational Behavior and Human Performance,* Vol. 19, 1977, pp. 89–105.

Figure 2.4

Stimulus Generalization
and Discrimination

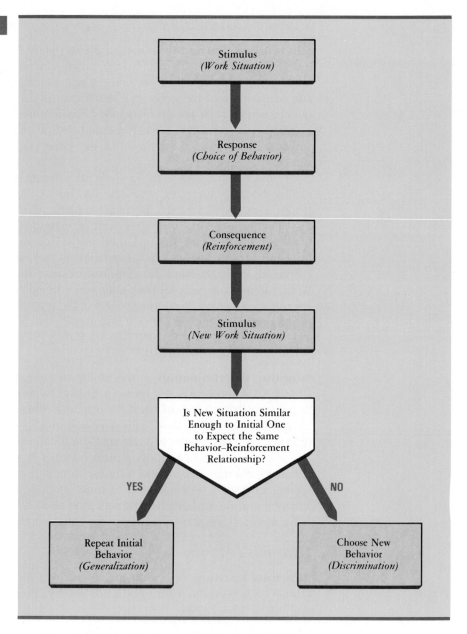

or by watching videotapes. And recall the earlier example where an employee learned not to be late by watching his boss chew out fellow workers.

Several conditions must be met for vicarious learning to take place. The behavior being modeled must be relatively simple. Although we can learn by watching someone else how to push three or four buttons to set specifications on a machine, we probably cannot learn a complicated sequence of operations without also practicing the various steps ourselves.

Second, the behavior being modeled must usually be concrete, not intellectual. We can learn by watching others how to respond to the different behaviors of a particular manager or how to assemble a few components into a final assembly. But we probably cannot learn through simple observation how to write a computer program or to conceptualize or think abstractly. Finally, to learn a job vicariously, we must possess the physical ability needed to do the job. Most of us, for instance, can watch televised baseball games or tennis matches every weekend but still will not be able to hit a curveball like Don Mattingly or a backhand like Martina Navratilova.

In recent years, considerable attention has been devoted to a specific type of vicarious learning called **social learning**. Social learning theory suggests that behavior is determined by a person's cognitions and social environment.[13] More specifically, people are presumed to learn behaviors and attitudes at least partially in response to what others expect of them.

Suppose that a new employee joins an existing work group. She already has some basis for knowing how to behave (i.e., education and previous experience). The group provides a set of very specific cues, however, that help the person see how her behavior needs to be tailored to fit the specific situation she is now in. The group may indicate how the organization expects its members to dress, how people are "supposed" to feel about the boss, and so forth. Hence the new employee learns how to behave in the new situation partially in response to what she already knows and partially in response to what others suggest and demonstrate. *A Look at Research* describes other elements of social learning theory in more detail.

Punishment

Punishment was defined earlier as the presentation of an unpleasant, or aversive, consequence after an individual engages in undesired behavior.[14] Thus, any unpleasant consequence that follows behavior can be called punishment. When an attempt to punish is structured, official, and organizationally sanctioned, it is called **discipline**. When a boss yells at an employee who drops a bottle of solvent, punishment has taken place. If the boss formally reprimands the worker and puts a written account of the reprimand in the employee's personnel folder, this action would represent an attempt at discipline.

---

[13] A. Bandura, *Principles of Behavior Modification* (New York: Holt, 1969). See also Henry P. Sims, Jr., and Dennis Gioia, *The Thinking Organization* (San Francisco: Jossey-Bass, 1986).

[14] See Richard Arvey and John M. Ivancevich, "Punishment in Organization: A Review, Propositions, and Research Suggestions," *Academy of Management Review*, April 1980, pp. 123–132 for a recent discussion of punishment.

A LOOK AT

RESEARCH

Social Learning Theory and Scripts

Social learning theory suggests that behavior is determined by cognitions and the social environment of the individual. Vicarious learning is one form of social learning, albeit a relatively simple one. As yet, we have learned little about the cognitive processes involved in either vicarious or social learning. One fairly new approach that has the potential to yield valuable insights into these processes is the notion of scripts.

A script in this context is a form of schema. A schema is a basic concept in cognitive processing and represents a knowledge base that guides the individual's interpretation of information. A script, in turn, is a schema held in memory by the individual for describing events or behaviors appropriate for a particular context.

For example, suppose a newcomer to an organization observes that whenever the district manager visits the office, people tend to dress more formally, be at their desks earlier, and have less social interaction during the day. The newcomer quickly develops a script for understanding why this happens (the district manager is important and someone you need to try to impress) and how she should behave (she should do the same things everyone else does).

Scripts have several potential areas of application in organizational settings. A fairly specialized application is in the area of employee training. If researchers and managers can develop a better understanding of how scripts are created, modified, and retained, they should be able to enhance the quality of employee training programs. In a more general area, scripts can also play a major role in the formation and maintenance of organizational cultures. (Chapter 16 explores the concept of organizational culture.) In addition, scripts may apply to other areas like decision making and performance appraisal.

Sources: Dennis A. Gioia and Peter P. Poole, "Scripts in Organizational Behavior," *Academy of Management Review,* July 1984, pp. 449–459; and Dennis A. Gioia and Charles C. Manz, "Linking Cognition and Behavior: A Script Processing Interpretation of Vicarious Learning," *Academy of Management Review,* July 1985, pp. 527–539.

To be effective, discipline must be perceived as punishing, but in fact, it may not always be seen as such. For example, a subordinate planning to quit in the near future might find the supervisor's written reprimand amusing.

Although punishment is common in organizations, many managers and researchers question its practical value for influencing employee behavior. They argue that punishment cannot be effective unless employee behavior is continually observed. Punishment is likely to suppress behavior temporarily, rather than permanently extinguish it, and the side effects of punishment, such as hostility and anger, may outweigh any potential benefits. Furthermore, undesirable behavior can often be changed through extinction or environmental engineering. For example, if two employees who must frequently interact are constantly arguing with each other, it may be possible to stop the bickering without punishing. The manager might alter their environment by having them deal with each other through a neutral third party.

Punishment may be an appropriate tool for altering behavior in some situations, however. Many of life's events teach us what to do by means of punishment. Falling off a bike, drinking too much, or going out in the rain without an umbrella all lead to punishing consequences (getting bruised, having a hangover, and getting wet), and we often learn to change our behavior as a result. Furthermore, certain types of undesirable behavior may have far-reaching negative effects if they go unpunished. For instance, an employee who sexually harasses a coworker, a clerk who steals money from the petty cash account, and an executive who engages in illegal stock transactions should all be punished.

When punishment is needed, how is it most effectively meted out and how can its negative consequences be reduced? First, punishment should be applied before the undesired behavior has been strongly reinforced. Thus, punishment should work better the second time an employee is late, rather than the tenth time. Second, the punishment should immediately follow the undesired behavior to emphasize the connection between the behavior and the consequence in the person's mind. Third, punishment should focus on the behavior, not the person; thus, it should be impersonal, consistent across time, and impartial. Finally, the punishment should have as much information value as possible. The employee should know exactly what he or she did to warrant the punishment, the reason why punishment follows such an action, and the consequences of repeating the same behavior.

OTHER MANAGERIAL IMPLICATIONS OF LEARNING

Beyond the day-to-day implications of learning already noted, there are others that relate to more general managerial practice. As shown in Figure 2.5, these implications relate most closely to the areas of motivation, performance evaluation and rewards, and employee training.

Motivation

Motivation is related in several ways to learning. The extent to which valued rewards follow high performance, for example, will affect an employee's willingness to work hard in the future, and the cause-and-effect linkage needs to be clear. That is, employees should recognize that certain behaviors (such as hard work) cause certain outcomes (desired rewards). Similarly, if rewards do not follow performance, an employee may be less inclined to work hard in the future. A lot of research on the learning process in organizations has been done recently. These studies have led to the development of a motivational perspective called organizational behavior modification.[15] This perspective is discussed in Chapter 5.

---

[15] Luthans and Kreitner, *Organizational Behavior Modification and Beyond.*

Figure 2.5

Managerial Implications
of Learning

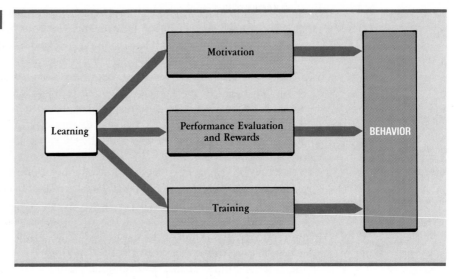

Performance Evaluation and Rewards

Learning also links up with organizational practices in the performance evaluation and reward system. Performance evaluation is how managers assess the work behavior of individuals and groups; rewards are the positive reinforcements (salary, promotion, public recognition) that companies give for desirable behavior.[16] Chapter 19 covers performance evaluation; Chapter 6 discusses rewards.

Training

Learning is the major goal of employee training.[17] Many organizations devote vast resources to training and development to expand the skills and abilities of their employees. Andrew Grove, president of Intel Corporation, heartily believes in the importance of employee training. Intel's employees spend from 2 to 4 percent of their time in the classroom. Much of this training, handled by Intel's own managers, focuses on how employees can benefit the organization while enhancing their own rewards.[18] *International Perspective* describes how one highly successful Japanese company, Honda, approached the training of American workers in plants the company opened in the United States.

---

[16] See Gary P. Latham, "Job Performance and Appraisal," in Cary Cooper and Ivan Robertson, eds., *International Review of Industrial and Organizational Psychology,* Vol. 1 (London: Wiley, 1986), pp. 117–156, for a recent review.

[17] See Kenneth N. Wexley, "Personnel Training," *Annual Review of Psychology,* 1984, pp. 519–553, for a review.

[18] Andrew S. Grove, "Why Training is the Boss's Job," *Fortune,* January 23, 1984, pp. 93–96.

International Perspective

Honda's Approach to Employee Training

Almost everyone is familiar with both the facts and the myths about Japanese automakers. We hear of their fanatical concern for quality, their participative management styles, and their highly motivated and committed work forces. Companies like Nissan, Toyota, and Honda have become major forces in the American automobile industry in a fairly short time and have in recent years begun to manufacture cars on American soil.

No company exemplifies more than Honda the push by Japanese firms into the American marketplace. Honda's Marysville, Ohio, plant builds about one-third of the cars the company sells in the United States, and Honda recently became the first foreign manufacturer to produce all of its cars' major components in this country.

A question long asked by many has been the extent to which American workers can demonstrate the same level of commitment as their Japanese counterparts. To help build this commitment, Honda has gone to extreme lengths to train its American workers in how things need to be done. For example, when a new model of the popular Accord was being introduced, the company flew two hundred American workers representing all parts of the factory to Japan, where the new model was already in production. Working in small groups, the Americans stayed from two weeks to three months observing and learning from their Japanese counterparts. Back at home in Marysville, these employees are given lots of responsibility and are expected to help train others.

Sources: "Honda: Made in the U.S.A.," *Newsweek,* January 19, 1987, p. 42; "Honda is Turning Red, White, and Blue," *Business Week,* October 5, 1987, p. 38; and "Honda Motor Planning Large U.S. Expansion," *Wall Street Journal,* January 9, 1987, p. 2.

Besides motivation, performance evaluation and rewards, and training, there are still other implications that can be drawn from learning theory. First, learning theory can explain certain forms of managerial behavior toward subordinates. Suppose a manager always delivers bad news to subordinates in a certain way. If the subordinates receive the news graciously and constructively, they are giving the manager positive reinforcement, so she will probably use the same mode of delivery in the future. Second, many aspects of the learning process underscore the manager's role as a teacher and the subordinate's role as a learner. Finally, learning processes clearly influence the day-to-day interactions, both official and casual, between people in organizations. Almost everything we do in responding to others, for example, has reinforcing consequences for them.

THE ROLE OF PERCEPTION

Another very important facet of individual behavior in organizations is perception. The introductory incident for this chapter, describing John Malone and TCI, clearly demonstrates both the importance and the complexity of perception.

If everyone perceived everything the same way, things would be a lot simpler (and a lot less exciting!). Of course, just the opposite is true—people perceive the same things in very different ways. The remainder of this chapter is devoted to perception and attribution.

Perception Defined

Perception is the set of the processes by which the individual becomes aware of and interprets information about the environment. A general discussion of behavioral concepts and processes might identify perception as a single process, but it actually consists of several distinct processes. Moreover, in perceiving, we receive information in many guises, from spoken words or visual images to movement and form. Through the perceptual processes, the receiver assimilates the varied types of incoming information for the purpose of interpreting it.

People often tend to assume that reality is objective, that we all perceive the same things in the same way. To test this idea, we could ask students at the Universities of Oklahoma and Nebraska to describe the most recent football game between their schools. We would probably hear two quite conflicting stories. These differences arise primarily because of perception. The fans "saw" the same things but interpreted them in very contrasting ways. Factors underlying these differences are perhaps best explained by the perceptual framework shown in Figure 2.6.[19] An object—another person, an event, an activity—is the focal point for perception. A stimulus makes the individual aware of the object. Next, the object is recognized for what it is. The meaning of the object must then be interpreted. Finally, interpretation triggers a response. Responses may include overt behavior, changes in attitudes, or both.

Perceptual Processes

The framework described in Figure 2.6 is useful in a general introduction to perception. It is also useful, however, to understand more specific characteristics and processes that affect perception. As indicated by Figure 2.7, perception is influenced by characteristics of the object (what is being perceived), characteristics of the person (the perceiver), and situational processes.[20]

---

[19] See Sheldon S. Zalkind and Timothy W. Costello, "Perception: Some Recent Research and Implications for Administration," *Administrative Science Quarterly,* September 1962, pp. 218–235, for a classic review. See Robert G. Lord, "An Information Processing Approach to Social Perceptions, Leadership and Behavioral Measurement in Organizations," in L. L. Cummings and B. M. Staw, eds., *Research in Organizational Behavior,* Vol. 7 (Greenwich, Conn.: JAI Press, 1985), pp. 87–128, for a more recent review.

[20] M. W. Levine and J. M. Shefner, *Fundamentals of Sensation and Perception* (Reading, Mass.: Addison-Wesley, 1981). For recent applications and research, see Georgia T. Chao and Steve W. J. Kozlowski, "Employee Perceptions on the Implementation of Robotic Manufacturing Technology," *Journal of Applied Psychology,*

Figure 2.6

The Perceptual
Framework

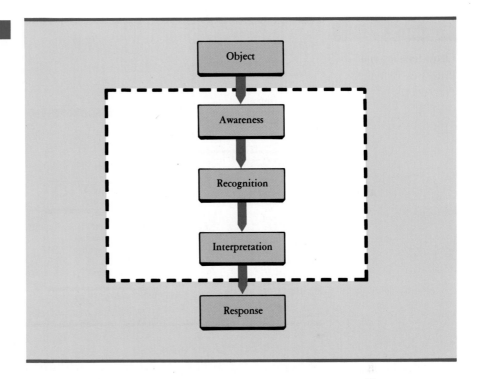

CHARACTERISTICS OF THE OBJECT   Perception is influenced by things about the object that set it apart from its surroundings or cause the perceiver to be more or less aware of it than would otherwise be the case. Such characteristics include contrast, intensity, movement, repetition, and novelty.

If an object in some way contrasts with its surroundings, it is more noticeable. A manager who interviews twenty women and one man for a job will tend to remember the man first simply because he posed such a contrast. Similarly, if one person in an office is dressed very casually and everyone else is dressed very formally, we will be most likely to notice the person in casual attire. Objects may also vary in their intensity—in features such as brightness, color, depth, or sound. For instance, we tend to listen carefully to someone who is yelling—or whispering—because the intensity of the utterance is unusual.

We also tend to focus our attention first on objects that are moving or changing. We notice a flashing neon sign on a dark street, a person walking through a group of standing people, or a single car moving along next to two lanes of stalled traffic. Movement stimulates our awareness of an object before we become aware of its surroundings. Repetition can also increase our awareness

Vol. 71, No. 1, 1986, pp. 70–76; and Steven F. Cronshaw and Robert G. Lord, "Effects of Categorization, Attribution, and Encoding Processes on Leadership Perceptions," *Journal of Applied Psychology,* Vol. 72, No. 1, 1987, pp. 97–106.

Figure 2.7

Characteristics and
Processes That Affect
Perception

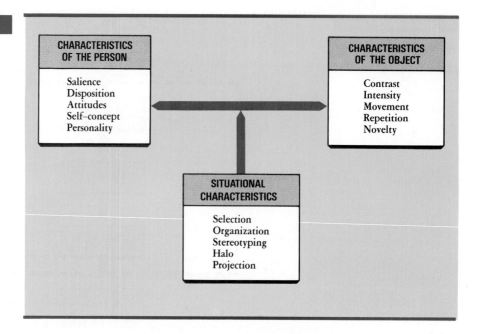

of objects. Most people can recall the most recent advertising jingles for McDonald's and Coca-Cola, because they are repeated over and over on television and the radio. Likewise, if one of our subordinates repeats a request for additional budget support over and over again, we are more likely to remember the request than if it had only been made once.

An object's novelty can also stimulate our perception of it. People wearing unusual clothing, books that have strange covers, and athletic teams with peculiar names all tend to attract our attention. Similarly, we are likely to remember people whose behavior or appearance is unexpected. Hence, a manager who has always worn gray suits to work will be noticed by everyone the day he wears a brown one. Even though the brown suit is not unusual, it is novel for that manager.

For various reasons, managers invest considerable time and energy in shaping how people perceive their organizations, products, and services. For example, most people think of Phillips Petroleum Company as just a petroleum refiner. The company recently undertook a series of commercials to increase people's awareness of other products it has introduced.

CHARACTERISTICS OF THE PERSON   A person's own characteristics also affect how he or she perceives and interprets things. The most important characteristics are salience, disposition, attitudes, self-concept, and personality.[21]

---

[21] Levine and Shefner, *Fundamentals of Sensation and Perception.*

Salience is the individual's feeling about how important the object is. The more salient the object is to you, the more attention you are likely to pay to it. If the local paper this morning contained an article about a dramatic tuition increase at a specific university, students at that university would probably read it carefully. Someone not affiliated with the school, however, might skim right past the article without a second glance. The reason is simple: the information contained in the article would be far more salient to the student than to the other person. Thus a marketing manager for IBM would eagerly read an article about a new advertising campaign by Hewlett-Packard but would probably show significantly less interest in a new stock offering by Sears.

An individual's disposition also affects how he or she perceives things. *Disposition* is a short-term emotional response triggered by various environmental stimuli. Suppose a manager has just been told that she will receive no pay raise next year because of low performance in her work group. Back in her office, no doubt in a lousy mood, she discovers that one of her subordinates has made an error in calculating unit costs. She promptly berates the subordinate for what she perceives as slipshod work. The manager's disposition made her more aware of the subordinate's performance as well as less tolerant of it.

Whereas our disposition tends to be a short-term mood or emotional response, our *attitudes* are longer-lasting feelings about things. Attitudes can affect perceptions in dramatic ways. Consider that when President Reagan was riding a wave of popularity in 1986, *Time* magazine called him "one of the strongest leaders of the 20th century." People had positive attitudes about him and, therefore, saw him in a favorable light. Sixteen months later, when his popularity had eroded because of the Iran-Contra affair, the same publication noted that "the nation calls for leadership and there is no one home" in the White House.[22] Because peoples' attitudes changed, so did their perceptions. Chapter 3 discusses attitudes.

Self-concept can also affect perception. *Self-concept* is a person's perception of himself or herself. A person who has a good self-concept tends to see things in a positive and enriching light. A negative self-concept, on the other hand, can give a person's perceptions an unfavorable or limiting cast.

A final characteristic that influences perception is a person's personality. A person's *personality* is the set of distinctive traits and features that make that person unique. Different personality traits can cause differences in the way individuals recognize and interpret their surroundings. An extrovert, for example, may eagerly respond to conversation. An introvert, in contrast, may be less interested in what others are talking about. There is more detail on personality in Chapter 3.

SITUATIONAL PROCESSES   In a sense, situational processes act as filters. That is, objective information from the environment is interpreted and shaped

---

[22] "Has Reagan Changed?" *Newsweek,* November 23, 1987, p. 20.

as it is perceived by the individual. The individual's cognitions of the environment are influenced, as described earlier, by characteristics of both the object and the individual. Subtle interactions that are unique to particular situations may also occur between person and object. This means that the same object may be perceived differently by the same person in different situations. The major situational processes are selection, organization, attribution, stereotyping, the halo effect, and projection.[23]

Through the process of *selection*, we pay attention to objects we are comfortable with and filter out those that cause us discomfort. A classic study by DeWitt Dearborn and Herbert Simon clearly demonstrated the effects of selection on managerial behavior.[24] Twenty-three executives were asked to read a case describing various problems faced by a company. Afterward, each executive was instructed to identify the case's single most important problem. Almost without exception, the executive's choices reflected their own functional specialties. Five of six marketing executives saw sales as the major problem, and four of five production managers identified production problems. The researchers concluded that the managers' selection process filtered in the problems they were most comfortable with, because of their functional expertise, and filtered out the problems they were less familiar with.

When used to describe an element of perception, the term *organization* refers to our tendency to order our perceptions so that they fit logical, consistent systems of meaning. As with selection, as we organize we often filter out stimuli that do not jibe with our view of reality. Take the case of a manager who believes a particular subordinate is hard working, conscientious, and loyal. One day the manager notices the worker goofing off. Because this perception does not fit into the manager's image of the worker, he may "choose" to see the behavior as a well-earned rest after hard work. Organization also causes us to group and label things. Almost unconsciously, employees develop attitudes about many individual features of the workplace, such as pay, benefits, their supervisor, their coworkers, working conditions, promotion opportunities, and organizational practices. But when asked to describe how they feel about their jobs, employees tend to collapse these attitudes into an overall impression such as "I can't stand it" or "It couldn't be better."

Stereotyping is the process of categorizing people into groups on the basis of certain presumed traits or qualities. Suppose you walk into the reception area of an executive suite. There you notice a man and woman talking beside a secretary's desk. Unfortunately, a typical reaction, owing to a firmly entrenched stereotype, is to assume that the woman is the secretary and the man is the executive. Stereotyping consists of three steps. First, we identify categories by which we will sort people (race, region, sex). Next, we associate attributes with

---

[23] Levine and Shefner, *Fundamentals of Sensation and Perception.*
[24] DeWitt C. Dearborn and Herbert A. Simon, "Selective Perception: A Note on the Departmental Identification of Executives," *Sociometry,* 1958, pp. 140—144.

those categories (athletic ability, speech patterns, occupations). Finally, we infer that all people in certain categories take on the attributes we have decided on (all blacks are athletic; all people from Boston talk funny; all secretaries are women; all people pursuing an MBA are aggressive and career-oriented.) Needless to say, stereotypes are almost always inaccurate.

In recent years, many researchers have studied stereotyping. Much of the research has been on either sex-role or age stereotyping. One study, for example, found that publishing company recruiters clearly assumed that female job applicants were suited for such positions as supervising other women and working as editorial assistants, whereas male applicants were thought to be better suited for jobs such as supervising men and working as editors.[25] Another study found that business students tended to stereotype older workers as less creative, more resistant to change, and less interested in learning new skills.[26]

The halo effect influences our perceptions when we let a single characteristic override our assessment of an individual's other characteristics. For example, if we consider a person friendly and outgoing, we may also assume that the person is diligent, conscientious, and punctual, even though we might be faced with evidence to the contrary. In a classic study conducted in the 1940s, two groups of people were given a list of personality traits and asked to describe the individual portrayed. The two lists were the same, except one contained the word *warm* and the other the word *cold*. This one-word difference led to significantly different descriptions. People working with the list containing the word *warm* said the individual must be humorous, intelligent, and popular. The other group said the person was serious and aloof and did not have many friends.[27] Sometimes people even consciously manipulate their own halos, as shown in *Management in Action,* which describes how executives can make people think they have performed better than they actually have.

Finally, perception may be influenced by the process of projection. *Projection* occurs when we see ourselves in others. If we are aggressive, power hungry, and status conscious, we may rationalize these traits by telling ourselves that everyone else is the same and that to get ahead we must take care of ourselves. We focus on examples of behavior by others that reinforce this view. When a colleague asks for another assistant, we see this request as yet another attempt to build a power base. In reality, of course, power may be the furthest thing from our colleague's mind. The request might even indicate that he is so inefficient that he cannot get his job done by himself. Projection, then, can cause misunderstandings, or worse.

---

[25] S. L. Cohen and K. A. Binker, "Subtle Effects of Sex Role Stereotypes on Recruiters' Hiring Decisions," *Journal of Applied Psychology,* Vol. 60, 1975, pp. 566–572.

[26] B. Rosen and T. H. Jerdee, "The Influence of Age Stereotypes on Managerial Decisions," *Journal of Applied Psychology,* Vol. 61, 1976, pp. 428–432.

[27] S. Asch, "Forming Impressions of Personality," *Journal of Abnormal and Social Psychology,* Vol. 41, 1946, pp. 258–290.

Distorting Reality

After the women's final at [1985's] U.S. Open, spectators waited anxiously: How would Martina Navratilova behave after having just lost to the superior skills of someone else? Would she blame her defeat on the stifling heat? On dubious calls by the judges? On the bad day that even champions are entitled to once in a while? Ms. Navratilova did none of these things. She stepped to the microphones and said: "I did my darndest, but I came up a little short."

Most corporate executives are in the same philosophical camp as Ms. Navratilova. They do their darndest and, if they come up short, accept the result with stoicism and equanimity. They recognize that the principle of pay for performance cuts both ways, that if performance is bad, bonuses have to be reduced, sometimes to zero. But too many executives are a lot less gracious.

First, we have the rationalizers. Having set a profit goal and missed it badly, you hear nothing about how they did their darndest. Instead, you hear why the lousy performance actually was super.

Consider one chief executive who has developed rationalization to a high art. In his company, bonuses are supposed to be based on the budgeted profit for the year. Meet the budget and you get a handsome bonus. Exceed it and you get a marvelous one. Fall short and you still get something unless you fall below 80% of budget; then you're out in the cold. In one recent year, profits came to only 60% of budget. No bonus, right? Wrong.

Our C.E.O., in a four-color, two-projector slide presentation to his board, first noted that labor costs had soared over budget because of an unexpectedly large industry-wide union settlement. The chief executive showed that the company would have achieved 90% of the budgeted profit had the labor settlement come in as expected.

Next, he turned his rhetoric loose on materials prices. Seems the price of the principal ingredient of the company's product has risen when the chief executive had predicted it would fall. Had the

THE ROLE OF ATTRIBUTIONS

Attribution theory, a relatively new addition to the field of organizational behavior, has links to perception, motivation, and leadership.[28] Here we only discuss its implications for perception. (For attribution theory's relationship to motivation and leadership, see Chapters 5 and 11, respectively.)

Fritz Heider and H. H. Kelley are the best known of the scholars who have contributed to what we call **attribution theory**,[29] which suggests, essentially,

---

[28] Cronshaw and Lord, "Effects of Categorization, Attribution, and Encoding Processes;" Mark J. Martinko and William L. Gardner, "The Leader/Member Attribution Process," *Academy of Management Review,* April 1987, pp. 235–249; and Jeffrey D. Ford, "The Effects of Causal Attributions on Decision Makers' Responses to Performance Downturns," *Academy of Management Review,* October 1985, pp. 770–786.

[29] Fritz Heider, *The Psychology of Interpersonal Relations* (New York: Wiley, 1958); and H. H. Kelley, *Attribution in Social Interaction* (Morristown, N.J.: General Learning Press, 1971).

labor settlement come in on budget and materials prices fallen, as predicted, the company would have earned a rather spectacular 115% of the budgeted profit.

The C.E.O. polished off the presentation with a rousing discourse on the fact that the company had just received an unexpected ruling from the Internal Revenue Service that raised its tax bill $10 million. The result: Profits would have come in at 125% of budget had the ruling gone in favor of the company and the other two items not been adverse as well. The board, instead of granting no bonuses to the C.E.O. and his subordinates, authorized an above-normal fund.

Like Babe Ruth, chief executives in this category stand at the plate and point confidently to the center-field bleachers. But their center-field walls have wheels. With a wall that can speed into the infield whenever required, even a pop fly makes history.

A second group of ungracious C.E.O.s is the revisionist historians. These executives aren't going to show you why dismal performance isn't dismal after all. They face up honestly to falling far short. But without a pause they inform you that achieving the profit budget is not really what performance is all about. Instead, they note that return on equity is very high and direct your attention to the fact that even though the company took it on the chin, its competitors are on the mat. Directors, grateful for something to brag about, hand out decent bonuses even though the bonus plan specifies that only budgeted performance is to be considered.

Finally, we have some chief executives who turn logic topsy-turvy. Like Ms. Navratilova, they start out proclaiming, "We did our darndest." But they finish with, "And that's why we should be rewarded." They conveniently forget that bonuses are supposed to be paid for output, not input. They provide the board with heart-tugging anecdotes of how Smith finished the year with an ulcer (doubtless his only tangible accomplishment) and how Jones ended up with a broken marriage (his spouse, on the evidence, is no dummy). Once again, the board comes across with the bucks.

Fortunately, most chief executives preach and practice pay for performance. They do not try to switch to other measures the minute their preferred ones turn sour. They stress long-term accomplishments. And most important, they never confuse input with output.

Source: Excerpted from Graef S. Crystal, "Too Many Make-Any-Excuses C.E.O's," *Fortune,* July 21, 1986, pp. 116–117. Reprinted by permission.

that we observe behavior and then attribute causes to it. That is, we attempt to explain *why* people behave as they do. The process of attribution is based on perceptions of reality, and these perceptions may vary widely from individual to individual.

Figure 2.8 illustrates the basic attribution theory framework. To start the process, we observe behavior, our own or someone else's. We then evaluate the behavior in terms of its degrees of consensus, consistency, and distinctiveness. *Consensus* is the extent to which other people in the same situation behave in the same way. *Consistency* is the extent to which the same person behaves in the same way at different times. *Distinctiveness* is the extent to which the same person behaves in the same way in other situations. As a result of various combinations of consensus, consistency, and distinctiveness, we form impressions or attributions as to the causes of behavior. We may believe that the

Figure 2.8

The Attribution Process

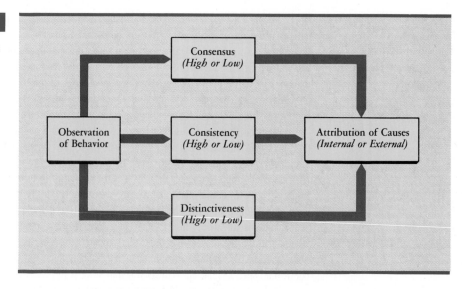

behavior is caused internally (by forces within the person) or externally (by forces in the person's environment).

For example, you might observe that one of your subordinates is being rowdy, disrupting the work of others and generally making a nuisance of herself. If you can understand the causes of this behavior, you may be able to change it. If the employee is the only one engaging in the disruptive behavior (low consensus), if she behaves like this several times each week (high consistency), and if you have seen her behave like this in other settings (low distinctiveness), a logical conclusion you could reach would be that internal factors are causing her behavior.

You might, however, observe a different pattern. Perhaps everyone in the person's work group is rowdy (high consensus), and although the particular employee is often rowdy at work (high consistency), you have never seen her behave this way in other settings (high distinctiveness). This pattern indicates that something in the situation is causing the behavior, that is, that the causes of the employee's behavior are external.

Attributions of behavior have important implications for managers. If we attribute poor performance to internal factors, such as ability or motivation, we will develop certain strategies to improve these factors. On the other hand, if we attribute poor performance to external factors, such as resource constraints or a poorly designed job, we will take different steps to enhance performance. Examples of different alternatives are shown in Table 2.2.

We also make attributions regarding ourselves. If we attribute a pay raise to our hard work, we may continue to work hard. On the other hand, if we

Table 2.2	**Attributions About Success**
Possible Alternative Responses to Different Attributions	Internal Attribution: "Sam is successful because he works hard and has lots of ability."
	Possible Responses: Give Sam positive reinforcement, promote him, hold him up as an example to others.
	External Attribution: "Sam is successful because he has an easy job and a strong work group."
	Possible Responses: Give Sam more work to do, promote some of his work group.
	Attributions About Failure
	Internal Attribution: "Sally is doing a poor job because she lacks ability and motivation."
	Possible Responses: Send Sally to a training program or change the incentive structure.
	External Attribution: "Sally is doing a poor job because she lacks the proper resources and has a weak work group."
	Possible Responses: Increase her resources and strengthen her work group.

think we were given the raise because the boss liked us, we may put more effort into cementing that friendship.

Attribution theory is currently getting a great deal of attention from organizational behavior researchers in the areas of leadership, motivation, performance appraisal, communication, reward systems, and a variety of other fields.[30] It holds considerable promise for increasing our understanding of behavior in organizational settings.

MANAGERIAL IMPLICATIONS OF PERCEPTION

Perception has many implications for managers in organizations, particularly in motivation, hiring, and performance appraisal.

Perception and Motivation

As we discuss in Chapters 4 and 5, perceptions of the workplace play a major role in motivation. Suppose an employee is experiencing some unexpected money trouble. Because of her disposition (she is worried) and the salience of money (it is unusually important to her at the moment), she will be especially sensitive to issues of compensation. Through projection, she may assume that

---

[30] For current examples, see Brendan D. Bannister, "Performance Outcome Feedback and Attributional Feedback: Interactive Effects on Recipient Responses," *Journal of Applied Psychology*, Vol. 71, No. 2, 1987, pp. 203–210; and Dennis A. Gioia and Henry P. Sims, Jr., "Cognition-Behavior Connections: Attribution and Verbal Behavior in Leader-Subordinate Interactions," *Organizational Behavior and Human Decision Processes*, Vol. 37, 1986, pp. 197–229.

everyone in the organization also cares mainly about money. A large pay raise given to another employee will seem frustrating and will intensify her efforts to get a pay raise of her own, focusing even more attention on her own pay, the pay of others, and how they compare to one another.

Obviously, attribution is also relevant to motivation, as suggested earlier. A person who believes her pay raise is attributable to effort (internal) rather than to her being the boss's niece (external) will choose to continue to work hard.

Perception and Hiring

Hiring new employees can be affected by perception in many ways. Contrast or novelty in the job applicant can affect his or her chances of getting the job. The person doing the hiring may stereotype applicants on the basis of race or sex or may allow the halo effect to color an overall perception of an applicant.

An interviewer's disposition during an interview or attitudes toward certain of the applicant's attributes can also affect the interviewer's perceptions of an applicant. For example, a manager with a toothache who believes that people should dress professionally for a job interview is likely to be unimpressed by an applicant who shows up wearing sunglasses and a flowered sport coat.

Perception and Performance Evaluation

Performance evaluation is the assessment of an employee's performance to correct shortcomings, identify strengths, and provide a basis for giving rewards. (Performance evaluation is the topic of Chapter 19.) Several areas of performance evaluation are especially susceptible to perceptual distortion.[31] The contrast between two employees can affect the evaluation. Suppose, for instance, that a manager prepares several performance evaluations of her subordinates in one afternoon, one right after the other. The first two employees receive extremely good evaluations. The next person, however, is only a marginal performer. If the manager is influenced by the high evaluations given to the first two people, the third employee may suffer in comparison. That is, his evaluation may be lower than it would have been if the first two employees had been unsatisfactory workers.

Selection also may affect performance evaluation. When we have a particularly favorable impression of an employee, we may ignore instances of poor performance. The halo effect and stereotyping, too, come into play as do the evaluator's characteristics, such as salience, disposition, and attitudes. In this way, a manager who emphasizes punctuality may weight it heavily as a standard of performance. Another manager may consider punctuality relatively unimportant and may barely mention it in a performance evaluation.

---

[31] Kenneth N. Wexley and Elaine D. Pulakos, "The Effects of Perceptual Congruence and Sex on Subordinates' Performance Appraisals of Their Managers," *Academy of Management Journal,* December 1983, pp. 666–676.

SUMMARY OF KEY POINTS

Learning is a relatively permanent change in behavior or potential behavior that results from direct or indirect experience. Learning is a cognitive process involving experiences and choices about behavior.

Reinforcement theory is the learning perspective most relevent for organizations. Types of reinforcement are positive reinforcement, avoidance, extinction, and punishment. Schedules of reinforcement include continuous, fixed interval, variable interval, fixed ratio, and variable ratio.

Important related aspects of learning are stimulus generalization, stimulus discrimination, vicarious learning, and punishment. Key implications that can be drawn from learning theory bear importantly on motivation, performance evaluation and rewards, and training.

Perception is the set of processes by which individuals become aware of information about their environment. Basic steps involving perception are awareness, recognition, interpretation, and response.

Basic perceptual processes are associated with characteristics of the object being perceived, the person perceiving it, and the situational processes. Characteristics of the object are contrast, intensity, movement, repetition, and novelty. Characteristics of the person include salience, disposition, attitudes, self-concept, and personality. Situational processes are selection, organization, attribution, stereotyping, the halo effect, and projection.

Attribution theory involves the processes by which we perceive and then attribute meaning to the behavior of others. We evaluate such behavior in terms of its consensus, consistency, and distinctiveness and then attribute internal or external causes to it.

Important managerial implications of perception bear on motivation, hiring, and performance evaluation.

DISCUSSION QUESTIONS

1. Can you think of instances when you have been classically conditioned to do something? Describe them.

2. How might an instructor use reinforcement theory to get students to come to class on time, turn in assignments on time, and take proper notes?

3. Think of a local business and imagine you are its manager. How might you use positive reinforcement, avoidance, extinction, and punishment to affect your employees' behavior?

4. In the context of your role as a student, identify examples of each schedule of reinforcement that influence your behavior.

5. Have you ever learned something vicariously? What? Have you ever practiced stimulus generalization or discrimination? In what situation?

6. Do you agree with the chapter's discussion of punishment? Why or why not?

7. Use the perceptual framework from the chapter to describe how you recently perceived something important.

8. Recall and describe recent situations when your perceptions were influenced by salience, disposition, and attitudes.

9. In what ways are selection, organization, and stereotyping different? In what ways are they similar?

10. Can you recall a recent instance in which you made attributions about someone else's behavior? How can you use attribution theory to explain those attributions?

11. How are learning and perception related? That is, how does one affect the other?

Case 2.1   Pillsbury's Learning and Health Center

When most people think of Pillsbury, they think of flour and other baking goods. In reality, however, Pillsbury is much more than just a home for the Doughboy. In addition to its baking goods business, Pillsbury owns Totino's Frozen Pizza; Green Giant Company, the vegetable company; Haagen-Dazs, the premium ice cream maker; and Van de Kamp's frozen entrees business. The company also owns one of the world's largest set of restaurant chains, including Burger King, Godfather's Pizza, Steak & Ale, and several smaller regional chains.

Until 1973, Pillsbury actually was only a small nondescript flour maker. CEO William Spoor began that year with an ambitious plan for growth that led the company to its current position. Accordingly, sales have increased from less than $300 million in 1983 to over $450 million in 1987.

To guard against stagnation and complacency, the Minneapolis-based giant has recently built an innovative and successful program for developing its human resources. Several organizations have in recent years come to recognize the importance of employee physical fitness. Employee fitness centers, some as lavish and comprehensive as private clubs, have become almost common. Pillsbury, though, has gone one step further. The company's human resource managers decided that stretching the mind is as important as stretching the muscles. So they planned and developed a Learning and Fitness Center focusing on the total person. They believe that when employees learn, both the employee and the company benefit.

In particular, the center's founders think that cognitive processes like learning positively affect the individual not only with the knowledge being learned but through improvement in the person's overall ability to think and reason. The center opened in 1985 and occupies 12,400 square feet in Pillsbury's corporate headquarters building. Adjacent to it is a 6,000-square-foot health center and a 1,000-square-foot medical services area.

By almost any set of standards, the Learning Center is top of the line. The physical components of the center include the most comfortable chairs made, a computer-based learning system, individual study carrels, and audio and video cassette hookups. There is also an extensive library, a battery of computers, and a large software selection.

The center is open during normal working hours, as well as several hours before and after. Its stated purpose is to encourage individual learning and self-development. However, the company's training personnel can also use it for training and development programs and seminars.

How well has the center worked? At this point, it is too early to tell. The early evidence, however, looks promising. Employees pay $5 per month to use the entire center. This nominal fee is supposed to build commitment from users, as well as help defray costs of operation. When the center first opened, 650 employees signed up to use it. As of 1986 its enrollment had grown to 3,500. Most of the users report that they think the center is a good idea and that both they and the company have gained from it.

Case Questions

1. Can you identify any elements of learning theory in this case? If so, elaborate.

2. Should other companies adopt Pillsbury's approach to employee learning? How might it be improved and made more effective?

3. Are there any activities at Pillsbury that can be explained by individual perception?

Case Sources

Brian Dumaine, "A CEO Bake-Off at Pillsbury," *Fortune*, November 23, 1987, pp. 109–116; Diana Doshan, "Pillsbury's Learning and Health Center: A Holistic Approach to Employee Development," *Personnel Administrator*, April 1986, pp. 133–141; and Subrata N. Chakravarty, "Pizzas, Anyone? Hamburgers? Trout Amandine?" *Forbes*, September 9, 1985, pp. 74–75.

Case 2.2

Differing Perceptions at Clarkston Industries

Bill Harrington continued to drum his fingers on his desk. He had a real problem, and wasn't sure what to do next. He had a lot of confidence in Jack Reed, but he suspected he was about the last person in the office that did. Perhaps if he ran through the entire story again in his mind he would see the solution . . .

Bill had been distribution manager for Clarkston for almost twenty years. An early brush with the law and a short stay in prison had made him realize the importance of honesty and hard work. Henry Clarkston had given him a chance in spite of his record, and Bill had made the most of it. He was now one of the most respected managers in the company. Few people knew of his background.

Bill had hired Jack Reed fresh out of prison six months ago. Bill understood how Jack felt when he tried to explain his past and asked for another chance. Bill decided to give him that chance, just has Henry Clarkston had given him his. Jack eagerly accepted the job on the loading docks and was soon able to load a truck as fast as anyone else in the crew.

Things had gone well at first. Everyone seemed to like Jack, and he made several new friends. Bill had been vaguely disturbed about two months ago, though, when another dock worker reported her wallet missing. He confronted Jack about it and was pleasantly surprised when Jack understood his concern and earnestly but calmly explained his innocence. Bill was especially relieved when the wallet was found a few days later.

Events of last week, however, had brewed serious trouble. First, a new personnel clerk came across records about Jack's past while updating employee files. Assuming the information was common knowledge, the clerk mentioned to several employees what a good thing it was to give ex-convicts like Jack a chance. The next day, a woman in bookkeeping discovered that some money was missing from petty cash. Another worker claimed to have seen Jack in the area around the office strong box, which was open during working hours, earlier that same day.

Most people assumed Jack was the thief. The worker whose wallet had earlier been misplaced suggested that perhaps Jack had indeed stolen it but had then returned it when questioned. Several employees had approached Bill and requested that Jack be fired. Meanwhile, when Bill had discussed the problem with Jack, he had been defensive and sullen and said little about the situation other than to deny stealing the money.

To Bill's dismay, he found that thinking over the story again did little to solve his problem. Should he fire Jack, he wondered? The evidence, of course, was purely circumstantial. Yet everybody else seemed to see things quite clearly. He feared that if he did not fire Jack, he would lose everyone's trust and that some people might even begin to question his own motives.

Case Questions

1. Can you explain the events in this case in terms of perceptual processes? Identify as many characteristics of the person, the object, and the situation as possible.

2. What should Bill do?

Experiential Exercise

Purpose: This exercise will give you insights into the problems and mechanisms of providing reinforcement to people.

Format: Your instructor will divide the class into groups of three. Each group will develop a reinforcement system that the instructor might use to reinforce student behavior in the classroom.

Procedure: First, develop a list of desirable and undesirable behaviors that students might exhibit in the classroom. Second, identify various kinds of reinforcement that the instructor might use to increase the frequency of the desired behaviors and decrease the undesired behaviors. Next, develop appropriate schedules for the various kinds of reinforcement. Your instructor will then select a few groups at random to present their systems to the rest of the class. (A variation might involve having a member from a group role-play an instructor using the reinforcement system developed by his or her group.)

Follow-Up Questions

1. How useful do you think your system would actually be if your instructor used it?
2. How much easier or more difficult would it be to do the same thing in a work setting?

CHAPTER
3

Individual Differences

Chapter Objectives

After reading this chapter, you should be able to

- describe the nature of individual differences.
- discuss personality and individual differences.
- discuss attitudes and attitude formation.
- identify and describe job-related attitudes.

- relate attitudes to behaviors.
- summarize the managerial implications of individual differences.

H. Ross Perot liked to be in charge. He founded Electronic Data Systems (EDS) because he hated working for someone else. EDS eventually became one of the largest computer service firms in the world. Along the way, Perot acquired a reputation for flamboyance and independence.

It came as somewhat of a surprise when Perot sold EDS to staid General Motors in 1984. In return for EDS, the mammoth automaker gave Perot enough stock to make him the corporation's largest stockholder and also granted him a seat on the board of directors. At the time, many observers wondered how Perot would fit in at GM.

It didn't take long to find out. Perot simply couldn't suppress his need to be in control, and he voiced his opinions far and wide. He saw many things at General Motors that were, in his opinion, in need of repair. He criticized the company's management philosophies, strategies, and organization. Charging that the company was inefficient in its operations, he argued against its bonus program. Finally, GM reached its breaking point. Perot was bought out in 1987 for $700 million. Even then, he announced to GM stockholders that the company had paid too much to get rid of him![1]

*P*erot's story offers many insights into organizational behavior, especially in terms of individual differences. General Motors has long been noted as a company that allows little room for individuality. Its employees are always expected to do things the "GM way." H. Ross Perot, however, is so strong-willed that he was unable to adapt to the GM approach. He just could not function effectively within the GM system.

This chapter is about differences among individuals. Simply stated, it focuses on key dimensions that distinguish people from one another. While learning and perception vary from person to person, even stronger differences exist in personalities and attitudes among people.

First we fully explore the nature of individual differences, then describe the role of personality in individual differences. Next we address the nature of attitudes and their effect on individuals, following up with a discussion of several important job-related attitudes. Finally, we relate attitudes to behaviors and summarize several important managerial implications.

THE NATURE OF INDIVIDUAL DIFFERENCES

Each person is much like everyone else in many important ways. Our biological systems, for example, are all quite similar, as is our basic appearance. Each person is also very different from everyone else, however. The ways we think,

---

[1] Thomas Moore, "Make-or-Break Time for General Motors," *Fortune,* February 15, 1988, pp. 32–42.

Figure 3.1

The Uniqueness of
People

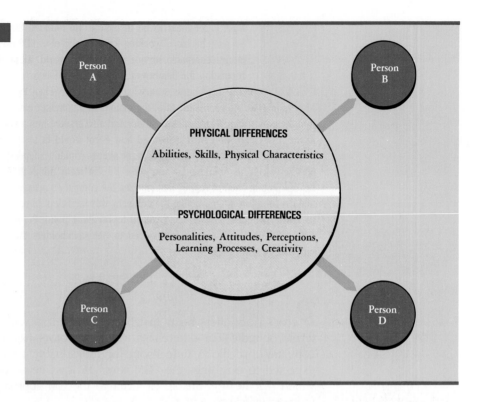

PHYSICAL DIFFERENCES

Abilities, Skills, Physical Characteristics

PSYCHOLOGICAL DIFFERENCES

Personalities, Attitudes, Perceptions,
Learning Processes, Creativity

Person
A

Person
B

Person
C

Person
D

the ways we interpret our environment, and the ways we respond to that environment are unique. We call this set of factors **individual differences.**

People Are Unique

People are like jigsaw puzzles. Just as a puzzle is a picture assembled by putting various pieces together in a certain way, a person is composed of various attributes fitted together in a certain way. Just as puzzles have pieces that fit together to form a whole, each of us has a unique set of attributes, or characteristics, that together represent the essence of what we are. Furthermore, although a person may resemble some people more than others, no two persons are exactly alike.

Figure 3.1 shows several of the most common attributes that differentiate people from one another. Some differences are physical and others are psychological. As previously noted, our focus here is on two critical psychological variables: personality and attitudes.

People and Situations

People do not function independently of their environment or the situation in which they find themselves. Situational differences can affect how people respond in a variety of ways. Consider a typical manager working for a large company. His attitudes and behaviors have always been essentially positive and he has been effective on the job. One day, however, his life takes a major change in direction. He gets a big promotion, he gets terminated because of a major cutback, or he and his wife decide to divorce. Any of these changes will place him in a quite different situation, and as a result his attitudes and behaviors may change. He may become happier, more upbeat, and work even harder than in the past. Or he may become moody, depressed, and withdrawn.

Our individuality is partially shaped by our environment. Groups of people in one situation behave differently than do similar groups in other situations. For example, *International Perspective* shows that workers in the United States and England see some features of their respective workplaces in very similar ways but see other features quite differently. Likewise, an individual person whose situation changes will also respond differently to the new situation than he or she did to the old one.

AN OVERVIEW OF PERSONALITY

One critical component of individual differences is a person's personality. We can define **personality** as the set of distinctive traits and characteristics that can be used to compare and contrast individuals.[2] In the next few pages we take a close look at the determinants of an individual's personality and then relate personality to the workplace.

The Nature of Personality

The word *personality* is one of the most misused in our language. When you describe someone as having "no personality," you mean that they have a particular kind of personality: one that is bland and colorless. When you describe a friend as having a "good personality," you mean that she is warm, friendly, and outgoing.

Why is the concept of personality important to managers? Although not everyone agrees, personality seems to play a major role in how a person perceives his or her work environment, evaluates it, and responds to it. The concept of interactional psychology we introduce in Chapter 1 relates directly to this assertion.[3] Interactional psychology suggests that individual behavior is a function of continuous interaction between the person and the situation.

---

[2] See Walter Mischel, *Introduction to Personality* (New York: Holt, 1971), for a classic treatment; and Lawrence Pervin, "Personality" in Mark Rosenzweig and Lyman Porter, eds., *Annual Review of Psychology*, Vol. 36 (Palo Alto, Calif.: Annual Reviews, 1985), pp. 83–114, for a recent review.

[3] James Terborg, "Interactional Psychology and Research on Human Behavior in Organizations," *Academy of Management Review*, October 1981, pp. 569–576.

International Perspective

Individual Differences in the United States and England

We all know that each of us is different from everyone else. Some of us see the world one way, while others have a different outlook altogether. Some are motivated by one set of factors, and others work for other reasons. Recent research has begun to examine how these differences vary across national boundaries.

P. Christopher Earley, an American professor, recently began to examine patterns of individual differences among American and British workers. In one study, he looked at what happens when workers receive information from their supervisor as opposed to their union shop steward. He also examined how the nature of the information affected their reactions.

His study was restricted to sixty American and sixty British workers in automobile tire manufacturing plants. He found that the basic processes surrounding goal setting and goal acceptance were the same for both samples. However, in the British sample, information had a much greater impact when it came from the shop steward instead of the supervisor. For American workers, where the information came from made no difference.

In another study, Earley examined the usefulness of performance feedback in shaping American and British workers' behaviors. Again, differences were found. For example, American workers responded favorably to both praise and criticism, whereas British workers responded favorably only to praise.

The bare-bones explanation for these findings has to do with employee attitudes toward management. While the union-management relationship in the United States has not always been positive, it has been considerably less hostile than in England. Thus, American workers are likely to have at least moderately positive attitudes toward their supervisors and to respond favorably to them. British workers, in contrast, are more likely to hold hostile attitudes toward their supervisors. Consequently, they may respond less favorably to information and feedback they get from the boss.

Sources: P. Christopher Earley, "Supervisors and Shop Stewards as Sources of Contextual Information in Goal Setting: A Comparison of the United States with England," *Journal of Applied Psychology,* Vol. 71, 1986, pp. 111–117; and P. Christopher Earley, "Trust, Perceived Importance of Praise and Criticism, and Work Performance: An Examination of Feedback in the United States and England," *Journal of Management,* Winter 1986; pp. 457–474.

Characteristics of the person—each a manifestation of personality—influence and are influenced by various factors in the workplace. For example, a person with a strong desire for status will analyze her work setting in terms of its opportunities to gain more status. She will view the situation as either facilitating or hindering the acquisition of status. And depending on the level of status achieved, such an employee may want even more status in the future, leave the situation in frustration, or be at least temporarily satisfied.

Figure 3.2

Personality Formation

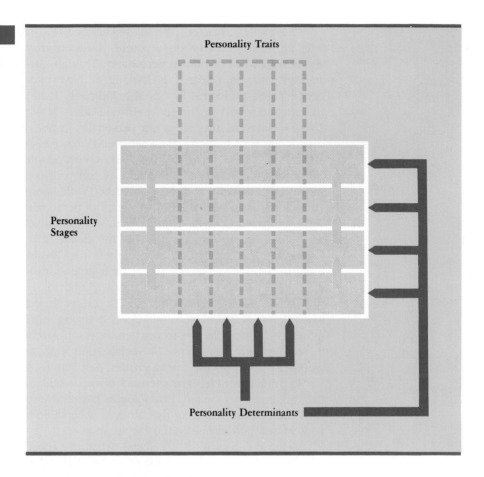

Personality Traits

Personality Stages

Personality Determinants

Personality Formation

Comparing individual differences to a jigsaw puzzle leaves an important question unanswered: What is the source of the pieces and their interrelationships? In other words, how is a person's personality formed? Although we do not have all the answers, the prevailing opinion, as shown in Figure 3.2, suggests that personality formation is best understood from the standpoint of three factors: determinants, stages, and traits.[4]

DETERMINANTS   A determinant of personality is a key objective variable that plays a role in determining a person's personality. The most widely studied determinants are biological factors, social factors, and cultural factors.

---

[4] Mischel, *Introduction to Personality.* See also Robert G. L. Pryor, "Differences Among Differences: In Search of General Work Preference Dimensions," *Journal of Applied Psychology,* August 1987, pp. 426–433.

One biological factor to be studied has been the extent to which personality traits are inherited from one's parents. Genetics may influence the formation and development of human personality. Though questions greatly outnumber answers, current research is looking at how biological factors affect our personalities. Biological factors also indirectly influence personality. Physical characteristics such as height and build affect how we feel about ourselves. These feelings, in turn, affect our personality. A person who is teased because she is considerably shorter than her friends may feel defensive about her height and choose activities particularly suited to short people—gymnastics rather than basketball, for example. But scientists today discount an early theory that suggested personality is directly correlated with a person's overall body shape.[5]

Social factors also are a determinant of personality. Our early experiences with our parents play a major role in our later lives. For example, children who suffer major traumas such as the death of a parent may experience emotional repercussions throughout their lives. As children grow, they develop friendship groups at school and in their neighborhoods. The kinds of people they interact with may influence their own behavior. For instance, a child whose own family is not religious but who develops close friendships with children whose families are religious may develop strong religious beliefs. Nor does the influence of social factors stop when a person reaches adulthood. Indeed, an increasing body of literature on socialization suggests that social forces in the workplace affect people's personalities, perceptions, and behaviors.[6]

Cultural factors are characteristics of the broader, sociocultural environment that influences personality. Psychologists have only recently begun to investigate these factors, but it is clear that motives, acceptable behaviors, and respect for authority vary from one country to another.

Cultural factors influence social dynamics. The English and Germans, for example, stand farther apart when talking than do Americans, whereas Arabs, Japanese, and Mexicans stand closer together. Culture also instills values. A strong sense of competitiveness may characterize people from some cultures, while those from others may be more comfortable with cooperation.[7]

In addition to the biological, social, and cultural determinants of personality, situational factors also affect personality, often in unpredictable or unknown ways. These may shape personality or bring out hidden characteristics. A good example of situational influences is the research of Stanley Milgram.[8] Milgram

---

[5] William H. Sheldon. *Atlas to Men: A Guide for Somatotyping the Adult Male at All Ages* (New York: Harper, 1954).

[6] John P. Wanous, Arnon E. Reichers, and S. D. Malik, "Organizational Socialization and Group Development: Toward an Integrative Perspective," *Academy of Management Review,* October 1984, pp. 670–683, provide a thorough review of the socialization literature.

[7] Nancy J. Adler, *International Dimensions of Organizational Behavior* (Boston: Kent, 1986).

[8] Stanley Milgram, "Some Conditions of Obedience and Disobedience to Authority," *Human Relations,* February 1965, pp. 57–76.

asked subjects to administer what they believed to be an electric shock to a person in another room. As the shocks became stronger, the other person began to scream in pain and beg the subject to stop. The experimenter, however, ordered the subject to continue. More than half the subjects were willing, when ordered, to administer a shock clearly labeled as dangerous and possibly life threatening.

The results of this and follow-up studies indicated that people have personality characteristics that are revealed only in specific situations. Real-life examples range from people who spontaneously perform heroic acts without thinking of their own personal welfare to people who engage in unethical or illegal behavior when under extreme pressure. As with culture, research into the situational determinants of personality is still in its infancy.

STAGES   A second major approach to personality formation considers each person's personality as developing in stages. The major proponents of stage approaches are Sigmund Freud, Erik Erikson, and Jean Piaget.

The pioneer of psychoanalytic theory, Freud argued that behavior is primarily caused by unconscious motives.[9] These motives are shaped by a variety of stages of personality development, each of which has sexual undertones. According to Freud, the four stages of personality development are dependent, compulsive, oedipal, and mature. The precise stages suggested by Freud, however, are not generally accepted by contemporary theorists.

Erik Erikson accepted the Freudian concept of personality stages but rejected Freud's stages as being too heavily slanted toward biological and sexual factors.[10] Instead, Erikson focused on the social adaptations people have to make as they grow older. He argued that we progress through eight basic stages of development, including such phases as mouth and senses (stage 1), latency (stage 4), early adulthood (stage 6), and mature adulthood (stage 8). The progression from one stage to the next is marked by a crisis. Healthy personality development is said to depend on the extent to which the individual copes effectively with each crisis. In organizational settings, parallels to Erikson's stages may appear in the form of the crises people pass through as they move from being a newcomer to being a mature and then a senior member of the organization.

Like Freud, Jean Piaget suggested that we pass through stages of personality development.[11] However, Piaget believed that the stages and the progressions between them are conscious activities. The precise stages suggested by Piaget are not specifically relevant to organizational settings. His more important

---

[9] Sigmund Freud, "Lecture XXXIII," *New Introductory Lectures on Psychoanalysis* (New York: Norton, 1933), pp. 153–186.

[10] Erik Erikson, *Childhood and Society,* 2nd ed. (New York: Norton, 1963).

[11] Jean Piaget, "The General Problems of the Psychological Development of the Child," in J. M. Tanner and B. Inhelder (Eds.), *Discussions on Child Development* (New York: International Universities Press, 1960), pp. 3–27.

contribution for our purposes was the argument that the conscious elements of personality formation are at least as important as the unconscious elements. Of the three stage approaches, the work of Piaget is perhaps best supported by empirical research.[12]

In terms of the organizational behavior, the main thing to be learned from these perspectives is the notion of development. As time passes, people change, and they change in ways that are at least somewhat predictable, rather than purely random and unstable. Furthermore, change is seen as healthy and desirable for both the person and the social system. More than likely, both conscious and unconscious stages, all marked with various crises of transition, typify most employees as they enter, participate in, and eventually leave organizations.

TRAITS   Trait approaches to personality formation try to identify a configuration of traits that best reflect personality. The most widely known of the trait theorists are Gordon Allport and Raymond Cattell.

Gordon Allport, a noted psychologist, suggested that everyone has a set of common personality traits, but that individuals also have and can be differentiated by a set of unique traits, called personal dispositions.[13] Allport's common traits include social, political, religious, and esthetic propensities. By definition, personal dispositions vary from one person to the next. For instance, one person might be very outgoing and friendly but not interested in politics. A second person, on the other hand, might be withdrawn but fascinated by politics.

Raymond Cattell, another pioneering psychologist, also advocated a trait framework for understanding personality.[14] In his view, everyone can be described and characterized along two specific sets of personality traits, or dimensions. Surface traits reflect the observable and consistent behaviors of people (honest or dishonest, warm or cold). Source traits (trusting or suspicious, mature or immature, dominant or submissive) are more difficult to discern because we often keep them hidden.

ARGYRIS'S MATURITY-IMMATURITY MODEL   In addition to the various theories and models of personality formation developed by psychologists, there is a model of personality formation developed specifically for the context of organizational behavior. Chris Argyris has proposed a model of the workplace personality that combines the stage and trait approaches.[15] His model, summarized in Table 3.1, focuses almost exclusively on people in organizational settings. According to Argyris, an individual's personality develops from immature to mature along seven basic dimensions. Argyris suggests that as people

---

[12] Mischel, *Introduction to Personality.*

[13] Gordon Allport, *Pattern and Growth in Personality* (New York: Holt, 1961).

[14] Raymond Cattell, *The Scientific Analysis of Personality* (Chicago: Aldine, 1965).

[15] Chris Argyris, *Personality and Organization* (New York: Harper & Row, 1957).

Table 3.1	Immature Characteristics	Mature Characteristics
Argyris's Maturity–Immaturity Model	Passive ————————————→	Active
	Dependent ————————————→	Independent
	Few Behaviors ————————————→	Many Behaviors
	Shallow Interests ————————————→	Deep Interests
	Short-Term Perspective ————————————→	Long-Term Perspective
	Subordinate Position ————————————→	Superordinate Position
	Little Self-Awareness ————————————→	More Self-Awareness and Control

Source: Adapted from page 50 in *Personality and Organization: The Conflict Between System and the Individual* by Chris Argyris. Copyright © 1957 by Harper & Row, Publishers, Inc. Reprinted by permission of the publisher.

gain experience and self-confidence in their jobs, they tend to move from the immature end to the mature end of each dimension. Thus, they move from passive to active, from having short-term perspectives to developing long-term perspectives, and so forth. Unfortunately, Argyris contends, organizations are typically designed to foster and reward immaturity and to stifle and punish maturity. If he is correct, then a basic conflict exists between people and the organizations in which they work.

Personality and Work

The most direct applications of personality theory for the field of organizational behavior have been through the identification and study of several traits that have direct relevance for the workplace. Three widely studied traits are locus of control, authoritarianism, and self-monitoring.

LOCUS OF CONTROL   *Locus of control* is the extent to which a person believes that his or her behavior has a direct impact on the consequences of that behavior.[16] Some people believe they can control what happens to them— that if they work hard, for instance, they will be successful. These people, called internals, are said to have an internal locus of control. Externals, or people who have an external locus of control, tend to think that what happens to them is a function of fate or luck. They see little or no connection between their own behavior and subsequent events. Like attribution theory, locus of control concepts focus on people's interpretations of what happens to them.

Locus of control concepts have some significant managerial implications. Internals are likely to want a voice in how they perform their jobs because they

[16] J. B. Rotter, "Generalized Expectancies for Internal vs. External Control of Reinforcement," *Psychological Monographs,* Vol. 80, 1966, pp. 1–28. See also Paul Spector, "Behavior in Organizations as a Function of Employee's Locus of Control," *Psychological Bulletin,* Vol. 91, No. 3, 1982, pp. 482–497; and Marilyn E. Gist, "Self-Efficacy: Implications for Organizational Behavior and Human Resource Management," *Academy of Management Review,* July 1987, pp. 472–485.

believe that what happens to them will depend on how well they control their environment. Externals, in contrast, may be less inclined to participate in decision making. A good example of an internal in business is Harry Gray, former chief executive officer of United Technologies Corp. In his years at UTC, Gray consistently sought to control his environment through such techniques as grooming potential successors and then driving them off with pressure tactics, dictating corporate policy from the executive suite, and going to unusual lengths to ensure that things would always be done his way.[17] Of course, not all internals are so extreme; many simply want a voice in determining what happens to them.

AUTHORITARIANISM   *Authoritarianism* is the extent to which a person believes that power and status differences should exist within a social system like an organization.[18] The stronger the belief, the more authoritarian the individual is said to be.

The literature on authoritarianism holds several helpful implications for managers. Subordinates who are highly authoritarian may be more willing to accept a directive style of supervision; they are also less likely to argue with a manager's suggestions. Researchers have also found some interesting tie-ins between the authoritarian personality and the Milgram studies summarized earlier. In particular, highly authoritarian people are more likely to obey orders from someone with authority without raising any serious objections, even if they recognize potential dangers or pitfalls.

SELF-MONITORING   *Self-monitoring,* a fairly new concept,[19] is the extent to which people emulate the behavior of others. A person who is a high self-monitor tends to pay close attention to the behaviors of others and to model his or her own behavior after that of the people observed. A high self-monitor might note the way a colleague acts when talking to the boss and then attempt to imitate this behavior when she or he next interacts with the boss.

A person who is low on the self-monitoring dimension pays considerably less attention to the behavior of others. Such a person tends to react to situations without looking to others for behavioral cues. The study of self-monitoring is just beginning, but the construct appears to have potential as a meaningful contribution to the literature on personality.[20]

---

[17] Geoffrey Colvin, "Why Harry Gray Can't Let Go at United Technologies," *Fortune,* November 12, 1984, pp. 16–19; and "Coming Attractions," *Fortune,* February 15, 1988, pp. 119–120.

[18] T. W. Adorno, E. Frenkel-Brunswik, D. J. Levinson, and R. N. Sanford, *The Authoritarian Personality* (New York: Harper & Row, 1950).

[19] Mark Snyder and Nancy Cantor, "Thinking About Ourselves and Others: Self-Monitoring and Social Knowledge," *Journal of Personality and Social Psychology,* Vol. 39, No. 2, 1980, pp. 222–234.

[20] Mark Snyder, Steve Gangestad, and Jeffrey A. Simpson, "Choosing Friends as Activity Partners: The Role of Self-Monitoring," *Journal of Personality and Social Psychology,* November 1983, pp. 1061–1071; and Aron W. Siegman and Mark A.

OTHER TRAITS   In addition to the three key traits just described, several other traits may also apply to organization behavior. Self-esteem, recognized as an important personality trait in recent years, is the extent to which a person believes that he or she is a worthwhile and deserving individual. Recent studies have linked self-esteem to job performance, job satisfaction, and the job search process. For example, a person with high self-esteem may be likely to seek a higher-status job, whereas a person with low self-esteem may be satisfied with the status quo.[21] Likewise, higher levels of self-esteem might lead to higher levels of performance and satisfaction from having attained that performance.

Besides self-esteem, certain traits that may be important for managers include how willing a person is to make a risky decision; a person's degree of motivation to accomplish his or her own selfish ends; and a person's tendency to be withdrawn, outgoing, open-minded, or intolerant.

ATTITUDES AND ATTITUDE FORMATION

Another individual difference of utmost importance to managers is employee attitudes. We sometimes speak of "attitude problems" or say that someone has a "bad attitude." But what is an attitude? How is one formed? What *is* a "bad attitude" or an "attitude problem"? This section attempts to provide some insight into these questions. After a summary of the dispositional and situational perspectives on attitudes, we address the processes involved in attitude formation. We conclude the section by explaining the concepts of cognitive dissonance and attitude change.

The Dispositional View

Historically, attitudes were viewed as stable dispositions to behave toward objects in a certain way as a result of experience.[22] For any number of reasons, a person might decide that he or she did not like a particular political figure or a certain restaurant (a disposition). That person would then be expected to express consistently negative opinions of the candidate or restaurant and to maintain the consistent and predictable intention of not voting for the political

---

Reynolds, "Self-Monitoring and Speech in Feigned and Unfeigned Lying," *Journal of Personality and Social Psychology,* December 1983, pp. 1325–1333.

[21] Phyllis Tharenou and Phillip Harker, "Moderating Influences of Self-Esteem on Relationships Between Job Complexity, Performance, and Satisfaction," *Journal of Applied Psychology,* November 1984, pp. 623–632; and Rebecca A. Ellis and M. Susan Taylor, "Role of Self-Esteem Within the Job Search Process," *Journal of Applied Psychology,* November 1983, pp. 632–640.

[22] Gordon W. Allport, "Attitudes," in C. Murchison, ed., *Handbook of Social Psychology* (Worcester, Mass.: Clark University Press, 1935), pp. 798–844. See Barry Gerhart, "How Important Are Dispositional Factors as Determinants of Job Satisfaction? Implications for Job Design and Other Personnel Programs," *Journal of Applied Psychology,* August 1987, pp. 366–373.

Figure 3.3

The Dispositional View
of Attitudes

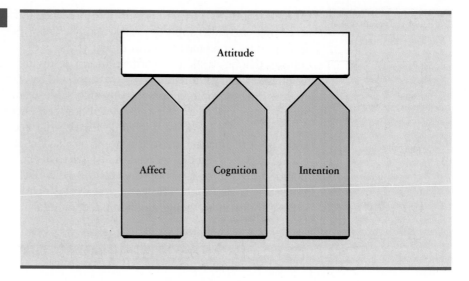

candidate or patronizing the restaurant. In the traditional **dispositional view of attitudes,** illustrated in Figure 3.3, attitudes are composed of three components: affect, cognition, and intention.

AFFECT   *Affect* refers to the individual's feelings toward something. In many ways, affect is similar to emotion—it is something we have little or no conscious control over. For example, most people react to words such as love, hate, sex, and war in a manner that reflects their feelings about what those words convey. In a similar way, you may like one of your classes, dislike another, and be indifferent toward a third. If the class you dislike is an elective, you may not be particularly concerned. But if it is the first course in your chosen major, your affective reaction may cause you considerable anxiety.

COGNITION   The *cognitive* component of an attitude is the knowledge a person presumes to have about something. You may believe you like a class because the textbook is excellent, it meets at your favorite time, the instructor is outstanding, and the workload is light. This "knowledge" may be true, partially true, or totally false. For example, you may intend to vote for a particular candidate because you think you know where she stands on several issues. In reality, depending on the candidate's honesty and your understanding of her statements, her thinking on the issues may be exactly the same as yours, partly the same as yours, or totally different. Cognitions are based on perceptions of truth and reality, and as we noted in Chapter 2, perceptions have varying degrees of agreement with reality.

INTENTION   *Intention* guides your behavior toward something. If you like your instructor, you may intend to take another class from him next semester.

Figure 3.4   The Situational View of Attitudes

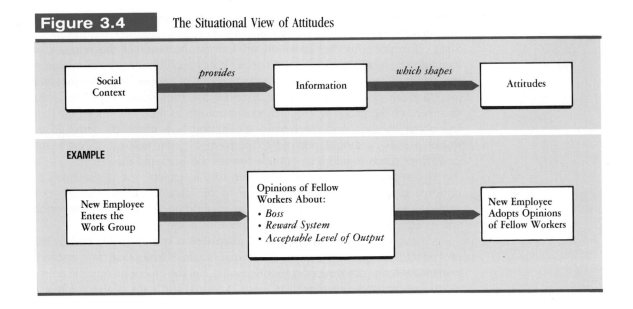

Intentions are not always translated into actual behavior, however. For example, if the instructor's course next semester is scheduled for 8:00 A.M., you might decide that another teacher is just as good! Some attitudes, and their corresponding intentions, are much more central and significant to an individual than others. A person may intend to do one thing (take a particular class), but later alter his or her intentions because of a more significant and central attitude (fondness for sleeping late).[23]

The Situational View

The dispositional view of attitudes has recently been challenged by Gerald Salancik and Jeffrey Pfeffer.[24] They contend that research has not clearly demonstrated that attitudes are stable dispositions composed of precise components that are consistently reflected in individual responses. Instead, they argue, attitudes evolve from socially constructed realities. Figure 3.4 illustrates the situational view.

Salancik and Pfeffer believe the social context delivers information that

---

[23] Bobby J. Calder and Paul H. Schurr, "Attitudinal Processes in Organizations," in Larry L. Cummings and Barry M. Staw, eds., *Research in Organizational Behavior,* Vol. 3 (Greenwich, Conn.: JAI Press, 1981), pp. 283–302.

[24] Gerald Salancik and Jeffrey Pfeffer, "An Examination of Need-Satisfaction Models of Job Attitudes," *Administrative Science Quarterly,* Vol. 22, 1977, pp. 427–456; and Gerald Salancik and Jeffrey Pfeffer, "A Social Information Processing Approach to Job Attitudes and Task Design," *Administrative Science Quarterly,* Vol. 23, 1978, pp. 224–253.

shapes the individual's attitudes. By means of cues and guides, social information provides a specific prescription for socially acceptable attitudes and behaviors. Such information focuses attention on specific attributes of the setting (for example, the workplace), thus making behaviors and attitudes that dominate in that setting more salient (important to the individual). Suppose a new employee joins a work group that has been together for some time. Very likely, the members of the group will quickly communicate to the newcomer how they feel about the boss and the reward system and how much effort the group thinks members should put out to perform a given task. As a result, the newcomer tends to adopt an attitude toward the boss and the reward system that is consistent with what she has been told to expect. She is also likely to perform at a level of effort acceptable to the group. The new employee's attitudes and behaviors, then, have been partly shaped by social information and its effects on the individual's perception of reality.

Although the **situational view of attitudes** is comparatively new, it has proved interesting to researchers and managers alike.[25] In general, most research provides at least partial support for this model, but the emerging opinion seems to be that attitudes are shaped by both objective attributes of the workplace and social information. (This perspective will be discussed from another viewpoint in Chapter 8.)

Cognitive Dissonance

Cognitive dissonance is the anxiety a person experiences when two sets of knowledge or perceptions are contradictory or incongruent. Cognitive dissonance also occurs when a person behaves in a fashion that is inconsistent with her or his attitudes.[26] For example, a person may realize that smoking and overeating are dangerous yet continue to do both. Because the attitudes and behaviors are not consistent with each other, the person will probably experience tension and discomfort and may engage in **dissonance reduction**—seeking ways to reduce the dissonance and the tension it causes. The dissonance associated with smoking might be resolved by rationalizing "Just a pack a day won't affect my health," or "I can quit when I have to." With regard to overeating, the person might decide to go on a diet "next week." In general, then, the person attempts to change the attitude, change the behavior, or perceptually distort the circumstances to reduce tension and discomfort.

A classic study by Barry M. Staw provided a very insightful example of the processes of dissonance reduction.[27] His subjects were male college students

---

[25] Ricky W. Griffin, "Toward an Integrated Theory of Task Design," in Larry L. Cummings and Barry M. Staw, eds., *Research in Organizational Behavior,* Vol. 9 (Greenwich, Conn.: JAI Press, 1987, pp. 79–120.

[26] Leon Festinger, *A Theory of Cognitive Dissonance* (Palo Alto, Calif.: Stanford University Press, 1957).

[27] Barry M. Staw, "Attitudinal and Behavioral Consequences of Changing a Major

who joined the Reserve Officers Training Corps (ROTC) between 1969 and 1971. During that turbulent period, many male students joined ROTC to avoid being drafted and sent to serve in the Vietnam War. The legally binding commitment to ROTC involved on-campus military training while in college and a commission in the reserve forces after graduation. Just after this period, the Selective Service Administration instituted an annual lottery to determine who would be drafted. Each lottery number corresponded to a birthday; the lower the lottery number, the higher the odds of being drafted.

Staw reasoned that ROTC students whose lottery numbers were high enough to keep them out of the draft would begin to experience cognitive dissonance. That is, they had made a commitment that turned out to be unnecessary. He predicted that those who received low numbers would experience less dissonance because their commitment continued to serve its intended purpose, namely to spare them active duty in the military. Staw asked a group of ROTC students to fill out questionnaires designed to measure their satisfaction with the ROTC program. As predicted, students with high lottery numbers—that is, those who now had the least to gain by being in the program—indicated the most satisfaction. They apparently used satisfaction as a reason to justify their ROTC commitment, given that it no longer served its original purpose.

Cognitive dissonance affects people in a variety of ways. We frequently encounter situations in which our attitudes conflict with our behaviors or with each other. Dissonance reduction is the way we deal with these feelings of discomfort and tension. In organizational settings, people contemplating leaving the organization may wonder why they continue to stay and work hard—as a result of this dissonance, they may conclude that the company is not so bad after all, that they have no immediate options elsewhere, or that they will leave "soon."

Attitude Change

How can managers initiate attitude change among employees? Suppose that employees are greatly dissatisfied with their pay; it may be necessary to change this attitude to prevent a mass exodus of valuable employees. One approach would be to inform employees that the organization is paying all it can now but hopes to increase wages in the near future. Another would be to demonstrate that no other organization pays more. A third way to change the attitudes would be to actually increase wages, thus eliminating the cause of the attitude. Employee attitude change is the goal of many organizational change and development techniques, which we discuss in Chapters 22 and 23.

Organizational Reward: A Natural Field Experiment," *Journal of Personality and Social Psychology,* Vol. 9, 1974, pp. 742–751.

JOB-RELATED ATTITUDES

Attitudes are an important consideration for managers. Employee attitudes may be related to behaviors critical to the organization—dissatisfied employees, for instance, are more likely to be absent from work or to leave for better opportunities elsewhere. Negative attitudes toward the organization can also spur employees to consider forming or joining a labor union. Theory and research on attitudes can help managers understand employee attitudes about the workplace. In general, employees develop consistent and identifiable sets of attitudes toward such job attributes as pay, working conditions, and the job's tasks.

Job Satisfaction

Job satisfaction or dissatisfaction—an individual's attitude toward his or her job—is undoubtedly one of the most widely studied variables in the entire field of organizational behavior. When this attitude is positive, employees are said to be satisfied. Dissatisfaction exists when the attitude is negative.

Literally thousands of studies have been published that deal with some aspect of job satisfaction.[28] Obviously, all managers should be concerned about the satisfaction or dissatisfaction of their employees.

Figure 3.5 summarizes the primary causes and consequences of job satisfaction and dissatisfaction. The key causes can be grouped into three categories: organizational factors, group factors, and personal factors. The two primary consequences of satisfaction or dissatisfaction are absenteeism and turnover.

CAUSES OF SATISFACTION AND DISSATISFACTION   There are five major organizational factors about which employees form attitudes: pay, opportunities for promotion, the nature of the work itself, policies and procedures of the organization, and working conditions. Clearly, a person may feel different levels of satisfaction toward each factor. An employee might feel he is underpaid (dissatisfied with pay) but simultaneously feel very positive about the other organizational factors.

The job satisfaction of individuals within a work group may also be influenced by both their coworkers and their supervisor or manager. Although the supervisor could be regarded as an organizational factor, since the position is described and defined by the organization, it is often his or her individual

---

[28] Edwin A. Locke, "The Nature and Causes of Job Satisfaction," in Marvin Dunnette, ed., *Handbook of Industrial and Organizational Psychology* (Chicago: Rand McNally, 1976), pp. 1297–1350. See also Ricky W. Griffin and Thomas S. Bateman, "Job Satisfaction and Organizational Commitment," in Cary L. Cooper and Ivan T. Robertson, eds., *International Review of Industrial and Organizational Psychology* (New York: Wiley, 1986), pp. 157–188.

Figure 3.5   Causes and Consequences of Job Satisfaction/Dissatisfaction

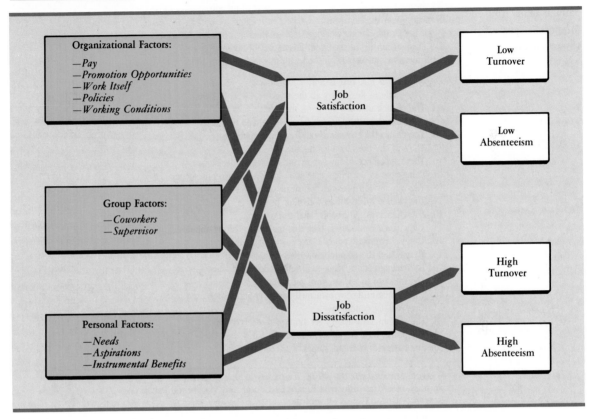

characteristics (warmth, understanding, or integrity) that most influence employee attitudes.

A person's needs and aspirations can also affect satisfaction. If a person wants to be in a high-status position, gaining such a position will probably enhance that person's level of job satisfaction. Also important are the instrumental benefits of the job, or the extent to which it enables the employee to achieve other ends. A person finishing her college degree might take a particular job on a temporary basis because it allows flexible scheduling while paying enough to cover her tuition. She may be quite satisfied with the job as long as she is in school but might be considerably less satisfied with the same job on a permanent basis.

CONSEQUENCES OF SATISFACTION AND DISSATISFACTION   As also shown in Figure 3.5, employee satisfaction affects turnover and absenteeism. When people are dissatisfied with their jobs, they are more likely to call in sick

Table 3.2

Sample Items from the
Minnesota Satisfaction
Questionnaire

Ask yourself: How satisfied am I with this aspect of my job?
VS means I am very satisfied with this aspect of my job.
S means I am satisfied with this aspect of my job.
N means I can't decide whether I am satisfied or not with this aspect of my job.
DS means I am dissatisfied with this aspect of my job.
VDS means I am very dissatisfied with this aspect of my job.

On my present job, this is how I feel about:

	VDS	DS	N	S	VS
1. Being able to keep busy all the time	☐	☐	☐	☐	☐
2. The chance to work alone on the job	☐	☐	☐	☐	☐
3. The chance to do different things from time to time	☐	☐	☐	☐	☐
4. The chance to be "somebody" in the community	☐	☐	☐	☐	☐
5. The way my boss handles his men	☐	☐	☐	☐	☐
6. The competence of my supervisor in making decisions	☐	☐	☐	☐	☐
7. Being able to do things that don't go against my conscience	☐	☐	☐	☐	☐
8. The way my job provides for steady employment	☐	☐	☐	☐	☐
9. The chance to do things for other people	☐	☐	☐	☐	☐
10. The chance to tell people what to do	☐	☐	☐	☐	☐
11. The chance to do something that makes use of my abilities	☐	☐	☐	☐	☐
12. The way company policies are put into practice	☐	☐	☐	☐	☐
13. My pay and the amount of work I do	☐	☐	☐	☐	☐
14. The chances for advancement on this job	☐	☐	☐	☐	☐
15. The freedom to use my own judgment	☐	☐	☐	☐	☐
16. The chance to try my own methods of doing the job	☐	☐	☐	☐	☐
17. The working conditions	☐	☐	☐	☐	☐
18. The way my co-workers get along with each other	☐	☐	☐	☐	☐
19. The praise I get for doing a good job	☐	☐	☐	☐	☐
20. The feeling of accomplishment I get from the job	☐	☐	☐	☐	☐

Source: *Manual for the Minnesota Satisfaction Questionnaire.* Used by
permission of the Industrial Relations Center and Vocational Psychology
Research, University of Minnesota.

when they really feel fine and may even leave the organization for more
attractive jobs elsewhere. Conversely, when employees are satisfied, they come
to work more regularly and are less likely to seek other employment.

MEASURING SATISFACTION   How do managers measure job satisfaction?
Several techniques have been developed, including interviews and critical
incidents, but by far the most popular approach has been to use questionnaires,
often called attitude or opinion surveys. Table 3.2 presents questions from one
popular measure.

Most organizations conduct attitude surveys fairly regularly. Basically, attitude
questionnaires ask how the person feels about various aspects of his or her
job. *A Look at Research* summarizes recent findings about common measures
used to assess job satisfaction.

Job satisfaction measures can give both managers and researchers a lot of
information about worker attitudes. But the picture provided by such instruments
may not be entirely accurate. Because instruments measure perceptions of the

A LOOK AT

RESEARCH

Pros and Cons of Job Satisfaction Measures

For many years, organizational behavior researchers have attempted to develop new and better ways to measure job satisfaction. While job satisfaction could be measured through interviews, use of a questionnaire is by far the most popular approach. In this approach, workers are given a survey form including several different questions about how they feel about their jobs. Their answers are presumed to indicate their level of job satisfaction.

Some questionnaires pose questions regarding satisfaction with specific facets of the workplace such as pay, working conditions, promotion opportunities, and so forth. Answers are then combined in various ways to provide an indication of overall satisfaction. Other questionnaires focus on general, overall attitudes to begin with. A typical question in their type of questionnaire might be: "How much do you like your job?" Still other questionnaires use a combination of these approaches.

One recent journal review identified a total of seventeen questionnaires developed to measure overall job satisfaction and twenty-nine more intended to measure satisfaction with various facets of a person's job. The most commonly used instruments are the Minnesota Satisfaction Questionnaire, the Job Diagnostic Survey, the Index of Organizational Reactions, and the Job Descriptive Index.

There are several advantages to these instruments. They can be administered easily and inexpensively to large numbers of people, scores can be tabulated easily, and there are known norms for each that can be used for comparisons. On the other hand, there are also disadvantages: they are based purely on perceptions, some suffer from psychometric deficiencies, and some might not be appropriate in various settings.

Organizations are increasingly using job satisfaction questionnaires (in spite of their imperfections) to monitor employee attitudes. Some larger companies like IBM and Hewlett-Packard routinely conduct their own surveys of employee attitudes. Others, like Leaseway Transportation and Wells Fargo, pay consulting firms to survey their employees. In all likelihood, the measurement of employee job satisfaction will become even more widespread in the future. So, too, will the techniques used to measure it.

Sources: John D. Cook, Sue J. Hepworth, Toby D. Wall, and Peter B. Warr, *The Experience of Work: A Compendium and Review of 249 Measures and Their Use* (London: Academic Press, 1981); Ricky W. Griffin and Thomas S. Bateman, "Job Satisfaction and Organizational Commitment," in Cary L. Cooper and Ivan T. Robertson (eds.) *International Review of Industrial and Organizational Psychology 1986* (New York: Wiley, 1986), pp. 157–188; "A Finger on the Pulse: Companies Expand Use of Employee Surveys," *Wall Street Journal,* October 27, 1986, p. 23.

workplace, rather than actual circumstances, results may be influenced by the wording of questions and the choice of topics covered by the survey. Moreover, the results may be contaminated by individual attitudes toward other dimensions of the workplace that are only tangentially related to the job. For example, a person might indicate low job satisfaction because of having to fight rush hour traffic every day. Short-term feelings, such as anxiety about a looming deadline, may also distort a person's responses, thereby giving an inaccurate impression of long-term attitudes.

Still, attitude surveys can be a valuable tool for managers. Normative data are available for certain questionnaires, indicating the distribution of responses in a representative population. The manager who uses those surveys can compare the attitudes of his or her employees with those of employees in similar organizations. Surveys can also point to major employee concerns that can then be remedied. At the least, they can provide a forum for constructive feedback from employees to managers.

JOB SATISFACTION IN THE UNITED STATES   In recent years, much debate has gone on about the general satisfaction of American workers. Movies (*Nine to Five*), songs ("Take This Job and Shove It"), and clichés ("the blue-collar blues") give the impression that most American workers are bored and dissatisfied with their jobs. From a more scientific vantage point, a large-scale government study also concluded that millions of workers were indeed unhappy with their jobs.[29] This study asked workers how satisfied they were with their jobs and whether, given the opportunity, they would prefer to change to a different line of work.

In most respects, however, the evidence about overall patterns of job satisfaction is mixed. There is some reliable evidence that most American workers are fairly satisfied with their work. For years, studies conducted by Gallup, the University of Michigan's Institute for Survey Research, and the National Opinion Research Center have consistently found that between 80 and 90 percent of all workers polled are more satisfied than dissatisfied with their jobs.[30] Yet the government study cited above found that more than half of those surveyed would choose a different kind of work if they could start their careers over again.[31] This finding is often taken as evidence that many people dislike their jobs.

Cognitive dissonance offers a possible explanation for this pattern of findings. If you ask a person who has worked at the same job for ten years or so how satisfied he or she is, a negative response would clearly contradict the behavior of keeping the job. A positive evaluation might be a way to reduce the tension. Some people may simply rationalize that they must not be too dissatisfied, or else they would have already changed jobs. Of course, some people will be more candid in their assessments, and this explanation does not hold for younger workers and others who have not been working at the same job as long.

---

[29] *Work in America: Report of a Special Task Force to the Secretary of Health, Education, and Welfare* (Cambridge, Mass.: MIT Press, 1973).

[30] C. N. Weaver, "Job Satisfaction in the United States in the 1970s," *Journal of Applied Psychology,* Vol. 65, 1980, pp. 364–367.

[31] *Work in America.*

Other Kinds of Satisfaction

Many kinds of attitudes exist in the workplace, and some matter far more to people than others do.[32] A worker who feels underpaid is fairly likely to do something about it, such as quit or ask for a pay raise. But although employees form attitudes about virtually everything, very few will take drastic action simply because they feel prices in the employee cafeteria are too high, or because they dislike the color of the company softball team's uniforms. Such dissatisfactions are not likely to be terribly significant to anyone.

Most research and theory on workplace attitudes has been limited to job satisfaction and has typically viewed satisfaction with other facets of organizational life as a subpart or determinant of job satisfaction. It is important to recognize, though, that reactions to the workplace may come from a variety of sources beyond the job itself.[33] And, beyond the routine examples noted earlier, the effects can be quite serious. For example, a worker who has been quite satisfied with his job may become very dissatisfied after being turned down for a promotion, or receiving only a small increase in salary when a larger one was expected.

Commitment and Involvement

Like job satisfaction, commitment and involvement, two closely related employee attitudes, influence important behaviors such as turnover and absenteeism.[34] **Commitment** can be defined as the individual's feelings of identification with and attachment to the organization. **Involvement** refers to a person's willingness, as an organizational "citizen," to go beyond the standard demands of his or her job.

Several factors have been found to lead to commitment and involvement. Richard M. Steers has suggested that commitment and involvement are enhanced both by personal factors such as age and years of tenure in the organization and by organizational characteristics such as the degree of participation allowed in decision making and the level of security employees feel.[35] Thus managers should be able to encourage commitment and involvement by allowing participation whenever possible and providing reasonable levels of job security for employees.

---

[32] Thomas S. Bateman and Dennis W. Organ, "Job Satisfaction and the Good Soldier: The Relationship Between Affect and Employee 'Citizenship'," *Academy of Management Journal*, December 1983, pp. 587–595.

[33] Griffin and Bateman, "Job Satisfaction and Organizational Commitment."

[34] Richard T. Mowday, Lyman W. Porter, and Richard M. Steers, *Employee-Organization Linkages—The Psychology of Commitment, Absenteeism, and Turnover* (New York: Academic Press, 1982).

[35] Richard M. Steers, "Antecedents and Outcomes of Organizational Commitment," *Administrative Science Quarterly*, Vol. 22, 1977, pp. 46–56.

Commitment and involvement can lead to several positive outcomes. More committed and involved employees show up for work more regularly, are more likely to stay with the organization, and work harder. Managers clearly should nurture and sustain such outcomes. Unfortunately, as described more fully in *Management in Action,* recent cutbacks at many organizations have dramatically reduced employee commitment.

Attitudes and Behaviors

There is currently considerable disagreement about the relationship between attitudes—such as job satisfaction—and behaviors—such as performance, turnover, and absenteeism. However, carefully constructed analyses by scholars such as Icek Ajzen and Martin Fishbein[36] and Cynthia D. Fisher[37] yield promising insights into these relationships.

These writers argue that it is not appropriate to investigate relationships between a general attitude such as job satisfaction and specific behaviors such as productivity. Instead, a more logical focus, as shown in Figure 3.6, might be on overall job satisfaction and its relationship to a broad view of job performance encompassing a variety of work-related behaviors. Alternatively, logical relationships might exist between a specific attitude, say, an employee's attitude toward working hard on a given day, and the actual behavior reflected by work produced on that day. That is, specific attitudes toward certain behaviors are more likely to be associated with those behaviors, whereas more general attitudes toward a set of behaviors are more likely to be associated with the entire set of behaviors, rather than individual ones. Hence, it is important to keep the attitude and behavior properly focused in terms of their relative specificity.[38]

MANAGERIAL IMPLICATIONS OF INDIVIDUAL DIFFERENCES

While managers can draw many implications from the research and theories on individual differences, there is one especially important message: we should always remember that people are, in fact, different. For example, a manager may have one worker who is determined to advance her career with the company. That worker will be very motivated by the opportunity to work on a special project that enhances her chances for promotion. Another worker,

---

[36] Icek Ajzen and Martin Fishbein, "Attitude-Behavior Relations: A Theoretical Analysis and Review of Empirical Research," *Psychological Bulletin,* Vol. 84, 1977, pp. 888–918.

[37] Cynthia D. Fisher, "On the Dubious Wisdom of Expecting Job Satisfaction to Correlate with Performance," *Academy of Management Review,* Vol. 5, 1980, pp. 607–612.

[38] M. M. Petty, Gail W. McGee, and Jerry W. Cavender, "A Meta-Analysis of the Relationships Between Individual Job Satisfaction and Individual Performance," *Academy of Management Review,* October 1984, pp. 712–721.

Management
in
ACTION

The Downside of Downsizing

American corporations have recently been laying off a large number of employees. In a two-year period in the mid-1980s, 500,000 white collar workers were let go; AT&T alone cut its work force by over 35,000. Some companies fire workers because of financial problems. Other, healthier companies are letting workers go to "downsize"—to do the same job with fewer employees, to cut costs, to become more lean and efficient in order to compete with foreign rivals, or to please investors on Wall Street. Such cutbacks often achieve their immediate goal of increased efficiency, but they have a price; the relationship between remaining workers and company may never be the same.

The commitment of employees to their company has long been seen as an essential element of a successful corporation. In fact, many who study Japanese businesses contend that one secret to their success is their emphasis on ensuring that workers' interests match those of their companies, so that everyone is working together toward a common goal. Employees who see their colleagues being let go all around them are much less likely to stay loyal to their company. Persons who feel that their jobs are on the line may start thinking more about their personal security than about company loyalty.

Downsizing and the resulting change in employee commitment threaten to change the way American workers view themselves and their jobs. Afraid of being laid off, many employees are now more concerned with how their skills will look out on the job market than with how well they're climbing the corporate ladder. Like free agents in professional baseball, many Americans now see themselves as committed to an industry or a profession, not to a particular company.

To fight this trend, many companies are doing everything they can to ease the stress on those people who are laid off and to reassure those who stay on. Rather than fire people outright, some corporations prefer to encourage older, high-paid workers to retire early by giving them retirement bonuses and better pensions. Such plans often reduce the need to fire anyone, but they also drain companies of some of their most experienced and valuable people. It may take years before American companies learn—perhaps from their Japanese rivals—how to be lean and efficient *and* inspire commitment.

Sources: Bruce Nussbaum, "The End of Corporate Loyalty?" *Business Week,* August 4, 1986, 42; John Bussey, "GM Workers Face Job Losses With a Savvy Pragmatism," *The Wall Street Journal,* November 14, 1986, 8; Walter Kiechel III, "Resurrecting Corporate Loyalty," *Fortune,* December 9, 1985, 207.

however, may be working for the organization simply until he can find an opening in another city. He will be indifferent to the same special project.

Similarly, the things that make one employee extremely satisfied may irritate another. Suppose two workers call in sick on the same day. Their boss decides to call each of them at home. One may genuinely appreciate the boss's concern, while another may resent being checked up on. And of course either one may be right!

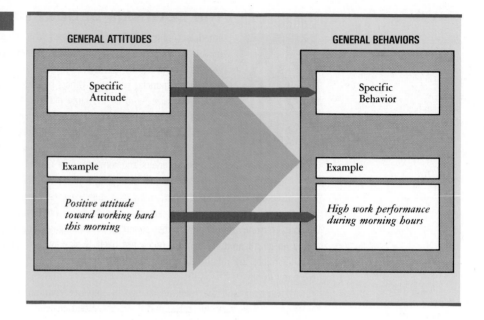

Figure 3.6

Attitude-Behavior
Relationships

GENERAL ATTITUDES

GENERAL BEHAVIORS

Specific
Attitude

Specific
Behavior

Example

Example

*Positive attitude
toward working hard
this morning*

*High work performance
during morning hours*

Thus, it is important for a manager, first, to recognize that such differences exist, and then to act accordingly. In general, managers should make as few assumptions as possible about people, instead treating and understanding people as the individuals that they are.

SUMMARY OF KEY POINTS

Individual differences are a set of unique factors that differentiate people from one another. It is also true that even the same person may act or feel differently in different situations.

One important individual difference is personality. Personality can be viewed from the standpoint of determinants, stages, and traits. The maturity-immaturity model is sometimes used to characterize workplace personalities. Personality traits that are especially relevant to the workplace are locus of control, authoritarianism, and self-monitoring.

Another important individual difference is a person's attitude. The dispositional view of attitude formation includes affect, cognition, and intention, while the situational view considers a person's social context.

Cognitive dissonance occurs when our attitudes conflict with our behaviors or with each other. Dissonance reduction is used to resolve the inner conflict that results.

Attitude change is generally undertaken via organizational change and development activities.

Job satisfaction is perhaps the most important work-related attitude, having multiple causes and consequences. Satisfaction can be measured (albeit imperfectly) with questionnaires. Other workplace attitudes include other kinds of satisfaction and commitment and involvement.

The relationships between attitudes and behaviors are quite complex. In their behavior and their own attitudes managers need to recognize and accept that people are different.

DISCUSSION QUESTIONS

1. Do you agree or disagree with the major personality determinants cited in this chapter? Why? Note examples that support or refute those determinants.

2. Do you think that stage approaches or trait approaches best explain personality? Why?

3. Argyris's maturity-immaturity model applies to the workplace personality. Does it also apply to your experiences as a student? Why or why not?

4. In terms of locus of control, are you primarily an internal or an external person? How can you tell? Cite some examples.

5. Give an example of how self-monitoring has affected either your own behavior or that of someone you know.

6. Prepare a brief personality profile of yourself. The profile should include each of the major personality traits discussed in this chapter—locus of control, authoritarianism, and self-monitoring.

7. Debate the relative merits of the dispositional perspectives on attitudes.

8. Can you recall an instance when you experienced cognitive dissonance? How did you resolve it?

9. What are your opinions about the general level of job satisfaction among American workers? What are the weaknesses in statements like "x% are satisfied"?

10. In what ways might personality and attitudes be related?

Case 3.1   Keeping the Family Business Flying

McDonnell Douglas Corporation, with 106,000 employees and more than $12 billion in sales in 1986, is far from an ordinary family business. But then, the McDonnells, who founded the business in 1939 and will probably take it into the next century, are not an ordinary family. Their differences—and the unique ways their character have been reflected in their company—provide a study in management individuality.

James S. McDonnell, Jr. (affectionately known as Mr. Mac) ran the company from its founding until his death in 1980 at age 81. He officially gave the title of chief executive officer to his nephew, Sanford McDonnell, some years before his death, when the head of Continental Airlines, unhappy with a McDonnell Douglas airplane, demanded to see McDonnell's CEO. Sanford took the job and the heat, but later his uncle told him, "You may be chief executive, but I'm still the boss."

During his reign, Mr. Mac was the boss in every way. Although he called his employees "teammates," he seldom asked anyone for advice. In his 40 years at the top he built McDonnell into an aerospace giant, but his tight control over the company gradually became a bottleneck because of his refusal to share decision making.

While Mr. Mac's non-technical interests included the paranormal (he funded research on the ability of the human mind to bend metal objects and named some of the company's planes Voodoo, Devil, and Phantom); Sanford, a born-again Christian, plays the bagpipes, quotes Albert Schweitzer, and makes clay sculptures. He also has his own ideas about management. When he took over the company, he was inspired by a book by John W. Gardner, *Self Renewal: The Individual and the Innovative Society.* The book argues that organizations, like people, grow old; they become inflexible and unreasoning, and without an infusion of youth, often they die.

With the help of his cousin, John McDonnell, the company's president, Sanford abstracted from the book five key ideas that became central to the company's new attitude: strategic management, human resources management, participative management, ethical decision-making, and quality/productivity. McDonnell now encourages its workers to split into "cells" and set their own productivity targets. Some managers work from desks on the factory floor to emphasize their participation in the cells. The executive dining room is open to everyone on Thursdays, although the menu is scaled down for the occasion. And everyone—including John—participates in "skip-level evaluations": all employees discuss their boss's performance with their boss's boss. Sanford, therefore, gets to hear what the vice presidents think of John.

On crucial issues, Sanford and John have worked together and kept the company growing. Over the objections of some board members who wanted the company to get out of commercial aviation and others who wanted to build an entirely new aircraft, the cousins steered a successful middle course. McDonnell's latest planes have been selling particularly well overseas, and its $1 billion deal to sell planes to China is the biggest agreement ever between an American company and China.

The company's course may change if, as expected, John takes over from Sanford. Unlike Sanford, who became interested in engineering only after the Army drafted him into the Manhattan Project during World War II, John always wanted to be an engineer, although he got an MBA soon after he joined the company. He's a quieter man than his cousin, and his interests reflect this—he likes to canoe and ski and gaze at the stars from the glass-walled turret on top of his house. In a few years he may engineer his own revolution at McDonnell. But chances are his employees will still be calling each other "teammates."

Case Questions

1. How far can you take the analogy between an aging person and an aging company? What are its uses and limitations?

2. To what extent should a company's policies reflect the beliefs and interests of its leaders?

Case Source

Based on "The Odd Couple at McDonnell Douglas" by Colin Leinster, *Fortune*, June 22, 1987. © 1987 Time Inc. All rights reserved.

Case 3.2   Back to the Old Saw

The employees at Henderson Manufacturing Company were unhappy. When they met outside the building, away from the noise of the big saws, workers would grumble to each other and talk about looking for different work. Management found that workers were punching in later in the mornings, and several times the vice president, Jack Macnam, had to go across the street to the pizza parlor to get employees back to work after their lunch break.

Oddly enough, the trouble seemed to start on a banner day for Henderson, the day the company began using its new high-tech saws. The company's principal product is cedar shingles used for roofing and siding and for 20 years the heart of its manufacturing process had been its huge circular saws. No one was ever allowed to tour the plant because management was afraid that people would be nervous when they saw the workers' hands moving like lightning around the deadly gleaming metal. Major accidents were rare, but few workers who worked by the saws had a complete set of fingers, and the company's owners lived in fear that a worker would cut off an arm, or worse. So when a new generation of virtually fool-proof saws came out, the company took a big step and invested in three.

The first sign of trouble was a little grumbling on the factory floor, but management had expected that. The workers had not been told about the new saws, and they were likely to resist any change. Then, during the second week with the new machines, two saw operators had close calls, and both had to be taken to the hospital for stitches. The saw's advanced safety brake saved both arms, but the next day some of the workers began talking about a jinx. Management brought the saw manufacturer's representatives in for a lecture about safe use of the new machines, but by the end of the week the saws had led to a total of 20 more stitches.

Over the weekend, management got an anonymous tip that drugs might be involved in the accidents, so on Monday it began a new policy of unannounced spot tests for drugs. The grumblings on the shop floor turned to outright hostility. Some of the employees refused to take the tests, and when one employee who'd never had an accident was fired for testing positive, the entire workforce walked off the job.

Frustrated, Macnam called in Bruce Ballenge, one of the senior employees, to talk about the problems. They both were tense; used to the constant scream of the saws, they felt uneasy in the silence. "Bruce," Jack said, "You've been working here 30 years and I know you're good at what you do and don't want to lose your job. What's gone wrong down there?"

"I don't know if those boys are using drugs," Bruce said, "but that's not the problem." He paused and looked around, not sure whether he should go on. "The problem's those new saws."

Macnam nearly fell off his stool. "But we spent $5,000 each on those saws. They're the best money can buy! They're so safe a child could run them."

"I know that," Bruce replied, "but that's your problem, not ours. Working with those old things, you know they'll just as easy cut your wrist as a stick of cedar, so you're on your toes all the time, you don't mess with them. But with those new saws, you can just about do it one-handed, you don't pay attention all the time, you get careless."

Jack was astonished, but he had faith in Bruce's experience. Now that he knew what the problem was and could deal with it directly, he suspected that it might not be too difficult to solve. He called a meeting with the plant manager to discuss the issue, and was able shortly afterward to tell the workers that only those who had proved their carefulness over the years would be allowed to work with the saws. In addition, drug testing would stop and the fired worker would be rehired.

The grumbling did not stop right away, but soon you again could not hear yourself think on the shop floor of Henderson Manufacturing.

Case Questions

1. What mistakes did the Henderson company make that led to the walkout?

2. Jack Macnam seems to have solved the problem of the new saws. Is there anything else he should do to improve worker morale?

Experiential Exercise

Purpose: This exercise should give you an appreciation for the complexities involved in applying personality theory to organizational settings.

Format: The class will be broken up into small groups of three or four members. Each group is to consider itself the personnel department for a regional department store chain. In recent months, the company has decided that it has not done a good job of hiring either department or stockroom managers. The existing job descriptions for the two positions are as follows:

> *Department Manager:* The department manager has full responsibility for keeping merchandise shelves stocked in the department, for managing the inventory, and for supervising and developing the departmental sales staff. The department manager also spends approximately half of his or her time on the sales floor working with customers.

> *Stockroom Manager:* The stockroom manager has full responsibility for receiving incoming shipments of merchandise, for properly storing it in the stockroom, and for delivering needed merchandise to the sales floor as requested by department managers.

Your task is to determine how these positions might be more effectively filled in the future.

Procedure: First, your group should develop a personality profile for the person needed for each position. This profile should specify the key personality traits likely to lead to success in the job. Next, the group should draft a set of questions for job applicants that will show how well their personalities match the desired profile.

Follow-up Questions

1. How effective do you think managers can be in developing optimal personality profiles for different kinds of jobs? Why?
2. How well do you think managers can measure personality traits? Explain.
3. Do you think it would be easier to measure attitudes than personalities? Why or why not?

CHAPTER

4

Motivation–
Basic Concepts

Chapter Objectives

After reading this chapter, you should be able to

▶ define the concept of *needs* and describe the basic motivational process.

▶ describe several historical perspectives on motivation.

▶ discuss three important need theories of motivation.

▶ discuss Herzberg's two-factor theory of motivation.

▶ identify and summarize three other important individual
   needs.

▶ describe parallels among the need theories.

B ack in the "old days," the United Auto Workers Union continually battled the American auto giants for hefty wage increases and more and more benefits. It seemed as though every new contract negotiation focused almost exclusively on employee compensation. And strikes were common.

In recent years, though, things have changed dramatically. The auto companies cut back their work forces massively to become more competitive with foreign auto manufacturers like Toyota and Nissan. It didn't take the UAW long to realize that it did little good to get higher wages for its members only to see large numbers of them being laid off.

Consequently, the union recently began to focus less on wages and more on job security. In 1987, for example, in a new contract negotiated with Ford, the union accepted three-year wage and benefit increases barely above the expected level of inflation. In return, Ford agreed not to cut any of its remaining 104,000 union jobs unless profits slumped, and to keep at least one job of every three vacated through attrition.[1]

W hat can we learn from this example? The Ford-UAW situation actually illustrates several points about employee motivation. For one thing, people are motivated by lots of different things, including money and benefits, but also including other things like job security. Another point is that the importance of different needs can change over time. When wages were relatively low and jobs secure, workers demanded more money. After wages reached acceptable levels but layoffs grew more common, workers scaled back their demands for money and, instead, were motivated to seek greater job security.

As will be apparent throughout this chapter, motivation is of vital importance to all organizations and thus to their managers. Very often, the difference between highly effective organizations and less effective ones lies in the motivational profiles of their members. Hence, managers need to understand the nature of individual motivation, especially as it applies to work situations.

This is the first of two chapters dealing with employee motivation. Here we examine basic concepts and theories of motivation. In the next chapter, we describe advanced concepts and applications.

THE NATURE OF MOTIVATION

Motivation can be defined as the forces that cause people to behave in certain ways.[2] The student who stays up all night to ensure that his term paper is the

---

[1] Thomas Moore, "Make-Or-Break Time for General Motors," *Fortune,* February 15, 1988, pp. 32–42.

[2] Richard M. Steers and Lyman W. Porter, *Motivation and Work Behavior,* 4th ed. (New York: McGraw-Hill, 1987), pp. 5–6. See also Frank J. Landy and Wendy S. Becker, "Motivation Theory Reconsidered," in L. L. Cummings and B. M. Staw, eds., *Research in Organizational Behavior,* Vol. 9 (Greenwich, Conn.: JAI Press, 1987), pp. 1–38.

best it can be, the salesman who works on Saturdays to get ahead, and the doctor who makes follow-up phone calls to her patients to check on their conditions are all motivated. Of course, the student who avoids her term paper by spending the day at the beach and the salesman who goes home early to escape a tedious sales call are also motivated—they are simply motivated to achieve different types of things than the first three. From the manager's viewpoint the objective is to motivate people to behave in ways that are in the organization's best interest.

The Importance of Motivation

One of the manager's primary tasks is to motivate people in the organization to perform at high levels. This means getting them to work hard, to be at work regularly, and to make positive contributions to the organization's mission. But job performance depends on ability and environment as well as motivation. The relationship can be stated as follows:

$P = f(M, A, \text{and } E)$

Where P = performance

M = motivation

A = ability

E = environment

To reach high levels of performance, an employee must want to do the job (motivation), be able to do the job (ability), and have the right materials and equipment to do the job (environment). A deficiency in any one of these areas will hurt performance. A manager should thus strive to ensure that all three of these conditions are met.[3]

The Motivation Framework

Current thinking on motivation rests on the concepts of need deficiencies and goal-directed behaviors. Figure 4.1 shows the basic motivational framework we will use to organize our discussion.

The starting point in the process is a need. A **need** is simply a deficiency experienced by an individual. For example, a person might feel her salary and position are deficient because they do not reflect the importance to the organization of the work she does. (As described in *International Perspective*, the kinds of needs likely to motivate behavior vary across cultures.)

A need triggers a search for ways to satisfy it. The person just described might consider three such options: to simply ask for a raise and promotion, to

---

[3] Victor H. Vroom, *Work and Motivation* (New York: Wiley, 1964). See also Benjamin Schneider, "The People Make the Place," *Personnel Psychology,* Autumn 1987, pp. 437–454.

Figure 4.1

The Basic Motivation Framework

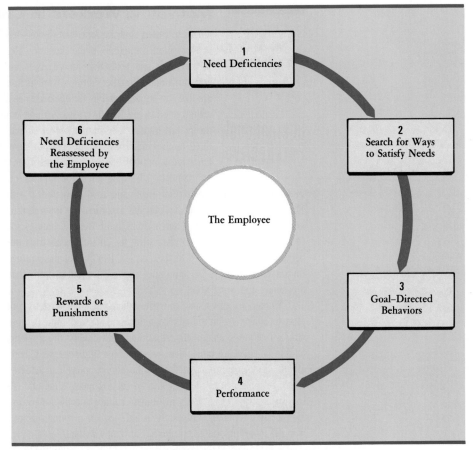

Source: From J. L. Gibson, J. M. Ivancevich, and J. H. Donnelly, *Organizations: Behavior, Structure, Processes,* 6th ed. © Business Publications, Inc., 1973, 1976, 1979, 1982, 1985, and 1988. Reprinted by permission.

work harder in hopes of earning a raise and promotion, or to look for a new job with a higher salary and more prestigious title.

Next comes a choice of goal-directed behaviors. While a person might actually pursue more than one option at the same time, most effort will likely be directed at only one option.

In step four, the person actually carries out the behavior chosen to satisfy the need. Suppose, for example, the person in our example decides to work harder. At this point, she will likely put in longer hours, work harder, and so forth.

As a result of the performance, rewards or punishment will follow. In this instance, of course, the person will most likely get the raise and promotion because of the higher performance.

International Perspective

Motivating Workers in China

American writers studying American workers have developed most of the theories of motivation commonly in the literature. Researchers have found that many of the needs and goals that Americans accept as universal do not have the same importance in other cultures. Workers in collectivist countries like Pakistan are likely to be motivated by filling social needs rather than individualistic self-actualization needs. Results of New Zealand studies using Herzberg's two-factory theory vary significantly from those of similar American studies. McClelland's three motives may be hard to apply to non-Western cultures because many languages don't have an exact equivalent for the word "achievement."

Studying the motivations of workers outside the United States can be instructive both about motivation theory and about how to deal with foreign workers and customers. The People's Republic of China provides a particularly interesting case because it is both culturally and developmentally very different from most Western nations. Studies of motivation in modern China show that workers do often strive for different goals than their Western counterparts. In fact, because of the importance to the People's Republic of the writings of Marx, Lenin, and Mao, the motivation of workers in communist China often differs from that of Chinese peoples in Taiwan, Singapore, and Hong Kong.

Workers in all Chinese countries differ from their Western counterparts in the importance they place on challenge, individual recognition, and nonwork time. Because Chinese culture has traditionally emphasized group attainment rather than individuality, the challenges that motivate Chinese workers tend to be collective rather than personal. For similar reasons, both traditional Chinese culture and Maoist ideology frown upon the glorification of individual achievement. Chinese workers also tend not to be motivated by the possibility of gaining more "time off." That might seem surprising, given the importance of the family in Chinese culture and the American idea that "leisure time" is time for the family. But the Chinese have little use for personal leisure time; they view work as making a much more important contribution to family welfare.

The ideology of the People's Republic of China's long-time leader Mao Zedong has led communist Chinese workers to be motivated by some factors that don't drive non-communist Chinese. For instance, Mao wrote that a person's ability "to find his bearing independently" should be rewarded; therefore personal autonomy is a more important motivator for communist than for non-communist Chinese. On the other hand, Mao departed from the traditional Confucian idea of "elevating the worthy," so the special clothes and colors that mark advancements in the ranks of traditional Chinese societies are banned in the People's Republic.

Such differences between cultures, and between groups with different political ideologies within cultures, may seem confusing for an American trying to deal with workers from other countries. But one point is clear: American business people cannot assume that what motivates a worker in New York will have the same effect on a worker in Beijing.

Source: Based on "Structure and Importance of Work Goals Among Managers in the People's Republic of China" by Oded Shenkar and Simcha Ronen, *Academy of Management Journal*, Vol. 39, No. 3, 1987, pp. 564–576. Reprinted by permission.

Finally, the person assesses the extent to which the need has been satisfied. Suppose, for example, the person wanted a 10-percent raise and a promotion to vice president. If she gets both, she should be satisfied. On the other hand, suppose she only gets a 7-percent raise and a promotion to assistant vice president. The person will have to decide whether to keep trying, accept what she did get, or choose one of the other options considered earlier. (Sometimes, of course, a need may go unsatisfied altogether, despite a person's efforts.)

HISTORICAL PERSPECTIVES ON MOTIVATION

Historical views on motivation are of interest for several reasons, even though they were not always accurate. For one thing, they provide a foundation for contemporary thinking about motivation. For another, since they were generally based on common sense and intuition, an appreciation of their strengths and weaknesses can help managers learn useful insights into employee motivation in the workplace.

Early Views of Motivation

The earliest views on human motivation were dominated by the concept of **hedonism:** the idea that people seek pleasure and comfort and try to avoid pain and discomfort.[4] Although this view seems reasonable as far as it goes, there are many kinds of behavior it cannot explain. Why do recreational athletes exert themselves willingly and regularly, when a hedonist would prefer to relax? Why do people occasionally risk their own lives for others in time of crisis? And why do volunteers give tirelessly of their own time to collect money for charitable causes?

It was the recognition that hedonism is an extremely limited view of human behavior, and one that is frequently wrong, that prompted the emergence of other perspectives. William James, for one, argued that instinctive behavior and unconscious motivation are also important in human behavior.[5] Although many of James's ideas were eventually supplanted by other views, they helped reshape contemporary motivation theory.

The Scientific Management View

As noted in Chapter 1, Frederick W. Taylor, the chief proponent of scientific management, assumed that employees are economically motivated and work so as to earn as much money as they can.[6] Taylor once used the case of a pig-iron handler named Schmidt to illustrate the concepts of scientific management.

---

[4] Craig Pinder, *Work Motivation* (Glenview, Ill.: Scott, Foresman, 1984).

[5] Ernest R. Hilgard and Richard C. Atkinson, *Introduction to Psychology,* 4th ed. (New York: Harcourt, Brace and World, 1967).

[6] Frederick W. Taylor, *Principles of Scientific Management* (New York: Harper, 1911).

Schmidt's job consisted of moving heavy pieces of iron from one pile to another. He appeared to be doing an adequate job and regularly met the standard of 12.5 tons per day. Taylor, however, believed that Schmidt was strong enough to do much more. To test his ideas, Taylor designed a piece-rate pay system that would award Schmidt a fixed sum of money for each ton of iron he loaded. Taylor reported that he then had the following conversation with Schmidt and observed his work:

> "Schmidt, are you a high-priced man?"
>
> "Well, I don't know what you mean." [Several minutes of conversation ensue.]
>
> "Well, if you are a high-priced man, you will do exactly as this man tells you tomorrow, from morning until night. When he tells you to pick up a pig and walk, you pick it up and walk, and when he tells you to sit down and rest, you sit down and rest. You do that right straight through the day. And what's more, no back talk. Do you understand that?"
>
> Schmidt started to work, and all day long, and at regular intervals, was told by the man who stood over him with a watch, "Now pick up a pig and walk. Now sit down and rest. Now walk, now rest . . . . " He worked when he was told to work, and rested when he was told to rest and at half-past five in the afternoon, had his 47.5 tons loaded on the car. And he practically never failed to work at this pace and do the task that was set him during the three years the writer was at Bethlehem.[7]

Recent evidence suggests that Taylor may have fabricated the conversation just related; Schmidt himself may have been an invention.[8] If so, this willingness to fabricate shows how strongly Taylor believed in his economic view of human motivation and in the need to spread the doctrine. But it was soon recognized that scientific management theorists' assumptions about motivation could not explain complex human behavior. The next perspective on motivation to emerge in the management literature was associated with the human relations movement.

The Human Relations View

The human relations view (also discussed in Chapter 1) arose as a product of the Hawthorne studies.[9] This perspective suggested that people are motivated by things besides money, in particular that employees, as social beings, are motivated by and respond to the social environment at work. Favorable employee attitudes, such as job satisfaction, were presumed to result in increased employee

---

[7] Taylor, *Principles of Scientific Management,* pp. 46–47.

[8] See Charles D. Wrege and Amedeo G. Perroni, "Taylor's Pig-Tale: A Historical Analysis of Frederick W. Taylor's Pig-Iron Experiment," *Academy of Management Journal,* March 1974, pp. 6–27.

[9] Pinder, *Work Motivation.* See also Daniel Wren, *The Evolution of Management Thought,* 2nd ed. (New York: Wiley, 1979).

performance. Chapter 5 explores this relationship in more detail. It is sufficient to say here, as we did in Chapter 1, that the human relations viewpoint left most questions about human behavior unanswered.[10] However, one of the primary theorists associated with this movement, Abraham Maslow, helped develop an important need theory of motivation.

NEED THEORIES OF MOTIVATION

Need theories represent the starting point for most contemporary thought on motivation,[11] although these theories, too, attracted critics.[12] The basic premise of need theories is that human motivation is caused primarily by deficiencies in one or more important needs or need categories. Need theorists have attempted to identify and categorize the most salient needs, that is, those that are most important to people. The best-known need theories are Maslow's hierarchy of needs, Murray's manifest needs, and Alderfer's ERG theory.

Maslow's Hierarchy of Needs

Abraham Maslow, a psychologist, first presented his needs hierarchy in the 1940s.[13] Influenced by the human relations school of thought, Maslow argued that human beings are "wanting" animals: they have innate desires to satisfy a given set of needs. Furthermore, Maslow believed these needs are arranged in a hierarchy of importance, with the most basic ones being at the bottom of the hierarchy. Maslow's **hierarchy of needs** is shown in Figure 4.2.

The three sets of needs at the bottom of the hierarchy are called *deficiency needs,* because they must be satisfied if the individual is to be fundamentally comfortable. The top two sets of needs are termed *growth needs,* because they focus on personal growth and development.

The most basic needs in the hierarchy are *physiological.* They include the needs for food, sex, and air. Next in the hierarchy are the *security needs:* things that offer safety and security, such as adequate housing and clothing and freedom from worry and anxiety. *A Look at Research* demonstrates the importance of security needs.

Belongingness needs, the third level in the hierarchy, are primarily social and include, for example, the need for love and affection and the need to be accepted by peers. The fourth level, *esteem needs,* actually takes in two slightly

---

[10] Wren, *The Evolution of Management Thought.*

[11] Steers and Porter, *Motivation and Work Behavior.*

[12] Gerald R. Salancik and Jeffrey Pfeffer, "An Examination of Need-Satisfaction Models of Job Attitudes," *Administrative Science Quarterly,* September 1977, pp. 427–456.

[13] Abraham H. Maslow, "A Theory of Human Motivation," *Psychological Review,* Vol. 50, 1943, pp. 370–396; and Abraham H. Maslow, *Motivation and Personality* (New York: Harper & Row, 1954).

| Figure 4.2 | Maslow's Hierarchy of Human Needs |

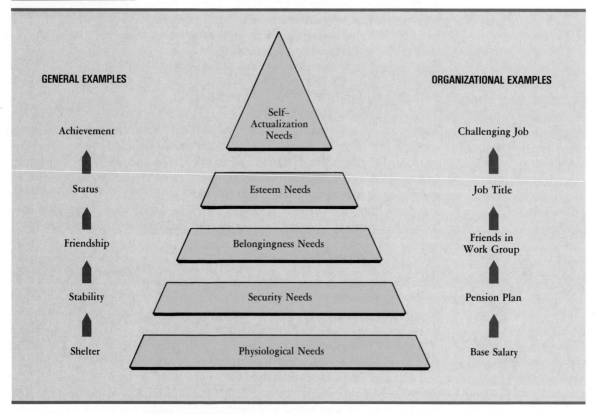

Source: Adapted from Abraham H. Maslow, "A Theory of Human Motivation," *Psychological Review*, Vol 50, 1943, pp. 374–396. Copyright 1943 by the American Psychological Association. Used with permission.

different kinds of needs: the need for a positive self-image and self-respect and the need to be respected by others. At the top of the hierarchy are what Maslow termed the *self-actualization needs*. They involve realizing our full potential and becoming all that we are able to be.

Maslow ranked the needs in his hierarchy according to their apparent importance. He placed the most important ones—physiological needs—at the bottom, or foundation, of the hierarchy. Until these needs are satisfied, the other needs do not play a large role in motivation.

Once physiological needs have been satisfied, however, they cease to be as important, and security needs emerge as the primary sources of motivation. This escalation up the hierarchy continues until the self-actualization needs become the primary motivators. But whenever a previously satisfied lower-level set of needs becomes deficient again, the individual returns to that level.

A LOOK AT

RESEARCH

Job security: A healthy bonus

As every employee who depends on a regular paycheck knows, job security is paramount when it comes to maintaining financial well-being. What they may not know, however, is that such security is related to their physical and mental health as well.

Psychologist Karl W. Kuhnert surveyed more than 200 employees in two similar manufacturing companies to see if job attitudes—including job satisfaction, job security and work involvement—were predictive of employee health. The participants were asked to agree or disagree with statements such as "I can keep my job for as long as I want it," "Everything is an effort for me" and "I experience chest pains."

Kuhnert found that there was a strong relationship between perceived job security and health. The more permanent the employees thought their position was, the greater their physical and mental well-being. Surprisingly, perceived job security was found to be a better predictor of employees' health than any other factor.

Further, the study showed that the workers' assessment of their own job performance was tied directly to their belief about how secure their job was. In other words, the higher the workers perceived the quality of their work to be, the more permanent they saw their position, regardless of their actual job performance.

It's no secret that organizations suffer financially as a result of employee stress and ill health. With skyrocketing medical costs, rising insurance claims and worker-compensation laws, it's in employers' best interest to keep their employees happy and healthy, Kuhnert says.

Kuhnert suggests that companies can combat the problem of worker insecurity by letting their employees know how well they're doing. "Since employees believe that if they do good work they'll be able to keep their jobs, and a key feature in job insecurity is not knowing where you stand, organizations can help their employees by giving them regular feedback."

Karl W. Kuhnert, Ph.D., is at Ohio State University, Columbus. He presented his work at last year's meeting of the American Psychological Association.

Source: Mindy Schanback, *Psychology Today*, May 1987, p. 16. Reprinted by permission of the American Psychological Association.

For example, a person who loses his or her job is likely to stop worrying about self-actualization and to concentrate on finding another job to satisfy now-deficient security needs.

In most organizational settings, physiological needs are satisfied by things like adequate wages, restrooms, ventilation and comfortable temperatures, and the like. Security needs in organizational settings can be satisfied by job continuity (no layoffs), a grievance system (to protect against arbitrary super-visory actions), and an adequate insurance and retirement system (to guard against financial loss from illness and to ensure retirement income).

Most peoples' belongingness needs are satisfied by family ties and group relationships inside and outside the workplace. In the workplace, for example, people usually develop friendships that provide a basis for social interaction and can play a major role in satisfying social needs. The manager can encourage this need satisfaction by fostering a sense of group identity and interaction among employees. At the same time, the manager can also be sensitive to the probable effects (such as low performance and absenteeism) on an employee when she or he has family problems or is not accepted by others in the workplace.

Esteem needs in the workplace are met by job titles, choice offices, merit pay increases, awards, and other forms of recognition. Of course if they are to be sources of long-term motivation, tangible rewards like these must be given out equitably and must be based on performance.

Self-actualization needs are perhaps the hardest to understand and the most difficult to satisfy. Clearly, few people ever become all they could become. In most cases, a person who is doing well on Maslow's hierarchy will have satisfied his or her esteem needs and will be moving toward self-actualization.

Maslow's needs hierarchy makes a certain amount of intuitive sense. Because it was the first motivation theory to be popularized, it is also one of the best known in management circles. Yet research has revealed a number of deficiencies in the theory. Five levels of needs are not always present; the actual hierarchy of needs does not always conform to Maslow's model; and need structures are more dynamic, unstable, and variable than the theory would lead us to believe.[14] Thus, the theory's primary contribution seems to be in providing a general framework for categorizing needs.[15]

Murray's Manifest Needs

Another interesting need construct is H. A. Murray's **manifest needs theory.** Although the theory was first presented by Murray in 1938,[16] its present conceptualization owes much to the work of J. W. Atkinson.[17] That is, Murray identified these needs, but only at an abstract level. Atkinson translated Murray's ideas into a more concrete, operational framework.

Like Maslow's needs hierarchy, the manifest needs theory assumes people have a set of needs that motivates behavior. The mechanisms by which needs operate, however, are somewhat more complex in this view. Murray suggests

---

[14] Mahmond A. Wahba and Lawrence G. Bridwell, "Maslow Reconsidered: A Review of Research on the Need Hierarchy Theory," *Organizational Behavior and Human Performance,* April 1976, pp. 212–240.

[15] Howard S. Schwartz, "Maslow and Hierarchical Enactment of Organizational Reality," *Human Relations,* Vol. 36, No. 10, 1983, pp. 933–956.

[16] H. A. Murray, *Explanation in Personality* (New York: Oxford University Press, 1938).

[17] J. W. Atkinson, *An Introduction to Motivation* (Princeton, N.J.: Van Nostrand, 1964).

that several categories of needs are important to most people and that any number of needs may be operating in varying degrees at the same time. That is, multiple needs motivate behavior simultaneously rather than in some preset order. Several of the needs that Murray sees as most powerful are summarized in Table 4.1.

Unlike Maslow, Murray did not arrange the needs he identified in any particular order of importance. (It is interesting to note that all of the manifest needs are learned needs. That is, we are not born with any of them—we learn

Table 4.1

Murray's Manifest Needs

Need	Characteristics
Achievement	Individual aspires to accomplish difficult tasks; maintains high standards and is willing to work toward distant goals; responds positively to competition; willing to put forth effort to attain excellence.
Affiliation	Enjoys being with friends and people in general; accepts people readily; makes efforts to win friendships and maintain associations with people.
Aggression	Enjoys combat and argument; easily annoyed; sometimes willing to hurt people to get his or her way; may seek to "get even" with people perceived as having harmed him or her.
Autonomy	Tries to break away from restraints, confinement, or restrictions of any kind; enjoys being unattached, free, not tied to people, places, or obligations; may be rebellious when faced with restraints.
Exhibition	Wants to be the center of attention; enjoys having an audience; engages in behavior that wins the notice of others; may enjoy being dramatic or witty.
Impulsivity	Tends to act on the "spur of the moment" and without deliberation; gives vent readily to feelings and wishes; speaks freely; may be volatile in emotional expression.
Nurturance	Gives sympathy and comfort; assists others whenever possible, interested in caring for children, the disabled, or the infirm; offers a "helping hand" to those in need; readily performs favors for others.
Order	Concerned with keeping personal effects and surroundings neat and organized; dislikes clutter, confusion, lack of organization; interested in developing methods for keeping materials methodically organized.
Power	Attempts to control the environment and to influence or direct other people; expresses opinions forcefully; enjoys the role of leader and may assume it spontaneously.
Understanding	Wants to understand many areas of knowledge; values synthesis of ideas, verifiable generalization, logical thought, particularly when directed or satisfying intellectual curiosity.

Source: Adapted from the *Personality Research Form Manual,* published by Research Psychologists Press, Inc., P.O. Box 984, Part Huron, Michigan 48060. Copyright © 1967, 1974, 1984, by Douglas N. Jackson.

them as we grow.)[18] In addition, Murray believed that each need has two components: direction and intensity. Direction refers to the object or person that is expected to satisfy the need. If you are hungry, getting to a local eating establishment may represent the direction of the need. Intensity represents the importance of the need. If you are very hungry, the need to get to a restaurant may be very great; if you are only moderately hungry, the intensity is not as strong.

Appropriate environmental conditions are necessary for a need to become manifest. For example, if someone with a high need for power works in a job setting where power is irrelevant, the need may remain latent, not influencing his behavior. But if conditions change, increasing the importance of power, the need for power may then manifest itself, and the employee will begin to work toward increasing his power.

Little research has been done to evaluate Murray's theory. However, some of the specific needs defined by Murray have been the subject of much research, as we discuss later in this chapter.

Alderfer's ERG Theory

A third important need theory of motivation is Clayton Alderfer's **ERG theory.**[19] In many respects, ERG theory extends and refines Maslow's needs hierarchy, although there are several important differences between the two. The E, R, and G in ERG stand for existence, relatedness, and growth—Alderfer's three basic need categories. *Existence needs,* seen as necessary for basic human existence, roughly correspond to the physiological and security needs of Maslow's hierarchy. *Relatedness needs,* involving the need to relate to others, are similar to the Maslow's belongingness and esteem needs. Finally, *growth needs* are analogous to Maslow's needs for self-esteem and self-actualization.

Like Murray, Alderfer suggested that more than one kind of need may motivate someone at the same time—for example, both relatedness and growth needs might be working on a person. A more important difference from Maslow's hierarchy is that ERG theory includes a frustration-regression component and a satisfaction-progression component (see Figure 4.3). The satisfaction-progression process suggests that after satisfying one category of needs, a person progresses to the next level. On this point Maslow's and Alderfer's theories agree. Maslow, however, assumed that the individual will remain at the next level until its needs are satisfied. Alderfer argued that a person who is frustrated in trying to satisfy a higher level of needs will eventually regress to the previous level.[20]

---

[18] Atkinson, *An Introduction to Motivation.*

[19] Clayton P. Alderfer, *Existence, Relatedness, and Growth* (New York: Free Press, 1972).

[20] Alderfer, *Existence, Relatedness, and Growth.*

Figure 4.3

Alderfer's ERG Theory

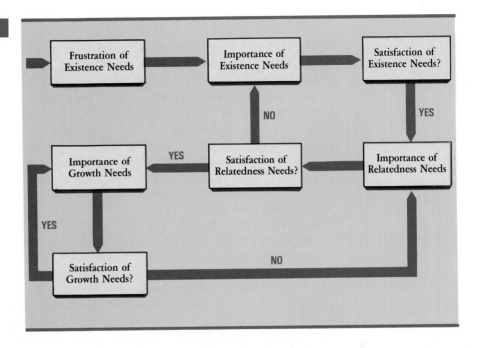

Suppose a manager has satisfied her basic needs at the relatedness level and is now trying to satisfy her growth needs. For a variety of reasons, such as organizational constraints (i.e., few challenging jobs) and the absence of opportunities to advance, she is unable to satisfy those needs. According to Alderfer, frustration of her growth needs will cause the manager's relatedness needs to once again dominate as motivators. Since Alderfer's theory is a fairly new addition to motivation literature, it has not been studied very much. Preliminary evidence suggests, though, that ERG theory may be a more economical and powerful explanation of human motivation than either of the other need theories.[21]

THE TWO-FACTOR THEORY

Another important seminal theory of motivation is Herzberg's two-factor theory, which in many ways is similar to the need theories just discussed. Herzberg's theory has played a major role in managerial thinking about motivation.

---

[21] Clayton P. Alderfer, "An Empirical Test of a New Theory of Human Needs," *Organizational Behavior and Human Performance*, Vol. 4, 1969, pp. 142–175.

Development of the Theory

Frederick Herzberg and his associates developed the **two-factor theory** in the late 1950s and early 1960s.[22] Herzberg began by interviewing approximately two hundred accountants and engineers in Pittsburgh. He asked them to recall times when they felt especially satisfied and motivated by their jobs and times when they felt especially dissatisfied and unmotivated. He then asked them to describe what caused the good and bad feelings. The responses to the questions were recorded by the interviewers and later subjected to content analysis. (In a content analysis, the words, phrases, and sentences used by respondents are analyzed and categorized according to their meanings.)

Somewhat to his surprise, Herzberg found that entirely different sets of factors were associated with the two kinds of feelings about work. For example, a person who indicated "low pay" as a cause of dissatisfaction would not necessarily identify "high pay" as a cause of satisfaction and motivation. Instead, respondents associated entirely different causes, such as recognition or achievement, with satisfaction and motivation.

The findings led Herzberg to conclude that the traditional model of satisfaction and motivation was incorrect. As shown in Figure 4.4, job satisfaction had up until then been viewed as one-dimensional, ranging from satisfaction to dissatisfaction. If this were the case, Herzberg reasoned, a single set of factors should influence movement back and forth along the continuum. But because his research had identified influences from two different sets of factors, Herzberg argued that two different dimensions must be involved.

Figure 4.4 also illustrates Herzberg's inference that there is one dimension ranging from satisfaction to no satisfaction and another ranging from dissatisfaction to no dissatisfaction. Presumably, the two dimensions must be associated with the two sets of factors identified in the initial interviews. Thus, Herzberg proposed, employees might be either satisfied or not satisfied and, at the same time, dissatisfied or not dissatisfied.[23]

Table 4.2 lists the primary factors identified in Herzberg's interviews. *Motivation factors,* such as achievement and recognition, were often cited by people in the original study as primary causes of satisfaction and motivation. When present in a job, these factors apparently could cause satisfaction and motivation; when they were absent, the result was feelings of no satisfaction, as opposed to dissatisfaction.

The other set of factors, *hygiene factors,* came out in response to the question about dissatisfaction and lack of motivation. The respondents suggested that pay, security, supervisors, and working conditions, if seen as inadequate,

---

[22] Frederick Herzberg, Bernard Mausner, and Barbara Snyderman, *The Motivation to Work* (New York: Wiley, 1959); and Frederick Herzberg, "One More Time: How Do You Motivate Employees?" *Harvard Business Review,* January–February 1968, pp. 53–62.

[23] Herzberg et al., *The Motivation to Work.*

Figure 4.4

Herzberg's View of Job
Satisfaction

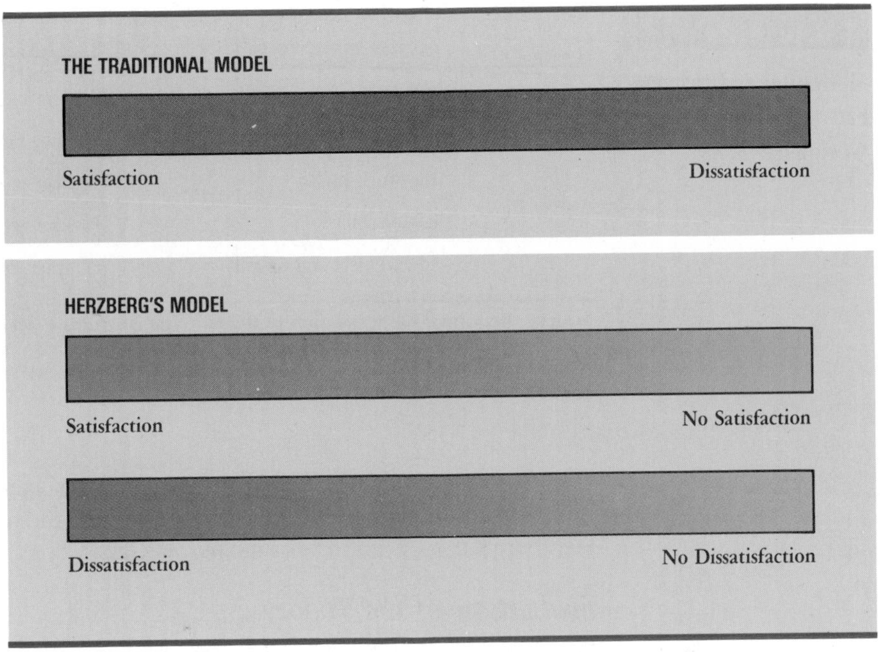

THE TRADITIONAL MODEL

Satisfaction   Dissatisfaction

HERZBERG'S MODEL

Satisfaction   No Satisfaction

Dissatisfaction   No Dissatisfaction

could lead to feelings of dissatisfaction. When these factors were considered acceptable, however, the person was still not necessarily satisfied. Instead, she or he was simply not dissatisfied.[24]

To use the two-factor theory in the workplace, Herzberg recommended a two-stage process. First, the manager should try to eliminate situations that cause dissatisfaction, which Herzberg assumed to be the more basic of the two dimensions. To reach this goal—achieving a state of no dissatisfaction—the manager presumably needs to take care of hygiene factors, for instance, by making certain that pay and job security are adequate, working conditions are reasonable, and so forth. According to Herzberg, once a state of no dissatisfaction exists, trying to further improve motivation through the hygiene factors is a waste of time. It is then that the motivation factors enter the picture. By increasing opportunities for achievement, recognition, responsibility, advancement, and growth, the manager can help subordinates feel satisfied and motivated.

Unlike many other theorists, Herzberg described quite explicitly how managers could apply his theory. He advocated a technique, called job enrichment, for structuring employee tasks.[25] (We discuss job enrichment in

---

[24] Herzberg et al., *The Motivation to Work*.

[25] Herzberg, "One More Time: How Do You Motivate Employees?" and Ricky W. Griffin, *Task Design: An Integrative Approach* (Glenview, Ill.: Scott, Foresman, 1982).

Table 4.2

Motivation and Hygiene
Factors in the
Workplace

Motivation Factors	Hygiene Factors
Achievement	Supervision
Recognition	Working Conditions
The Work Itself	Interpersonal Relationships
Responsibility	Pay and Security
Advancement and Growth	Company Policies

Source: Reprinted by permission of the *Harvard Business Review.* An exhibit
from "One More Time: How Do You Motivate Employees?" by Frederick
Herzberg (January–February, 1968). Copyright © 1968 by the President and
Fellows of Harvard College; all rights reserved.

Chapter 8.) This technique was tailored to his key motivation factors. This
unusual attention to application may explain the widespread popularity of
Herzberg's theory among practicing managers.

Evaluation of the Theory

Because it gained popularity so quickly, Herzberg's theory has been scientifically
scrutinized more often than most other theories in the field of organizational
behavior.[26] The results have been contradictory to say the least.

The initial study by Herzberg and his associates supported the basic
premises of the theory, as did a few follow-up studies.[27] In general, studies that
use the same methodology as Herzberg did (content analysis of recalled
incidents) tend to support the theory.[28] However, this methodology has itself
come under attack. Studies that use other methods for measuring satisfaction
and dissatisfaction frequently find results quite different from Herzberg's.[29] If
the theory is "method bound," as it appears to be, its validity is, at best,
questionable.

---

[26] Pinder, *Work Motivation.*

[27] Frederick Herzberg, *Work and the Nature of Man* (Cleveland: World, 1966);
Valerie M. Bookman, "The Herzberg Controversy" *Personnel Psychology,* Summer
1971, pp. 155–189; and Benedict Grigaliunas and Frederick Herzberg, "Relevance in
the Test of Motivation-Hygiene Theory," *Journal of Applied Psychology,* February
1971, pp. 73–79.

[28] Pinder, *Work Motivation.*

[29] Marvin Dunnette, John Campbell, and Milton Hakel, "Factors Contributing to Job
Satisfaction and Job Dissatisfaction in Six Occupational Groups," *Organizational
Behavior and Human Performance,* May 1967, pp. 143–174; and Charles L. Hulin
and Patricia Smith, "An Empirical Investigation of Two Implications of the Two-
Factor Theory of Job Satisfaction," *Journal of Applied Psychology,* October 1967,
pp. 396–402.

Several other criticisms have also been directed against the theory. Critics say the original sample of accountants and engineers may not represent the general working population. And they maintain that the theory fails to account for individual differences. Also, subsequent research has found that a given factor such as pay may bear on satisfaction in one sample and dissatisfaction in another, and research has found that the effect of a given factor depends on the individual's age and organizational level. Finally, say its critics, the theory does not define the relationship between satisfaction and motivation.[30]

It is not surprising, then, that Herzberg's theory is no longer held in very high esteem by organizational behavior researchers.[31] Indeed, the field has since adopted far more complex and valid conceptualizations of motivation, most of which are discussed in Chapter 5. But because of its initial popularity and its specific guidance for application, the two-factor theory merits a special place in the history of motivation research.

OTHER IMPORTANT NEEDS

Each of the theories discussed thus far describes interrelated sets of important individual needs. Several other key needs have been identified. As noted earlier, J. W. Atkinson has recently incorporated several of them into Murray's manifest needs framework. However, they have most often been studied as independent needs apart from these theories. The three most frequently cited are the needs for achievement, affiliation, and power.[32]

The Need for Achievement

The **need for achievement** is most frequently associated with the work of David McClelland.[33] This need arises from an individual's desire to accomplish a goal or task more effectively than in the past. Need for achievement has been studied at both the individual and societal levels. At the individual level, the primary aim of research has been to pinpoint characteristics of high-need achievers, the outcomes associated with high-need achievement, and methods for increasing the need for achievement. Figure 4.5 illustrates the principal traits of high-need achievers.

---

[30] Nathan King, "A Clarification and Evaluation of the Two-Factor Theory of Job Satisfaction," *Psychological Bulletin,* July 1970, pp. 18–31. See also Dunnette et al. "Factors Contributing to Job Satisfaction and Job Dissatisfaction in Six Occupational Groups"; and R. J. House and L. Wigdor, "Herzberg's Dual-Factor Theory of Job Satisfaction and Motivation: A Review of the Evidence and a Criticism," *Personnel Psychology,* Summer 1967, pp. 369–389.

[31] Pinder, *Work Motivation.*

[32] Pinder, *Work Motivation.*

[33] David McClelland, *The Achieving Society* (Princeton, N.J.: Van Nostrand, 1961).

Figure 4.5

Characteristics of High-Need Achievers

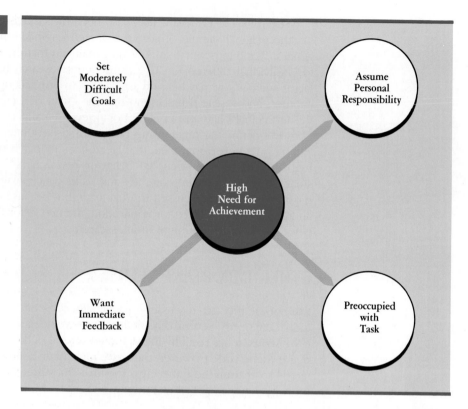

CHARACTERISTICS OF HIGH-NEED ACHIEVERS   High-need achievers tend to set moderately difficult goals and to make moderately risky decisions. For example, when people are asked to play ring toss and are allowed to stand anywhere they want to, people with a low need for achievement tend to stand either so close to the target that there is no challenge or so far away that they have little chance of hitting the mark. High-need achievers stand at a distance that is challenging but also allows frequent success.

High-need achievers also want immediate and specific feedback on their performance. They want to know how well they have done something as quickly after finishing it as possible. For this reason, high-need achievers frequently take jobs in sales, where they get almost immediate feedback from customers, and they avoid jobs in areas such as research and development, where tangible progress is slower and feedback comes at longer intervals.

Preoccupation with their work is another characteristic of high-need achievers. They think about it on their way to work, during lunch, and at home. They find putting their work aside difficult, and they become frustrated when they must stop working on a partly completed project.

Finally, high-need achievers tend to assume personal responsibility for getting things done. They often volunteer for extra duties and find it difficult to delegate part of a job to someone else. Accordingly, they get a feeling of accomplishment when they have done more work than their peers without the assistance of others.

CONSEQUENCES OF ACHIEVEMENT   Although high-need achievers tend to be quite successful, they do not often achieve top management posts. The most common explanation is that high need for achievement helps people advance quickly through the ranks, but the traits associated with the need often conflict with the requirements of high-level management positions. Because of the amount of work they are expected to do, top executives must be able to delegate tasks to others; they also seldom receive immediate feedback; and they often must make decisions that are either more or less risky than a high-need achiever would be comfortable with.[34]

LEARNING ACHIEVEMENT   McClelland estimated that only around 10 percent of the American population has a high need for achievement. Nevertheless, he argued that proper training could boost an individual's need for achievement to a high level.[35] The training program developed by McClelland and his associates tries to teach trainees to think like high-need achievers, to increase personal feedback to trainees about themselves, and to develop a group esprit de corps that supports high effort and success. That is, the trainers work to create a group feeling that reinforces the characteristics of high-need achievers.

High-need achievers tend to do quite well as individual entrepreneurs with little or no group reinforcement. Steven Jobs, the cofounder of Apple Computer, and Nolan Bushnell, a pioneer in electronic video games and founder of Atari, are both recognized as high-need achievers, and each has done quite well for himself.

ACHIEVEMENT AND ECONOMIC DEVELOPMENT   McClelland also conducted research on the need for achievement at the societal level. He believed that a nation's level of economic prosperity correlates with its people's need for achievement.[36] The higher the percentage of a country's population having a high need for achievement, the stronger and more prosperous its economy. Conversely, the lower the percentage, the weaker the economy. The reason for this correlation is that high-need achievers tend toward entrepreneurial success. Hence, one would expect a country with many high-need achievers to have a high level of business activity and economic stimulation.

---

[34] Michael J. Stahl, "Achievement, Power, and Managerial Motivation: Selecting Managerial Talent With the Job Choice Exercise," *Personnel Psychology,* Winter 1983, pp. 775–790.

[35] David McClelland, "Achievement Motivation Can Be Learned," *Harvard Business Review,* November–December 1965, pp. 6–24. See also Robert L. Helmreich, Linda L. Sawin, and Alan L. Carsrud, "The Honeymoon Effect in Job Performance: Temporal Increases in the Predictive Power of Achievement Motivation," *Journal of Applied Psychology,* May 1986, pp. 185–188.

[36] McClelland, *The Achieving Society.*

The Need for Affiliation

Individuals also feel the **need for affiliation,** that is, the need for human companionship.[37] Not much research has been done on the need for affiliation, but researchers do recognize several ways in which people with a high need for affiliation differ from those with a lower need. Individuals with a high need tend to want reassurance and approval from others and are usually genuinely concerned about others' feelings. They are likely to act and think as they believe others want them to, especially those with whom they strongly identify and desire friendship. As we might expect, people with a strong need for affiliation most often work in jobs with a lot of interpersonal contact, such as sales and teaching positions.

The Need for Power

A third major individual need is the **need for power,** that is, the desire to control one's environment, including financial resources, material resources, information, and other people.[38] People vary greatly along this dimension. Some people spend time and energy seeking power; others avoid power if at all possible. People with a high need for power can be successful managers if three conditions are met. They must seek power for the betterment of the organization, rather than for their own interests. They must also have a fairly low need for affiliation. (Fulfilling a personal need for power may very well alienate others in the workplace.) Finally, they need plenty of self-control, so they can curb their desire for power when it threatens to interfere with effective organizational or interpersonal relationships.[39] *Management in Action* illustrates what can happen when these conditions are not met.

INTEGRATING NEED PERSPECTIVES

This chapter has described several views of individual motives and needs. Despite their differences, the theories intersect at several points. Both Maslow and Alderfer, for instance, determined a hierarchy of needs, while Herzberg proposed two discrete continua for two need categories. The individual needs identified by each of the three theories are strikingly similar. Figure 4.6 illustrates the major likenesses among three need theories.

The hygiene factors described by Herzberg correspond well with the lower three levels of Maslow's hierarchy. In particular, pay and working conditions

---

[37] Stanley Schachter, *The Psychology of Affiliation* (Stanford, Calif.: Stanford University Press, 1959).

[38] David McClelland and David H. Burnham, "Power Is the Great Motivator," *Harvard Business Review,* March–April 1976, pp. 100–110.

[39] Pinder, *Work Motivation;* and McClellan and Burnham, "Power is the Great Motivator."

Tripping on the Top Steps of Power

Power is both celebrated and feared in our society, especially in the corporate world. Those without power tend to mistrust power itself as well as those who wield it. Those driven by a need for power often find that it becomes intoxicating and sometimes self-destructive just when they are on the verge of attaining it.

To many in the business world, becoming chief executive officer is a lifetime goal, something for which rising executives are often willing to sacrifice years of their time and effort. For such people, the drive towards the top often takes precedence over their families, their private lives, sometimes even their health. Ironically, the drive itself often keeps them from their goal.

Personality often plays a major role in that final promotion. The current CEO often chooses a successor, so the prospective leader's relationship to the top person may be crucial. Sometimes chief executives, recognizing their own personal defects, may give the company's number two spot to someone who has complementary strengths and weaknesses. This may allow the two to work well as a team, but also may make the chief executive hesitant to turn over the reins to someone so different. Such a scenario apparently took place recently at Kroger, the supermarket company: President William Kagler did much of the dirty work for Chairman Lyle Everingham when the company was restructuring and closing stores, but then Everingham fired the younger man rather than give him the top job.

People in the number two position often get overconfident, feeling that their goal is inevitably in sight. Such people suffer from "goal gradient syndrome," the same tendency that makes horses speed up as they approach the barn and prisoners try to escape when their sentence is almost up. After repressing certain behaviors and being careful not to offend all the way up the ladder, some people let loose a little too soon.

Management consultant Charles M. Kelly has coined the term "destructive achiever" to describe one type of power-hungry executive who has become common recently. The destructive achiever usually has the charisma, appearance, knowledge, energy, and drive of the true leader and is often promoted up the corporate ladder because of these attributes. But destructive achievers lack the constructive leader's values and ethical standards, and therefore they often fall short of their goal, sometimes exposed or sabotaged by people who they stepped upon during their rapid climb.

Learning to channel their drive for power into a constructive force is clearly a major challenge for future business leaders. Those who lust for the top spot might want to keep in a prominent place a quote from Will and Ariel Durant: "Power dements even more than it corrupts, lowering the guard of foresight and raising the haste of action."

Sources: Charles M. Kelly, "The Interrelationship of Ethics and Power in Today's Organizations," *Organizational Dynamics*, Summer 1987, 5; Christopher Farrell, "Gutfreund Gives Salomon's Young Lions More Power," *Business Week*, October 20, 1986, 32; Jolie Solomon, "Heirs Apparent to Chief Executives Often Trip Over Prospect of Power," *The Wall Street Journal*, March 24, 1987, 29.

Figure 4.6   Parallels Among Need Theories of Motivation

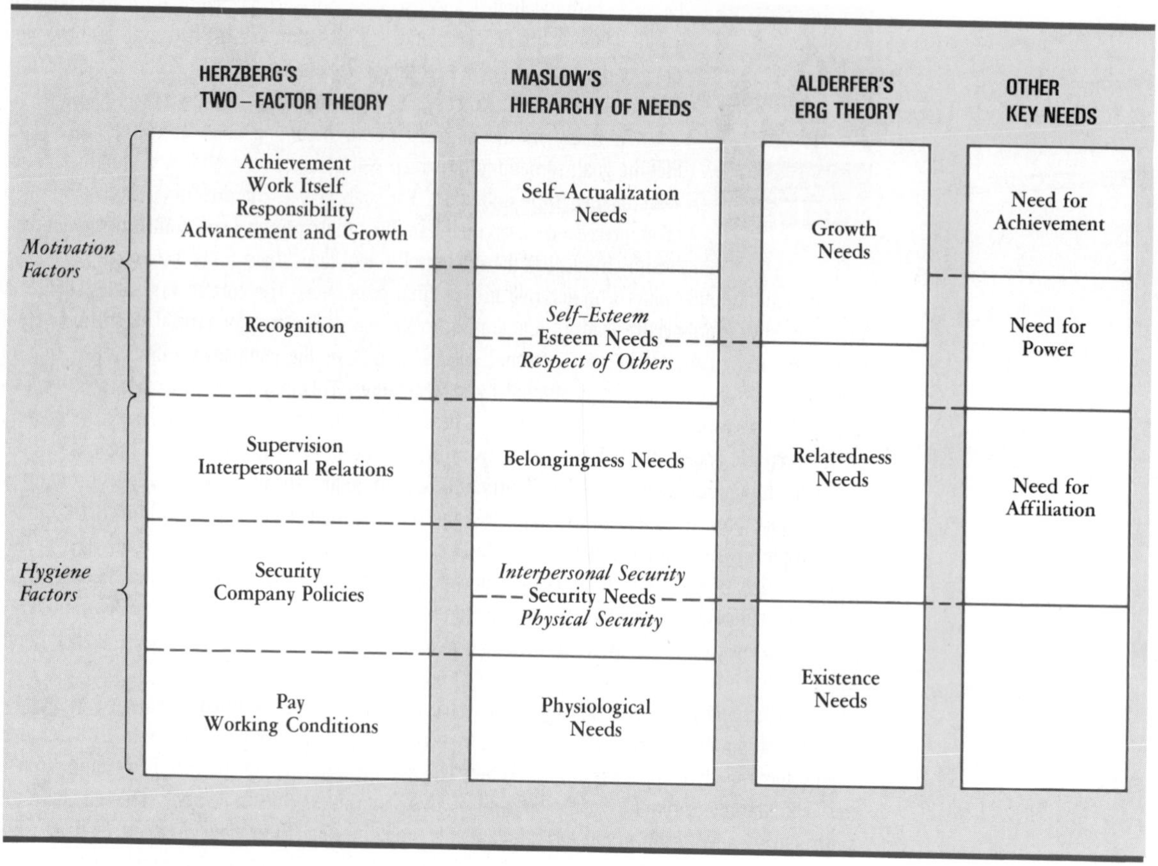

	HERZBERG'S TWO–FACTOR THEORY	MASLOW'S HIERARCHY OF NEEDS	ALDERFER'S ERG THEORY	OTHER KEY NEEDS
Motivation Factors	Achievement Work Itself Responsibility Advancement and Growth	Self–Actualization Needs	Growth Needs	Need for Achievement
	Recognition	*Self-Esteem* Esteem Needs *Respect of Others*		Need for Power
	Supervision Interpersonal Relations	Belongingness Needs	Relatedness Needs	Need for Affiliation
Hygiene Factors	Security Company Policies	*Interpersonal Security* Security Needs *Physical Security*		
	Pay Working Conditions	Physiological Needs	Existence Needs	

correspond to Maslow's physiological needs, security and company policies correspond to his security needs, and supervision and interpersonal relations correspond to belongingness needs. Herzberg's motivation factors parallel the two top levels of Maslow's hierarchy. Recognition, for example, is equivalent to esteem; achievement, the work itself, responsibility, and advancement and growth might all be categorized as part of the self-actualization process.

There are also clear similarities between Maslow's hierarchy and Alderfer's ERG theory. The existence needs in the ERG theory correspond to the physiological and physical security needs in the hierarchy. The relatedness needs overlap with the interpersonal security needs, the belongingness needs, and the need for respect from others in Maslow's theory. Finally, the growth needs correspond to Maslow's self-esteem and self-actualization needs.

The independent individual needs we discussed can also be correlated with the need theories. The need for affiliation is clearly analogous to relatedness needs in the ERG theory, belongingness needs in Maslow's hierarchy, and interpersonal relations in Herzberg's theory. The need for power overlaps with Alderfer's relatedness and growth needs, while the need for achievement resembles Alderfer's growth needs and Maslow's self-actualization needs.

Despite the many conceptual similarities among the need theories that have emerged over the years, the theories also share an inherent weakness.[40] They do an adequate job of telling us what factors motivate behavior, but they tell us very little about the actual processes of motivation.[41] Even if two people are obviously motivated by interpersonal needs, they may pursue quite different paths to satisfy those needs. In Chapter 5, we describe several theories that try to solve that part of the motivation puzzle.

SUMMARY OF KEY POINTS

Motivation is the set of forces that cause people to behave in various ways. Motivation starts with a need. People search for ways to satisfy their needs and then behave accordingly. Their performance of this behavior results in rewards or punishments. To varying degrees, a favorable outcome may satisfy the original need.

The earliest view of motivation was based on the concept of hedonism, the view that people seek pleasure and comfort and seek to avoid pain and discomfort. Scientific management extended this view by asserting that money is the primary human motivator in the workplace. The human relations view suggested that social factors were primary motivators.

According to Abraham Maslow, human needs are arranged in a hierarchy of importance, from physiological, to security, to belongingness, to esteem, and finally to self-actualization. Murray's manifest needs include many work-related needs that may operate simultaneously. Alderfer's ERG theory is a refinement of Maslow's original hierarchy that also includes the regression component.

In Herzberg's theory, satisfaction and dissatisfaction are two distinct dimensions instead of opposite ends of the same dimension. Motivation factors are presumed to affect satisfaction, and hygiene factors are presumed to affect dissatisfaction. Herzberg's theory is well known among managers but has several deficiencies.

Other important individual needs include the needs for achievement, affiliation, and power. These needs are part of Murray's theory, but have been most widely studied in isolation.

---

[40] Salancik and Pfeffer, "An Examination of Need—Satisfaction Models of Job Attitudes."
[41] Pinder, *Work Motivation.*

DISCUSSION QUESTIONS

1. Can you think of other definitions of motivation besides the one presented in the chapter? Suggest as many alternative definitions as possible.

2. Is it useful to characterize motivation in terms of a deficiency? Why?

3. When in your experience has your level of performance been directly affected by motivation? By your ability? By the environment?

4. What are the similarities between the views of human motivation taken by the scientific management theorists and those taken by the human relations theorists? How are they different?

5. Identify examples from your own experience that support, and others that refute, Maslow's hierarchy of needs.

6. Which theory do you think has the greatest value, Maslow's hierarchy, Murray's manifest needs theory, or Alderfer's ERG model?

7. Do you agree or disagree with the basic assumption of Herzberg's two-factor theory? Why?

8. Which of the need theories discussed in this chapter has the most practical value for managers? Which one has the least practical value?

9. How do you evaluate yourself in terms of your needs for achievement, affiliation, and power?

10. Do you agree or disagree with the assertion that the need for achievement can be learned? Do you think it might be easier to learn it as a young child or as an adult?

11. What other important needs might emerge as topics for managerial consideration in the future?

Case 4.1   The Big Brown Team

To many workers, the scene reads like a nightmare: everywhere package deliverer Clay Bois goes, a supervisor follows with a stopwatch, calculating the time it takes him to walk to a customer's door (is he keeping to the standard three-feet-per-second pace?) and noting whether he knocks immediately, as he is supposed to, or whether he wastes precious seconds searching for the doorbell. To get the packages to drivers like Bois for delivery, sorters must handle 1,124 packages an hour and make a mistake less than once every two hours, and loaders are expected to fill the delivery vans at the rate of at least 500 packages per hour. What keeps these people going?

That is the secret of the United Parcel Service, the nation's largest and most profitable transportation company. Of course, supervisors only occasionally ride with drivers, but they have been known to goad slow drivers by asking them if they'd like a sleeping bag. The entire company is run on stopwatches, an approach that began in the 1920s when the company's founder, James E.

Casey, turned to time-study engineers to help make his business 30 percent more efficient. Yet rather than create burnout and high turnover, UPS's approach has earned the company a consistently high corporate reputation, and its employee turnover rate is only 4 percent.

Much of the company's success with its workers can be attributed to what one UPS board member calls "managerial socialism." In return for their three-feet-per-second pace, UPS workers earn substantial pieces of a company that turns $700 million in profits per year. Attracted to UPS by its high wages, many workers stay because they like the feeling of being an integral part of a team that's working hard and doing a superb job. Because the company seldom hires outside executives, drivers can often work their way up to supervisory and management levels, and many retire as millionaires.

Drivers start off earning over $15 an hour, about a dollar more than they could expect from other trucking companies. After ten years in the company, a middle-level manager might be earning $54,000 augmented by a $7500 dividend and $14,000 in stock. Founder Casey declared that he wanted the company to be "owned by its managers and managed by its owners," and in fact most of the stock is held by 15,000 managers and supervisors, who must sell their stock to the company when they leave or retire. So people who work for the company for any length of time get the feeling of being driven not by a faceless, impersonal organization but by themselves. As in any good team, everyone's success depends on everyone else.

The lack of status symbols at UPS promotes workers' feeling of being an equal part of an important group. Top executives battle everyone else for parking spaces, stand in the same cafeteria lines, and do their own photocopying. Not even the chairman has his own secretary. Office workers have standards as strict as those for drivers and loaders: no one is allowed to drink beverages at a desk, and everyone follows tough grooming standards, including a rule against beards and long mustaches.

Rather than seeing themselves as the drudge workers, UPS's drivers often see themselves as the company's heros. The company, in turn, recognizes them as being, in effect, small businesspeople, creating their own business by doing their jobs well. Workers' identification with the company is so strong that as much as eighty percent of the workforce shows up for voluntary workshops after hours.

The Teamsters Union, which represents over 100,000 UPS workers, often gripes about the stopwatches and the tension of the constant rush to move things even faster. UPS is in the midst of moving into high technology package-tracking equipment, in part to compete with Federal Express in the airmail package market, and it may in the future find it more profitable to improve efficiency through pushing machines rather than people. But at the moment the company stands as a fine example of how to improve workers' productivity by filling their needs.

Case Questions

1. How does UPS manage to keep its workers from resenting the rigidity of some of its rules?

2. Could UPS use methods other than supervisors with stopwatches to keep its workers efficient?

3. What employee needs are most and least likely to be satisfied by UPS's approach?

Case Sources

Kenneth Labich, "Big Changes at Big Brown," *Fortune,* January 18, 1988, 56–64; Larry Reibstein, "Federal Express Faces Challenges to Its Grip on Overnight Delivery," *The Wall Street Journal,* January 8, 1988, 1; Daniel Machalaba, "Up to Speed: United Parcel Service Gets Deliveries Done By Driving Its Workers," *The Wall Street Journal,* April 22, 1986, 1.

Case 4.2   More Than a Paycheck

Lemuel Greene was a trainer for National Home Manufacturers, a huge builder of prefabricated homes. National Home had hired Greene fresh from graduate school with a master's degree in English. At first the company put him to work writing and revising company brochures and helping with the most important correspondence at the senior level. But soon both Greene and senior management officials began to notice how well he worked with executives on their writing, how he made them feel more confident and less anxious about it, and how, after he'd worked with an executive on a report, that executive was often much more eager to take on the next writing task.

So National Home moved Greene into its respected and prestigious training department. The company's trainers worked with thousands of supervisors, managers, and executives, helping them learn everything from a new computer language to time management skills to how to get the most out of the workers on the plant floor, many of whom were unmotivated high school dropouts. Soon Greene was spending his weeks giving small seminars in executive writing as well as coaching his students, helping them perfect their memos and letters.

Greene's move into training meant a big increase in salary, and when he started working exclusively with the company's top brass, he seemed to get a bonus every month. Greene's supervisor, Mirela Albert, knew he was making more than many executives who had been with the company three times as long, and probably twice as much as any of his graduate school classmates who concentrated in English. Yet in her bi-weekly meetings with him, she could tell that Greene wasn't happy.

When she asked him about it, he said that he was in a bit of a rut, that he had to keep saying the same things over and over in his seminars, that business memos weren't as interesting as the literature he had been trained on. But then after trailing off for a moment, he looked up at her and blurted out: "They don't need me." The fact that the memos filtering down through the company were now flawlessly polished, or that the annual report was 20 percent shorter yet said everything it needed to, didn't fulfill Greene's desire to be needed.

The next week, Greene came to Albert with a proposal: what if he started holding classes for some of the floor workers, many of whom had no future in the company or outside of it because they could often write nothing but their own names? Albert took the idea to her superiors, who told her that they wouldn't oppose it, but that Greene couldn't possibly keep drawing such a high salary if he were to work with people whose contribution to the company was compensated at $4 an hour.

Greene agreed to a reduced salary and began offering English classes on the factory floor, billed by management (who hoped to avoid a wage hike that year) as an added benefit of the job. At first only two or three workers showed up, and they, Greene thought, just wanted an excuse to get away from the nailing guns for a while. But gradually word got around that Greene was serious about what he was doing and didn't treat the workers like stupid kids in a remedial class.

At the end of the year, Greene got a bonus from a new source—the vice-president in charge of production. Although Greene's course took workers off the job for a couple of hours a week, productivity had actually improved since his course began, employee turnover had dropped, and for the first time in over a year some of the floor workers had begun to apply for supervisory positions. Greene was pleased with the bonus, but when Albert saw him grinning as he walked around the building, she knew he wasn't thinking about his bank account.

Case Questions

1. What needs theories would explain Mr. Greene's unhappiness despite his high income level?

2. Mr. Greene seems to have drifted into being a teacher. Given his needs and motivations, do you think teaching is an appropriate profession for him?

Experiential Exercise

Purpose: This exercise asks you to apply the theories discussed in the chapter to your own needs and motives.

Format: You will first develop a list of things you want from life and then categorize them according to one of the theories in the chapter. Next, you will discuss your results with a small group of classmates.

Procedure: Prepare a list of approximately fifteen things you want. These things can be very specific (such as a new car) or very general (such as a feeling of accomplishment in school). Next, choose the one motivational theory discussed in the chapter that best fits your set of needs. Classify each of the things from your "wish list" in terms of the need or needs it might satisfy.

Your instructor will then divide the class into groups of three people. Spend a few minutes in the group discussing each person's list and its classification according to needs.

After the small group discussions, your instructor will reconvene the entire class. Discussion should center on the extent to which each theory can serve as a useful framework for classifying individual needs. People who found that their needs could be very neatly categorized or who found little correlation between their needs and the theories are especially encouraged to share their results.

Follow-up Questions

1. As a result of this exercise, do you now place more or less trust in the needs theories as valuable management tools?

2. Could a manager use some form of this exercise in an organizational setting to enhance employee motivation?

C H A P T E R

5

Motivation–Advanced Concepts

Chapter Objectives

After reading this chapter, you should be able to

- ▶ describe equity theory.
- ▶ describe expectancy theory.
- ▶ discuss organizational behavior modification.

- ▶ describe participative management.
- ▶ relate attribution theory to motivation.
- ▶ identify and describe the consequences of motivation.

n 1982, the General Motors plant in Fremont, California, was a management disaster waiting to happen. The plant had an average daily absenteeism rate of 20 percent, five thousand worker grievances were outstanding, and labor and management relations were extremely tense. GM finally gave up and closed the plant.

Shortly after the shutdown, GM entered into a joint venture with Toyota called NUMMI. The Fremont plant was subsequently reopened with a Japanese management team in charge. The new managers rehired many of the former workers, including several of the most militant.

This time, however, things were different. Workers were organized into teams and given a much greater voice in how to do their jobs. Closed offices, private parking spaces, and the executive dining room were eliminated. Everyone was made to feel like they were working together in a cooperative venture.

By mid-1985, half as many workers were producing twice as many cars. Absenteeism was around 2 percent and only two grievances had been filed all year. Moreover, the quality of the cars being produced was higher than at any other GM plant.

What had changed? The clearest difference was the relationship between management and the workers. The new system treated workers as equals. They had a voice in what was being done in the plant and were made to feel part of a team as with management.[1]

*I*n short, the new Japanese managers were doing a much better job of motivating the workers than GM's managers had. However, it takes more than a simplistic need perspective like the ones discussed in the preceding chapter to explain the Fremont experience. Just as this example clearly demonstrates the need for complex representations of human motivation in the workplace, this chapter presents several such approaches.

Motivation theory is in a state of flux.[2] Managers and researchers now realize that employee motivation simply cannot be addressed with simplistic models and concepts. Consider the case of two close friends who grew up together, went to the same college, and now work in the same office. Each wants to get ahead. The first devotes all her time and energy to doing the best

---

[1] A. Bernstein, D. Cook, P. Engardio, and G. L. Miles, "The Difference Japanese Management Makes," *Business Week*, July 14, 1986, pp. 47–50; Andrea Gabor and Jack A. Seamonds, "GM's Bootstrap Battle: The Factory Floor View," *U.S. News and World Report*, September 21, 1987, pp. 52–53; "The Toyota Touch," *The Economist*, December 13, 1986, pp. 76–77.

[2] Terence R. Mitchell, "Motivation: New Directions for Theory, Research and Practice," *Academy of Management Review*, January 1982, pp. 80–88. See also Martin Evans, "Organizational Behavior: The Central Role of Motivation," *Journal of Management*, Summer 1986, pp. 203–222; and Jeremiah J. Sullivan, "Three Roles of Language in Motivation Theory," *Academy of Management Review*, January 1988, pp. 104–115.

job possible. She works late, takes work home at night, and is frequently in the office on weekends. She interacts with others only if it is necessary to get her job done more effectively. The second friend believes he can best get ahead by playing politics. He spends a lot of time cultivating his relationship with the boss and evaluates new job assignments in terms of how they will increase his visibility in the organization. He also goes to great lengths to be seen with the right people.

These two friends come from similar backgrounds, they share many of the same experiences, and they have the same goal. Yet they have adopted dramatically different strategies to attain that goal. For a motivational framework to have true value, it must capture the range of complexity that typifies human behavior, a range illustrated by this example. Basic need theories are limited in this respect; so the field of organizational behavior has turned to more sophisticated conceptualizations of motivation to understand its causes in work settings.

The so-called **content-process distinction** differentiates the need theories described in Chapter 4 and the newer, more complex models addressed here.[3] Need theories try to describe the causes of motivated behavior; they are basically content oriented. Process theories try to describe the processes by which motivated behavior occurs. In other words, they say how people satisfy their needs. Process theories also describe how people choose between behavioral alternatives. With respect to our example, content theories could explain that the two friends have the need to succeed. Process theories, however, would describe how each person decided on the best way to satisfy that need and why the two chose different behaviors. The equity theory of motivation was one of the first such process theories.

EQUITY THEORY

First articulated by J. Stacey Adams, **equity theory** is based on the simple premise that people want to be treated fairly.[4] The theory defines **equity** as the belief that we are being treated fairly in relation to others, and **inequity** as the belief that we are being treated unfairly in relation to others. Equity

---

[3] John P. Campbell, Marvin D. Dunnette, Edward E. Lawler, and Karl E. Weick, *Managerial Behavior, Performance, and Effectiveness* (New York: McGraw-Hill, 1970).

[4] J. Stacey Adams, "Toward an Understanding of Inequity," *Journal of Abnormal and Social Psychology*, November 1963, pp. 422–436. See also Richard T. Mowday, "Equity Theory Predictions of Behavior in Organizations," in Richard M. Steers and Lyman W. Porter, eds., *Motivation and Work Behavior*, 4th ed. (New York: McGraw-Hill, 1987), pp. 89–110; and Richard C. Huseman, John D. Hatfield, and Edward W. Miles, "A New Perspective on Equity Theory: The Equity Sensitivity Construct," *Academy of Management Review*, October 1987, pp. 222–234.

Figure 5.1

The Formation of Equity
Perceptions

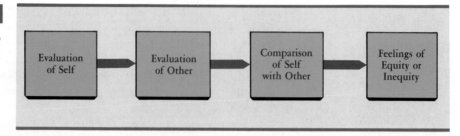

theory is just one of several theoretical formulations derived from social comparison processes.[5] Social comparisons involve evaluating our own situation in the context of the situation of others. This chapter focuses mainly on equity theory because it is the best developed of the social comparison conceptualizations and the one that applies most directly to motivation.

Equity Perceptions

Figure 5.1 illustrates the four-step process by which people form equity perceptions. Putting this in an organizational setting, the individual first evaluates how she or he is being treated by the organization. Next, the individual develops an evaluation of how a "comparison-other" is being treated. This comparison-other might be a person in the same work group, someone in another part of the organization, or even a composite of several people scattered throughout the organization. After evaluating the treatment of self and other, the individual compares the two. That is, the person looks at his or her own situation relative to the situation of the other. As a consequence of this comparison, the individual tends to feel either equity or inequity. Depending on the strength of this feeling, the person may choose to pursue any of the several alternatives discussed in the next section.

Adams describes the equity comparison process in terms of input/outcome ratios. **Inputs** are an individual's contributions to the organization, such as education, experience, effort, and loyalty. **Outcomes** are what he or she receives in return, such as pay, recognition, social relationships, and intrinsic rewards.[6] A person's assessment of inputs and outcomes for both self and other are based partially on objective data (for example, the person's own salary) and partially on perceptions (such as the comparison-other's level of recognition). The equity comparison thus takes the form:

---

[5] Paul S. Goodman, "Social Comparison Processes in Organizations," in Barry M. Staw and Gerald R. Salancik, eds., *New Directions in Organizational Behavior* (Chicago: St. Clair, 1977), pp. 97–131.

[6] Jerald Greenberg and Suzyn Ornstein, "High Job Status as Compensation for Underpayment: A Test of Equity Theory," *Journal of Applied Psychology*, May 1983, pp. 285–297.

Figure 5.2

Responses to Equity and
Inequity

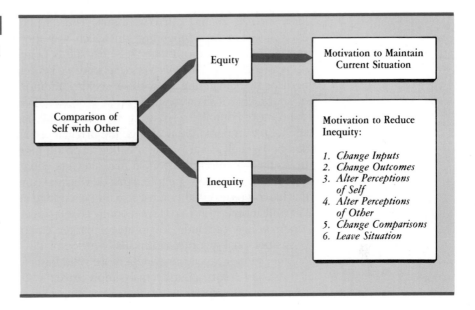

$$\frac{\text{Outcomes (self)}}{\text{Inputs (self)}} \quad \text{compared to} \quad \frac{\text{Outcomes (other)}}{\text{Inputs (other)}}$$

The person compares his or her own input-to-outcome ratio with the corresponding ratio of the comparison-other.

A feeling of equity does not require that the perceived outcomes and inputs
be equal, only that their ratios be the same. A person may believe that his
comparison-other deserves to make more money because she works harder;
then her higher outcome/input ratio is acceptable. Only if the other's outcomes
seem disproportionate to her inputs will the comparison provoke a feeling of
inequity.

Responses to Equity/Inequity

Figure 5.2 summarizes the results of an equity comparison. A feeling of equity
motivates the person to maintain the status quo. She or he will continue to
make the same level of input to the organization, at least as long as her or his
outcomes do not change and the inputs and outcomes of the comparison-other
also do not change. A person who feels inequity, however, is motivated to
reduce it—the greater the inequity, the stronger the level of motivation.

Adams has suggested six common methods people use to reduce inequity.[7]

[7] J. Stacey Adams, "Inequity in Social Exchange," in L. Berkowitz, ed., *Advances in
Experimental Social Psychology*, Vol. 2 (New York: Academic Press, 1965),
pp. 267–299.

First, we may change our own inputs. Thus, a person may put more or less effort into the job, depending on which way the inequity lies, as a way of altering her own ratio. If she feels that she is being underrewarded, she may decrease her effort, and vice versa. Second, we may change our own outcomes—perhaps by demanding a pay raise, seeking additional avenues for growth and development, or even stealing.

A more complex response is to alter our perceptions of self. After finding an inequity, a person may change the original self-assessment, and thus decide that he is really contributing less but receiving more than originally believed. In a similar fashion, the person may alter his perception of the other's inputs and/or outcomes. For example, a person who feels underrewarded may conclude that his comparison-other must actually be working more hours than it appeared.

Still another way to reduce inequity is by changing the object of comparison. A person may conclude, for instance, that the current comparison-other is the boss's personal favorite, is unusually lucky, or has special skills and abilities. Another person would provide a more valid basis for comparison.

As a last resort, a person may simply leave the situation. That is, transferring to another department or quitting altogether may seem to be the only way to reduce inequity.

Evaluation of Equity Theory

Equity theory has been the subject of much research. However, most studies have been somewhat narrowly focused,[8] dealing with only one ratio—pay (both hourly and piece-rate) versus the quality and/or quantity of worker output given overpayment and underpayment.[9] Findings support the predictions of equity theory pretty consistently, especially in conditions of underpayment. When people experience inequity while paid on a piece-rate basis, they tend to reduce their inputs by decreasing quality and to increase their outcomes by producing more units of work. When a person experiences inequity while paid by the hour, the theory predicts an increase in quality and quantity if the person feels overpaid and a decrease in quality and quantity if the person feels underpaid. Research evidence provides stronger support for responses to underpayment than for responses to overpayment, but overall, most studies seem to uphold the basic premises of the theory.[10] And an interesting finding of recent research, as detailed in *A Look at Research,* suggests that males and females react differently in inequity.

---

[8] Goodman, "Social Comparison Processes in Organizations"; and Mowday, "Equity Theory Predictions of Behavior in Organizations."

[9] Craig Pinder, *Work Motivation* (Glenview, Ill.: Scott, Foresman, 1984).

[10] Richard A. Cosier and Dan R. Dalton, "Equity Theory and Time: A Reformulation," *Academy of Management Review*, April 1983, pp. 311–319.

A LOOK AT

RESEARCH

Equity versus Equality

Equity theory posits that people generally like to feel that they get as much out of a relationship as they put into it. Laboratory studies have tended to confirm the theory. Subjects are likely to give the greatest rewards to those who have contributed the most. And they feel dissatisfied if they perceive that they are getting less out of a relationship than they put into it. Studies are less conclusive about how people feel when they are getting more than they feel they deserve; "egocentric bias" apparently allows people to feel satisfied with at least a moderate degree of inequity in their favor.

A study conducted in 1985 by Joel Brockner of Columbia University's Graduate School of Business and Laury Adsit of the University of Arizona focused on the question of whether men and women react the same way to situations of inequity. The participants were members of Business Lead and Referral Clubs, organizations founded specifically to encourage profitable exchanges and interactions between club members. The members were asked to rate the amount of effort they put into their interactions, the usefulness of the leads they'd gotten from other members, and their satisfaction with the exchanges.

The results confirmed earlier studies. When they felt that they were getting less than they deserved out of an interaction, men were significantly more disturbed than were women. Women, it seems, tend to be more interested in *equality* than in *equity*, that is, they're more likely than men to be satisfied when all participants in an interaction are rewarded equally, regardless of their inputs. Moreover, the differences between the male and female reactions become more extreme when the participants in the interactions are of the same sex. Men feel particularly dissatisfied when they feel they haven't received their just rewards in an interaction with other men. Women seem to worry about inequity least when they're dealing with other women.

The researchers were careful not to declare either sex more "fair" in reward allocation situations. What their research seems to show is that men and women tend to have different definitions of what constitutes fairness. They suggested that sex role stereotyping may play some role in developing these different concepts of fairness. Men, trained to value competence, logically feel that such competence should be rewarded. Stereotypical female behavior, on the other hand, values interpersonal warmth, something that can be facilitated by minimizing status differences and treating everyone equally.

Source: Joel Brockner and Laury Adsit, "The Moderating Impact of Sex on the Equity-Satisfaction Relationship: A Field Study," *Journal of Applied Psychology*, 1986, Volume 71, Number 4, 585–590.

Management Implications of Equity Theory

For managers, the most important implication of equity theory relates to organizational rewards and reward systems. Since "formal" organizational rewards (such as pay and office assignments) are more easily observable than "informal" rewards (intrinsic satisfaction, feelings of accomplishment, and the like), they are often at the center of a person's equity perceptions. Social comparisons are clearly a powerful factor in the workplace.

Equity theory offers managers three messages. First, everyone in the organization needs to understand the basis for the rewards. If people are to be rewarded more for high-quality work than for quantity of work, the fact needs to be clearly communicated. Second, people tend to take a multifaceted view of their rewards; they perceive and experience a variety of rewards, some tangible and others intangible. Finally, people base their actions on their perceptions of reality—if two people make exactly the same salary but each thinks the other makes more, they will each base their feelings of equity on the perception, rather than on reality. Hence, if a manager thinks two employees are fairly rewarded, the employees themselves may not necessarily agree.

EXPECTANCY THEORY

Expectancy theory is a complex, more encompassing model of motivation than equity theory, and over the years since its original formulation, the theory's scope and complexity have continued to grow.

The Basic Model

The basic expectancy theory model emerged from the work of Edward Tolman and Kurt Lewin.[11] Victor Vroom, however, is generally credited with first applying the theory to motivation in the workplace.[12] The theory is concerned with determining how individuals choose among alternative behaviors. Its premise is that motivation depends on how much we want something and how likely we think we are to get it. The following simple example illustrates this premise.

A new college graduate is looking for her first managerial job. While scanning the want ads, she sees that Exxon is seeking a new executive vice president to oversee its foreign operations. The starting salary is $200,000. The student would love to have the job, but does not bother to apply because she recognizes that she has no chance of getting it. Continuing, she sees a position that involves scraping bubble gum from underneath desks in college classroom buildings. The starting salary is $3.00 an hour, no experience necessary. Again, however, the student is unlikely to apply. Even though she thinks she could get the job, she does not want it. Then she comes across an advertisement for a management training position with a large company. No experience is necessary, the primary requirement is a college degree, and the starting salary is $25,000. She will probably apply for this position, first, because she wants it and, second, because she thinks she may have a reasonable chance of getting it. (This example understates the true complexity of most choices. Job-seeking

---

[11] E. C. Tolman, *Purposive Behavior in Animals* (New York: Appleton-Century-Crofts, 1932); and Kurt Lewin, *The Conceptual Representation and the Measurement of Psychological Forces* (Durham, N.C.: Duke University Press, 1938).

[12] Victor Vroom, *Work and Motivation* (New York: Wiley, 1964).

Figure 5.3

The Expectancy Theory
of Motivation

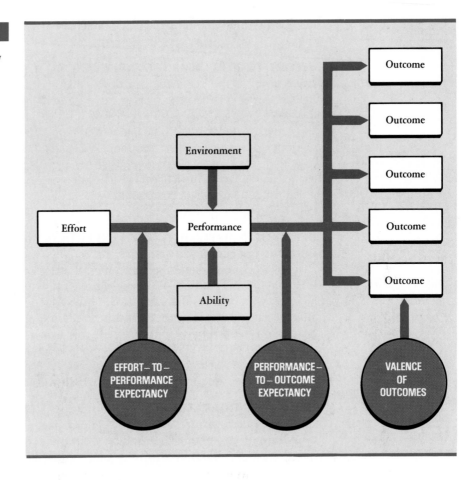

students may have strong geographic preferences, they may have other job opportunities, and they may also be considering graduate school. Most decisions, in fact, are quite complex.)[13]

Figure 5.3 summarizes the expectancy model. Its basic ingredients are effort (the result of motivation), performance, and outcomes. (Note that performance is considered a joint function of effort, environment, and ability—consistent with our discussions in Chapter 4.) Expectancy theory emphasizes

[13] Michael J. Stahl and Adrian M. Harrell, "Using Decision Modeling to Measure Second Level Valences in Expectancy Theory," *Organizational Behavior and Human Performance*, August 1983, pp. 23–34; John Wanous, Thomas L. Keon, and Janina C. Latack, "Expectancy Theory and Occupational/Organizational Choices: A Review and Test," *Organizational Behavior and Human Performance*, August 1983, pp. 66–86; and Adrian Harrell and Michael Stahl, "Additive Information Processing and the Relationship Between Expectancy of Success and Motivational Force," *Academy of Management Journal*, June 1986, pp. 424–433.

the linkages between these elements, which are described as expectancies and valences.

EFFORT-TO-PERFORMANCE EXPECTANCY   The **effort-to-performance expectancy** is the perceived probability that effort will lead to performance. In a person who believes that his or her effort will lead to higher performance, this expectancy is very strong, perhaps approaching 1.0 (where 1.0 equals absolute certainty that the outcome will occur). In a person who feels that his or her performance will be the same no matter how much effort he or she makes, the expectancy is very low, close to 0.0 (where 0.0 equals absolutely no chance that the outcome will occur). The person who thinks there is a moderate relationship between effort and performance has an expectancy somewhere in between.

PERFORMANCE-TO-OUTCOME EXPECTANCY   The **performance-to-outcome expectancy** is a person's perception of the probability that performance will lead to certain other outcomes. If a person thinks a high performer is certain to get a pay raise, this expectancy is close to 1.0. At the other extreme, a person who believes that raises are entirely independent of performance has an expectancy close to zero. Finally, if a person thinks performance has some bearing on the prospects for a pay raise, his or her expectancy is somewhere between 1.0 and 0.0. In a work setting, several performance-to-outcome expectancies are relevant because, as shown in Figure 5.3, several outcomes might logically result from performance. Each will have its own expectancy.

OUTCOMES AND VALENCES   An **outcome** is anything that might possibly result from performance. High-level performance might conceivably produce a pay raise, a promotion, recognition from the boss, fatigue, stress, and less time to rest. The **valence** of an outcome is how attractive or unattractive that outcome is to the person. Pay raises, promotions, and recognition might all have positive valences, whereas fatigue, stress, and less time to rest might all have negative valences. People vary in the strength of their outcome valences. Stress may be a significant negative factor for one person but only a slight annoyance for another. Similarly, a pay increase may have a strong positive valence for someone desperately in need of money, a slight positive valence for someone interested mostly in getting a promotion, and even a negative valence for someone in an unfavorable tax position!

The basic expectancy framework suggests that three conditions must be met before motivated behavior will occur. First, the effort-to-performance expectancy must be well above zero. That is, an individual must have a reasonable expectation that an exertion of effort will produce high levels of performance. Second, the performance-to-outcome expectancies must also be well above zero. An individual must feel that performance may realistically result in valued outcomes. Third, the sum of all the valences for the potential outcomes relevant to the person must be positive. One or more valences may be negative, so long as the positives outweigh the negatives. For example, stress and fatigue may have moderately negative valences, but if pay, promotion, and recognition have very high positive valences, the overall valence of the set of outcomes associated with performance will still be positive.

Conceptually, the valences of all relevant outcomes and the corresponding pattern of expectancies are assumed to interact in an almost mathematical sense to determine the level of motivation. Most people do assess likelihoods and preferences for various consequences of behaviors, but they seldom approach them in such a calculating manner.

Management in Action provides a good example of how expectancy theory works in the real world. Management at A & P offered employees an opportunity to achieve outcomes they wanted (job security and money) and showed them how to do it (by maximizing the expectancies).

The Porter-Lawler Extension

Vroom's original presentation of expectancy theory placed it in the mainstream of contemporary motivation theory. Since then, the model has been refined and extended. Most modifications have focused on the identification and measurement of outcomes and expectancies.[14] An exception was the version of expectancy theory presented by Lyman W. Porter and Edward E. Lawler, which takes a novel view of the relationship between employee satisfaction and performance.[15] Although the conventional wisdom was that satisfaction led to performance, Porter and Lawler argued the reverse. Under the right conditions, they suggested, high levels of performance may lead to satisfaction, not the other way around.

The **Porter-Lawler model** appears in Figure 5.4. Some of its features are quite different from the original formulation of expectancy theory. For example, the extended model includes ability, traits, and role perceptions (how well the individual understands his or her job; see Chapter 8). At the beginning of the motivational cycle, effort is a function of the value of the potential reward for the employee (its valence) and the perceived effort-reward probability (an expectancy). Effort then combines with abilities, traits, and role perceptions to determine performance.

Performance results in two kinds of rewards. *Intrinsic rewards* are intangible—a feeling of accomplishment, a sense of achievement, and so forth.

---

[14] Jay Galbraith and Larry Cummings, "An Empirical Investigation of the Motivational Determinants of Task Performance: Interactive Effects Between Valence-Instrumentality and Motivation-Ability," *Organizational Behavior and Human Performance*, Vol. 2, 1967, pp. 237–258; George Graen, "Instrumentality Theory of Work Motivation: Some Experimental Results and Suggested Modifications," *Journal of Applied Psychology Monograph*, Vol. 53, 1969, pp. 1–25; and Campbell, Dunnette, Lawler, and Weick, *Managerial Behavior, Performance, and Effectiveness*.

[15] Lyman W. Porter and Edward E. Lawler, *Managerial Attitudes and Performance* (Homewood, Ill.: Dorsey Press, 1968).

Management in ACTION

A "Super Fresh" Idea

In the late 1970s many industry analysts thought A&P—officially the Great Atlantic & Pacific Tea Company—was doomed. The company had only 1,016 stores in 1982, down from 3,468 in 1974. Things looked particularly bleak for A&P employees in the Philadelphia area when the company closed all 81 of its stores there at the end of 1981. The United Food & Commercial Workers struggled to buy some of the stores and save jobs and then proposed an unusual worker participation idea to A&P. The company's chairman, James Wood, bought the scheme, saying: "The idea of people getting a piece of what they are trying to achieve has always appealed to me enormously."

The company revived 60 of its stores in the Philadelphia area—most under the new name Super Fresh—as a result of a unique bargain. A&P wanted to cut labor costs: it had been spending 13 to 15 percent of its stores' sales on labor, and it wanted to get that figure down below the industry average of 12 percent. To do so, it slashed workers' pay up to 25 percent.

In return, employees received an unusual collection of promises and incentives. First, they got their jobs back, and with labor costs down to 11 percent of sales, they felt reasonably secure that the stores would survive and the jobs would last. To encourage workers to find ways to cut costs further, A&P offered them bonuses: employees at a store that lowered labor costs to 10 percent of sales would share a bonus equal to 1 percent of the store's sales. Employees would actually keep about two-thirds of the bonus, and one-third would go into a worker fund. If A&P should decide to sell a particular store, its workers would have the right of first refusal to buy it, and the fund would provide the necessary cash.

To provide workers with an opportunity to institute cost-cutting measures, the company has given employees a greater voice in management decisions. Workers have a say in deciding what to stock, when to open, how to arrange the store. The employees of one store in a black and Italian neighborhood persuaded management to break with A&P tradition and stock large sections of ethnic food. Workers at another store convinced management that extra space between store shelves and checkouts would increase sales because customers wouldn't become frustrated with the congestion at peak hours.

These and other ideas have paid off, it seems, for everyone. The base pay of Philadelphia-area workers is still lower than that of workers in other food stores, but their bonuses often are the envy of the industry. And the company's profits, stock price, and per-store sales have all risen dramatically. Not surprisingly, other food stores have begun to take notice.

Sources: David I. Diamond, "A & P's Worker-Managers," *The New York Times*, May 21, 1983, 37; Christopher S. Eklund, "How A&P Fattens Profits by Sharing Them," *Business Week*, December 22, 1986, 44; Ellen Uzelac, "A&P Become Dead Letters Here Sunday," *The Baltimore Sun*, November 25, 1986, 10D.

Figure 5.4   The Porter-Lawler Extension of Expectancy Theory

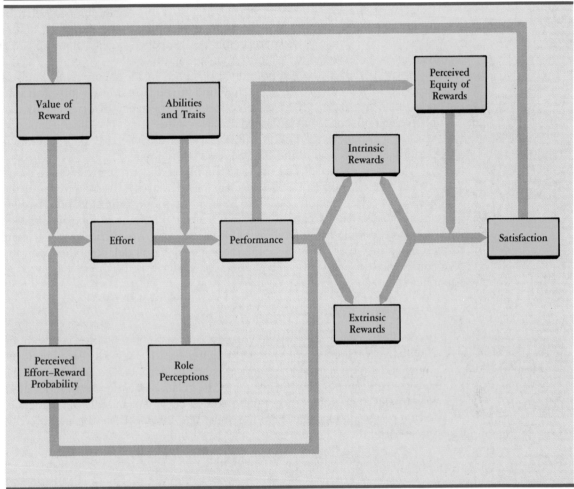

Source: From Lyman W. Porter and Edward E. Lawler: *Managerial Attitudes and Performance.* © Richard D. Irwin, Inc., 1968. Reprinted by permission.

Extrinsic rewards are such tangible outcomes as pay and promotion. The individual judges the value of his or her performance to the organization, and uses social comparison processes to form an impression of the equity of the rewards received. If the rewards are regarded as equitable, the employee feels satisfied. In subsequent cycles, satisfaction with rewards influences the value of the rewards anticipated, and actual performance following effort influences future perceived effort-reward probabilities.

Evaluation of Expectancy Theory

Expectancy theory has been repeatedly tested by organizational behavior researchers.[16] As noted earlier, the complexity of the theory has been both a blessing and a curse.[17] Nowhere is this double-edged quality more apparent than in the research undertaken to evaluate the theory.

Several studies have supported various parts of the theory. Both kinds of expectancy and valence have been found to be associated with effort and performance.[18] Research has also confirmed expectancy theory's claims that people will not engage in motivated behavior unless they (1) value the expected rewards, (2) believe their effort will lead to performance, and (3) believe their performance will lead to the desired rewards.[19]

However, expectancy theory is so complicated that researchers have found it quite difficult to test.[20] In particular, the measures of various parts of the model may lack validity, and the procedures for investigating relationships among the variables have not always been as scientific as one would like. Moreover, people are seldom as rational and objective in choosing behaviors as expectancy theory implies. Still, the logic of the model, combined with the consistent, if modest, research support for it, suggests the theory has much to offer.[21]

Management Implications of Expectancy Theory

Because expectancy theory is so complex, it is difficult to apply directly in the workplace. A manager would need to figure out what rewards each employee wants and how valuable those rewards are to each individual, measure the various expectancies, and finally adjust the relationships to create motivation. Nevertheless, expectancy theory offers several important and relevant guidelines for the practicing manager. David A. Nader and Edward E. Lawler have recently summarized these guidelines:

1. Determine the primary outcomes each employee wants.

---

[16] Terence R. Mitchell, "Expectancy Models of Job Satisfaction, Occupational Preference, and Effort: A Theoretical, Methodological, and Empirical Appraisal," *Psychological Bulletin*, Vol. 81, 1974, pp. 1096–1112; and John P. Campbell and Robert D. Pritchard, "Motivation Theory in Industrial and Organizational Psychology," in Marvin D. Dunnette, ed., *Handbook of Industrial and Organizational Psychology* (Chicago: Rand McNally, 1976), pp. 63–130.

[17] Wanous et al., "Expectancy Theory and Occupational/Organizational Choices: A Review and Test"; and Pinder, *Work Motivation*.

[18] Pinder, *Work Motivation*.

[19] Campbell and Pritchard, "Motivation Theory in Industrial and Organizational Psychology."

[20] Pinder, *Work Motivation*.

[21] Campbell and Pritchard, "Motivation Theory in Industrial and Organizational Psychology"; and Pinder, *Work Motivation*.

2. Decide what levels and kinds of performance are needed to meet organizational goals.
3. Make sure the desired levels of performance are possible.
4. Link desired outcomes and desired performance.
5. Analyze the situation for conflicting expectancies.
6. Make sure the rewards are large enough.
7. Make sure the overall system is equitable for everyone.[22]

ORGANIZATIONAL BEHAVIOR MODIFICATION

Chapter 2's discussion of learning and reinforcement theory notes that we treat the managerial implications of learning theory, especially as they relate to motivation, in this chapter. The major organizational application of learning theory is **organizational behavior modification (OB Mod).**[23]

Behavior Modification

OB Mod. is the application of reinforcement theory to people in organizational settings. As Chapter 2 explains, reinforcement theory says that we can increase the frequency of desired behaviors by linking those behaviors with positive consequences and decrease undesired behaviors by linking them with negative consequences. OB Mod. characteristically uses positive reinforcement to encourage employees in desired behaviors. Figure 5.5 illustrates the basic steps used in OB Mod.

The first step is to identify *performance-related behavioral events* (i.e., desired and undesired behaviors). A manager of an electronics store, for example, might decide that the most important behavior for salespeople working on commission is to greet customers warmly and show them the merchandise they came in to see. Note in Figure 5.5 that three kinds of organizational activity are associated with this behavior: the behavioral event itself, the performance that results, and organizational consequences that befall the individual.

The manager next measures *baseline performance*—the existing level of performance for each individual. This is usually stated in terms of a percentage frequency across different time intervals. For example, the electronics store manager may observe that a particular salesperson is presently greeting around 40 percent of the customers each day, as desired. The third step is identifying the existing *behavioral contingencies,* or consequences, of performance. That

---

[22] David A. Nadler and Edward E. Lawler, "Motivation: A Diagnostic Approach," in J. Richard Hackman, Edward E. Lawler, and Lyman W. Porter, eds., *Perspectives on Behavior in Organizations*, 2nd ed. (New York: McGraw-Hill, 1983), pp. 67–78.

[23] Fred Luthans and Robert Kreitner, *Organizational Behavior Modification* (Glenview, Ill.: Scott, Foresman, 1975); and Fred Luthans and Robert Kreitner, *Organizational Behavior Modification and Beyond* (Glenview, Ill.: Scott, Foresman, 1985).

Figure 5.5   The Steps in OB Mod.

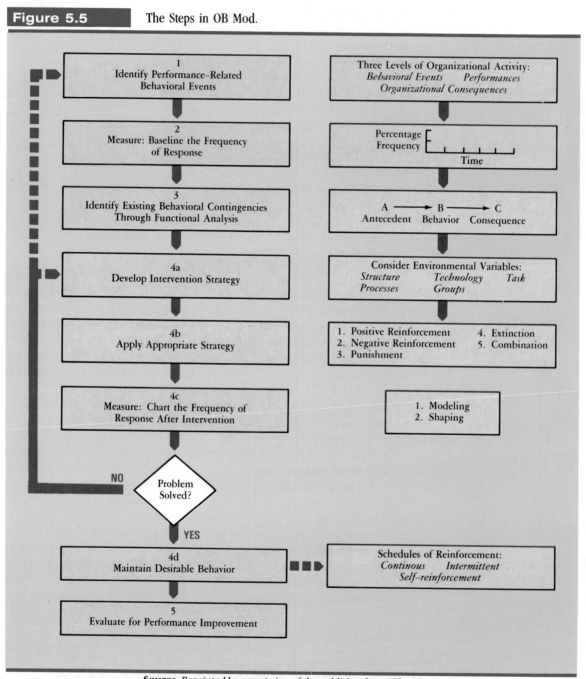

is, what now happens to employees who perform at various levels? If an employee works hard, does he or she get a reward or just get tired? For example, the electronics store manager may observe that when customers are greeted warmly and assisted, they buy something 40 percent of the time, while those that are not properly greeted make a purchase only 20 percent of the time. Thus, the salesperson earns both gratification from the sales, as well as higher commissions.

At this point, the manager develops and applies an appropriate *intervention strategy*. That is, some element of the performance-reward linkage—structure, process, technology, groups, or the task—is changed with the goal of making high-level performance more rewarding. Various kinds of positive reinforcement are used to guide employee behavior in desired directions. The electronics store manager, for example, might offer a sales commission whereby salespeople earn a percentage of the dollar amount taken in by each sale. He might also compliment salespeople who give appropriate greetings and ignore those who don't.

After the intervention step, the manager again measures performance to determine whether the desired effect has been achieved. If not, the manager must redesign the intervention or repeat the entire process. Suppose the salespeople in the electronics store still are not greeting customers nicely. The manager might need to look for other forms of positive reinforcement, perhaps a higher-percentage commission.

If performance has increased, the manager must try to maintain the desired behavior through some schedule of positive reinforcement. For example, higher commissions might be granted for every other sale, for sales over a certain dollar amount, and so forth. (As Chapter 2 explains, a schedule defines the interval at which reinforcement will be given.) Finally, the manager looks for improvements in individual employees' behavior. Here, the emphasis is on offering significant longer-term rewards, such as promotions and salary adjustments, to encourage ongoing efforts to improve performance.[24]

Results of OB Mod.

OB Mod. is relatively simple, and so it has been used by many different kinds of organizations, with varying levels of success.[25] A program at Emery Air Freight prompted much of the initial enthusiasm for OB Mod., and other success stories have also caught the attention of practicing managers.[26] For example, B.F. Goodrich increased productivity over 300 percent and Weyerhauser Company

---

[24] Luthans and Kreitner, *Organizational Behavior Modification and Beyond*.

[25] W. Clay Hamner and Ellen P. Hamner, "Organizational Behavior Modification on the Bottom Line," *Organizational Dynamics*, Spring 1976, pp. 2–21.

[26] "At Emery Air Freight: Positive Reinforcement Boosts Performance," *Organizational Dynamics*, Winter 1973, pp. 41–50; and Hamner and Hamner, "Behavior Modification on the Bottom Line."

increased productivity by at least 8 percent in three different work groups.[27] These results seem to show that OB Mod. is a valuable method for improving employee motivation in many situations.

OB Mod. also has certain drawbacks, however. Not all applications have worked—for example, a program at Standard Oil of Ohio was discontinued because it failed to meet its objectives, and another at Michigan Bell was only modestly successful. Further, managers frequently have limited ways to provide meaningful reinforcement for their employees, and some people have argued that OB Mod. is manipulative because it tries to suppress individual freedom of behavioral choice. Much of the research testing OB Mod. has gone on in laboratories and so is hard to generalize to the real world. And even if OB Mod. works for a while, after the novelty has worn off, the impact of the positive reinforcement may wane, and employees may come to view it as a part of the normal compensation system.[28]

PARTICIPATIVE MANAGEMENT

Participative Management, another applied approach to employee motivation, is a way of thinking about the human resources of an organization. A historical perspective is necessary to fully understand participative management.

Historical Perspectives

The human relations movement in vogue from the 1930s through the 1950s (see Chapter 1) assumed that employees who are happy and satisfied will work harder.[29] The movement stimulated general interest in worker participation in various organizational activities. The hope was that if employees were given the opportunity to participate in decision making about their work environment, they would be satisfied, and satisfaction was supposed to result in improved performance. But managers tended to see employee participation merely as a way to increase satisfaction, not as a source of potentially valuable input. Eventually, managers began to recognize the employee input was useful in itself, apart from its presumed effect on satisfaction. Employees came to be seen as valued resources who contribute to organizational effectiveness.[30]

The role of participation in motivation can be expressed in terms of both the need theories discussed in Chapter 4 and expectancy theory. Employees

---

[27] Hamner and Hamner, "Behavior Modification on the Bottom Line."

[28] Edwin Locke, "The Myths of Behavior Mod in Organizations," *Academy of Management Review*, Vol. 2, 1977, pp. 543–553.

[29] Daniel Wren, *The Evolution of Management Thought*, 2nd ed. (New York: Wiley, 1979).

[30] Raymond E. Miles, "Conflicting Elements in Managerial Ideologies," *Industrial Relations*, October 1964, pp. 77–91.

who participate in decisions may feel more committed to executing them properly. Further, the successful process of making a decision, executing it, and then seeing the positive consequences can help satisfy one's need for achievement, provide recognition and responsibility, and enhance self-esteem. Simply being asked to participate in organizational decisions may also enhance an employee's sense of self-esteem. And participation should help clarify expectancies. That is, by participating in decisions, employees may better understand the linkage between their performance and the rewards they want most.

Areas of Participation

At one level, employees can participate in questions and decisions about their own individual jobs. Instead of just telling them how to do their jobs, for example, managers can ask employees to make their own decisions about how to do them. Based on their own expertise and experience with their tasks, workers might be able to improve their own productivity. In many situations, they might also be well qualified to make decisions about what materials to use, what tools to use, and so forth.

It might also be helpful to let workers make decisions about administrative things—work schedules, for instance. If jobs are relatively independent of one another, people might be able to decide when to change shifts, take breaks, go to lunch, and so forth. A work group might also be able to schedule vacations and days off for all its members.

More and more, too, employees are getting opportunities to participate in broader issues of product quality. Such participation has been seen as a hallmark of successful Japanese firms, so American companies have followed suit. *International Perspective* illustrates how Japanese companies pay attention to hiring the "right" employees, even when doing business in this country. In this instance, "right" means having the right set of attitudes—being motivated and interested in participating. Another increasingly popular approach for managing employee participation is through the use of quality circles.

Quality Circles

Quality circles became popular in the United States in the early 1980s. Widely used in Japan, they were presumed to have played a role in that country's rapid economic and technological growth. **Quality circles (QCs)** are usually defined as small groups of volunteers who meet regularly to identify, analyze, and solve quality and related problems that pertain to their work.[31]

The mechanics of quality circles are summarized in Figure 5.6. The first step is to seek volunteers. Recruitment usually stresses the circle's potential to

---

[31] G. Munchus, "Employer-Employee Based Quality Circles in Japan: Human Resource Implications for American Firms," *Academy of Management Review*, April, 1983, pp. 255–261.

International Perspective

Wanted: People Who Need Toyota

Times have changed for workers in the auto industry. In the period when Detroit was king, a job applicant took a few minutes to list previous experience and contacts within the company and was often hired on the spot. But now many car manufacturers, particularly Japanese car makers who have built plants in the United States, are being much more careful in choosing workers whose skills and needs match those of the company. Honda puts job candidates through three interviews. Nissan gives potential new workers 40 hours of training without pay to see if the worker and the company are compatible.

By far the most rigorous screening program is being conducted by Toyota, Japan's leading auto maker, as it hires American workers for jobs like those at its new auto-assembly plant in Georgetown, Kentucky. The company puts job applicants through up to 25 hours of tests to find workers who are not just willing to adopt the company's philosophy, but who also *need* to feel versatile in their work and who hunger for the sense of mutual commitment brought about by working on a team with a common goal. These are key parts of the Japanese business ethic.

To find such employees, even for assembly-line jobs, Toyota is using the kind of testing that used to be reserved for management positions. Applicants start by taking tests in reading, math, and manual dexterity. Skilled workers are tested on their technical knowledge. Then everyone participates in workplace simulations. Groups are presented with problems like ranking customers' reactions to particular automobile features or judging manufacturing and repairing processes. The company's advisors listen to the conversations and take notes on who says what. The company also tests applicants' alertness and ability to spot problems by putting them on a flawed mock assembly line and asking them how to improve the line.

Perhaps the key step in the attempt to find workers whose needs match the company's is a job-fitness test. Applicants are asked to agree or disagree with 100 statements like "It's important for workers to work past quitting time to get the job done when necessary" and "Management will take advantage of employees whenever possible." Through such testing of attitudes, Toyota hopes to find workers who will not just do a good job, but also be happy doing it.

Not everyone is enthusiastic about Toyota's testing. Union officials worry that the company may use the tests as a way of screening out those people who would be most likely to join a union. In addition, groups like the Urban League are closely watching the company's hiring of minorities and women.

Despite such worries, if current trends continue, more workers can count on taking such tests in the future. Because of the yen's strength relative to the dollar and talk in Washington about trade protectionism, Japanese manufacturers are likely to continue building plants in the United States. American companies are therefore being increasingly influenced by Japanese screening procedures. General Motors, for instance, after working on a joint venture with Toyota in California, is now applying more rigorous hiring standards for its new Saturn plant in Tennessee.

The companies' motives behind the testing may be complex, but workers can at least hope that perfecting such testing will enable future employers to locate job applicants whose needs will fit perfectly with the company's. That would make everyone happy.

Source: Richard Koenig, "Toyota Takes Pains, And Time, Filling Jobs At Its Kentucky Plant," *The Wall Street Journal*, December 1, 1987, 1. Reprinted by permission of *The Wall Street Journal.* © Dow Jones & Company, Inc. (1987). All rights reserved.

Figure 5.6

The Mechanics of
Quality Circles

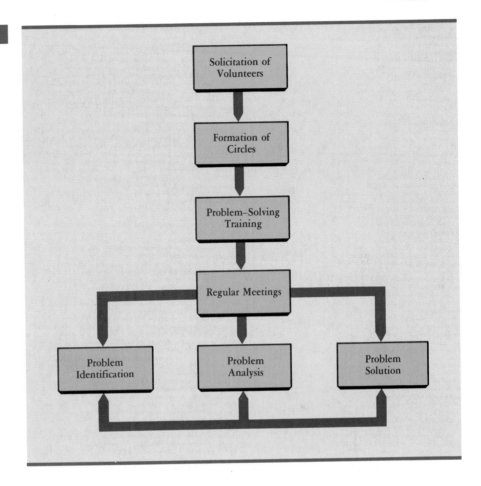

help the organization and influence its future. It is crucial, of course, that the participants be true volunteers—participation through coercion will probably have more negative than positive consequences. Circles usually have eight to ten members drawn from the same work area or from related areas so that they have a common frame of reference. A circle's membership is ordinarily fixed, although people may be added or dropped as appropriate. The circle usually receives some form of problem-solving training to help it deal with work problems. Training may be provided only at the outset or as an ongoing process.

Quality circle meetings are almost always held on company premises and on company time. One meeting a week is standard, with each meeting lasting about one hour, but there is variation from company to company. During meetings, the circle identifies, analyzes, and solves quality problems in its areas of responsibility. Problems may range from eliminating vandalism to reducing

Figure 5.7

An Attributional View of
Employee Motivation

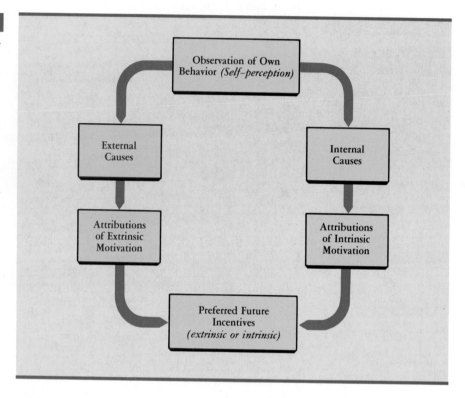

defects in a particular production process. Since quality circles were "discovered" by American firms, many have adopted them, including Westinghouse, Hewlett-Packard, Texas Instruments, Eastman Kodak, and Procter and Gamble. Many firms report positive results from quality circles, although not much research has been done to assess their effectiveness.[32]

ATTRIBUTION THEORY

Chapter 2 discusses the role of attribution in perception. Here we explore the motivational implications of attribution theory.[33] According to the **attributional view of employee motivation,** summarized in Figure 5.7, employees observe their own behavior through the processes of self-perception. On the basis of

---

[32] Ricky W. Griffin, "Consequences of Quality Circles in an Industrial Setting: A Longitudinal Assessment," *Academy of Management Journal,* June 1988, pp. 338–358.
[33] H. H. Kelley, *Attribution in Social Interaction* (Morristown, N.J.: General Learning Press, 1971).

these perceptions, the individual decides whether his or her behavior is a response primarily to external or internal factors.[34]

Through this attribution of causes, the individual decides whether he or she is basically extrinsically or intrinsically motivated and develops a preferred pattern of future incentives. A person who believes he is extrinsically motivated will seek extrinsic rewards, such as pay or status symbols, as future incentives. One who feels she is intrinsically motivated will look more for intrinsic incentives in the future.

Although relatively little work has been done on attribution theory's applications to motivation, there have been some intriguing findings. For example, E. L. Deci reasoned that paying an intrinsically motivated person on an incentive basis (that is, providing extrinsic rewards) would make him or her become more extrinsically motivated and less intrinsically motivated. Deci's research has indicated that if people are paid to do something they already like to do (that is, they are intrinsically motivated), their level of "liking" declines. Furthermore, if the pay is later withheld, their level of effort also declines. Thus, attributional processes appear to play a meaningful role in employee motivation in the workplace.[35]

CONSEQUENCES OF MOTIVATION

At the beginning of Chapter 4, we note that all behavior is motivated. The manager's job is to channel the motivation of her or his employees such that their behaviors enhance the effectiveness of the overall organization. In this section, we take a brief look at the behaviors that are key to organizational effectiveness.

Performance and Productivity

Since the early 1960s in the United States, business, government, and the academic community have been worrying about performance and productivity. Much of this concern has been prompted by decreases in American productivity growth compared to other industrial countries, most notably Japan.[36] Although the gap has narrowed slightly in the 1980s, the issue still deserves attention.

---

[34] Craig A. Anderson, "Motivational and Performance Deficits in Interpersonal Settings: The Effect of Attributional Style," *Journal of Personality and Social Psychology*, November 1983, pp. 1136–1147.

[35] See E. L. Deci, "Effects of Externally Mediated Rewards on Intrinsic Motivation," *Journal of Applied Psychology*, Vol. 18, 1971, pp. 105–115. See also Paul C. Jordan, "Effects of an Extrinsic Reward on Intrinsic Motivation: A Field Experiment," *Academy of Management Journal*, June 1986, pp. 405–412.

[36] W. Bruce Chew, "No-Nonsense Guide to Productivity," *Harvard Business Review*, January–February 1988, pp. 110–119.

Productivity refers to how many goods and services an organization creates from its resources. If one worker produces 100 units, 3 of which are defective, she is more productive than a worker who produces 90 units with 5 defects, and less productive than a worker who produces 105 units with no defects. Similarly, a bank that can process an average of 75 customers an hour with 3 teller stations is more productive than a bank that can only process 70 customers an hour with the same number of teller stations. Productivity is the level of outputs relative to inputs; it can be assessed at the level of the individual, the work group, or the organization itself.

Performance, a broader concept, can be defined as the total set of job-related behaviors employees engage in. If worker A can produce 20 units an hour, then worker A is more productive than worker B. Yet suppose that worker B is always willing to work late, assists in training new employees, looks for opportunities to help the organization, always comes to work on time, and has not missed a day of work in three years. Worker A, on the other hand, insists on leaving at promptly 5:00 P.M. every day, ignores new employees, never shows any initiative, is often several minutes late for work, and misses an average of one day of work per month.

Although worker A is more productive, it might be argued that worker B is the better performer across a wider array of activities. Of course, it is up to the manager and the organization to determine exactly what the appropriate job-related behaviors are and how they should be weighted in determining performance. The point is that performance goes beyond the mere level of outputs. (Performance appraisal is discussed in Chapter 19.)

Absenteeism and Turnover

Two intimately related employee behaviors of great interest to managers and researchers are absenteeism and turnover. Both are forms of withdrawal from the workplace. **Absenteeism** occurs when employees are absent from work, for whatever reason. **Turnover** occurs when employees permanently quit working for an organization. Absenteeism is an important dimension of performance, for an absent employee's responsibilities fall on others in the organization. Turnover is also critical, since organizations must usually spend considerable time and money recruiting, hiring, and training new employees to replace those who leave.

Figure 5.8 shows a simplified model of employee absenteeism. The model, based on the work of Steers and Rhodes, suggests that job satisfaction and pressures to attend work interact to determine attendance motivation. Actual attendance depends on both motivation and ability to attend.[37]

---

[37] Richard M. Steers and Susan R. Rhodes, "Major Influences on Employee Attendance: A Process Model," *Journal of Applied Psychology,* Vol. 63, 1978, pp. 391–407.

Figure 5.8

A Model of Employee
Absenteeism

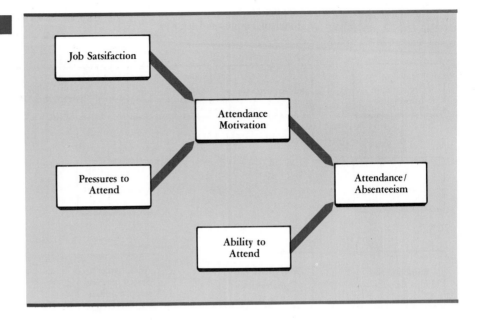

Working with Richard Mowday, Steers has also formulated an integrated model of employee turnover.[38] Figure 5.9 presents a simplified form of this model. Individual characteristics interact with information about the job and the organization to determine job expectations and values, and with economic and market conditions to determine alternative job opportunities. Expectations, job performance, and organizational characteristics and experiences then determine job satisfaction.

Satisfaction interacts with nonwork factors that support staying or leaving, such as job transfer for a spouse, to influence the employee's desire to stay or leave. A person searching for another job may end the search if offered some kind of accommodation. For example, if the boss learns that a valued employee is thinking about leaving to take a new job with a higher salary, a pay raise may persuade the employee to stay. But if no such accommodation is offered, the employee will continue to ponder the choice of leaving.

Although the complete model has not been tested, it summarizes a considerable amount of research on employee turnover and can serve as a useful framework for understanding this important phenomenon.

---

[38] Richard Steers and Richard Mowday, "A Model of Voluntary Employee Turnover," in L. L. Cummings and B. M. Staw, eds., *Research in Organizational Behavior*, Vol. 3 (Greenwich, Conn.: JAI Press, 1981).

Figure 5.9   A Model of Employee Turnover

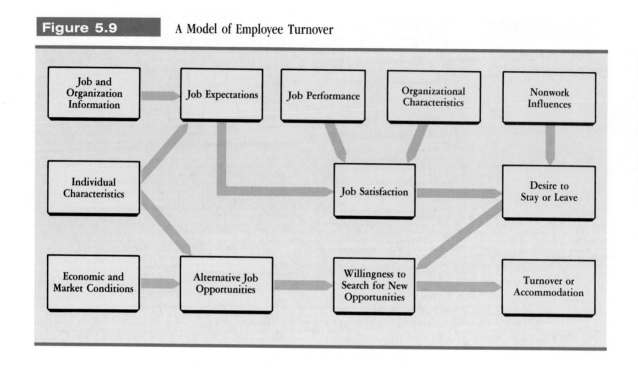

CONCLUDING PERSPECTIVES ON MOTIVATION

Many of the most important managerial implications of motivation are self-evident. Like the content theories discussed in Chapter 4, each of the process theories presented in this chapter has potential uses in the workplace. Equity theory provides useful guidelines for managing reward systems, and expectancy theory partially explains why people put different levels of effort into their jobs. OB Mod. and participative management each provide practical guidelines for the implementation of motivational strategies. Finally, attribution theory is a promising new perspective on motivation.

Yet each of these theories only offers a piece or two of the motivation puzzle. Managers should recognize that no single theory explains or predicts employee motivation completely. The primary message is to understand the value of each viewpoint while guarding against its shortcomings.

SUMMARY OF KEY POINTS

The equity theory of motivation assumes that people want to be treated fairly. Equity theory hypothesizes that people compare their own input-to-outcome ratio in the organization to the ratio of a comparison-other. If they feel their treatment has been relatively inequitable, they take steps to reduce the inequity.

Expectancy theory, a somewhat more complicated model, follows from the assumption that people are motivated to work toward a goal if they want it and think they have a reasonable chance of achieving it. The effort-to-performance expectancy is the belief that effort will lead to performance. The performance-to-outcome expectancy is the belief that performance will lead to certain outcomes. Valence is the desirability to the individual of the various possible outcomes of performance.

The Porter-Lawler extension of expectancy theory provides useful insights into the relationship between satisfaction and performance. This model suggests that performance may lead to a variety of intrinsic and extrinsic rewards. When perceived as being equitable, these rewards lead to satisfaction.

Organizational behavior modification is the application of reinforcement principles and concepts to organizational settings. Using a variety of reinforcers and reinforcement contingencies, several organizations have achieved impressive motivational improvements through OB Mod.

Participative management can help improve employee motivation in many business settings. Quality circles have received a lot of attention in recent years as a useful way to increase employee participation.

Attribution theory has also been applied to employee motivation. The theory suggests that employees perceive their behavior as stemming from either external or internal causes and are motivated by rewards that correspond to the causes of their behavior.

From a managerial standpoint, motivation theory is primarily intended to help channel employee behavior toward high performance, high productivity, low absenteeism, and low turnover.

DISCUSSION QUESTIONS

1. What other ways besides the content-process distinction might categorize the various motivation theories discussed in Chapters 4 and 5?

2. Apply equity theory to a classroom setting. Specify your inputs and potential outcomes. Choose a likely comparison-other and judge whether you should feel equity or inequity.

3. What might be some other managerial implications of equity theory beyond those discussed in the chapter?

4. Do you think that expectancy theory is too complex for direct use in organizational settings? Why or why not?

5. Do you agree or disagree with the relationships between performance and satisfaction suggested by Porter and Lawler? Can you cite both examples that support the model and ones that refute it?

6. The OB Mod. theory of motivation seems to be more application based than the equity or expectancy theories. It is also rather narrow in scope. What are the advantages and disadvantages of a theory that has these characteristics?

7. What are some of the ways in which your instructor might be able to use OB Mod. in the classroom to shape your behavior? Are there ways you can shape his or her behavior through some of the same techniques?

8. What are the motivational consequences of participative management—specifically, quality circles—from the frame of reference of another theory or theories?

9. What motivational problems might result from an organization's attempt to set up quality circles?

10. Cite personal examples of attributional processes and motivation.

Case 5.1

Motivation Through Commitment

The mid-1980s were lean times for many high-tech firms, particularly computer companies. Faced with decreasing demand and a growing list of domestic and foreign competitors, many computer and electronics manufacturers made drastic cuts in their workforce to become more efficient and competitive. [See *Management in Action,* Chapter 3.] Like most companies in the industry, Hewlett-Packard had a rough year in 1985, with orders rising only 1 percent and per-share earnings dropping 10 percent from 1984. It was forced to cut back on hiring, trim travel and overtime, and offer voluntary time off programs. Yet Hewlett-Packard did not fire a single worker.

Such commitment of the company to its workers reflects a management outlook that has nurtured thousands of creative engineers and their products and has resulted in an employee turnover rate of less than half the industry average. Other companies seek to hire former Hewlett-Packard employees because they have a reputation for being talented and loyal. Yet, as a high-tech specialist at an executive search firm put it, "It's not easy getting people to leave H-P."

The promise of a stable job is just a small part of Hewlett-Packard's people-oriented philosophy. The company's founders, William Hewlett and David Packard, were clever, entrepreneurial engineers, and for the last 50 years Hewlett-Packard has been attracting similar people and providing them with an environment in which to do their best work.

The company follows a management by objectives policy, hiring people who are goal oriented, telling them what their objective is, and then letting them figure out the best way to attain it. Although the company has necessarily become more structured as it has expanded, the atmosphere is still informal—work areas are open, dress is casual, and everyone's on a first-name basis. The company puts its trust in individuals, not in a system of close supervision and work regimentation. It offers ample room for advancement; instead of letting individual departments get larger and larger, Hewlett-Packard creates new departments, opening up positions for new supervisors and managers. Each of the fifty-five manufacturing divisions is run like a small independent company. Employees rarely feel they need to leave the company to advance their careers.

The atmosphere of flexibility and innovation has always been reflected in the company's products. Recently some industry analysts were forecasting that Hewlett-Packard would be forced out of the mid-range computer market by IBM and Digital. But the company gambled, apparently successfully, on its own flexibility. Rather than build new, more complex, incompatible systems, Hewlett-Packard has focused on products that are simpler and cheaper than those of their competitors and that can easily be adapted to other companies' hardware and software. Two of the results look promising: Spectrum, a computer system that's faster than Digital's comparable system but costs half as much; and a new, less expensive terminal, sales of which were 150 percent above the company's previous levels in the first four months.

The terminal required a unique team effort, including cooperation from engineers asked to change "finished" blueprints to accommodate different components. At other companies, engineers might have balked at the constant re-designing, but Hewlett-Packard's employees, with their eyes on the goal, came through with a product that uses 40 percent fewer parts and costs up to 45 percent less than competing products.

Whether asked to make such cooperative sacrifices or to create individual innovations, Hewlett-Packard workers do the job because the company gives them the freedom and encouragement they need. Hewlett-Packard treats its workers as valuable, talented, trusted individuals; in such a company, apparently, motivation is not an issue.

Case Questions

1. What are the motivating factors at Hewlett-Packard?

2. Would Hewlett-Packard's formula for successful motivation work at other companies?

Case Sources

Bob Weinstein, "What It's Like to Work for Hewlett-Packard," *Business Week Careers*, November 1986, 14; Jonathon B. Levine, "Mild-Mannered Hewlett-Packard is Making Like Superman," *Business Week*, March 7, 1988, 110; Jonathon B. Levine, "How HP Built a Better Terminal," *Business Week*, March 7, 1988, 114.

Case 5.2   Academic Equity

When the last student left Melinda Wilkerson's office at 5:30, the young English professor sat for a few minutes, too exhausted to move. Her desk was piled high with student papers, journals, and recommendation forms. "There's my weekend," she thought to herself, knowing that reading and commenting on the 30 journals alone would take up all of Saturday. She liked reading the journals, getting a glimpse of how the young women and men in her classes were reacting to the novels and poems she had them read, watching them grow and change. But recently, as she picked up another journal from the endless pile or greeted another student with a smile, she often wondered whether it was all worth it.

She'd had such a moment about an hour earlier, when Ron Agua, whose office was across the hall, had waved to her as he walked past her door, putting on his coat. "I'm off to the Rat," he said, a note of friendly sympathy in his voice. "Come join us if you ever get free." For a moment she had stared blankly at the stack before her, thinking of the scene at the Ratskellar, the university's favorite restaurant and meeting place. Ron would be there with four or five of the department's senior members, including Alice Brody, the department chair. They would all be glad to have her join them ... if only she didn't have so much work.

For the first few months of her first year as an assistant professor, Melinda had accepted her overwhelming workload as simply part of the territory. Her paycheck was smaller and her hours longer than she had expected, but Ron and the other two new faculty members all seemed to be suffering equally under the same burdens.

But now, in her second semester, Melinda was beginning to feel that things weren't right. While the stream of students knocking on her door continued unabated, she noticed that Ron was spending less time talking, and more time typing, than he had first semester. When asked, Ron told her that he had had his course load reduced because of his extra work on the department's hiring and library committees. He seemed surprised when Melinda admitted that she didn't know there was such a thing as a course reduction.

As the semester progressed, she realized that there was a lot she didn't know about the way the department functioned. Ron would disappear once a week or so to give talks to groups around the state, and then would turn those talks into papers for scholarly journals, something Melinda didn't dream of having time to do. She and Ron were still best of friends, but she began to see differences in their approaches. "I cut down my office hours this semester," he told her one day. "With all those students around all the time, I just never had a chance to get my work done."

Melinda had pondered that statement for a few weeks. She thought that dealing with students was "getting work done." But when salaries were announced for the next year, she realized what he meant. Ron would be making almost $1000 more than she would; the personnel committee viewed his committee work as a valuable asset to the department, his talks around the state had already earned him quite a reputation, and his three upcoming publications clearly put him ahead of the other first-year professors.

Melinda was confused. Ron hadn't done anything sneaky or immoral—in fact, everything he did was admirable, things she would like to do. His trips to the Rat seemed to give him the inside scoop on what to do and who to talk to, but she couldn't blame him for that either. She could have done exactly the same thing. They worked, she thought, equally hard; yet Ron was already the highly paid star, while she was just another overworked teacher.

As she began piling all the books, papers, and journals into her bag, Melinda thought about what she could do. She could quit and go somewhere else where she might be more appreciated, but jobs were hard to find and she had a sneaking suspicion that the same thing might happen there. She could charge sex discrimination and demand to be paid as much as Ron, but that would be unfair to him, and she didn't really feel discriminated against for being a woman. The university simply didn't value what she did with her time as highly as they valued what Ron did with his.

While putting her coat on, Melinda noticed a piece of paper that had dropped out of one of the journals. She picked it up and saw it was a note from Wendy Martin, one of her freshman students. "Professor Wilkerson," it read, "I just wanted to thank you for taking the time to talk to me last week. I really needed to talk to someone older about it, and all my other professors are men, and I just couldn't have talked to them. You helped me a whole lot."

Melinda sighed, folded the note, put it in her bag, and closed her office. Suddenly the pile of journals and the thousand dollars didn't look so big.

Case Questions

1. What do you think Melinda will do? Is she satisfied with the way she is being treated?

2. Do you think Melinda is being discriminated against because she's female?

Experiential Exercise

Purpose: This exercise will help you recognize both the potential value and the complexity of expectancy theory.

Format: Working alone, you will be asked to identify the various aspects of expectancy theory that are pertinent to your class. You will then share your thoughts with some of your classmates.

Procedure: Using your class as a surrogate for a workplace and your effort in the class as a surrogate for a job, do the following:

1. Identify six or seven things that might happen as a result of good performance in your class.
2. Using a value of 10 for extremely desirable and a value of minus 10 for extremely undesirable, assign a valence to each of the outcomes.
3. Assume that you are a high performer. On that basis, estimate the probability of each potential outcome. Express the probability as a percentage.

4. Multiply each valence by its associated probability and sum the results. This total is your overall valence for high performance.
5. Assess the probability that if you exert effort, you will be a high performer. Express the probability as a percentage.
6. Multiply this probability by the overall valence for high performance calculated in step 4. This score reflects your motivational force—that is, your motivation to exert high effort.

Now, form groups of three or four people. Compare your scores on motivational force. Discuss why some scores are so different. Also note whether any group members had similar force scores but different combinations of factors leading to those scores.

Follow-up Questions

1. What does the exercise tell you about the strengths and limitations of expectancy theory?
2. Would this exercise be useful for a manager to run with a group of subordinates? Why or why not?

CHAPTER

6

Goal Setting and Rewards

Chapter Objectives

After reading this chapter, you should be able to

- ▶ discuss the role of goal setting in the workplace.
- ▶ describe goal setting theory.
- ▶ summarize management by objectives.
- ▶ discuss reward systems in organizations.

- ▶ identify several different types of rewards.
- ▶ summarize issues regarding the management of reward systems.

ypress Semiconductor Corporation is a hot young Silicon Valley semiconductor manufacturer. The company's 1986 profit margin of 28 percent sales of $51 million represents an astonishing return in the dynamic electronics industry. Cypress's sales surged to $86 million in 1987 and are forecasted at $143 million for 1988. Its profits continue to be just as robust.

One key factor in the company's success is its goal setting system. Every Monday morning, management groups set goals for all six hundred of the company's employees. The goals are entered into an elaborate computer system designed so that everyone can check their personal progress at any time. Management reviews results every day.

The goal setting system at Cypress is the brain child of the company's founder and CEO, T. J. Rodgers. Rodgers wanted a system that would simultaneously allow employees to know exactly what was expected of them and managers to know exactly where every project and activity in the company stood.[1]

The experiences of Cypress provide several interesting insights into organizational behavior. The goals used by the company are apparently working to direct employee motivation toward accomplishing the things deemed most important by management. And they are also apparently facilitating control by providing an ongoing check on progress.

Goals are one of several things an organization can use to provide this guidance and direction for its members. Another important tool is the rewards offered by the organization. This chapter is about goals and rewards and their role in shaping employee behavior.

First, we explore the role of goals in the workplace. We next examine the goal setting theory of motivation. Management by objectives, another important approach to goal setting is examined next. We then turn our attention to reward systems and their role in motivation. Important types of rewards are identified, and perspectives on managing reward systems are discussed. Finally, we look at useful managerial implications.

GOAL SETTING IN THE ORGANIZATION

Almost everyone sets goals. A **goal** is simply a desirable objective to be achieved. Athletes have performance goals, politicians have goals for winning elected office, students have goals for their grades, and executives have goals for the growth of their organizations. Clearly, then, goal setting is an important dimension of human behavior.

---

[1] Steven B. Kaufman, "The Goal System That Drives Cypress," *Business Month*, July 1987, pp. 30–32.

The Role of Goal Setting

Bandura's social learning theory perhaps best describes the role of goal setting in organizational settings.[2] This perspective suggests that the extent to which people achieve their goals results in feelings of pride or shame for performance. That is, a person who achieves a goal will be proud of having done so, while a person who fails to achieve a goal will feel shame. The degree of pride or shame a person experiences is also affected by the feeling that he or she can or cannot function at the desired level of performance. This feeling is called **self-efficacy.** Having a sense of self-efficacy is believing that we can still accomplish our goals, even if we have failed in the past.

Evans has recently presented this perspective in the context of a model of motivation.[3] Figure 6.1 shows a simplified version of this approach. As a starting point, a goal is set (either by the individual or by a superior) and accepted. This goal influences the individual's degree of attention, effort, and persistence, as well as the strategy adopted to achieve the goal. These factors, along with constraints on performance and the individual's ability, determine actual performance.

When performance has been completed, the individual compares actual performance with the original goal. If the goal has been reached, the person is ready for another goal. However, if the goal has not been reached, the individual cognitively evaluates the discrepancy between the goal and what has actually been achieved. This evaluation determines the person's subsequent level of satisfaction with the performance and his or her sense of self-efficacy. Finally, these attitudes also influence future goal-directed behavior.

Goal Setting, Motivation, and Control

In most organizational settings, goals are used for two purposes. First, they are a useful framework for managing motivation. Managers and employees can set goals for themselves and then work toward those goals. The goal serves as a target, an objective. As illustrated by *International Perspective,* goal setting may be a universal phenomenon.

Goals are also an effective control device.[4] *Control* is the management activity directed at monitoring how well the organization is performing. Thus, if the organization's goal is to increase sales by 10 percent, the manager can use individual goals to help attain the overall goal. Further, comparing people's short-term performance with their goals can be an effective way to monitor the organization's long-run performance.

---

[2] A. Bandura, *Social Learning Theory* (Englewood Cliffs, N.J.: Prentice-Hall, 1977).

[3] Martin G. Evans, "Organizational Behavior: The Central Role of Motivation," *Journal of Management,* Summer 1986, pp. 203–222.

[4] William G. Ouchi, "A Conceptual Framework for the Design of Organizational Control Systems," *Management Science,* September 1979, pp. 833–848.

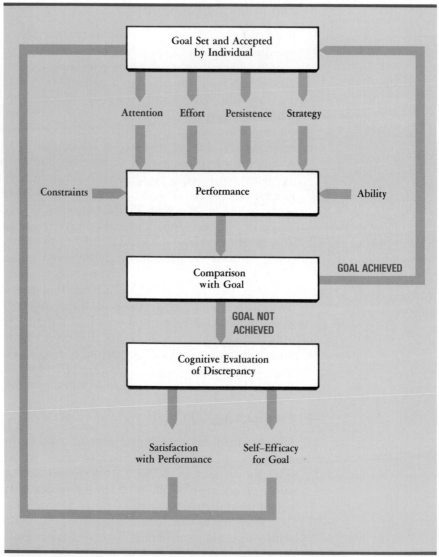

Figure 6.1

The Role of Goal Setting in Organizations

Source: Adapted from Martin G. Evans, "Organizational Behavior: The Central Role of Motivation," *Journal of Management*, Summer 1986, p. 206. Reprinted by permission.

GOAL SETTING THEORY

Bandura's social learning theory and its motivational derivative are general views of human behavior. Another much more specific and applied approach to goal setting is called the **goal setting theory of motivation.** Edwin A. Locke

International Perspective

Setting Goals in the Caribbean

Most research that has established the validity of goal setting theory has been conducted in North America. As we discuss in Chapter 4, theories based on research in a certain cultural and economic setting don't always apply when some of the variables in the setting are changed. To see whether goal-setting theory would extend to a significantly different culture, Betty Jane Punnett of New York University performed a study in the Caribbean in 1984. Her results suggest that the theory applies beyond the borders of the United States.

For her study, Punnett chose a small eastern Caribbean island with characteristics of a "lesser developed country": widespread poverty, unequal distribution of income, little industry, a balance of payments problem, and few ways for people to fulfill their aspirations. Her subjects were 92 women who worked at home doing ornamental sewing on children's clothes. Each worker picked up and dropped off the clothes at a central location and was paid for each piece completed. The conditions were perfect for a goal-setting study, for while the workers were paid for their work and given feedback about it, prior to the study they had no quotas. They could do as much or as little sewing as they wished.

The study divided the women into three groups: a control group given no instructions, a second group asked to do their best, and a third group assigned the specific goal of 20 percent above their previous high production. Punnett compared the groups' earnings per day. The control group averaged $.96, the "do your best" group averaged 35 percent higher, $1.30 per day, and the group given a specific, difficult goal averaged $1.91, almost double the earnings of the control group and 47 percent higher than the "do your best" group.

While certainly not conclusive, this study offers strong evidence that goal-setting theory applies in social and economic settings outside of the typical American business. The conditions in the study area were radically different from those in, for instance, a General Motors plant; yet the group given a specific, difficult goal performed at a level perhaps even higher than the theory would have predicted. If further studies corroborate these findings, international businesspeople will be able to feel confident of at least one of their tools for increasing the productivity of their foreign employees.

Source: Betty Jane Punnett, "Goal Setting: An Extension of the Research," *Journal of Applied Psychology*, 1986, Volume 71, Number 1, 171–172.

was the researcher who most decisively showed the utility of goal setting theory in a motivational context.[5]

The Basic Model

Goal setting theory assumes that behavior is a result of conscious goals and intentions. Therefore, by setting goals for people in an organization, a manager should influence their behavior. Given this premise, the challenge is to develop

---

[5] Edwin Locke, "Toward a Theory of Task Performance and Incentives," *Organizational Behavior and Human Performance*, Vol. 3, 1968, pp. 157–189.

Figure 6.2

The Basic Goal Setting
Model

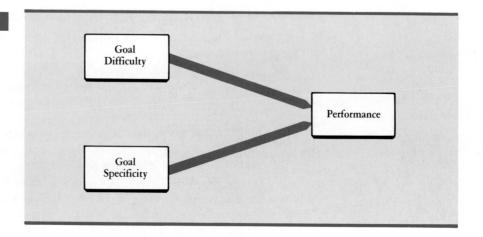

a thorough understanding of the processes by which people set goals and then work to reach them. Figure 6.2 presents a model of goal setting consistent with Locke's original presentation.[6] In the model, goal difficulty and goal specificity shape performance.

GOAL DIFFICULTY   **Goal difficulty** is the extent to which a goal is challenging and requires effort. If people work to achieve goals, it is reasonable to assume that they will work harder to achieve more difficult goals. But a goal must not be so difficult that it is unattainable. If a new manager asks her sales force to increase sales by 300 percent, the group may become disillusioned. A more realistic but still difficult goal—say, a 50-percent increase—would be a better incentive. Reinforcement also fosters motivation toward difficult goals. A person who is rewarded for achieving a difficult goal will be more inclined to strive toward the next difficult goal than will someone who has received no reward after reaching the first goal.

A fairly large body of research supports the importance of goal difficulty.[7] In one study, Gary P. Latham and J. J. Baldes set difficult goals for truck drivers hauling loads of timber from cutting sites to wood yards.[8] Over a nine-month

---

[6] Locke, "Toward a Theory of Task Performance and Incentives." See also Gary Latham, "The Role of Goal Setting in Human Resources Management," in Kendrith M. Rowland and Gerald R. Ferris, eds., *Research in Personnel and Human Resource Management*, Vol. 1 (Greenwich, Conn.: JAI Press, 1983), pp. 169–200; and James C. Naylor and Daniel R. Ilgen, "Goal Setting: A Theoretical Analysis, A Motivational Technology," in Barry M. Staw and L. L. Cummings, eds., *Research in Organizational Behavior*, Vol. 6 (Greenwich, Conn.: JAI Press, 1984), pp. 95–140.

[7] Gary P. Latham and Gary Yukl, "A Review of Research on the Application of Goal-Setting in Organizations," *Academy of Management Journal*, Vol. 18, 1975, pp. 824–845. See also Mark E. Tubbs, "Goal Setting: A Meta-Analytic Examination of the Empirical Evidence," *Journal of Applied Psychology*, Vol. 71, 1986, pp. 474–483.

[8] Gary P. Latham and J. J. Baldes, "The Practical Significance of Locke's Theory of Goal Setting," *Journal of Applied Psychology*, Vol. 60, 1975, pp. 187–191.

period, the drivers improved the quantity of wood they delivered by an amount that would have required $250,000 worth of new trucks at the previous per-truck average load.

GOAL SPECIFICITY   **Goal specificity** relates to the definition of the target for performance. Specificity usually means stating a goal in quantitative terms. For example, cutting costs by 10 percent and hiring twenty new minority employees are each specific goals. In areas such as employee satisfaction, however, specificity is difficult.

Specificity has also been shown to be consistently related to performance.[9] The previously cited study by Latham and Baldes also examined specificity.[10] The initial loads drivers were carrying were found to be 60 percent of the maximum weight each truck could haul. The researchers set a new goal for drivers of 94 percent. The goal was thus quite specific as well as difficult.

The Expanded Model

Because his theory has attracted widespread interest and research support, Locke has recently proposed an expanded model of the goal setting process.[11] The expanded model, shown in Figure 6.3, is an attempt to capture more fully the complexities of goal setting in organizations.

Locke assumes that goal-directed effort is initially a function of four goal attributes: difficulty and specificity and also acceptance and commitment. **Goal acceptance** is the extent to which a person accepts a goal as his or her own. **Goal commitment** is the extent to which he or she is personally interested in reaching the goal. The manager who vows to take whatever steps are necessary to cut costs by 10 percent has made a commitment to achieve the goal. Factors that can foster goal acceptance and commitment include participating in the goal setting process, making goals challenging but realistic, and believing that goal achievement will lead to valued rewards.[12]

Actual performance is determined by the interaction of goal-directed effort, organizational support, and individual abilities and traits. *Organizational support* is whatever the organization does to help or hinder performance. Positive support might mean making available adequate personnel and a sufficient supply of raw materials; negative support might mean failing to fix damaged equipment. *Individual abilities and traits* are the skills and other personal characteristics necessary to do a job. As a result of performance, a person

---

[9] Latham and Yukl, "A Review of Research on the Application of Goal Setting Theory in Organizations."

[10] Latham and Baldes, "The Practical Significance of Locke's Theory of Goal Setting."

[11] Gary P. Latham and Edwin Locke, "Goal Setting—A Motivational Technique That Works," *Organizational Dynamics*, Autumn 1979, pp. 68–80.

[12] Gary P. Latham and Timothy P. Steele, "The Motivational Effects of Participation Versus Goal Setting on Performance," *Academy of Management Journal*, September 1983, pp. 406–417.

| Figure 6.3 | The Extended Goal Setting Model |

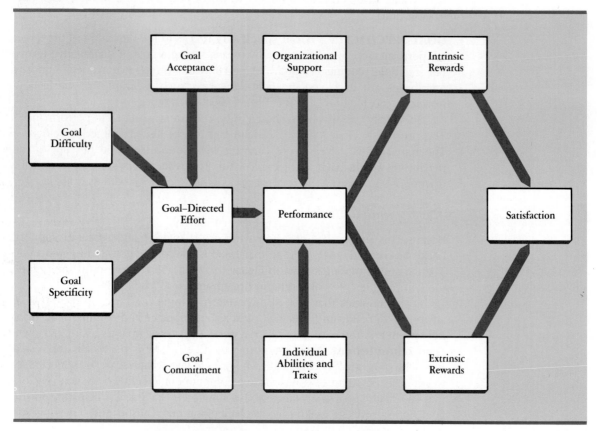

receives various intrinsic and extrinsic rewards, which in turn influence satisfaction. Note that the latter stages of Locke's extended model are quite similar to the Porter and Lawler expectancy model discussed in Chapter 5.[13]

Research Evidence

Goal setting theory has been widely tested in a variety of surroundings.[14] Research has demonstrated fairly consistently that goal difficulty and specificity

---

[13] Lyman W. Porter and Edward E. Lawler, *Managerial Attitudes and Performance* (Homewood, Ill.: Dorsey Press, 1968).

[14] Latham and Yukl, "A Review of Research on the Application of Goal Setting Theory

are closely associated with performance. Other elements of the theory, such as acceptance and commitment, have not been studied as widely. A few studies have shown the importance of acceptance and commitment, but little is currently known about how people adopt acceptance and commitment. More details about the evidence for and against goal setting theory are summarized in *A Look at Research*.

It has been argued that goal setting theory is not really a theory at all but simply an effective motivational technique. The goal setting process may also be a narrow and unnecessarily rigid view of employee behavior. Some important aspects of behavior cannot be quantified easily, and goal setting may focus too much attention on the short run at the expense of long-term consideration. Despite these objections, goal setting appears to be a useful approach to motivation. The next section examines a related approach through which goal setting is applied in organizational settings.

MANAGEMENT BY OBJECTIVES

Management by objectives, or MBO, is a popular technique for managing the goal setting process in organizations. Figure 6.4 illustrates the basic MBO process.[15]

The MBO Process

Management by objectives (MBO) is essentially a collaborative goal setting process through which organizational goals systematically cascade down through the organization. It is implemented through a series of discrete steps. The following discussion describes the steps in a general way. Many organizations have adopted variations to suit their own purposes.

STARTING MBO   MBO must start at the top to be successful. Top management must stand behind the program and take the first step by establishing overall goals for the organization.

ESTABLISHMENT OF ORGANIZATIONAL GOALS   The initial goals are, of course, set by upper-level managers. Goals might relate to sales growth, market share growth, costs, productivity, employee absenteeism and turnover, or any other area important to the organization.

COLLABORATIVE GOAL SETTING   Superiors and subordinates then collaborate in setting goals. First, the organizational goals are communicated to

---

in Organizations"; and Tubbs, "Goal Setting." See also John R. Hollenbeck and Howard J. Klein, "Goal Commitment and the Goal-Setting Process: Problems, Prospects, and Proposals for Future Research," *Journal of Applied Psychology*, Vol. 72, 1987, pp. 212–220.

[15] See Stephen J. Carroll and Henry L. Tosi, *Management by Objectives* (New York: MacMillan, 1973).

A LOOK AT

RESEARCH

Goal Setting Theory Continues to Expand

Recent research and surveys of past studies have confirmed the most important components of goal-setting theory and have further refined the theory in ways useful to managers and workers alike. In "A Meta-Analytic Examination of the Empirical Evidence," Mark E. Tubbs concludes that the evidence supporting the importance of goal difficulty and goal specificity is so strong as to make further studies focusing on these effects unnecessary. He also finds that the evidence supports the positive effects of worker participation in goal setting, although not enough studies have yet been done which hold the goal level constant while testing groups assigned a goal versus groups who participated in setting it. The effects of feedback on the results of goal setting also need more investigation.

In a study of department store salespeople, John R. Hollenbeck and Charles R. Williams tested the relationship between goal importance, goal level, and self-focus. They found that when subjects perceive difficult goals to be important, and when they tend to focus attention inward toward the self rather than outward toward the environment, they are much more likely to monitor carefully their progress toward those goals.

In what may be the most important recent article about the subject, Hollenbeck and Howard J. Klein focus on goal commitment. They argue that goal commitment has not received adequate attention in the research on goal setting. They see the commitment of a person to the goal as crucial to that person's performance, and, using expectancy theory, they have developed a model of the factors that influence goal commitment. In their model, both situational and personal factors contribute to the attractiveness and expectancy of goal attainment, which together determine the level of goal commitment.

According to their model, people see goal attainment as attractive when they make their commitment public, explicit, and voluntary, and if they have a high need for achievement, tend to persevere, are Type A individuals (aggressive and competitive) involved in their jobs, and see that their organization backs the goal attainment. People expect to attain their goal if they see others committed to attainment, if their supervisors support the goal, if they perceive the link between effort and performance to be strong, if they feel they have the ability, if they have high self-esteem, and if they have succeeded in similar situations in the past.

If further research confirms the importance of goal commitment to task performance, managers and workers alike should take note of the factors this model identifies. The factors can help managers both select employees who are likely to commit themselves to goals, and adjust situational factors to improve the possibilities for such commitment.

Sources: John R. Hollenbeck and Howard J. Klein, "Goal Commitment and the Goal-Setting Process: Problems, Prospects, and Proposals for Future Research," *Journal of Applied Psychology*, 1987, Volume 72, Number 2, 212–220; John R. Hollenbeck and Charles R. Williams, "Goal Importance, Self-Focus, and the Goal-Setting Process," *Journal of Applied Psychology*, 1987, Volume 72, Number 2, 204–211; Mark E. Tubbs, "Goal Setting: A Meta-Analytic Examination of the Empirical Evidence," *Journal of Applied Psychology*, 1986, Volume 71, Number 3, 474–483.

Figure 6.4   The MBO Process

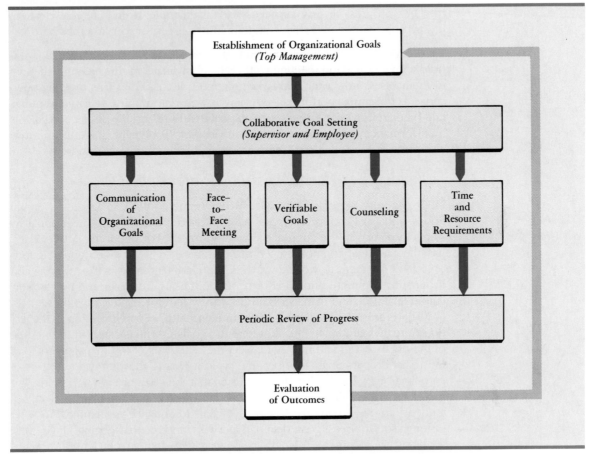

Source: Adapted from Ricky W. Griffin, *Management*, 2nd ed. (Boston: Houghton Mifflin, 1987), p. 128. Reprinted by permission.

everyone. Every manager then meets with each subordinate. During this meeting, the manager explains the unit goals to the subordinate and the two of them determine together how the subordinate can most effectively contribute to those goals. The manager acts as a counselor, and helps make sure the subordinate develops goals that are *verifiable*. For example, a goal of "cutting costs by 5 percent" is verifiable, whereas a goal of "doing my best" is not. Finally, the two of them ensure that the subordinate has the resources needed to reach his or her goals. This entire process spirals downward as each subordinate meets with his or her own subordinates to develop their goals. Thus, as noted earlier, the initial goals set at the top cascade down throughout the entire organization.

PERIODIC REVIEW   During the period of time set for goal attainment (usually one year), the manager periodically meets with each subordinate again to check progress. It may be necessary, for example, to modify goals in light of new information, to provide additional resources, or to take other action.

EVALUATION   Finally, at the end of the specified time period, managers hold a final evaluation meeting with each subordinate. At this meeting, the two of them assess how well goals were met and discuss why. This meeting often serves as the annual performance review as well, determining salary adjustments and other rewards based on reaching goals. (MBO is briefly discussed again as a performance evaluation technique in Chapter 19.) Finally, this meeting may also serve as the initial goal setting meeting for the next year's cycle.

Evaluation and Management Implications of MBO

MBO is a very popular technique. Alcoa, Tenneco, Black & Decker, General Foods, and Du Pont, for example, have all used it extensively. This popularity stems in part from the approach's many strengths. For one thing, MBO clearly has the potential to motivate employees because it provides unambiguous objectives for them to work toward. It also clarifies the basis for rewards, and it can spur communication. Performance appraisals are easier and more clear-cut under MBO, and managers can use the system for control purposes.[16]

There are also, however, pitfalls in using MBO. Sometimes top managers do not really participate, meaning that the goals essentially start in the middle of the organization and may not reflect the real goals of top management, and those that do participate may become cynical. That is, they interpret the lack of participation by top management as a sign that the goals are not important, and therefore view their own involvement as a waste of time. There is also a tendency to overemphasize quantitative goals to enhance verifiability. An MBO system also requires a great deal of paperwork and record keeping, since every goal must be documented. Finally, some managers do not really let subordinates participate in goal setting but, instead, assign goals and order subordinates to accept them.

On balance, MBO is often an effective and useful system for managing goal setting in organizations. Research suggests that it can actually do many of the things its advocates claim, but it must also be handled carefully. In particular, most organizations would need to tailor it to their own unique circumstances. Properly used, MBO can be an effective approach to managing an organization's reward system, the area we turn to now.[17]

---

[16] See Stephen J. Carroll and Henry L. Tosi, *Management by Objectives* (New York: Macmillan, 1973).

[17] Jack N. Kondrasuk, "Studies in MBO Effectiveness," *Academy of Management Review*, July 1981, pp. 419–430.

REWARD SYSTEMS

Obviously reward systems are an important tool that managers can use to channel employee motivation in desired ways. The **reward system** consists of all organizational components—including people, processes, rules and procedures, and decision-making activities—involved in the allocation of compensation and benefits to employees in exchange for their contributions to the organization.

As we examine organizational reward systems, it is important to keep in mind their relationship to employee motivation (covered in Chapters 4 and 5). Reinforcement theory and theories of perception and learning (covered in Chapter 2) also relate to the study of organizational rewards. In short, reward systems in an organizational context cannot be studied apart from their effects on individuals.[18]

The Exchange Process

The organizational reward system and the performance appraisal system are the key links in the exchange process between individual employees and the organization. Employees contribute many resources to the organization: time, effort, knowledge, skills, creativity, and energy. In turn, the organization rewards its employees with both tangible and intangible compensation. *Tangible compensation* consists of rewards that have a definite value, such as pay, pension plans, life and health insurance, and vacation. *Intangible compensation* refers to rewards whose value is less easily defined, such as status symbols, opportunities to be creative, and a sense of self-esteem. Figure 6.5 illustrates this exchange process.

As is typical of most areas in the field of organizational behavior, the exchange process is dynamic, not static. If either party feels the exchange is not equitable, the parties may attempt to reach agreement on an equitable relationship, or they may terminate the exchange relationship. Nor does the exchange relationship exist in a vacuum. Both parties are at least somewhat aware of the exchange relationship between employees and other organizations. Because an organization's reward system is the one part of the exchange process that the organization can control, the system must be properly designed and carefully managed.

---

[18] Edward E. Lawler, *Pay and Organization Development* (Reading, Mass.: Addison-Wesley, 1981). See also Edward E. Lawler, "The Design of Effective Reward Systems," in Jay W. Lorsch, ed., *Handbook of Organizational Behavior* (Englewood Cliffs, N.J.: Prentice-Hall, 1987), pp. 255–271; and Jeffrey Pfeffer and Alison Davis-Blake, "Understanding Organizational Wage Structures," *Academy of Management Journal*, Vol. 30, 1987, pp. 437–455.

Figure 6.5

The Individual-
Organization Exchange
Process

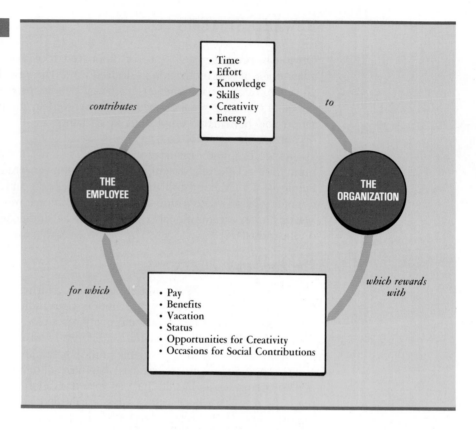

The Roles, Purposes, and Meanings of Rewards

In most organizations the purpose of the reward system is to attract, retain, and motivate qualified employees.[19] Compensation philosophy centers on three issues: the concept of fairness and equality of rewards, the importance of each employee's contribution to the organization, and the status of the external labor market.

The organization's compensation structure must be equitable and consistent to ensure equality of treatment and compliance with the law. In addition, compensation should be a fair reward for the individual's contributions to the organization, although in most cases these contributions are difficult if not impossible to measure objectively. Given this limitation, managers should be as fair and equitable as possible. Finally, the system must be competitive in the

[19] Douglas B. Gehrman, "Beyond Today's Compensation and Performance Appraisal Systems," *Personnel Administrator*, March 1984, pp. 21–33. See also Jeffrey Kerr and John W. Slocum, Jr., "Managing Corporate Culture Through Reward Systems," *Academy of Management Executive*, Vol. 1, No. 2, 1987, pp. 99–108.

external labor market if the organization is to attract and retain competent workers in appropriate fields.

Beyond these broad considerations, however, an organization must develop its own philosophy of compensation based on its own conditions and needs. And this philosophy must be defined and built into the actual reward system. For example, the compensation philosophy of Lincoln Electric Company is that all employees should receive compensation in accordance with their accomplishments and should share in the profits that they helped create.[20] As a result, Lincoln employees earn about twice as much as similar workers at other companies, yet the labor costs per sales dollar at Lincoln are well below industry averages.

A well-developed compensation philosophy articulates the purpose of the system and provides a building framework for making compensation decisions. It can serve as a point of stability in changing economic, technological, and labor market conditions. In addition, a clearly stated philosophy can give the system credibility among those most affected by it—the employees. The organization needs to decide what types of behaviors or performance it wants to encourage with a reward system, because what is rewarded tends to recur. There are many possibilities: performance, longevity, attendance, loyalty, contributions to the "bottom line," responsibility, and conformity.

Performance appraisal measures these behaviors, but the choice of which ones to reward is a function of the compensation system. A reward system must also take into account volatile economic issues such as inflation, market conditions, technology, labor union activities, and others.

It is also important for the organization to recognize that organizational rewards have many meanings for employees. As shown in Figure 6.6, intrinsic and extrinsic rewards carry with them both surface and symbolic value. The *surface value* of a reward to an employee is the meaning it has at an objective level. A salary increase of 5 percent, for example, means that an individual has 5 percent more spending power than before, while a promotion, on the surface, means new duties and responsibilities.

But rewards also carry *symbolic meanings.* Consider what frequently happens when a pro football or basketball team signs a top prospect from college for loads of money. The new player often feels enormous pressure to live up to his salary, and veteran players may argue that their pay should be increased to keep the salary structure in balance. Rewards convey to people how much they are valued by the organization, as well as their importance relative to others. Consider again a 5 percent salary increase. If the recipient later finds out that everyone else got 3 percent or less, he will see himself as

---

[20] James F. Lincoln, *A New Approach to Industrial Economics* (New York: Devin-Adair, 1961), reprinted in Arthur A. Thompson, Jr. and A. J. Strickland, III, *Strategic Management: Concepts and Cases*, 3rd ed. (Plano, Tex.: Business Publications, 1984), p. 948.

Figure 6.6

The Meaning of
Organizational Rewards

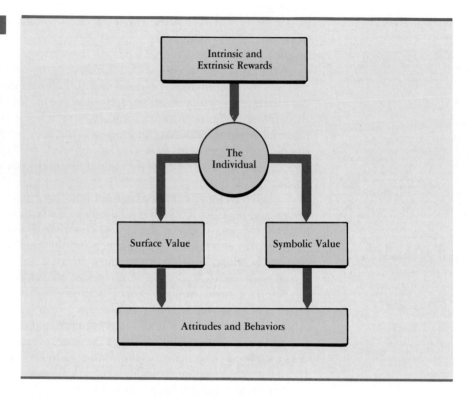

vitally important to the organization—someone whose contributions are recognized and valued. On the other hand, if everyone else got at least 8 percent, he probably will feel like the organization places little value on his contributions. In short, then, managers need to tune in to the many meanings rewards can have, not only the surface messages, but the symbolic messages as well.[21]

TYPES OF REWARDS

Most organizations use several different types of rewards, although the primary ones are money (wages, salary, commission), benefits, perquisites, awards, and incentive plans. The rewards are combined in a compensation package, as shown in Figure 6.7.

---

[21] See Richard T. Mowday, "Equity Theory Predictions of Behavior in Organizations," in Richard M. Steers and Lyman W. Porter, eds., *Motivation and Work Behavior*, 4th ed. (New York: McGraw-Hill, 1987), pp. 89–110. See also Rabindra N. Kanungo and Jon Hartwick, "An Alternative to the Intrinsic-Extrinsic Dichotomy of Work Rewards," *Journal of Management*, Vol. 13, pp. 751–766.

Figure 6.7

A Total Compensation
Package

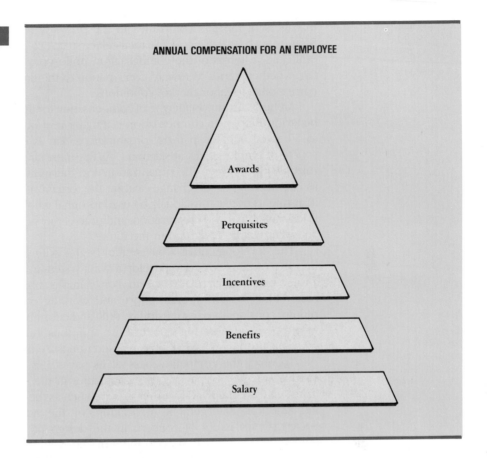

Money

The most important organizational reward for most people is money. Money is obviously important because of the things it can buy but, as just noted, it can also symbolize an employee's worth. *Business Week* conducts an annual survey of executive compensation. It recently reported that among companies who responded to the survey, the highest-paid executive was T. Boone Pickens, chairman and president of Mesa Petroleum Company. He made $22.8 million in salary, bonus, and long-term compensation.[22] The company clearly regarded Pickens as a very valuable employee, but we might ask whether he is 1,000 times more valuable to the company than lower-level employees who make $20,000 per year. Pickens may not be a fair example, since he is the major stockholder in the company, but other CEOs are also highly compensated. The average salary and bonus (not including long-term incentive income) for top

---

[22] "The CEO 1000," *Business Week*, October 23, 1987, pp. 99–350.

managers of the 259 companies in the *Business Week* survey was $653,000. Salaries such as these and the total salary structure of a company can only be evaluated in terms of the compensation philosophy—whether it is equal and fair, whether it tries to reward contribution to the organization, and whether it corresponds to labor market conditions.

Money is an important type of compensation for the student of organizational behavior. Employee compensation is a major cost of doing business—as much as 50 to 60 percent in many organizations. Pay is considered to be a major source of employee dissatisfaction.[23] As the most tangible part of the exchange relationship between the organization and the individual, it also can be used as an instrument of change within the organization. For example, salary adjustments might consciously be used to signal who is more valuable and who is less valuable to the organization, and/or to clarify norms as to what is expected and what will be rewarded in the future.

The development of a pay system begins with **job analysis.** Job analysis information can be used to develop a point system in which each job is assigned a value based on its relative worth. For example, jobs can be compared on the basis of responsibility, skill, effort, and working conditions. Those jobs that require considerable responsibility, skill, and effort in harsh working conditions would be assigned a high point value and, thus, high pay. Point systems and other means of comparing jobs are used to ensure the internal fairness of pay.

To verify the competitiveness of its pay scales, an organization can also conduct a survey of pay at other companies in the same industry or use data from surveys conducted by other groups, such as the Bureau of Labor Statistics, the American Management Association, or the Administrative Management Society. Other issues of concern in the design of a pay system include the number of pay grades and the number of steps within each grade; the minimum, midpoint, and maximum pay levels for each grade and for the organization as a whole; the amount of overlap between grades; the way in which an employee moves from one step or grade to the next; and the effect on the pay system of changes in external conditions (for example, labor supply and demand or inflation).[24]

Benefits

The second major component of the compensation package is the employee benefit plan. Benefits are often called indirect compensation. Typical benefits provided by organizations include the following:

---

[23] See Lawler, *Pay and Organization Development*, for a more detailed discussion of organizational pay issues.

[24] See Richard I. Henderson, *Performance Appraisal* (Reston, Va.: Reston, 1984), for more information on the design of a pay structure.

1. *Payment for time not worked,* both on-the-job and off-the-job. On-the-job free time includes lunch periods, rest periods, coffee breaks, wash-up time, and get-ready time. Off-the-job time not worked includes vacations, sick leave, holidays, and personal days.

2. *Social Security contributions.* The employer contributes half of money paid into the system established under the Federal Insurance Contributions Act (FICA). The employee pays the other half, making a total of approximately $3,045 per year for the average employee. The employee receives Social Security income when she or he retires.

3. *Unemployment compensation.* People who have lost their job or are temporarily laid off get a percentage of their wages from the state. Funds come from payments by companies, as regulated by state laws.

4. *Disability and workers' compensation benefits.* Employers contribute funds to assist workers who are ill or injured and cannot work owing to occupational injury or ailment. These benefits are regulated by federal and state laws.

5. *Life and health insurance programs.* Most organizations offer insurance at a cost far below what individuals would pay to buy insurance by themselves.

6. *Pension plans.* Most organizations offer plans to provide supplementary income to employees after they retire. These company-paid or joint employee-and-company-paid programs are meant to supplement Social Security.

A company's Social Security, unemployment, and worker's compensation contributions are set by law. But how much to contribute for other kinds of benefits is up to each company. Some organizations contribute more to the cost of these benefits than others do. Some companies pay the entire cost, others pay a percentage of the cost of certain benefits, such as health insurance, and bear the entire cost of others. Offering benefits beyond wages became a standard component of compensation during World War II, as a way of increasing employee compensation when wage controls were in effect. Since then, competition for employees and employee demands (expressed, for instance, in union bargaining) have caused companies to increase these benefits. In many organizations, they now account for 30 to 40 percent of payroll. They are therefore of major concern to businesses, some of which are trying to reduce the costs of indirect compensation. The motivational power of benefits is unknown; however, weak or poorly designed benefit packages have been known to cause employee dissatisfaction.

Perquisites

Perquisites are an aspect of the exchange relationship that has received little theoretical consideration but much legal attention and media coverage. For years the top executives of many organizations were allowed such privileges as unlimited use of the company airplane, motor home, vacation home, and executive dining room. Eventually, the Internal Revenue Service ruled that some "perks" were a form of income and thus could be taxed. The IRS decision has substantially changed the nature of these benefits, but they have not entirely disappeared—nor are they likely to. More than anything else, perquisites seem to add to the status of those who receive them and thus serve to increase job satisfaction and reduce turnover.

Awards

In many companies, employees receive awards for everything from seniority to perfect attendance, from zero defects (quality work) to cost reduction suggestions. Award programs can be costly in the time required to run them and in money if cash awards are given.

Award systems can improve performance under the right conditions. For instance, in one medium-sized manufacturing company, careless work habits were pushing up the costs of scrap and rework (that is, the cost of scrapping defective parts or reworking them to meet standards.) Management instituted a zero-defects program to recognize employees who did perfect or near-perfect work. The first month two workers in shipping caused only one defect in over two thousand parts handled. Division management called a meeting in the lunch room and recognized each worker with a plaque and a ribbon. The next month the same two workers had two defects and there was no award. The following month the two workers had zero defects and, once again, top management called a meeting to give out plaques and ribbons. Elsewhere in the plant, defects, scrap, and rework decreased dramatically as workers evidently sought recognition for quality work. What worked in this particular plant might or might not work in other plants. The effects of award programs can be explained by reinforcement theory (Chapter 2) or the various need theories (Chapter 4).

Incentive Systems

Incentive systems usually promise additional money for certain types of performance. Examples of incentive programs include the following:

1. *Piecework* programs that tie a worker's earnings to the number of units produced
2. *Gain-sharing* programs that grant additional earnings to employees or work groups for cost-reduction efforts or ideas

3. *Commission* programs that provide sales personnel with earnings based on the number of units they sell
4. *Bonus* systems whereby management personnel receive lump sums from a special bonus pool based on the financial performance of the organization or a unit of the organization
5. *Long-term compensation* that provides management personnel with substantial additional income based on stick price performance, earnings per share, or return on equity
6. *Merit pay* plans that base raises on the employee's performance, as determined by objectivity measured productivity or by the results of performance appraisal
7. *Profit-sharing* plans that distribute a percentage of the profits of the organization to all employees at a predetermined rate
8. *Employee stock option* plans that, most often, set aside a block of stock in the company for employees to purchase at a reduced rate, the expectation being that employees who own part of the company are more committed to it and work harder to increase the value of their stock

Plans oriented mainly toward individual employees may cause increased competition for the awards and some possibly disruptive behaviors, such as sabotaging a coworker's performance, sacrificing quality for quantity, or fighting over customers. A group incentive plan, on the other hand, requires that employees trust each other and work together. Of course, incentive systems have advantages and disadvantages. Long-term compensation for executives is particularly controversial because of the large sums of money involved and the basis for the payments.[25] The successful implementation of an incentive program depends on the history and traditions of the organization; the nature of the organization's products or services; current political, economic, and legal conditions; and employee needs and perceptions of the system.

MANAGING REWARD SYSTEMS

Much of our discussion to this point in the chapter has focused on reward systems from a general perspective. As Figure 6.8 shows, however, there are also several other issues to be confronted in the management of organizational reward systems. The figure suggests that after a reward system is developed and implemented, three additional factors may need to be considered for it to remain effective. These factors are pay secrecy, participation, and flexibility.

---

[25] Arthur M. Louis, "Business Is Bungling Long-Term Compensation," *Fortune*, July 23, 1984, pp. 64–69.

Figure 6.8

Managing Reward
Systems

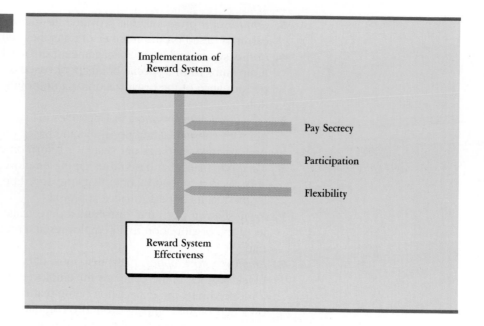

Pay Secrecy

A policy of open salary information means that the exact salary amounts for employees are public knowledge. State governments, for instance, make public the salaries of everyone on their payrolls. Complete secrecy means that no information is available to employees regarding other employees' salaries, average or percentage raises, or salary ranges. Although a few organizations have a completely public or a completely secret system, most are somewhere in the middle.

Diverse issues surround the question of secret versus open pay.[26] Some workers feel that their pay is their business and no one else's; others prefer knowing exactly where they stand in relation to other employees. (The latter is a concrete example of an equity perception issue.) In an open pay system, managers must be able to defend the pay differences to those who are paid less. From a motivational point of view, an open system may clarify the relationship between pay and performance for all concerned. Moreover, research evidence suggests that in a secret system, employees tend to overestimate the pay of coworkers, thus causing motivational problems.[27] In light of these considerations, many organizations have elected a compromise solution: a

---

[26] See Lawler, *Pay and Organization Development*, pp. 43–50, for more discussion of the secret versus open pay system.

[27] Lawler, *Pay and Organization Development*.

partially open system that lets employees know the salary ranges of jobs and average increases within each range.

Participative Pay Systems

In keeping with the current trend toward worker involvement in organizational decision making, employee participation in the pay process is also increasing. A **participative pay system** may involve the employee in the system's design, administration, or both. A pay system can be designed by staff members of the organization's human resources department, by a committee of managers in the organization, by an outside consultant, by the employees, or by a combination of these sources. Organizations that have used a joint management-employee task force to design the compensation system have generally succeeded in designing and implementing a plan that managers could use and that employees believed in.[28]

Employee participation in administering the pay system is a natural extension of having employees participate in its design. Examples of companies that have involved employees in the administration of the pay system include Romac Industries, where employees vote on the pay of other employees; Graphic Controls, where each managers' pay is determined by a group of peers; and the Friedman-Jacobs Company, where employees set their own wages based on their perception of their performance.[29] Allowing individuals and work groups to set their own salaries may not be appropriate for all organizations, but it can be successful in organizations characterized by a climate of trust, joint problem solving, and a participative management style.

Flexible Reward Systems

Flexible, or cafeteria style, reward systems are a recent and increasingly popular variation on the standard compensation system.[30] A **flexible reward system** allows employees to choose the combination of benefits that best suits their needs. For example, younger workers starting a family may prefer additional maternity or paternity benefits or a family medical plan that pays 100 percent, whereas a worker nearing retirement may want to maximize pension benefits. Organizations even get more for their benefit dollar by using the flexible approach. Flexible systems generally require more administrative time and effort to develop and maintain than the standard approach, but the benefits of the flexible approach seem to outweigh these costs. In fact, most companies

---

[28] Lawler, *Pay and Organization Development*, pp. 101–111. See also Jack C. Horn, "Bigger Pay for Better Work," *Psychology Today*, July 1987, pp. 54–57.

[29] Lawler, *Pay and Organization Development*, pp. 109–110.

[30] See Dale Gifford, "The Status of Flexible Compensation," *Personnel Administrator*, May 1984, pp. 19–25, for a recent discussion of flexible compensation systems.

Can Everyone Win With Flexible Benefits?

Under flexible benefit plans, workers may often choose between various options—health plans, dental plans, dependent care accounts, tax-deferred savings plans, or extra vacation days. Often each option includes a number of variables—deductibles, limits, the amounts paid by employee and employer, ways of dealing with inflation. Some companies allot a certain amount of money per year for each employee's benefits and let the employee choose. Other companies allot a percentage of each employee's salary for benefits, an option that favors highly paid employees. Still others figure in an employee's family status or length of employment.

Most standard benefit plans were created to serve the needs of a male worker with a non-working wife and dependent children at home. Yet today fewer than 10 percent of the work force fits that stereotype. In the traditional plans, when the company gives the same benefits to all, younger workers without dependents subsidize workers with large families: the actual cost to the company of insurance for a large family could be over twice the cost of insuring a single employee. Such plans are costly to employers and unfair to most employees, so both management and workers have tended to welcome flexible benefit plans enthusiastically; the number of large companies with these plans has been doubling every two years.

On the surface, the concept of flexible benefits sounds too good to be true: employees get exactly what they want and the employer saves money. In fact, a majority of employees at companies with flexible benefits do seem to favor the new plans, but not everyone is happy. Such plans allow companies to distribute benefits more equitably and employees to choose what they most need. But they also put more of a burden on employees to determine their real needs and to scrutinize the various options offered.

Employees faced with the choices offered by a flexible benefit plan need to study the options and consider the potential drawbacks. In some plans, employees share with the company the rising costs of health care; PepsiCo employees, for instance, pay half of the yearly increases. Many companies use the switchover to flexible plans as an opportunity to get employees to shoulder more of the financial burden regardless of the options they choose, so employees may have to get used to larger copayments and deductibles. Balancing the relative worth of various options can be very difficult. For instance, is $300 extra in dental benefits worth more than 2 extra vacation days?

The biggest losers in almost all flexible benefit plans are employees with lots of dependents, i.e. employees with "traditional" families. Therefore it seems possible that flexible benefits—like the advent of two-career marriages—will not only reflect but also change the career and family decisions that employees make.

Sources: Aaron Bernstein, "Benefits Are Getting More Flexible—But *Caveat Emptor*," *Business Week*, September 8, 1986, 64–66; Larry Reibstein, "To Each According to His Needs: Flexible Benefits Plans Gain Favor," *The Wall Street Journal*, September 16, 1986, 29; Ross D. Spencer, "Flexible Benefits Can Reduce Inequities Between Married and Single Coverages," *Employee Benefit Plan Review*, January 1988, 52.

save enough money to pay back the initial investment in a few years.[31] *Management in Action* provides some additional insights into flexible benefits.

Some organizations are starting to apply the flexible approach to pay. For example, employees sometimes have the option of taking an annual salary increase in one lump sum rather than in monthly increments. General Electric recently implemented such a system for some of its managers.[32] Although lump-sum payments necessitate special provisions for taxes and for payback if the employee quits during the year of the raise, this alternative lets the employee lay hands on the full amount of the increase at one time, possibly resulting in a greater motivational impact. In a totally flexible reward system, employees are able to trade off salary increases for benefit increases and vice versa.

SUMMARY OF KEY POINTS

Goal setting is an important dimension of human behavior in organizations. Pride or shame may follow success or failure to reach goals. Goal setting is also important to motivation and control.

The goal setting theory of motivation suggests that goal difficulty, specificity, acceptance, and commitment are important determinants of performance. This view is generally supported by research.

Management by objectives is another useful approach to goal setting. It is based on collaboratively setting verifiable goals and tying rewards to goal attainment. Again, this approach is often supported by research.

Another major part of managing people in organizations is the reward system. The purpose of the reward system is to attract, retain, and motivate qualified employees and to maintain a pay structure that is internally equitable and externally competitive. Rewards have both surface and symbolic meanings.

Rewards take the form of pay, benefits, perquisites, awards, and incentives. Factors such as motivational impact, cost, and fit with the organizational system must be considered when designing or analyzing a reward system. Other issues related to reward systems are the openness of pay systems, employee participation in the pay system, and flexible (or cafeteria style) reward systems.

---

[31] Lance D. Tane and Michael E. Treacy, "Benefits That Bend With Employees' Needs," *Nation's Business*, April 1984, pp. 80–82; and Henderson, *Performance Appraisal*. See also "Benefits are Getting More Flexible—But Caveat Emptor," *Business Week*, September 8, 1986, pp. 64–66.

[32] "How'd You Like a Big Fat Bonus—But No Raise?" *Business Week*, November 3, 1986, pp. 30–31.

DISCUSSION QUESTIONS

1. Do you set goals for yourself? In what areas? How do you feel when you have been successful or unsuccessful in reaching your goals?

2. Do goals motivate you? Can you cite instances of personal goals that were difficult or specific?

3. Would you like to work in an organization that uses MBO? Why or why not?

4. Can a person set too many goals? What are the implications of this question for managers?

5. The chapter implies that goals and rewards are linked. Can you think of cases where they are not or should not be linked?

6. What are the pros and cons of participative goal setting?

7. As a student in this class, what "rewards" do you receive in exchange for your time and effort? What are the rewards for the professor who teaches this class? How do your contributions and rewards differ from those of some other student in the class?

8. Do you expect to obtain the rewards you discussed in question 7 on the basis of your intelligence, your hard work, the number of hours you spend in the library, your height, your good looks, your work experience, or some other personal factor?

9. What do Herzberg's two-factor theory and the expectancy theory of motivation (discussed in Chapters 4 and 5 respectively) tell us about rewarding employees?

10. Quite often institutions in federal and state government give the same percentage pay raise to all of their employees. What is the effect of this type of pay raise on employee motivation?

| Case 6.1 | **American Divides Workers to Conquer Costs** |

During the hard economic times of 1983, many unions made concessions to companies that complained that high union wages were driving them towards bankruptcy. As no one likes to take a cut in pay, a number of unions, including those representing American Airlines' employees, settled for a relatively new form of wage agreement, the "two-tier" contract, thereby saving money for the companies without reducing wages for current employees. This radically different form of reward system is economical for the companies, but has wide-ranging effects on the ways employees view their jobs.

In a two-tier system, all employees hired before the signing of the new contract stay on the old wage scale, while new workers are hired on a new scale that may be as much as 50 percent lower. Some two-tier systems are temporary: the pay of a lower-tier worker who stays on the job long enough (from one to twelve years) eventually rises to the level of the higher tier. Other systems are permanent: a lower-tier worker will never catch up with a higher-tier employee who might have been hired only a month earlier.

Like many other large, traditional airlines, American was feeling squeezed in the early 1980s by the high wages it paid its unionized employees and the competition from low-cost airlines that had sprung up since airline deregulation. In 1983 American spent over 37 percent of its revenue on wages and fringe benefits, compared to about 21 percent spent by cut-rate carriers like People Express and Continental. The company persuaded its unions that it couldn't keep paying so much more for labor.

The differences between the two tiers in the 1983 contract were drastic. A top senior pilot on the old wage scale could make over $125,000 a year. Pilots hired under the new contract would never earn even half of that, no matter how long they flew. New flight attendants began at $972 a month and reached their peak at $1,199 a month, as compared to the high-tier peak of $2,217. Analysts estimated that the company saved $100 million in labor costs in 1984 alone, and the savings grew each year as well-paid old timers retired and new, less expensive workers were hired. As American became healthier in the following years, first pilots and then flight attendants fought to change the two-tier system. But most unions have found that companies are very reluctant to give up such substantial savings.

Bitterness seems inevitable among workers doing the same job for significantly different pay. Some senior flight attendants report that the low-tier employees sometimes refuse to do chores, saying in effect: "Why don't you do it? You make more." Other employees worry that companies are trying to get workers to quarrel among themselves, and they fear as well that their employers will try to force out veteran workers and replace them with less expensive new ones.

The two-tier systems often affect morale, turnover, and even the ability of the company to find new employees. Researchers investigating the effects of two-tier contracts using equity theory have found that low-tier workers feel their pay is inequitable, have less commitment to their employers, and have less faith in their union than do high-tier workers.

A number of supermarkets have instituted a third tier of employees, sometimes titled "service" or "nonfood clerks," who may make only a third as much as someone doing almost exactly the same job. When Giant Food instituted such a lower tier in Baltimore and Washington, it found that the turnover rate grew unacceptably high—within three months of being hired, two-thirds of its new employees quit. In the tight labor market of Santa Clara County, California, Lockheed has been unable to find people who want to work at its low-tier wages.

Only the strongest of unions seem able to reverse the trend to two-tier contracts. Some don't even try, for perhaps the most divisive effect of the contracts is that they separate the interests of new union members from those of senior members who generally control the unions and negotiate new contracts. Future negotiations by employees of companies like American Airlines may determine whether the 100-year-old American union movement will abandon for good the principle of "equal pay for equal work."

Case Questions

1. What are the likely long-term effects of two-tier contracts?

2. In what ways does a two-tier contract succeed as a reward system? In what ways does it fail?

Case Source

Case 6.2　No More Dawdling Over Dishes

Andy Davis was proud of his restaurant, The Golden Bow. Its location was perfect, its decor tasteful, its clientele generous and distinguished. When he had first taken over the business a year ago, Davis had worried that the local labor shortage might make it difficult to hire good workers, but he had made some contacts at a local college and hired a group of waiters and waitresses who did good work and enjoyed being with each other. The only problem he still hadn't solved involved the dishwasher.

At first he had felt lucky when he found Eddie Munz, a local high school dropout who had some experience washing dishes. Davis couldn't afford to pay a dishwasher more than $4 an hour, and Eddie did not seem to mind that. Moreover Eddie did seem to get the dishes clean. But he was so slow! At first Davis thought that Eddie just wasn't quick about anything, but he changed his mind as he observed his behavior in the kitchen. Eddie loved to talk to the cooks, often turning his back on the dishes for minutes at a time to explain and gesture. He also nibbled desserts off of dirty plates and sprayed the waitresses when they got near him, a habit which did not make him popular. The kitchen was always a mess, and dishes would pile up so much that often two hours after closing time, when everything else was ready for the next day, Eddie would still be scraping and squirting and talking. Davis began to wonder if there was a method to Eddie's madness—he was getting paid by the hour, after all, so why shouldn't he dawdle? But Davis didn't like having a kitchen that looked sloppy all the time, so he determined to have a talk with Eddie.

Davis decided that what Eddie needed was a goal. He figured out what Eddie had been making on his reasonably efficient nights—$28—and then he met with Eddie and made Eddie a proposal. First he asked Eddie how soon after the last customer left he thought he could finish. Eddie said an hour and a quarter. When Davis asked if he would be interested in getting off forty-five minutes earlier than he had been, Eddie seemed excited. And when he offered to pay Eddie the $28 for a complete job every night, regardless of when he finished, Eddie could hardly contain himself. It turned out he didn't like to work until 2:00 in the morning, but he needed every dollar he could get.

The next week a new chalkboard appeared next to the kitchen door leading out to the dining room. On the top it read "Eddie's Goal for a Record Time," and by the end of the first week, Davis printed on the bottom "$1\frac{1}{4}$." Davis took to inspecting the dishes more often than usual, but he found no decrease in the quality of Eddie's work. So on Sunday, he said to Eddie, "Let's try for an hour."

A month later, the board read "42 minutes." The situation in the kitchen had changed radically. Formerly sloppy Eddie had become Eddie the Perfectionist. He was often waiting, his area spotless, when someone came from the dining room with a stack of dirty plates, and he took it as a personal affront if anyone found a spot on a plate he had washed. Instead of complaining about Eddie squirting them, the waitresses kidded Eddie about what a worker he'd become, and they stacked the plates and separated the silver in order to help him break his record. And the first time Eddie got done at 12:42, they all went out for an hour on the town together.

Case Questions

1. What elements of goal setting did Andy Davis employ?

2. Could Mr. Davis have used a different system of rewards to get the same results from Eddie Munz?

Experiential Exercise

Purpose: The purpose of this exercise is to enable you to see the potential benefits as well as the limitations of applying goal setting and rewards to a real situation.

Format: Working alone, develop a set of goals for yourself in this class. You should develop a range of goals of varying time horizons (i.e., grade on next quiz, grade at end of course, etc.). Next, identify appropriate rewards that you would like to receive for achieving each of your goals.

Develop a framework (a picture) linking goals and rewards for the course. That is, in one column list your goals. In another column list the rewards. Then connect each goal with its associated rewards.

Finally, meet with two of your classmates and compare notes. What are the similarities and differences between your goals and rewards? What are the similarities and differences in how you see goals linked to various rewards?

Follow-Up Questions

1. Would a formal MBO system work in a classroom? Why or why not?

2. What are the rewards available to you in a classroom setting? How do those rewards differ in their surface and symbolic meanings?

CHAPTER

7

Work Stress

Chapter Objectives

After reading this chapter, you should be able to

▶ discuss the nature of work stress.

▶ identify and discuss several causes of stress.

▶ identify and discuss several consequences of stress.

▶ describe Type A and Type B personality profiles.

▶ explain ways in which stress can be managed.

F ran Gennarelli is a sales representative for MMT Sales Inc., a Minneapolis firm that sells television time to advertisers. During busy periods, a workday can easily stretch to twelve hours or more. Clients call constantly, critical decisions must be made, and the pressure becomes almost unbearable.

Gennarelli says that his work is the main source of stress in his life. If he didn't work hard to cope with it, the stress in his job could become a real problem. So how *does* he cope with it? For one thing, he forces himself to mentally relax and to not take things too seriously. For another, he runs or lifts weights every night to let off steam.[1]

T he situation confronted by Fran Gennarelli is not unlike that faced by millions of American workers every day. Stress has become an inescapable part of most jobs. It can also be quite a dangerous part if not properly managed. This chapter offers a number of insights into stress in the workplace. First, we explore the nature of stress. We next identify and discuss a number of causes of stress and then outline its potential consequences. Then we describe Type A and Type B personality profiles, an approach to understanding why some people are more prone to stress than others. Finally, we highlight several things people and organizations can do to effectively manage stress at work.

THE NATURE OF STRESS

Many people think they understand stress. In reality, however, stress is complex and often misunderstood. To learn how job stress truly works, we must first define it and then relate it to the individual in the workplace.

Stress Defined

Although stress has been defined in many ways,[2] a common ground of most definitions is that stress is caused by a stimulus, that the stimulus can be either physical or psychological, and that the individual responds to the stimulus in some way. Here, then, we define **stress** as a person's adaptive response to a stimulus that places excessive psychological or physical demands on that person.[3]

Let us look at each component of this definition. First is the notion of adaptation. As we discuss shortly, people adapt to stressful circumstances in

---

[1] "Don't Let Stress Get the Best of You," *USA Today*, June 16, 1987, p. 7B.

[2] See James C. Quick and Jonathan D. Quick, *Organizational Stress and Preventive Management* (New York: McGraw-Hill, 1984), for a review.

[3] James L. Gibson, John M. Ivancevich, and James H. Donnelly, Jr., *Organizations— Behavior, Structure, Processes*, 6th ed. (Plano, Tex.: BPI, 1988), p. 230.

Figure 7.1   The General Adaptation Syndrome

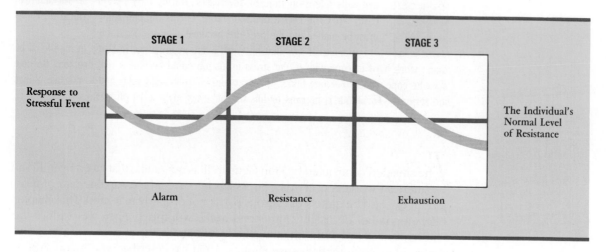

any of several different ways. Second is the role of the stimulus. This stimulus is generally called a stressor. That is, a *stressor* is anything that induces stress. The definition also notes that stressors can be either psychological or physical. Finally, the demands placed on the individual by the stressor must be excessive for stress to result. Of course, what is excessive for one person may be perfectly tolerable for another. So the point is simply that a person must view the demands as excessive or stress does not result.

Stress and the Individual

Much of what we know about stress today can be traced to the pioneering work of Dr. Hans Selye.[4] Selye identified what he called general adaptation syndrome and the notions of eustress and distress.

GENERAL ADAPTATION SYNDROME   Figure 7.1 graphically shows the **general adaptation syndrome (GAS).** According to this view, we each have a normal level of resistance to stressful events. Some of us can tolerate a great deal of stress, while others can handle much less, but everyone has a basic threshold at which stress starts to affect us.

The GAS begins when a person first encounters a stressor. The first stage is called *alarm.* At this point, the person may feel some degree of panic, may wonder how to cope, and so forth. For example, suppose a manager is assigned a lengthy report to write overnight. His first reaction may be, "How will I ever get this done by tomorrow?"

If the stressor is too extreme, the person may simply be unable to cope

[4] Hans Selye, *The Stress of Life* (New York: McGraw-Hill, 1976).

with it at first. In most cases, however, the individual gathers his or her strength (physical or emotional) and *resists* the negative effects of the stressor. For example, the manager with the long report to write may calm down, call home to say he's working late, role up his sleeves, order out for dinner, and set to work. Thus, at stage 2 of the GAS, the person is resisting the effects of the stressor.

In many cases, the resistance phase may end the GAS. If, for example, the manager is able to complete the report earlier than expected, he may drop it in his briefcase, smile to himself, and head home tired but happy. On the other hand, prolonged exposure to a stressor, without resolution, may bring on phase 3 of the GAS—*exhaustion*. At this stage, the person literally gives up and can no longer fight the stressor. The manager, for example, might fall asleep at his desk at 3 A.M. and not get the report finished.

DISTRESS AND EUSTRESS   Selye also pointed out that the sources of stress need not be bad.[5] For example, receiving a bonus and then having to decide what to do with the money can be stressful. So, too, can getting a promotion, gaining recognition, getting married, and similar "good" things. Selye called this type of stress **eustress.**

Of course, there is also negative stress. Called **distress,** this is what most people think of when they hear the word stress. Excessive pressure, unreasonable demands on our time, bad news, and so forth, all fall into this category.

For purposes of simplicity, we will continue to use the simple term stress. It is important to remember throughout the discussion, though, that stress can be either good or bad. It can motivate and stimulate us, or it can lead to any number of dangerous side effects.

INDIVIDUAL DIFFERENCES   It is also important to note the effects of individual differences on stress. We have already noted, for example, that people differ in their normal levels of resistance to stressors. The distinction between Type A and Type B personalities, discussed more fully later, is important in this regard.

Cultural differences are also important. For example, as detailed more fully in *International Perspective,* research by Cary Cooper suggests that American executives may have less stress than executives in many other countries, including Japan and Brazil.

Other research suggests that women are perhaps more prone to experience the psychological effects of stress, whereas men may report more physical effects.[6] Finally, it has also been suggested that people who see themselves as

---

[5] Selye, *The Stress of Life.*

[6] Todd D. Jick and Linda F. Mitz, "Sex Differences in Work Stress," *Academy of Management Review*, October 1985, pp. 408–420; and Debra L. Nelson and James C. Quick, "Professional Women: Are Distress and Disease Inevitable?" *Academy of Management Review*, April 1985, pp. 206–218.

International Perspective

U.S. Executives Less Stressed than Those of Other Nations

Executive stress is considered something that only afflicts U.S. chief executive officers and general managers.

The stereotype of top-ranking U.S. executives portrays the workaholic rushing around all day, smoking and drinking excessively, always under pressure and frequently headed toward a stress-related heart attack.

Work-related stress does cost corporations big bucks: In lost employment and decreased productivity, alcoholism costs U.S. industry $55 billion a year, according to a report of the National Institute for Occupational Safety and Health's symposium on strategy for reducing psychological disorders in the workplace.

But executives aren't the only ones afflicted with stress.

In fact, the United States "comes out pretty good," when compared with other countries, said Dr. Cary L. Cooper, professor of organizational psychology at the University of Manchester's Institute of Science and Technology in Great Britain.

Based on data he collected from 1,100 senior executives in 10 countries, the professor, chairman of the university's department of management sciences, says executive stress has no geographical boundaries and isn't limited to the Western world.

"The pressures on managers to perform in a climate of rapid sociological, technological and economic change in emerging countries such as Brazil, Nigeria, Egypt and Singapore, as well as Japan, are beginning to produce negative effects," Cooper said in the introduction to his research, "Executive Stress: A Ten-Country Comparison."

Surprisingly, the countries that emerge with good ratings for mental health and job satisfaction, he says, are Britain, Sweden, West Germany and the United States.

"The country whose executives suffer the least stress is Sweden," Cooper said in a telephone interview from Manchester. "They have the best mental health and are most satisfied with their lifestyles."

Cooper says he was surprised about the findings concerning Japanese executives and stress.

"Everyone assumes the Japanese are so productive that they should be in good shape," he said. "But in terms of mental health, 32 percent of the Japanese executives had mental ill-health scores that came close to . . . those of psychiatric outpatients."

being very complex are better able to handle stress than are people who have a simpler view of themselves.[7] We should add, though, that the study of individual differences in stress is still in its infancy; it would be premature to draw rigid conclusions about how different types of people handle stress.

---

[7] "Complex Characters Handle Stress Better," *Psychology Today*, October 1987, p. 26.

On the other hand, the United States, West Germany and Sweden reflect overall mental health and well-being.

Cooper bases his mental-health percentages on the results of a questionnaire devised to measure depression, anxiety and psychosomatic tendencies.

It includes such questions as: Do you feel that life is too much effort? Do you often feel upset for no obvious reason? Do you feel unduly tired or exhausted?

In job-related questions, 34 percent of Japanese, Egyptian and Brazilian executives reported unhappiness, a major cause of stress.

"It's interesting to note the high levels of dissatisfaction among Japanese executives, who are internationally stereotyped as 'committed and job-satisfied,'" Cooper said.

"Japan's social institutions support executives and encourage hard work and loyalty, but many Japanese executives are beginning to experience the competitiveness of Americans and Western Europeans."

Even though U.S. executives "look good" in terms of mental health, they complain about sources of presssure at work, the study shows.

U.S. executives feel considerable pressure related to business ethics, Cooper said. The United States leads the world, at 30 percent, he says, "with stress from what executives internally believe is right and just, contrasted with having to adhere to corporate expectations."

The major causes of stress among executives in the other nations reported in Cooper's survey:

- Sweden: encroachment of work on private lives.
- West Germany: time pressures and deadlines.
- Britain: keeping up with technology.
- South Africa: long hours.
- Nigeria: inadequately trained underlings.
- Brazil: time pressures and deadlines.
- Egypt: work overload and taking work home.

Source: By Carol Kleiman, from *The Chicago Tribune, March 31, 1988.* © *Copyrighted, Chicago Tribune* Company, all rights reserved, used with permission.

CAUSES OF STRESS

Many different things can cause stress. Figure 7.2 shows two broad categories: life stressors and organizational stressors. Also shown in the figure are three categories of stress consequences: individual and organizational consequences and burnout.

Organizational Stressors

Organizational stressors are factors in the workplace that can cause stress. Obviously, anything from a broken pencil sharpener to an argument

| Figure 7.2 | Causes and Consequences of Stress |

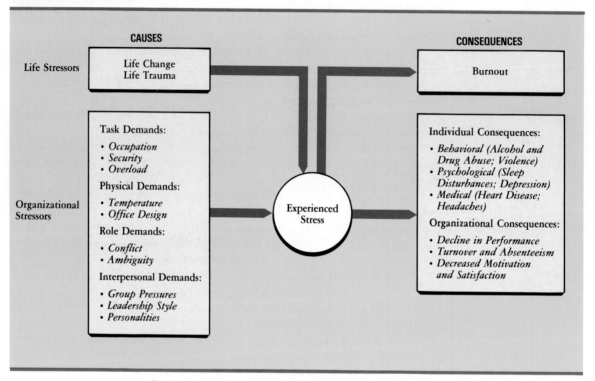

Source: Adapted from James C. Quick and Jonathan D. Quick, *Organizational Stress and Prevention Management*, McGraw-Hill, 1984, pp. 19, 44, and 76.

with one's boss can lead to stress. Four general sets of organizational stressors are task demands, physical demands, role demands, and interpersonal demands.[8]

TASK DEMANDS   **Task demands** are stressors associated with the specific job a person is performing. For example, some occupations are simply more stressful than others. The jobs of surgeon, air traffic controller, and professional football coach are comparatively more stressful than are the jobs of general practitioner, airplane baggage loader, and team trainer.

Beyond task-related pressure, other task demands may amount to physical threats to a person's health. Such conditions are found in occupations like coal mining, toxic waste handling, and so forth.

[8] Selye, *The Stress of Life*. See also Stephan J. Motowidlo, John S. Packard, and Michael R. Manning, "Occupational Stress: Its Causes and Consequences for Job Performance," *Journal of Applied Psychology*, Vol. 71, 1986, pp. 618–629.

Figure 7.3

Workload, Stress and
Performance

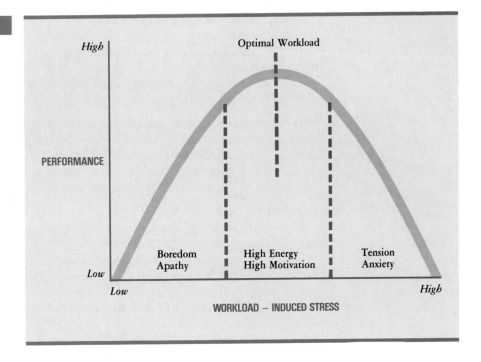

Security is also an important task demand that can cause stress. Someone in a relatively secure job is not likely to worry a lot about losing that job. On the other hand, if job security is threatened, stress can increase dramatically. For example, stress generally increases throughout an organization during a period of layoffs or immediately following a merger with another firm.[9]

The final task demand stressor is overload. Overload occurs when a person simply has more work to do than he or she can handle. The overload can be either quantitative (the individual has too many tasks to perform or too little time in which to perform them) or qualitative (the individual may feel that she or he lacks the ability to do the job). We should also note, however, that the opposite of overload may also be undesirable. As shown in Figure 7.3, low task demands can result in boredom and apathy, just as overload can cause tension and anxiety. Thus, a moderate degree of workload-related stress is optimal, since it leads to high levels of energy and motivation.

PHYSICAL DEMANDS   **Physical demands** relate to the setting of the job. One important element is temperature. Working outdoors in extreme temperatures, for example, can result in stress, as can even an improperly heated or cooled office.

[9] "Corporate Mergers Take a Toll on Employees in Lost Jobs and Family Strain," *Wall Street Journal*, September 9, 1986, p. 1.

Office design can also be a problem. A poorly designed office, for example, can make it difficult for people to have privacy or can promise too much or too little social interaction. Too much interaction might cause a person to be distracted from his or her task, while too little could lead to boredom or loneliness. Likewise, poor lighting, inadequate work surfaces, and so forth can also lead to stress.[10]

ROLE DEMANDS   **Role demands** can also be stressful to people in organizations. A role is a set of expected behaviors associated with a particular position in a group or organization. A person may experience stress from either *role ambiguity* (a lack of clarity as to what is expected) or *role conflict* (incongruence among two or more roles). We say more about roles in Chapter 8.[11]

INTERPERSONAL DEMANDS   A final set of organizational stressors consists of three **interpersonal demands** that may confront people in organizational settings. *Group pressures* include such things as pressure to restrict output, pressure to conform to the group's norms, and so forth. (Groups are covered in Chapter 9.) For instance, it is quite common, as we have noted before, for a work group to arrive at an informal agreement about how much each member will produce. Individuals who produce much more or much less than this level may be pressured by the group to get back in line. An individual who feels a strong need to vary from the group's expectations (perhaps to get a pay raise or promotion) will experience a great deal of stress, especially if acceptance by the group is also important to him or her.

Leadership style may also cause stress. Suppose an employee needs a great deal of social support from his leader. His leader, however, is quite brusque and refuses to show any concern or compassion of him. He will likely feel stressed. Similarly, an employee may feel a strong need to participate in decision making and to be active in all aspects of management. Her boss, though, who is very autocratic, refuses to consult subordinates about anything. Once again, stress is likely.[12]

Finally, personalities and behaviors may also cause stress. Conflict can occur when two or more people must work together even though their personalities, attitudes, and behaviors differ. For example, a person with an internal locus of control, always wanting to control how things turn out, might be frustrated

---

[10] Robert I. Sutton and Anat Rafaeli, "Characteristics of Work Stations as Potential Occupational Stressors," *Academy of Management Journal*, June 1987, pp. 260–276.

[11] See Edward R. Kemery, Arthur G. Bedeian, Kevin W. Mossholder, and John Touliatos, "Outcomes of Role Stress: A Multisample Constructive Replication," *Academy of Management Journal*, June 1985, pp. 363–375, for a recent examination of the effects of role demands.

[12] See Gary M. Kaufman and Terry A. Beehr, "Interactions Between Job Stressors and Social Support: Some Counterintuitive Results," *Journal of Applied Psychology*, Vol. 71, 1986, pp. 522–526, for an interesting study in this area.

working with an external person who likes to wait and just let things happen. Likewise, suppose a smoker and nonsmoker are assigned adjacent offices. The potential for stress on the part of each is apparent.[13]

Life Stressors

Stress in organizational settings can also be influenced by events that take place outside the organization. Common approaches categorize these events in terms of life change and life trauma.[14]

LIFE CHANGE   Holmes and Rahe first developed and popularized the notion of life change as a source of stress.[15] **Life change** is any meaningful change in a person's personal or work situation. Holmes and Rahe reasoned that major changes in a person's life can lead to stress and, eventually, disease. Table 7.1 summarizes their findings on major life change events. Note that several of these events relate directly (i.e. fired at work, retirement) or indirectly (i.e. change in residence) to work.

Each event's point value is supposed to reflect its impact on the individual. At one extreme, a spouse's death, assumed to be the most traumatic event considered, is assigned a point value of 100. At the other extreme, minor violations of the law carry only 11 points. The points themselves represent life change units, or LCUs. Note also that the list includes negative events (like divorce and trouble with the boss) as well as positive ones (like marriage and vacations).

Holmes and Rahe argued that a person can handle a certain threshold of LCUs, but beyond that threshold, problems can set in. In particular, they suggest that people who encounter more than 150 LCUs in a given year will experience a decline in their health the following year. A score of between 150 and 300 LCUs supposedly carries a 50-percent chance of major illness, while the chance of major illness is said to increase to 70 percent if the LCUs exceed 300.

These ideas offer some insight into the potential impact of stress and underscore our limitations in coping with stressful events. However, research on Holmes and Rahe's proposals has provided only mixed support. One avenue that does seem promising, however, is based on the notion of hardiness.

This view suggests that some people have hardier personalities than others do. People with hardy personalities have an internal locus of control, are committed to the activities in their lives, and view change as an opportunity.

---

[13] David R. Frew and Nealia S. Bruning, "Perceived Organizational Characteristics and Personality Measures as Predictors of Stress/Strain in the Work Place," *Academy of Management Journal*, December 1987, pp. 633–646.

[14] Quick and Quick, *Organizational Stress and Preventive Management*.

[15] T. H. Holmes and R. H. Rahe, "Social Readjustment Rating Scale," *Journal of Psychosomatic Research*, Vol. 29, 1967, pp. 213–218.

	Rank	Life Event	Mean Value
Table 7.1	1	Death of spouse	100
	2	Divorce	73
Life Changes and Life	3	Marital separation	65
Change Units	4	Jail term	63
	5	Death of close family member	63
	6	Personal injury or illness	53
	7	Marriage	50
	8	Fired at work	47
	9	Marital reconciliation	45
	10	Retirement	45
	11	Change in health of family member	44
	12	Pregnancy	40
	13	Sex difficulties	39
	14	Gain of new family member	39
	15	Business readjustment	39
	16	Change in financial state	38
	17	Death of close friend	37
	18	Change to different line of work	36
	19	Change in number of arguments with spouse	35
	20	Mortgage over $10,000	31
	21	Foreclosure of mortgage or loan	30
	22	Change in responsibilities at work	29
	23	Son or daughter leaving home	29
	24	Trouble with in-laws	29
	25	Outstanding personal achievement	28

Such people are seen as less likely to suffer illness if they experience high levels of LCUs, while people with low hardiness may indeed be more susceptible to the predicted effects of high LCUs.[16]

LIFE TRAUMA   Approaching individual stress in terms of life trauma is similar to using the notion of life change but has a narrower, more direct, and shorter-term focus. A **life trauma** is any single upheaval in an individual's life that disrupts his or her attitudes, emotions, or behaviors.

To elaborate, under the life change view, a divorce adds to a person's potential for health problems in the next year. At the same time, however, it should be obvious that the person will also experience emotional turmoil

---

[16] Susan C. Kobasa, "Stressful Life Events, Personality, and Health: An Inquiry into Hardiness," *Journal of Personality and Social Psychology*, January 1979, pp. 1–11; and Susan C. Kobasa, S. R. Maddi, and S. Kahn, "Hardiness and Health: A Prospective Study," *Journal of Personality and Social Psychology*, January 1982, pp. 168–177.

Table 7.1 (continued)

Rank	Life Event	Mean Value
26	Spouse beginning or stopping work	26
27	Beginning or ending school	26
28	Change in living conditions	25
29	Revision of personal habits	24
30	Trouble with boss	23
31	Change in work hours or conditions	20
32	Change in residence	20
33	Change in schools	20
34	Change in recreation	19
35	Change in church activities	19
36	Change in social activities	18
37	Mortgage or loan less than $10,000	17
38	Change in sleeping habits	16
39	Change in number of family get-togethers	15
40	Change in eating habits	15
41	Vacation	13
42	Christmas	12
43	Minor violations of the law	11

The amount of life stress that a person has experienced in a given period of time, say one year, is measured by the total number of life change units (LCUs). These units result from the addition of the values (shown in the right-hand column) associated with events that the person has experienced during the target time period.
Source: Reprinted with permission from *Journal of Psychosomatic Research*, Vol. II, pp. 213–218, Thomas H. Holmes and Richard H. Rahe, "The Social Adjustment Rating Scale," Copyright 1967, Pergamon Press plc.

during the divorce process itself. This turmoil, the focus of the term *life trauma*, will clearly cause stress, much of which may spill over into the workplace.[17]

Major life traumas that may cause stress include marital problems, family problems, other personal problems, and health problems initially unrelated to stress. For example, suppose a person learns she has developed arthritis that will limit her favorite activity, perhaps skiing. Her disappointment over the news may translate into stress at work.

CONSEQUENCES OF STRESS

A number of consequences can result from stress. As already noted, if the stress is positive, the result may be more energy, enthusiasm, and motivation. Of

---

[17] Evelyn J. Bromet, Mary Amanda Dew, David K. Parkinson, and Herbert C. Schulberg, "Predictive Effects of Occupational and Marital Stress on the Mental Health of a Male Workforce," *Journal of Organizational Behavior*, Vol. 9, 1988, pp. 1–13.

more concern, of course, are the negative consequences of stress. Referring back to Figure 7.2, three sets of consequences that can result from stress are individual consequences, organizational consequences, and burnout.[18]

Observe that many of the factors listed are interrelated. For example, alcohol abuse is shown as an individual consequence. Yet alcohol abuse by an employee is also a consequence to the organization; for one thing it may directly affect performance. If the category for a consequence seems somewhat arbitrary, be aware that each consequence is categorized according to its *primary* constituent.

Individual Consequences

Individual consequences of stress, then, are those outcomes that mainly affect the individual. The organization may also suffer, either directly or indirectly, but it is the individual who pays the real price. Three categories of individual consequences of stress are behavioral, psychological, and medical.

BEHAVIORAL CONSEQUENCES   Behavioral consequences of stress are responses that may harm the person under stress or others. One such behavior is smoking. Research has clearly documented that people who smoke tend to smoke more when they experience stress. There is also evidence that alcohol and drug abuse are linked to stress, although this relationship is not as well established.[19] Other behavioral consequences may include accident proneness, violence, and appetite disorders.

PSYCHOLOGICAL CONSEQUENCES   Psychological consequences of stress relate to an individual's mental health and well-being. When people experience too much stress at work, they may become depressed or may find themselves sleeping too much or not enough. Stress may also lead to family problems and sexual difficulties.[20]

MEDICAL CONSEQUENCES   Finally, stress can lead to medical disorders. These medical consequences of stress affect a person's physical well-being. Heart disease and stroke, for example, have been linked to stress. Other common medical problems resulting from too much stress may include headaches, backaches, ulcers and related stomach and intestinal disorders, and skin conditions like acne and hives.[21]

---

[18] Quick and Quick, *Organizational Stress and Preventive Management.* See also John M. Ivancevich and Michael T. Matteson, *Stress and Work: a Managerial Perspective* (Glenview, Ill.: Scott, Foresman, 1980).

[19] Quick and Quick, *Organizational Stress and Preventive Management.*

[20] Quick and Quick, *Organizational Stress and Preventive Management.*

[21] Quick and Quick, *Organizational Stress and Preventive Management.*

Organizational Consequences

Clearly, any of the individual consequences just discussed can also affect the organization. Still other consequences of stress, however, have even more direct consequences for the organization.

PERFORMANCE   One clear organizational consequence of too much stress is a decline in performance. For operating workers, such a decline can translate into poor-quality work or a drop in productivity. For managers, it can mean faulty decision making or disruptions in working relationships as people become irritable and hard to get along with.

WITHDRAWAL   Withdrawal behaviors can also result from stress. The two most important are absenteeism and quitting. People who are having a hard time coping with stress in their jobs are more likely to call in sick or consider leaving the organization for good.

Other, more subtle forms of withdrawal can result from stress. A manager may start missing deadlines, for example, or taking longer lunch breaks. An employee may also withdraw psychologically by ceasing to care about the organization and the job.[22]

ATTITUDES   Another direct organizational consequence of employee stress relates to attitudes. As just implied, job satisfaction, morale, and organizational commitment, can all suffer, along with motivation to perform at high levels.

Burnout

A final consequence of stress has potential impact on both people and organizations. **Burnout** is a general feeling of exhaustion that may develop when an individual simultaneously experiences too much pressure and too few sources of satisfaction.[23]

Figure 7.4 illustrates in a very general way how burnout develops.[24] First, people with high aspirations and strong motivation to get things done are prime candidates for burnout under certain conditions. They are especially vulnerable when they find themselves in an organization that suppresses or limits their own initiative while constantly demanding that they serve the organization's own ends. In such a situation, the individual is likely to put too

---

[22] Quick and Quick, *Organizational Stress and Preventive Management.* See also "Stress: The Test Americans are Failing," *Business Week*, April 18, 1988, pp. 74–76.

[23] Leonard Moss, *Management Stress* (Reading, Mass.: Addison-Wesley, 1981).

[24] See Susan E. Jackson, Richard L. Schwab, and Randall S. Schuler, "Toward an Understanding of the Burnout Phenomenon," *Journal of Applied Psychology*, Vol. 71, 1986, pp. 630–640; and Daniel W. Russell, Elizabeth Altmaier, and Dawn Van Velzen, "Job-Related Stress, Social Support, and Burnout Among Classroom Teachers," *Journal of Applied Psychology*, Vol. 72, 1987, pp. 269–274.

Figure 7.4

The Process of Burnout

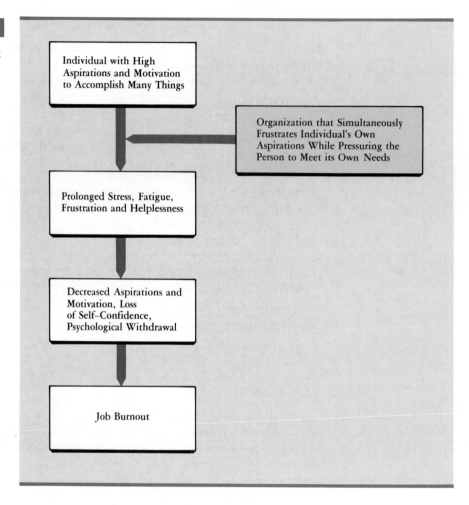

much of himself or herself into the job. That is, the person may well keep trying to accomplish his or her own agenda while simultaneously trying to fulfill the organization's expectations. The most likely effects of this are fatigue, frustration, and helplessness under the burden of overwhelming demands. The person literally exhausts his or her aspirations and motivation, much as a candle burns itself out. Ultimately, burnout results.

At this point, the individual may start dreading going to work in the morning, may put in longer hours but get less accomplished than before, and may generally display mental and physical exhaustion. *A Look at Research* provides additional insights into the burnout phenomenon.

A LOOK AT

RESEARCH

Trying to Understand Burnout

"Burnout" has become part of our national vocabulary since it was coined by psychologist Herbert Freudenberger in 1974. There is not doubt that its use has become so widespread in part because so many people feel, at times, burned out from their jobs, and therefore feel that they know intuitively what it means. Yet the research to measure and analyze burnout effectively has been scarce.

A 1985 study by Susan E. Jackson, Richard L. Schwab, and Randall S. Schuler attempted to isolate some of the causes and effects associated with burnout. The researchers studied school teachers in New Hampshire. They chose teachers because burnout has been most often associated with professionals like nurses, social workers, and police officers who spend a large amount of time working with others who need help. Freudenberger originally observed the syndrome in staff members working in free clinics and halfway houses.

The researchers in the New Hampshire study defined burnout as a combination of emotional exhaustion, depersonalization (the tendency to distance oneself from a student, client, or patient and treat that person as an object), and feelings of low personal accomplishment. They hypothesized that these three elements of burnout are linked to unmet expectations (the difference between a person's expectations of a job and its realities) and a number of conditions of the job itself, among them large caseloads, role conflict (having to react to many incompatible demands), lack of support, lack of autonomy, and lack of rewards related to performance. They also expected to find that the symptoms of burnout would lead people to think about leaving their particular job or the entire teaching profession.

Some of their findings surprised the researchers. The unmet expectations of the teachers did not correlate with any of the signs of burnout. The researchers cautioned, however, that asking people to recall their expectations of years before was not necessarily a reliable way to measure such expectations. They were also surprised to find that while people who were burned out thought about moving to other jobs, those teachers wanting to move into educational administration tended to have low burnout scores. One might conclude that school principals are not, as some have argued, burned out teachers.

The findings did confirm some hypotheses, however. Emotional exhaustion seems to be the primary component of burnout. The primary source of emotional exhaustion appears to be role conflict. The teachers reported feelings of depersonalization only when they felt a lack of support from their principals. Also not surprisingly, teachers in supportive environments, particularly ones with supportive principals, reported the greatest feelings of personal accomplishments.

Source: Susan E. Jackson, Richard L. Schwab, and Randall S. Schuler, "Toward an Understanding of the Burnout Phenomenon," *Journal of Applied Psychology,* 1986, Volume 71, Number 4, 630–640.

TYPE A AND TYPE B PERSONALITY PROFILES

As noted at the beginning of this chapter, not everyone responds to stress in the same way. In fact, virtually every aspect of stress, from what triggers it to its consequences, can vary from person to person. One line of thinking about systematic differences between people has been in terms of Type A and Type B personality profiles.

The Type A and B profiles were first observed by two cardiologists, Meyer Friedman and Ray Rosenman.[25] The idea started when a worker repairing the upholstery on their waiting room chairs noted that many of the chairs were worn only on the front. This suggested to the two cardiologists that many heart patients were anxious and had a hard time sitting still.

Using this observation as a starting point, and based on their own clinical practice, Friedman and Rosenman concluded that their patients seemed to exhibit two very different types of behavior patterns. Their research led them to conclude that the differences were personality based. The basic behavioral characteristics of Type A and Type B individuals are shown in Figure 7.5.

The **Type A** individual is one who is extremely competitive, very devoted to work, and has a strong sense of urgency. Moreover, this individual is likely to be aggressive, impatient, and very work oriented. He or she has a lot of drive and wants to accomplish as much as possible in as short a time as possible.

The **Type B** person, in contrast, is less competitive, less devoted to work, and has a weaker sense of urgency. This person feels less conflict with either people or time and has a more balanced, relaxed approach to life. She or he has more confidence and is able to work at a constant pace. Finally, the Type B person is not necessarily any more or less successful than is a Type A person.

Friedman and Rosenman point out that people are not purely Type A or Type B. Instead, people are presumed to tend toward one or the other type. This is reflected in our figure by the overlap between the profiles. For example, an individual might exhibit marked Type A characteristics much of the time but still be able to relax once in a while and even forget about work in a few situations.

Early research by Freidman and Rosenman on the Type A and B profile differences yielded some alarming findings. In particular, it was argued that Type As were much more likely to experience coronary heart disease than were Type Bs.[26] In recent years, though, follow-up research by other scientists suggests that the relationship between Type A behavior and the risk of coronary heart disease is not all that straightforward.[27]

---

[25] M. Friedman and R. H. Rosenman, *Type A Behavior and Your Heart* (New York: Alfred A. Knopf, 1974).

[26] Friedman and Rosenman, *Type A Behavior and Your Heart*.

[27] Joshua Fischman, "Type A on Trial," *Psychology Today*, February 1987, pp. 42–50.

Figure 7.5

Type A and Type B
Personality Profiles

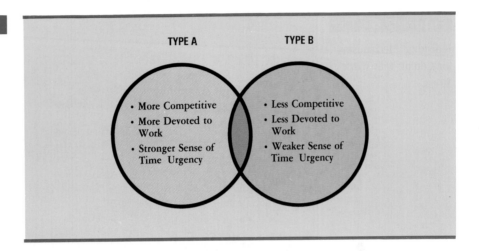

TYPE A

- More Competitive
- More Devoted to Work
- Stronger Sense of Time Urgency

TYPE B

- Less Competitive
- Less Devoted to Work
- Weaker Sense of Time Urgency

Although the reasons are unclear, recent findings suggest that Type As are much more complex than originally thought. Not only do they have the traits noted in Figure 7.5; they are also likely to be depressed and hostile. And it could be any or all of these feelings that lead to heart problems. Moreover, different approaches to measuring Type A tendencies yield different results.

Finally, in one study that found Type As to be *less* susceptible to heart problems than Type Bs, researchers still offered an explanation consistent with earlier thinking: they reasoned that since Type As are compulsive, they seek treatment earlier and are more likely to follow doctor's orders![28]

MANAGING STRESS IN THE WORKPLACE

Given that stress is widespread and potentially so disruptive in organizations, it follows that people and organizations should be concerned about how to manage it more effectively. And in fact they are. Many strategies have been developed to help manage stress in the workplace. Some are strategies for individuals; others are geared toward organizations.[29]

---

[28] "Prognosis for the 'Type A' Personality Improves in a New Heart Disease Study," *Wall Street Journal*, January 14, 1988, p. 27.

[29] Quick and Quick, *Organizational Stress and Preventive Management*.

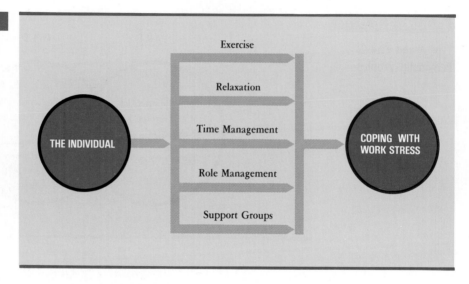

Figure 7.6

Individual Mechanisms for Coping with Work Stress

Individual Coping Strategies

Of the many strategies proposed to help individuals manage stress, five of the more popular ones are illustrated in Figure 7.6.

EXERCISE   One method by which individuals can manage their stress is through exercise. People who exercise regularly are less likely to have heart attacks than inactive people are. More directly, it has also been suggested that people who exercise regularly feel less tension and stress, are more self-confident, and show greater optimism. People who don't exercise regularly, on the other hand, feel more stress, are more likely to be depressed, and so forth.[30]

RELAXATION   A related method individuals can use to manage stress is relaxation. We noted at the beginning of the chapter that coping with stress requires adaptation. Proper relaxation is an effective way to adapt.

Relaxation can take many forms. One way to relax is to take regular vacations. A recent study found that people's attitudes toward a variety of workplace characteristics improved significantly following a vacation.[31] People can also relax while on the job. For example, it has been recommended that people take regular rest breaks during their normal workday. A popular way of resting is to sit quietly with closed eyes for ten minutes every afternoon.

[30] C. Folkins, "Effects of Physical Training on Mood," *Journal of Clinical Psychology*, April 1976, pp. 385–390.

[31] John W. Lounsbury and Linda L. Hoopes, "A Vacation From Work: Changes in Work and Nonwork Outcomes," *Journal of Applied Psychology*, Vol. 71, 1986, pp. 392–401.

TIME MANAGEMENT   Time management is often recommended as a method for managing stress. The idea is that many daily pressures can be eased or eliminated if a person does a better job of managing time. One popular approach to time management is to make a list every morning of the things to be done that day. You then group the items on the list into three categories: critical activities that must be performed, important activities that should be performed, and optional or trivial things that can be delegated or postponed. Then, of course, you do the things on the list in their order of importance. This strategy helps get more of the important things done every day. It also promotes delegating less important activities to others.

ROLE MANAGEMENT   Somewhat related to time management is the idea of role management, in which the individual actively works to avoid overload, ambiguity, and conflict. For example, if you do not know what is expected of you, you should not sit and worry about it. Instead, ask for clarification from your boss.

Another strategy in role management is learning to say no. As simple as saying no might sound, a lot of people create problems for themselves by always saying yes. Besides their own regular jobs, they agree to serve on committees, volunteer for extra duties, and accept extra assignments. Sometimes, of course, we may have no choice but to accept an extra obligation (if our boss tells us to complete a new project, we most likely will have to do it). In many cases, though, saying no is a viable option.[32]

SUPPORT GROUPS   A final method for managing stress is to develop and maintain support groups. A support group is simply a group of family members or friends that a person can spend time with. Going out after work with a couple of coworkers to a basketball game, for example, can help relieve the stress that built up during the day. Supportive family and friends can help us deal with normal stress on an ongoing basis.

Support groups can also be particularly useful during times of crisis. For example, suppose an employee has just learned that she did not get the promotion she has been working toward for months. It may help her tremendously if she has good friends to lean on, be it to talk to or to yell at.[33]

Organizational Coping Strategies

Organizations are realizing that they should be involved in managing their employees' stress. There are two different rationales for this view. One is that since the organization is at least partially responsible for creating the stress, it

---

[32] "Eight Ways to Help You Reduce the Stress in Your Life," *Business Week Careers*, November 1986, p. 78.

[33] Daniel C. Ganster, Marcelline R. Fusilier, and Bronston T. Mayes, "Role of Social Support in the Experiences of Stress at Work," *Journal of Applied Psychology*, Vol. 71, 1986, pp. 102–110.

Management in ACTION

Stress on the job? Ask yourself.

How to take this quiz

This quiz will help you recognize your level of stress on the job. Take the test, figure your score and then see if your stress level is normal, beginning to be a problem, or dangerous. Answer the following statements by putting a number in front of each:

1—seldom true
2—sometimes true
3—mostly true

_____ 1. Even over minor problems, I lose my temper and do embarassing things, like yell or kick a garbage can.

_____ 2. I hear every piece of information or question as criticism of my work.

_____ 3. If someone criticizes my work, I take it as a personal attack.

_____ 4. My emotions seem flat whether I'm told good news or bad news about my performance.

_____ 5. Sunday nights are the worst time of the week.

_____ 6. To avoid going to work, I'd even call in sick when I'm feeling fine.

_____ 7. I feel powerless to lighten my work load or schedule, even though I've always got far too much to do.

_____ 8. I respond irritably to any request from co-workers.

_____ 9. On the job and off, I get highly emotional over minor accidents, like typos, spilt coffee.

_____ 10. I tell people about sports or hobbies that I'd like to do, but say I never have time because of the hours I spend at work.

_____ 11. I work overtime consistently, yet never feel caught up.

_____ 12. My health is running down; I often have headaches, backaches, stomachaches.

_____ 13. If I even eat lunch, I do it at my desk while working.

_____ 14. I see time as my enemy.

_____ 15. I can't tell the difference between work and play; it all feels like a drain on my energy.

_____ 16. Everything I do feels like a drain of my energy.

_____ 17. I feel like I want to pull the covers over my head and hide.

_____ 18. I seem off center, distracted—I do things like walk into mirrored pillars in department stores and excuse myself.

_____ 19. I blame my family—because of them, I have to stay in this job and location.

_____ 20. I have ruined my relationship with co-workers whom I feel I compete against.

Scoring:

20–29—You have normal amounts of stress.

30–49—Stress is becoming a problem. You should try to identify its source and manage it.

50–60—Stress is at dangerous levels. Seek help or it could result in worse symptoms, such as alcoholism or illness.

Source: From *USA Today*, June 16, 1987. Copyright 1987, *USA Today*. Excerpted with permission.

Figure 7.7

Organizational Strategies
for Helping Employees
Cope with Stress

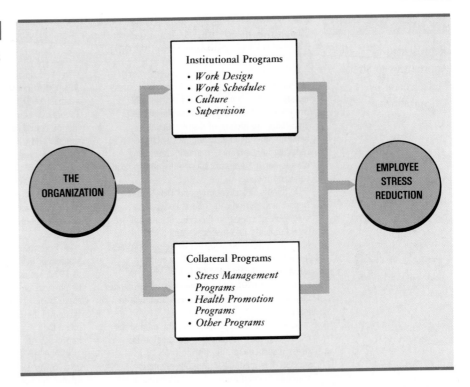

Institutional Programs
- *Work Design*
- *Work Schedules*
- *Culture*
- *Supervision*

THE
ORGANIZATION

EMPLOYEE
STRESS
REDUCTION

Collateral Programs
- *Stress Management Programs*
- *Health Promotion Programs*
- *Other Programs*

should also help relieve it. The other is that workers experiencing lower levels of harmful stress will be able to function more effectively. *Management in Action* provides some additional insights into stress management at the organizational level. In addition, Figure 7.7 shows some of the more common organizational methods for helping employees deal with stress.

INSTITUTIONAL PROGRAMS   *Institutional programs* to manage stress are undertaken through established organizational mechanisms.[34] For example, properly designed jobs (discussed more fully in Chapter 8) and work schedules can help ease stress. Shift work, in particular, can cause major problems for employees, as they constantly have to adjust their sleep and relaxation patterns. So the design of work and work schedules should be a focus of organizational efforts to reduce stress.[35]

The organization's culture (covered in Chapter 16) can also be used to help manage stress. Consider that in some organizations there is a strong norm

[34] Randall S. Schuler and Susan E. Jackson, "Managing Stress Through PHRM Practices: An Uncertainty Interpretation," in K. Rowland and G. Ferris, *Research in Personnel and Human Resources Management*, Vol. 4 (Greenwich, Conn.: JAI Press, 1986), pp. 183–224.

[35] Quick and Quick, *Organizational Stress and Preventive Management*.

Table 7.2	Examples of Stress Management Programs	Examples of Employee Fitness Programs
Representative Approaches to Stress Management by Organizations	• Metropolitan Life Insurance Center for Health Help offers a program in worksite stress management to employees and markets the program to other corporations. The program emphasizes reduction of distress through behavior modification techniques such as reducing time urgency pressure, developing interpersonal communication skills, and relaxing voluntary muscle. • Illinois Bell's Training and Development Department periodically offers a stress management course at the request of employees. • Equitable Life Insurance Emotional Health Program utilizes biofeedback to help employees learn to ease their tensions. The company informally estimates that each $15 which it spends on a treatment session relieves symptoms that would have cost three times that much in lost productivity. • New York Telephone Company piloted the use of Clinically Standardized Meditation for stress management and, on the basis of its success, has made CSM training regularly available to employees. • B. F. Goodrich Tire's Group Learning Center has prepared a training program entitled "Manage Your Stress," a nine-hour program in three sessions designed to teach employees to identify their own stress responses and to assume responsibility for altering their responses.	• Weyerhaeuser Company in 1972 invested $73,000 to construct and equip a colorful gymnasium at the company's headquarters in Tacoma, Washington. The facility, which includes indoor courts, a well-equipped exercise room, saunas, and a locker room, is open daily to employees and their families. • Johns-Manville spent $17,000 to equip a small company gym at its Denver headquarters. Like many corporate fitness programs, participants must have a medical examination before beginning and are given specific guidelines. • Exxon Corporation, when it planned its Manhattan headquarters building which opened in 1972, set aside a 2,900-square-foot area for its physical fitness laboratory. Under the supervision of the medical department, over 300 executives have participated in regular prescribed exercise, achieving significant improvements in several health parameters. • The Life Insurance Company of Georgia set up a Tower Health Club atop its building in Atlanta. Its executives, over 200 of whom are members, pay a subsidized membership fee which is about one-third of the fee for other tenants in the building. Facilities, which include handball and squash courts, massage and exercise rooms, and a rooftop track, are open twelve hours daily on weekdays.

Source: Based on James C. Quick and Jonathan D. Quick, *Organizational Stress and Preventive Management,* McGraw-Hill, 1984, pp. 256–287.

against ever taking time off or going on vacation. In the long run, such a norm can cause major stress. Thus the organization should strive to foster a culture that reinforces a healthy mix of work and nonwork activities.

Finally, supervision can play an important institutional role in managing stress. A supervisor is potentially a major source of overload. If made aware of their potential for assigning stressful amounts of work, supervisors can do a better job of keeping workloads reasonable.

COLLATERAL PROGRAMS   In addition to their institutional efforts aimed at reducing stress, many organizations are turning to collateral programs. A *collateral stress program* is an organizational program specifically created to help employees deal with stress. As noted in Figure 7.7, organizations have adopted stress management programs, health promotion programs, and other kinds of programs for this purpose.

Table 7.2 summarizes several examples of stress management programs that have been adopted. More and more companies are developing their own programs or adopting existing programs of this type.[36]

Table 7.2 also gives examples of firms that have employee fitness programs. These kinds of programs attack stress indirectly by encouraging employees to exercise, which in turn is presumed to reduce stress. On the negative side, this kind of effort costs considerably more money than stress management programs, since the firm must invest in physical facilities. Still, more and more companies are also exploring this option.[37]

Finally, organizations also try to help employees cope with stress through other kinds of programs. For example, existing career development programs, like one at General Electric, are used for this purpose. Other companies use programs promoting everything from humor to massage as antidotes for stress.[38] Of course, there is little or no research to support some of the claims made by advocates of these programs. Thus the manager must take steps to ensure that any organizational effort to help employees cope with stress is at least reasonably effective.

SUMMARY OF KEY POINTS

Stress is a person's adaptive response to a stimulus that places excessive psychological or physical demands on that person. According to the general adaptation syndrome, the three stages of response to stress are alarm, resistance, and exhaustion. Two important forms of stress are eustress and distress.

Stress can be caused by many different factors. Major organizational stressors are task demands, physical demands, role demands, and interpersonal demands. Life stressors are life change and life trauma.

Stress has many consequences. Individual consequences can be behavioral, psychological, and medical problems. Organizational consequences can affect performance and attitudes or cause withdrawal. Burnout is also possible.

Type A personalities are more competitive and time driven than Type B personalities. Initial evidence suggested that Type As are more susceptible to coronary heart disease, but recent findings provide less support.

---

[36] Quick and Quick, *Organizational Stress and Preventive Management.*

[37] Richard A. Wolfe, David O. Ulrich, and Donald F. Parker, "Employee Health Management Programs: Review, Critique, and Research Agenda," *Journal of Management*, Winter 1987, pp. 603–615.

[38] "A Cure for Stress?" *Newsweek*, October 12, 1987, pp. 64–65.

Primary individual mechanisms for managing stress are exercise, relaxation, time management, role management, and support groups. Organizations use both institutional and collateral programs for this purpose.

DISCUSSION QUESTIONS

1. Can you describe recent times when stress had both good and bad consequences for you?

2. Describe a time when you successfully avoided stage 3 of the GAS and another time when you did go to stage 3.

3. What are the major stressors for a student?

4. Which is likely to be more powerful, an organizational stressor or a life stressor?

5. What consequences are students most likely to suffer as a result of too much stress?

6. Do you agree with the assertion that a certain degree of stress is necessary to induce high energy and motivation?

7. What can be done to prevent burnout? If someone you knew had suffered burnout, how would you advise them to recover from it?

8. Do you consider yourself a Type A or a Type B person? Why?

9. Can a person who is a Type A change? How?

10. Do you practice any of the stress reduction methods discussed in the text? Which one(s)? Are there others you use?

Case 7.1   Work Stress at Texas Air

Flying a commercial aircraft is a stressful job under any circumstances. Pilots have to contend with changing and uncontrollable weather conditions while bearing almost total responsibility for the lives of sometimes hundreds of people. And, as one pilot put it, "We can't just pull over for a cup of coffee when things get too tense."

Imagine, then, the stress experienced by pilots working for a company in the midst of radical changes, many lawsuits, and sharp spending cutbacks, a company run by a man disliked by most in the industry and in the company itself. This is the fate of pilots flying for Eastern and Continental Airlines, two of the major wings of Frank Lorenzo's Texas Air Corporation.

In less than a decade, formerly tiny Texas Air has grown to control more than 20 percent of the market by gobbling up larger airlines, including Continental, Eastern, People Express, Frontier, and New York Air. To do so, it has had to take on large debts and find ways to cut costs substantially. Texas Air's chairman, Frank Lorenzo, made himself unpopular with many people in the industry when he broke the strike—and the union—at Continental in 1983 by taking the company into bankruptcy and firing many of the strikers. His goal is to build the nation's largest and lowest-fare airline, and in pursuing this goal, he has had to make further cuts.

All this creates a variety of stresses for Texas Air employees, especially for Eastern and Continental pilots. In 1987 Continental captains with 10 years' experience were making $52,500, less than half the industry average of $108,000. Continental pilots also fly more hours than their counterparts at other airlines— 90 hours a month versus the industry average of 80 to 85 hours—and unlike most in the industry, they get no pay for the time they spend on the ground before a return flight. Because Continental has expanded so fast, the company sometimes books more flights than it can fly. During Easter weekend in 1987, flight instructors had to return to normal pilot duty to meet Continental's schedules. Pilots at Eastern complain that the company pushes them to violate Federal Aviation Administration rules about such things as the 30-hour-per-week flying time limit.

The merger of pilots from so many airlines, all with various levels of seniority, has also created tension. Some pilots who had been captains were demoted to first officers after the merger. Because of the personnel shuffling and the fact that the union has held on to Eastern, some of Texas Air's cockpits contain a union pilot and a non-union pilot, a striker and a strike-breaker, or a captain and a former captain.

Pilots worry about what's going on outside the cockpit as well. Low pay and a high turnover rate among Continental's flight attendants, mechanics, and baggage handlers has resulted in some of the poorest service in the industry, and customers often take out their irritation on pilots. Although in 1987 Lorenzo pledged to improve the company's service and public image, many in the industry don't know how he can do that while still cutting pay. To keep good mechanics and ease worries about the safety of its airplanes, Continental raised the pay of its senior mechanics by 5 percent in 1987, but a starting mechanic's salary is still well below the industry average.

"I assume Frank Lorenzo wants the pilot group to be as divided and confused as possible," one of Lorenzo's pilots says. Whether or not this assessment is true, so far Lorenzo's strategies have succeeded at cutting costs. The long-term effects of pilot stress, however, remain to be seen.

Case Questions

1. How many different sources of stress can you identify for the Continental and Eastern pilots?

2. Could Texas Air Corporation cut down on some of the sources of stress without spending large amounts of money?

Case Sources

Paulette Thomas, "Bumpy Ride: Pilots Feel the Stress of Turmoil in the Airline Industry," *The Wall Street Journal*, April 24, 1987, 33; Jo Ellen Davis, "What It's Like To Work For Frank Lorenzo," *Business Week*, May 18, 1987, 76–78; Doug Carroll, "Lorenzo Rallies His Airline Crews," *USA Today*, September 23, 1987, 1B.

Case 7.2

Stress Takes Its Toll

Larry Field had a lot of fun in high school. He was a fairly good student, especially in math, he worked harder than most of his friends, and somehow he ended up going steady with Alice Shiflette, class valedictorian. He worked summers for a local surveyor, William Loude, and when he graduated Mr. Loude offered him a job as number-three man on one of his survey crews. The pay wasn't very high, but Field was already good at the work, and he felt that all he needed was a steady job to boost his confidence sufficiently to ask Alice to marry him. Once he did, the sequence of events which followed happened rapidly. He started work in June, he and Alice were married in October, Alice took a job as a secretary in a local company that made business forms, and a year later they had their first child.

The baby came as something of a shock to Larry Field. He had come to enjoy the independence that his own pay check afforded him every week. Food and rent took up most of it, but he still enjoyed playing basketball a few nights a week with his high school buddies and spending Sunday afternoons on the softball field. When the baby came, though, Larry's brow began to furrow a bit. He was only 20 years old, and he still wasn't making much money. He asked Mr. Loude for a raise and got it—his first.

Two months later, one of the crew chiefs quit just when Mr. Loude's crews had more work than they could handle. Mr. Loude hated to turn down work, so he made Larry Field into a crew chief, giving his crew some of the old instruments that weren't good enough for the precision work of the top crews, and assigned him the easy title surveys in town. Since it meant a jump in salary, Larry had no choice but to accept the crew chief position, but it scared him. He had never been very ambitious or curious, so he hadn't paid much attention to the training of his former crew chief. He knew how to run the instruments— the basics anyway—but every morning he woke up terrified that he would be sent on a job he couldn't handle.

During his first few months as a crew chief, Larry Field began doing things that his wife Alice thought he had grown out of. He would try to talk so fast that he would stumble over his own words, stammer, turn red in the face, and have to start all over again. He began smoking, as well—something he had not done since they had started going out together. He told his crew members that it kept his hands from shaking when he was working on an instrument. Neither of them smoked, and when he began lighting up in the truck when they were waiting for the rain to stop, they would become resentful and complain that he had no right to ruin their lungs, too.

Larry found it particularly hard to adjust to being "boss," especially since one of his workers was getting an engineering degree at night school and both were as old as he was. He felt sure that Alfonso Reyes, the scholar, would take over his position in no time. He kept feeling that Alfonso was looking over his shoulder, and Larry began snapping any time they worked close together.

Things were getting tense at home, too. Alice had to give up her full-time day job to take care of the baby, so she had started working nights. They hardly ever saw each other, and it seemed as though her only topic of conversation was how they should move to California or Alaska where she had heard that surveyors were paid five times what Larry made. Larry knew she was dissatisfied with her work and felt her intelligence was being wasted, but he didn't know what he could do about it. He was disconcerted when he realized that drinking and worrying about the next day at work while sitting at home with the baby at night had become a pattern.

Case Questions

1. What signs of stress was Larry Field exhibiting?

2. How was Larry Field trying to cope with his stress? Can you suggest more effective methods?

Experiential Exercise

Purpose: This exercise is intended to help you assess the current and potential future levels of stress you might encounter and to help you plan ahead for confronting stress.

Format: Working alone, do two things. First, look back to the list of life change factors in Table 7.1. Write down each one that you have experienced during the last twelve months and total the LCUs you have accumulated. Next, project ahead to the time you expect to finish school. (If you are not in school, use the year ahead.) Write down a second list of changes you anticipate facing then. Total those LCUs.

Meet as a group with two or three of your classmates. Discuss the LCU totals for the current year and the projected totals for your future period. Discuss things you can do to prepare now for any stress in your life. Share the best solutions with the rest of the class.

Follow-up Questions

1. How valid do you think the LCU concept is?

2. Is it possible to anticipate stress ahead of time and plan ways to help manage it?

Individual-Organizational Interface

PART III

Part Contents

CHAPTER

8

Job Design and Role Dynamics

Chapter Objectives

After reading this chapter, you should be able to

- ▸ summarize the historical development of job design.
- ▸ discuss the job characteristics approach to job design.
- ▸ describe how jobs can be designed for groups.

- ▸ discuss the social information processing model.
- ▸ identify other contemporary approaches to job design.
- ▸ discuss role dynamics.

*O*utside of Kalmar, Sweden, sits an automobile plant. The plant makes Volvos and is unlike almost every other automobile plant in the world. The typical auto plant has long assembly lines. Along each line, hundreds of workers stand or sit and perform some small function on a partially assembled automobile as it passes along in front of them. At Kalmar, however, workers are assigned to teams of fifteen to twenty-five members. Each team works in a certain section of the plant. Cars pass from section to section on computer-guided platforms. While a car is in their work station, the members of a team perform a large number of operations, each member doing a variety of tasks, with very little supervision.

Each work group sets its own pace, and hourly productivity rates are flashed to all groups via computer terminals. During breaks, each group can relax in its own private lounge area. Large windows provide plenty of light.

How did this plant come to be? Volvo built it as an experiment in combating the high turnover, absenteeism, and poor performance prevailing at its existing plants. Company management felt that workers would respond more favorably to jobs made more challenging and meaningful. In general, the experiment has worked.[1]

*T*he basic difference between Kalmar and other plants is in how employee jobs are designed. Job design, which this chapter considers in detail, is a crucial element in managing an organization's human resources. **Job design** is the specification of an employee's task-related activities, including both structural and interpersonal aspects of the job. The specification is determined by the needs and requirements of both the organization and the individual. After reviewing historical approaches to task design, this chapter discusses job enrichment, a more recent method based on a particular motivational theory. We then examine the job characteristics approach, how to design jobs for groups, and the social information processing model. We next consider some additional developments in contemporary job design. Finally, we discuss role dynamics, another perspective on jobs.

HISTORICAL APPROACHES TO JOB DESIGN

To understand job design, we must first trace how approaches to work have evolved. At first, the trend was toward increasing specialization and standardization of jobs. Eventually, however, this trend slowed and reversed. This section summarizes the reasons for this developmental pattern, as well as the dominant approaches to job design that emerged along the way.

---

[1] Ricky W. Griffin, *Task Design: An Integrative Approach* (Glenview, Ill.: Scott, Foresman, 1982).

Figure 8.1   The Historical Development of Job Design

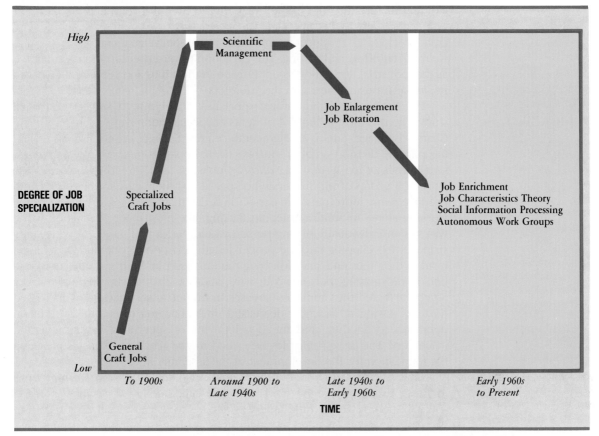

Source: Adapted from *Managerial Process and Organizational Behavior*, 2nd ed. by Alan C. Filley, Robert J. House, and Steven Kerr. Copyright © 1976, 1969 by Scott, Foresman and Company. Reprinted by permission.

The Evolution of Job Design

Although formal theories of job design are fairly recent, attempting to design work has a long history. The construction of the pyramids in Egypt was founded on job specialization grouping jobs together by function. The ancient Romans devoted much attention to designing jobs in the production sector.[2] Figure 8.1 traces the historical trends of job design in this country from the mid-1800s to the present. Before the general craft stage (the opening point on the figure), many families made and produced all the things they needed, above all, food.

---

[2] Daniel A. Wren, *The Evolution of Management Thought*, 2nd ed. (New York: Wiley, 1979).

General craft jobs came about as individuals ceased or reduced their own food production, invested their labor in the production of other necessities such as clothing or furniture, and traded or bartered them for food and goods. Over time, people's work became increasingly specialized. For example, the general craft of clothing production splintered into specialized craft jobs such as weaving, tailoring, and sewing. This evolution toward specialization accelerated as the Industrial Revolution swept Europe in the 1700s and 1800s and followed in similar form in America in the later 1800s.

Eventually, the trend toward specialization became a subject of formal study. The two most influential students of specialization were Adam Smith and Charles Babbage. Smith, an eighteenth-century Scottish economist, originated the phrase "division of labor" in his classic book *An Inquiry into the Nature and Causes of the Wealth of Nations,* published in 1776.[3] The book tells the story of a group of pin makers who specialized their jobs so that they could produce many more pins per person in a day than each could have made by working alone. In Smith's time, pin making, like most other production work, was still an individual job. One person would perform all tasks, drawing out a strip of wire, clipping it to the proper length, sharpening one end, attaching a head to the other end, and polishing the finished pin. With specialization, one person did nothing but draw out wire, another did the clipping, and so on. Smith attributed the dramatic increases in output to such factors as increased dexterity owing to practice, decreased time changing from one production operation to another, and the development of specialized equipment and machinery. The basic principles described in *The Wealth of Nations* provided the foundation for the development of the assembly line.

Charles Babbage wrote *On the Economy of Machinery and Manufactures* in 1832.[4] Extending Smith's work, Babbage cited additional advantages of job specialization: relatively little time was needed to learn specialized jobs, waste decreased, workers needed to make fewer tool and equipment changes, and workers' skills improved through frequent repetition of tasks.

As the Industrial Revolution spread to America, job specialization spread throughout its industry. While it began in the mid-1880s, as shown in Figure 8.1, job specialization reached its peak with the development of scientific management in the early 1900s.

Job Specialization

The chief proponent of scientific management, Frederick W. Taylor,[5] argued that jobs should be scientifically studied, broken down into their smallest

---

[3] Adam Smith, *An Inquiry into the Nature and Causes of the Wealth of Nations* (New York: Modern Library, 1937). Orginally published in 1776.

[4] Charles Babbage, *On the Economy of Machinery and Manufactures* (London: Charles Knight, 1832).

[5] Frederick W. Taylor, *The Principles of Scientific Management* (New York: Harper & Row, 1911).

component tasks, and then standardized across all workers doing the jobs. (See Chapter 1 for a full discussion of scientific management.) Taylor's view was consistent with the premises of the division of labor as discussed by Smith and Babbage. In practice, **job specialization** generally brought most, if not all, of the advantages its advocates claimed. Specialization paved the way for large-scale assembly lines and was at least partly responsible for the dramatic gains in output achieved by American industry for several decades after the turn of the century.

On paper, job specialization is a rational, seemingly efficient way to organize both manufacturing and nonmanufacturing jobs. But in practice it can cause problems for the individuals who do the work. Foremost among them is the extreme monotony of highly specialized, standardized tasks. Consider the job of assembling color televisions. A person who does the entire assembly will find the job complex and challenging, but such a process is inefficient. If the job is specialized so that the worker simply inserts one circuit board into the television set as it passes along on an assembly line, the process may be efficient, but it is unlikely to interest or challenge the worker. A worker numbed by boredom and monotony may be less motivated to work hard and more inclined to be absent, to complain about the job, and to look elsewhere for more interesting employment. For these reasons, managers began to search for job design alternatives to specialization. One of the primary catalysts for this search was a famous study of jobs in the automobile industry.

In 1952, C. R. Walker and R. Guest published a study of 180 workers in a Detroit automobile assembly plant.[6] The purpose of the study was to assess how satisfied the workers were with various aspects of their jobs. The workers indicated that, in general, they were reasonably satisfied with such things as pay, working conditions, and the quality of their supervision. However, they expressed extreme dissatisfaction with the actual work they did. During that era, automobile plants were very noisy places where the moving assembly line dictated a rigid, grueling pace and jobs were highly specialized and standardized. The workers in the study cited six facets of the work as causing dissatisfaction: mechanical pacing by an assembly line (over which they had no control), repetitiveness, low skill requirements, involvement with only a small portion of the total production cycle, limited social interaction with others in the workplace, and no control over the tools and techniques used in the job. Each of these sources of dissatisfaction is directly or indirectly a consequence of the job design prescriptions of scientific management.

In response to Walker and Guest's findings, as well as other reported problems with job specialization and a general desire to explore ways of creating less monotonous jobs, managers formulated two alternative approaches, job enlargement and job rotation.

---

[6] R. Walker and R. Guest, *The Man on the Assembly Line* (Cambridge, Mass.: Harvard University Press, 1952).

Figure 8.2

Job Enlargement

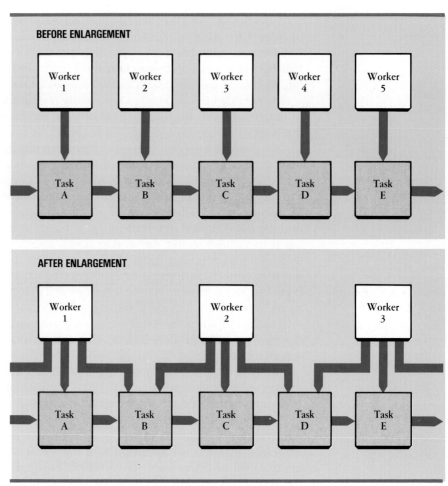

Source: Ricky W. Griffin, *Task Design: An Integrative Approach* (Glenview, Ill.: Scott, Foresman, 1982), p. 22. Reprinted by permission.

Early Alternatives to Specialization

JOB ENLARGEMENT   Job enlargement, or *horizontal job loading,* means that the worker's job is expanded to include tasks previously performed by other workers. This process is illustrated in Figure 8.2. Before enlargement, each worker performs a narrowly defined, specialized task; afterward, he or she has a "larger" job to do. Thus, Worker 2 in the figure does Task B, as before, but also does a portion of Tasks A and C. The logic behind this kind of change was that the increased number of tasks would reduce monotony and boredom.

Maytag was one of the first companies to use job enlargement.[7] In the assembly of washing machine water pumps, for example, jobs done sequentially by six workers at a conveyor belt were modified so that each worker completed an entire pump alone. Other organizations that implemented job enlargement were the American Telephone & Telegraph Company, the U.S. Civil Service, and Colonial Life Insurance Company.

Unfortunately, job enlargement often failed to have the desired effects. Generally, if the entire production sequence consisted of simple, easy-to-master tasks, simply doing more of them did not significantly change the worker's job. That is, if the task of putting two bolts on a piece of machinery was "enlarged" to putting on three bolts and connecting two wires, the monotony of the original job essentially remained.

JOB ROTATION   **Job rotation** involves systematically shifting workers from one job to another, with the goal of sustaining worker motivation and interest. Figure 8.3 shows the basic steps in job rotation. Worker A, for example, starts out with Job 1. On a regular basis (perhaps weekly or monthly), she or he is systematically rotated to Job 2, to Job 3, to Job 4, and back to Job 1.

At various times, job rotation has been used by numerous firms, including American Cyanamid, Baker International, Ford Motor Company, and The Prudential Insurance Company of America. However, like job enlargement, it has not entirely lived up to expectations.[8] For the disappointing results, we can once again blame the fundamental problem of narrowly defined, routine jobs. If a rotation cycle takes workers through the same old jobs the workers simply experience several routine and boring jobs instead of just one. Although a worker may begin each job shift with renewed enthusiasm, the effect is usually short-lived.

Rotation may also decrease efficiency. The practice clearly sacrifices the proficiency and expertise that grow from specialization. Often, though, job rotation is a very effective training technique because a worker rotated through a variety of related jobs acquires a larger set of job skills. Thus, there is increased flexibility in transferring workers to new jobs. Many American companies now use job rotation for training, but few rely on it to enhance employee motivation.

Job Enrichment

Job enlargement and job rotation seemed promising but eventually disappointed managers looking for answers to the ill effects of extreme specialization. They failed partly because they were intuitive, narrow approaches, rather than more fully developed, theory-driven methods. As a result, a new, more complex approach to task design—job enrichment—was developed in the late 1950s.

---

[7] H. Conant and M. Kilbridge, "An Interdisciplinary Analysis of Job Enlargement: Technology, Cost Behavioral Implications," *Industrial and Labor Relations Review*, 7, Vol. 18, 1965, pp. 377–395.

[8] Griffin, *Task Design*.

Figure 8.3

Job Rotation

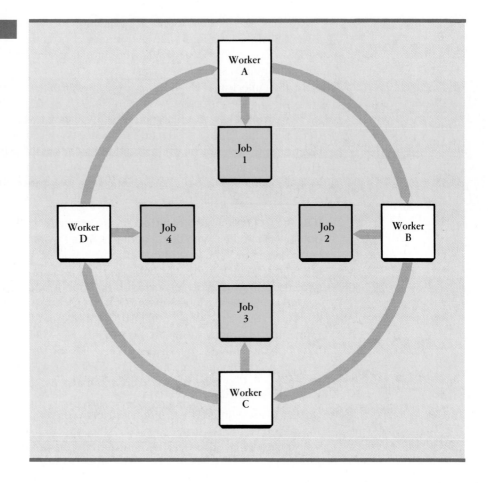

Job enrichment is based on Herzberg's two-factor theory of motivation (discussed in Chapter 4). Herzberg thought that employees could be motivated by positive job-related experiences such as feelings of achievement, responsibility, and recognition. To this end, he advocated *vertical job loading:* not only adding more tasks to a job, as in horizontal loading, but also giving the employee more control over those tasks. Vertical job loading should enrich a job in six ways:

1. *Accountability.* Workers should be held responsible for their performance.
2. *Achievement.* Workers should feel that they are doing something worthwhile.
3. *Feedback.* Workers should receive direct and clear information about their performance.

Table 8.1	**Principles of Vertical Job Loading**	
	Principle	*Motivators Involved*
Using Herzberg's Two-Factor Theory of Motivation	A. Removing some controls while retaining accountability.	Responsibility and personal achievement
	B. Increasing the accountability of individuals for own work	Responsibility and recognition
	C. Giving a person a complete natural unit of work (module, division, area, and so on)	Responsibility, achievement, and recognition
	D. Granting additional authority to an employee in his activity; job freedom	Responsibility, achievement, and recognition
	E. Making periodic reports directly available to the worker himself rather than to the supervisor	Internal recognition
	F. Introducing new and more difficult tasks not previously handled	Growth and learning
	G. Assigning individuals specific or specialized tasks, enabling them to become experts	Responsibility, growth, and advancement

Source: Reprinted by permission of the *Harvard Business Review.* Exhibit from "One More Time—How Do You Motivate Employees?" by Frederick Herzberg (January–February 1968). Copyright © 1968 by the President and Fellows of Harvard College; all rights reserved.

4. *Work pace.* To the extent possible, workers should be able to set their own work pace.

5. *Control over resources.* If possible, workers should have control over the resources used in their jobs.

6. *Personal growth and development.* Workers should have the opportunity to learn new skills.[9]

Table 8.1 outlines how Herzberg proposed to incorporate these characteristics into a job.

Various job enrichment programs have been reported by managers. Companies with noteworthy programs include AT&T, Texas Instruments, IBM, and General Foods. To show how job enrichment actually operates, we will describe two of these programs in some detail.

R. N. Ford has described several different job enrichment programs used by AT&T.[10] One involved a group of eight typists who were responsible for preparing service orders. Managers felt that turnover in the group was too high and performance too low; an analysis of the situation revealed several deficiencies

---

[9] Frederick Herzberg, "One More Time: How Do You Motivate Employees?" *Harvard Business Review*, January–February 1968, pp. 53–62; and Frederick Herzberg, "The Wise Old Turk," *Harvard Business Review*, September–October 1974, pp. 70–80.

[10] R. N. Ford, "Job Enrichment Lessons from AT&T," *Harvard Business Review*, January–February 1973, pp. 96–106.

in the work. The typists worked in relative isolation, and any service representative could ask them to type work orders. They felt they had little client contact or responsibility, and they received scant feedback on their job performance. The job enrichment program focused on creating a typing team. Each member of the team was paired with a service representative, and the tasks were restructured: ten discrete steps were replaced with three more complex ones. In addition, the typists began to get specific feedback about performance, and their job titles were changed to reflect their greater responsibility and status. As a result of these changes, the number of orders delivered on time increased from 27 percent to 90 percent, accuracy improved, and turnover dropped significantly.

Texas Instruments used job enrichment to improve janitorial jobs. The company gave janitors more control over their schedules and let them sequence their own cleaning jobs and purchase their own supplies. The outcome? Turnover dropped; things got dramatically cleaner; and the company reported estimated cost savings of approximately $103,000.[11]

Nevertheless, many job enrichment programs have failed. Some companies have found them to be cost-ineffective, and others have found that they simply did not produce the expected results.[12] Several programs at Prudential Insurance, for example, were abandoned because managers felt they were not benefiting anyone. Several reasons for this pattern have been offered.

Some of the criticism is associated with Herzberg's two-factor theory of motivation, on which job enrichment is based. In Chapter 4 we reviewed the major objections: the theory confuses employee satisfaction with motivation, is fraught with methodological flaws, ignores situational factors, and is not convincingly supported by research.[13] Thus, there are still many unanswered questions about the usefulness of job enrichment.

Several difficulties have also been associated with job enrichment. Richard Hackman has identified five major problem areas:[14]

1. Many reports of the success of job enrichment programs have been evangelical in nature. That is, the authors of these studies overstate the potential benefits of job enrichment and minimize its pitfalls.

2. Evaluations of job enrichment programs have often been methodologically flawed. Many studies have been poorly designed, so that results are subject to alternative explanation.

---

[11] E. D. Weed, "Job Enrichment 'Cleans Up' at Texas Instruments," in J. R. Maher, ed., *New Perspectives in Job Enrichment* (New York: Van Nostrand, 1971).

[12] Griffin, *Task Design*.

[13] Griffin, *Task Design*. See also Robert J. House and L. Wigdor, "Herzberg's Dual-Factor Theory of Job Satisfaction and Motivation: A Review of the Evidence and a Criticism," *Personnel Psychology*, Vol. 20, 1967, pp. 369–389.

[14] J. Richard Hackman, "On the Coming Demise of Job Enrichment," in E. L. Cass and F. G. Zimmer, eds., *Man and Work in Society* (New York: Van Nostrand, 1975).

3. Few failures have been reported in the literature, although it is probable that some job enrichment programs have not achieved their goals. Without information about these failures it is difficult to develop a full understanding of job enrichment.

4. Situational factors have seldom been assessed. Some situations are probably more favorable to job enrichment efforts than others. Unfortunately we have not developed an understanding of the factors that lead to success or failure.

5. Economic data pertaining to the effectiveness of job enrichment have rarely been presented. Because job enrichment is often an expensive proposition, managers need a carefully developed procedure for evaluating the technique's costs and benefits. Such procedures have not been developed.

Because of these and other troubles, job enrichment has recently fallen into disfavor among managers. Yet some valuable aspects of the concept can be salvaged. The efforts of managers and academic theorists ultimately led to more complex and sophisticated viewpoints. Many of these advances are evident in the job characteristics approach, which we consider next.

THE JOB CHARACTERISTICS APPROACH

The **job characteristics approach** to job design dominated in the 1970s and early 1980s. It evolved from work on the motivational attributes of jobs (such as autonomy and feedback), was expanded to include explicit consideration of individual differences in employee responses to a job, and was eventually codified in the Job Characteristics Theory.[15]

Job Characteristics

The job characteristics approach began with the pioneering work of A. N. Turner and P. R. Lawrence, who conducted a large-scale project to assess employee responses to different kinds of jobs.[16] Turner and Lawrence believed that workers would prefer complex, challenging tasks to monotonous, boring ones. They predicted that job complexity would be associated with employee

---

[15] J. Richard Hackman and Greg Oldham, "Motivation Through the Design of Work: Test of Theory," *Organizational Behavior and Human Performance*, Vol. 16, 1976, pp. 250–279. See also Michael A. Campion and Paul W. Thayer, "Job Design: Approaches, Outcomes, and Trade-Offs," *Organizational Dynamics*, Winter 1987, pp. 66–78.

[16] N. Turner and P. R. Lawrence, *Industrial Jobs and the Worker* (Boston: Harvard School of Business, 1965).

satisfaction and attendance. Tasks were described in terms of six job character-istics assumed to be desirable motivational properties of jobs: (1) variety, (2) autonomy, (3) required social interaction, (4) opportunities for social interaction, (5) knowledge and skill requirements, and (6) responsibility. Thus, a worker whose job was rated high on all six characteristics would be expected to have relatively high levels of satisfaction and attendance. If the job rated low on all attributes, the job-holder would be expected to be less satisfied and more frequently absent.

These predictions were tested on 470 employees holding 47 different jobs in several manufacturing plants. Field observations and interviews were used to measure the relevant variables. Measures of the six job characteristics were combined into a single measure of task complexity, which was correlated with measures of satisfaction and attendance. The results confirmed the predicted relationship between task complexity and attendance, but showed no relation between task complexity and satisfaction.

Because of this second unexpected finding, Turner and Lawrence analyzed their data further. They found a positive relationship between task complexity and the satisfaction of workers from factories in small towns, but not in larger towns. To explain this pattern, the researchers concluded that workers in larger communities had a variety of nonwork interests and consequently were less involved and motivated by their work. Workers in smaller towns, they argued, had fewer nonwork interests and were therefore more receptive to the positive features of their jobs.

This explanation was suspiciously pat, but the original study was not designed to assess individual differences. Recall that the implicit assumption of the study had been that everyone would respond to job conditions in the same way. An individual difference perspective, on the other hand, would have allowed for the possibility of variations in people's reactions. Hence, the explanations were necessarily imprecise and speculative. The chief value of the unexpected findings was perhaps to call attention to the role of individual differences in the workplace.

Individual Differences

Among the first researchers to explore the role of individual differences among job-holders were Charles L. Hulin and Milton R. Blood.[17] As a starting point, they developed a more precise explanation of Turner and Lawrence's findings, arguing that rural-urban differences reflected varying adherence to middle-class work norms such as the Protestant work ethic. They theorized that people governed by the work ethic would be highly motivated by challenging, complex

---

[17] Charles L. Hulin and Milton R. Blood, "Job Enlargement, Individual Differences, and Worker Responses," *Psychological Bulletin*, Vol. 69, 1968, pp. 41–55; and Milton R. Blood and Charles L. Hulin, "Alienation, Environmental Characteristics, and Worker Responses," *Journal of Applied Psychology*, Vol. 51, 1967, pp. 284–290.

jobs, whereas people who believed less strongly in the ethic would be less interested and motivated by the same kind of job. The Protestant work ethic was also assumed to influence rural workers more than urban workers. A preliminary study of this explanation provided reasonable but not total support for it.[18]

In light of this mixed evidence, other researchers also tried to develop ways of understanding individual differences.[19] Foremost among these efforts was the work of J. Richard Hackman and Edward E. Lawler, who suggested that psychological or motivational characteristics are what really matter in how people react to jobs.[20] Specifically, they borrowed from the need theories of motivation (discussed in Chapter 4). They reasoned that people motivated by higher-order needs, such as the needs for self-actualization and personal growth and development, would be enthused by complex, challenging jobs, whereas those with weak higher-order needs would be less motivated by those kinds of jobs. The initial test of this interpretation was promising enough to encourage the development of another formal theory of job design.[21]

The Job Characteristics Theory

Working with Greg Oldham, Hackman used the findings from the test of the individual differences interpretation to develop the **Job Characteristics Theory,** the basic features of which are shown in Figure 8.4.[22]

At the center of the theory are what Hackman and Oldham termed critical psychological states. These states, they said, determine the extent to which characteristics of the job enhance employee responses to that task. They defined the three critical psychological states as follows:

1. *Experienced meaningfulness of the work.* The degree to which the individual experiences the job as generally meaningful, valuable, and worthwhile.
2. *Experienced responsibility for work outcomes.* The degree to which the individual feels personally accountable and responsible for results of the work she or he does.
3. *Knowledge of results.* The degree to which the individual continuously understands how effectively he or she is performing the job.[23]

---

[18] Blood and Hulin, "Alienation, Environmental Characteristics, and Worker Responses."

[19] Griffin, *Task Design.*

[20] J. Richard Hackman and Edward E. Lawler, "Employee Reactions to Job Characteristics," *Journal of Applied Psychology*, Vol. 55, 1971, pp. 259–286.

[21] Hackman and Lawler, "Employee Reactions to Job Characteristics."

[22] Hackman and Oldham, "Motivation Through the Design of Work"; and J. Richard Hackman and Greg Oldham, *Work Redesign* (Reading, Mass.: Addison-Wesley, 1980).

[23] Hackman and Oldham, "Motivation Through the Design of Work," pp. 256–257.

Figure 8.4

The Job Characteristics
Theory

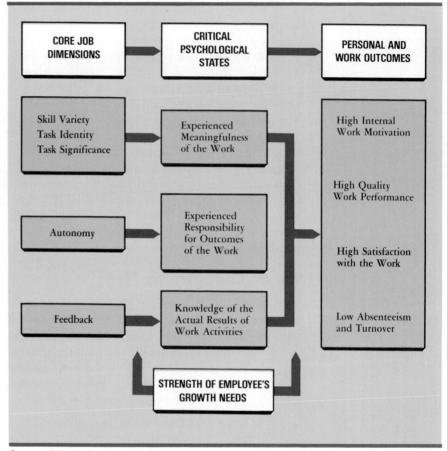

Source: J. R. Hackman and G. R. Oldham, "Motivation Through the Design of
Work: Test of a Theory," *Organizational Behavior and Human Performance*,
Vol. 16, 1976, pp. 250–279. Used by permission.

If employees experience these states to an adequate degree, they are
expected to feel good about themselves and to respond favorably to their jobs.

Hackman and Oldham further argued that the three critical psychological
states are triggered by five characteristics of the job, or *core job dimensions*.
These characteristics are as follows:

1. *Skill variety.* The degree to which the job requires a variety
   of activities that involve different skills and talents.
2. *Task Identity.* The degree to which the job requires completion of a "whole" and identifiable piece of work, that is, a
   job that has a beginning and an end with a tangible outcome.

3. *Task significance.* The degree to which the job affects the lives or work of other people, whether in the immediate organization or in the external environment.
4. *Autonomy.* The degree to which the job allows the individual substantial freedom, independence, and discretion to schedule the work and determine the procedures for carrying it out.
5. *Feedback.* The degree to which the job activities give the individual direct and clear information about the effectiveness of his or her performance.[24]

Figure 8.4 shows how the core job dimensions stimulate the psychological states: skill variety, task identity, and task significance are expected to affect the person's experienced meaningfulness of the work; autonomy is expected to influence the experienced responsibility for outcomes of the work; and feedback contributes to knowledge of the actual results of work activities. The critical psychological states then determine a variety of personal and work outcomes—high internal work motivation (that is, intrinsic motivation), high-quality work performance, high satisfaction with the work, and low absenteeism. Finally, the strength of the employee's growth needs is expected to influence the effects of other elements of the theory. The earlier findings of Hackman and Lawler suggested that the effects would be very strong in people whose higher-order needs are strong and weaker in people whose higher-order needs are weak.[25]

To test the Job Characteristics Theory, Hackman and Oldham developed the *Job Diagnostic Survey,* or *JDS.*[26] This questionnaire measures employee perceptions of job characteristics, the various psychological states, personal and work outcomes, and strength of growth needs. Figure 8.5 illustrates the use of data obtained from the JDS. The graph on the left summarizes the level of each of the five job characteristics for two hypothetical jobs. Job A clearly has higher levels of each of the five characteristics. The chart on the right shows each job's *motivating potential score,* or *MPS,* which is calculated according to the following formula:

$$\text{MPS} = \frac{(\text{Variety} + \text{Identity} + \text{Significance})}{3} \times \text{Autonomy} \times \text{Feedback}$$

The MPS provides a summary index of a job's overall potential for motivating employees, and the JDS can thus be used to identify jobs in the organization with high and low motivating potential. Jobs with a low MPS index are candidates for redesign to improve their potential for motivating job-holders.

[24] Hackman and Oldham, "Motivation Through the Design of Work," pp. 257–258.

[25] Hackman and Lawler, "Employee Reactions to Job Characteristics."

[26] J. Richard Hackman and Greg Oldham, "Development of the Job Diagnostic Survey," *Journal of Applied Psychology,* Vol. 60, 1975, pp. 159–170.

Figure 8.5

JDS Profile of a "Good" Job and a "Bad" Job

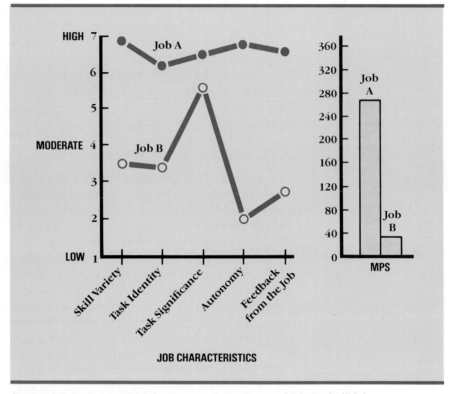

Source: J. R. Hackman, "Work Design," in J. R. Hackman and J. L. Suttle (Eds.), *Improving Life at Work: Behavioral Science Approaches to Organizational Change* (Santa Monica, Calif.: Goodyear, 1977), p. 135. Used by permission.

Hackman, with assistance from J. L. Suttle, has also developed a general set of guidelines to help managers implement the theory,[27] as set forth in Figure 8.6. Managers can do such things as form natural work units (that is, group similar tasks together), combine existing tasks into more complex ones, establish direct relationships between workers and clients, increase worker autonomy through vertical job loading, and open feedback channels. Theoretically, such actions should enhance the MPS of each task.

Using these guidelines, sometimes in adapted form, several organizations have implemented job design changes in accordance with the Job Characteristics Theory. 3M, Volvo, AT&T, Xerox, Texas Instruments, and Motorola have all tried this approach.[28] *International Perspective* summarizes how the model works in Hong Kong.

[27] J. Richard Hackman, "Work Design," in J. Richard Hackman and J. L. Suttle, eds., *Improving Life at Work: Behavioral Science Approaches to Organizational Change* (Santa Monica, Calif.: Goodyear, 1977).

[28] Griffin, *Task Design*.

Figure 8.6   Implementing the Job Characteristics Theory

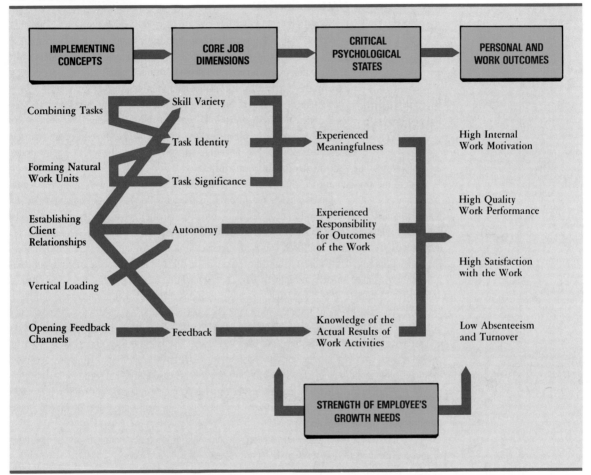

Source: J. R. Hackman, G. R. Oldham, R. Janson, and K. Purdy, "A New Stage for Job Enrichment." © 1975 by the Regents of the University of California. Reprinted from *California Management Review,* Vol. 17, No. 4, p. 62, by permission of the Regents.

International Perspective

Testing the Job Characteristics Model in Hong Kong

A recent study using the job characteristics model in Hong Kong produced interesting results. Rather than draw conclusions about international variations in the perceptions of job characteristics from these results, the authors called into question some aspects of Hackman and Oldham's five-trait model and some of the methods used to gather data for studies using the model.

Philip H. Birnbaum, Jiing-Lih Farh, and Gilbert Y. Y. Wong analyzed data on 57 different jobs in Hong Kong. One criterion in choosing the jobs was that they use well-defined job classification systems. Workers in these particular jobs completed both the Job Diagnostic Survey (JDS) and the Job Descriptive Index; their supervisors filled out the Job Rating Form (JRF).

Using the five-trait model, the researchers found that supervisors and workers agreed on the amount of task variety and task autonomy involved in the jobs. However, they concluded that the Hackman and Oldham model did not fit the data; in particular the trait of job significance yielded very poor correlations. They therefore used a second model, a four-trait model without the significance trait, to analyze the data. In justifying such an approach, they pointed out that significance had not been one of the core dimensions included in Hackman's and Lawler's 1971 model, nor was it present in a number of other models currently in use. They argued that a job's significance is not so much an intrinsic characteristic of a particular job but a measure of the relation of one job to others.

The four-trait model fit the data much more satisfactorily, and the results led the researchers to two other important conclusions. They found that the JRF was a much better statistical measure of job characteristics than was the JDS. They speculated that because they are removed from the particular jobs and see all the jobs in relation to each other, supervisors can more accurately distinguish the dimensions of jobs than can job holders. They also found that some of the job traits, particularly autonomy and variety, were highly correlated for any one job, and might possibly be two aspects of the same trait. It was unusual to find a job that had a good deal of variety without an equivalent amount of autonomy.

The researchers concluded with calls for further study of job traits, noting that "the usefulness of this classification for job redesign is highly suspect."

Source: Philip H. Birnbaum, Jiing-Lih Farh, and Gilbert Y. Y. Wong, "The Job Characteristics Model in Hong Kong," *Journal of Applied Psychology*, 1986, Volume 71, Number 4, 598–605.

Evaluation and Management Implications of the Job Characteristics Theory

Much research has been devoted to the job characteristics view of job design.[29] This research has generally supported the Job Characteristics Theory, although performance has seldom been found to correlate with job characteristics.[30] Several apparent weaknesses in the theory have also come to light, though. First, the JDS is not always as valid and reliable as it should be. Further, the role of individual differences has frequently not been supported by scientific assessment. Finally, implementation guidelines are not terribly specific and managers usually must modify at least part of the theory to use them.[31]

DESIGNING JOBS FOR GROUPS

The job design perspectives we have talked about to this point have focused almost exclusively on individual jobs. Many situations, however, may call for designing jobs for groups.

Group Tasks

Considering a group-based approach to job design may be appropriate under either of two circumstances. For one thing, some jobs are simply better suited to a group than to an individual. For example, it may be more efficient for American Airlines to use a team to service a 747 than to assign the job to a set of individuals. The other situation when group-based job design might be best is when the organization wants to use groups as a mechanism for enhancing individual attitudes and behaviors, as was done by Volvo. An increasingly popular form of this approach is autonomous work groups.

Autonomous Work Groups

In **autonomous work groups,** jobs are structured for groups rather than for individuals. The group itself is then given considerable discretion in scheduling, individual work assignments, and other matters that have traditionally been management prerogatives—even to the extent of hiring new members and determining members' pay increases.

---

[29] Griffin, *Task Design*. See also Karlene H. Roberts and William Glick, "The Job Characteristics Approach to Task Design: A Critical Review," *Journal of Applied Psychology*, Vol. 66, 1981, pp. 193–217; and Ricky W. Griffin, "Toward an Integrated Theory of Task Design," in L. L. Cummings and B. M. Staw, eds., *Research in Organizational Behavior*, Vol. 9 (Greenwich, Conn.: JAI Press, 1987), pp. 79–120.

[30] Ricky W. Griffin, M. Ann Welsh, and Gregory Moorhead, "Perceived Task Characteristics and Employee Performance: A Literature Review," *Academy of Management Review*, October 1981, pp. 655–664.

[31] Roberts and Glick, "The Job Characteristics Approach to Task Design."

Figure 8.7   An Autonomous Work Group at Volvo's Kalmar Plant

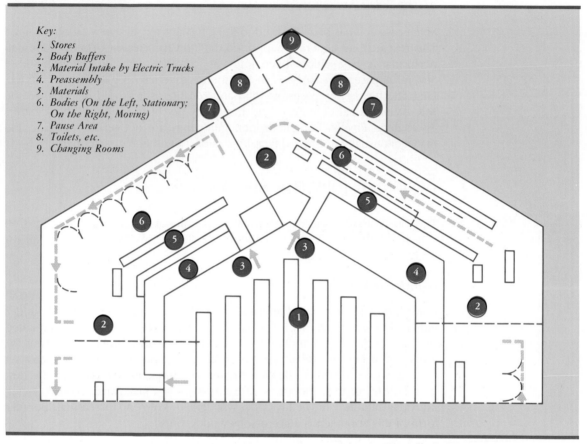

Key:
1. *Stores*
2. *Body Buffers*
3. *Material Intake by Electric Trucks*
4. *Preassembly*
5. *Materials*
6. *Bodies (On the Left, Stationary; On the Right, Moving)*
7. *Pause Area*
8. *Toilets, etc.*
9. *Changing Rooms*

Source: Reprinted by permission of the publisher from "Job Redesign on the Assembly Line: Farewell to Blue-Collar Blues," by William F. Dowling, *Organizational Dynamics,* Autumn 1973, p. 62. © 1973 American Management Association, New York. All rights reserved.

Several organizations have instituted autonomous work groups, including Westinghouse, General Foods, and as noted, Volvo. Figure 8.7 shows a layout of one autonomous work group at Volvo's Kalmar plant. The group has its own inventory area (labeled "stores" in the figure), toilets, changing rooms, and so on. The intended effect is that workers feel as though they work in a small machine shop rather than in a huge factory. Each group is responsible for a complete set of tasks, such as wiring or upholstery. The group itself decides who will perform each task and can control the speed at which incoming cars enter its work area. The group thus functions fairly autonomously.

More and more companies are experimenting with autonomous work groups, although technological constraints and costs can be problematic. The Kalmar plant, for instance, cost more to build and produces fewer cars than a conventional plant.[32]

Other Group Applications

There are also other situations in which groups are used as a basis for designing jobs. Even committees are essentially work groups with a task to perform. So, too, are work teams (discussed more fully in Chapter 15) and quality circles (discussed in Chapter 5). In each instance where these or other kinds of groups are the work unit, the manager must recognize the basis for using a group task design and arrange things accordingly.[33] *A Look at Research* offers some additional insights into how social patterns and task design are interrelated. Still other insights are provided in our next section.

THE SOCIAL INFORMATION PROCESSING MODEL

Gerald Salancik and Jeffrey Pfeffer recently reviewed the theoretical and empirical literature from which the job characteristics approach to job design has grown.[34] They question the validity of two basic assumptions of the approach: (1) that people have basic and stable needs that can be satisfied, at least partially, by their jobs; and (2) that tasks have stable and objective characteristics that people perceive and respond to consistently and predictably. They claim, for example, that people probably do not think of their jobs in terms of dimensions such as variety and autonomy. Only when a questionnaire inquires about the variety and autonomy of their jobs do those dimensions come to mind. Salancik and Pfeffer also point to alleged flaws in earlier approaches to job design, such as measurement deficiencies.

Salancik and Pfeffer believe individual needs, task perceptions, and reactions are a result of socially constructed realities. That is, social information in the workplace shapes the individual's perception of the job and responses to it. For example, if a newcomer to the organization is told, "You're really going to like it here because everybody gets along so well," he or she may begin to think that the job should be evaluated in terms of social interactions and that those interactions are satisfactory. But if the message is, "You won't like it here because the boss is lousy and the pay is worse," the newcomer may think that

---

[32] Griffin, *Task Design.*

[33] Griffin, *Task Design.*

[34] Gerald Salancik and Jeffrey Pfeffer "An Examination of Need-Satisfaction Models of Job Attitudes," *Administrative Science Quarterly*, Vol. 22, 1977, pp. 427–456; and Gerald Salancik and Jeffrey Pfeffer, "A Social Information Processing Approach to Job Attitudes and Task Design," *Administrative Science Quarterly*, Vol. 23, 1978, pp. 224–253.

A LOOK AT RESEARCH

Different Perceptions of Open Offices

What happens to the way employees view their jobs when their work setting changes from traditional offices with floor-to-ceiling walls and doors to open or "landscaped" offices, separated only by doorless partitions? The answer to this question is very important to modern American businesses because the concept of open offices has taken hold so strongly over the last decade, particularly in large organizations. Supporters of open offices say that the openness promotes communication, increases work efficiency, lowers operating costs, and in general improves working conditions. Some studies, however, have shown that the open office can lead to lower work motivation, dissatisfaction with the aesthetics of the office, and a loss of the sense of privacy.

In an attempt to answer some of the questions about open offices, Mary D. Zalesny and Richard V. Farace studied the effects of a shift from traditional to open office space on employees of a government agency. Unlike some previous studies of the effects of office environment, Zalesny and Farace divided employees into three groups—clerical, professional, and managerial. They hypothesized that employees with high status in the organization would be unhappy with the change to an open office, while low-status clerical workers would generally have a positive reaction to the change.

In fact, clerical workers did have more positive reactions to the new offices than did managers. However, all three groups reported getting less feedback in the new offices. The overall job satisfaction of both clerical workers and managers dropped as a result of the change, while the job satisfaction of professionals remained about the same.

The researchers suggested an explanation for this somewhat surprising result by pointing out that professionals, whose work is generally specialized and requires specific training and college degrees, cannot directly compare their work to that of other professionals. Their satisfaction will generally depend on their job characteristics. Clerical workers and managers, on the other hand, can readily compare their work with that being done by others in similar positions and may rely on these comparisons to define their own jobs. Therefore, while professionals can be relatively oblivious to changes in working environment, a new environment may have a strong effect on the job satisfaction of managers and clerical workers.

The researchers did not try to draw any conclusions about the overall value of open offices. But their study does show that organizations planning to change their office environments should consider how the change will affect people in varying job classifications, and not assume that everyone will react the same way.

Source: Based on "Traditional Versus Open Offices: A Comparison of Sociotechnical, Social Relations, and Symbolic Meaning Perspectives" by Mary D. Zalesky and Richard V. Farace, *Academy of Management Journal*, Vol. 30, No. 2, 1987, pp. 240–259. Reprinted by permission.

the job's most important aspects are interactions with the boss and pay, and that both areas are deficient.[35]

Figure 8.8 shows the complete **social information processing model.** The model obviously is quite complex. Basically, it suggests that through a variety of processes, *commitment* (discussed in Chapter 3), *rationalization* (self-interpretation of behavior), and *information saliency* (or importance) are defined. These processes include the following:

1. *Choice.* The freedom to choose different behaviors
2. *Revocability.* The ability to change behaviors
3. *Publicness.* The degree of visibility to others
4. *Explicitness.* The ability to be clear and obvious
5. *Social norms and expectations.* The knowledge of what others expect from someone
6. *External priming.* The receiving of cues from others

Attributional and enactment processes then combine with social reality construction processes to influence perceptions, attitudes, and behaviors.

To date, the social information processing model has gotten mixed support from empirical research.[36] Laboratory experiments and field studies have often found that social information influences task perceptions and attitudes, but they have also shown the importance of job characteristics.[37] The findings suggest that task perceptions may be a joint function of objective task properties and social information.[38] For example, positive social information and a well-designed task may produce more favorable responses than either information or task properties alone produce. Conversely, negative information and a poorly designed task may produce more negative reactions than either social information or job properties would by themselves. In situations where social information and task conditions do not reinforce each other, they may cancel each other out, as when negative social information may diminish the positive effects of a well-designed task. Similarly, positive information may at least partially offset the negative consequences of a poorly designed task. At present,

---

[35] Salancik and Pfeffer, "A Social Information Processing Approach to Job Attitudes and Task Design."

[36] Joe Thomas and Ricky W. Griffin, "The Social Information Processing Model of Task Design: A Review of the Literature," *Academy of Management Review*, October 1983, pp. 672–682. See also Griffin, "Toward an Integrated Theory of Task Design."

[37] Charles A. O'Reilly and D. F. Caldwell, "Informational Influence as a Determinant of Perceived Task Characteristics and Job Satisfaction," *Journal of Applied Psychology*, Vol. 64, 1979, pp. 157–165; and Ricky W. Griffin, "Objective and Social Sources of Information in Task Redesign: A Field Experiment," *Administrative Science Quarterly*, June 1983, pp. 184–200.

[38] Griffin, "Objective and Social Sources of Information in Task Redesign." See also Griffin, "Toward an Integrated Theory of Task Design"; and Donald J. Campbell, "Task Complexity: A Review and Analysis," *Academy of Management Review*, January 1988, pp. 40–52.

Figure 8.8   The Social Information Processing Model of Job Design

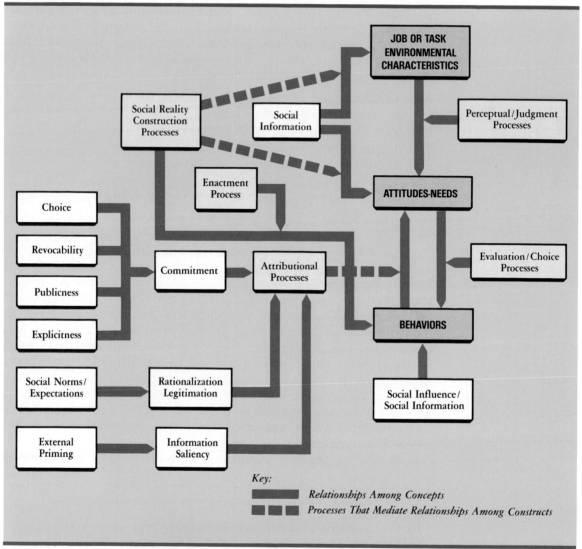

there is considerable debate as to which of the three views—the job characteristics model, the social information processing model, or a model combining both—is correct.

OTHER CONTEMPORARY APPROACHES TO JOB DESIGN

Two other issues pertaining to job design that are not tied to any particular theory are employee work schedules and automation and robotics.

Work Schedules

Employee work schedules are not related to job design in the strictest sense, but they are a direct point of contact between the employee and the job. Managers have been seeking new work scheduling methods that improve the employee's work-related experiences and at the same time improve attendance, motivation, and attitudes. Three relatively new approaches to work scheduling are the compressed workweek, flexible work schedules, and job sharing.

COMPRESSED WORKWEEK   An employee following a **compressed workweek** schedule works a full forty-hour week in less than the traditional five days. Most typically, this schedule involves working ten hours a day for four days, leaving an extra day off. Another alternative is for employees to work slightly fewer than ten hours a day, but to complete the forty hours by lunch time on Friday. Organizations that have used the compressed workweek include John Hancock, Atlantic Richfield, and R.J. Reynolds. However, research has found little evidence that a compressed workweek does anything for motivation or attendance.[39]

FLEXIBLE WORK SCHEDULES   **Flexible work schedules,** or **flextime,** may be more promising. Flextime gives employees some control over their working hours and thus, from a task design point of view, contributes to employee autonomy. Research evidence suggests that flextime may be an effective motivational strategy.[40] Figure 8.9 illustrates how flextime works.

The work day is broken down into two categories: flexible time and core time. All employees must be at their work stations during core time, but they can choose their own schedules during flexible time. Thus, one employee may choose to start work early in the morning and leave in midafternoon, another to start in the late morning and work until late afternoon, and still another to start early in the morning, take a long lunch break, and work until late afternoon. Organizations that have used this method include Control Data Corp., Metropolitan Life, and the federal government.

---

[39] A. R. Cohen and H. Gadon, *Alternative Work Schedules: Integrating Individual and Organizational Needs* (Reading, Mass.: Addison-Wesley, 1978).

[40] Cohen and Gadon, *Alternative Work Schedules.*

Figure 8.9

Flexible Work Schedules

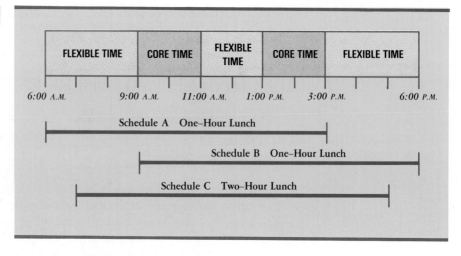

JOB SHARING   In **job sharing,** two part-time employees share one full-time job. One person may perform the job from 8:00 A.M. to noon, the other from 1:00 P.M. to 5:00 P.M. Job sharing may be desirable for people who want to work only part-time or when job markets are tight. For its part, the organization can accommodate the preferences of a broader range of employees and may benefit from the talents of more people. Although job sharing has not been scientifically evaluated, it appears to be a useful alternative to traditional work scheduling.

Another work scheduling variation is an increasing movement toward permanent part-time, or *contingent* workers. Organizations often don't have to pay benefits to part-time workers and can use them to easily cut back or expand the work force as needed. *Management in Action* offers additional information about this trend.

Automation and Robotics

American industry's growing reliance on automation and robotics has a variety of implications for job design, some positive and others perhaps negative.[41] In general, these implications relate to the potential changes that automation and robotics may bring to existing jobs.

Automation may eliminate many boring, routine, and hazardous jobs from the workplace, theoretically allowing workers to move into more interesting and challenging jobs. But automation may also dehumanize jobs. Witness the many grocery stores that are adopting opti-scan technology that reads prices from printed bar codes as the check-out clerk passes products over a screen.

---

[41] Hackman, "Work Design"; Griffin, *Task Design*; and Hackman and Oldham, *Work Redesign*.

Contingent Workers—The Dispensable Become Indispensable

As many as 25 million Americans, one-quarter of the total American workforce, could be labeled contingent workers—meaning that their jobs are contingent upon the fortunes and needs of an employer or employers at any given time. Some people choose such work because they like the lifestyle, the variety and flexibility it allows them. Others are forced to take contingent jobs when their regular jobs disappear or in some cases are transformed into part-time positions. Recently so many companies have come to count on these workers to help them cut costs and increase efficiency that the contingent work force, which had been by definition dispensable, has become an important part of the American scene. An indicator of this is that in 1984, over 18 percent of all workers worked on a part-time basis.

Among those forced to become contingent workers are former full-time employees of USX, the steel-making giant. In 1982, the company needed ten in-house hours of labor to produce a ton of steel. It now manages with four. Subcontractors make up much of the difference, filling various staffing holes that USX creates. For instance, the company fired a number of pipe fitters at its Gary Works steel plant in 1984, hiring a subcontractor to do the work. The subcontractor in turn hired many of the laid-off workers for $5 an hour and no benefits, less than one-half of what some of the pipe fitters had been making. Because subcontractors can represent such savings for big companies—and sometimes break unions in the process—they have proliferated in recent years and now employ over 7.5 percent of the steel industry's work force, compared to 3 percent a decade ago.

Many who have no stable employer do not feel as manipulated as the pipe fitters at USX. Instead, they often feel that they are using the flexibility of their positions to live the way they want to. More and more people choose to work at home, some on computers that are often hooked up to company headquarters, others doing some kind of piecework task on their own schedule. Often they get paid less than they would to do the same work at the office, but being able to keep their own hours, avoid commuting, or be with their children compensates for the difference in pay. The Bureau of Labor Statistics estimates that several million people choose to work part-time.

Perhaps the greatest advantage to companies hiring contingent employees comes in the area of benefits. Benefits constitute as much as 40 percent of many companies' payroll costs, so companies can afford to pay a part-timer good wages and still save money by not spending a cent on benefits. For most people making a living on their own, living without an employer-funded health plan raises fears and represents considerable expense. New laws may one day force employers to give all workers some basic benefits. Or it may be, as one observer put it, that "We're creating a second-class tier in the labor force."

Sources: Ellen F. Jackofsky and Lawrence H. Peters, "Part-time versus Full-time Employment Status Differences: A Replication and Extension," *Journal of Occupational Behaviour*, Volume 8, January 1987, 1–9; Susan Lee and Stuart Flack, "Hi ho, silver," *Forbes*, March 9, 1987, 90–98; Michael A. Pollock, "The Disposable Employee Is Becoming A Fact of Corporate Life," *Business Week*, December 15, 1986, 52.

The Role Episode

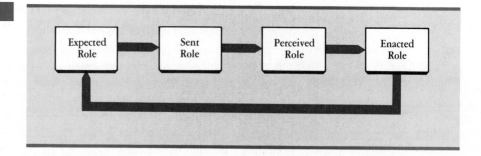

The clerk may well be more efficient but also has much less to do. Some newer units even have audio capabilities: they call out the prices, the total bill, and the customer's change and even say "Thank you"! Required only to pass items over the scanner, the clerk becomes merely an adjunct to the technology.

ROLE DYNAMICS

Another useful perspective on the design of jobs in organizations is role theory. A **role** is the part an individual plays in the work group. As such, it has formal (i.e., job-related and explicit) requirements as well as informal (i.e., social and implicit) requirements. Figure 8.10 illustrates the basic role episode. This sequence suggests that people in a group expect a person in a particular role to act in certain ways. They transmit these expectations formally and informally by the way of the *sent role.* The individual perceives the role expectations with varying levels of accuracy, and then enacts his or her role. When "errors" creep into the role episode, however, either role ambiguity or role conflict can result. (Role expectations can also lead to overload, discussed in the preceding chapter.)[42]

Role Ambiguity

Role ambiguity occurs when a person is uncertain as to the exact nature of a particular role. It arises when the sent role is unclear. Poor job descriptions, vague instructions from a supervisor, or unclear cues from coworkers can all result in role ambiguity.

Role Conflict

Another possible disruption in the role episode is **role conflict,** which arises when demands of or messages about roles are essentially clear but also

---

[42] Daniel Katz and Robert L. Kahn, *The Social Psychology of Organizations,* 2nd ed. (New York: Wiley, 1978).

contradict each other somewhat. *Interrole conflict* can occur when a person experiences conflict among two or more roles. A part-time student being told by an instructor that there will be an exam tomorrow and also being told by his boss that he has to work late tonight will experience interrole conflict.

Intrarole conflict can happen when a person gets contradictory messages from different people in the same role. Suppose that one of your subordinates tells you that another subordinate is loafing and needs to be told to work harder. The second subordinate, meanwhile, expresses concern that the first is working too hard and needs to be told to ease up before he collapses from exhaustion. It will take astute investigation to find out which set of messages is most accurate.

In *intrasender conflict,* the same person provides contradictory messages. A worker might tell her boss right before Christmas that she would appreciate chances to earn extra money but then refuse the first offer of overtime. The manager will be uncertain as to her true preferences.

Finally, *person-role conflict* can result if there is some basic incongruence between the person and his or her job. A peace activist working in a factory that makes weapons, for example, will feel this form of conflict. So, too, will people who are pressured to do illegal or unethical things or something distasteful like firing a favorite employee.

SUMMARY OF KEY POINTS

Historical trends showed a general movement toward increasingly specialized jobs until about the 1950s. Since then, there has been a consistent move away from extreme specialization. Two early alternatives to specialization were job enlargement and job rotation. Job enrichment stimulated considerable interest in job design.

Job Characteristics Theory grew from the early work on job enrichment. The basic premises of this theory are that jobs can be described in terms of a specific set of motivational characteristics and that managers should work to enhance the presence of those motivational characteristics in jobs, but that individual differences must also be taken into account. It is sometimes appropriate to design jobs for groups rather than for individuals.

Advocates of the social information processing view question some basic premises of the job characteristics approach. Social information processing theorists argue that neither employee needs nor task perceptions are stable, consistently predictable properties, but instead are socially constructed realities. Today, the emerging opinion is that employees' task perceptions and attitudes are jointly determined by objective task properties and social information.

New issues also have emerged in the area of task design. Compressed workweeks, flexible work schedules, and job sharing are scheduling innovations. Automation and robotics also have implications for job design.

Finally, it is important to consider role dynamics. If problems arise during the role episode, ambiguity or various forms of conflict can arise.

DISCUSSION QUESTIONS

1. What are the primary advantages and disadvantages of job specialization? Were they the same in the early days of mass production?

2. When might job enlargement be especially effective and especially ineffective? How about job rotation?

3. What trends today might suggest a return to job specialization?

4. What are the strengths and weaknesses of job enrichment? When might it be useful?

5. Do you agree or disagree with the idea that individual differences affect how people respond to their jobs? Explain.

6. What are the primary similarities and differences between job enrichment and the Job Characteristics Theory?

7. Are you familiar with other alternative work schedules besides those discussed in the chapter? Can you create one?

8. How do automation and robotics make work easier? How do they make it more difficult?

9. What other job design alternatives can you envision that might emerge in the future?

10. How do role dynamics relate to job design?

Case 8.1   Job Changes at IBM

From the factory floor to corporate headquarters, jobs at International Business Machines, the nation's largest computer company, have been undergoing radical changes. After a slump in 1985-1986, the only two-year period in the company's history during which profits declined, IBM has made public the development of several new products and new production technologies, and in early 1988 chairman John Akers announced a major restructuring of the giant company. Through this period, IBM has stuck to a policy that has helped keep it at the top of the "most respected corporations" list: no layoffs. As has been true for over thirty years, IBM's strategies and successes are the talk of the business world.

In 1986, when IBM's PC Convertible laptop computer hit the market, the product itself drew only limited attention. It wasn't the first laptop, nor the cheapest, nor, by some estimates, the best. But it may be the only one that is untouched by human hands until the customer takes it out of its box. The Convertible is the most prominent example of IBM's new approach to production technology: cutting costs by automating. It is not, however, just a matter of replacing people with robots. IBM has redesigned many of its products with an automated assembly line in mind, slashing the number of parts involved (the Compatible has only 70), using new superchips that do the job of a number of previous chips, and altering some designs so that they can be more easily assembled by computer arms.

The thirteen robots on the Convertible's assembly line in Austin, Texas can handle up to twelve separate steps each; the line turns out a computer every two minutes. The robots "see" spaces, pieces, and instructions with video eyes and bar code readers, grip with claws objects that are barely one-hundredth of an inch thick, and turn screws with pneumatic screwdrivers.

In other companies, factory workers have fought against such automation, afraid that jobs for humans will disappear. But the reality at IBM has been that robots have taken over the tedious jobs and allowed factory workers to take on more interesting, challenging jobs. Many employees have taken advantage of IBM's impressive employee education opportunities and have become programmers, sales agents, or customer consultants. During the period of change between 1985 and 1988, over 45,000 people, more than one-tenth of IBM's workforce, went through IBM's informal training programs, and 9,400 took formal courses lasting up to 18 months. In the process, 21,000 IBM employees changed locations and 4,300 had to move when their offices closed.

These tremors in Big Blue were felt—and in fact began—at the top. When IBM began to see its sales slowing, it cut new hiring to a trickle and instituted voluntary early retirement programs, in the process cutting its total workforce from over 405,000 to under 390,000 in less than three years. Even more important was chairman John Akers's reorganization plan.

IBM has a history of undergoing a major reorganization every five years or so. This is part of what keeps executives on their toes and interested in what they're doing. The previous reorganization had taken place in 1983, so in 1988 past experience indicated another change was due. The problem was not just that the company's profits weren't growing as quickly as usual. The plague of all big institutions—red tape and slow-moving bureaucracies—threatened to make IBM into a follower, not a leader. Many worried that IBM was becoming arrogant and flabby, and not responding to customer needs as it used to.

Akers shook things up by creating a new division—IBM United States—which will oversee five new businesses which Akers hopes will have the entrepreneurial spirit of much smaller organizations. Each new business has a different set of products and competitors, but their goal is the same: shorten product cycles. Akers has also reversed IBM's policy of developing new products in secret and then convincing people to buy them. Both he and his managers are reaching out to customers, touring their organizations, asking them what they need, and getting a read of the marketplace. If Akers's reorganization is successful, within a short time executives from those same companies may be approaching him to learn how he keeps such a big organization together, even as it undergoes such rapid change.

Case Questions

1. What connection is there between changes initiated at the top of an organization like IBM and the job changes on the factory floor?

2. Should other big American businesses follow IBM's lead and undergo a significant reorganization every five years?

3. In what ways are automation and job design related?

Case Sources

Geoff Lewis, "Big Changes at Big Blue," *Business Week*, February 15, 1988, 92–98; Aaron Bernstein, "How IBM Cut 16,200 Employees—Without An Ax," *Business Week*, February 15, 1988, 98; John Hillkirk, "How Akers Reshaped IBM," *USA Today*, January 29, 1988, 4B; Mark Lewyn, "Import War Goes to Factory Floor," *USA Today*, August 8, 1987, 1B; Bill Saporito, "IBM's No-Hands Assembly Line," *Fortune*, September 15, 1986, 105.

Case 8.2   Enriching the Jobs at Standard Decoy

Standard Decoy Company in Witchell, Maine, has been making traditional wooden hunting decoys since 1927. Cyrus Witchell began the business by carving a couple of ducks a day by hand, but demand and competition have long since driven the company to use modern machinery and assembly line techniques, turning out 200 ducks a day even on the slowest days.

When Stewart Alcorn, Cyrus Witchell's grandson, took over the business, he knew things needed to change. Output hadn't fallen, and the company was surviving financially despite competition from what he called "plastic ducks" from the Far East. But Alcorn noticed that productivity per worker had stayed the same for ten years, even in the time since the company bought the latest equipment. While taking a tour of the plant, he noticed many employees yawning, and found himself doing the same. No one quit. No one complained. They all gave him a smile when he walked by. But no one seemed excited with the work.

Alcorn decided to take a survey. He appointed a respected worker at each step in the production process to ask each of his or her co-worker's questions and to fill in response sheets. One conclusion emerged from the survey—the fine-tuners, as Alcorn thought of them, were the most content. That is, those who used fine tools and brushes to get the heads and expressions and feathers just so seemed to enjoy their work. The people who planed and cut the wood into blocks, those who rough-cut the body shapes and spray-painted the body color and applied the varnish were all pretty bored.

Having heard about a technique called job rotation, Alcorn decided to try it out. He gave all workers a taste of the "fun" jobs. He asked for volunteers to exchange jobs for one morning a week. The fine-tuners were skeptical, and the other workers only slightly more enthusiastic; the whole program turned out to be a disaster. Even with guidance, the planers and spray-painters could not seem to master the more delicate techniques, and it seemed as though the fine tuners only wanted to give them a limited amount of assistance. After one trial week, Alcorn gave up.

During lunch break that Friday, as Alcorn was wandering around outside the plant bemoaning his failure, he noticed one of the younger workers, Al Price, a rough-cutter, whittling at something with a regular pocket knife. It turned out to be a block of wood that he had cut wrong and would normally have thrown in the scrap heap. But as Price said, "It kind of looked like a duck, in a odd way," and he had started whittling on it in spare moments.

Alcorn liked what he saw and asked Price if he would be willing to sell him the duck when he got through with it. Price looked surprised, but agreed. The next week Alcorn noticed that Price had finished the whittling and was getting one of the fine-tuners to help him paint the duck in a way that made it look even odder. When it was finished, Alcorn offered it to one of his regular customers, who took a look at it, said, "You've got hand made?" and asked if he could order a gross.

By the middle of the next month, Alcorn's "Odd Ducks" program was in full swing. Workers were held responsible for producing their usual number of conventional ducks, but they were allowed to use company tools and materials any time they wanted to work on their own projects. There were no quotas or expectations on the Odd Ducks. Some employees worked on one for weeks; others collaborated and produced one or two a day. Some wouldn't sell their ducks, but crafted them in order to improve their skills, and brought them home to display on their mantles. Those who would sell kept half the selling price. That did not usually amount to more than their regular hourly wage, but no one seemed to care about the precise amount of income.

The response to the ducks was so great that Alcorn put up a bulletin board with the title "Odd Letters," where he posted appreciative notes from customers, most of whom, it seemed, had no interest in hunting but just liked to have the ducks around. And when he found that some of his customers were in turn selling the ducks as "Cyrus Witchell's Olde Time Odd Ducks" he did not complain.

Case Questions

1. How has the "Odd Ducks" program enriched the jobs at Standard Decoy?

2. What motivates workers to participate in making the Odd Ducks?

Experiential Exercise

Purpose: This exercise will help you assess the processes involved in redesigning employee jobs.

Format: Working in small groups, you will diagnose an existing job in terms of its motivating potential, analyze its motivating potential in comparison to other jobs, suggest ways to redesign it, and then assess the effects of your redesign suggestions on other elements in the workplace.

Procedure: Your instructor will divide the class into groups of three or four people. In assessing the characteristics of jobs, use a scale value of 1 (for very little) to 7 (for very high).

1. Using the scale values, assign scores on each of the job dimensions in the Job Characteristics Theory (on pages 236–237) to the following jobs: secretary, professor, waitress or waiter, auto mechanic, lawyer, short-order cook, department store clerk, construction worker, newspaper reporter.
2. Calculate the motivating potential score (MPS) (see page 237) for each of the jobs and rank-order them from highest to lowest.
3. Your instructor will now assign your group one of the jobs from the list. Discuss how you might reasonably go about enriching the job.
4. Calculate the new MPS score for the redesigned job and check its new position in the rank-ordering.
5. Discuss the feasibility of your redesign suggestions. Especially, look at how your recommended changes might necessitate organizational change, such as changes in other jobs, the reward system, and the selection criteria used in hiring people for the job.
6. Briefly discuss your observations with the rest of the class.

Follow-up Questions

1. How might the social information processing model have explained some of your own perceptions in this exercise?
2. Are some jobs simply impossible to redesign?

CHAPTER

9

Group Dynamics

Chapter Objectives

After reading this chapter, you should be able to

- ▶ define the term *group* and discuss why the study of groups is important in managing organizations.
- ▶ describe the differences between formal and informal groups in organizations.
- ▶ discuss the reasons for group formation and their impact on managing groups.

- ▶ trace the stages of development of groups from initial introduction to a mature stage of productivity and control.
- ▶ summarize the key factors affecting group performance.
- ▶ discuss several things managers can do to manage group performance.

ould you spit at a fellow group member for doing something the group did not approve of, especially if he were a 6-foot 5-inch, 235-pound coworker? That is what happened to Mark Gastineau, the New York Jets' defensive end, during the NFL strike in 1987. Gastineau is a big, fast, enormously talented, and extremely well-paid member of what had been a highly cohesive work group. During the brief strike, players who on the field rely on close working relationships, cohesiveness, and trust found themselves fighting with teammates. The strike was called over several issues that were deemed important for all members of the union. Many players, however, crossed the picket lines, often amid a hail of eggs and cries of "scabs" from their striking teammates.[1]

Football stresses teamwork in every phase of the game. There is a need to be unified in a strike, too. It was essential that all players stay on strike if better pay, benefits, and working conditions were to be forthcoming from the owners. Football, obviously, is also very physical. Collisions and injury are a normal part of the job, and there was some concern following the strike that scab players might become the target of cheap shots. Randy White, star defensive lineman for the Dallas Cowboys, crossed the picket line to avoid losing the $31,000 salary he makes for each game. He did so recognizing that he was inviting animosity and might have to step down as captain of the team. He also realized that some players might attempt to end his career through violence on the field.[2]

Football teams share the characteristics of work groups that are found in every organization. A team is a very powerful work group with expected behaviors for members, leadership, and group loyalties, all of which are necessary for the group to achieve its goals. The composition of the team is a strong determinant of its performance, just as in other organizations. Football teams have summer camp and preseason games to practice plays and give the group time to get to know each other and develop into a performing unit.

This chapter is about work groups in organizations—whether a football team, an engineering work group, a task force on new product development, or a group of nurses working the night shift at your local hospital. We first define a group and summarize the importance of groups in organizations. We then describe different types of groups and discuss the stages that groups go through as they develop from initial introduction to mature, high-performing units. Next, we identify four key factors that are important in group performance. Finally, we summarize the important elements in managing groups within organizations.

To set the stage for our discussion of groups in organizations, Figure 9.1 presents a general model of group dynamics. We show a three-phase view of group dynamics. The first phase includes the type of group and the reasons for

---

[1] Bill Saporito, "The Life of a Scab," *Fortune*, October 26, 1987, pp. 91–94.
[2] Jill Lieber, "A Test of Loyalty." *Sports Illustrated*. October 5, 1987, pp. 41–43.

Figure 9.1   General Model of Group Dynamics

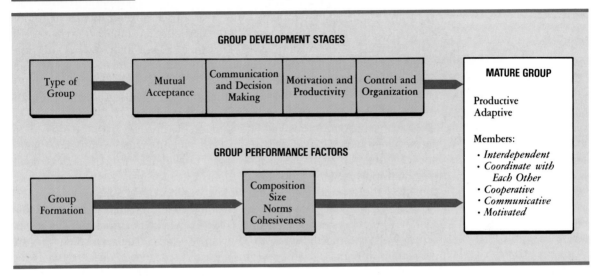

group formation. The second phase includes a four-step process of group development and the four primary group performance factors. The final phase shows a mature group that is productive and adaptive. This model serves as the framework for the discussion of groups in this chapter.

OVERVIEW OF GROUPS AND GROUP DYNAMICS

Work groups are made up of people trying to make a living for themselves and their families, and the group often becomes a person's primary source of identification with the organization. A group in an organization may seem to take on a life of its own that transcends the individual members. Let us, therefore, try to define what we mean by the entity *group*.

Definition of a Group

Definitions of groups are as plentiful as the people who write about groups. Groups can be defined in terms of perceptions, motivation, organization, interdependencies, and interactions.[3] A simple and comprehensive definition has been offered by Marvin Shaw: "A **group** is two or more persons who are interacting with one another in such a manner that each person influences and

---

[3] Marvin E. Shaw, *Group Dynamics: The Psychology of Small Group Behavior*, 3rd ed. (New York: McGraw-Hill, 1981).

is influenced by each other person."[4] The concept of interaction is essential to this definition. Two people who are physically near each other and even "look like a group" to other people are not a group, according to this definition, unless they interact and have some influence on each other. Coworkers may work side by side on related tasks, but if they do not interact, they are not a group. The presence of others may influence the performance of a group: an audience may stimulate the performance of actors, or an evaluator may inhibit the behavior of employees.[5] However, the audience or the evaluator cannot be considered part of the group unless there is interaction.

Note that the definition makes no mention of a group goal or the motivations of group members. This omission implies that members of a group may identify little or not at all with the group's goal. Consider a team in an essentially individual sport, a high school golf or tennis team, for instance. A star performer who joins the school team to attract scholarship offers may not care much about the group goal of winning the regional championship. In fact, the entire team may be composed of individuals like that whose personal motives are just to play well, without thought of the group purpose. The team members still interact and influence each other, though, and so can be considered a group. Of course, the quality of the interactions and the group's performance may be affected by the members' lack of interest in the group goal. But a goal can exist even if it is secondary to certain group members.

Shaw's definition of a group also suggests a limit on group size. A collection of people so large that its members cannot interact and influence each other does not meet this definition. And in reality the dynamics of large assemblies of people usually differ significantly from those of small groups. Our focus in this chapter is on small groups in which the members interact and influence each other.

Importance of Studying Groups

For several reasons, we cannot study behavior in organizations without endeavoring to understand the behavior of people in group settings. Groups are everywhere in our society. Most people belong to several groups—a family, a bowling team, a church group, a fraternity or sorority, a regular work group at the office.[6] Some may be formally established groups in a work or social organization, and others may be more loosely knit associations of people.

In order to understand the behavior of people in organizations, it is

---

[4] Shaw, *Group Dynamics*, p. 11.

[5] Gerald R. Ferris and Kendrith M. Rowland, "Social Facilitation Effects on Behavioral and Perceptual Task Performance Measures: Implications for Work Behavior," *Group & Organization Studies*, December 1983, pp. 421–438; and Jeff Meer, "Loafing Through a Tough Job," *Psychology Today*, January 1985, p. 72.

[6] J. Paul Sorrels and Bettye Myers, "Comparison of Group and Family Dynamics," *Human Relations*, May 1983, pp. 477–490.

Table 9.1

Classification Scheme
for Types of Groups

	Permanence	
	Relatively Permanent	*Relatively Temporary*
Formal	Command groups	Task groups
Informal	Friendship groups	Interest groups

necessary to understand the forces that affect individuals as well as the ways that individuals affect the organization. The behaviors of individuals both affect, and are affected by, the group.

The accomplishments of groups are strongly influenced by the behavior of their individual members. For example, the addition of one key all-star player to a basketball team may be the difference between a bad season and a league championship. At the same time, however, a group has a profound effect on the behaviors of its members.[7] In the football strike, some players crossed the picket line, but others who needed the money and thought about crossing the picket line did not, because they feared reprisal. Thus, the behavior of many individuals was affected by factors within the group. We discuss this further in the section on group norms.

From a managerial perspective, the work group is the primary means by which managers coordinate individual behavior to achieve organizational goals. Managers direct the activities of individuals, but they also direct and coordinate the interactions within groups. The behavior of individuals is key to the success or failure of a group. This means that the manager must be aware of individual needs and interpersonal dynamics to manage groups effectively and efficiently.

TYPES OF GROUPS

Our first task in understanding group processes is to develop a typology of groups that provides insight into their dynamics. Groups may be loosely categorized according to their degrees of formalization (formal or informal) and permanence (relatively permanent or relatively temporary). Table 9.1 shows this classification scheme.

Formal Groups

Formal groups are established by the organization to do its work and are usually identifiable on an organization chart. Formal groups include the

---

[7] Alfred W. Clark and Robert J. Powell, "Changing Drivers' Attitudes Through Peer Group Decision," *Human Relations*, February 1984, pp. 155–162.

Figure 9.2

Command Groups on an Organization Chart

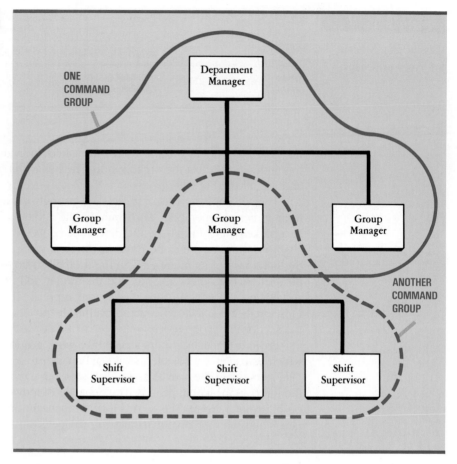

command (or functional) **group,** which is relatively permanent, and the **task group,** which is relatively temporary. In business organizations, most employees work in command groups, typically specified on an official organization chart. Figure 9.2 shows a simple organization chart with two command groups circled. The size, shape, and organization of a company's command groups can vary quite a bit.

Typical command groups in organizations include the quality assurance department, the industrial engineering department, the cost accounting department, and the personnel department. Other types of command groups include work teams organized as in the Japanese style of management, in which subsections of manufacturing and assembly processes are assigned to a team of workers to complete. The team members decide among themselves who will do each task. At People Express Airlines, the entire organization is based on teams empowered to make a wide range of decisions.[8] Teams are also becoming widespread in automobile manufacturing. General Motors is organizing its highly automated assembly lines into work teams of between five and twenty workers.[9] Command groups, whether they be entire departments or sophisticated work teams, are the dominant type of work groups in organizations.

Task or special project groups are usually temporary. Task groups are often established to solve a particular problem. Once such a group solves the problem or makes recommendations, the group is usually dissolved. While serving in a task group, people typically remain members of their command groups, or functional departments, and continue to carry out the normal duties of their jobs. If the task group requires a great deal of time and effort, the command group duties of the members may be temporarily reduced. Task groups exist in organizations around the world. For an example, see *International Perspective.*

Informal Groups

Whereas formal groups are established by an organization, **informal groups** are formed by their members. They consist of the **friendship group,** which is relatively permanent, and the **interest group,** which may be less long-lived. Friendship groups arise from friendly relationships among members and the pleasure they get from being together. Interest groups, on the other hand, are organized around a common activity or interest, although friendships may develop among members.

Good examples of interest groups are the networks of working women that have developed during the past few years. Many of these groups began as informal social gatherings of women wanting to meet with other women working in male-dominated organizations, but they soon developed into interest groups whose benefits went far beyond the initial social purposes. The networks became information systems for counseling, job placements, and management training. Some networks were eventually established as formal, permanent associations; some remained informal groups based more on social relationships than on any specific interest; and others were dissolved. These groups may be partly responsible for the past decade's dramatic increase in the percentage of women in managerial and administrative jobs.[10]

Although the distinction between friendship and interest groups can be hazy, the relative permanence of the association usually helps mark the difference. For example, the common interests and activities of a well- established friendship group may change over time, but the group stays together. Friendship and companionship are strong and durable ties. An interest group, though, may break up if its members' interests change.

---

[8] "Growing Pains at People Express," *Business Week,* January 28, 1985, pp. 90–91.

[9] "Detroit vs. The UAW: At Odds Over Teamwork," *Business Week,* August 24, 1987, pp. 54–55.

[10] "Women at Work," *Business Week,* January 28, 1985, pp. 80–85.

International Perspective

Task Force for the Vatican

As the headquarters of the Roman Catholic Church, the Vatican is viewed as the center of religious influence for over 840 million followers and affects the lives of millions of non-Catholics as well. As a large bureaucratic organization it is divided into two separate administrative units: the Vatican City-State, entirely inside the city of Rome, and the Holy See. The Vatican City-State functions as a governmental organization and supervises municipal services for the 108.7-acre city within a city. The world's smallest sovereign state, it maintains the Vatican's museum as well as its two-hundred-man security force. The Holy See, on the other hand, rules the Church, operates 116 diplomatic missions around the world, organizes the Pope's trips abroad, and oversees 40 commissions that carry out Church policy. These commissions are organized into congregations, secretariats, and councils.

The Vatican has a major problem: it is running out of money. The Vatican City-State is in good financial shape for a municipal authority. Its income exceeded expenses by $6 million in 1986. The Holy See, however, is another story. In 1986 it spent over $112 million on income of only $57.3 million. The revenue shortfall was partially covered by diverting money from the "Peter's Pence" collection for the Pope that normally goes to charities and missions. Most experts point to expansion of the administrative bureaucracy within the Holy See following the Second Vatican Council in 1962–1965 as the origin of the current financial troubles.

In 1981 the Pope appointed a special task force of fifteen cardinals to investigate the problem and develop new ways to raise money. This task force, called a council, is separate from the normal administrative hierarchy of the Holy See and reports directly to the Pope. Cardinals appointed to the council, who continue to carry out their normal duties, meet twice each year to discuss and evaluate various ways to increase Church revenues. In one attempt at a short-run solution, the council in 1987 sent letters to over three thousand bishops and heads of religious orders to make them aware of the financial problems and ask them to increase their contributions to the Peter's Pence collection. Longer-term solutions have not been decided upon, although a proposal for creating a pension fund has been investigated. The Pope, meanwhile, seems to be losing patience with the council. During one of its 1987 meetings in Rome, the Pope met with the council over lunch and strongly urged them to get busy and balance the budget.

Thus, the Pope has created a special task force, separate from the Holy See's normal hierarchy and the command groups that exist within it. The task force reports to the Pope and will presumably be disbanded once its task is completed, and the Pope clearly seems anxious for the group to achieve its goal.

Sources: Shawn Tully, "The Vatican's Finances," *Fortune*, December 21, 1987, pp. 28–40; Jean-Pierre Clerc, "The Vatican's Money Troubles," from the daily *Le Monde* of Paris, reprinted in *World Press Review*, September 1987, p. 46; Laura Colby, "Vatican Bank Played A Central Role in Fall of Banco Ambrosiano," *The Wall Street Journal*, April 27, 1987, pp. 1, 16; and Laura Colby, "Warrant Details Accusation Against Vatican Officials," *The Wall Street Journal*, June 22, 1987, p. 22.

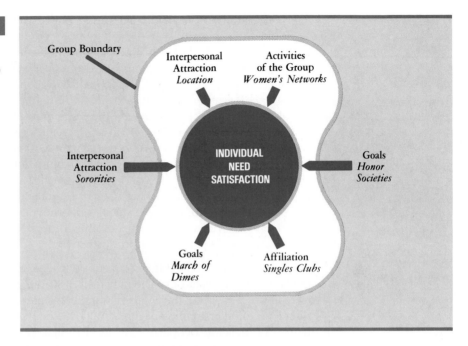

Figure 9.3

Sources of Need
Satisfaction from Group
Membership

REASONS FOR GROUP FORMATION

Command groups are formed because managers expect that organizational
tasks can be better completed and coordinated with each other if people work
together in work groups. On the other hand, individuals may form an informal
group or join an existing one for many different reasons, one of the most
important being that members expect affiliation with the group to satisfy a
need. The sources of need satisfaction can be classified in two categories:
sources inside the group (internal sources) and sources outside the group
(external sources)[11] as shown in Figure 9.3.

Internal Sources of Need Satisfaction

Internal sources of individual need satisfaction fall into four categories:
interpersonal attraction, the group's activities, the group's goals, and social
affiliation. Although these sources may overlap somewhat, it is useful to explain
each and give an example.

INTERPERSONAL ATTRACTION   Interpersonal attraction is probably the
most obvious reason for group formation—people join or form a group because
they are attracted to other people in the group. Several factors may influence

---

[11] Shaw, *Group Dynamics*, pp. 82–98.

interpersonal attraction, including location, physical attraction, perceived ability, and similarities in attitudes, beliefs, sex, race, and personality.

A very common factor in interpersonal attraction is location, or physical proximity. Proximity may mean nearby desks or offices or neighboring houses; it is certainly not unusual for people to form a group of coworkers or neighbors.[12] Location not only provides a setting for interpersonal attraction but also can reinforce it. Nearness increases the opportunity for interactions and, in turn, for the discovery of attractive characteristics.

When people who need to coordinate their work have offices close together, informal groups may develop, leading to more interaction and feelings of closeness. From there it is a short step to better working relationships and coordination on the job. Grouping offices together may improve the performance of executive teams, for example.[13] With opportunities to interact in an informal group, busy executives may be better able to coordinate the operations of the organization and thus improve productivity.

THE GROUP'S ACTIVITIES   Group activities may also be a source of individual need satisfaction. The networks of working women discussed earlier were formed because the women wanted to interact with others in similar situations. Another example is a group that assembles regularly to play bridge. It may be that the people in the group enjoy playing bridge and like the competition. Or it may be that the members have little interest in who wins or in the intricacies of the game. Social chitchat about families, sporting events, and other subjects of mutual interest may be the group's actual basis.

THE GROUP'S GOALS   A third internal source of individual need satisfaction is identification with group goals that seem to merit a commitment of time and effort. For example, each year thousands of women throughout the United States go door to door requesting donations for the March of Dimes. The driving force behind this so-called Mothers' March is the goal of eliminating birth defects. This example also illustrates the difference between joining a group because of its activities and joining because of its goals.[14] Many of the women in the Mothers' March may not enjoy the activity itself—canvassing neighborhoods and knocking on doors—but their commitment to the goal overrides their personal preferences. This distinction is important in the analysis of individual behavior in the group, as discussed later in the chapter.

SOCIAL AFFILIATION   A final internal source of individual need satisfaction

---

[12] R. Robert Huckfeldt, "Social Contexts, Social Networks, and Urban Neighborhoods: Environmental Constraints of Friendship Choice," *American Journal of Sociology*, November 1983, pp. 651–669.

[13] Fritz Steele, "The Ecology of Executive Teams: A New View of the Top," *Organizational Dynamics*, Spring 1983, pp. 65–78.

[14] M. Sherif and C. W. Sherif, *Groups in Harmony and Tension* (New York: Harper & Row, 1953).

is the need for affiliation, or companionship[15] (a primary individual need, as noted in Chapter 4). Group membership may be the source of a good deal of personal value and emotional significance and may provide the foundation for a person's social identity.[16] The group's goals and activities may be largely irrelevant in satisfying the need for affiliation. For example, people who have recently lost a spouse and join a group to replace the lost companionship may care little about the group's purpose or activities.

External Sources of Need Satisfaction

People may also join groups for reasons that lie outside the group, either interpersonal attraction to people outside the group or the pursuit of goals outside the group. Although this may sound somewhat contradictory, several examples exist to support it.

INTERPERSONAL ATTRACTION   By interpersonal attraction to people outside the group, we mean a person may be able to gain access to certain people only by affiliation with a group apart from those people. Say, for example, that a young woman at college wishes to meet men who are in a certain fraternity. She may find that being a member of a certain women's sorority might help her meet these young men. Thus, she joins a group because of her attraction to people outside of the group she joins.

GOALS OUTSIDE THE GROUP   A person may join a group because of the status or prestige that comes with being a member. For example, a student may accept an invitation to join an honor society at college because membership in the society will "look good" on his or her resumé when he or she looks for a job. He or she may not identify with the goals of the society or even seek to interact with its members because his or her reasons for joining are external to the group.

Implications of Group Formation

Understanding why a group forms is important in studying individual behavior in groups. Suppose people join a bridge group primarily for social contact. If a more competitive player substitutes one evening for an absent regular player, she or he joins the group (temporarily) with a different goal in mind. The substitute may be annoyed when the game slows down or stops altogether because the other players are absorbed in a discussion. The regular members, on the other hand, may be irritated when the substitute impatiently interrupts the discussion and rebukes her or his partner for faulty technique. Someone

---

[15] Stanley Schacter, *The Psychology of Affiliation* (Stanford, Calif.: Stanford University Press, 1959).

[16] Rupert Brown and Jennifer Williams, "Group Identification: The Same Thing to All People?" *Human Relations*, July 1984, pp. 547–560.

who wants to resolve the resulting conflict between the members will have to understand the differences in why the people joined the group. The inconsistencies in behavior are probably resulting because members are seeking the satisfaction of different needs. Settling the spat may require that the regulars and the substitute be more tolerant of each other's behavior, at least for the rest of the evening. Then the substitute player may not be asked back the next time a regular member cannot attend.

Thus, understanding why people have joined a group sheds light on apparent inconsistencies in behavior and the tensions likely to result from them. With such an understanding, we may be better able to manage certain kinds of conflict that arise in groups in organizations. For example, the president of a community college created a task force to study and recommend changes in employee health insurance benefits. Some members of the task force volunteered to serve because they wanted to improve the benefit package. Other members were assigned to the task force by their department managers. Repeatedly, the members who had been assigned to the task force were late for meetings and in a hurry to adjourn because of their lack of interest in the group's goals. In effect, their goals were to superficially complete the group's work quickly and go back to other duties, rather than to realistically study alternative insurance plans. The volunteers, on the other hand, were frustrated by the assigned members' lack of cooperation. Conflict arose over many seemingly minor issues. At first, the chair of the group did not understand the source of conflict and just kept pleading for the members to cooperate. The group made little progress until the chair figured out the source of the bickering and asked to have the membership changed. Clearly, why people ended up in this group had a significant impact on how the group functioned.

STAGES OF GROUP DEVELOPMENT

Groups are not static. Characteristically they develop through a four-stage process: (1) mutual acceptance, (2) communication and decision making, (3) motivation and productivity, and (4) control and organization.[17] The stages and the activities that typify them are shown in Table 9.2. We discuss the stages as if they were separate and distinct, but because their activities overlap, it is difficult to pinpoint exactly when a group moves from one stage to another.

Mutual Acceptance

In the first stage of group development, members get to know each other by sharing information about themselves. They often test each other's opinions by

---

[17] Bernard M. Bass and Edward C. Ryterband, *Organizational Psychology*, 2nd ed. (Boston: Allyn and Bacon, 1979), pp. 252–254.

	Stages	Typical Characteristics
Table 9.2 Stages of Group Development and Typical Characteristics of Each	1. Mutual acceptance	Making acquaintances Sharing information Discussing subjects unrelated to task Testing each other Being defensive, quibbling
	2. Communication and decision making	Expressing attitudes Establishing norms Establishing goals Openly discussing tasks
	3. Motivation and productivity	Cooperating Working actively on tasks Being creative
	4. Control and organization	Working interdependently Assigning tasks based on ability Acting spontaneously Being flexible

discussing subjects that have little to do with the group, such as the weather, sports, or recent happenings within the organization. Some aspects of the group's task, such as its formal objectives, may also be discussed at this stage. However, such discussion will probably not be very productive because the members are unfamiliar with each other and do not know how to evaluate each other's comments. If the members do happen to know each other already, this stage may be brief, but it is unlikely to be skipped altogether, since this is a new group with a new purpose. Besides, there are always likely to be a few members that the others do not know well or at all.[18]

As the members get to know each other better, discussion may turn to more sensitive issues, such as the organization's politics or recent controversial decisions. In this way the participants explore each other's reactions, knowledge, and expertise. From the discussion, members may be able to learn each other's views on a variety of issues, how similar their beliefs and values are, and the extent to which they can trust each other. Members may discuss their expectations about the group's activities in terms of their previous group and organizational experience.[19] Eventually, the conversation will turn to the business of the group. When this discussion becomes serious, the group is moving to the next stage of development.

[18] John P. Wanous, Arnon E. Reichers, and S. D. Malik, "Organizational Socialization and Group Development: Toward an Integrative Perspective," *Academy of Management Review*, October 1984, pp. 670–683.

[19] Susan Long, "Early Integration in Groups: A Group To Join and a Group To Create," *Human Relations*, April 1984, pp. 311–332.

Communication and Decision Making

Once group members have begun to accept each other, the group discusses feelings and opinions more openly. During this stage the members may show tolerance for opposing viewpoints and explore different ideas to bring about a good solution or decision. Members discuss and eventually agree on the group's goals. They are then assigned roles and tasks to accomplish the goals.

Motivation and Productivity

At this stage, emphasis shifts away from personal concerns and viewpoints to activities that will benefit the group. Members cooperate and actively help others accomplish their goals. The members are highly motivated and may carry out their tasks creatively. In this stage the group's work is being accomplished, and the group itself is moving toward the final stage of development.

Control and Organization

In the fourth stage the group works effectively toward accomplishing its goals. Tasks are assigned by mutual agreement and according to ability. In a mature group the activities of the members are relatively spontaneous and flexible, rather than subject to rigid structural restraints. Mature groups can evaluate their activities and potential outcomes and take corrective actions if necessary. The characteristics of flexibility, spontaneity, and self-correction are very important if the group is to remain productive over an extended period.

Not all groups go through all four stages and become effective; some groups may disband before reaching the final stage, and others may do a poor job of completing a stage.[20] Rather than spend the time necessary to get to know each other and build trust, for example, a group may cut short the first stage of development because of pressure from its leader, from deadlines, or from an outside threat (such as the boss). If members are forced into activities typical of a later stage while the work of an earlier stage remains incomplete, they are likely to become frustrated; the group will not develop completely and will be less productive than it might.[21] Group productivity depends on successful development at each stage. A group that evolves fully through the four stages of development will become a mature, effective group.[22] Its members will be interdependent, coordinated, cooperative, capable of doing their jobs, motivated to do them, and in communication with one another.[23]

---

[20] Wanous, Reichers, and Malik, "Organizational Socialization and Group Development: Toward an Integrative Perspective."

[21] Steven L. Obert, "Developmental Patterns of Organizational Task Groups: A Preliminary Study," *Human Relations*, January 1983, pp. 37–52.

[22] Bass and Ryterband, *Organizational Psychology*, pp. 252–254.

[23] Bernard M. Bass, "The Leaderless Group Discussion," *Psychological Bulletin*, September 1954, pp. 465–492.

Groups in organizations are often given the time and resources needed for development. For example, some top executive teams go on retreats periodically. Retreats provide a few days in an environment free from telephone calls, meetings, and other daily work pressures for the group to study information, get to know each other, and make plans for the future. A retreat may be especially useful when the membership of an executive team has changed, because it provides time for the mutual adjustment phase of the development process. By allowing the group to get away from normal day-to-day burdens and focus on itself and its tasks, the organization can improve group productivity.

Fully developed groups are making contributions in many different ways. Chapter 5 notes the growing popularity of quality circles as a group management technique. A *quality circle* (*QC*) is a group of employees who meet, usually on company time and property, to discuss ways to improve quality and productivity. Circles are usually trained in information sharing and problem solving. A first-level supervisor usually leads the discussion, but anyone can take the role of leader. Other types of groups are becoming popular in many organizations. Some examples are discussed in *Management in Action*.

Finally, as working conditions and relationships change, groups may need to re-experience one or more of the stages of development if the feeling of cohesiveness and productivity that usually exists in a well-developed group is to be maintained. The San Francisco Forty-Niners, for example, found their return from the NFL strike in 1987 to be a very uncomfortable period filled with apprehension. Their coach, Bill Walsh, conducted very difficult practices but also allowed time for players to get together to air their feelings. Slowly, team unity returned, and players began joking and socializing again as they prepared for the rest of the 1987 season.[24]

GROUP PERFORMANCE FACTORS

The performance of any group is affected by several factors other than the reasons for its formation and the stages of its development. In a high-performing group, a group synergy often develops in which the group's performance is more than the sum of the individual contributions of its members. Several additional factors may account for this accelerated performance.[25] Figure 9.4 shows the four basic **group performance factors**—composition, size, norms, and cohesiveness.

---

[24] Jill Lieber "Time to Heal the Wounds" *Sports Illustrated,* November 2, 1987, pp. 86–91.

[25] James H. Davis, *Group Performance*, (Reading, Mass.: Addison-Wesley, 1964), pp. 82–86.

Management in ACTION

The Power of Groups in Manufacturing

Groups formed to make decisions and enhance productivity are showing up in some unusual places. In traditionally organized manufacturing plants that are union dominated, group decision making and joint labor-management efforts are having significant impacts, especially in the automobile and steel industries. The traditional mass production manufacturing system has been characterized by highly specialized jobs and worker-management antagonism. But now some plants are creating teams and joint decision-making groups to improve both productivity and quality.

Eight steel companies have agreed to a joint effort with the industry's dominant union, the United Steel Workers of America (USW), to create *labor management participation teams (LMPT)* throughout the industry. LMPTs have been used in some steel companies since 1980, but the current effort is designed to improve the industry as a whole by harnessing the talents of those who know the work the best: the workers. Teams are similar to what are often called quality circles in other industries and usually consist of ten to fifteen workers who meet regularly to discuss and recommend solutions to production and quality problems. In the new effort, workers and managers will participate in a training program designed to teach them how to put participation in teams to best use.

National Steel Company, where 1,200 of 8,225 union employees currently participate in LMPTs, is convinced of their benefits, citing one LMPT's suggestion that a simpler method of refilling a caustic-cleaning-solution tank would prevent injuries and save money. A company official estimates that National saves more than $40,000 per month and reduces the threat of injuries by 90 percent owing to the implementation of the LMPT's recommendation.

At the Toledo, Ohio, plant of General Motors, management and labor have found that formal work rule changes have not been necessary because workers are willingly becoming more flexible through "employee involvement" groups. One such group of fourteen skilled trade workers met voluntarily to discuss and assist in the movement of their work area to another section of the plant. And management at the plant in Shreveport, Louisiana, consulted a work team for help in determining how to cut one job from the team, which installs rear bumpers. The team switched tasks around and experimented with various systems and will soon make its recommendation. The person whose job is cut will be moved to another part of the plant. The productivity of the Shreveport plant, which is organized almost entirely around the team concept, is among the highest of all 175 GM plants. Furthermore, GM has decided to adopt the team concept at all of its auto assembly plants and many of its component-part plants.

Sources: "Steelmakers Want to Make Teamwork an Institution," *Business Week*, May 11, 1987, p. 84; Jacob M. Schlesinger, "Auto Firms and UAW Find That Cooperation Can Get Complicated," *The Wall Street Journal*, August 25, 1987, pp. 1, 14; and "Detroit vs. the UAW: At Odds Over Teamwork," *Business Week*, August 24, 1987, pp. 54–55.

Figure 9.4

Four Factors that Affect Group Performance

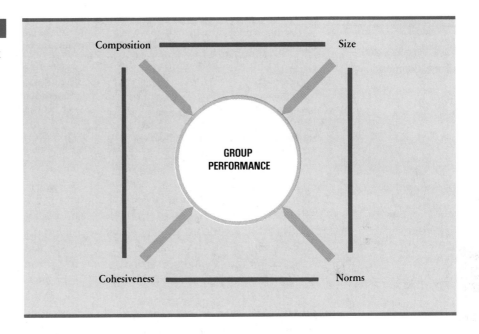

Composition

The composition of a group plays an important role in determining group productivity.[26] **Group composition** is most often described in terms of the homogeneity or heterogeneity of the members. A group is *homogeneous* if the members are similar in one or several ways that are critical to the work of the group, such as age, work experience, education, technical specialty, or cultural background. In *heterogeneous* groups, the members are different in one or more ways that are critical to the work of the group. Homogeneous groups are often created in organizations when people are assigned to command groups based on a similar technical specialty. Although the people who work in such command groups may differ on some factors, such as age or work experience, they are homogeneous in terms of a critical work performance variable— technical specialty. The assignment of nurses to work groups in hospitals is a good example of this.[27]

Much research has explored the relationship between a group's composition and its productivity. Table 9.3 summarizes task variables that make a homogeneous or a hetergeneous group advantageous over its counterpart. A homogeneous group is likely to be most productive in situations where the group

---

[26] Shaw, *Group Dynamics*.

[27] Peggy Leatt and Rodney Schneck, "Criteria for Grouping Nursing Subunits in Hospitals," *Academy of Management Journal*, March 1984, pp. 150–165.

Table 9.3	A homogeneous group is more useful for:	A heterogeneous group is more useful for:
Task Variables and Group Composition	Simple tasks	Complex tasks
	Sequential tasks	Collective tasks
	Cooperation required	Creativity required
	Speed required	Speed not important

Source: Based on discussion in Bernard M. Bass and Edward C. Ryterband, *Organizational Psychology,* 2nd. ed. (Boston: Allyn and Bacon, 1979). Reprinted by permission.

task is simple, cooperation is needed, the group tasks are sequential, or quick action is required. Teams of firefighters who put out summer forest fires are relatively homogeneous groups—usually college students majoring in forestry and working in the Forest Service for the season. Although no two fires are the same, all require swift, coordinated action to get the blaze under control.

A heterogeneous group is most likely to be productive in situations where the task is complex, requires a collective effort (that is, each member does a different task and the sum of these efforts constitutes the group output), and demands creativity, or where speed is less important than thorough deliberations. For example, a group asked to generate ideas for marketing a new product probably needs to be heterogeneous to develop as many different ideas as possible.

The link between group composition and type of task is explained by the interactions typical of homogeneous and heterogeneous groups. A homogeneous group tends to have less conflict, fewer differences of opinion, easier communication, and more interaction. A task that requires cooperation and speed therefore makes a homogeneous group more desirable. If, however, the task requires complex analysis of information and creativity in arriving at the best possible solution, a heterogeneous group may be more appropriate because a wide range of viewpoints are represented. More discussion and more conflict are likely, both potentially improving the group's decision.

Size

According to Shaw's definition, a group can have as few as two members or as many as can interact and influence each other. **Group size** can have an important effect on performance: a group with many members has more resources available and may be able to complete a large number of relatively independent tasks. Among groups established to generate ideas, those with more members tend to produce more ideas, although the *rate of increase* in the number of ideas diminishes rapidly as the group grows.[28] Beyond a certain

---

[28] Shaw, *Group Dynamics*, pp. 173–177.

point, the greater complexity of interactions and communication may make it more difficult for a large group to achieve agreement.

Interactions and communication are much more likely to be formalized in larger groups. Large groups tend to set agendas for meetings and to follow a protocol or parliamentary procedure to control discussion. As a result, some time that might otherwise be available for task accomplishment is taken up in administrative duties such as organizing and structuring the interactions and communications within the group. Also, the large size of a group may inhibit participation of some people[29] and increase absenteeism[30] because so many people are trying to contribute. If repeated attempts to contribute or participate are thwarted by the sheer number of similar efforts by other members, some people may give up on making a meaningful contribution and may even stop coming to group meetings. Furthermore, large groups may present more opportunities for interpersonal attraction, leading to more social interactions and fewer task interactions. How much of a problem this becomes depends on the nature of the task and the characteristics of the people involved.

Figure 9.5 illustrates and summarizes the differences between large- and small-group interactions. In small groups people can interact frequently. In large groups, however, subgroups often develop because frequent interaction among all members is impossible. Subgroups tend to take in those people who interact together most often. The effects of this subgrouping may be either good or bad for the group, depending on its mission. If the group's tasks can be subdivided into smaller tasks that can be accomplished by the subgroups, the formation of subgroups may be beneficial. (Of course, the results must eventually be pooled into a group product.) On the other hand, if the group needs to function as a whole, the subgroups have to be integrated in performing the group's tasks.

Norms

A **norm** is a standard against which the appropriateness of a behavior is judged.[31] Thus a norm is the expected behavior or behavioral pattern in a certain situation. Group norms are usually established during the second stage of group development (communication and decision making) and carried forward into the maturity stage.[32] People often have expectations about the behavior of others. By providing a basis for predicting the behaviors of others, norms enable people to formulate response behaviors. Without norms, the activities within a group would be chaotic.

---

[29] Davis, *Group Performance*, p. 73.

[30] Steven E. Markham, Fred Dansereau, Jr., and Joseph A. Alutto, "Group Size and Absenteeism Rates: A Longitudinal Analysis", *Academy of Management Journal*, December 1982, pp. 921–927.

[31] Davis, *Group Performance*, p. 82.

[32] Bass and Ryterband, *Organizational Psychology*, pp. 252–254.

Figure 9.5

Group Size and
Interpersonal
Interactions

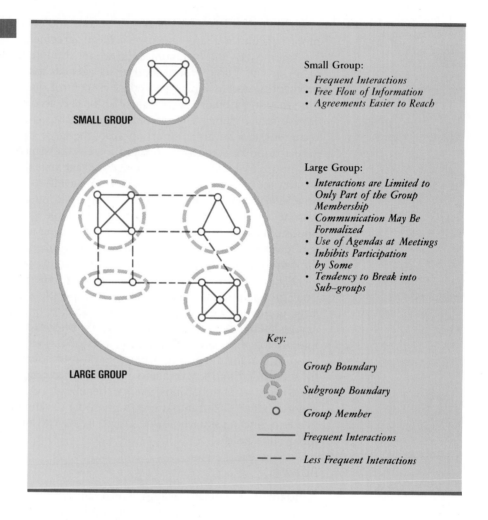

SMALL GROUP

Small Group:
- *Frequent Interactions*
- *Free Flow of Information*
- *Agreements Easier to Reach*

Large Group:
- *Interactions are Limited to Only Part of the Group Membership*
- *Communication May Be Formalized*
- *Use of Agendas at Meetings*
- *Inhibits Participation by Some*
- *Tendency to Break into Sub-groups*

LARGE GROUP

Key:

Group Boundary

Subgroup Boundary

Group Member

Frequent Interactions

Less Frequent Interactions

Norms result from the combination of members' personality characteristics, the situation, the task, and the historical traditions of the group. Lack of conformity to group norms may result in verbal abuse, physical threats, ostracism, or ejection from the group. Group norms are enforced, however, only for actions that are important to group members.[33] For example, if the office norm is that employees should wear suits to convey a professional image to clients, a staff member who wears blue jeans and a sweatshirt violates the group norm and will hear about it quickly. But if the norm is that dress is unimportant (because, for example, little contact with clients occurs in the office), someone wearing blue jeans may not be noticed.

---

[33] Shaw, *Group Dynamics*, pp. 280–293.

Norms serve four purposes.

1. Norms help the group survive. Groups tend to reject deviant behavior that does not contribute to accomplishing group goals or to the survival of the group if it is threatened. Accordingly, a successful group that is not under threat may be more tolerant of deviant behavior.

2. Norms simplify and make more predictable the behaviors expected of group members. Norms mean that members do not have to analyze each behavior and decide on a response. Members can anticipate the actions of others on the basis of group norms. When members do what is expected of them, the group is more likely to be productive and to reach its goals.

3. Norms help the group avoid embarrassing situations. Group members often want to avoid damaging other members' self-images and are likely to avoid certain subjects that might hurt a member's feelings.

4. Norms express the central values of the group and identify the group to others. Certain clothes, mannerisms, or behaviors in particular situations may be a rallying point for members and may signify to others the nature of the group.[34]

Norms usually regulate the behavior of group members rather than their thoughts or feelings.[35] Members may thus believe one thing but do another to maintain membership in a group. For example, during the Iran-Contra affair in 1985–1987, there were several meetings in which the president and aides, such as Lt. Col. Oliver North, National Security Advisor Robert McFarlane, and Central Intelligence Agency Director William Casey discussed the sale of arms to Iran in exchange for American hostages.[36] Secretary of State George P. Schultz and Secretary of Defense Caspar W. Weinberger were known to be against the sale of arms to Iran, even indirectly through Israel. The president and others strongly favored such arms sales and were eager to achieve the release of American hostages held in Iran. Thus, Schultz and Weinberger were not in attendance at meetings in which further arms sales were authorized.[37] Although it is not clear

---

[34] Daniel C. Feldman, "The Development and Enforcement of Group Norms," *Academy of Management Review*, January 1984, pp. 47–53.

[35] J. Richard Hackman, "Group Influences on Individuals," in Marvin D. Dunnette, ed., *Handbook of Industrial and Organizational Psychology* (Chicago: Rand McNally, 1976), pp. 1455–1525.

[36] John Tower, Edmund Muskie, and Brent Skowcroft, *The Tower Commission Report*, (New York: Joint publication of Bantam Books and Times Books, 1987); and *Taking the Stand: The Testimony of Lieutenant Colonel Oliver L. North*, (New York: Pocket Books, 1987).

[37] *The Tower Commission Report*, pp. 37–38.

whether they were excluded by the members or they excluded themselves by not attending, norms clearly affected the meetings and outcomes. From the group's perspective, the norms were to approve the arms transfer and not argue against it. Anyone who continued to argue against the transfer would not be in the group. Thus, Schultz and Weinberger did not attend. From their perspective, they knew that they were in the minority and were making it uncomfortable for the president. If they wanted to maintain their valued membership in the president's cabinet as heads of two of the most powerful agencies of the executive branch, they knew that they should not continue to cause trouble. Thus, the group norms regarding how presidential advisors are supposed to act may have led them to not attend.

Pressures to conform to group norms can be powerful determinants of group performance. Norms affect setting goals, defining behaviors that are appropriate for members, and restricting behaviors of members.[38] Conformity to group norms may result in serious problems at work, such as unsafe work practices. For example, at a manufacturing plant strict rules were in place regarding the use of gloves in the drill press area. Company safety regulations prohibited the use of gloves for certain tasks because of the safety hazard involved if the gloves (and the worker's hands along with them) were caught in the rapidly--spinning drill bit. However, the norms of the group dictated the common practice for drill press operators, which was to use gloves for several steps of the drilling process. On-the-job training, health and safety training classes, and numerous strict warnings were given to the drill press operators, but the group norms were very strong. Finally, one Monday morning an operator's glove got caught in a spinning drill bit, grabbing two of his fingers with it and seriously twisting them. Obviously, this worker and the company paid a very high price for conformance to group norms.

Cohesiveness

Group cohesiveness results from "all forces acting on the members to remain in the group."[39] The forces that create cohesiveness are attraction to the group, resistance to leaving the group, and the motivation to remain a member of the group.[40] As shown in Figure 9.6, group cohesiveness is related to many aspects of group dynamics that we have already discussed—maturity, homogeneity, and manageable size.

---

[38] Robert J. Lichtman and Irving M. Lane, "Effects of Group Norms and Goal Setting on Productivity," *Group & Organization Studies*, December 1983, pp. 406–420.

[39] L. Festinger, "Informal Social Communication," *Psychological Review*, September 1950, p. 274.

[40] William E. Piper, Myriam Marrache, Renee Lacroix, Astrid M. Richardson, and Barry D. Jones, "Cohesion as a Basic Bond in Groups," *Human Relations*, February 1983, pp. 93–108.

Figure 9.6   Group Cohesiveness: Factors that Affect Group Cohesiveness;
Consequences of Group Cohesiveness

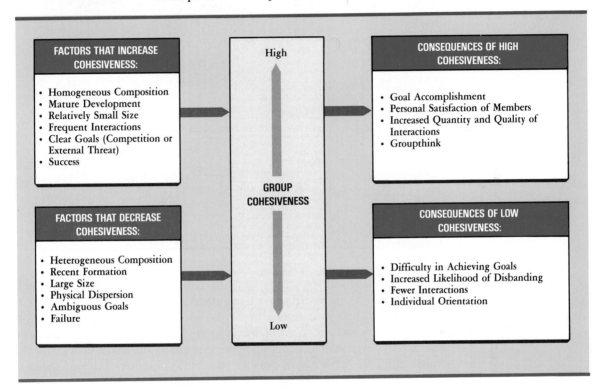

The figure also shows that group cohesiveness can be increased by competition or by the presence of an external threat.[41] Either competition with another group or an external threat can serve as a clearly defined goal that focuses members' attention on their task and increases their willingness to work together. The threat of NFL teams using replacement players for those on strike had an immediate effect of unifying the players against the owners. The players became more cohesive and vowed more strongly than ever to hold out.[42] Similarly, in the Iran-Contra affair, the inner group (Casey, North, McFarlane, and Vice Admiral Poindexter) became a cohesive group owing to the need for secrecy and threats of exposure by Congress and the media.[43]

---

[41] Davis, *Group Performance*, pp. 78–81.

[42] Paul Zimmerman, "When Push Came to Shove," *Sports Illustrated*, October 5, 1987, pp. 38–43.

[43] Tower, Muskie, and Skowcroft, *The Tower Commission Report*; and *Taking the Stand*.

Figure 9.7

Group Cohesiveness,
Goals, and Productivity

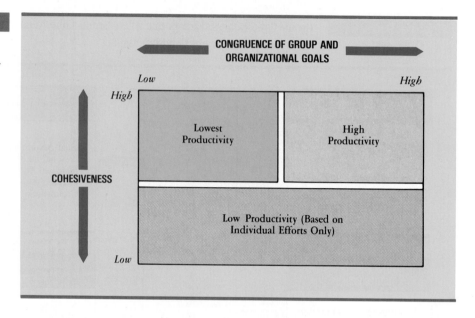

Finally, successfully reaching goals often increases the cohesiveness of a group because people are glad to be identified with a winner and to be thought of as competent and successful. This may be one reason for the popular phrase, "Success breeds success." A group that is successful may become more cohesive and possibly even more successful. One example is the initial success of the design group at Apple Computers in which the designers became so close through the hard work and success of the MacIntosh personal computer. These teams worked and partied together and became quite cohesive. (Of course, other factors can get in the way of continued success, such as personal differences and egos and the lure of more individual success in other activities.)

Research on group performance factors has focused on the relationship between cohesiveness and group productivity. Studies have shown that highly cohesive groups are more effective at achieving their goals than are groups low in cohesiveness.[44] But highly cohesive groups will not necessarily be more productive in an organizational sense than the groups with low cohesiveness. As illustrated in Figure 9.7, when a group's goals are compatible with the organization's, a cohesive group will probably be more productive than one that is not cohesive. In other words, if a highly cohesive group has the goal of contributing to the good of the organization, it is very likely to be productive in organizational terms. But if such a group decides on a goal that has little to do with the business of the organization, it will probably achieve its own goal, even at the expense of any organizational goal. For an example of the continuing

---

[44] Shaw, *Group Dynamics*, pp. 222–225.

A LOOK AT RESEARCH

Group Cohesiveness and Performance for R&D Project Groups

Industry, as it grows more complex and technologically sophisticated, is relying more and more on high-technology research and development to spur innovation and change. Often R&D groups are arranged into project groups, with the assignment of one specific project to each group. People who are members of these project groups usually have advanced degrees in engineering or some field of science. Responding to increasing interest in the management and success of R&D project groups, Robert T. Keller of Louisiana State University did research on the predictors of high performance by such groups.

In his study, in a major American corporation, Keller analyzed 32 single-project groups, consisting of 221 technical professionals. The people who participated in the study were about evenly split between engineers and scientists and were highly educated—over 60 percent held doctorates. Most were men (92 percent), and their average age was forty-three years. The varied projects assigned to the groups included basic research, applied research, product or process development, and technical service development.

Keller used a questionnaire to gather information about the groups. Members and managers evaluated their groups in terms of eighteen different descriptive factors. The factors included such things as type of project, education and age of members, group cohesiveness, group size, innovative orientation of members, physical distance between group members, job satisfaction of members, and several indicators of group performance such as project quality, budget and cost performance, meeting schedules, and value to the company.

The results of Keller's analysis showed group cohesiveness to be the only variable that was consistently related to the performance factors identified for the groups. This relationship held up for all types of R&D projects. The results showed that cohesive R&D project groups consistently met their goals, produced higher-quality projects, and met budget and schedules, regardless of the type of project or the size of the group. These results suggest that managers of R&D project groups should do their best to foster the development of group cohesiveness.

Source: Adapted from Robert T. Keller, "Predictors of the Performance of Project Groups in R&D Organizations," *Academy of Management Journal*, December 1986, pp. 715–726. Reprinted by permission.

efforts to understand the relationship between group cohesiveness and performance, see *A Look at Research*.

Cohesiveness may also be a primary factor in the development of certain problems for some decision-making groups, such as groupthink[45], which occurs when a group's overriding concern is a unanimous decision rather than the critical analysis of alternatives. Chapter 17 goes into groupthink in more detail. These problems, together with the evidence regarding group cohesiveness and

---

[45] Janis, *Groupthink*.

productivity, mean that a manager must carefully weigh the pros and cons of fostering highly cohesive groups.

MANAGING GROUP PERFORMANCE IN ORGANIZATIONS

Managing groups in organizations is difficult. Managers must, of course, know what types of groups—command or task, formal or informal—exist in the organization. If a certain command group is very large, there will probably be several informal subgroups to be managed. A manager might want to take advantage of existing informal groups, "formalizing" some of them into command or task groups based on a subset of the tasks to be performed. Other informal groups may need to be broken up to make task assignment easier. In assigning tasks to people and subgroups, the manager must also consider individual motivations for joining groups, as well as the composition of groups.

Quite often, a manager can help make sure a group develops into a productive unit by nurturing its activities in each stage of development. Helpful steps include encouraging open communication and trust among the members, stimulating discussion of important issues and providing task-relevant information at appropriate times, and assisting in the analysis of external factors, such as competition and external threats and opportunities. Managers might also encourge the development of norms and roles within the group to help out in development.

In managing a group, managers must consider the goals of the people in the group as well as those of the group as a whole. Developing a reward structure that lets people reach their own goals by working toward those of the group can result in a very productive group. A manager may also be able to influence some factors that affect group cohesiveness. For example, trying to stimulate competition, provoke an external threat to the group, establish a goal-setting system, or employ participative approaches might help harness the productive potential of high cohesiveness.

In summary, managers must be aware of the implications—organizational and social—of their attempts to manage people in groups in organizations. Groups affect the behavior of people and, individual efforts, when aggregated to the group level, are the source of group performance. As prevalent as groups are in our society, it is essential that managers strive to improve their understanding of people in the groups to which they belong.

SUMMARY OF KEY POINTS

A group is two or more people who interact so as to influence one another. It is important to study groups because they are everywhere in our society, they can profoundly affect individual behavior, and the behavior of individuals in a group is key to the group's success or failure. The work group is the primary means by which managers coordinate individual behavior to achieve organizational goals.

Groups may be differentiated on the basis of relative permanence and degree of formality. The two types of formal groups are command and task groups. Friendship and interest groups are the two types of informal groups. Command groups are relatively permanent work groups established by the organization and are usually specified on an organization chart. Task groups, although also established by the organization, are relatively temporary and exist only until the specific task is accomplished. In friendship groups, the affiliation among the people arises from close social relationships and the pleasure that comes from being together. The common bond in interest groups is the activity in which the members engage.

Group formation and development have important effects on a group's performance. Group formation depends on the expectation that a need will be satisfied as a result of membership. There are four types of need satisfactions that are internal to the group: interpersonal attraction, group activities, group goals, and the need for affiliation. The two types of need satisfaction that are external to the group are interpersonal attraction to people outside the group and goals external to the group.

Groups develop in four stages: mutual acceptance, communication and decision making, motivation and productivity, and control and organization. Although the stages are sequential, they may overlap. A group that does not fully develop within each stage will not fully develop as a group, resulting in lower group performance.

Incomplete group development can lead to member frustration and low group productivity. A group that fully realizes the four stages of development will become a mature, effective group in which the members are interdependent, coordinated, cooperative, capable of doing their jobs, motivated to do them, and in communication with one another.

Four additional factors affect group performance: composition, size, norms, and cohesiveness. The homogeneity of the people in the group affects the interactions that occur and the productivity of the group. The effect of increasing the size of the group depends on the nature of the tasks and the people in the group.

Norms help people function and relate to each other in predictable and efficient ways. Norms serve four purposes. They facilitate group survival, simplify and make more predictable the behaviors of group members, help the group avoid embarrassing situations, and express the central values of the group and identify the group to others.

The relationships between group cohesiveness, productivity, and other group factors are very complex. The most organizationally productive groups are highly cohesive and have goals that are compatible with the organization's. In managing groups in organizations, the manager should consider the goals of groups as well as the factors that affect group cohesiveness.

DISCUSSION QUESTIONS

1. Why is it useful for a manager to be familiar with the concepts of group behavior? Why is it useful for an employee to be familiar with the concepts of group behavior?

2. Our definition of a group is a rather broad one. Would you classify each of the following collections of people as a group or as something else? Explain why.

   70,000 people at a football game

   the people taking this course

   people in an elevator

   people on an escalator

   employees of IBM

   employees of your local college bookstore

3. List four different groups to which you belong. Identify each as formal or informal.

4. For each group you just listed, describe the reasons for its formation. Why did you join each group? Why might others have decided to join each group?

5. In which stage of development is each of your four groups? Did any group move too quickly through any of the stages? Explain.

6. Analyze the composition of two of the groups to which you belong. How are they similar and different in composition?

7. Is any one of the groups to which you belong too large or too small to get its work done? If so, is there anything that the leader or the members can do to alleviate the problem?

8. List two norms of two of the groups to which you belong. How are these norms enforced?

9. Discuss the following statement: Group cohesiveness is the good, warm feeling that we get from working in groups and is something that all group leaders should strive to develop in the groups they lead.

Case 9.1   The Group that Points the Finger

When an airplane crashes in the United States, the National Transportation Safety Board (NTSB) puts together a group of people to determine who or what was responsible for the accident. The group faces a daunting task, examining evidence that is often incomplete and possibly burned or in small scattered pieces. It tries to judge what combination of human error, mechanical failure, weather, and other factors led to the tragedy. The task is complex, often urgent, and complicated by diverse political pressures. It demands a hetero-geneous investigating group composed of a number of experts and interested parties. Because the group's conclusions can have such an impact on particular companies, unions, and individuals, the composition of the group itself can become a major issue, even before it begins its work.

A 1987 Continental Airlines crash created just such a situation in which political considerations may have affected group composition and optimal functioning. A Continental DC-9 crashed during takeoff at Denver's Stapleton International Airport on November 15, 1987, killing 28 people. The law requires the NTSB to work with the Federal Aviation Administration in its investigation of such accidents, and the NTSB chooses other members of the crash investigation team on the basis of their expertise and specific interest in the factors that might have contributed to the accident. In this case, the NTSB asked for participation from the makers of the plane and the engines, McDonnell Douglas Corporation and Pratt & Whitney Group; from the city and county of Denver; and from groups representing air traffic controllers, airport executives, and flight attendants. But the safety board's refusal to include members of the Air Line Pilots Association in this diverse group drew strong criticism from the pilots.

The NTSB defended its action by saying that the Association no longer represents Continental pilots. (Continental broke its pilots union in 1985 after a bitter two-year strike.) The Pilots Association charged that the NTSB yielded to Continental pressure in excluding the union. The Association pointed out that it represents the vast majority of DC-9 pilots throughout the nation and that the pilot who died in the crash, Frank Zvonek, was an active union member.

The crash team's neglect of the union members' DC-9 expertise may have encouraged Continental to attempt to blame the crash on a peculiar kind of air turbulence induced by large aircraft. While the safety board was considering the turbulence along with ice buildup on the wings, pilot experience, and many other factors that might have contributed to the crash, Continental issued a memo to its pilots to delay take-offs for up to five minutes after large planes had landed nearby. The memo implied that the turbulence—known as "wing-tip vortex"—caused by the landing of a large Boeing 767 before the smaller DC-9 took off might have caused the DC-9 to crash.

Turbulence experts dismissed the idea, an NTSB spokesman said that Continental was "trying to sell" the theory, and an FAA terminal procedures specialist said "The reason for their memo ... could be more political than technical." The whole incident suggests how group functioning can suffer when political pressures override a group's need for expertise and input from a variety of sources.

Case Questions

1. If you were the director of the NTSB, would you change the composition of the investigation team because of the demands of the pilots union? Why or why not?

2. What are the advantages and disadvantages of having such a heterogeneous group probing the crash?

3. What recommendations would you make to the NTSB director regarding the make-up of future crash investigation teams?

Case Sources:

David Ashenfelter, "Crash Probe Omits Pilots Union," *Detroit Free Press*, November 23, 1987, 1; Robert Kowalski, "Continental Jets To Avoid Nearby Wing-Tip Vortex," *The Denver Post*, December 2, 1987, B1; Robert Kowalski, "Officials Doubt Air Turbulence Caused Crash," *The Denver Post*, December 3, 1987, C1.

Case 9.2   A Difficult Task Force

As chair of a task force on in-process materials handling, Jim had scheduled an initial meeting for 10:00 A.M. A month earlier, quality assurance at the large manufacturing company where Jim works had noticed that a significant number of parts were scratched when they arrived at the assembly room. A fact-finding committee (of which Jim was a member) had determined that the problem was caused by rough handling of the parts as they were moved around the plant. The committee's solution was to transport the parts in special divider trays. Representatives of the departments involved in the processing and transportation of the parts—including process engineering, plant transportation, industrial engineering, product design, and quality assurance—had been appointed to a task force responsible for designing the trays. The members, most of whom had been with the company for a decade or more, were chosen for their expertise and familiarity with these parts and their manufacture. All had agreed to work on the project, but they had not been asked what they thought of the fact-finding committee's report.

When the task force members arrived, Jim started the meeting by reviewing the history of the problem and the activities of the fact-finding committee. He stressed that the task force was to come up with a design concept for the special divider trays. He then opened the meeting for comments and suggestions.

Bob, from industrial engineering, spoke first. "In my opinion the solution to the problem is to make sure the workers are more careful in handling the parts, rather than in designing some new contraption to get in the way." Mary, from product design, agreed. She urged the committee to recommend that new handling procedures be written and enforced. Jim interrupted the discussion: "The earlier fact-finding committee already decided, with the approval of top management, that new divider trays will be designed and used." He knew that the earlier committee had considered new handling procedures with better enforcement but had rejected this solution because of the extent of the damage and the very expensive parts involved. He told the task force this and reminded them that the purpose of this committee was to design the new dividers, not to question the fact-finding committee's solution.

The task force members then began discussing the design of the dividers. But the discussion always returned to the issue of handling procedures and enforcement. Finally, George, from plant transportation, spoke up: "I think we ought to do what Mary suggested earlier. It makes no sense to me to design dividers when written procedures will solve the problem." The other members nodded their heads in agreement. Jim again reminded them of the task force's purpose and said a new recommendation would not be well received by top management. Nevertheless, the group insisted that Jim write a memo to the vice president of manufacturing with the recommendation. The meeting adjourned at 10:45 A.M.

Jim started to write the memo, but he knew that it would anger several of his supervisors. He hoped that he would not be held responsible for the actions of the task force, even though he was its chair. He sat wondering what had gone wrong and what he could have done to prevent it.

Case Questions

1. Which characteristics of group behavior discussed in the chapter can be identified in this case?

2. If you were in Jim's position, what would you have done differently?

3. If you were in Jim's position, what would you do now?

Experiential Exercise*

Purpose: This exercise demonstrates the benefits a group can bring to accomplishing a task.

Format: You will be asked to do the same task individually and as part of a group.

Procedure: Part 1—You need a pen or pencil and an 8½ × 11 inch sheet of paper. Working alone, do the following:

    1. Write the letters of the alphabet in a vertical column down the left-hand side of the paper.

    2. Your instructor will randomly select a sentence from any written document and read out loud the first 26 letters in

---

*Source: Adapted from John E. Jones and J. William Pfeiffer, eds., *The 1979 Annual Handbook for Group Facilitators* (San Diego, Calif.: University Associates, 1979), pp. 19–20.

that sentence. Write these letters in a vertical column immediately to the right of the alphabet column. Everyone should
have identical sets of 26 two-letter combinations.

3. Working alone, think of a famous person whose initials
correspond to each pair of letters and write the name next
to the letters, for example, M T   Mark Twain. You will have
ten minutes. Only one name per set is allowed. One point is
awarded for each legitimate name, so the maximum score is
26 points.

4. After time expires, exchange your paper with another member of the class and score each other's work. Disputes about
the legitimacy of names will be settled by the instructor.
Keep your score for use later in the exercise.

Part 2—Your instructor will divide the class into groups of five to ten people
each. All groups should have approximately the same number of members.
Each group should now follow the procedure given in Part 1. Again write the
letters of the alphabet down the left-hand side of a sheet of paper; your
instructor will dictate a new set of letters for the second column. The time
limit and scoring procedure are the same. The only difference is that the
groups will generate the names.

Part 3—Each team should calculate the average individual score of its members on Part 1 and compare it with the team score. Your instructor will put
the average individual score and the team score for each group on the board.

Follow-up Questions

1. Are there differences in the average individual scores and the team
scores? What are the reasons for the differences?

2. Although the team scores in this exercise are usually higher than the
average individual scores, under what conditions might individual averages exceed a group score?

CHAPTER

10

Intergroup Dynamics

Chapter Objectives

After reading this chapter, you should be able to

▶ discuss the importance of the organizational setting and specific group factors in understanding interactions between and among groups in organizations.

▶ describe several factors that make a difference in the way groups interact.

▶ discuss the several types of group interactions that can occur in organizations and explain what makes them different from each other.

▶ explain how managers can do a better job of making group interactions more productive.

etween 1970 and 1972 a leading company in the oil field supplies industry found itself in a troubling predicament. The firm had major backlogs of orders for some of its primary products—twenty-two months in the case of pipe connectors. Thus drilling companies placing orders for the product during the period were told they could not expect delivery for almost two years. Although it may seem desirable to have so much demand for the company's products, the situation had several troubling effects within the company.

Over time, the company's sales representatives had developed very good relationships with drilling company buyers. The buyers and sales representatives socialized as well as worked together and helped each other in ways that went far beyond the normal buyer-seller relationship. This familiarity encouraged the buyers to lobby their sales reps for quicker delivery. The sales reps would then try to arrange better delivery dates for their "special" customers. As the number of these special customers increased, the company was besieged by its own sales force, individually and collectively demanding faster delivery times on every part the company made.

These demands had a domino effect inside the company. Sales demanded that the scheduling group give priority to the parts needed by special customers. Marketing claimed that the long-term survival of the company depended on meeting the demands of all its customers. Production, on the other hand, wanted a stable manufacturing schedule, and industrial engineering asserted that the company could cut costs if production runs were long and uninterrupted. While these groups were debating the issue of long production runs for increased efficiency versus short runs to meet the needs of customers, quality assurance said it wanted production equipment shut down on a rotating basis for preventive maintenance. Incensed, the product manager replied, "We can't shut down any of those machines when we're two years behind in delivery!"

*T*his company was faced with growing internal turmoil, owing primarily to the order backlog. This external event stimulated more intensive interactions among operating and staff groups in the organization. It put more pressure on the interactions among the different work groups as they struggled to do their normal jobs. Increased pressure on intergroup interactions, as typified by this case, can affect group and organizational goal accomplishment.

The foregoing chapter discusses small group dynamics and performance. But the contribution of a group to an organization depends on its interaction with other groups as well as on its own internal productivity. In this chapter we deal with the dynamics of **intergroup behavior,** that is, the ways groups interact with each other. The groups that interact may be formally established work groups, task forces, departments, or even major organizational divisions. We first define intergroup interactions and then present a framework for understanding interactions and their importance to organizational performance. We close with a discussion of strategies for managing intergroup behavior. We use the oil field equipment supplier throughout this chapter as a continuing example of intergroup behavior.

There are many possible relationships among groups in organizations. Interactions may be frequent, regular, and routine, like those between waiters and cooks in a restaurant. These two groups must interact in predictable ways if hungry customers are to get their food in good time. But given the close working relationships between cooks and waiters and the demands for speed and accuracy, the potential for friction between the two groups is quite high. If conflicts arise between waiters and cooks, the result may be lower-quality service to customers and, ultimately, loss of patronage for the restaurant.

On the other hand, some groups, such as bank tellers and the personnel who design new branch banks, may interact very infrequently. In this case the design personnel may occasionally consult with tellers for ideas on branch design, and tellers may contact the design people about rearranging office space or tearing down a wall. For the most part, however, the two groups rarely interact in the daily operation of the bank.

The interactions in these situations and in the opening case differ in many respects. But whether the groups interact regularly (such as the cooks and the waiters) or infrequently (such as the bank tellers and the designers), the interaction between them is crucial to the organization's success and the potential for problems between them always exists. It is management's responsibility to forestall such problems and to help groups work together constructively, and this chapter is about that responsibility.

A MODEL OF INTERGROUP DYNAMICS

The preceding examples show how interactions between groups in organizations can differ a great deal. Figure 10.1 presents a general model that can help us describe several types of group interactions and provide a basis for understanding how a manager can make intergroup interactions more effective.

Our model of intergroup behavior makes three assumptions and has three corresponding parts. First, we assume that there is an organizational need for the groups to interact. Thus, we must understand the organizational setting within which groups interact. Second, we assume that groups that interact are different from each other. Thus, we need to understand the key elements of these differences. Third, we assume that the relationship between the groups has some systematic basis or foundation in the work that needs to be done. Thus, we need to understand the bases of these interactions.

The first assumption of this model encompasses the probability that the work of the organization will be more productive if the groups interact, and may not get done if they do not. Group interactions occur within a specific organizational setting of groups, departments, and divisions. Interactions take place within a system of organizational rules and procedures; history, traditions, and culture; goals and reward systems; and decision-making processes.

After several years in the organization, people and work groups learn the

Figure 10.1 A Summary of the Factors Influencing Intergroup Interactions

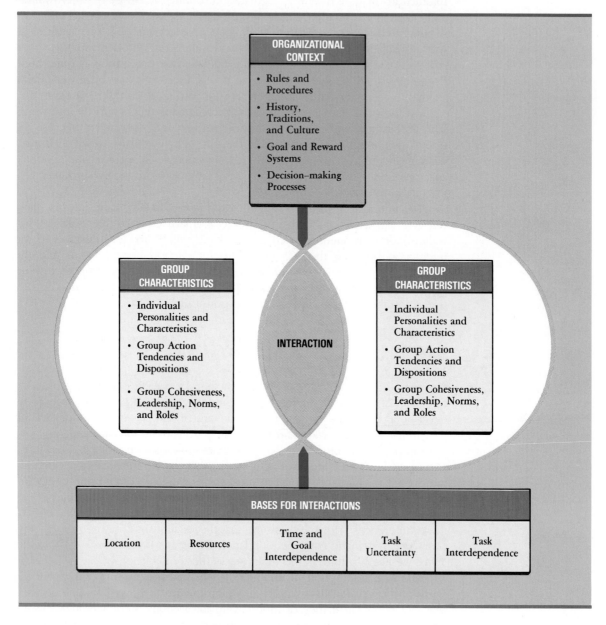

rules and procedures (both written and unwritten) that govern daily business. For example, official company procedures may require that designers get the approval of quality assurance before releasing design drawings to the shop floor. However, over the years the designers may have started to release the drawings without quality assurance approval because of the long delays that may occur. Thus, group interactions can be prescribed by company rules and by informal practices that have developed through many years of tradition. Certain actions may be allowed, whereas others may be absolutely forbidden.[1] In addition, the reward system may be established to reward certain behaviors and not others.[2] All of these factors, which are discussed in more detail in Part IV of the text, may affect the group interactions in the organization.

Group interactions can be especially important to the success of a new venture. Ford Motor Company, for example, attempted to build the Escort as a "world car" by creating a single design that could be produced all over the world. However, the company's design groups did not cooperate very well. The European and American versions of the car shared only one part, a water pump seal.[3] Policies have now been established to require much closer cooperation among design groups. Ford is also working with its unions to develop more cooperative relationships between departments and new work rules that provide ways for departments to interact.[4] In this way the organizational context in which the groups interact is affecting the relationships between groups at Ford.[5]

The second major part of our model emphasizes the uniqueness of interacting groups. At the center of the interaction model is the point where behaviors of the groups come together. Each group brings to the interaction situation a unique set of characteristics that influences its interactions with other groups. The individual personalities and characteristics of the members (discussed in Chapters 3 and 4) are important determinants of the group's aggregate actions. They are also important because a single member or a few members often represent a group in interactions with other groups.[6] The behavior of a group in its interactions with other groups is also influenced by

[1] Richard L. Daft, *Organization Theory and Design* (St. Paul, Minn.: West, 1986).

[2] Daniel Robey, *Designing Organizations: A Macro Perspective* (Homewood, Ill.: Irwin, 1982).

[3] "Now That It's Cruising, Can Ford Keep Its Foot to the Gas?" *Business Week*, February 11, 1985, pp. 48–52.

[4] "Ford's Mr. Turnaround: 'We Have More to Do,'" *Fortune*, March 4, 1985, pp. 83–84.

[5] Deborah L. Gladstone, "Groups in Context: A Model of Task Group Effectiveness," *Administrative Science Quarterly*, December 1984, pp. 499–517.

[6] See Michael N. Chanin and Joy A. Schneer, "A Study of the Relationship Between Jungian Personality Dimensions and Conflict-Handling Behavior," *Human Relations*, October 1984, pp. 863–880, for a study of how individual personality may affect interactions.

group characteristics like cohesiveness, norms, size, and composition, as discussed in Chapter 9.

The third major part of the model focuses on the working relationship between the interacting groups and on the reasons for the interaction. Because these reasons, shown at the bottom of the model, are so important, they are called the *bases* for group interaction and are discussed in more detail in the next section.

FACTORS INFLUENCING INTERGROUP BEHAVIOR

The bases of intergroup interactions configured at the bottom of Figure 10.1 both cause interactions and determine their characteristics: the frequency of interaction, the volume of information exchange between groups, and the type of coordination needed for the groups to interact and function. For example, if two groups greatly depend on each other in performing a task about which there is much uncertainty, they need a lot of information from each other to define and perform the task. Let us discuss each basis for interaction individually.

Task Interdependence

The most powerful basis for interaction among groups in organizations is **task interdependence,** or the degree to which the activities of separate groups force them to depend on each other, thereby requiring more coordination to reach organizational goals. The three types of task interdependence—pooled, sequential, and reciprocal—require increasing levels of group interaction.[7]

POOLED INTERDEPENDENCE   *Pooled interdependence* exists when two or more groups function with relative independence, but their aggregated or combined outputs contribute to the output and profitability of the total organization. This relationship is shown in Figure 10.2, part A. The oil field supply company described in the opening case had two major product lines: rock bits and threaded pipe connectors. The outputs, inputs, and manufacturing processes of each group were separate and distinct from one another. Their contributions to organizational goals were pooled only at the end of the process. Many companies have separate operating divisions that interact only when the operating profits are pooled at the end of the year. In both situations, the groups do not interact except to aggregate their outputs.

SEQUENTIAL INTERDEPENDENCE   When the outputs of one group are the inputs of a second group, but the outputs of the second group are not inputs of the first, *sequential interdependence* exists (see Figure 10.2, part B).

---

[7] James D. Thompson, *Organizations in Action* (New York: McGraw-Hill, 1967), pp. 54–56.

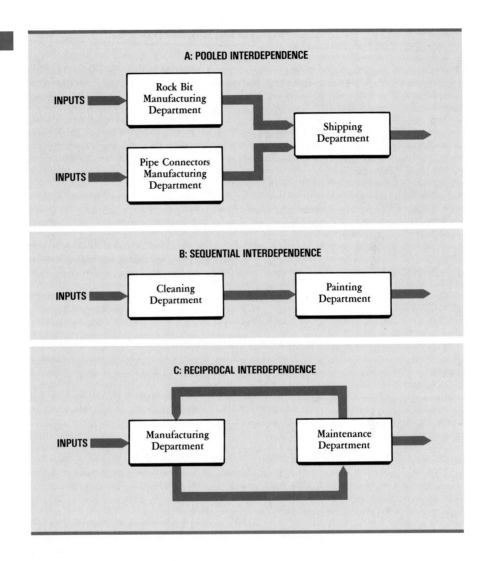

Figure 10.2

Three Types of Task
Interdependencies

The work of the second group is dependent on the first. If the outputs of the first group are interrupted, the outputs of the second group eventually stop as well.

In our oil field supply company, the relationship between the cleaning department and the painting department is an example of sequential interdependence. After the products are assembled and tested, they are sent to the finishing area, where they are cleaned, painted, and boxed for shipment. All parts must be cleaned before painting. Thus, the cleaning group's outputs are the painting group's inputs, but the outputs of the painting group are not the cleaning group's inputs.

RECIPROCAL INTERDEPENDENCE   *Reciprocal interdependence* occurs when the outputs of one group become inputs for another and vice versa, as in Figure 10.2, part C. In such situations groups are highly interdependent. This is the most complex of the three types of interdependence and the most difficult to manage because the groups are constantly interacting. Reciprocal interdependence can be illustrated by the relationships between the manufacturing and maintenance groups in the oil field supply company. These groups both are important to the production of high-quality products and are subject to compressed schedules caused by very high demand. Manufacturing provides inputs to the maintenance group in the form of machines needing preventive maintenance. The output of the maintenance group is machines for the manufacturing group to use in production. Therefore, the two groups are in reciprocal interdependence.

Many interacting groups are embedded within most large organizations. In fact, group interactions may be the foundation for an organization's structure.[8] For a novel way of viewing organizations and group interactions, see *Management in Action.*

Task Uncertainty

Uncertainty is a central problem of complex organizations.[9] **Task uncertainty** arises whenever employees or work groups lack information about what course of action to take or about future events that may affect them, the task, or the organization. Uncertainties may arise from changes in technology, government regulations, competition, supplier conditions, economic conditions, and other factors outside of the group's control.

In many cases, work groups deal with task uncertainties in relative isolation, facing them with little interaction from other groups. Sometimes, however, a work group seeks or is given assistance from other groups to help reduce uncertainties.

Consider an operating department that needs new employees. The task involves advertising the positions, recruiting candidates, screening and selecting the new employees, and arranging for them to be placed on the payroll. The manager knows the duties of the jobs to be filled, but the task also requires being up-to-date on Equal Employment Opportunity (EEO) and Affirmative Action regulations, the current labor market, salary ranges, and perhaps requirements of the company's labor contract and the workings of the internal job-bidding system. For a busy line manager, this task clearly may involve much uncertainty.

Therefore the personnel or human resources department often assists managers of operating departments by providing them with needed information.

---

[8] Clayton P. Alderfer and Ken K. Smith, "Studying Intergroup Relations Embedded in Organizations," *Administrative Science Quarterly,* March 1982, p. 35.

[9] Thompson, *Organizations in Action,* p. 159.

Management in ACTION

A Sporting Look at Business Groups

"Teamwork" and "team players" have become such clichés in the business world that people seldom stop to think about what the concepts really mean. Robert W. Keidel, a senior fellow at the University of Pennsylvania's Wharton Applied Research Center, has thought a lot about the connections between sports and business. In his scholarship and in the training sessions he conducts, he uses analogies between business organizations and football, baseball, and basketball teams. But before business people can make productive use of a sports analogy, Keidel feels they must answer one central question: Which sport are they playing?

As Keidel sees it, America's three major professional sports—baseball, basketball, and football—differ markedly in terms of their group organization and behavior. Baseball is largely an individualistic sport. While some of the game's best moments depend on coordination between two or three players, an individual pitcher or hitter can dominate a game. A baseball manager often makes his most important decisions during the off-season, making trades for the most talented individuals he can find. During the game itself, the manager is limited to hoping individuals will do their best, and replacing them when they do not.

Football, by contrast, is a game of sequences and units: offense, defense, and special teams. Individuals who handle the ball do stand out, but the team wins only if everyone works together with precision. Coaches tend to dominate their teams, planning both the game as a whole and each individual play.

In basketball, one of the coach's main functions is to integrate the players into a team that will function on its own on the court. Individual high-scoring stars often grab headlines in basketball, but teamwork and good passing win championships.

Problems occur when business leaders try to use the wrong model of teamwork for their organizations. A sales force most closely resembles a baseball team—each individual works largely alone and needs to be rewarded for individual efforts. A manager who tries to get a group of salespeople to become the "well-oiled machine" of football jargon will probably end up with frustrated, unmotivated employees.

The football analogy works well, however, for a manufacturing plant in which products move down an assembly line the way a football moves down the field, each step executed smoothly and precisely to prepare for the next. Planning is crucial, and the work unit—welders or machinists, for instance—is likely to be more important than team unity.

Advertising agencies or consulting firms can thrive using a basketball metaphor. The individuals on the team need to work together, thinking spontaneously and playing off each other's ideas. The manager's main job is to create the most productive group interaction.

Business groups can learn a lot from watching successful sports teams, Keidel concludes. But first they need to determine which sport to watch.

Source: Reprinted, by permission of the publisher, from "Baseball, Football, and Basketball: Models for Business" by R. K. Keidel, *Organizational Dynamics*, Winter 1984, © 1984 American Management Association, New York. All rights reserved.

Without this information, a manager might make mistakes that could frustrate the search for qualified employees. The personnel department can make a special effort to integrate its own activities with those of operating departments, such as assigning a special liaison to help department managers in recruiting, interviewing, and selecting new employees. The liaison's role is primarily to enhance communication between the groups. In this case the personnel or human resource department has absorbed some of the manager's uncertainty.[10] In such a situation, the two departments generally interact on a regular basis as long as the need exists.

Time and Goal Interdependence

Most organizations use some type of goals to give the organization direction and to serve as performance targets.[11] Usually initiated at the top level, goals filter down through an organization and are divided into subgoals that become the goals of work groups. In addition, the work of managers and work groups is usually subject to a certain time frame that involves deadlines for completing a project or task. These two factors combine to force interactions among groups in organizations.[12]

For example, in many companies engineers in the research department work on long-term projects, where results might not be applied to products or production processes for several months or years. In contrast, engineers in a production department may be concerned about keeping the machines on the shop floor going to ensure that finished products are shipped on schedule. Although these different time frames are entirely appropriate to the groups' different tasks, they can brew problems if the two groups have to work together. If the production engineers on the shop floor encounter a metallurgical problem in the machining of a piece of steel, they might call the research department for help. The production engineers would expect an immediate solution to the problem so that production could resume. But the research engineers might approach the problem from a scientific point of view and spend hours, days, or even weeks analyzing it and pondering the best possible solution. Thus, while one group of engineers grows frantic for an answer, the other group might come to resent the pressure for a quick and less than ideal "fix."

In this case, the time and goal differences between the two groups are major factors in influencing the interactions between them. Managers responsible

---

[10] Jay R. Galbraith, *Organization Design* (Reading, Mass.: Addison-Wesley, 1977), pp. 152–158.

[11] See Richard H. Hall, *Organizations: Structure and Process,* 3rd ed. (Englewood Cliffs, N.J.: Prentice-Hall, 1982), pp. 278–294, for a more detailed discussion of goals and organizational effectiveness.

[12] Paul R. Lawrence and Jay W. Lorsch, *Organization and Environment* (Homewood, Ill.: Irwin, 1969), pp. 34–39.

for coordinating diverse groups need to be sensitive to such differences and to resolve them so as to promote productive interactions.

Resources

Organizations have material, human, financial, and information resources, and groups must have their proper share of these resources to accomplish their tasks. Naturally, when resources are finite but the demands on groups increase, the groups will interact over the available resources. The potential for interaction increases if the groups use the same or similar resources or if one group can affect the availability of the resources needed by another group. Consider a state government office building where only a certain amount of office space was available when two agencies each hired several new college graduates. Each agency assumed that it could somehow find office space for the new workers by making small adjustments and squeezing other agencies a little. When the new people came on board in June, though, neither agency had been able to come up with the space. Several heated discussions ensued, and interactions between the groups were extremely awkward for several months. Other typical situations in which resources cause group interactions include budget meetings, personnel assignments, and placement of computers and office equipment.

Interactions having to do with resources need not always be hostile. In times of a budget crunch, for instance, several government agencies may work together to help each other with paperwork processing and other activities.

Location

The closer groups are to each other physically, the more chance there is that group members, and thus the groups themselves, will interact with each other. Some interactions based on physical location may be primarily interpersonal in nature, as opposed to formal and work related.[13] They may occur initially because of physical interaction (for example, seeing members of another group in a common office area or in the hall), but over time they may develop into regularly occurring interactions between the groups. On the other hand, groups that are physically separated may find that their interactions are infrequent, as might be the case in a decentralized sales organization with offices distributed around the country. More frequent contact with other groups affects their interactions, as discussed in *A Look at Research*.

The pattern of group interactions can sometimes be changed by altering the arrangement of offices and the location of various departments. The offices

---

[13] See Marvin E. Shaw, *Group Dynamics: The Psychology of Small Group Behavior,* 3rd ed. (New York: McGraw-Hill, 1981), pp. 83–85, for a discussion of physical proximity and group interactions.

A LOOK AT

RESEARCH

Group Identification and Intergroup Contact

How does an individual's identification with a particular group affect that person's perceptions of similar, rival groups? And how does contact between two groups' members affect the groups' perceptions of each other? A 1986 study of nurses in three British hospitals attempted to answer these questions and came up with some surprising results.

The study focused on two groups of nurses, "general" nurses working in medical, surgical, or orthopedic wards, and "specialist" nurses working in intensive care, accident, and emergency departments. The two groups were equally qualified and received equal pay, but the researchers found that both groups thought of the specialist nurses as having higher status.

The researchers hypothesized that, in keeping with social identity theory, nurses who most closely identified themselves with their particular group would see the largest number of differences between their group and the other group. The researchers also expected to find that nurses who had more contact with members of the other group would see less of a gap between the two groups.

The research results supported neither of these hypotheses. Nurses in the two groups did display identification with and loyalty to their own group, as expected. However, nurses with the strongest identification with their own group did not favor their own group and tended to see fewer differences between the groups. The researchers speculated that nurses who identified closely with their group may actually have been indicating a loyalty to nursing as a profession. Someone committed to nursing as a whole would, according to this theory, tend not to stress distinctions between generalists and specialists. The researchers found some support for this theory in the fact that the nurses, when explaining why they identified with their own group, spoke more about the jobs they were doing than about their closeness to the others in their group. Therefore a loyal generalist nurse was really more committed to good health care than to the other generalist nurses.

The researchers were also surprised to find that contact between the two groups did not lead to feelings of trust and closeness between the specialists and generalists. Many theorists have viewed formal and informal contact between rival groups as the surest way to bring the groups together; yet the research showed that results of such contact were uneven. The overall conclusion of this research seems to be that group loyalty and differentiation are more complex matters than some theories have assumed.

Source: Gillian Oaker and Rupert Brown, "Intergroup Relations in a Hospital Setting: A Further Test of Social Identity Theory," *Human Relations*, Volume 39, Number 8, 1986, 767–778.

of work groups can be moved nearer to each other to promote helpful interactions. Conversely, it may be appropriate to separate groups who squabble, in order to decrease the frequency of interactions between the groups, as long as they are not too dependent on each other.

TYPES OF GROUP INTERACTIONS

The purpose of this section is to help you understand the most common of the many types of interactions that occur in organizations. Some interactions are everyday occurrences and may be treated very casually by employees. Others may occur infrequently but routinely, and may be special occasions accompanied with great fanfare. Some types of interactions are associated with antagonistic behaviors and may result in open conflict. (Conflict is a special type of interaction between people or groups and is discussed in more detail in Chapter 12.) The most common types of interactions are avoidance, accommodation, competition, collaboration, and compromise.[14]

Any time that groups interact, it is really the people in the groups who are interacting. Still, in most cases the people are acting as representatives of the groups to which they belong. In effect, they work together representing their group as they strive to do their part in helping the group achieve its goals. Thus, the five types of interactions discussed here can be analyzed in terms of relationships between the goals of the interacting groups.

Interactions can be differentiated according to the importance of the interaction to the attainment of each group's goals and the degree of compatibility between the groups' goals, as shown in Figure 10.3. The importance of the interaction to the goal attainment of each of the interacting groups ranges from very high to very low. The degree of goal *compatibility* is the extent to which the goals of the groups can be achieved simultaneously. In other words, the goals of interacting groups are compatible if one group can accomplish its goals without preventing the other group from accomplishing its goals. The goals of interacting groups are incompatible if one group's accomplishment of its goals prohibits the other group from accomplishing its goals. The degree of goal compatibility can vary from very incompatible to very compatible. At the midpoint of each continuum, goals are neither very important nor very unimportant and neither very incompatible nor very compatible.

Avoidance

Avoidance happens when an interaction is not very important to either group's goals and the groups' goals are incompatible, as in the bottom left-hand corner of Figure 10.3. Because the groups are not striving toward compatible goals and the issues in question do not seem to be important, the groups just try to avoid interacting with one another. One state agency may simply ignore another agency's requests for information. The requesting agency may then practice its own form of avoidance by not following up on the requests.

---

[14] Kenneth Thomas, "Conflict and Conflict Management," in Marvin Dunnette, ed., *Handbook of Industrial and Organizational Psychology* (New York: Rand McNally, 1976), pp. 889–935.

Figure 10.3

Five Types of Group
Interactions as a
Function of Goal
Importance and the
Degree of Goal
Compatibility

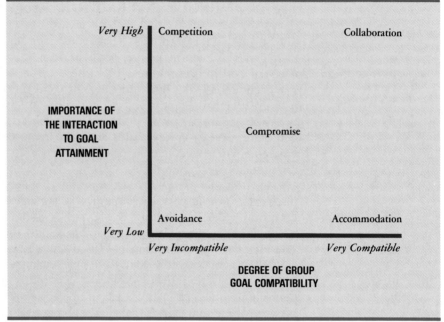

Source: Adapted from Kenneth Thomas, "Conflict and Conflict Management," in
Marvin Dunnette, ed., *Handbook of Industrial and Organizational Psychology*
(New York: Rand McNally, 1976), pp. 889–935. Reprinted by permission.

Accommodation

Accommodation is when the two groups' goals are compatible but the
interactions are not considered to be very important to overall goal attainment,
as in the bottom right-hand corner of Figure 10.3. Interactions of this type may
involve discussions that center on how the two groups can accomplish their
interdependent tasks with the least expenditure of time and effort. Accommodation occurs because the groups agree on goals but do not feel the issues
creating the interaction are extremely important. This type of interaction tends
to be very friendly.[15]

Departments in a manufacturing company often engage in accommodation.
In a large computer manufacturing firm, the maintenance department and the
production department needed to work out a procedure for reporting machine
and equipment malfunctions. Production employees and supervisors felt that
anyone noticing a need for repairs should be able to call the maintenance
group. Maintenance, however, wanted production supervisors to investigate
each situation first and place the calls personally. To the production department

[15] Robert R. Blake, Herbert A. Shepard, and Jane S. Mouton, *Managing Intergroup
Conflict in Industry* (Houston, Tex.: Gulf, 1964).

the issue was not extremely important, and the two groups' goals seemed compatible. It therefore accommodated the maintenance group by agreeing that supervisors would investigate and report maintenance needs.

Competition

Competition occurs when the goals of interacting groups are incompatible and the interactions are important to the goal attainment of each group, as in the top left-hand corner of Figure 10.3. If both groups are striving for a goal, such that only one group can reach its goal, the groups may be in competition. In one freight warehouse and storage firm, the first, second, and third shifts each sought the weekly productivity record, each trying to post the highest productivity. Workers on the winning shift received recognition in the company newspaper. Since the issue was important to each group and the interests of the groups were incompatible, the result was competition.

Bear in mind, though, that although this was a situation in which only one shift could win and the other two shifts would lose, all groups realized some gain from the competition. The competition encouraged each shift to produce more per week, which increased the company's output and eventually improved its overall welfare (and thus the welfare of each group). Also, the company and the groups benefited from the competition because it fostered innovative and creative work methods, which further boosted productivity.

Collaboration

Collaboration occurs when the interaction is very important to group goal attainment and the goals of the groups are compatible, as in the top right-hand corner of Figure 10.3. At first glance this may seem to be a simple interaction in which groups participate jointly in activities to accomplish goals after agreeing on the goals and their importance. In many situations, however, it is no easy matter to agree on goals, their importance, and especially, the means for achieving them. In a collaborative interaction, group goals may not be the same, but are compatible. Groups may initially have difficulty working out the ways that both can achieve their goals. However, because the interactions are important to goal attainment, the groups are willing to continue to try to work together to achieve the goals. Collaborative relationships can lead to new and innovative ideas and solutions to any differences between the groups.[16]

At the oil field supplies company, suppose the sales, production, industrial engineering, and quality assurance groups all recognized the importance of the production issue and were genuinely concerned about each other's interests. In effect, they realized that they all had the same corporate, very compatible goals and that their interactions were very important to reaching those goals.

---

[16] Andrew S. Grove, "How to Make Confrontation Work for You," *Fortune*, July 23, 1984, pp. 73–75.

Thus, the representatives of all the groups might have met and engaged in problem-solving activities, discussing and questioning the issues and concerns of each department. The result would have been a set of production priorities that balanced the high output and equipment maintenance necessary for high-quality production. By collaborating, the groups would have developed solutions that might not have been identified through any other form of interaction.

Compromise

The final type of intergroup interaction is **compromise**, which occurs when the interactions are of moderate importance to goal attainment and goals are neither completely compatible nor incompatible. In a compromise situation, groups interact with other groups striving to achieve goals, but the groups may not aggressively pursue goal attainment in either a competitive or a collaborative manner, because the interactions are not that important to goal attainment. On the other hand, they may not avoid each other or be accommodating either, because the interactions are somewhat important. Quite often each group gives up something, but because the interactions are only moderately important, people do not become upset over what they have given up.

Contract negotiations between union and management are an example of compromise. Each side brings to the bargaining table numerous issues of varying importance. Through rounds of offers and counteroffers, the two sides give and take on the issues. Typically, each side "gives" most on issues of little importance to it so that it can "take" on the important issues; workers may thus give in on their demands for a better vacation benefit plan in exchange for an increase in wages. See *International Perspective* for an example of how international compromises are reached.

To sum up, then, if the goals of two groups are very compatible, the groups may engage in mutually supportive interactions, that is, collaboration or accommodation. If the goals of the groups are very incompatible, each group may be expected to foster its own success at the expense of others, such as in competition or avoidance.

MANAGING INTERGROUP BEHAVIOR IN ORGANIZATIONS

Strategies for dealing with interactions among groups must be carefully chosen, following thorough examination and analysis of the groups, their goals, their unique characteristics, and the organizational setting in which the interactions occur. Managers can use a variety of strategies to increase the efficiency of intergroup interactions. Five such choices are goal-based strategies, location-based strategies, resource-based strategies, people and group strategies, and organization-based strategies. These strategies are based on the model of intergroup behavior presented in Figure 10.1. You may want to review the model before proceeding.

International
Perspective

International Automakers and Their Unions

Both worker groups and management groups around the world are finding themselves increasingly affected by what similar groups are doing in other countries. Recent negotiations between top automakers and their unions have highlighted the complex intergroup interactions and patterns that will likely become more prevalent as more companies and industries become international.

Negotiations between Canadian, American, and British unions and automakers have reflected a curious mixture of solidarity and mistrust. The general aim of the companies, pressed by Japanese competition and impressed by Japanese techniques, is to cut their workforces, raise productivity, and adopt Japanese management practices such as quality circles and work groups. Unions, on the other hand, have been negotiating largely for job security.

Yet despite the similarities in their overall goals, neither the managements nor the unions of the different automakers have been able to present a united front free of competitiveness and mistrust. In both the United States and Canada, unions like to make an agreement with one company first, then pressure the other companies to sign similar contracts. In the United States, the United Auto Workers first signed with Ford, then asked General Motors to approve similar terms. But GM executives balked, worrying that because Ford is already a leaner company with higher productivity per worker, a contract that preserved the status quo at healthy Ford would be dangerous for ailing GM. On the Canadian side of the border, unions won pension increases from Chrysler's Canadian unit, then demanded similar increases from Ford of Canada.

Unions, too, can feel pressure from the agreements signed by their colleagues in other companies and other countries. The United Auto Workers negotiated a contract requiring Ford to pay workers if it shifted work to non-UAW plants. But what looked good to the UAW worried the Canadian Auto Workers union, which feared that the new contract clause would force Ford to close Canadian plants rather than American ones.

In Britain, meanwhile, both Ford and GM are pressuring their unions to accept new work guidelines similar to those followed by employees at the new Nissan plant in northeast England. Nissan's workers are largely non-union, young, and flexible; they are more productive than Ford's and GM's workforces and more willing to change jobs and join in workplace reorganization and quality circles. Such proposals to institute Japanese-style workplace changes have the potential to pit one plant against another.

Each side, therefore, is playing the game of divide and conquer with the other. Yet at the moment in the auto industry, neither side can win, in part because intragroup rivalries sometimes become as fierce as those between groups.

Sources: Gary Lamphier, "Ford of Canada Reaches Tentative Pact With Union Similar to Chrysler Contract," *The Wall Street Journal*, October 2, 1987, 5; Gary Lamphier, "Ford Canada Offers Workers 3-Year Contract," *The Wall Street Journal*, September 30, 1987, 16; Richard A. Melcher, "What's Throwing A Wrench Into Britain's Assembly Lines," *Business Week*, February 29, 1988, 41; Jacob M. Schlesinger, "GM Looks for UAW-Contract Loopholes," *The Wall Street Journal*, October 2, 1987, 5.

Goal-Based Strategies

The five types of interactions discussed in the previous section (avoidance, accommodation, competition, collaboration, and compromise) may be viewed as goal-based strategies to manage group interactions.[17] Remember that the five types of interactions are based on the compatibility of the groups' goals and the importance of the interaction to achieving those goals.

In a situation in which a manager believes interactions could be improved, the manager should analyze the goals of the groups. For example, when two groups are not working well together, they may be experiencing goal displacement. **Goal displacement** occurs when groups overemphasize their own goals at the expense of the organization's. When two or more groups do this, their activities may interfere with one another.

The solution to goal displacement is straightforward: the groups need to be redirected toward the overall organizational goals. A **superordinate goal** is usually a goal of the overall organization and is more important to the well-being of the organization and its members than the more specific goals of interacting groups. It can serve as a guide for integrating the interacting groups by redirecting their activities.

In most organizational situations, however, the problems of interacting groups are not obvious because of the complexity of the circumstances. Groups and their leaders may be too close to the situation, often believing that their progress toward their own goals furthers the goals of the organization. In fact, as Figure 10.4 shows, groups generally do pursue organizational goals but may get sidetracked and work at cross-purposes with other groups. At this point the manager can redirect the efforts of the groups by reminding them of a superordinate goal that both are trying to accomplish for the organization. In effect, the manager reminds the groups of the inherent compatibility of their goals and tries to foster collaborative interaction between them. The use of a superordinate goal to manage interactions can be useful when the groups' tasks are interdependent, as long as the groups really do view the goal as superordinate—as important to themselves and to the organization.

In a medium-sized manufacturer of automobile parts, the quality assurance group was guilty of goal displacement. Aspiring to be the best QA department in the industry, it designed unnecessarily elaborate test equipment, established inspection requirements that were very severe, and had significant cost overruns. Eventually the group was reminded that the organization's goal was to make a profit by producing quality products at reasonable prices, and it had to work with manufacturing for the good of the organization, not the glory of the QA department.

Other strategies for managing interactions may follow from an analysis of the situation. For example, if the interacting groups' goals are incompatible

---

[17] Blake, Shepard, and Mouton, *Managing Intergroup Conflict in Industry.*

Figure 10.4   Goal Displacement and Superordinate Goals

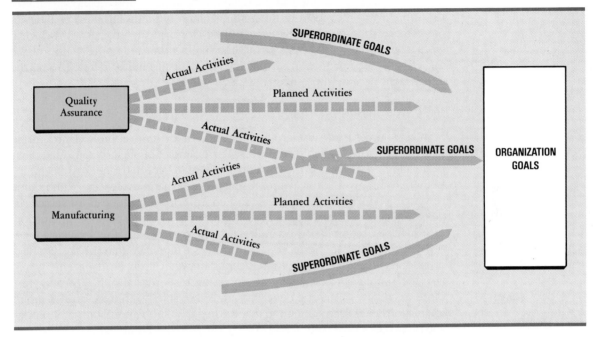

and affected little by the interaction, the manager may suggest that the groups avoid each other. Or if the goals are compatible but affected little by the interaction, the manager may suggest that one group accommodate the other's wishes. Thus, the five types of interactions can be used to manage interactions between groups.

Location-Based Strategies

Physical location is a very simple basis of interaction among groups in organizations. Since groups located near each other tend to interact more than groups that are far apart, the most basic strategy for managing interactions is to examine and consider altering this factor. If the basis for group interaction is largely physical proximity, then the interactions may decrease if the distance between the groups is increased, but the quality of the interactions or the degree of cooperation between the groups may also change. On the other hand, if the physical location of groups is not important to their interactions, altering it may have unexpected effects on the interactions. The groups may find other ways to communicate, such as by telephone or computer hookup, that may be less efficient and more expensive.

Organizations rarely rearrange their employees solely to reduce interactions among certain groups. However, they often shift groups to improve interactions and coordination. In the oil field supply company, the quality assurance department was moved from the administration building into new facilities in the center of the plant so that it would be closer to the groups with which it worked on a daily basis. As a result, the interactions and coordination of the QA efforts with production and maintenance departments increased and the department became more effective.

Resource-Based Strategies

Scarce resources may cause group interactions to be more complex by requiring that groups share available resources. For example, budgetary constraints may make it impossible for each sales representative to have his or her own secretary. But it may be possible for five representatives to share a secretary. With limited resources, then, the staff members must coordinate their requests for secretarial help. Having to coordinate their requests may require direct personal interaction, or it may be accomplished by indirect interaction through the secretary.

Management can therefore use resources to regulate interactions. If a lack of resources causes complex interactions between groups, management may take the simple but costly step of increasing resources and, in this case, hire more secretaries. Management may thus be able to reduce the complex interactions over secretarial time that cause delays in the preparation of reports and proposals. Conversely, it is possible to increase the complexity of interactions by making organizational resources more scarce (although management seldom seeks this effect deliberately).

People and Group Strategies

Individual and group characteristics are a major influence on group interaction in our model. People strategies include attempts to train individuals in human relations, organizational practices, or group dynamics. The expectation is that individual behavior in the group interactions will be different after the training.[18] Organizations often hire consultants to develop a training program to teach people how to deal with group interactions. Other types of strategies include techniques intended to alter people's values and attitudes, thus affecting the ways they deal with individuals in other work groups. (Chapter 23 discusses training programs.)

The preceding chapter explained group performance in terms of such factors as cohesiveness, size, composition, and norms. These group characteristics, as well as the group's leadership, combine to determine how the group interacts with other groups; they can make a group very antagonistic or very

---

[18] Pamela S. Shockley-Zalabak, "Current Conflict Management Training: An Examination of Practices in Ten Large American Corporations," *Group & Organizational Studies,* December 1984, pp. 491–508.

congenial toward other groups. "Groupthink" (also discussed in Chapters 9 and 17), a mode of thinking in which striving for unanimity replaces critical evaluation of alternatives, can develop in a highly cohesive group that is insulated from expert opinions and whose leader expresses his or her preferred decision. One of the symptoms of groupthink is a stereotypical view of other groups as stupid, slow, or evil, which naturally affects the interactions with other groups.[19] Therefore, one strategy for managing a group's interactions with other groups is to properly manage the internal dynamics of the group such that interactions with other groups are more favorable.

Organization-Based Strategies

There are five organization-based strategies for managing group interactions: linking roles, rules and procedures, task forces, member exchange, and decoupling. Figure 10.5 shows these strategies in order of complexity. The simplest strategy is to create a new position or department that serves a linking role; the most complicated mechanism is the decoupling of interdependent activities.

Linking roles are established in appropriate positions in the organizational hierarchy.[20] A **linking role** is a position for a person or a group that serves to coordinate the activities of two or more organizational groups. A neutral third party may serve as a bridge between interacting groups.[21] More formally established positions or groups are generally referred to as integrating mechanisms because they bring together groups that have become extremely specialized or narrow in their focus.[22] If the interactions among some groups are especially complex or important, management may create a new position to serve as a focal point for the interactions, mediating interactions, settling disputes, and resolving conflict. A simple linking role is the shared supervisor, as shown in Figure 10.6.

A more sophisticated device is the integrating department. Complex interactions may demand a position or department wholly devoted to managing the integration of work groups (see Figure 10.7). This position or department may carry such titles as project management or product management. The role of this linking group is to increase information flow, coordinate the activities of several departments that relate to a product or project, provide interacting groups with better functional understanding of each other, and facilitate intergroup relations and decision making. In many multiproduct companies, a

---

[19] See Irving L. Janis, *Groupthink,* 2nd ed. (Boston: Houghton Mifflin, 1982), for more discussion of the symptoms of groupthink.

[20] Rolf P. Lynton, "Linking an Innovative Subsystem into the System," *Administrative Science Quarterly,* September 1969, pp. 398–416.

[21] Robert R. Blake and Jane S. Mouton, "Overcoming Group Warfare," *Harvard Business Review,* November–December 1984, pp. 98–108.

[22] Lawrence and Lorsch, *Organization and Environment,* pp. 58–62.

Figure 10.5

Organization-Based Strategies for Managing Intergroup Interactions

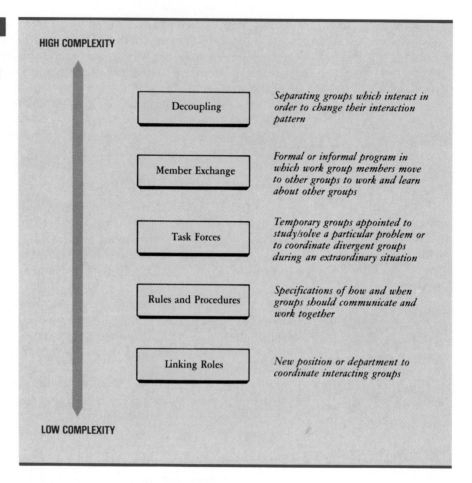

HIGH COMPLEXITY

| Decoupling | Separating groups which interact in order to change their interaction pattern |

| Member Exchange | Formal or informal program in which work group members move to other groups to work and learn about other groups |

| Task Forces | Temporary groups appointed to study/solve a particular problem or to coordinate divergent groups during an extraordinary situation |

| Rules and Procedures | Specifications of how and when groups should communicate and work together |

| Linking Roles | New position or department to coordinate interacting groups |

LOW COMPLEXITY

product manager's office coordinates all intergroup activities involved in the production of the company's various products. One person or a small group in the product manager's office is assigned to each product type. The responsible person or group is expected to know the details of every order for that product type and to manage the interactions among the groups in the plant that deal with that particular product line.

Another organizational method for managing group interactions is to establish rules and procedures governing how groups are to deal with each other in certain situations. Groups may be required to interact in very specific ways; one work group may have to notify another when a certain point is reached in a process, or the drafting group may have to have all production drawings approved by quality assurance. Rules may force groups to interact or limit their interaction to prescribed situations. However, where interactions are very dynamic or where there is a high degree of task uncertainty, rules and procedures may not be effective. Returning to the product manager's office, we

Figure 10.6

A Simple Organization-
Based Strategy: A
Shared Supervisor to
Integrate Interactions
Between Work Groups

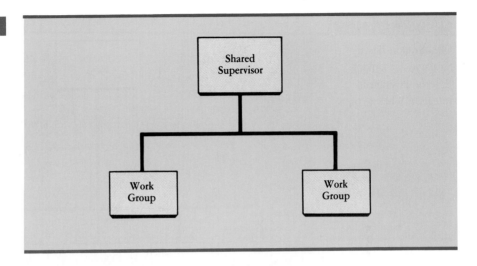

might find that the office created a rule to cover repetitive situations and solutions. For instance, for one manufacturing process that was experiencing many problems, the product manager's office authorized the quality assurance group to shut down an operation whenever it discovered a manufacturing problem that might affect the field serviceability of certain high-visibility products. The only condition was that the product manager's office had to be notified immediately.

A less permanent way of managing intergroup interactions is to create task forces to handle short-term issues. A task force may be formed to study a particular situation or to act as arbitrator or coordinator of group interaction during a particularly busy period or while a permanent solution to an intergroup problem is being studied. A task force is generally appointed by a manager higher in the organizational hierarchy than the members of the interacting groups.

St. Luke's Hospital in Phoenix, Arizona recently expanded by adding a new wing of surgical suites and four hundred patient rooms onto its existing building. The expansion required blocking off its main entrance and tearing up its existing parking lot, thus interrupting the normal flow of traffic into and out of the hospital. To minimize disturbance of normal hospital operations, the hospital administrator appointed a task force to coordinate the necessary adjustments. The task force, headed up by the assistant administrator, was made up of one middle-level manager from each affected group in the hospital—nursing, maintenance, food services, clinic, emergency room, and others. The task force worked with the contractor and the various internal departments during each successive phase of construction to control the construction work's impact on hospital operations. Like most task forces, the group disbanded after the new wing was finished.

Figure 10.7

Organization-Based
Strategies: A Linking
Role or Position to
Integrate Work Groups

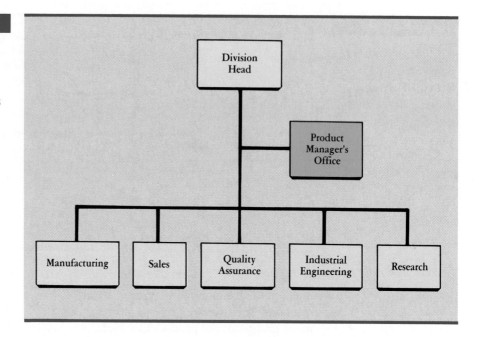

A more elaborate strategy is to have interacting groups exchange members. Member exchange can be a highly formal rotation program[23] or a temporary transfer of an employee from one group to another. An exchange program increases information flow and promotes better understanding among groups. By working in another group, employees may better appreciate the types of problems other groups face in pursuing organizational goals. Many companies have an informal exchange program in which staff project engineers move to positions in other groups. In one typical case, an engineer in the production engineering group went over to the quality assurance department. The move was a lateral one, with the engineer retaining the same title, Project Engineer, and getting a small raise. As a result of the transfer, coordination and communication between the two departments increased dramatically. The engineer soon understood the concerns of both departments and knew whom to contact on every issue, thus helping the two groups to interact more smoothly and productively.

The final organizational mechanism for managing intergroup interactions is decoupling.[24] **Decoupling** means that two groups whose tasks require that

---

[23] Eric H. Nellsen, "Understanding and Managing Intergroup Conflict," in Jay W. Lorsch and Paul R. Lawrence, eds., *Managing Group and Intergroup Relations,* (Homewood, Ill.: Irwin, 1972), pp. 329–343.

[24] Jeffrey Pfeffer, *Organizations and Organization Theory,* (Boston: Pitman, 1982), pp. 244–245.

they interact are functionally separated in some way. Decoupling may be needed when two groups have difficulty interacting positively. Going back to the oil field supplier, for example, the drilling machine group worked on most parts immediately following the milling operation. Since the outputs of the milling group were the inputs to the drilling group, the two groups were sequentially interdependent. Late delivery of parts by the milling group disrupted the drilling group's operations. So one time when the milling group experienced a rash of machine failures, its interactions with the drilling group became less than congenial. The solution to the hostile interactions was to increase the work-in-process inventory between the two groups, thus decoupling them. Slowdowns in the milling group then had little or no effect on the drilling group.

SUMMARY OF KEY POINTS

A model of intergroup behavior assumes that group interactions reflect certain needs for interaction, that they occur within a specific organizational setting, and that they occur between unique groups. The five bases of intergroup interactions determine the characteristics of the interactions, including frequency, the volume of information exchanged, and the type of interaction.

Interactions among work groups involve some of the most complex relationships in organizations. They are based on five factors: task interdependence, task uncertainty, time and goal interdependence, resources, and location. Being near each other naturally increases groups' opportunities for interactions. If groups use the same or similar resources, or if one group can affect the availability of the resources needed by another group, the potential for frequent interactions increases. The nature of the tasks groups perform further affects the interactions among them through time and goal orientation, the uncertainties of the task, and group interdependencies.

Five types of group interactions can occur: avoidance, accommodation, competition, collaboration, and compromise. The types of interactions are determined by the compatibility of goals and the importance of the interaction to group goal attainment.

Strategies for dealing with interactions among groups must be carefully chosen, following thorough examination and analysis of the groups, their goals, their unique characteristics, and the organizational setting in which the interactions occur. A lot of strategies have been developed for managing group interactions in organizations. They include goal-based strategies, location-based strategies, resource-based strategies, people and group strategies, and organization-based strategies. Goal-based strategies include those that might lead to competition, collaboration, compromise, accommodation, or avoidance. Location-based strategies use the physical location or the arrangement of desks, offices, or departments either to reduce or to promote group interactions. Resource-based strategies alter resource allocation either to reduce or to force more resource sharing among groups. People and group strategies focus on the characteristics of the people and the dynamics of the interacting groups. Organization-based strategies range from the creation of simple linking roles and groups to the very complex decoupling of tasks.

DISCUSSION QUESTIONS

1. Some individuals have asserted that people, not groups, interact and that interpersonal interactions, not group interactions, should therefore be the focus of study for group dynamics. Do you agree or disagree with this point of view? Why?

2. List four different groups to which you belong that have recently been involved in interactions with another group or groups. Describe the interactions in terms of the five bases of intergroup behavior discussed in the chapter.

3. If any of the interacting groups you discussed in question 2 are related by task interdependence, discuss which type of interdependence exists—pooled, sequential, or reciprocal.

4. How do the group performance factors of cohesiveness, group norms, composition, and leadership affect the interactions between the groups you discussed in question 2?

5. Each of the groups you discussed in question 2 probably has different goals. List each group and give a brief statement describing each group's goals. Compare these goals to the goals of the groups with which each interacts. Are the goals compatible? How important are the goals in terms of the interactions? Which of the five types of interactions are represented by the groups to which you belong?

6. The five strategies for managing intergroup interactions differ in the situations in which they may be appropriate as well as in the amount of money, time, and effort required to implement them. How might each of these be applied in the interactions discussed in the previous questions?

7. It would be a lot simpler if there were one strategy for managing intergroup interactions. Why isn't there such an all-encompassing strategy?

Case 10.1   When Workers Take Over

In 1985 the 225 employees of Seymour Specialty Wire Company bought the factory for $10 million from National Distillers & Chemical Corporation and began what may be a unique experiment in American business. Workers own stock in at least 8,000 American companies, and they are the majority stockholders in about 1,500 of those. Full control is exercised by employees in just 200 companies. Yet in most employee-owned companies, a majority of the board members is still appointed by banks and outsiders. Seymour Specialty Wire may be the only company in the country with a board of directors controlled by its workers. The workers elect five of the board's nine members.

This unusual situation is not resulting in the chaos of workers trying to make management decisions, as some had feared, nor does the board split 5–4 on every vote. Instead, worker representatives are learning how to compromise when group loyalties come into conflict, and the workers themselves are having to rethink their traditional adversarial relationship with management.

As has been the case on other corporate boards, employee representatives on the Seymour board have shied away from trying to take over managerial functions and control. Directors are required, by law, to represent all shareholders equally, so workers on the board who had previously thought in terms of "What's best for the workers?" have begun asking "What's best for the company?" They have realized that the company still needed professional management, and that some decisions they as board members made for the good of the company would not be popular with their fellow employees.

The learning has been slower on the factory floor, where workers have trouble thinking of managers and directors as anything but "the enemy," even though some of those directors are now their friends. Many of the workers howled when the board voted a 40 percent pay increase for the former plant manager who is now the company's president. One of the worker-directors protested that the president had had much more responsibility as an independent manager, but the board stuck to its decision. Equally unpopular was the board's hiring of an outside consultant to advise the company on production methods. Workers worried that the consultant would conduct time studies and cut jobs and incentives. The board argued that its aim was simply to improve quality, cut costs, and "put more money in the workers' pockets."*

Worker-owners generally tend to be conservative in their management outlook, because when they make decisions about the company, they are making decisions about their own money. It has taken a while for Seymour's workers to realize this fact, to understand that, as the company's president put it, management and workers were "negotiating with ourselves."**

Both groups—management and workers—have had to change their attitudes at Seymour. Managers listen more, while workers pay more attention to management decisions and voice their opinions more often. It will probably take years for the two groups to forget the historically adversarial nature of their relationship. Having the head of the local union sit on the board of directors certainly has helped at Seymour. And so have the company's wage hikes, bonuses, and debt reduction. At least so far, the experiment in overcoming traditional group boundaries seems to be working.

* Hoerr, "Blue Collars in the Boardroom," p. 126.
** Daniel, "What It Takes To Succeed," p. 48.

Case Questions

1. What group pressures and loyalties are likely to influence the decisions of a worker-owner on the board of directors?

2. Would a normal (not worker-owned) company benefit from workers on its board?

Case Sources

Missy Daniel, "What It Takes to Succeed," *U.S. News & World Report*, June 8, 1987, 48; Clemens P. Work, "When Workers Get in the Takeover Game," *U.S. News & World Report*, June 8, 1987, 47; John Hoerr, "Blue Collars in the Boardroom: Putting Business First," *Business Week*, December 14, 1987, 126–128.

Case 10.2

Seeing Where the Other Half Works

Shaun Somers was a graduate student in history at Crozet State University. Like most history graduate students at Crozet, Somers was given a teaching assistantship to help him pay his tuition. For $800 a semester, Shaun and Professor Menster's other t.a.'s attended all of Professor Menster's lectures on Mondays and Wednesdays. Then on Fridays each t.a. led a discussion section. Besides preparing the topics for discussion, the t.a.'s were expected to help the students in their sections write their papers and to grade both papers and exams. So along with their $800, the teaching assistants were given offices on the third floor of the history building.

Everyone who had an office on the third floor called it the ghetto; three or four t.a.'s shared small offices, and the big ones were partitioned into half a dozen small cubicles. Since the building had no elevators, everyone had to walk the three flights up, arriving at the top out of breath, to be greeted by the buckets perpetually lined up on the landing to catch leaks from the roof above.

Conversations between t.a.'s in the ghetto tended to begin with complaints about the offices and then move on to how boring the professors were, how insensitive the administration was, how little anyone in the department did to make the graduate students feel welcome. The third floor group was a tight little society, the members of which were happy with each other but bitter and jealous of everyone else in the building. "Us" was everyone on the third floor; "them" was anyone on the floors below. "They" all had more power, more respect, more pay, and more space than "we" had.

At the start of his second year, Somers received a surprise in his mailbox—he had been moved down to the first floor to share an office with a new assistant professor. Complaints about the overcrowding in "the ghetto" had apparently reached the fire marshall, who had put a cap on the number of people the department could cram into the third floor offices.

Somers's first meeting with his new officemate was awkward. He felt nervous and defensive, sure that this new professor would resent having to share an office. He was ready to say, "Yeah, I'm a graduate student, what of it?" But his officemate, Bill Peters, actually seemed glad to have Somers around. "You can show me the ropes," he said when they first met.

Somers did not use his new office much for the first few weeks of the semester, preferring to visit his friends on the third floor. But gradually he came to like Peters, and to get a new perspective on the department through talking to him. He had never realized how small assistant professors' salaries were, or how much pressure they were under to do everything right—teach, publish, spend hours on committee work. Through Peters, Somers met other new assistant professors and began going out to lunch with them. Through their eyes, Somers began to see the life of a graduate student as relatively carefree. They were not making any money, but they also had relatively few responsibilities and did not have to worry about real jobs until they graduated.

Because of their friendship, Peters and Somers began to draw together two groups that had never paid any attention to each others' existence. New junior faculty members went to graduate student parties and then returned the invitation. The groups found they had much in common, especially the feeling of being at the bottom of a very heavy hierarchy and of getting no respect from anyone. By the end of the year, the ghetto was still the ghetto, but it was no longer "the only place in the building a faculty member has never seen." The chair of the department was so pleased with the positive interactions between graduate students and junior faculty that he considered moving Somers into his own office the following semester, to see if senior faculty, too, could be brought into the act.

Case Questions

1. What factors would be likely to draw graduate students and new professors together? What factors would keep them apart?

2. Would the department chair be wise to mix graduate students and junior and senior faculty members in future office assignments?

3. How might the lessons learned about graduate students and new professors be applied to the situation where a new worker joins a company and finds similar barriers to interaction? How does the location of the new person's office affect her or his assimilation into the normal work activities?

Experiential Exercise

Purpose: This exercise will help you recognize the complexities of intergroup dynamics.

Format: Your objective in this exercise is to earn as much money as possible. There will be eight decision situations, or rounds. Your group will earn positive and negative points based on your decisions in each round. Each point is worth a $100,000 profit or loss.

Procedures: The class will be divided into four teams of approximately equal size. Your instructor will provide each team with a red card, a blue card, and an envelope. In each round your team will have three minutes to choose either red or blue. Indicate your decision by placing the appropriate card in the envelope and handing it to the instructor.

When everyone is ready, the instructor will direct the teams to begin the three-minute deliberation period for the first decision. At the end of the period, the instructor will announce each team's decision and record it on the Tally Sheet. Points are assigned according to the Payoff Table, which follows. The instructor will then announce the beginning of the next three-minute deliberation period and return the cards and envelopes to the teams.

At three different times during the exercise, designated representatives of the teams will have an opportunity to meet for three minutes. The meetings of representatives should take place just outside the classroom. The representatives may discuss anything they wish at the meetings. During the meetings, the representatives may talk only among themselves. There should be no communication between teams other than during the meetings of the representatives. Note that point values are greater for rounds preceded by the meetings.

After the eight rounds, the profits and losses of each team will be totaled and displayed. Positive points are profits, and negative points are losses.

Tally Sheet

Round	Choices				Round Points				Cumulative Points			
	1	2	3	4	1	2	3	4	1	2	3	4
1												
2												
3*												
4												
5												
6**												
7												
8***												

*Representatives meet for three minutes before team decisions for third round. Point values are multiplied by 2 for this round.
**Representatives meet for three minutes before team decisions for the sixth round. All point values are multiplied by 3 for this round.
***Representatives meet for three minutes before team decisions for the last round. All points are multiplied by 4 for this round.

Payoff Table

In each round, the point payoffs for each team are as follows:

4 Blue, 0 Red: All four teams receive +2 points each.

3 Blue, 1 Red: Teams choosing Blue receive −4 points each, and the team choosing Red receives +4 points.

2 Blue, 2 Red: Teams choosing Blue receive −6 points each, and teams choosing Red receive +6 points each.

1 Blue, 3 Red: The team choosing Blue receives +4 points, and the teams choosing Red receive −4 points each.

0 Blue, 4 Red: All four teams receive −2 points each.

Follow-up Questions

1. Did some of the teams have positive points and some negative? Did the participants figure out how all teams could have received positive points?

2. What would have happened if the teams had viewed themselves as subgroups of a larger organization with an organizational goal of maximizing the total profits for the organization?

3. What factor is most necessary for these teams to work together?

CHAPTER
11

Leadership

Chapter Objectives

After reading this chapter, you should be able to

- ▶ describe the general nature of leadership.
- ▶ summarize early approaches to leadership.
- ▶ describe the contingency theory.
- ▶ describe the path-goal theory.

- ▶ describe the Vroom-Yetton-Jago model.
- ▶ identify and summarize two other contemporary theories of leadership.
- ▶ discuss emerging perspectives on leadership.

ack Welch became chief executive officer of General Electric in 1981. Since then, he has reduced the company's work force by 100,000 employees and increased revenues by 48 percent. He has taken GE out of its traditional businesses like electronics and housewares and moved it into new areas like broadcasting and high-tech manufacturing. He has reduced corporate bureaucracy and increased decentralization.

Along the way, Welch has gained many admirers and many detractors. His fans argue that he has created the model corporation of the future, one that is cost-conscious while also being growth oriented. Welch's detractors charge that he has undermined corporate loyalty and built an unwieldy mix of poorly integrated businesses.[1]

Welch is clearly a manager. He is also a leader, at least in the eyes of many. He has been forced to make hard decisions and to take bold risks. He has also inspired strong emotions among those who follow him.

Leadership has long concerned both researchers and managers.[2] Managers talk about the factors that make an effective leader, and organizational scientists have extensively researched the same issue. Unfortunately, neither group has definitively answered the many questions concerning leadership.

In some situations, a leader has no significant effect on the organization at all. In other situations, the leader makes the difference between enormous success or overwhelming failure. Some leaders are effective in one organization but not in others. Other leaders are successful no matter where they go. Despite hundreds of studies on leadership, researchers cannot fully explain these contradictions and inconsistencies. Why, then, should we study leadership? There are two main reasons: because leadership is of great practical importance to organizations and because some variables influencing leadership effectiveness have been isolated and verified.[3]

This chapter begins with a discussion of the meaning of leadership, including a definition of the concept and a framework of leadership perspectives. We then turn to historical views of leadership, focusing on the trait approaches and the behavioral approaches. Thereafter the chapter examines three important leadership theories that form the basis for most leadership research: the contingency theory initiated by Fiedler, the path-goal theory, and the Vroom-

---

[1] "Jack Welch: How Good a Manager?" *Business Week,* December 14, 1987, pp. 92–103.

[2] Bernard M. Bass, *Stogdill's Handbook of Leadership,* rev. ed. (Riverside, N.J.: Free Press, 1981). See also James R. Meindl and Sanford B. Ehrlich, "The Romance of Leadership and the Evaluation of Organizational Performance, "*Academy of Management Review,* January 1987, pp. 91–109.

[3] Ralph M. Stogdill, *Handbook of Leadership* (New York: Free Press, 1974). See also Bass, *Stogdill's Handbook of Leadership.*

Yetton-Jago model. We conclude by describing a number of contemporary perspectives on leadership.

THE NATURE OF LEADERSHIP

Before defining leadership, it is useful to make two key distinctions. First, management and leadership are not the same. Management relies on formal position power to influence people, whereas leadership stems from a social influence process. Thus, a person may be a manager or a leader or both. A leader can also be formal, someone appointed to head a group, or informal, one who emerges from the ranks of the group according to a consensus of the members. *Management in Action* underscores the value organizations place on leadership.

Leadership Defined

Many definitions of leadership have been offered, but none has won wide acceptance.[4] We will define **leadership** as both a process and a property. As a process, leadership is the use of noncoercive influence to direct and coordinate the activities of group members toward goal accomplishment. As a property, leadership is the set of characteristics attributed to those who are perceived to employ such influence successfully.[5] From an organizational viewpoint, leadership is vitally important because it has such a powerful influence on individual and group behavior. Moreover, because the goal toward which the group directs its effort is the desired goal of the leader, it may or may not mesh with organizational goals.

Leadership does not involve force or coercion. A manager who relies on force to direct subordinates' behaviors is not exercising leadership. So, as noted earlier, a manager or supervisor may or may not also be a leader. It is important to note, too, that the set of characteristics attributed to a leader may be characteristics the individual really does possess, but they might also be ones he or she is merely perceived to possess.

A Framework of Leadership Perspectives

Leadership theory has its base in several different perspectives. Arthur Jago recently developed a framework for organizing the predominant leadership perspectives.[6] The framework consists of two dimensions: focus and approach.

---

[4] Stogdill, *Handbook of Leadership* and Bass, *Stogdill's Handbook of Leadership.*

[5] Arthur G. Jago, "Leadership: Perspectives in Theory and Research, " *Management Science,* March 1982, pp. 315–336.

[6] Jago, "Leadership."

Management in ACTION

America's Corporate Leaders

Corporate America is fascinated with the concept of "leader." Abraham Zaleznik's influential 1977 article about the differences between leaders and managers shook many corporations out of the belief that a CEO who was "managing" was doing just fine. The recent celebrity of business people like Lee Iacocca has helped make the business leader of the 1980s into a hero and cult figure of sorts, in some eyes. Corporate America seems convinced that it wants leaders, but is somewhat less sure of what the term means.

One recent article argues that corporate courage—the willingness to defend an unpopular policy because it's good for the corporation—is the mark of a good leader. Managers who try to protect themselves and the status quo are, in this view, contributing to the death of good ideas and of innovation within the corporation.

A related and widespread view is that a corporate leader must have a passion for change, what one management consultant calls "a divine discontent with the status quo." Yet while continuously shaking things up, the leader of today's corporation is also supposed to have a vision of what the future holds for the company—a vision so strong, attractive, and convincing that everyone at all levels of the company will buy into it.

Jack Welch of General Electric is, according to his admirers, such a man. He generally shares the top of the list with Lee Iacocca when business leaders are asked to name the colleagues they most admire. They like his toughness, the single-mindedness of his vision, his proven capabilities in turning GE into a lean, profitable enterprise. Since he took over, GE has cut its workforce by one-quarter, while its revenues have grown 48 percent. On the other hand, some of GE's employees view him as a tyrant who has destroyed employee loyalty and who will stop at nothing to cut costs and make a profit.

One element that many insist must be a part of today's corporate leader is a strong set of values, including a concern for employees, customers, honesty, and fairness. Such values are necessary, in this view, to keep the leaders and their companies free of the taint of recent ethical scandals in business, religion, and government. Yet others wonder if such values are compatible with the single-minded pursuit of profit. Jesse Jackson won widespread support in his 1988 campaign for attacking corporate America's habit of exporting jobs, using Jack Welch's GE as a prime example of what is wrong with America's corporations and economy. And Lee Iacocca's public admission that Chrysler had been selling as "new" cars its dealers had been driving was but one of a series of incidents that left many wondering about his qualifications to be one of America's new heros. It remains to be seen whether any one person can meet all the criteria required of America's true corporate leader.

Sources: Harvey A. Hornstein, "When Corporate Courage Counts," *Psychology Today,* September 1986, 56–60; Jeremy Main, "Wanted: Leaders Who Can Make a Difference," *Fortune,* September 28, 1987, 92; Russell Mitchell, "Jack Welch: How Good A Manager?," *Business Week,* December 14, 1987, 92–103; Alex Taylor, "Iacocca's Time of Trouble," *Fortune,* March 14, 1988, 79.

		Table 11.1

Table 11.1

A Framework of
Leadership Perspectives

		Approach	
		Universal	*Contingent*
Focus	*Leader Traits*	Type I Trait theories	Type III Fiedler's contingency model
	Leader Behaviors	Type II Michigan studies Ohio State studies	Type IV Path-goal Theory Vroom-Yetton-Jago model

Source: Arthur G. Jago, "Leadership Perspectives in Theory and Researrch," *Management Science*, Vol. 22, 1982, p. 316. Used by permission.

Focus refers to the decision of whether to view leadership as a set of traits *(trait perspective)* or as a set of behaviors *(behavioral perspective)*. Those working from the trait perspective see leadership primarily in terms of relatively stable and enduring individual characteristics. That is, leaders are believed to have certain innate characteristics that are important for leader effectiveness.[7] On the other hand, supporters of the behavioral perspective focus on observable leader behaviors—that is, the actions of the leader—rather than on unobservable and/or inherent traits.[8]

The second dimension of Jago's framework is *approach*. This dimension defines whether a universal or contingency perspective is adopted. The *universal perspective* assumes that there is "one best way" to lead, that effective leadership always conforms to this ideal, and that effective leadership in one situation or organization will also be effective in a different situation or organization. The *contingency perspective* assumes that the situation in which leadership is exercised is crucial. Because effective leadership depends on the situation, leadership is contingent on situational factors.

When combined, the two dimensions yield the four ways of viewing leadership that are shown in Table 11.1. From a Type I perspective, leadership is seen as a set of traits possessed by the effective leader in any group or organizational context. Early research on leadership, referred to as *trait theories,* took this perspective. From a Type II viewpoint, leadership is a set of behaviors displayed by the effective leader, again in any group or organizational setting. The Michigan and Ohio State studies, to be described shortly, were based on this perspective. The Type III perspective assumes that leadership traits vary with the situation. Fiedler's contingency model represents this view. Leadership from a Type IV perspective is a set of behaviors that are contingent on the

---

[7] Gary A. Yukl, *Leadership in Organizations* (Englewood Cliffs, N.J.: Prentice-Hall, 1981).

[8] Yukl, *Leadership in Organizations.*

situation. The path-goal theory and the Vroom-Yetton-Jago model illustrate this perspective.

EARLY APPROACHES TO LEADERSHIP

Although leaders and leadership have profoundly influenced the course of human events, it was not until the twentieth century that scientific research on leadership began. The first efforts examined traits, or personal characteristics, of leaders. Because this line of inquiry did not produce consistent findings and occasionally degenerated into absurd speculation, the second phase of research began to examine leader behaviors.

Trait Approaches

The earliest leadership researchers thought that leaders like Napoleon, Gandhi, and Lincoln had some unique set of qualities or traits that distinguished them from their peers. These traits were presumed to be relatively stable and enduring. The research agenda was thus to identify **leadership traits,** develop techniques for measuring them, and use these techniques to select leaders.[9]

Hundreds of studies guided by this agenda were conducted during the first several decades of this century. The earliest writers thought that leadership traits might include intelligence, dominance, self-confidence, energy, activity, and task-relevant knowledge. The results of ensuing studies gave rise to a long list of additional traits. Unfortunately, in fact, the list quickly became so long that it was of little practical value. In addition, the results of many studies were inconsistent. For example, some found that effective leaders tended to be taller than ineffective leaders, while others came to the opposite conclusion. Some writers even suggested leadership traits based on body shape, astrological sign, or handwriting characteristics! The trait approach also had a significant theoretical problem: it could not specify or prove how presumed leadership traits were connected to leadership per se.[10]

Behavioral Approaches

In the late 1940s, some researchers began to look at leadership as an observable process or activity. The goal of this **behavioral approach** was to determine what behaviors were associated with effective leadership. The researchers assumed that the behaviors of effective leaders were somehow different from the behaviors of less effective leaders, and that the behaviors of effective leaders

---

[9] Bass, *Stogdill's Handbook of Leadership.*

[10] Bass, *Stogdill's Handbook of Leadership.* See also Walter Kiechel III, "Beauty and the Managerial Beast," *Fortune,* November 10, 1986, pp. 201–203, for a recent discussion about leadership traits.

would be the same for all situations. Behavioral approaches to the study of leadership included the Michigan studies, the Ohio State studies, and the Managerial Grid.

THE MICHIGAN STUDIES   The **Michigan leadership studies** were a program of research on leadership behavior conducted at the University of Michigan under the direction of Rensis Likert.[11] The goal was to determine what pattern of leadership behavior results in effective group performance. From interviews with supervisors and subordinates of high- and low-productivity groups in several organizations, the researchers collected and analyzed descriptions of supervisory behavior to determine how effective supervisors differed from ineffective ones. Two basic forms of leader behavior were identified— job-centered and employee-centered—as shown in Figure 11.1, part A.

In *job-centered leader behavior,* the leader pays close attention to the work of subordinates, explains work procedures, and is interested mainly in performance. The leader's main concern is the efficient completion of the task. In *employee-centered leader behavior,* the leader is interested in developing a cohesive work group and ensuring that employees are basically satisfied with their jobs. The leader's main concern is the well-being of subordinates.

These two styles of leader behavior were presumed to be at opposite ends of a single dimension. Thus, a leader was thought to exhibit either job-centered or employee-centered leader behavior, but not both.

THE OHIO STATE STUDIES   The **Ohio State leadership studies** were conducted about the same time as the Michigan studies in the late 1940s and early 1950s.[12] Researchers at Ohio State University designed a questionnaire, which was administered in both military and industrial settings, to assess subordinates' perceptions of their leaders' actual behavior. The Ohio State studies also identified two major factors of leadership behavior, which were labeled consideration and initiating structure.

In *consideration behavior,* the leader is concerned about the feelings of subordinates and respects subordinates' ideas. The leader-subordinate relationship is characterized by mutual trust, respect, and two-way communication. In *initiating structure behavior,* the leader clearly defines the leader-subordinate roles so that subordinates know what is expected of them. The leader also establishes channels of communication and determines the methods for accomplishing the group's task.

Unlike the employee-centered and job-centered leader behaviors, consideration and initiating structure were not thought to be located on the same behavioral dimension. Instead, as shown in Figure 11.1, part B, they were seen as independent dimensions. As a result, a leader could exhibit high initiating

---

[11] Rensis Likert, *New Patterns of Management* (New York: McGraw-Hill, 1961).

[12] Edwin Fleishman, E. F. Harris, and H. E. Burtt, *Leadership and Supervision in Industry* (Columbus: Bureau of Educational Research, Ohio State University, 1955).

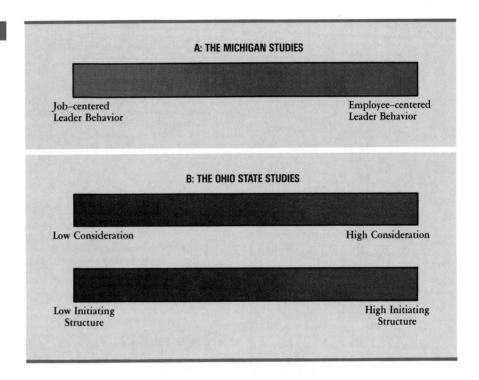

Figure 11.1

Early Behavioral
Approaches to
Leadership

structure and low consideration or low initiating structure and high consideration. A leader could also exhibit high or low levels of each behavior simultaneously. For example, a leader might do a good job of defining subordinate's roles and expectations while exhibiting little concern for their feelings. Alternatively, she or he might be concerned about subordinate's feelings but do a bad job of defining roles and expectations. Finally, the leader might do both, or neither.

The Ohio State researchers also investigated the stability of leader behaviors over time. They found that a given individual's leadership pattern did not seem to change very much as long as the situation remained fairly constant.[13] They also looked at the combinations of initiating-structure and consideration behaviors that were related to effectiveness. At first, it was believed that leaders who exhibited high levels of both behaviors would be most effective. A study at International Harvester, however, found that employees of supervisors who ranked high on initiating structure were higher performers but also expressed lower levels of satisfaction. Conversely, employees of supervisors who ranked high on consideration had lower performance ratings but also had fewer

[13] See Edwin A. Fleishman, "Twenty Years of Consideration and Structure," in Edwin A. Fleishman and James G. Hunt, eds., *Current Developments in the Study of Leadership,* (Carbondale, Ill.: Southern Illinois University Press, 1973), pp. 1–40.

Figure 11.2

The Managerial Grid®

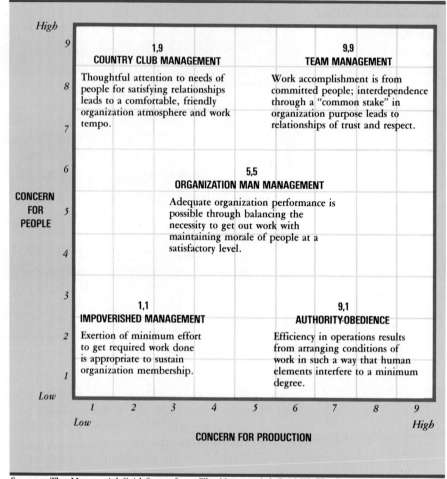

Source: The Managerial Grid figure from *The Managerial Grid III: The Key to Leadership Excellence,* by Robert R. Blake and Jane Srygley Mouton. Houston: Gulf Publishing Company, Copyright © 1985, page 12. Reproduced by permission.

absences from work.[14] Later research (covered in this chapter) showed that these conclusions are misleading because other variables were at work. That is, contingency variables limit the extent to which consistent and uniform relationships exist between leader behaviors and subordinate responses.

THE MANAGERIAL GRID   The **Managerial Grid**® was developed by Robert R. Blake and Jane Srygley Mouton as a framework for examining types of

---

[14] Fleishman, Harris, and Burtt, *Leadership and Supervision in Industry.*

supervision.[15] As shown in Figure 11.2, the grid consists of two dimensions similar to the leader behaviors described by the Michigan and Ohio State studies. The first dimension, concern for production, is parallel to initiating-structure and task-centered behaviors. A manager's concern for production is rated along a nine-point scale, where 9 represents high concern and 1 indicates low concern. A manager who has high concern for production is task-oriented and focuses on getting results or accomplishing the mission. The second dimension is concern for people, also rated on a nine-point scale with 9 high and 1 low. Concern for people is similar to consideration and employee-centered behaviors. As might be expected, a manager who has a high concern for people avoids conflict and strives for friendly relations with subordinates.

The two dimensions are integrated to form the grid. The grid, in turn, identifies an array of possible leader behaviors. Blake and Mouton suggested that the 9,9 position in the upper right corner is the most effective leadership style. That is, a manager who has a high concern for both people and production will be a very effective leader.

These behavioral models and theories attracted considerable attention from researchers, but unfortunately further research revealed significant limitations and weaknesses.[16] The behavioral approaches were valuable in identifying important leader behaviors and freeing leadership research from the traditional trait theory approach. However, in trying to specify a set of leader behaviors effective in all situations, the studies ran afoul of the enormous complexities of individual behavior in organizational settings. In the end, they all failed to identify universal leader-behavior/follower-response relationships. A different approach was needed to accommodate the complexities of leadership, and the contingency theory was advanced for just this purpose.

THE CONTINGENCY THEORY

The **contingency theory of leadership** was described by Fred Fiedler in 1967 to do justice to both the personality of the leader and the complexities of the situation.[17] The theory contends that a leader's effectiveness will depend on the situation and that, as a result, some leaders may be effective in one situation or organization, but not in another. The theory also explains why this discrepancy may occur and identifies leader-situation matches that should result in effective performance.

---

[15] See Robert R. Blake and Jane S. Mouton, *The Managerial Grid* (Houston: Gulf, 1964).

[16] See Yukl, *Leadership in Organizations.*

[17] See Fred E. Fiedler, *A Theory of Leadership Effectiveness* (New York: McGraw-Hill, 1967).

Basic Premises

Fiedler and his associates maintained that leadership effectiveness depends on the match between the leader's personality and the situation. Fiedler devised a special term to describe the leader's basic personality trait: task versus relationship motivation. He described the situation in terms of its favorableness for the leader, ranging from highly favorable to highly unfavorable.

TASK VERSUS RELATIONSHIP MOTIVATION   In some respects, task versus relationship motivation is similar to the concepts identified in the behavioral approaches. *Task motivation* parallels job-centered and initiating-structure leader behavior, and *relationship motivation* is similar to employee-centered and consideration leader behavior. A major difference is that Fiedler viewed task versus relationship motivation as a trait that is basically constant for any given person.

The degree of task or relationship motivation is measured by the *Least Perferred Coworker scale (LPC)*. The LPC instructions ask respondents (leaders) to think of all the persons with whom they have ever worked and to select their least preferred coworker. Respondents then describe their least preferred coworker by marking a series of sixteen scales anchored at each end by a positive or negative quality. For example, three of the items Fiedler uses in the LPC are:[18]

Pleasant									Unpleasant
	8	7	6	5	4	3	2	1	
Inefficient									Efficient
	1	2	3	4	5	6	7	8	
Unfriendly									Friendly
	1	2	3	4	5	6	7	8	

High numbers on the scales are associated with a positive evaluation of the least preferred coworker. (Note that the higher scale numbers are associated with the more favorable term and that some items reverse both the terms and the scale values. The latter feature forces the respondent to read the scales more carefully and to provide more valid answers.) Respondents who describe their least preferred coworker in consistently positive terms receive a high LPC score, while those who use consistently negative terms receive a low LPC score.

Fiedler assumed that a respondent's descriptions say more about the respondent than about the least preferred coworker. He believed, for example, that everyone's least preferred coworker is about equally "unpleasant" and that differences in descriptions actually reflect differences in a personality trait

---

[18] From Fred E. Fiedler, *A Theory of Leadership Effectiveness* (New York: McGraw-Hill, 1967). Reprinted by permission of the author.

among the respondents. Fiedler contended that high LPC leaders are basically more concerned with interpersonal relations, whereas low LPC leaders are more concerned with task-relevant problems.

Much controversy has surrounded the LPC scale. Researchers have offered several different interpretations of the LPC score, arguing that it may be an index of behavior, personality, or some other unknown factor.[19] Nevertheless, we are still asking the question: What does the LPC scale measure?

Situational Favorableness

Fiedler identified three factors that determine the favorableness of the situation. In decreasing order of influence they are leader-member relations, task structure, and leader position power.

Leader-member relations refers to the personal relationship between the leader and subordinates. It includes the degree to which subordinates trust, respect, and have confidence in the leader, and vice versa—a high degree, obviously, signals good relations and a low degree means relations are poor.

Task structure has four components:

1. *Goal-path multiplicity.* The number of different ways in which the job can be performed
2. *Decision verifiability.* How well the job provides feedback on results
3. *Decision specificity.* The degree to which a task has an optimal solution or outcome
4. *Goal clarity.* How clearly the requirements of the job are stated.

Tasks that have low multiplicity and high verifiability, specificity, and clarity are considered structured. Jobs of this type are routine, easily understood, and unambiguous. As a result, contingency theory presumes structured tasks to be more favorable because the leader does not have to be closely involved in defining activities and can devote time to other matters. On the other hand, tasks that have high multiplicity and low verifiability, specificity, and clarity are unstructured—nonroutine, ambiguous, complex, and presumed to be more unfavorable, since the leader must play a major role in guiding and directing the activities of subordinates.

Position power is the power inherent in the leader's role itself. If the leader has the power to assign work, reward and punish employees, and recommend them for promotion, position power is high and favorable. If, however, the leader must have job assignments approved by someone else, does not give

---

[19] See Chester A. Schriesheim, B. D. Bannister, and W. H. Money, "Psychometric Properties of the LPC Scale: An Extension of Rice's Review," *Academy of Management Review,* April 1979, pp. 287–294.

rewards and punishment, and has no voice in promotions, position power is low and unfavorable, since so many decisions are out of the leader's control.

LEADER MOTIVATION AND SITUATION FAVORABLENESS   Fiedler and his associates conducted several studies examining the relationships among leader motivation, situation favorableness, and group performance. Figure 11.3 summarizes the results of these studies.

Before we interpret the results, examine the situational favorableness dimensions shown at the bottom of the figure. The various combinations of these three dimensions result in eight different situations. The left side of the diagram describes the most favorable situation, where leader-member relations are good, the task is structured, and the leader has high position power. The far right side of the diagram shows the least favorable situation, characterized by poor leader-member relations, an unstructured task, and low leader position power. The other situational combinations represent intermediate levels of favorableness.

The line graph identifies the leadership approach that is supposed to achieve high group performance in each of the eight situations. A task-oriented leader is appropriate for very favorable as well as very unfavorable situations. For example, if leader-member relations are poor, the task is unstructured, and leader position power is low, the model predicts that a task-oriented leader will be effective. It also predicts that a task-oriented leader will be effective if leader-member relations are good, the task is structured, and leader position power is high. In cases of intermediate favorability, the theory suggests a person-oriented leader will be most likely to get high group performance.

LEADER-SITUATION MATCH   What happens if a person-oriented leader faces a very favorable or very unfavorable situation or a task-oriented leader faces a situation of intermediate favorability? Fiedler refers to these leader-situation combinations as mismatches. A basic premise of his theory is that leadership behavior is a personality trait, and he believes the mismatched leader cannot adapt to the situation and achieve effectiveness. Fiedler contends that when a leader's style and the situation do not match, the only available course of action is to change the situation through "job engineering."[20]

If a person-oriented leader ends up in a situation that is very unfavorable, Fiedler suggests that the manager attempt to improve matters by spending more time with subordinates to improve leader-member relations and by laying down rules and procedures to provide more task structure. Fiedler has developed a training program for supervisors on how to assess situation favorability and change the situation to achieve a better match.[21]

---

[20] See Fred E. Fiedler, "Engineering the Job to Fit the Manager," *Harvard Business Review,* September–October 1965, pp. 115–122.

[21] See Fred E. Fiedler, Martin M. Chemers, and Linda Mahar, *Improving Leadership Effectiveness: The Leader Match Concept* (New York: John Wiley, 1976).

| Figure 11.3 | Fiedler's Contingency Theory |

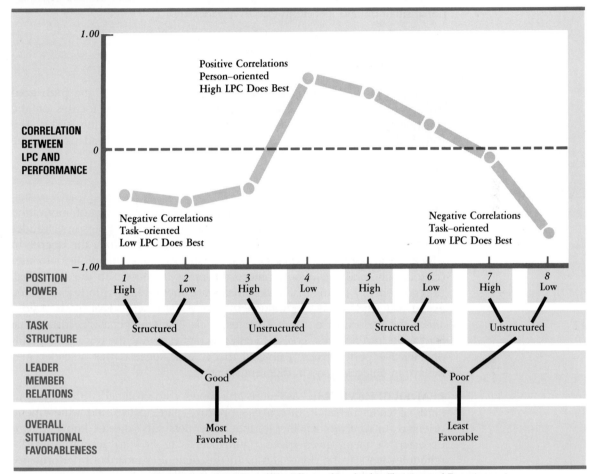

Source: Reprinted from "The Effects of Leadership Training and Experience: A Contingency Model Interpretation" by Fred E. Fiedler, published by *Administrative Science Quarterly,* Vol. 17, No. 4 (Dec. 1972), p. 455 by permission of *Administrative Science Quarterly.* Copyright © 1972 by Cornell University.

Scientific Evidence

The validity of Fiedler's contingency model has been heatedly debated, since research results are inconsistent. Apparent shortcomings of the contingency theory are that the LPC measure lacks validity, the theory is not always supported by research, and Fiedler's assumptions about the inflexibility of leader behavior are unrealistic.[22] The theory itself, however, is an advance over previous leadership approaches because it gives explicit consideration to the organizational situation and its role in effective leadership.

THE PATH-GOAL THEORY

Developed in the 1970s by Martin Evans and Robert House,[23] the **path-goal theory of leadership** is also a contingency approach but focuses on the situation and leader behaviors rather than on fixed traits of the leader. The path-goal theory thus allows for the possibility of adapting leadership to the situation.

Basic Premises

The path-goal theory has its roots in the expectancy theory of motivation discussed in Chapter 5. Basically, expectancy theory says that a person's attitudes and behaviors can be predicted from two interrelated factors: the degree to which the person believes that job performance will lead to various outcomes (expectancy), and the value of these outcomes (valences) to the individual. Path-goal theory claims that subordinates are motivated by the leader to the extent that leader behavior influences their expectancies. That is, the leader affects the performance of subordinates by clarifying the behaviors (paths) that lead to desired rewards (goals). Ideally, of course, getting the rewards depends on effective performance. Path-goal theory also suggests that a leader may behave in different ways in different situations.

LEADER BEHAVIORS   As Figure 11.4 shows, path-goal theory identifies four kinds of leader behavior: directive, supportive, participative, and achievement-oriented. In *directive* leadership, the leader lets subordinates know what is expected of them, gives specific guidance as to how to accomplish tasks, schedules work to be done, and maintains definite standards of performance for subordinates. The *supportive* leader is friendly and shows concern for the

---

[22] See Schriesheim et al., "Psychometric Properties of the LPC Scale"; George Graen, K. M. Alvares, J. B. Orris, and J. A. Martella, "Contingency Model of Leadership Effectiveness: Antecedent and Evidential Results," *Psychological Bulletin,* October 1970, pp. 285–296; and J. Timothy McMahon, "The Contingency Theory: Logic and Method Revisited," *Personnel Psychology,* Winter 1972, pp. 697–711. See also Lawrence H. Peters, Darrell D. Hartke, and John T. Pohlmann, "Fiedler's Contingency Theory of Leadership: An Application of the Meta-Analysis Procedures of Schmidt and Hunter," *Psychological Bulletin,* April 1985, pp. 274–285.

[23] See Martin G. Evans, "The Effects of Supervisory Behavior on the Path-Goal Relationship," *Organizational Behavior and Human Performance,* May 1970, pp. 277–298; Robert J. House, "A Path Goal Theory of Leadership Effectiveness," *Administrative Science Quarterly,* September 1971, pp. 321–339; and Robert J. House and Terence R. Mitchell, "Path-Goal Theory of Leadership," *Journal of Contemporary Business,* Autumn 1974, pp. 81–98.

Figure 11.4   The Path–Goal Theory

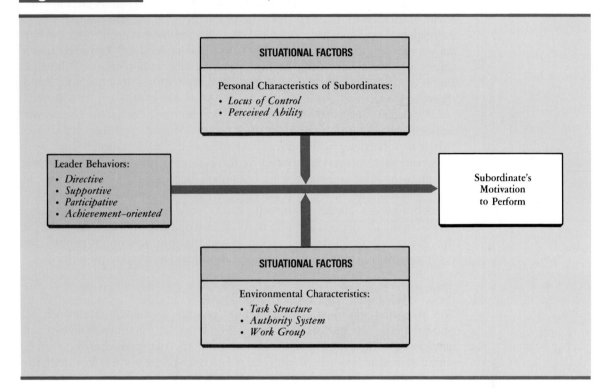

status, well-being, and needs of subordinates. In *participative* leadership, the leader consults with subordinates about issues and takes their suggestions into account before making a decision. And the *achievement-oriented* leader sets challenging goals, expects subordinates to perform at their highest level, and shows strong confidence that the subordinates will put forth effort and accomplish the goals.[24]

Unlike Fiedler's contingency theory, path-goal theory assumes that the same leader may display any or all of these leadership styles depending on the situation.

SITUATIONAL FACTORS   The theory proposes two types of situational factors that influence how leader behavior relates with subordinate satisfaction: the personal characteristics of the subordinates and the characteristics of the environment (see Figure 11.4).

Two important personal characteristics of subordinates are locus of control and perceived ability. *Locus of control* (discussed in Chapter 3) refers to the

---

[24] See House and Mitchell, "Path-Goal Theory of Leadership."

extent to which individuals think that what happens to them results from their own behavior or from external causes. Research indicates that individuals who attribute outcomes to their own behavior may be more satisfied with a participative leader, whereas individuals who attribute outcomes to external causes may respond more favorably to a directive leader.[25] *Perceived ability* refers to how a person views his or her ability with respect to the task. Employees who rate their own ability relatively high are less likely to accept directive leadership.

Important environmental characteristics are task structure, the formal authority system, and the primary work group. The path-goal theory proposes that leader behavior will motivate subordinates if it helps them cope with environmental uncertainty created by these factors. However, in some cases certain forms of leadership will be redundant, decreasing subordinate satisfaction. For example, when task structure is high, directive leadership is less needed and less effective; similarly, if the work group gives the individual plenty of social support, a supportive leader won't be especially attractive. So the extent to which leader behavior matches the situation's people and environment is presumed to influence subordinate motivation to perform.

Scientific Evidence

The path-goal theory was designed to provide a general framework for understanding how leader behavior and situational factors influence subordinate attitudes and behaviors. But the intention of the path-goal theorists was to stimulate research on the theory's major propositions, not to offer definitive answers. Researchers hoped that a more fully developed, formal theory of leadership might emerge from continued study, and further work actually has supported the theory's major predictions, but it has not validated the entire model.[26]

THE VROOM-YETTON-JAGO MODEL

The third major contemporary theory of leadership is the **Vroom-Yetton-Jago model,** first proposed by Victor Vroom and Philip Yetton in 1973 and recently expanded by Vroom and Arthur G. Jago.[27] Like the path-goal theory it attempts to prescribe a leadership style appropriate to a given situation, and it assumes that one leader may display various leadership styles. But the Vroom-Yetton-

---

[25] See Terence R. Mitchell, "Motivation and Participation: An Integration," *Academy of Management Journal,* 1973, pp. 160–179.

[26] See Yukl, Leadership in Organizations.

[27] See Victor H. Vroom and Philip H. Yetton, *Leadership and Decision Making* (Pittsburgh, Penn.: University of Pittsburgh Press, 1973); and Victor H. Vroom and Arthur G. Jago, *The New Leadership* (Englewood Cliffs, N.J.: Prentice-Hall, 1988).

International Perspective

Dr. Inaba's Autocracy

The recent American fascination with Japanese management techniques has focused mostly on aspects of participative management and collective decision-making. There is, however, a very different side to Japanese management that is perhaps best personified by Dr. Seiuemon Inaba, the head of Fanuc, the world's leading producer of industrial robots and of the controls and motors for machines in automated factories. Only giants like GM and GE participate in the industry *with* Dr. Inaba, and even they may not be able to keep that up for long.

"I hate meetings and conferences," Dr. Inaba says. "They're a waste of time." His distaste is mirrored throughout Fanuc's huge complex near Mt. Fuji. Employees are not allowed to roam the corridors during working hours. Memos are delivered by facsimile machine, not by hand. Executives normally gather only once a day, in the dining room. When he does have to hold a meeting, Inaba does all the talking unless he calls on someone.

Inaba's leadership style can be seen as a reflection of his motto—precision—and of what he sees as the key to the company's success—"walking a narrow path." It might be hard to imagine a company that has joint ventures with General Motors, General Electric, and the West German company Siemens being on a "narrow path," but in fact control devices and robots bring in three-quarters of Fanuc's revenues. In its joint ventures with the American giants, Fanuc has not so much broadened its product line as it has increased its access to the best in automation and robotic technology, areas in which the American companies were at first leaders, then competitors, and may one day simply be customers.

Comparisons between Fanuc's business and its corporate culture seem inevitable. Robots outnumber production workers, and when the factory is making machine tool parts at night, only a single human is on duty, monitoring a TV screen. Many workers whose families live in Tokyo, seventy-five miles away, stay in company dormitories during the week, some of them putting in fifteen-hour days. Inaba says proudly of his son, a Fanuc research engineer, "I've never seen him taking days off. I've never seen him resting."

In return for this almost fanatical loyalty, Fanuc pays its workers well. Managers earn up to 50 percent more than their counterparts in other Japanese organizations, and engineers up to 30 percent more. Many Americans might balk at working for the autocratic Dr. Inaba, even for such high wages. But Inaba's methods—and his company's success—clearly demonstrate that American companies trying to compete with Japan have more than just quality circles to worry about.

Sources: Gene Bylinsky, "Japan's Robot King Wins Again," *Fortune*, May 25, 1987, 53–58; Lee Smith, "Japan's Autocratic Managers," *Fortune*, January 7, 1985, 56–64; "Fanuc Chief: GE Deal Won't Hurt Any Other," *MIS Week*, June 30, 1986, 11.

Jago model concerns itself with only a single aspect of leader behavior—subordinate participation in decision making. The goals of the model are to protect the quality of the decision while also ensuring decision acceptance by subordinates. (*International Perspective* illustrates a quite different approach to decision making practiced by one prominent Japanese manager.)

Basic Premises

The Vroom-Yetton-Jago model assumes that how much subordinates should be encouraged to participate in decisions depends on characteristics of the situation. In other words, no one decision-making process is best for all situations. After evaluating each of the *problem attributes* (characteristics of the problem or decision), the leader determines an appropriate decision style that specifies the amount of subordinate participation.

Vroom and Jago's expansion of the original model requires the use of a decision tree.[28] The manager assesses his or her situation in terms of several variables and, based on those variables, follows the paths through the tree to a recommended course of action. There are actually four trees, two for group-level decisions and two for individual-level decisions. One of each of these is for use when time is important and the other for when time is less important and the manager wants to develop the subordinate's decision-making abilities.

The model for time-driven group problems is shown in Figure 11.5. The problem attributes (situational variables) are arranged along the top of the decision tree and are expressed as questions. To use the model, the decision maker starts at the left-hand side of the diagram and asks the first question. For instance, the manager first decides whether the problem involves a quality requirement. That is, are there quality differences in the alternatives and do they matter? The answer determines the path to the second node on the decision tree, where the question pertaining to that attribute is asked. This process continues until a terminal node is reached. In this way, the manager identifies an effective decision-making style.

The various decision styles reflected at the ends of the tree branches represent different levels of subordinate participation the manager should strive for in a given situation. The five styles are defined as follows:

> AI: The manager makes the decision alone.

> AII: The manager asks for information from subordinates but makes the decision alone. Subordinates may or may not be informed about the situation.

> CI: The manager shares the situation with individual subordinates and asks for information and evaluation. Subordinates do not meet as a group, and the manager alone makes the decision.

---

[28] Vroom and Jago, *The New Leadership*.

Figure 11.5   The Vroom-Yetton-Jago Model (Time-Driven Group Problems)

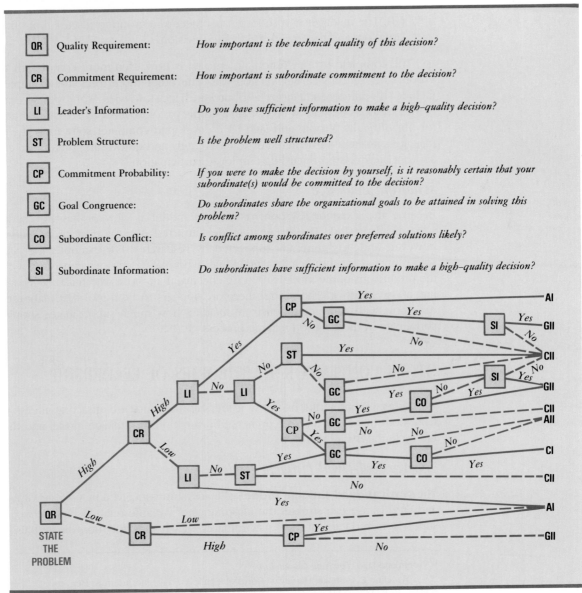

QR	Quality Requirement:	*How important is the technical quality of this decision?*
CR	Commitment Requirement:	*How important is subordinate commitment to the decision?*
LI	Leader's Information:	*Do you have sufficient information to make a high-quality decision?*
ST	Problem Structure:	*Is the problem well structured?*
CP	Commitment Probability:	*If you were to make the decision by yourself, is it reasonably certain that your subordinate(s) would be committed to the decision?*
GC	Goal Congruence:	*Do subordinates share the organizational goals to be attained in solving this problem?*
CO	Subordinate Conflict:	*Is conflict among subordinates over preferred solutions likely?*
SI	Subordinate Information:	*Do subordinates have sufficient information to make a high-quality decision?*

Source: Reprinted from *The New Leadership* by Victor H. Vroom and Arthur G. Jago. Prentice-Hall, 1988. Used by permission of the authors.

CII: The manager and subordinates meet as a group to discuss the situation but the manager makes the decision.

GII: The manager and subordinates meet as a group to discuss the situation, and the group makes the decision.

The complete Vroom-Yetton-Jago model is now even more complex than Vroom and Yetton's earlier version was. The other three trees, for example, include still different situational attributes and decision styles. Moreover, several of the questions now allow more than a simple yes or no answer. To compensate for this difficulty, Vroom and Jago have developed computer software to help managers assess a particular situation accurately and quickly and then make an appropriate decision regarding employee participation.[29]

Scientific Evidence

Because the expanded Vroom-Yetton-Jago model is new, it has not been scientifically tested. The original model attracted a great deal of attention, however, and was generally supported by research.[30] For example, there is some support for the idea that individuals who make decisions consistent with the predictions of the model are more effective than those who make decisions inconsistent with it. The model therefore appears to be a tool that managers can apply with some confidence in deciding how much subordinates should participate in the decision-making process.

OTHER CONTEMPORARY THEORIES OF LEADERSHIP

Two other recent additions to the leadership literature are attracting attention from both managers and researchers: the vertical-dyad linkage model and the life cycle theory.

The Vertical-Dyad Linkage Model

The **vertical-dyad linkage model** of leadership conceived by George Graen and Fred Dansereau stresses the importance of variable relationships between supervisors and each of their subordinates.[31] Each superior-subordinate pair is

---

[29] Vroom and Jago, *The New Leadership.*

[30] See Madeline E. Heilman, Harvey A. Hornstein, Jack H. Cage, and Judith K. Herschlag, "Reactions to Prescribed Leader Behavior as a Function of Role Perspective: The Case of the Vroom-Yetton Model," *Journal of Applied Psychology,* February 1984, pp. 50–60; R. H. George Field, "A Test of the Vroom-Yetton Normative Model of Leadership," *Journal of Applied Psychology,* 1982, pp. 523–532.

[31] George Graen and J. F. Cashman, "A Role Making Model of Leadership in Formal Organizations: A Developmental Approach," in J. G. Hunt and L. L. Larson, eds.,

Figure 11.6   The Vertical-Dyad Linkage Model of Leadership

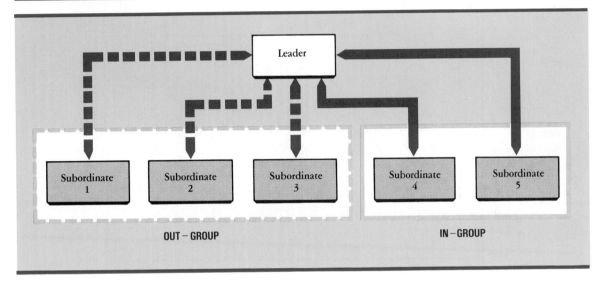

referred to as a vertical dyad. The model differs dramatically from earlier approaches in that it does not assume that a supervisor behaves in the same way toward each subordinate. Figure 11.6 shows the basic concepts of the vertical-dyad linkage model.

The model suggests that supervisors establish a special relationship with a small number of trusted subordinates referred to as the in-group. The in-group usually receives special duties requiring responsibility and autonomy and may also receive special privileges. Those subordinates who are not a part of this group are called the out-group, and they receive less of the supervisor's time or attention. Note in the figure that the leader has a dyadic, or one-to-one, relationship with each of the five subordinates.

Early in his or her interaction with a given subordinate, the supervisor initiates either an in-group or out-group relationship. It is not clear how a leader selects members of the in-group, but the decision may be based on personal compatibility and subordinate competence. Research studies have confirmed the existence of in-groups and out-groups; they have, in addition,

Leadership Frontiers (Kent, Ohio: Kent State University Press, 1975), pp. 143–165; and Fred Dansereau, George Graen, and W. J. Haga, "A Vertical Dyad Linkage Approach to Leadership Within Formal Organizations: A Longitudinal Investigation of the Role-Making Process," *Organizational Behavior and Human Performance*, Vol. 15, 1975, pp. 46–78.

Figure 11.7   The Life Cycle of Leadership

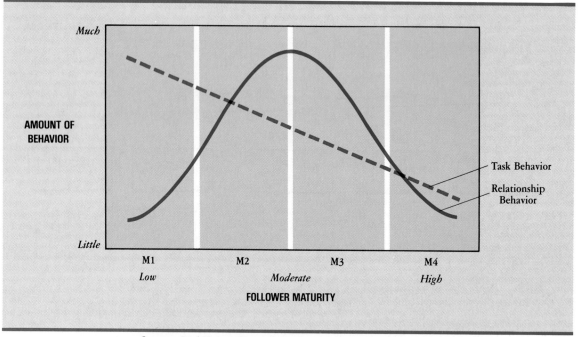

Source: Paul Hersey, Kenneth H. Blanchard, *Management of Organizational Behavior: Utilizing Human Resources,* 3/e, © 1977, p. 165. Adapted by permission of Prentice Hall, Inc., Englewood Cliffs, New Jersey.

generally found the in-group members to have a higher level of performance and satisfaction than out-group members.[32]

The Life Cycle Theory

Another popular theory is the **life cycle theory,**[33] based on the notion that appropriate leader behavior depends on the maturity of the leader's followers. In this instance, maturity refers to how motivated, competent, experienced, and interested in accepting responsibility the subordinate is.

The basic life cycle model is shown in Figure 11.7. As follower maturity increases from low to high, the leader needs to move gradually from high task-

[32] See Robert P. Vecchio and Bruce C. Gobdel, "The Vertical-Dyad Linkage Model of Leadership: Problems and Prospects," *Organizational Behavior and Human Performance,* Vol. 34, 1984, pp. 5–20. See also Dennis Duchon, Stephen G. Green, and Thomas D. Taber, "Vertical Dyad Linkage: A Longitudinal Assessment of Antecedents, Measures, and Consequences, " *Journal of Applied Psychology,* Vol. 71, 1986, pp. 56–60.

[33] Paul Hersey and Kenneth H. Blanchard, *Management of Organizational Behavior,* 3rd ed. (Englewood Cliffs, N.J.: Prentice-Hall, 1977).

oriented behavior to low task-oriented behavior. At the same time, person-oriented behavior (labeled *relationship behavior* on the figure) should start low, rise at a moderate rate, and then decline again.

The life cycle theory has much appeal to managers. However, it has not been truly tested by scientific researchers. Hence, while it may shed some interesting light on the leadership process, managers should be cautious about adopting it too mechanistically.

EMERGING PERSPECTIVES ON LEADERSHIP

In addition to the various theories of leadership that have been offered, several other perspectives provide insights into the leadership process.

Leadership Substitutes

Leadership substitutes are individual, task, and organizational characteristics that tend to outweigh the leader's ability to affect subordinate satisfaction and performance.[34] That is, if certain factors are present, the employee will perform his or her job capably, without the direction of the leader. In contrast to traditional theories, which assume that hierarchical leadership is always important, the premise of the leadership substitutes perspective is that in many situations leader behaviors are irrelevant. Figure 11.8 schematically represents this concept.

Individual characteristics that may neutralize leader behaviors are ability, experience, training, knowledge, need for independence, professional orientation, and indifference toward organizational rewards. For example, an employee who has the skills and abilities to perform her job and a high need for independence may not need, and may resent, a leader who provides direction and structure.

A task characterized by routineness, a high degree of structure, frequent feedback, and intrinsic satisfaction may also render leader behavior irrelevant. Thus, if the task provides the subordinate with an adequate level of intrinsic satisfaction, she or he may not need support from a leader.

Characteristics of the organization that may substitute for leadership include explicit plans and goals, rules and procedures, cohesive work groups, a rigid reward structure, and physical distance between supervisor and subordinate. For example, if job goals are explicit and there are many rules and procedures for task performance, a leader providing directions may not be necessary.

---

[34] See Steven Kerr and John M. Jermier, "Substitutes for Leadership: Their Meaning and Measurement," *Organizational Behavior and Human Performance*, Vo. 22, 1978, pp. 375–403. See also Charles C. Manz and Henry P. Sims, Jr., "Leading Workers to Lead Themselves: The External Leadership of Self-Managing Work Teams," *Administrative Science Quarterly*, March 1987, pp. 106–129.

Figure 11.8

Leadership Substitutes

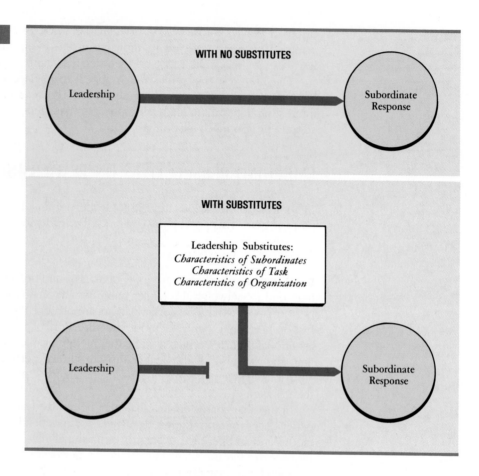

WITH NO SUBSTITUTES

Leadership

Subordinate Response

WITH SUBSTITUTES

Leadership Substitutes:
Characteristics of Subordinates
Characteristics of Task
Characteristics of Organization

Leadership

Subordinate Response

Preliminary research has provided support for the concept of leadership substitutes, but additional research is needed to identify other potential substitutes and their impact on leadership effectiveness. *A Look at Research* illustrates some of the findings to date.

Charismatic Leadership

The notion of **charismatic leadership,** like trait theories, assumes that charisma is an individual characteristic of the leader. Charisma is a form of interpersonal attraction that inspires support and acceptance and is likely to make a supervisor who is very charismatic more successful in influencing subordinate behavior than a supervisor lacking charisma. Robert House proposed a theory of charismatic leadership in 1977, based on research findings from a variety of

A LOOK AT

RESEARCH

Supervisors Need Not Apply

American telephone companies have never been accused of giving their employees too much leeway. Supervisors keep track of how long an operator takes on each call, and they listen in randomly to see how a customer is greeted. Computerization of the phone system has increased the pressure on operators to answer more calls in less time and has enabled even closer scrutiny by supervisors. Therefore, when Mountain Bell, part of the old Bell system, created in 1983 a facility with 100 operators and only one supervisor, the experiment became important not just for the company and people involved but for the concept of working without supervison itself.

The facility, the Hotel Billing Information System (HOBIS) was actually a joint development of Mountain Bell and the Communications Workers of America. Its operators, available around the clock, handled about 11,500 calls per day, arranging refunds and credits and providing hotels with information about the cost of calls dialed by their customers. At most equivalent facilities, eight to ten supervisors and one manager would have been on duty.

Without such extensive supervision, operators at HOBIS took on responsibility for training, productivity, office procedures, attendance, and service quality. The experiment did encounter problems, many of which were compounded by the turmoil resulting from AT&T's divestiture when HOBIS was less than a year old. Yet most operators felt more satisfied and less stressed than they had in traditional offices. They liked being part of something, being able to put quality service over speed, having a voice in decisions, and feeling that they were trusted to do good work. By more objective standards, the project was also successful: HOBIS workers were absent less often, filed fewer grievances, and received fewer customer complaints than operators at similar facilities. Both morale and productivity were high.

The AT&T task force set up to study the experiment concluded that nonmanagement employees could perform many traditional management functions and that investing in their training paid off in the long run. It also established guidelines and qualifications about such projects: they require careful planning; they need more than one manager (the operators reported not getting enough positive feedback); and they don't solve all problems. The operators experienced frustration and burnout just like their colleagues in more supervised environments. But they also proved that they could do a very good job without Ma Bell staring over their shoulders.

Source: Based on "Operating Without Supervisors: An Experiment," Thomas O. Taylor, Donald J. Friedman, and Dennis Couture, *Organizational Dynamics,* Winter 1987, pp. 26–29. © 1987 American Management Association, New York. By permission of the publisher: all rights reserved.

social science disciplines.[35] The following characteristics are believed to contribute to charisma:

1. The followers trust the correctness of the leader's beliefs.
2. The followers' beliefs are similar to the leader's beliefs.
3. The followers accept the leader unquestioningly.
4. The followers feel affection for the leader.
5. The followers obey the leader willingly.
6. The followers feel an emotional involvement in the mission of the organization.
7. The followers have heightened performance goals.
8. The followers believe that they can contribute to the success of the group's mission.

The theory also suggests behaviors and traits of charismatic leaders. For example, charismatic leaders are likely to have a lot of self-confidence, a strong conviction in their own beliefs and ideals, and a strong need to influence people. They also tend to communicate high expectations about follower performance and express confidence in followers.

Charismatic leadership ideas are a synthesis of social science research, but few studies have specifically attempted to test the theory's propositions. The theory's major contribution is that it explains charismatic leadership in terms of a set of testable propositions.

Attributional Perspectives

Attribution theory, discussed in Chapter 2, has also recently been applied to the study of leadership. Recall that *attribution theory* suggests that we observe the behavior of others and then attribute causes to it. Thus, if a leader attributes subordinates' poor performance to low effort or to a lack of ability, responses might include a reprimand, training, or dismissal. On the other hand, if attributions are to such external factors as a poorly designed task or a work overload, the leader might instead concentrate on correcting those problems, rather than giving the subordinate negative feedback. Research on this perspective is still in its infancy.[36]

Leadership as Symbolic Action

Finally, some writers have recently argued that the true meaning of leadership lies in its symbolic nature as opposed to its substance. That is, this view suggests

---

[35] See Robert J. House, "A 1976 Theory of Charismatic Leadership," in J. G. Hunt and L. L. Larson, eds., *Leadership: The Cutting Edge* (Carbondale, Ill. Southern Illinois University Press, 1977), pp. 189–207. See also Jay A. Conger and Rabindra N. Kanungo, "Toward a Behavioral Theory of Charismatic Leadership in Organizational Settings," *Academy of Management Review,* October 1987, pp. 637–647.

[36] Mark J. Martinko and William L. Gardner, "The Leader/Member Attribution Process," *Academy of Management Review,* April 1987, pp. 235–249.

that the actual decisions and actions taken by leaders matter very little. More important is the symbolic aura that the behavior of the leader carries with it. Suppose a manager always tries to remember to send each subordinate a birthday card. Traditional leadership theorists would consider this a part of considerate behavior and would assume it would result in employee satisfaction. The symbolic view, however, would see a more complex picture. If the cards are always on time and personally signed, for example, this would symbolically indicate caring and concern. To the extent that other behaviors are consistent with this interpretation, the manager will be respected. On the other hand, suppose the cards are often late and obviously signed by a secretary. Worse still, imagine that the subordinate's name is misspelled! This sequence of events would denote a lack of attention and concern by the manager and would likely result in resentment or disrespect. Thus, it may not be the content of the decisions (i.e., the decision to send the card) but the symbolism of the act (i.e., how it is carried out) that truly matters.[37]

To sum up, several potentially useful leadership models are beginning to emerge. As theories and research techniques become more refined, some of these new perspectives may start to dominate the area of leadership research. Eventually they may be integrated with one or more of the major models into a more complex and valid view of leadership in organizational settings.

SUMMARY OF KEY POINTS

Leadership is both a process and a property. Leadership as a process is the use of noncoercive influence to direct and coordinate the activities of group members toward goal accomplishment. As a property, leadership is the set of characteristics attributed to those who are perceived to employ such influence successfully. Leadership theories concern themselves with either leader traits or leader behaviors and approach the concept from either a universal or contingent perspective.

Early leadership research was dominated by attempts to identify important traits of leaders. The problems of the trait approach prompted researchers to examine leader behaviors in an effort to identify universally applicable forms of leadership behavior. The Michigan studies defined two kinds of leader behavior: job-centered and employee-centered. These behaviors were viewed as points on a single continuum. At about the same time, studies at Ohio State recognized consideration and initiating structure as basic leader behaviors. These behaviors

---

[37] Jeffrey Pfeffer, "Management as Symbolic Action: The Creation and Maintenance of Organizational Paradigms," in L. L. Cummings and B. M. Staw, eds., *Research in Organizational Behavior,* Vol. 3 (Greenwich, Conn.: JAI Press, 1981), pp. 1–52. See also Ricky W. Griffin, Kristen Dahlen Skivington, and Gregory Moorhead, "Symbolic and Interactional Perspectives on Leadership: An Integrative Framework," *Human Relations,* Vol. 40, 1987, pp. 199–218.

were viewed as separate dimensions. The managerial grid suggested that the most effective leaders were those who had a high concern for both people and production.

The contingency theories tried to identify appropriate leadership style on the basis of the situation. Leadership style was viewed as a trait of the leader. Fiedler's contingency theory stated that leadership effectiveness depended on a match between the leader's style and the favorableness of the situation, determined by task structure, leader-member relations, and leader position power.

Two other theories, the path-goal theory and the Vroom-Yetton-Jago model, focus on appropriate leader behavior for various situations. The path-goal theory suggests that directive, supportive, participative, or achievement-oriented leader behavior may be appropriate, depending on the personal characteristics of subordinates and on characteristics of the environment. Using the same perspective, the Vroom-Yetton-Jago model suggests appropriate decision-making styles based on situation characteristics. The Vroom-Yetton-Jago theory is essentially a model for deciding on how much subordinates should participate in the decision-making process. The model is designed to protect the quality of the decision and ensure decision acceptance by subordinates.

Six recent perspectives that do not have their roots in traditional leadership theories are the vertical-dyad linkage model, the life cycle theory, leadership substitutes, charismatic leadership, attributional perspectives, and symbolic action. More research is needed to validate these approaches to the study of leadership.

DISCUSSION QUESTIONS

1. Can you propose other definitions of leadership besides the one offered in the chapter?

2. Cite examples of managers who are not leaders and leaders who are not managers. What makes them one and not the other? Also, cite examples of both formal and informal leaders.

3. What traits do you think characterize successful leaders?

4. What other forms of leader behavior are there besides those cited in the chapter?

5. Critique Fiedler's contingency theory. Are there other elements of the situation that are important? Do you think Fiedler's assertion about the inflexibility of leader behavior makes sense? Why?

6. Do you agree with Fiedler's belief that leadership motivation is basically a personality trait? Why or why not?

7. Compare and contrast the contingency and path-goal theories of leadership. What are the strengths and weaknesses of each?

8. Of the three major leadership theories (the contingency theory, the path-goal theory, and the Vroom-Yetton-Jago model), which is the most comprehensive? Which is the narrowest? Which has the most practical value?

9. How realistic do you think it is for managers to attempt to use the Vroom-Yetton-Jago model as prescribed? Explain.

10. Which of the six contemporary and emerging perspectives do you think holds the most promise for future research? Which holds the least promise? Why?

11. Can any of the six contemporary perspectives be integrated with any of the three major theories? How could this be done?

Case 11.1

An About-Face for Citicorp

Walter Wriston, Citicorp's chairman until 1985 and the man who personified banking in his time, led American banks into making huge loans to Third World countries with his famous statement that sovereign nations don't default on loans. Now, when very few Third World nations have proven able to keep up with their interest payments, Citicorp's new chairman, John Reed, is trying to lead America's banks in a very different direction. His leadership style and his bank's policies have won both support and criticism in the banking world and have made him one of the single most influential forces in current American banking.

Ironically, today's international banking problems spring in large measure from what can be seen as transactions between Third World countries in which American banks served as an intermediary. In the mid-1970s, OPEC nations, loaded with money from the profits of selling oil at suddenly inflated prices, invested a lot of that money in American banks. Many of these banks, in turn, loaned the money to developing Third World nations like Mexico and Brazil, foreseeing high profits and, according to Wriston's pronouncement, little risk. But the growth of the debtor nations was not as strong as had been predicted, much of the money loaned to those countries ended up in the pockets of the wealthy, who often reinvested it in the United States, and when interest rates rose drastically in the late 1970s, the debtor nations began to say that they simply could not pay.

For almost a decade, American banks have wrestled with how to handle the loans to Third World countries. Without granting the countries some relief from their debt, many in the industry feared that countries would simply repudiate their loans or set a cap on how much they would repay, as Peru has done. The banks have been reluctant simply to write off the loans, because that would show up as massive amounts of red ink on the banks' books and could threaten the stability of the whole banking system. So the most popular approach has been to allow debtor nations to refinance their loans at lower rates over longer terms, in effect giving the countries back some of the profits that the banks have made from the loans.

As chairman of the bank with the largest loans to Third World nations, John Reed has participated in many negotiations about such loans. He fought a losing battle against a settlement allowing Mexico to renegotiate its loans and then refused to go along with other banks in reducing interest rates to the Philippines. Then, in May 1987, Reed dropped the bombshell that is still having effects on American banking: he announced that Citicorp was adding $3 billion to its reserves against losses on its Third World loans.

The move was especially dramatic because Mr. Reed is a less public, more secretive and brash person than was his predecessor. He warned regulators at home and abroad of the move and flew in representatives from the Third World nations so that they would all learn of it at the same moment. He waited until minutes before the public announcement to tell other bankers and then held a news conference from which Wall Streeters hurried to place orders on Citicorp's future.

What made the move so bold is that it was the first public admission of a truth everyone else had refused to admit: that much of the money owed to banks by Third World countries was never going to be repaid. By breaking the pretense and putting money into the reserves, Reed and Citicorp took a huge loss—$2.5 billion for the second quarter—but put themselves in a stronger position to deal with the loans in the future. Wall Street liked what it heard, and the price of Citicorp stock rose, despite the huge loss. Other banks trembled, fearing pressure to make the same kind of commitment to reserves. No doubt Reed's move will be debated for years, but it was a stunning step that many feel someone had to make. And it will probably mean that John Reed will be remembered not just as a banker but as a leader.

Case Questions:

1. Is there a difference between being the leader of a company and the leader of an industry?

2. Is risk-taking a necessary quality for all leaders? Could John Reed have risen to the top of Citicorp if he wasn't willing to take risks?

3. Which theory of leadership best explains Reed's success?

Case Sources:

Sarah Bartlett, "A Stunner From The Citi," *Business Week,* June 1, 1987, 42–43; Sarah Bartlett, "John Reed's Citicorp," *Business Week,* December 8, 1986, 90–96; Jaclyn Fierman, "John Reed's Bold Stroke, " *Fortune,* June 22, 1987, 26–32; "Banking Gamble Citicorp Sharply Lifts Loss Reserves, Putting Its Rivals on The Spot," *The Wall Street Journal,* May 20, 1987, pp. 1 and 18.

Case 11.2

Right Boss, Wrong Company

James Kesmer was on top of things. In school, he had always been at the top of his class. When he went to work for his uncle's shoe business, Fancy Footwear Inc., he had been singled out as the most productive employee with the best attendance. The company had been so impressed with him that it had sent him to get an MBA, grooming him for a top management position. In school again, and with three years of practical experience to draw from, Kesmer had gobbled up every idea put in front of him, relating many of them to the work he'd done at Fancy Footwear. Kesmer graduated, as usual, at the top of his class. When he returned to Fancy Footwear no one was surprised to find that when the head of the company's largest division took advantage of its early retirement plan, Kesmer was given his position.

Kesmer knew the pitfalls of suddenly being catapulted to a leadership position, and he was determined to avoid them. He'd read cases in business school about family businesses that fell apart when the young family member arrived and wielded an iron fist, giving orders, cutting personnel, and destroying morale. Kesmer knew a lot about participative management, and he wasn't going to be stuck with the label of arrogant know-it-all.

His predecessor, Max Worthy, had run the division from an office at the top of the building, far above the factory floor. Two or three times a day he would summon a messenger or a secretary from the offices on the second floor and have a memo sent out to one group of workers or another. But mostly he was, as Kesmer saw it, an absentee autocrat, making all the decisions from above and spending most of his time at extended lunches with his friends from the Elks club.

Kesmer's first move was to change all that. He set up his office on the second floor. From his always-open doorway he could see down onto the factory floor, and as he sat behind his desk he could see anyone walking by in the hall. He never ate lunch himself, but spent the time from 11 to 2 down on the floor, walking around, talking, organizing groups. The workers, many of whom had 20 years of seniority at the plant, seemed surprised by this new policy and reluctant to volunteer for any groups. But in fairly short order, Kesmer had established a worker productivity group, a "Suggestion of the Week" committee, an environmental group, a worker award group, and a management relations group. Each group held two meetings a week, one without him and one with him. He encouraged each to set up goals in its particular focus area and to develop plans for reaching those goals. He promised any support that was within his power to give.

The group work seemed agonizingly slow at first, but Kesmer had been well trained as a facilitator, and he soon took on that role in their meetings, writing down ideas on a big board, organizing them, and later communicating them in notices to other employees. He got everyone to call him Jim and set himself the task of learning all their names. By the end of the first month, Fancy Footwear was stirred up.

But as it turned out, that was the last thing most employees wanted. The truth finally hit Kesmer when the entire management relations committee resigned at the start of their fourth meeting. "I'm sorry, Mr. Kesmer," one of them said. "We're good at making shoes, but not at this management stuff. A lot of us are heading towards retirement. We don't want to be supervisors."

Astonished, Kesmer went around to talk to the workers with whom he felt he had built good relations. Yes, they told him, reluctantly, all these changes did make them uneasy. They liked him, so they did not want to complain. But given the choice, they would rather go back to the way Mr. Worthy ran things. They never saw him much, but he never got in their hair. He did his work, whatever that was, and they did theirs. "After you've been in a place doing one thing for so long," one of them concluded, "the last thing you want to do is learn a new way of doing it."

Case Questions:

1. What factors should have alerted Kesmer to the problems that eventually came up at Fancy Footwear?

2. Could Kesmer have instituted the changes he was interested in without getting such a negative reaction from the workers? How?

Experiential Exercise

Purpose: This exercise will help you better understand the behaviors of successful and unsuccessful leaders.

Format: You will be asked to find articles and case studies of both successful and unsuccessful leaders and then to describe how these leaders differ.

Procedure:

1. Working in small groups, go to the library and find brief biographies, case studies, or articles about various leaders. Sources might include the annual *Fortune* article presenting its Business Hall of Fame; biographies of such famous and infamous personalities as Vince Lombardi, Adolf Hitler, and Abraham Lincoln; or articles about managers in other business periodicals besides *Fortune*.

2. Choose two leaders most people would consider to be very successful and two who seem unsuccessful.

3. Identify similarities and differences between each pair of leaders. That is, compare the two successful leaders with one another, and the two unsuccessful leaders with one another.

4. Identify similarities and differences between the two successful and the two unsuccessful leaders.
5. Relate the successes and failures to at least one theory or perspective discussed in the chapter.
6. Select one group member to report your findings to the rest of the class.

Follow-up Questions

1. What role does luck play in leadership?
2. Are there factors about the leaders you researched that might have predicted their success or failure before they achieved leadership roles?
3. What are some of the criteria of successful leadership?

CHAPTER

12

Power, Politics, and Conflict

Chapter Objectives

After reading this chapter, you should be able to

- describe the nature of power.
- identify and discuss various types of power.
- explain how to use different kinds of power.
- discuss politics and political behavior.
- describe the nature of conflict in organizations.

*I*n the early 1980s, Steven Jobs, cofounder of Apple Computer, realized that his company needed professional managerial guidance. He recruited John Sculley away from PepsiCo and appointed him president and CEO. Jobs remained on as chairman of the board. At first, things worked just as planned.

Sculley reorganized Apple into three product divisions. Jobs chose to head up one of them. Jobs's group soon ran into scheduling and product development trouble, however, and other members of the board began pressuring Sculley to replace Jobs. He finally did so, precipitating a herculean power struggle for control of the company.

Sculley won. Jobs was subsequently forced to resign as chairman of the board. For a time, he stayed on in an advisory capacity, but soon gave that up as well. He is currently developing a new company focusing on networking personal computers with large mainframes.[1]

*T*his incident reveals much about the power, political behavior, and conflict that pervade practically all organizations. This chapter begins by characterizing the nature of power. We then identify types of power and discuss how each should be used. Politics and political behavior are explored next, and we conclude with a discussion of conflict in organizations.

THE NATURE OF POWER

Our opening incident illustrates several facets of power. It demonstrates, for example, that two or more people are usually involved when a power struggle occurs, often resulting in conflict, and there is usually a winner and a loser. Exactly what is power? And how pervasive is it? Let us review some opinions.

Power Defined

Many definitions of power have been advanced. Here are a few:

The capacity to effect (or affect) organizational outcomes.[2]

A force sufficient to change the probability of an individual's behavior from what it would have been in the absence of the force.[3]

The possibility of imposing one's will on the behavior of others.[4]

---

[1] Brian O'Reilly, "Growing Apple Anew for the Business Market," *Fortune*, January 4, 1988, pp. 36–37.

[2] Henry Mintzberg, *Power In and Around Organizations* (Englewood Cliffs, N.J.: Prentice-Hall, 1983).

[3] Jeffrey Pfeffer, *Power in Organizations* (Marshfield, Mass.: Pitman Publishing, 1981).

[4] John Kenneth Galbraith, *The Anatomy of Power* (Boston: Houghton Mifflin, 1983).

An agent's potential at a given time to influence the attitudes and/or behavior of one or more specified target persons in the direction desired by the agent.[5]

Although these definitions each have certain unique elements, they also have some conceptual similarities from which we can synthesize an acceptable working definition. We will define **power** as the potential ability of a person or group to influence another person or group.

Our definition expresses power in terms of potential. That is, we may be able to influence others but may choose not to exercise that ability. Nevertheless, simply having the potential may be sufficient in some settings to influence others. Power may reside in individuals, such as managers and informal leaders; informal groups, such as departments and committees; and in informal groups. Finally, we should note the definition's use of the word *influence* as the mechanism for affecting others. If a person can convince another person to change his or her opinion on some issue, to engage in or refrain from some behavior, or to view circumstances in a certain way, influence has been exercised. And power has been used.

The Pervasiveness of Power

Considerable difference of opinion exists about how thoroughly power pervades organizations. Some people argue that virtually all interpersonal relations are influenced by power, while others feel that it is confined only to certain situations. Whatever the case, power is without a doubt a pervasive part of organizational life. It affects decisions ranging from choice of strategies to color of the new office carpet. It makes or breaks careers. And it enhances or limits organizational effectiveness. *International Perspective* clearly illustrates one situation where power and political forces play a major role.

TYPES OF POWER

Within the broad framework of our definition, there are obviously many different types of power. These types are usually described in terms of bases of power and position versus personal power.

Bases of Power

The most widely used and recognized analysis of the bases of power is the framework developed by John R. P. French and Bertram Raven.[6] French and

---

[5] Gary A. Yukl, *Leadership in Organizations* (Englewood Cliffs, N.J.: Prentice-Hall, 1981).

[6] John R. P. French and Bertram Raven, "The Bases of Social Power," in Darwin Cartwright, ed., *Studies in Social Power* (Ann Arbor: University of Michigan Press, 1959), pp. 150–167. See also Philip M. Podsakoff and Chester A. Schriesheim, "Field Studies of French and Raven's Bases of Power: Critique, Reanalysis, and Suggestions for Future Research," *Psychological Bulletin*, Vol. 97, pp. 387–411.

International Perspective

Japanese Competition Comes to America

Recently, a number of American companies, particularly in the auto industry, have begun to face a new kind of Japanese competition—competition from Japanese companies that have built plants in the United States. This new battle being waged on American soil confuses traditional loyalties and leads to some unusual power struggles.

The Japanese companies that make news when they move to the United States are the big automakers like Toyota and Nissan. But some of the latest skirmishes involve companies that supply automakers with parts. The automotive parts industry is one of the five largest in the country; with over $100 billion in annual sales, it is about twice the size of GM, Ford, and Chrysler combined. Until a few years ago, the parts manufacturers have not had reason to fear Japanese competition. They have figured that even if GM lost sales to Toyotas being made in Kentucky, at least those Toyotas would use American parts.

But now some of those manufacturers are furious because Japanese automakers are buying many of their parts from the more than fifty Japanese parts suppliers that have moved to the United States since 1979. Two interesting types of power dynamics have surfaced as a result of this new source of competition.

The first involves Japanese companies' loyalty to their suppliers. American parts manufacturers are used to battling with each other to come up with the lowest bid for supplying GM or Ford with a part; quality and efficiency have been secondary. Japanese automakers tend to have a much closer working relationship with their suppliers, a relationship strengthened by long-standing ties in Japan. The automakers often own stock in the suppliers, and auto executives often sit on the suppliers' boards of directors. The two companies work closely together and know what to expect from each other. While American parts manufacturers complain that Japanese companies give them inadequate specifications for the car parts they want, these vague specs are sufficient for a Japanese manufacturer with a long history of working with a particular company's designs.

Interesting dynamics also develop when American executives go to work for Japanese companies. Often these executives end up echoing words that many Americans find so irritating when coming from Japanese mouths. For instance, when explaining why his company buys from so many Japanese suppliers, A. Darrell Shown, Honda's American purchasing manager, says "our quality name isn't going to take a back seat to anything." A Nissan executive who used to work for Ford faults U.S. companies' attitudes, which presume that the quality that has always satisfied the big three is good enough for Nissan.

These new kinds of international power dynamics will certainly multiply as more Japanese manufacturers move their plants to the U.S.

Source: Based on "Are Japanese Managers Biased Against Americans?" by Edward Boyer, *Fortune*, September 1, 1986. © 1986 Time Inc. All rights reserved.

Figure 12.1

Five Bases of
Organizational Power

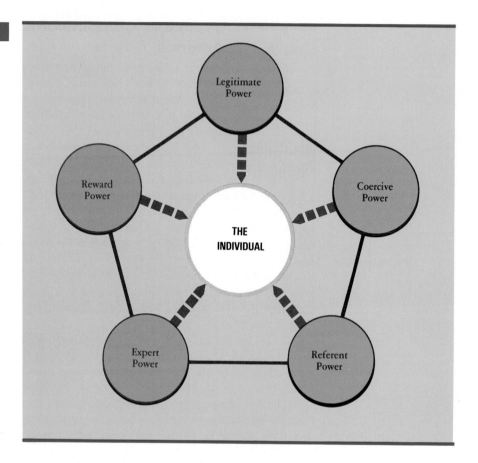

Raven identified five general bases of power in organizational settings (see Figure 12.1).

LEGITIMATE POWER   Legitimate power is granted by virtue of one's position in the organization. The organization itself thus provides the power. A manager has **legitimate power** over his or her subordinates, as well as over their subordinates, and so on. The organization declares that it is proper, or legitimate, for the designated individual to direct the activities of others. The bounds of this legitimacy are defined partially by the formal nature of the positions involved and partially by informal norms and traditions. For example, it was once commonplace for managers to expect their secretaries not only to perform such work-related activities as typing and filing, but also to run personal errands including picking up laundry and buying gifts.

The degree of legitimate power varies from one organization to another. In highly mechanistic and bureaucratic organizations such as the military, the legitimate power inherent in each position is closely specified, widely known, and strictly followed. In more organic organizations, the lines of legitimate power are often blurry. Employees may work for more than one boss at the same time, and subordinates and superiors may be on a nearly equal footing.

REWARD POWER   A second base of power identified by French and Raven is the extent to which one person controls rewards that are valued by another. The most obvious examples of organizational rewards are pay, promotions, and work assignments. If a manager has almost total control over the pay her subordinates receive, can make recommendations about promotions, and has considerable discretion to make job assignments, she has a high level of **reward power.**

Reward power can extend beyond material rewards. As we noted in our discussions of motivation theory in Chapters 4 and 5, people work for a variety of reasons that include more than just pay. At a given time, for instance, some people may be primarily motivated by a desire for recognition and acceptance. To the extent that a manager's praise and acknowledgment satisfy those needs, the manager has an additional form of reward power.

COERCIVE POWER   Coercive power exists when someone has the ability to punish or physically or psychologically harm someone else. Some managers, for example, berate subordinates in front of everyone, belittling their efforts and generally making life miserable. To the degree that subordinates try to avoid such sanctions, the manager has **coercive power** over them.

Certain forms of coercion may be subtle. In some organizations, for example, a certain division may be notorious as a resting place for people who have no future with the company. Threatening to transfer someone to a dead-end branch or to a particularly unpleasant location can be a form of coercion.

Physical coercion is less common in organizations than it once was, although such force is still occasionally practiced in settings like factories, loading docks, prisons, merchant ships, athletic teams, and the military.

Clearly, the more negative the sanctions a person can bring to bear on others, the stronger is her or his coercive power. At the same time, the use of coercive power is used at the considerable cost of employee resentment and hostility.

EXPERT POWER   Control over expertise or, more precisely, over information can be a source of power. To the extent that, say, an inventory manager has information that a salesperson needs, the inventory manager has **expert power** over the salesperson. The more important the information and the fewer the alternative sources for getting it, the greater the power.

Expert power can reside in many niches in an organization—it transcends positions and jobs. Although legitimate, reward, and coercive power may not always correspond exactly to formal authority, they often do. Expert power, on the other hand, may be much less in keeping with formal authority. Upper-level managers usually decide an organization's strategic agenda. But individuals at lower levels in the organization may have the expertise those managers need to do so. A research scientist, for instance, may have crucial information about a technical breakthrough of great importance to the organization and its strategic decisions. Or secretaries or assistants may take on so many of their boss's routine and mundane activities that the boss loses track of such details and comes to depend on the assistant to keep things running smoothly.[7] In still other situations, lower-level participants are given power as a way to take advantage of their expertise. *A Look at Research* summarizes how this happened in one situation.

REFERENT POWER   Like expert power, referent power does not always correlate with formal organizational authority. **Referent power** is basically power through identification. If José is respected by Adam, then José has power over Adam. In some ways, referent power is similar to the concept of charisma discussed in Chapter 11. In particular, it often involves trust, similarity, acceptance, affection, willingness to follow, and emotional involvement.

Referent power usually surfaces as imitation. For example, suppose a new department manager is the youngest person in an organization to have reached that rank. Further, it is commonly thought that she is being groomed for the highest levels of the company. Other people in the department may begin to imitate her, thinking that they too may be able to advance. They may begin dressing like her, working the same hours, and trying to pick up as many work-related hints and pointers from her as possible. Thus she has referent power over them.

Position Power Versus Personal Power

The French and Raven analysis is not the only approach to the origins of organizational power. Another approach categorizes power in organizations as one of two types: position power or personal power. **Position power** resides in the position, regardless of the person holding the job. Thus, legitimate, reward, and some aspects of coercive and expert power can all contribute to position power. Position power is thus similar to authority.

In creating a position, the organization creates a sphere of power for the incumbent. He or she will generally have the power to direct the activities of subordinates in the performance of their jobs, to control some of their potential rewards, and to have a say in their punishment and discipline. There are, however, limits to a manager's position power. The manager cannot order or control activities falling outside his sphere of power; he cannot, for instance, direct a subordinate to commit crimes, perform personal services, or take on tasks that clearly are not part of the subordinate's job.

Personal power resides in the person, regardless of his or her position in the organization. Thus, the primary bases of personal power are referent

---

[7] Walter Kiechel III, "How to Manage Your Boss," *Fortune*, September 17, 1984, pp. 207–210.

A LOOK AT

RESEARCH

Power Sharing From the Bottom Up

In the Basque region of Spain, the Mondragon system of industrial cooperatives has created a success story whose lessons may ultimately be more important than all that Americans have tried to learn from Japan's example. For in an age in which more companies are sharing power and profits through participative decision-making and employee stock ownership plans, the Mondragon cooperatives stand out as the ultimate example of just how capable workers are of managing companies from below.

The Mondragon system consists of eighty-nine small- to medium-sized industrial companies. The first small co-op was founded in 1956. In 1960, Caja Laboral Popular (The People's Savings Bank) was created to attract money from the community and invest it in the cooperatives in order to provide capital for computer services, feasibility studies, designs, training, and loans. The companies themselves make everything from agricultural equipment to plastics and robots. One of the largest, with 3,400 members and six factories, is the leading manufacturer of appliances in Spain and markets 25 percent of its products internationally. Despite its strongly socialist nature, the Mondragon system earns twice the profits of traditional capitalist enterprises and has a higher productivity rate.

The members of the cooperative share the power in each organization. Anyone capable of providing the service offered by the particular company and willing to take on the responsibilities of membership may join by paying an initial cash fee of approximately $3,000, which in effect buys the worker a share of the cooperative. The entire membership elects a supervisory board which in turn appoints managers directly responsible for the co-op's administrative functions. The members also elect a management council of outside experts and executives, a social council that looks after personnel and safety matters, and a watchdog council that oversees the other councils. Each worker/owner has a single vote, regardless of the number of shares he or she owns. The cooperatives put a cap on the amount of money any one worker may make: the highest-paid manager cannot earn more than three times the salary of the lowest paid worker/owner.

The goals of the cooperatives are to provide employment and training and to help the local communities. Besides the bank, other institutions associated with the cooperatives are a social security system, a research and development center, a technical school, an engineering college, elementary schools, day-care centers, supermarkets, and housing cooperatives.

The degree of Mondragon's success was highlighted by its response to the 1974 OPEC oil crisis. No Mondragon business has yet failed, and when some industries slowed down during the crisis, workers were sent to schools for training and/or transferred to other, faster-growing companies, never losing a day's pay. During that period, when so many companies were suffering, the cooperatives' employment rose 7.5 percent, profits rose 26 percent, and exports increased 56 percent. Any power-sharing organization that was able to post such impressive results during a crisis, and has experienced 15 percent annual growth ever since, is sure to gain more attention from researchers and executives trying to find ways to share power and motivate workers.

Source: Based on "Managing from Below" by Warner P. Woodworth, *Journal of Management*, Vol. 12, No. 3 (Fall 1986), pp. 391–402. Reprinted by permission.

Figure 12.2

Position and Personal
Power

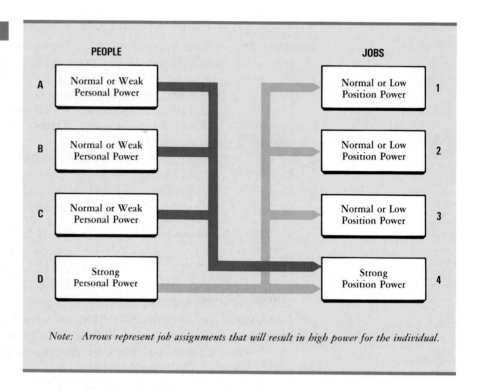

Note: Arrows represent job assignments that will result in high power for the individual.

and some traces of expert, coercive, and reward power. Someone usually exercises personal power through rational persuasion or through playing on followers' identification with him or her.

An individual with personal power can often inspire greater loyalty and dedication in followers than someone who has only position power. The stronger influence stems from the fact that the followers are acting more from choice than from necessity (as dictated, for example, by their organizational responsibilities) and thus will respond more readily to requests and appeals. Of course, the influence of a leader relying only on personal power is also limited since followers may freely decide not to accept her directives or orders.

Chapter 11 notes the distinction between formal and informal leaders. These two concepts are also related to position and personal power. A formal leader will have, at a minimum, position power, and an informal leader will have some measure of personal power. Just as a person may be both a formal and an informal leader, he or she can have both position and personal power simultaneously. Indeed, such a combination usually yields the greatest potential influence on the actions of others.

Figure 12.2 illustrates how personal and position power may characterize a situation. In particular, the position power of Job 4 exists regardless of whether person A, B, or C occupies it. On the other hand, person D has power no matter which job he or she holds.

THE USES OF POWER

Power can be used in many different ways. Gary Yukl has recently presented a useful perspective for understanding how power may be wielded.[8] His perspective has two closely related aspects. The first takes power bases, requests from individuals possessing power, and probable outcomes and correlates them in the form of prescriptions for the manager, as summarized in Table 12.1. The second aspect, summarized in Table 12.2, consists of general guidelines for the exercise of power.

Table 12.1 indicates the three potential outcomes that may result when a leader tries to exert power. These outcomes depend on the leader's base of power, how that base is operationalized, and the subordinate's individual characteristics (for example, personality traits or past interactions with the leader). *Commitment* will probably meet the attempt to exercise power if the subordinate accepts and identifies with the leader. Such an employee will be highly motivated by requests that seem important to the leader. For example, a leader might explain that developing a new piece of software will greatly benefit the organization if done as soon as possible. A committed subordinate will work just as hard as the leader to complete the project, even though that might mean working overtime. *Compliance* means the subordinate is willing to carry out the leader's wishes so long as doing so won't take extra effort and energy. Thus, the subordinate may work at a reasonable pace but refuse to work overtime, insisting instead that the job will still be there tomorrow. *Resistance* means the subordinate fights the leader's wishes. A resistant subordinate may even deliberately neglect the project to ensure that it is not done as the leader wants.

Using Referent Power

As is clear from Table 12.1, referent power can be a big help to a leader. Yukl's guidelines for building referent power are listed in Table 12.2.[9] Note that in a somewhat mechanistic method, a manager might enhance her referent power by choosing subordinates with backgrounds similar to her own. For example, she might build a referent power base by hiring several subordinates who went to the same college she did.

A more subtle way to exercise referent power is through role modeling: the leader behaves as he wants subordinates to behave. As noted earlier, since

---

[8] Yukl, *Leadership in Organizations*, Chapter 3.

[9] Yuki, *Leadership in Organizations*, pp. 44–47.

Table 12.1	Source of leader influence	Type of Outcome		
		Commitment	*Compliance*	*Resistance*
The Uses and Outcomes of Power	*Referent Power*	*Likely* If request is believed to be important to leader	*Possible* If request is perceived to be unimportant to leader	*Possible* If request is for something that will bring harm to leader
	Expert Power	*Likely* If request is persuasive and subordinates share leader's task goals	*Possible* If request is persuasive but subordinates are apathetic about task goals	*Possible* If leader is arrogant and insulting, or subordinates oppose task goals
	Legitimate Power	*Possible* If request is polite and very appropriate	*Likely* If request or order is seen as legitimate	*Possible* If arrogant demands are made or request does not appear proper
	Reward Power	*Possible* If used in a subtle, very personal way	*Likely* If used in a mechanical, impersonal way	*Possible* If used in a manipulative, arrogant way
	Coercive Power	*Very Unlikely*	*Possible* If used in a helpful, nonpunitive way	*Likely* If used in a hostile or manipulative way

Source: Table adapted by Gary A. Yukl from information in John R. P. French, Jr., and Bertram Raven, "The Bases of Social Power," in *Studies in Social Power*, Dorwin P. Cartwright, ed. (Ann Arbor: Institute for Social Research, the University of Michigan, 1959), pp. 150–167. Data used by permission of the Institute for Social Research.

subordinates relate to and identify with the leader with referent power, they may attempt to emulate his behavior.[10]

Using Expert Power

Yukl has also suggested several ways managers can use expert power,[11] as shown in Table 12.2. Managers can promote an image of expertise by subtly making others aware of their education, experience, and accomplishments. Maintaining credibility simply means that a leader should not pretend to know things that he really does not know. A leader whose pretensions are exposed will rapidly lose expert power. A confident and decisive leader demonstrates a firm grasp of situations and takes charge when circumstances dictate. To enhance her expert power, a manager should also keep herself informed about

[10] French and Raven, "Bases of Social Power."
[11] Yukl, *Leadership in Organizations*, pp. 47–49.

Table 12.2	Basis of Power	Guidelines for Use
Guidelines for Using Power	*Referent Power*	Treat subordinates fairly Defend subordinates' interests Be sensitive to subordinates' needs, feelings Select subordinates similar to oneself Engage in role modeling
	Expert Power	Promote image of expertise Maintain credibility Act confident and decisive Keep informed Recognize employee concerns Avoid threatening subordinates' self-esteem
	Legitimate Power	Be cordial and polite Be confident Be clear and follow up to verify understanding Make sure request is appropriate Explain reasons for request Follow proper channels Exercise power regularly Enforce compliance Be sensitive to subordinates' concerns
	Reward Power	Verify compliance Make feasible, reasonable requests Make only ethical, proper requests Offer rewards desired by subordinates Offer only credible rewards
	Coercive Power	Inform subordinates of rules and penalties Warn before punishing Administer punishment consistently and uniformly Understand the situation before acting Maintain credibility Fit punishment to the infraction Punish in private

Source: Reprinted from Gary A. Yukl, *Leadership in Organizations,* © 1981, pp. 44–58. Reprinted by permission of Prentice-Hall, Inc. Englewood Cliffs, N.J.

developments relevant to tasks and valuable to the organization and to her expertise.

As described by Yukl, a leader who recognizes employee concerns works to understand the underlying nature of a subordinate's concerns and takes appropriate steps to quiet them. For example, if employees feel threatened by rumors that they will lose office space after an impending move, the leader might ask people about this worry, then find out just how much office space there will be and tell the subordinates what he has found out. Finally, to avoid threatening subordinates' self-esteem, a leader with expert power should be careful not to flaunt expertise or behave like a know-it-all.

Using Legitimate Power

In general, a leader exercises legitimate power by formally requesting that subordinates do something. Once again, Yukl has provided several potentially valuable guidelines for using legitimate power. [12] The leader should be especially careful to make requests cordially and politely if the subordinate is sensitive about the relationship with the leader. This might be the case, for example, if the subordinate is older or more experienced than the leader. But though the request should be polite, it should be made confidently. The leader is in charge and needs to convey his or her command of the situation. A leader who says, "I'm not sure I have the authority to do this, but ... " is inviting lack of commitment or compliance. The request should also be clear; the leader may need to follow up to ensure that the subordinate has understood it properly.

To ensure that a request is seen as appropriate and legitimate to the situation, the leader may need to explain the reasons for it. Often subordinates do not understand the rationale for a request and consequently are unenthusiastic about it. It is important, too, to follow proper channels when dealing with subordinates. Suppose, for example, a manager has asked a subordinate to spend his day finishing an important report. Later, while the manager is out of the office, her boss comes by and asks the subordinate to drop that project and work on something else. The subordinate will then be in the awkward position of having to choose which of two higher-ranking individuals to obey. Yukl has also said that exercising authority regularly will reinforce its presence and legitimacy in the eyes of subordinates.

Compliance with legitimate power should be the norm because if employees resist a request, it will erode the leader's power base. Thus, if necessary, the leader must enforce compliance. Finally, the leader exerting legitimate power should always attempt to be responsive to subordinates problems and concerns in the same ways outlined for expert power.

Using Reward Power

Reward power is in some respects the easiest base of power to use. By observing Yukl's guidelines a manager can enhance its potential value.[13] Verifying compliance simply means that the leader should find out whether subordinates have carried out his request before giving rewards. Otherwise, the subordinates may not recognize a performance-reward linkage. The request to be rewarded must be both reasonable and feasible because even the promise of a reward

---

[12] Yukl, *Leadership in Organizations*, pp. 49–53.

[13] Yukl, *Leadership in Organizations*, pp. 53–55.

will not motivate a subordinate who thinks a request should not be or cannot be carried out. The same can be said for a request that seems improper or unethical. Among other things, this suggests that the reward must not be perceived as a bribe or other shady offering. Finally, if the leader promises rewards that subordinates know she cannot actually deliver, or if they have little use for rewards that she can deliver, they will not be motivated to carry out requests. In addition, they may grow skeptical of the leader's ability to deliver rewards that are worth anything to them.

Using Coercive Power

Coercion is certainly the most difficult form of power to exercise. Because coercive power is likely to cause resentment and to erode referent power, it should be used infrequently, if at all. Compliance is about all that can be expected from using coercive power, and that only if the power is used in a helpful, nonpunitive way—that is, if the sanction is mild and fits the situation and if the subordinate learns from it. Notably, resistance is the most likely outcome, especially if coercive power is used in a hostile or manipulative way.

Yukl's first guideline for using coercive power, that subordinates should be fully informed about rules and the penalties for violating them,[14] will prevent accidental violations of a rule, which pose an unpalatable dilemma for a leader. Overlooking the infraction on the grounds of ignorance may undermine the rule or the leader's legitimate power; yet carrying out the punishment will probably create resentment. As an example of providing reasonable warning before inflicting punishment, the first violation of a rule may simply be met by a warning about the consequences of another violation. Of course, a serious infraction such as theft or violence warrants immediate and severe punishment. The disciplinary action needs to be administered consistently and uniformly because doing so will show that punishment is both impartial and clearly linked to the infraction.

Leaders should obtain complete information about what has happened before they punish, because punishing the wrong person or uncalled-for punishment can stir great resentment among subordinates. Credibility must be maintained because a leader who continually makes threats but fails to carry them out will lose both respect and power. Similarly, if the leader uses threats that subordinates know are beyond his ability, the attempted use of power will be fruitless. Obviously, too, the severity of the punishment generally should match the seriousness of the infraction. Finally, punishing someone in front of others adds humiliation to the penalty, which reflects poorly on the leader and makes those who must watch and listen uncomfortable as well.

---

[14] Yukl, *Leadership in Organizations*, pp. 55–59.

POLITICS AND POLITICAL BEHAVIOR

A concept closely related to power in organizational settings is politics, or political behavior. Jeffrey Pfeffer has defined **organizational politics** as activities carried out by people to acquire, enhance, and use power and other resources to obtain their preferred outcomes in a situation where there is uncertainty or disagreement.[15] Thus, political behavior is the general means by which people attempt to obtain and use power. Put simply, the goal of such behavior is to get one's own way about things.

The Pervasiveness of Political Behavior

A recent survey provides some interesting insights about how managers perceive political behavior in organizations.[16] Roughly one-third of the 428 managers who responded believed that political behavior influenced salary decisions in their organizations, while 28 percent felt it affected hiring decisions. As Table 12.3 shows, three-quarters of the respondents also believed political behavior was more prevalent at higher levels of the organization than at lower levels. Over half of the respondents thought that politics were unfair, bad, unhealthy, and irrational, yet most also believed that successful executives have to be good politicians and that it is necessary to behave politically to get ahead. The survey results suggest that managers see political behavior as an undesirable but unavoidable facet of organizational life.

Politics are often viewed as synonymous with dirty tricks or back-stabbing, and therefore as something distasteful and best left to others. But the survey results demonstrate that political behavior in organizations, like its sidekick power, is pervasive. Thus, rather than ignoring or trying to eliminate political behavior, managers might more fruitfully consider when and how organizational politics can be used constructively.

Recently, Gerald F. Cavanaugh, Dennis J. Moberg, and Manuel Valasquez presented a model of the ethics of organizational politics, illustrated in Figure 12.3.[17] In the model, a political behavior alternative (PBA) is a given course of action, largely political in character, in a particular situation. Cavanaugh and his associates considered political behavior to be ethical and appropriate under two conditions: (1) if it respects the rights of all affected parties, and (2) if it respects the canons of justice (that is, a common-sense judgment of what is fair and equitable). Even if the political behavior does not meet these tests, it may

---

[15] Pfeffer, *Power in Organizations*.

[16] Victor Murray and Jeffrey Gandz, "Games Executives Play: Politics at Work," *Business Horizons*, December 1980, pp. 11–23. See also Gandz and Murray, "The Experience of Workplace Politics," *Academy of Management Journal*, June 1980, pp. 237–251.

[17] Gerald F. Cavanaugh, Dennis J. Moberg, and Manuel Velasquez, "The Ethics of Organizational Politics," *Academy of Management Review*, July 1981, pp. 363–374.

Table 12.3	Statement	Mean Score°	Standard Deviation	Strong or Moderate Agreement %
Management Perceptions of Political Behavior	(a) The existence of workplace politics is common to most organizations	1.59	.71	93.2
	(b) Successful executives must be good politicians	1.75	.88	89.0
	(c) The higher you go in organizations, the more political the climate becomes	1.99	1.10	76.2
	(d) Only organizationally weak people play politics[b]	2.21	1.17	68.5
	(e) Organizations free of politics are happier than those where there is a lot of politics	2.34	1.09	59.1
	(f) You have to be political to get ahead in organizations	2.37	1.13	69.8
	(g) Politics in organizations are detrimental to efficiency	2.57	1.14	55.1
	(h) Top management should try to get rid of politics within the organization	2.67	1.23	48.6
	(i) Politics help organizations function effectively[b]	2.76	1.13	42.1
	(j) Powerful executives don't act politically[b]	3.87	1.15	15.7

°Score: 1—strongly agree; 2—slightly agree; 3—neither agree nor disagree; 4—slightly disagree; 5—strongly disagree.
[b]Reverse scoring.
Source: Jeffrey Gandz and Victor Murray, "The Experience of Workplace Politics," *Academy of Management Journal*, June 1980, p. 244. Used by permission.

be ethical and appropriate under certain circumstances. For example, politics may play a part in the choice of which employees will be let go during a recessionary period of cutbacks, but it might provide the only possible basis for such decisions. But in all cases where non-political alternatives exist, the model recommends the rejection of political behavior that abrogates rights or justice.

To illustrate how the model works, consider the cases of Susan and Bill, two assistant professors of English. University regulations require that only one of the assistant professors may be tenured—the other must be let go. Both Susan and Bill submit their credentials for review. By most objective criteria, such as number of publications and teaching evaluations, the two faculty members' qualifications are roughly the same. Because he fears termination, Bill begins an active political campaign to support a tenure decision favoring him. He continually reminds the tenured faculty of his intangible contributions,

Figure 12.3   A Model of Ethical Political Behavior

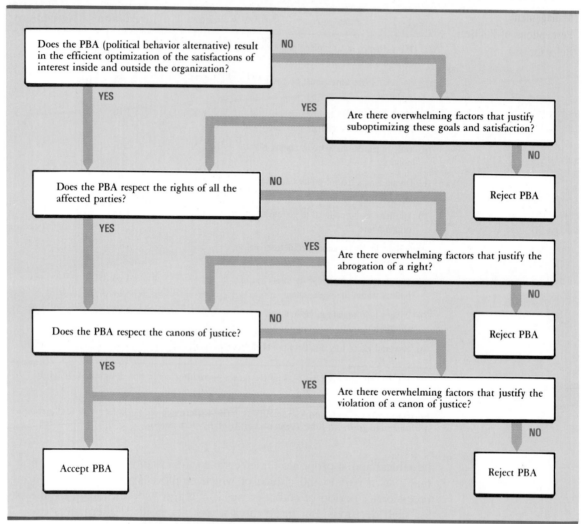

Source: Gerald F. Cavanaugh, Dennis J. Moberg, and Manuel Velasquez, "The Ethics of Organizational Politics," *Academy of Management Review,* July 1981, p. 368. Used by permission.

such as his friendship with influential campus administrators. Susan, on the other hand, decides to say nothing and let her qualifications speak for themselves. The department ultimately votes to tenure Bill and let Susan go.

Was Bill's behavior ethical? Assuming that his comments about himself were accurate and that he said nothing to disparage Susan, his behavior did not affect her rights. That is, she had equal opportunity to advance her own cause but chose not to do so. Bill's efforts did not directly hurt Susan, but only helped himself. On the other hand, it might be argued that Bill's actions did violate the canons of justice since clear and defined data were available on which to base the decision. It could thus be argued that his calculated introduction of additional information into the decision was unjust.

The model developed by Cavanaugh and his associates has not been tested empirically. Indeed, its very nature may make it impossible to test. Furthermore, as Bill and Susan's example attests, it is often difficult to give an unequivocal yes or no answer to the questions, even under the simplest of circumstances. Thus, the model can only serve as a general framework for understanding the ethical implications of various courses of action managers might take.

How, then, should managers approach the phenomenon of political behavior? Trying to eliminate political behavior will seldom, if ever, work. In fact, such action may well increase political behavior because of the uncertainty and ambiguity it creates. At the other extreme, universal and free-wheeling use of political behavior will probably lead to conflict, feuds, and turmoil.[18] In most cases, a position somewhere in between is best: the manager does not attempt to eliminate political activity, recognizing its inevitability, and may try to use it effectively, perhaps following the ethical model just described. At the same time, the manager can take certain steps to minimize the potential dysfunctions of abusive political behavior.

Managing Political Behavior

Managing organizational politics is no easy task. The very nature of political behavior makes it tricky to approach in a rational and systematic way. Success will require a basic understanding of three things: the reasons for political behavior, common techniques for behaving politically, and strategies to limit the effects of political behavior.[19]

REASONS FOR POLITICAL BEHAVIOR   Robert Miles has argued that political behavior occurs in organizations for five basic reasons: ambiguous goals, scarce resources, technology and environment, nonprogrammed decisions, and organizational change (see Figure 12.4).[20]

Most organizational goals are inherently ambiguous. Organizations frequently espouse such goals as "increasing our presence in certain new markets" or "increasing our market share." The ambiguity of such goals provides an

---

[18] Pfeffer, *Power in Organizations*.

[19] Anthony T. Cobb, " An Episodic Model of Power: Toward an Integration," *Academy of Management Review*, July 1984, pp. 482–493. See also Henry Mintzberg, "Power and Organizational Life Cycles," *Academy of Management Review*, April 1984, pp. 207–224.

[20] Robert H. Miles, *Macro Organizational Behavior* (Glenview, Ill.: Scott, Foresman, 1980). See also Carrie R. Leana, "Power Relinquishment Versus Power Sharing: Theoretical Clarification and Empirical Comparison of Delegation and Participation," *Journal of Applied Psychology*, Vol. 72, 1987, pp. 228–233.

Figure 12.4

Reasons for Political
Behavior

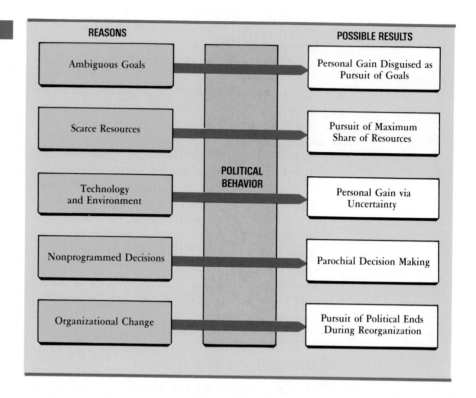

opportunity for political behavior because people can view a wide range of
behaviors as potentially contributing to goal accomplishment. In reality, of
course, many of these behaviors may actually be designed for the personal gain
of the individuals involved. For example, a top manager might argue that the
corporation should pursue its goal of entry into a new market by buying out
another firm instead of forming a new division. Seemingly, the manager has
the good of the corporation in mind. But what if he owns some of the target
firm's stock and stands to make money on a merger or acquisition?

Whenever resources are scarce, some people will not get everything they
think they deserve or need; and so they are likely to engage in political behavior
as a strategy to inflate their share of resources. In this way, a manager seeking
a larger budget might present accurate but misleading or incomplete statistics
to inflate the perceived importance of her department. Because no organization
has unlimited resources, incentives for this kind of political behavior are always
present. *Management in Action* offers details on one such situation.

As we discuss in Chapters 14 and 16, technology and environment may
influence the overall design of the organization and its activities.[21] The influence

---

[21] Joan Woodward, *Industrial Organization Theory and Practice* (London: Oxford
University Press, 1965); and Paul R. Lawrence and Jay W. Lorsch, *Organization and
Environment* (Homewood, Ill.: Irwin, 1967).

Management in ACTION

The Political Nature of Employee Appraisals

Employee performance appraisals are an important and often dreaded part of American worklife. Academics and businesspeople alike spend considerable time and energy analyzing appraisal instruments and trying to make them more accurate, scientific, and fair. Yet a recent study shows that evaluating employees is a very political business and that accuracy and fairness very often take a back seat to political expediency.

The researchers interviewed sixty executives who had an average of thirteen years of managerial experience and had conducted performance appraisals in a total of 197 organizations. The executives admitted that their knowledge of the effects of the appraisal nearly always influenced their ratings. Most executives used appraisals to send a message to their employees—inflating a rating to hearten an employee, to win a deserved raise for an employee, or to encourage the continuation of a recent streak of good work; or deflating a rating to shake an employee up, to get that employee moving, or perhaps to prepare the employee for a pink slip. The executives were very aware of the permanence of a written appraisal and the effect it has on an employee's pay, and indicated that they were reluctant to say anything in an appraisal that would hurt an employee financially, even if the employee's recent work had been below par. Many executives agreed that the oral part of an appraisal was more likely to be honest and include criticism than the permanent record.

The organization's culture generally influences how its executives view appraisals. Employees learn how to evaluate others by watching their bosses; if upper-level executives do not take the appraisals seriously, or seem to use them for political ends, then all appraisals by managers down the line are likely to reflect this outlook. Executives participating in the study generally viewed the appraisals as becoming less accurate and more political as the management level of the employee and the evaluator got higher.

Despite the evidence that politics influence almost all employee appraisals, the researchers did not condemn the general nature of the appraisals, nor did they call for radical changes in the appraisal process. Instead, they suggested some steps organizations can take to insure that the evaluations are as fair and effective as possible. To this end, they encouraged organizations to have their top executives model appropriate appraisal behavior, to encourage open discussion of the appraisal process, to foster openness and trust between managers and subordinates, to reward those executives who write particularly good appraisals, and to narrow the number of people who have access to written appraisals in order to limit the temptation of the rater to impress other executives with the employee's abilities. The crucial first step, however, is for organizations to admit and confront the fact that appraisals are political documents.

Source: Based on Clinton O. Longenecker, Henry P. Sims, Jr., and Dennis A. Gioia, "Behind The Mask: The Politics of Employee Appraisal," *The Academy of Management EXECUTIVE,* Vol. 1, No. 3, 1987. pp. 183–193. Reprinted by permission.

stems from the uncertainties associated with nonroutine technologies and dynamic, complex environments. These uncertainties favor the use of political behavior since in a dynamic and complex environment, it is imperative that an organization respond to change. An organization's response generally involves a wide range of activities, from true responses to uncertainty to the purely political, wherein, for instance, a manager might use an environmental shift as an argument for restructuring his department to increase his own power base.

Political behavior is also likely whenever many nonprogrammed decisions need to be made. Nonprogrammed decision situations involve ambiguous, ill-defined circumstances that allow plenty of opportunity for political maneuvering. The two faculty members competing for one tenured position is an example. The nature of the decision allowed political behavior, and in fact, from Bill's point of view, the nonprogrammed decision demanded political action.

As we discuss in Chapters 22 and 23, changes in organizations occur regularly and can take many shapes. Each such change introduces some uncertainty and ambiguity into the organizational system, at least until it has been completely institutionalized. This period usually affords ample opportunity for political activity. For instance, a manager worried about the consequences of a reorganization may resort to politics to protect the scope of her authority.

TECHNIQUES OF POLITICAL BEHAVIOR Several techniques are used in practicing political behavior. Unfortunately, since these techniques have not been systematically studied, our understanding of them is based primarily on informal observation and inference.[22] Further complicating this problem, the participants themselves may not even be aware that they are using particular techniques. The most frequently used techniques are listed in Figure 12.5.[23]

One technique of political behavior is to control as much information as possible. The more critical the information and the fewer the people who have it, the larger the power base and influence of those who do. A top manager, for example, may have a report compiled as a basis for future strategic plans. Rather than distribute the complete report to peers and subordinates, he shares only parts of it with those few managers who must have the information. Because on one but the manager has the complete picture, he has power and is engaging in politics to control decisions and activities according to his own wishes.

Similarly, some people create or exploit situations so that they control lines of communication, particularly access to others in the organization. Secretaries, for instance, frequently control access to their bosses. The secretary may put visitors in contact with the boss, may send them away, or may delay the contact by not having phone calls returned promptly, and so forth. People in these

---

[22] Pfeffer, *Power in Organizations*, and Mintzberg, *Power In and Around Organizations*.

[23] Pfeffer, *Power in Organizations*; Mintzberg, *Power In and Around Organizations*; and Galbraith, *The Anatomy of Power*.

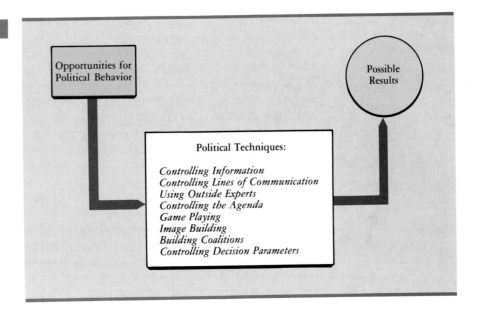

Figure 12.5

The Techniques of
Political Behavior

positions often find that they can use this type of political behavior quite effectively.

Using outside experts, such as consultants or advisors, can be an effective political technique. The manager who hires a consultant may select one whose views match her own. Since the consultant realizes that the manager was responsible for his selection, he may feel a certain obligation to her. Although the consultant may truly attempt to be objective and unbiased, he may unconsciously recommend courses of action favored by the manager. Given the consultant's presumed expertise and neutrality, others in the organization may accept his recommendations without challenge. By using an outside expert, the manager ultimately gets what she wants.

Controlling the agenda is also a common political technique. Suppose that a manager wants to prevent a committee from approving a certain proposal. The manager might first try to keep the decision off the agenda entirely, perhaps claiming that it is not yet ready for consideration, or he may try to have it placed last on the agenda. As other issues are decided, he might side with the same set of managers on each of them, building up a certain expectation that they are a team. When the controversial item comes up, he may be able to defeat it through a combination of fatigue and everyone's wish to get the meeting over with and the support of his carefully cultivated allies. This technique, then, involves group polarization (discussed in more detail in Chapter 17). A less sophisticated tactic is to prolong discussion of prior agenda items so that the group never reaches the controversial one. Or the manager may raise so many technicalities and new questions about the proposal that the committee decides to table it. In any of these cases, the manager will have used political behavior for his own ends.

Game playing is a complex technique that may take many different forms. When playing games, managers simply work within the rules of the organization to increase the probability that their preferred outcomes will come about. Suppose a manager is in a position to cast the deciding vote on an upcoming issue. She may not want to alienate either side by voting on it. One game she might play would be to arrange to be called out of town on a crucial business trip when the vote is to take place. Assuming that no one questions the need for the trip, she will have successfully maintained her position of neutrality and will not have angered either of the opposing camps.[24] Another game might be to employ any of the techniques of political behavior in a purely manipulative or deceitful way. For example, a manager soon to be making recommendations about promotions might tell each subordinate, in strictest confidence, that he or she is a leading candidate and needs only to increase his or her performance to have the inside track. Here, the manager is using his control over information to play games with his subordinates.

Image building, a subtle form of political behavior, is in most cases a means of enhancing one's power base for future activity. The methods discussed earlier for enhancing expert power are effective image-building techniques. Such behavior increases an individual's power base and thus his or her opportunity for political activities. Another, more manipulative set of techniques also falls under this heading: jockeying to be associated only with successful projects, taking credit for the work of others, and exaggerating one's personal accomplishments may all lead to an enhanced image.[25]

The technique of building coalitions has as its general goal convincing others that everyone should work together to get certain things accomplished. A manager who feels she does not control enough votes to pass an upcoming agenda item may visit with other managers before the meeting to urge them to side with her. If her preferences are in the best interests of the organization, this may be a laudable strategy for her to follow. But if she herself is the principal beneficiary, the technique is not desirable from the organization's perspective.

At its extreme, this technique, which is frequently used in political bodies, may take the form of blatant reciprocity. In return for Manager Kline's vote on an issue that concerns her, Manager Takeda may agree to vote for a measure that does not affect her group at all but is crucial to Manager Kline's group. Depending on the circumstances, this practice may benefit or hurt the organization as a whole.

---

[24] Michael Macoby, *The Gamesman* (New York: Simon and Schuster, 1976).

[25] Robert W. Allen and Lyman W. Porter, eds., *Organizational Influence Processes* (Glenview, Ill.: Scott, Foresman, 1983). See also Eric M. Eisenberg and Marsha G. Witten, "Reconsidering Openness in Organizational Communication," *Academy of Management Review*, Vol. 12, 1987, pp. 418–426.

Figure 12.6 Limiting the Effects of Political Behavior

Political Behavior

Constraining Techniques:
- *Open Communication*
- *Reduction of Uncertainty*
- *Awareness*

Effects of Political Behavior

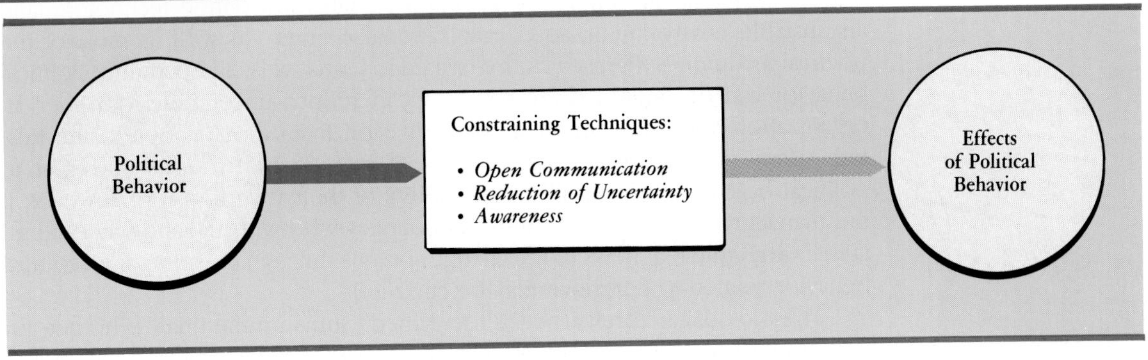

The technique of controlling decision parameters can be used only in certain situations and requires much subtlety. Instead of trying to control the actual decision, the manager backs up one step and tries to control the criteria and tests on which the decision is based. This allows him to take a less active role in the actual decison but still achieve his preferred outcome. For example, suppose a district manager wants a proposed new factory to be constructed on a site in his region. If he tries to influence the decision directly, his arguments will be seen as biased and self-serving. Instead he may take a very active role in defining the criteria on which the decision will be based, such as target population, access to rail transportation, tax rates, distance from other facilities, and the like. If he is a skillful negotiator, he may be able to influence the decision parameters in such a way that his desired location subsequently appears to be the ideal site, as determined by the criteria he has helped shape. Hence, he gets just what he wants without playing a prominent role in the actual decision.

LIMITING THE EFFECTS OF POLITICAL BEHAVIOR Although it is virtually impossible to eliminate political activity in organizations, the manager can limit its dysfunctional consequences. The techniques for checking political activity aim at the reasons why it occurs in the first place, as well as at the specific techniques that people use for political gain. Figure 12.6 summarizes the primary techniques for limiting political activity.

Open communication is one very effective technique for constraining the impact of political behavior. Open communication can, for instance, make the basis for allocating scarce resources known to everyone. This knowledge, in turn, tends to reduce the propensity to engage in political behavior to acquire those resources, since people already know how decisions will be made. Open communication also limits the ability of any single person to control information or lines of communication.

A related technique is to take steps to reduce uncertainty. Several of the reasons for political behavior—ambiguous goals, nonroutine technology and an unstable environment, and organizational change—as well as most of the political techniques themselves, are related to high levels of uncertainty. Political behavior can be limited if the manager can reduce uncertainty. Consider an organization about to transfer a major division from the Sun Belt to the Rust Belt. Many people will loathe the idea of moving north and may resort to political behavior to forestall the possibility of their own transfer. However, if the manager in charge of the move announces who will stay and who will go at the same time that news of the change spreads through the company, political behavior related to the move may be curtailed.

The old adage "forewarned is forearmed" sums up the final technique for controlling political activity. Simply being aware of the causes and techniques of political behavior can help a manager check their effects. For instance, a manager might anticipate that several impending organizational changes will cause the level of political activity to increase. As a result of this awareness, the manager might quickly infer that a particular subordinate is lobbying for the use of a certain consultant only because the subordinate thinks the consultant's recommendations will be in line with his own. Attempts to control the agenda, engage in game playing, build a certain image, and control decision parameters are often transparent to the knowledgeable observer. Recognizing such behaviors for what they are, an astute manager may be able to take appropriate steps to limit their impact.

CONFLICT IN ORGANIZATIONS

Related to power and politics in organizational life is conflict. **Conflict** can occur between individuals or between groups. And it is often started by political behavior. In particular, it often occurs when a group thinks its attempts to achieve its goal are being blocked by another group. For example, conflict may arise over financial resources, the number of authorized positions in work groups, or the number of microcomputers to be purchased for departments. Conflict may also result from anticipating trouble: a group may behave antagonistically toward another group that it expects to pose obstacles to its goal achievement.[26]

The Nature of Conflict

Figure 12.7 illustrates the basic nature of organizational conflict. When groups strive for the same goal, hold little or no antagonism toward each other, and

---

[26] See Stephen P. Robbins, *Managing Organizational Conflict* (Englewood Cliffs, N.J.: Prentice-Hall, 1974), for a classic review.

Figure 12.7

Conflict-Competition
Relationships

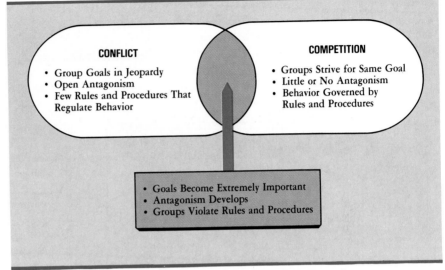

CONFLICT
- Group Goals in Jeopardy
- Open Antagonism
- Few Rules and Procedures That Regulate Behavior

COMPETITION
- Groups Strive for Same Goal
- Little or No Antagonism
- Behavior Governed by Rules and Procedures

- Goals Become Extremely Important
- Antagonism Develops
- Groups Violate Rules and Procedures

Source: S. P. Robbins, *Managing Organizational Conflict,* © 1974, p. 26.
Adapted by permission of Prentice-Hall, Inc., Englewood Cliffs, NJ.

behave according to rules and procedures, competition is the most likely outcome. Conflict is likely, however, when one group's goals jeopardize the other's, when there is open antagonism between the groups, and when few rules and procedures regulate their behavior. When this happens, the goals become extremely important, the antagonism increases, and rules and procedures are violated.[27]

Managing Conflict

Given the potentially disruptive effects of conflict, managers need to be sensitive to how it can be managed. When a potentially harmful conflict situation exists, a manager needs to engage in *conflict resolution*. As shown in Figure 12.8, conflict needs to be resolved when it causes major disruptions in the organization and absorbs time and effort that could be used more productively. In addition, conflict needs to be resolved when the focus of conflict is on the group's internal goals rather than the organizational goals.

We will describe the principal conflict-handling strategies in a moment. First, though, note that sometimes the manager should worry, too, about the absence of conflict. An absence of conflict may indicate that the organization is stagnant and employees are content with the status quo. It may also suggest that work groups are not motivated to challenge traditional and well-accepted ideas.[28] *Conflict stimulation* is the creation and constructive use of conflict by

---

[27] Robbins, *Managing Organizational Conflict.*
[28] Irving Janis, *Groupthink*, 2nd ed. (Boston: Houghton Mifflin, 1982).

Figure 12.8

Conflict Management
Alternatives

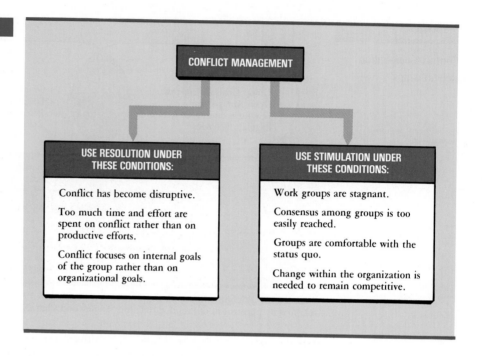

CONFLICT MANAGEMENT

USE RESOLUTION UNDER
THESE CONDITIONS:

Conflict has become disruptive.

Too much time and effort are
spent on conflict rather than on
productive efforts.

Conflict focuses on internal goals
of the group rather than on
organizational goals.

USE STIMULATION UNDER
THESE CONDITIONS:

Work groups are stagnant.

Consensus among groups is too
easily reached.

Groups are comfortable with the
status quo.

Change within the organization is
needed to remain competitive.

a manager.[29] Its purpose is to bring about situations where differences of opinion are exposed for examination by all. If, for example, competing organizations are making significant changes in products, markets, or technologies, it may be time for a manager to stimulate innovation and creativity by challenging the status quo. Stimulating conflict may provide employees with the motivation and opportunity to reveal differences of opinion that they previously had kept to themselves. When all parties to the conflict are interested enough in an issue to be somewhat antagonistic toward other groups, they often expose their hidden doubts or opinions. In turn, this allows the parties to get to the heart of the matter and, often, to develop unique solutions to a problem. Indeed, the interactions may cause the groups to acknowledge that there is in fact a problem. Conflict, then, can be a catalyst for creativity and change in the organization.

There are several methods available for stimulating conflict under controlled conditions.[30] These include altering the physical location of groups to stimulate more interaction, forcing more resource sharing, and other changes in relationships among groups. In addition, training programs can be used to increase

[29] Robbins, *Managing Organizational Conflict.*
[30] Robbins, *Managing Organizational Conflict.*

employee awareness of potential problems in group decision making and group interactions. Adopting the role of "devil's advocate" in discussion sessions is another method of stimulating conflict between groups. In this role a manager challenges the prevailing consensus of opinion in an effort to be sure that all alternatives have been critically appraised and analyzed. Although this role is often an unpopular one, it may be a good way to stimulate constructive conflict.

Of course, too much conflict is also a concern. If conflict becomes excessive or destructive, the manager needs to adopt a strategy for reducing or resolving it. The most common strategies were described in Chapter 10. In particular, any of the goal-based, location-based, resource-based, or organization-based strategies, as well as people or group strategies, can be used to reduce or resolve conflict between people or groups. For example, one organization strategy is decoupling. Thus, if conflict has become excessive, individuals or groups involved might be functionally separated.

Thus, conflict management is the process of recognizing the proper role of conflict among groups in organizations and using resolution and stimulation techniques appropriately for organizational effectiveness.

SUMMARY OF KEY POINTS

Power is the potential ability of a person or group to influence another person or group. French and Raven have identified five bases of power. Legitimate power is power granted by virtue of one's position in the organization. Reward power is the control of rewards valued by others. Coercive power is the ability to punish or harm. Expert power is control over organizationally valuable and relevant information. Finally, referent power is power through personal identification, often surfacing as imitation.

Another approach proposes two sources of power. Position power is tied to a position, regardless of the individual holding that position, whereas personal power is power that resides in a person regardless of position.

Attempts to use power can result in commitment, compliance, or resistance. Yukl's guidelines detail how managers can use the five bases of power to achieve commitment or compliance and to avoid resistance.

Organizational politics are activities carried out by people to acquire, enhance, and use power and other resources to obtain their preferred outcomes in a situation where there is uncertainty or disagreement. Survey results indicate that political behavior is not advocated by most managers but is seen as a necessity of organizational life. Cavanaugh and his associates have developed a model that attempts to specify conditions under which political behavior may or may not be ethical. Since managers cannot eliminate political activity in an organization, they must learn to cope with it.

Understanding how to manage political behavior requires an understanding of the reasons for political behavior, the techniques of political behavior, and techniques for limiting the effects of political behavior. There are several common causes of political activity, including ambiguous goals, scarce resources, technology and environment, nonprogrammed decisions, and organizational change. Common political techniques are controlling information, controlling lines of communication, using outside experts, controlling the agenda, game playing, image building, building coalitions, and controlling decision parameters. Ways to limit the effects of political behavior are open communication, the reduction of uncertainty, and vigilant awareness of causes and techniques of political behavior.

Conflict is common in organizations. This conflict is often a natural outgrowth of political behavior. Managers should recognize that conflict can be good in some situations and bad in others. Numerous techniques can be used to either stimulate or resolve conflict.

DISCUSSION QUESTIONS

1. Do you agree or disagree with the definition of power used in the chapter? What would you add or delete? Can you suggest an alternative?

2. What might happen if two people, each of whom has significant and equal power, attempt to influence each other?

3. Cite examples in a professor-student relationship to illustrate each of the five bases of organizational power.

4. Is there a logical sequence for the use of power bases that a manager might follow? That is, should the use of legitimate power usually precede the use of reward power or vice versa? In your opinion, is it possible to make such generalizations?

5. Choose a popular political figure and characterize his or her position and personal power. Which is stronger? Is it really possible to separate the two?

6. Cite examples in which you have been committed, compliant, and resistant as a result of efforts to influence you. Can you think of times when your attempts to influence others have led to commitment, compliance, and resistance?

7. Do you disagree with any guidelines for using power cited in the chapter? Can you suggest others? Can you recall situations in which you observed the successful use of one or more of them?

8. Do you agree or disagree with the assertion that political behavior is inevitable in organizational settings?

9. Given its general association with governmental bodies, why do you think the term politics has also come to be associated with behavior in organizations as described in the chapter?

10. Recall examples of how you have either used or observed others using the techniques of political behavior identified in the chapter. Can you suggest other techniques?

11. Do you agree or disagree with the assertion that conflict can be both good and bad? Cite examples of both.

Case 12.1

Power Politics At CBS

Most employees know what the word "politics" means when applied to a business, but few people ever get a chance to sit in on a board meeting that decides the fate of millions of dollars and thousands of jobs, careers, and reputations. In 1986, however, a top-level shakeup occurred that allowed the rest of the world to see what rarefied corporate politics is all about. As if someone had programmed it, the shakeup came at one of the nation's biggest media companies, CBS.

Although the showdown occurred on September 10, 1986, the story really began in 1980, when CBS's founder and chairman, William Paley, hired Thomas Wyman as the company's CEO. Three years later, CBS's board forced Paley out as chairman, giving the position to Wyman. Even if he didn't plan it that way, Paley got his revenge three years later.

In the meantime, CBS attracted a lot of attention, both in the media and on Wall Street. In 1985 a group led by Senator Jesse Helms announced that it was going to try to buy CBS. The company's stock rose and a number of America's financial heavyweights, including Ivan Boesky, Ted Turner, and Marvin Davis, made bids for the company. Turner, for example, wanted to divest the company of its non-broadcasting business. The latest to buy a big share of CBS was Laurence Tisch, chairman of Loews Corp., who bought just under 25 percent of the company and was appointed to its board of directors in October 1985. The company was not doing well at all, either financially or in the ratings, and everyone was waiting for something to break.

On September 10, during a nine-hour board meeting, it did. Most of the board had met for dinner the night before, and Paley had argued unsuccessfully that Wyman must go. Wyman had appointed some of the board members and a number of others supported him; only four or five joined Paley in opposing him. But Wyman apparently feared that Tisch intended to take over the company, or that another unfriendly raider would appear with an offer that CBS would not be able to fight off. Tisch had refused to sign a statement saying that he would not increase his holding in CBS, although he had given the other directors his word.

After a gloomy morning meeting about the company's market and financial positions, Wyman played his card: he announced that The Coca-Cola Company was willing to buy CBS. He apparently anticipated that the directors would be pleased to hear of a friendly offer for CBS or that Tisch would be forced to play his hand and reveal his own interest in buying the company. In fact, the directors were stunned and appalled. After fighting to keep the company independent for two years, Wyman was asking them to sell out to a company whose leaders were, they knew, personally friendly with Wyman. In addition, he apparently had been negotiating on his own, without telling anyone else on the board.

The move cost Wyman his credibility and, ultimately, his job. Tisch and Paley refused to consider the sale, and the other directors were even more unnerved when Wyman told them that he'd need some time to get an offer on the table. He hadn't brought along any lawyers or investment bankers to help him make his case. Wyman left the meeting at noon, Paley and Tisch soon after, and the remaining board members pondered the situation. By late afternoon two board members visited Wyman to tell him that his support among the board had disappeared. Wyman resigned, and the board asked Tisch to take over as CEO and Paley to return to his position as chairman. Both appointments were to be temporary.

The postscript to the September 10 showdown contained many ironies. Under Tisch's leadership, CBS began selling off its record, and book and magazine publishing businesses, exactly as Ted Turner, the spurned raider, had said he himself would do. Some of the news people who welcomed Tisch's takeover at a party that fateful night began to have their doubts when Tisch cut the news budget and staff. And it seemed that Thomas Wyman may have been right about Laurence Tisch's motives: two years after the shakeup, Tisch had firm control over the company, as firm as if he owned it.

Case Questions:

1. What kinds of power did the various participants in the CBS shakeup wield?

2. Is it inevitable that such a boardroom battle take on some of the aspects of a poker game?

3. Can you see any possible examples of political activities, as discussed in the chapter, that occurred at CBS?

Case Sources:

Peter W. Barnes, "Tisch Does What CBS Feared in Turner," *The Wall Street Journal*, November 20, 1987, 6; Peter W. Barnes, Laura Landro, James B. Stewart, "How The CBS Board Decided Chief Wyman Should Leave His Job," *The Wall Street Journal*, September 12, 1986, 1; Bill Powell and Jonathan Alter, "The Showdown at CBS," *Newsweek*, September 22, 1986, 54–59.

Case 12.2

The Struggle for Power at Ramsey Electronics

A vice president's position is about to open up at Ramsey Electronics, maker of components for audio and visual equipment and computers. Whoever fills the position will be one of the four most powerful people in the company and may one day become its executive officer. So the whole company has been watching the political skirmishes among the three leading candidates: Arnie Sander, Laura Prove, and Billy Evans.

Arnie Sander, currently the head of the reasearch and development division, worked his way up through the engineering ranks. Of the three candidates, he alone has a Ph.D. (in electrical engineering from MIT), and he is the acknowledged genius behind the company's most innovative products. One of the current vice presidents, Harley Learner, himself an engineer, has been pushing hard for Sander's case.

Laura Prove spent five years on the road, earning a reputation as an outstanding salesperson of Ramsey products before coming to the company headquarters and working her way up through the sales division. She knows only enough about what she calls the "guts" of Ramsey's electronic parts to get by, but she is very good at selling them and at motivating the people who work for her. Frank Barnwood, another of the current vice presidents, has been filling the Chief's ear with Prove's praises.

Of the three candidates, Billy Evans is the youngest, with the least experience at Ramsey. Like the Chief, he has an MBA from Harvard Business School and has a very sharp mind for finances. The Chief has credited him with turning the company's financial situation around, although others in the company feel that Sander's products or Prove's selling ability really deserves the credit. Evans has no particular champion among Ramsey's top executives, but he is the only other handball player that the Chief has located in the company, and the two of them play every Tuesday and Thursday after work. Learner and Barnwood have noticed that the company's financial decisions often seem to get made during the cooling-off period following a handball game.

In the month preceding the Chief's decision, the two vice presidents have been busy men. Learner, head of a national engineering association, worked to have Sander win an achievement award from the association, and two weeks before the naming of the new vice president he threw the most lavish banquet the company had ever seen to announce the award. When introducing Sander, Learner made a long, impassioned speech, detailing Sander's accomplishments and closing with the line, "the future of Ramsey Electronics."

Frank Barnwood has moved more slowly and subtly. The Chief had asked Barnwood years before to keep him updated on "all these gripes by women and minorities and such," and Barnwood did so by giving the Chief articles of particular interest. Recently he gave the Chief one from a psychology magazine about the cloning effect—the tendency of powerful executives to choose successors who are most like themselves. He also passed on to the Chief a

Fortune article arguing that many American corporations are floundering because they're being run by financial people, not by people who really know the company's business. He has made sure that the bulletin boards and the Chief's desk were flooded by news clippings about the values of having women and minorities at the top levels of a company.

Billy Evans has not seemed to care about the promotion. He has spent his days on the phone and in front of the computer screen, reporting to the Chief every other week about the company's latest financial successes, and never missing a handball game.

Case Questions:

1. Who do you think the Chief will pick as the new vice president?

2. Who do you think should get the job? Why?

3. Discuss political activities in which each candidate might engage to increase his or her chances for getting the promotion.

Experiential Exercise

Purpose: This exercise will help you appreciate some of the ambiguities in assessing the ethics of political activity in organizations.

Format: You will first create scenarios that you think represent different ethical perspectives. Your interpretations will then be assessed by others, while you, in turn, assess their perspectives.

Procedure: Your instructor will first divide the class into an even number of small groups (approximately three to four persons per group). Using the model of ethical political behavior presented in Figure 12.3, write several short scenarios that, to your group, represent different ethical perspectives. Write one scenario that follows all of the "yes" branches in the model, one that follow only "no" branches, and three that follow different combinations of "yes" "no" branches. For an example, reread the hypothetical case of the two professors up for a tenure vote.

Number your scenarios randomly from 1 to 5. Do not write down anything that might indicate which branches are to be followed. On a separate page, write a brief description of the rationale for the path your group thinks each scenario most logically follows.

Next, exchange scenarios with another group. Evaluate each of its scenarios and determine the most logical path through the model. Then exchange "answer sheets" and compare your interpretation of each scenario with that of the other group.

The two pairs of groups should then meet together to discuss their results. In particular, discussion should center on reasons for any disagreement between the two groups.

Follow-up Questions

1. How realistic was this exercise? What did you learn from it?
2. Could you assess real-life situations in this same way in deciding upon the ethics of political activity?

Organizational
Characteristics

PART IV

Part Contents

CHAPTER

13

Basic Organization Structure

Chapter Objectives

After reading this chapter, you should be able to

- define *organization structure* and discuss its purpose.
- describe structural configuration and summarize the four basic dimensions.
- summarize two structural policies that affect operations.
- explain the dual concept of authority and responsibility.

hen we think of jet engines, we think of those big powerful things hanging off the wings or tails of big commercial jets. Did you know that many other kinds of turbine, jet, and turbo-fan engines power modern aircraft? There are smaller engines made for private jets for business and personal use. There are specialized engines for military applications. And some turbine engines are used only for auxiliary power for the big commercial airplanes.

One of the largest manufacturers of jet and turbine engines is the Garrett Turbine Engine Co., a division of Allied-Signal Aerospace Co. Recently, Garrett changed its organization structure from a single integrated unit to two separate divisions: Garrett Engine Division and Garrett Auxiliary Power Division.[1] The Garrett Engine Division under president M. E. "Mal" Craig, formerly president of the whole company, will build aircraft engines for general aviation (private airplanes) and various military applications. The Engine Division will also include the Garrett General Aviation Services group, which will handle customer service and supply parts for private aircraft. The Engine Division will be one of the largest producers of engines for private and military aircraft.

The other new division, Garrett Auxiliary Power Division, will specialize in gas turbines for ground and airborne auxiliary power applications and will be run by divisional president, F. E. "Rick" Johnson. Garrett's auxiliary engines "are on almost every airliner produced since the 1970s," and this division will be the world's leader in manufacturing gas turbines for auxiliary applications. The division will also include a group for power-equipment repair and service and parts.[2]

*O*rganizations do not make major structural changes, such as the one just described, for the fun of it. There must be some compelling reason. In Garrett's case, the firm was already the industry leader; but its managers felt that reorganizing would help focus the company's efforts to serve customers with better products and services. In this chapter we explore how the structure of an organization can be a major factor in how well an organization achieves its goals.

An **organization** is a group of people working together to achieve common goals.[3] Top management sets the direction of an organization by defining its purpose, establishing the goals to meet that purpose, and formulating strategies to achieve the goals.[4]

---

[1] "Two New Units Created by Garrett," *The Arizona Republic,* January 12, 1988, p. 5.

[2] "Two New Units Created by Garrett," p. 5.

[3] See Richard Daft, *Organization Theory and Design,* 2nd ed. (St. Paul, Minn.: West, 1986), p. 9 for more discussion of the definition of organization.

[4] Arthur A. Thompson, Jr., and A. J. Strickland III. *Strategic Management,* 3rd ed. (Plano, Tex.: Business Publications. 1984), pp. 19–27.

The definition of purpose gives the organization reason to exist; in effect, it answers the question "What business are we in?" The establishment of goals converts the defined purpose into specific, measurable performance targets. **Organizational goals** are objectives that management seeks to achieve in pursuing the purpose of the firm. Goals motivate people to work together. Although each individual's goals are important to the organization, it is the organization's overall goals that are most important. Goals keep the organization on track by focusing the attention and actions of the members. They also provide the organization with a forward-looking orientation. They do not address past success or failure; rather, they force members to think about and plan for the future.

Finally, strategies are specific action plans that enable the organization to achieve its goals and thus its purpose. They involve the development of an organization structure and the processes to do the work of the organization.

In the first three parts of this book we discuss key elements of the individual and the factors that tie the individual and the organization together. In a given organization, these factors do their work within a common framework—the organization's structure. In this chapter, we define and analyze the basic elements of the structure of an organization.

OVERVIEW OF ORGANIZATION STRUCTURE

Organization structure is a system of task, reporting, and authority relationships within which the work of the organization is done. Thus, structure defines the form and function of the organization's activities. Structure also defines how the parts of an organization fit together (as in an organization chart).

The purpose of organization structure is to order and coordinate the actions of employees so as to achieve organizational goals. The premise of organized effort is that people can accomplish more by working together than they can separately. However, if the potential gains of collective effort are to be realized, the work must be coordinated. Suppose the thousands of employees at Ford Motor Company worked without any kind of structure. Each person might try to build a car that he or she thought would sell. No two automobiles would be alike, and each would take months or years to build. The costs of making the cars would be so high that no one could afford them. To produce automobiles that are both competitive in the marketplace and profitable for the company, Ford must have a structure in which its employees and managers work together in a coordinated way.

The task of coordinating the activities of thousands of workers to produce cars that are not only drivable but guaranteed for 60,000 miles may seem monumental. Yet whether for mass producing cars or making gas turbine engines, the requirements of organization structure are similar. First, the structure must divide the available labor according to the tasks to be performed. Even small organizations (those with fewer than one hundred employees) make use of division of labor.[5] Second, the structure must combine and coordinate the divided tasks to achieve a desired level of output. The more interdependent the divided tasks are, the more coordination is required.[6] Every organization structure addresses these two fundamental requirements.[7] The various ways they do so are what make one organization structure different from another.

Organization structure can be analyzed in three ways. First, we can examine its configuration, or its size and shape as depicted on an organization chart. Second, we can analyze its operational aspects or characteristics, such as separation of specialized tasks, rules and procedures, and decision making. Finally, we can analyze structure by examining responsibility and authority within the organization. In this chapter, we look at organization structure from all three of these points of view.

STRUCTURAL CONFIGURATION

The structure of an organization is most often described in terms of its organization chart. A complete **organization chart** shows all people, positions, reporting relationships, and lines of formal communication in the organization. (However, as discussed in Chapter 18, communication is not limited to these formal channels.) For large organizations, several charts may be necessary to show all positions. For example, one chart may show top management, including the board of directors, the chief executive officer, the president, all vice presidents, and important headquarters staff units. Subsequent charts may show the structure of each department and staff unit. Figure 13.1 depicts two organization charts for a large firm; top management is shown in part A and the manufacturing department is shown in part B. Notice in part B that the structure of the different manufacturing groups is given in separate charts.

An organization chart depicts reporting relationships and work group memberships and shows how positions and small work groups are combined into departments, which together make up the **configuration**, or shape, of the organization. The configuration of organizations can be analyzed in terms of how the two basic requiremets of structure—division of labor and coordination of the divided tasks—are fulfilled.

---

[5] A. Bryman, A. D. Beardsworth, E. T. Keil, and J. Ford, "Organizational Size and Specialization," *Organization Studies,* September 1983, pp. 271–278.

[6] Joseph L. C. Cheng, "Interdependence and Coordination in Organizations: A Role System Analysis," *Academy of Management Journal,* March 1983, pp. 156–162.

[7] See Henry Mintzberg, *The Structuring of Organizations* (Englewood Cliffs, N.J.: Prentice-Hall, 1979), for more discussion of the basic elements of structure.

Figure 13.1   Examples of Organization Charts

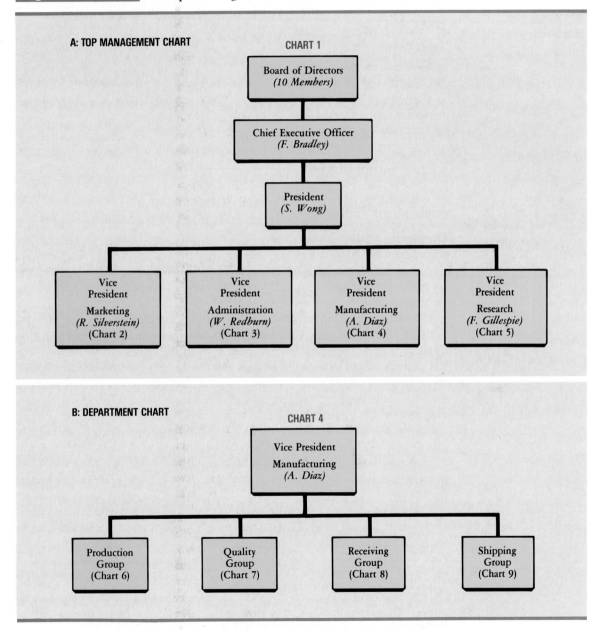

A: TOP MANAGEMENT CHART

CHART 1

Board of Directors
(10 Members)

Chief Executive Officer
(F. Bradley)

President
(S. Wong)

Vice President
Marketing
(R. Silverstein)
(Chart 2)

Vice President
Administration
(W. Redburn)
(Chart 3)

Vice President
Manufacturing
(A. Diaz)
(Chart 4)

Vice President
Research
(F. Gillespie)
(Chart 5)

B: DEPARTMENT CHART

CHART 4

Vice President
Manufacturing
(A. Diaz)

Production Group
(Chart 6)

Quality Group
(Chart 7)

Receiving Group
(Chart 8)

Shipping Group
(Chart 9)

Table 13.1	**Advantages**	**Disadvantages**
Advantages and Disadvantages of Division of Labor	Efficient use of labor	Routine, repetitive jobs
	Reduced training costs	Reduced job satisfaction
	Increased standardization and uniformity of output	Decreased worker involvement and commitment
	Increased expertise due to repetition of tasks	Increased worker alienation
		May not be compatible with computerized manufacturing technologies

Division of Labor

Division of labor is the extent to which the work of the organization is separated into different jobs to be done by different people. Division of labor is one of the seven primary characteristics of structuring described by Max Weber[8] (see Chapters 1 and 15) but the concept can be traced back to the eighteenth-century economist, Adam Smith. As noted in Chapter 1, Smith used a study of pin making to promote the idea of dividing production work to increase productivity.[9] Division of labor continued to increase in popularity as large organizations became more prevalent in a manufacturing society. This has continued, and most research indicates that large organizations usually have more division of labor than smaller ones.[10] Division of labor has also been found to have both advantages and disadvantages (see Table 13.1). Modern managers and organization theorists are still struggling with the primary disadvantage—division of labor often results in repetitive, routine, boring jobs that undercut worker satisfaction, involvement, and commitment.[11] In addition, extreme division of labor may not be compatible with new, integrated computerized manufacturing technologies that require teams of highly skilled workers.[12]

However, division of labor does not have to result in boredom. Visualized in terms of a small organization such as a basketball team, it can seem quite

---

[8] Max Weber, *The Theory of Social and Economic Organization*, A. M. Henderson and Talcott Parsons, trans. (New York: Free Press, 1947).

[9] Adam Smith, *An Inquiry into the Nature and Causes of The Wealth of Nations* (London: Dent, 1910).

[10] Nancy M. Carter and Thomas L. Keon, "The Rise and Fall of the Division of Labour, the Past 25 Years," *Organization Studies,* 1986, pp. 54–57.

[11] Glenn R. Carroll, "The Specialist Strategy," *California Management Review,* Spring 1984, pp. 126–137.

[12] "Management Discovers the Human Side of Automation," *Business Week,* September 29, 1986, pp. 70–75.

dynamic. A basketball team plays with five players, each of whom plays a different role on the team. In professional basketball the five positions are usually center, power forward, small forward, shooting guard, and point guard. The tasks of the players in each of these positions are quite different, resulting in players of different sizes and skills being on the floor at any one time. Consider one of the most successful professional basketball teams in the last decade, the Los Angeles Lakers. The team's center, Kareem Abdul-Jabbar, is over seven feet tall and is very good at rebounding, scoring from under the basket, and intimidating opponents. Point guard Earvin "Magic" Johnson, in contrast, is adept at dribbling, passing, and hitting shots from outside. The demands of these two positions are quite different, requiring different players with different skills to fulfill them. Similar differences exist for the other positions. Division of labor is thus important to a basketball team; players specialize in doing specified tasks, and they learn to do them very well. (Of course, some players have a pretty wide range of "specialties.")

Coordination of the Divided Tasks

Three basic mechanisms are used to help coordinate the divided tasks: departmentalization, span of control, and administrative hierarchy. These mechanisms focus on grouping tasks in some meaningful manner, on creating work groups of manageable size, and on establishing a system of reporting relationships among supervisors and managers.

DEPARTMENTALIZATION   Departmentalization describes the manner in which divided tasks are combined and allocated to work groups. It is a consequence of the division of labor. Because employees engaged in specialized activities can lose sight of overall organizational goals, their work must be coordinated to ensure that it contributes to the welfare of the organization. There are many possible ways to group, or departmentalize, tasks, but the five most used methods are by business function, by process, by product or service, by customer, and by geography. The first two, function and process, derive from the internal operations of the organization; the others are based on external factors. Most organizations tend to use a combination of methods, and departmentalization often changes as organizations evolve.[13]

Departmentalization by business function is based on the traditional business functions such as marketing, manufacturing, and personnel administration (see Figure 13.2). In this configuration employees most frequently associate with those engaged in the same function, which helps in communication and cooperation. In a functional group, employees who do similar work can learn from each other by sharing ideas about opportunities and problems they encounter on the job. Unfortunately, the functional grouping lacks an automatic

---

[13] See Robert H. Miles, *Macro Organizational Behavior* (Santa Monica, Calif.: Goodyear, 1980), pp. 28–34, for a discussion of departmentalization schemes.

Figure 13.2   Departmentalization by Business Function

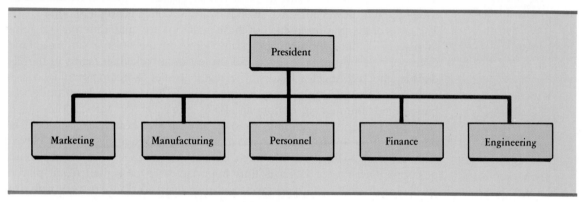

mechanism for coordinating the flow of work through the organization.[14] That is, employees in a functional structure tend to associate little with those in other parts of the organization. The result can be a narrowness of focus that limits the coordination of work among functional groups, as when the engineering department fails to provide marketing with product information because it is too busy testing materials to think about sales.

Departmentalization by process is similar to functional departmentalization, except the focus is much more on specific jobs grouped according to the activity engaged in by the workers. Thus, as illustrated in Figure 13.3, the firm's manufacturing jobs are divided into certain well-defined manufacturing processes: drilling, milling, heat treating, painting, and assembly. Hospitals often use process departmentalization, grouping the professional employees, such as therapists, according to the types of treatment they provide.

Process groupings encourage specialization and expertise among employees, who tend to concentrate on a single operation and share information with departmental colleagues. A process orientation may develop into an internal career path and managerial hierarchy within the department. As in functional grouping, however, narrowness of focus can be a problem in process departmentalization. Employees in a process group may become so absorbed in the requirements and execution of their operation that they disregard larger considerations such as overall product flow.[15]

Departmentalization by product or service occurs when employees who work on a particular product or service are members of the same department, regardless of their business function or the process they are engaged in. This configuration is shown in Figure 13.4. In this way, IBM recently reorganized its

---

[14] Mintzberg, *The Structuring of Organizations*, p. 125.

[15] Miles, *Macro Organizational Behavior*, pp. 122–133.

Figure 13.3	Departmentalization by Process

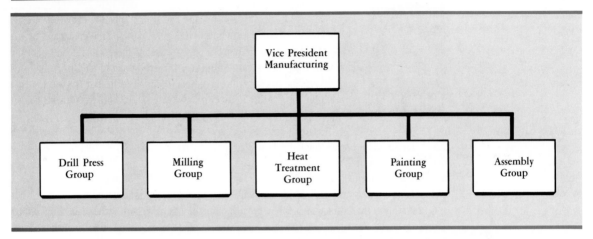

operations into five autonomous business units: personal computers, medium-sized office systems, mainframes, communications equipment, and components.[16]

Departmentalization according to product or service obviously enhances interaction and communication among employees producing the same product or providing the same service. Such a grouping may reduce product- or service-related coordination problems. In this type of configuration there may be less process specialization, but more specialization in the peculiarities of the specific product or service. IBM expects that the new alignment will allow all employees, from designers to manufacturing workers to marketing experts, to become specialists in a particular product line. The disadvantage is that employees may become so interested in their particular product or service that they miss technological improvements or innovations developed in other departments. Honda Motor Co. chose a product departmentalization strategy when it introduced the Acura. (See *Management in Action*.)

Departmentalization by customer is often referred to as departmentalization by market. Many lending institutions, in Texas for example, have separate departments for retail, commercial, agriculture, and petroleum loans, as shown in Figure 13.5. When significant groups of customers differ substantially from one another, organizing along customer lines may represent the most effective way of providing the best product or service possible. This is why hospital nurses are often grouped by the type of illness they handle, because the different maladies demand different treatment and specialized knowledge.[17]

[16] "Big Blue Wants to Loosen Its Collar," *Fortune*, February 29, 1988, p. 8.

[17] Peggy Leatt and Rodney Schneck, "Criteria for Grouping Nursing Subunits in Hospitals," *Academy of Management Review*, March 1984, pp. 150–165.

Management in ACTION

A New Department for Honda

Honda Motor Co., Ltd. sells more cars in America than any other foreign manufacturer. Its Accord model is the best-selling Japanese car in the United States and in surveys of automobile buyer satisfaction, the company has by-passed Mercedes-Benz as number one. Yet despite the good will and publicity that such a reputation carries with it, Honda chose not to lend its name to its new luxury line of cars, which it introduced in 1986. Instead, it created a new division for them. Acura's success shows that such product departmentalization can pay off.

According to Tetsuo Chino, president of American Honda, part of the reason for separating Acura from Honda was to keep life relatively simple for Honda dealers. "We don't want Honda dealers to get too complicated," Chino said at the time. "We want Honda dealers to be specialists in small cars."* The company may also have felt that it wanted to divorce the high-priced, luxury Acuras from the old Honda image—that of being inexpensive and tiny.

To achieve the distinction between product lines, Honda prohibited its dealers from selling Acuras in Honda showrooms. In fact, if a Honda dealer wants to sell Acuras, the Acura outlet must be at least 10 miles from that dealer's Honda showroom. Other Acura dealers, however, may be located within that ten-mile limit, a fact that does not please Honda dealers.

The decision to separate the two lines may also be tied to Honda's corporate culture. The company's founder, Soichiro Honda, was a maverick in Japanese industry who told employees to work not just for the company but also for themselves. This approach has become part of Honda's culture and has meant that traditional distinctions between jobs often get blurred. For example, there are only two job classifications for the over 3,000 workers in Honda's Marysville, Ohio, plant, compared to over 100 classifications for unionized workers at GM factories. Engineers, designers, salespeople, and marketers work together and trade suggestions for making a better car. Honda may have felt that with so few distinctions between job categories and functions, adding more cars to the Honda line would have led to chaos.

Whatever the reasons, the move was successful; in its second year, Acura sold 109,000 cars. And now Toyota and Nissan, playing catch-up with their formerly upstart rival, are creating their own luxury lines to sell through new dealer systems.

* Stewart Toy, "The Selling of Acura—A Honda That's Not a Honda," *Business Week*, March 17, 1986, 93.

Sources: Stephen Koepp, "Honda in a Hurry," *Time*, September 8, 1986, 48–49; Stewart Toy, "The Americanization of Honda," *Business Week*, April 25, 1988, 90–96; Stewart Toy, "The Selling of Acura—A Honda That's Not a Honda," *Business Week*, March 17, 1986, 93.

Figure 13.4   Departmentalization by Product

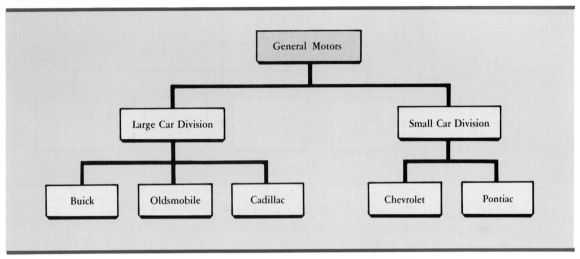

With customer departmentalization there is usually less process specialization because employees must remain flexible to do whatever is necessary to enhance the relationship with customers. This configuration offers the best coordination of the flow of work to the customer; however, it may isolate employees from others in their special areas of expertise. For example, if a company's three metallurgical specialists are each assigned to a different market-based group, they are not likely to have many opportunities to discuss the latest technological advances in metallurgy.

Departmentalization by geography means that groups are organized according to a region of the country or world. Sales or marketing groups are often arranged by geographic region. As illustrated in Figure 13.6, the marketing effort of a large multinational corporation can be divided according to major geographical divisions.

Using a geographically based configuration may result in significant cost savings and better market coverage. On the other hand, it may isolate work groups from activities in the organization's home office or in the technological community, because the focus of the work group is solely on the affairs within the region. This may foster loyalty to the work group that exceeds commitment to the larger organization. In addition, work-related communication and coordination among groups may not be particularly efficient.

Many large organizations use a mixed departmentalization scheme. Such organizations may have separate operating divisions based on products, but

Figure 13.5

Departmentalization by Customer

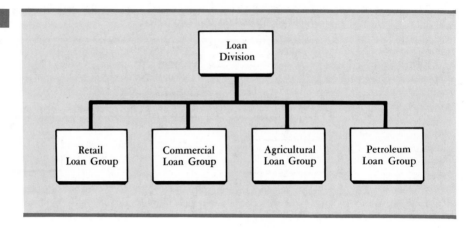

within each division departments may be based on business function, process, customers, or geographic region (see Figure 13.7). Which methods work best depends on the organization's activities, its communication needs, and its coordination requirements. Another type of mixed structure often occurs in joint ventures, which are becoming increasingly popular. (See *International Perspective.*)

SPAN OF CONTROL   The second dimension of organizational configuration, **span of control,** is the number of people reporting to a manager; thus it defines the size of the organization's work groups. Span of control is also referred to as *span of management.* A manager who has a small span of control can maintain close control over the workers and stay in contact with daily operations. If the span of control is large, close control is not possible. Figure 13.8 shows examples of small and large spans of control. Supervisors in part A have a span of control of 16, whereas in part B, their span of control is 8.

A number of formulas and rules have been offered for determining the optimal span of control in an organization,[18] but research on the topic has not conclusively identified a foolproof method.[19] Henry Mintzberg has concluded that the optimal unit size depends on the coordination requirements within the unit, including such things as the degree of job specialization in the unit, the similarity of the tasks in the unit, the type of information available or needed by unit members, differences in the members' need for autonomy, and how

---

[18] Lyndall F. Urwick, "The Manager's Span of Control," *Harvard Business Review,* May–June 1956, pp. 39–47.

[19] Dan R. Dalton, William D. Tudor, Michael J. Spendolini, Gordon J. Fielding, and Lyman W. Porter, "Organization Structure and Performance: A Critical Review," *Academy of Management Review,* January 1980, pp. 49–64.

International Perspective

Joint Ventures That Move the Earth

While the world focuses on the competitive skirmishes between Japanese and American automakers, other industrial giants from the two countries struggle for dominance in making construction equipment. As industry leader Caterpillar and challenger Komatsu vie for market share, they are both using the same tactic—joint ventures with companies on the other side of the Pacific.

Caterpillar has been making construction machinery for sixty years. It was formed in 1928 from the merger of two other companies, including one owned by Benjamin Holt, who invented the "Caterpillar" crawler track for working in California mud. Many American construction companies have been buying nothing but "Cats" for half a century.

Komatsu began its challenge against the giant in 1971 by importing to the United States its two best products. For a decade it sold nothing but crawler-tractors and crawler-loaders, building a reputation for reasonable price, high quality and good parts support. Given a strong dollar and an established name, Komatsu began importing a broader line of equipment in the 1980s, underselling Caterpillar by as much as 40 percent.

Fighting back, Caterpillar looked to overseas partners to replace weak links in its product line and to compete in areas where Komatsu was stronger. First it contracted Daewoo Heavy Industries of South Korea to make some of its trucks. Then it formed a joint venture, Shin Caterpillar-Mitsubishi, to make excavators. The new venture draws on Mitsubishi's experience in designing and manufacturing quality excavators and on Caterpillar's unrivaled dealer network and manufacturing capacity.

Komatsu struck back in 1988 by signing an agreement with Dresser Industries of Dallas. In this joint venture, Dresser workers will assemble parts made in Japan by Komatsu, giving the Japanese company a firmer grip on the American market. (It had already tried to fend off protectionist pressures by building a plant in Tennessee.) Analysts say that Komatsu needed to make the move because of the strong yen and because its Tennessee plant could not meet the American demand. It will be pouring a significant amount of money into the Dresser plants, especially older factories that Dresser bought from International Harvester. The companies will combine engineering and manufacturing activities and will keep their own distribution systems.

In their joint ventures, Caterpillar and Komatsu have each found another company with complementary strengths and weaknesses. The joint ventures are resulting in organization structures that involve unusual combinations of facilities—designed to meet the competitive challenge. Analysts are now betting on who will win the struggle to move the earth.

Sources: Tsukasa Furukawa, "Global Construction Machinery Battle Looms," *Metalworking News*, July 27, 1987, 5, 31; Bill Kelley, "Komatsu in a Cat Fight," *S&MM*, April 1986, 50–53; Kevin Kelly, "A Weakened Komatsu Tries To Come Back Swinging," *Business Week*, February 22, 1988, 48; Robert D. Franceschini, "It's a Dog Fight!" *Purchasing*, March 13, 1986, 48–55.

Figure 13.6   Departmentalization by Geographic Region

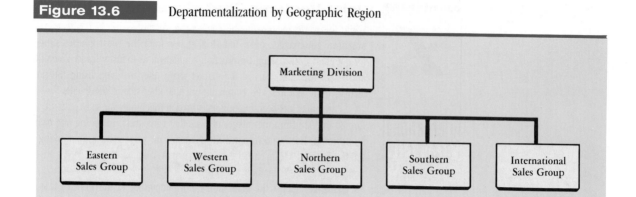

much the members need to have direct access to the supervisor.[20] Because results so far are inconclusive, research on span of control continues.[21]

ADMINISTRATIVE HIERARCHY   The **administrative hierarchy** is a system of reporting relationships in the organization, from the first level up through the president or CEO. It results from the need for supervisors and managers to coordinate the activities of employees. The size of the administrative hierarchy is inversely related to the span of control: in organizations where the span of control is small, there are many managers in the hierarchy; where it is large, the administrative hierarchy is smaller.

Using Figure 13.8, we can examine the effects of small and large spans of control on the number of hierarchical levels. The smaller span of control for the supervisors in part B requires that there be four supervisors rather than two. Correspondingly, another management layer is needed to keep the department head's span of control at two. In part B, then, the span of control is small, the workers are under tighter supervision, and there are more administrative levels. In part A, production workers are not closely supervised, and there are fewer administrative levels. As a measure of the number of management personnel, or administrators, in the organization, the administrative hierarchy is sometimes called the *administrative component*, *administrative intensity*, or *administrative ratio*.

The size of the administrative hierarchy also relates to the overall size of the organization. As an organization's size increases, so do its complexity and the requirements for coordination, necessitating proportionately more people

---

[20] Mintzberg, *The Structuring of Organizations*, pp. 133–147.
[21] See David Van Fleet, "Span of Management Research and Issues," *Academy of Management Journal*, September 1983, pp. 546–552, for a recent example of research on span of control.

Figure 13.7 Mixed Departmentalization

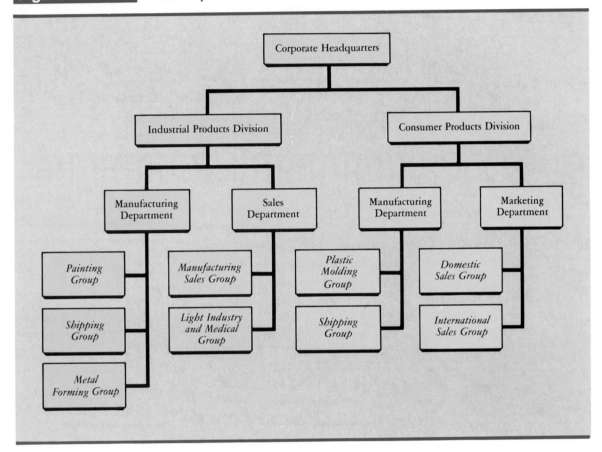

to manage the business.[22] However, this conclusion defines the administrative component as including all of the administrative hierarchy, that is, all of the support staff groups, such as personnel and financial services, legal staff, and others. Defined in this way, the administrative component in a large company may seem huge when compared to the number of production workers. On the other hand, research that separates the support staff and clerical functions from the management hierarchy has found that the ratio of managers to total employees actually decreases with increases in an organization's size.[23] Still

[22] John B. Cullen and Douglas D. Baker, "Administration Size and Organization Size: An Examination of the Lag Structure," *Academy of Management Journal,* September 1984, pp. 644–654.
[23] See Daft, *Organization Theory and Design,* 2nd ed., pp. 181–182, for a good discussion of the research on administrative hierarchy.

Figure 13.8

Span of Control

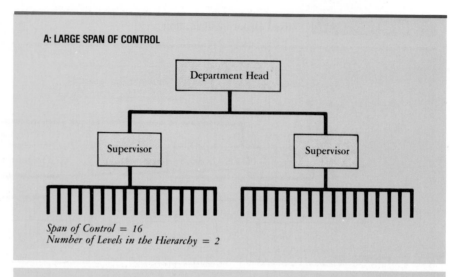

A: LARGE SPAN OF CONTROL

Span of Control = 16
Number of Levels in the Hierarchy = 2

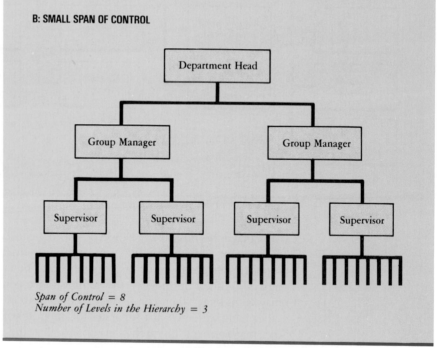

B: SMALL SPAN OF CONTROL

Span of Control = 8
Number of Levels in the Hierarchy = 3

other, more recent research has shown that the size of the administrative hierarchy and the overall size of the organization are not related in a simple manner, especially during periods of growth and decline.[24]

STRUCTURE AND OPERATIONS

Some important aspects of organization structure do not appear on the organization chart and thus are quite different from the configurational aspects discussed in the previous section. This section describes the structural policies that affect operations and prescribe or restrict how employees behave in their organizational activities.[25] The two primary aspects of these policies are formalization of rules and procedures and centralization of decision making.

Formalization

Formalization is the degree to which rules and procedures shape the jobs and activities of employees. The purpose of formalization is to predict and control how employees behave on the job.[26] Rules and procedures can be both explicit and implicit. *Explicit rules* are set down in job descriptions, policy and procedures manuals, or office memos. (In one large company that continually issues directives attempting to limit employee activities, workers refer to them as Gestapo memos because of their prescriptive tone.) *Implicit rules* may develop as employees become accustomed to doing things in a certain way over a period of time.[27] Though unwritten, these established ways of getting things done become standard operating procedures (SOPs) with the same effect on employee behavior as written rules.

We can assess formalization in organizations by looking at the proportion of jobs that are governed by rules and procedures and the extent to which variation is allowed within those rules. More formalized organizations have a higher proportion of rule-bound jobs and less tolerance for rule violations.[28] Increasing formalization may effect the design of jobs throughout the organization[29]

---

[24] John R. Montanari and Philip J. Adelman, "The Administrative Component of Organizations and the Rachet Effect: A Critique of Cross-Sectional Studies, *"Journal of Management Studies,* March 1987, pp. 113–123.

[25] Dalton et al., "Organization Structure and Performance."

[26] Mintzberg, *The Structuring of Organizations,* pp. 83–84.

[27] Arthur P. Brief and H. Kirk Downey, "Cognitive and Organizational Structures: A Conceptual Analysis of Implicit Organizing Theories," *Human Relations,* December 1983, pp. 1065–1090.

[28] Jerald Hage, "An Axiomatic Theory of Organizations," *Administrative Science Quarterly,* December 1965, pp. 289–320.

[29] See Gregory Moorhead, "Organizational Analysis: An Integration of the Macro and Micro Approaches," *Journal of Management Studies,* April 1981, pp. 191–218; and Ricky W. Griffin, *Task Design: An Integrative Approach* (Glenview, Ill.: Scott, Foresman, 1982), for more discussion of the complexities surrounding the relationships between formalization and job design.

as well as employee motivation[30] and work group interactions.[31] The specific effects of formalization on employees are still unclear, however.[32]

Organizations tend to add more rules and procedures as the need for control of operations increases. For example, Lotus, a developer of software for personal computers, instituted more rules and procedures, especially in the areas of hiring and personnel, to gain control of its operations in the face of rapid growth.[33] Some organizations have become so formalized that they have rules for how to make new rules. One large state university created such rules in the form of a three-page document entitled "Procedures for Rule Adoption" that was added to the 4-inch-thick "Policy and Procedures Manual." The new policy first defines terms such as *University, Board,* and *rule* and lists ten exceptions that describe when this policy on rule adoptions does not apply. It then presents a nine-step process for adopting a new rule within the university.

Other organizations are trying to become less formalized by reducing the number of rules and procedures that employees must follow. In this way, Chevron recently cut the number of its rules and procedures from over four hundred to eighteen. Highly detailed procedures for hiring were eliminated in favor of letting managers make hiring decisions based on common sense.[34]

A relatively new approach to organizational formalization attempts to describe how, when, and why good managers should bend or break a rule.[35] Although rules exist in some form in almost every organization, how strictly they are enforced may vary significantly from one organization to another, or even within a single organization. Some managers argue that "a rule is a rule" and all rules must be enforced to control employee behaviors and prevent chaos in the organization. Other managers act as if "all rules are made to be broken" and see rules as stumbling blocks to effective action. Neither point of view is best for the organization; a more balanced attitude is recommended. The test of a good manager in a formalized organization may be the use of appropriate judgment in making exceptions to rules.

A balanced approach to making exceptions to rules should do two things. First, it should recognize that individuals are unique and that the organization can benefit from making exceptions that capitalize on exceptional capabilities.

---

[30] J. Daniel Sherman and Howard L. Smith, "The Influence of Organizational Structure on Intrinsic Versus Extrinsic Motivation," *Academy of Management Journal,* December 1984, pp. 877–885.

[31] John A. Pearce II and Fred R. David, "A Social Network Approach to Organizational Design-Performance," *Academy of Management Review,* July 1983, pp. 436–444.

[32] Eileen Fairhurst, "Organizational Rules and the Accomplishment of Nursing Work on Geriatric Wards," *Journal of Management Studies,* July 1983, pp. 315–332.

[33] "Coming of Age at Lotus: Software's Child Prodigy Grows Up," *Business Week,* February 25, 1985, pp. 100–101.

[34] Amanda Bennett, "Chevron Corp. Has Big Challenge Coping With Worker Cutbacks," *The Wall Street Journal,* November 4, 1986, pp. 1, 25.

[35] F. Neil Brady, "Rules for Making Exceptions to Rules," *Academy of Management Review,* July 1987, pp. 436–444.

For example, an engineering design department with a rule mandating equal access to tools and equipment may acquire a limited amount of specialized equipment, such as personal computers. The department manager may decide to make an exception to the equal-access rule by assigning the computers to designers the manager thinks will use them most and with the best results, instead of making them available for use by all.

Second, a balanced approach should recognize the commonalities among employees. Managers should make exceptions to rules only when there is a true and meaningful difference between individuals, rather than base exceptions on features such as race, sex, appearance, or social factors.

Centralization

The second structural policy that affects operations is **centralization**, whereby decision-making authority is concentrated at the top of the organizational hierarchy. This structural aspect is opposed to *decentralization*, where decisions are made throughout the hierarchy.[36] Increasingly, centralization is discussed in terms of participation in decision making.[37] In decentralized organizations, lower-level employees participate in making decisions. The recent changes in the organization structure at IBM have decentralized the decision making in some areas. No longer will all marketing decisions be made at the corporate headquarters in Armonk, New York. Each product-centered division will make marketing decisions affecting its products.[38]

Decision making in organizations is more complex than indicated by the simple classification as centralized or decentralized. In Chapter 17 we discuss organizational decision making in more depth. One of the major distinctions we make there is that some decisions are relatively routine and require only the application of a decision rule. These decisions we call *programmed* decisions. Others that are not routine are called *nonprogrammed*. The decision rules for programmed decisions are formalized for the organization. This difference between programmed and nonprogrammed decisions tends to cloud the distinction between centralization and decentralization. For even if decision making is decentralized, the decisions themselves may be programmed and tightly circumscribed.

Figure 13.9 summarizes the three possible types of centralization and decentralization in organizations. If there is little participation in decision making, the organization structure is centralized, regardless of the nature of the decisions being made. In the other extreme situation, if individuals or

---

[36] See John Child, *Organization: A Guide to Problems and Practice,* 2nd ed. (New York: Harper & Row, 1984), pp. 145–153, for a good discussion of the concept of centralization.

[37] Richard H. Hall, *Organization: Structure and Process,* 3rd ed. (Englewood Cliffs, N.J.: Prentice-Hall, 1982), pp. 87–96.

[38] "Big Blue Wants to Loosen Its Collar."

Figure 13.9

Centralization

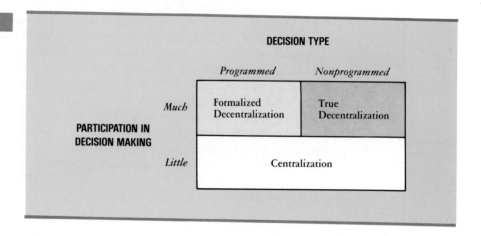

With a diagram titled **DECISION TYPE** showing categories *Programmed* and *Nonprogrammed* across the top, and **PARTICIPATION IN DECISION MAKING** on the left with *Much* and *Little*. The cells show "Formalized Decentralization" (Much/Programmed), "True Decentralization" (Much/Nonprogrammed), and "Centralization" (Little, spanning both).

groups participate extensively in making nonprogrammed decisions, the structure can be described as *truly* decentralized. If individuals or groups participate extensively in decision making but mainly in programmed decisions, the structure is said to be *formalized* decentralization. Formalized decentralization is a common way to provide decision-making involvement for employees at many different levels in the organization, while at the same time maintaining control and predictability.

Participative management (discussed in more detail in Chapter 5) has been described as a total management system in which people are involved in the daily decision making and management of the organization. As part of an organization's culture, it can contribute importantly to the long-run success of the organization.[39] It has been described as effective and in fact morally necessary in organizations.[40] In the thinking of many people, then, participation in decision making has become more than a simple aspect of organization structure.

The configurational and operational aspects of structure remain a source of interest, especially in comparisons between U.S. and Japanese companies. (See *A Look at Research*.)

RESPONSIBILITY AND AUTHORITY

Responsibility and authority are related to both configurational and operational aspects of structure. For example, the organization chart shows who reports to whom at all levels in the organization. From the operational perspective, the

[39] Daniel R. Denison, "Bringing Corporate Culture to the Bottom Line," *Organizational Dynamics*, Autumn 1984, pp. 4–22.

[40] Marshall Sashkin, "Participative Management Is an Ethical Imperative," *Organizational Dynamics*, Spring 1984, pp. 4–22.

A LOOK AT

RESEARCH

How Different Are Japanese Organizations?

Despite the fact that differences between American and Japanese organization structures are often cited, relatively little research has been done to measure and correlate the differences. A study published in 1986 sought to fill that gap and see if statistically significant differences exist between similar American and Japanese corporations. The researchers conducted surveys of 55 manufacturing plants in the United States and 51 Japanese plants in the same industries. Their results both confirmed and challenged popular hypotheses about differences in manufacturing companies in the two countries.

The researchers found five basic differences. They are enumerated in the following paragraphs.

Jobs are less specialized in Japan than in the United States. Of the twenty job functions listed on the survey, three-quarters were assigned to specialists in the United States, but only one-third were handled by Japanese specialists.

Japanese organizations tend to have taller organizational structures than their American counterparts; the average Japanese organizational chart contains one-half a rank more than the average American chart. However, contrary to some earlier findings, the researchers did not find that the span of control is narrower in Japanese than in American companies.

The ratios between management and production personnel in the two countries are roughly the same. However, Japanese corporations average 4 percent more clerical workers, a finding consistent with the common observation that Japanese companies tend to be very meticulous about record-keeping.

The management level at which decisions are made differs between companies in the two countries in interesting ways. Executives in the two sets of companies were given a list of thirty-seven decisions and asked to indicate what level of management had the authority to make each decision, and at what level the decision would typically actually be made. The Japanese executives surveyed said that the formal authority to make the decisions rests, on average, with plant managers, while in the United States the authority to make the same decisions would be found somewhere between the department head and plant manager levels. In both countries, such decisions are actually made at lower levels in the organizational hierarchy. But while the levels of formal and actual authority are nearly equal in the United States, decisions that plant managers are supposed to make actually get made at a much lower level in Japan, somewhere between the middle manager and department head levels.

As expected, many more Japanese employees (76 percent) reported being members of quality circles than did American employees (27 percent). The study indicated that in both countries, highly centralized organizations use quality circles more than do decentralized companies. Based on this evidence, the researchers speculated that companies may use quality circles more often to increase the perception that workers are participating in decision making, rather than to expand actual participation.

Source: James R. Lincoln, Mitsuyo Hanada, and Kerry McBride, "Organizational Structures in Japanese and U.S. Manufacturing," *Administrative Science Quarterly*, 31 (1986), 338–364.

amount of centralization defines the locus of decision-making authority in the organization. However, there is often some confusion about what responsibility and authority really mean for managers in an organization, and how the two terms relate to each other.

Responsibility

Responsibility is an obligation to do something under the expectation that some act or output will be achieved. For example, a manager may expect an employee to write and present a proposal for a new program by a certain date; thus, the employee is "responsible" for preparing the proposal.

Responsibility ultimately derives from the ownership of the organization. The owners hire or appoint a group, often called a board of directors, to be responsible for managing the organization, making the decisions, and reaching the goals set by the owners. A downward chain of responsibility is then established. The board hires a president to be responsible for running the organization. The president hires more people and holds them responsible for accomplishing designated tasks that enable the president to produce the results expected by the board and the owners. The chain extends throughout the organization, since each manager has an obligation to fulfill—to appropriately employ organizational resources (e.g., people, money, and equipment) to meet the owners' expectations. Although managers seemingly pass responsibility on to others to achieve results, each manager is still held responsible for the outputs of those to whom he or she delegates tasks.

A manager responsible for a work group assigns tasks to members of the group. Each group member is then responsible for doing his or her task. Yet the manager remains responsible for each task and for the work of the group as a whole. This means managers can take on the responsibility of others but cannot shed their own onto those below them in the hierarchy.

Authority

Authority is power that has been legitimized within a specific social context.[41] (Power is discussed in Chapter 12.) Only when power is part of an official organizational role does it become authority. Authority includes the legitimate right to use resources to accomplish expected outcomes. As we discussed in the previous section, the authority to make decisions may be restricted to the top levels of the organization or dispersed throughout the organization.

Like responsibility, authority originates in the ownership of the organization. The owners establish a group of directors who are responsible for managing the affairs of the organization. They, in turn, authorize people in the organization to make decisions and to use organizational resources. So they delegate authority, or power in a social context, to others.

---

[41] See Jeffrey Pfeffer, *Power in Organizations* (Boston: Pittman, 1981), pp. 4–6, for a good discussion of the relationship between power and authority.

Authority is linked to responsibility because an employee responsible for accomplishing certain results must have the authority to use resources to achieve the results.[42] The relationship between responsibility and authority must be one of *parity*; that is, the authority over resources must be sufficient to enable the employee to meet the output expectations of others.

But authority and responsibility differ in significant ways. Responsibility cannot be delegated down to others, but authority can be. One complaint often heard from employees is that they have too much responsibility but not enough authority to get the job done: this indicates a lack of parity between responsibility and authority. Managers are usually quite happy to hold individuals responsible for specific tasks, but are reluctant to delegate sufficient authority to do the job. In effect, managers try to rid themselves of responsibility for results (which they cannot do), yet they rarely like to give away their cherished authority over resources.

The Iran/Contra affair of 1987–88 is a good example of the difference between authority and responsibility. Drucker noted that the Reagan administration confused delegation of authority with abdication of responsibility.[43] President Reagan delegated a great deal of authority to subordinates, but did not require that they keep him informed. Neither did the subordinates make an effort to keep the President informed of their activities. Thus, delegation of authority by the administration is appropriate and necessary, but not to require progress reports to keep informed and in control of operations resulted in the administration trying to avoid responsibility. Although the President did hold his subordinates responsible for their actions, he ultimately—and rightfully—retained full responsibility.

An Alternative View of Authority

So far we have described authority as a "top-down" function in organizations. That is, authority originates at the top and is delegated downward as the managers at the top consider appropriate. In Chester Barnard's alternative perspective, authority is seen as originating in the individual, who can choose whether or not to follow a directive from above. The choice of whether to comply with a directive is based on the degree to which the individual understands it, feels able to carry it out, and believes it to be in the best interests of the organization and consistent with personal values.[44] This perspective has been called the **acceptance theory of authority** because it means that the authority of the manager depends on the subordinate's acceptance of the manager's right to give the directive and expect compliance.

---

[42] John B. Miner, *Theories of Organizational Structure and Process* (Chicago, Ill.: Dryden, 1982), p. 360.

[43] Peter F. Drucker, "Management Lesson of Irangate," *The Wall Street Journal*, March 24, 1987, p. 36.

[44] See Chester Barnard, *The Functions of the Executive* (Cambridge, Mass.: Harvard University Press, 1938), pp. 161–184, for a complete discussion of this perspective.

For example, suppose you are a sales analyst. Your company has a painting crew, but for some reason your manager has told you to repaint your own office over the weekend. You would probably question your manager's authority to make you do this work. In fact, you would probably refuse to do it. A similar request to work over the weekend to finish a report would more likely be accepted and carried out. So workers can either accept or reject the directives of a supervisor and thus limit supervisory authority.[45] In most organizational situations, employees accept a manager's right to expect compliance on normal, reasonable directives because of the manager's legitimate position in the organizational hierarchy or in the social context of the organization. When they do not accept the manager's right they may choose to disobey the directive and must accept the consequences.

SUMMARY OF KEY POINTS

The structure of an organization is a system of task, reporting, and authority relationships within which the work of the organization is done. The purpose of organization structure is to order and coordinate the actions of employees to achieve organizational goals. Every organization structure addresses two fundamental issues: the division of available labor according to the tasks to be performed, and the combination and coordination of divided tasks to assure the accomplishment of the tasks.

An organization chart shows reporting relationships, work group memberships, departments, and formal lines of communication. In a broader sense, an organization chart shows the configuration, or shape, of the organization. Configuration has four dimensions: division of labor, departmentalization, span of control, and the administrative hierarchy. Division of labor is the extent to which the work is separated into different jobs to be done by different people. Departmentalization is the manner in which the divided tasks are combined and allocated to work groups for coordination. Tasks can be combined into departments on the basis of business function, process, product, customer, and geographic region. Span of control is the number of people reporting to a manager; it also defines the size of work groups and is inversely related to the number of hierarchical levels in the organization. The administrative hierarchy is the system of reporting relationships in an organization.

Structural policies that affect operations prescribe how employees behave in their organizational activities. Such policies include formalization of rules and procedures and centralization of decision making. Formalization is the degree to which rules and procedures shape the jobs and activities of employees. The purpose of formalization is to predict and control how employees behave on the job. Explicit rules are set down in job descriptions, policy and procedures

---

[45] Pfeffer, *Power and Organizations,* pp. 366–367.

manuals, or office memos. Implicit rules develop over time as employees become accustomed to doing things in a certain way.

Centralization concentrates decision-making authority at the top of the organizational hierarchy as opposed to decentralization, where decisions are made throughout the hierarchy.

A final aspect of organization structure is the dual concept of authority and responsibility. Responsibility is an obligation to do something. Authority is defined as power that has been legitimized within a specific social context. Authority includes the legitimate right to use resources to accomplish expected outcomes. The relationship between responsibility and authority needs to be one of parity; that is, authority over resources must be adequate to enable the employee to meet the expectations of others.

DISCUSSION QUESTIONS

1. Define organization structure and explain how it fits into the process of managing the organization.

2. What is the purpose of organization structure? What would an organization be like without a structure?

3. In what ways are aspects of the organization structure similar to the structural parts of the human body?

4. How is labor divided in your college or university? In what other ways could your college or university be departmentalized?

5. What types of organizations could benefit from a small span of control? What types might benefit from a large span of control?

6. Discuss how increasing formalization might affect the role conflict and role ambiguity of employees. How might the impact of formalization differ for research scientists, machine operators, and bank tellers?

7. How might centralization or decentralization affect the job characteristics specified in job design?

8 When a group makes a decision, how is the responsibility for the decision apportioned among the members who make it?

9. Why do employees typically want more authority and less responsibility?

10. Considering the job you now hold or one that you have held some time in the past, did your boss have the authority to direct your work? Why did he or she have this authority?

Case 13.1   Bad Apples At Beech-Nut

Most people—and certainly most parents—would agree with Richard C. Theuer, president of Beech-Nut Nutrition Corporation, who says, "Feeding babies is a sacred trust."* Yet in 1987 Theuer's company pleaded guilty to 215 felony counts, and two of its top officers went on trial for selling adulterated apple juice for babies. The prosecutors charged that between 1981 and 1983—and perhaps as early as 1977—Beech-Nut knowingly sold fake apple juice under the label "100% fruit juice." Apparently at least a few people at Beech-Nut did not feel responsible for that sacred trust.

As is the case in many bad business choices, Beech-Nut's decision to ignore warnings about the juice concentrate its supplier was providing was made when the company was in severe financial difficulties. It had been stripped of its profitable operations and existed almost solely on sales of its baby food, which had never been profitable. The company was deeply in debt. So when Interjuice Trading Company offered to sell Beech-Nut apple juice concentrate at 20 percent below market prices, some top Beech-Nut executives were easily led to ignore the suspicions that there was something wrong with the juice.

Rumors of adulterated juice had already spread throughout the industry, and some of Beech-Nut's researchers became suspicious of the new supplier's juice because of the low price. At the time, they could not prove that the juice was fake—it eventually was determined to be made up almost entirely of synthetic ingredients—but they concluded that it was probably not all apple juice.

The company sent two employees to investigate the concentrate source in Queens, New York, but they were not allowed into the plant. Still, Beech-Nut kept buying the concentrate, representing 60 percent of Interjuice's sales. Jerome J. LiCari was one of several Beech-Nut chemists who advised the company to stop buying the concentrate, but neither operations chief John F. Lavery nor then president Neils L. Hoyvald took action.

In August 1981, LiCari sent a warning memo to his superiors, a document that became important in the trials as it proved that Beech-Nut's management knew about the problem and did nothing. In June 1982, a private investigator hired by Processed Apples Institute Inc. told Beech-Nut that the concentrate was fake and asked the company to join a law suit against the producer. Beech-Nut refused to cooperate and tried to sell off its supply of fake juice. Although it entered into its own suit against the juice maker in December 1982, it continued to sell the synthetic product as real juice until March 1983. In fact, prosecutors charged that Hoyvald, trying to avoid the confiscation of the $3.5 million inventory, sent 25,000 cases of the fake concentrate to Puerto Rico.

The Beech-Nut employees who knew about the fraud apparently soothed their consciences by telling themselves that the fake juice was harmless and that Beech-Nut was not the only company selling it. In fact, however, industry analysts say only about 5 percent of the apple juice being sold at the time was impure, and no one knows the long-term effects of the chemicals used in the synthetic juice. Like many officials in hot water, the Beech-Nut executives said they never had proof, tried to characterize their employees as "the only ones who knew what was going on,"** and said they got bad advice.

Beech-Nut's shameful handling of the fraud demonstrates what can happen when responsibility and authority are divorced. The people with the authority to do something about the problem ignored it, and now they are paying for it. Hoyvald was found guilty of 350 violations of the Food, Drug, and Cosmetic Act; Lavery was found guilty on 448 counts, including conspiracy and mail fraud. The company was hit with a $2 million fine, by far the largest in the history of the Act, and also paid $7.5 million to settle a class-action lawsuit brought by retailers and consumers. But the scandal came to light only when people without authority—like LiCari—took upon themselves the responsibility of the "sacred trust" and exposed what LiCari called at the trial "a chemical cocktail."

Case Questions

1. It is often said that an executive's main responsibility is to company shareholders. From that perspective, did the Beech-Nut executives act responsibly?

2. What kind of organizational structure might prevent the kind of scandal that Beech-Nut went through?

Case Sources

Rebecca Fannin, "A Juicy Bit of Bad News," *Marketing and Media Decisions*, January 1987, 8; Stonewalling at Beech-Nut," *Business Week*, February 22, 1988, 174; Chris Welles, "What Led Beech-Nut Down the Road to Disgrace," *Business Week*, February 22, 1988, 124–128; "Beech-Nut: The Case of the Ersatz Apple Juice," *Newsweek*, November 17, 1986, 66; Leonard Buder, "2 Former Executives of Beech-Nut Guilty in Phony Juice Case," *The New York Times*, February 18, 1988, 1.

* Chris Welles, "What Led Beech-Nut Down the Road to Disgrace," *Business Week*, February 22, 1988, p. 125.
** Ibid, p. 128.

Case 13.2 Changing the Rules At Cosmo Plastics

When Alice Thornton took over as Chief Executive Officer at Cosmo Plastics, the company was in trouble. Cosmo had started out as an innovative company, known for creating a new product just as the popularity of one of the industry's old stand-bys was fading. In two decades, it had become an established maker of plastics for the toy industry. Cosmo had grown from a dozen employees to 400, and its rules had grown haphazardly with it. Thornton's predecessor, Willard P. Blatz, had found the company's procedures chaotic, and he had instituted a uniform set of rules for all employees. Since then, both research output and manufacturing productivity had steadily declined. When the company's board of directors hired Thornton, they emphasized the need to evaluate and revise the company's formal procedures in an attempt to reverse the trends.

First, Thornton studied the rules that Blatz had implemented. She was impressed to find that the entire procedures manual was only twenty pages long. It began with the reasonable sentence "All employees of Cosmo Plastics shall be governed by the following...." Thornton had expected to find evidence that Blatz had been a tyrant who ran the company with an iron fist. But as she read through the manual, she found nothing to indicate this. In fact, some of the rules were rather flexible. Employees could punch in any time between 8:00 and 10:00 in the morning and leave nine hours later, between 5:00 and 7:00. Managers were expected to keep monthly notes on the people working for them and make yearly recommendations to the personnel committee about raises, bonuses, promotions, and firings. Except for their one-hour lunch break, which they could take at any time, employees were expected to be in the building at all times.

Puzzled, Thornton went down to the lounge where the research and development people gathered. She was surprised to find a time clock on the wall. Curious, she fed a time card into it, and became even more surprised when the machine chattered noisily, then spit it out. Apparently, R & D was none too pleased with the time clock and had found a way to rig it. When she looked up with astonishment, only two of the ten or twelve employees who had been in the room were still there. They said the others had "punched back in" when they saw the boss come.

Thornton asked the remaining pair to tell her what was wrong with company rules, and she got an earful. The researchers, mostly chemists and engineers with advanced graduate degrees, resented punching a time clock and having their work evaluated once a month, when they could not reasonably be expected to come up with something new and worth writing about more than twice a year. Before the implementation of the new rules, they had often gotten inspirations from going down to the local dimestore and picking up $5 worth of cheap toys, but now they felt they could only make such trips on their own time. And when a researcher came up with an innovative idea, it often took months for the proposal to work its way up the company hierarchy to get the attention of someone who could put it into production. In short, all these sharp minds felt shackled.

Concluding that maybe she had overlooked the rigidity of the rules, Thornton walked over to the manufacturing building to talk to the production supervisors. They responded to her questions with one word: "anarchy." With employees drifting in between 8:00 and 10:00 and then starting to drift out again by 11:00 for lunch, the supervisors never knew if they had enough people to run a particular operation. Employee turnover was high, but not high enough in some cases—supervisors felt the rules prevented them from firing all but the most incompetent workers before the end of the yearly evaluation period. The rules were so "humane" that discipline was impossible to enforce.

By the time Alice Thornton got back to her office, she had a plan. The next week she called in all the department managers and asked them to draft formal rules and procedures for their individual areas. She told them that she did not intend to lose control of the company, but she wanted to see if they could improve productivity and morale by each creating formal procedures for their department.

Case Questions

1. Do you think that Alice Thornton's proposal to decentralize the rules and procedures of Cosmo Plastics will work?

2. What risks will the company face if it establishes different procedures for different areas?

Experiential Exercise

Purpose: This exercise will help you understand the configurational and operational aspects of organization structure.

Format: You will interview employees of a small- to medium-sized organization and analyze its structure. (You may want to coordinate this exercise with the exercise in Chapter 15.)

Procedures: Your first task is to find a local organization with fifty to five hundred employees. (It should not be part of your college or university.) The organization should have more than two hierarchical levels, but it should not be too complex to understand in a short period of study. You may want to check with your professor before contacting the company. Your initial contact should be with the highest possible ranking manager. You should be sure that top management is aware of your project and gives its approval.

Using the material in this chapter, interview employees to obtain the following information on the structure of the organization:

1. The type of departmentalization (business function, process, product, customer, geographic region)
2. The typical span of control at each level in the organization
3. The number of levels in the hierarchy
4. The administrative ratio (number of managers to total employees and number of managers to production employees)
5. The degree of formalization (To what extent are rules and procedures written down in job descriptions, policy and procedures manuals, and memos?)
6. The degree of decentralization (To what extent are employees at all levels involved in making decisions?)

Interview at least three employees of the company at different levels and in different departments. One should hold a top-level position. Be sure to ask the questions in a way that is clear to the respondents. They may not be familiar with the terminology used in this chapter.

The result of the exercise should be a report with a paragraph on each configurational and operational aspect of structure listed in this exercise, an organization chart of the company, a discussion of differences in responses from the various employees that you interviewed, and a discussion of any unusual structural features (for example, a situation in which employees report to more than one person or to no one). You may want to send a copy of your report to the top management of the cooperating company.

Follow-up Questions

1. Which aspects of structure were the hardest to obtain information on? Why?

2. If there were differences in the responses of the employees you interviewed, how do you account for them?

3. If you were president of the organization you analyzed, would you structure it in the same way? Why or why not? If not, how would you structure it differently?

CHAPTER

14

Environment and Technology

Chapter Objectives

After reading this chapter, you should be able to

- define *organizational environment* and *technology* and discuss their importance to organizations.
- describe several components of the environment and explain the relationship of each to environmental uncertainty and its two basic dimensions.

- elaborate on the general principles of the structural contingency, resource dependence, and population perspectives of organizational environments.
- identify and discuss five different perspectives of organizational technology.

new activism is at work in the organizational environment. Shareholders of corporations such as General Motors Corp. are making demands of the companies' boards of directors in unprecedented ways. For example, GM shareholders recently demanded to know why management received big bonuses in a year when the company had earned less than Ford Motor Company and why the value of their stock had not been increasing. In response to pressure from shareholders, GM cut capital spending, cut back on production to reduce inventories, and changed the bonus system for top management to reflect long-term corporate performance.[1] Many shareholders, like those of GM, are now making demands of corporate management rather than sitting back and waiting for stock dividends.

Shareholders are not alone in their new activism. Increasingly, employees—many of whom are also shareholders—are stepping forward to demand a decision-making role. Whereas unions used to bargain over pay and work rules and let management do the managing, coalitions of employees are gaining influence over management decisions in many companies. One example involves Allegis Corporation (formerly United Airlines). The company's pilots, who are members of the Air Line Pilots Association (ALPA), disagree with management attempts to integrate the airline, hotel, and rental-car businesses. The pilots' protest has gone so far as an attempted buyout of the company.[2] In other cases, workers are claiming that they have a greater stake in decisions to shut down plants or merge with other companies than do shareholders, suppliers, managers, or customers. With more employees participating in Employee Stock Ownership Programs (ESOP), the movement toward employee activism is gaining force and is not likely to abate soon.

*N*ew pressures from shareholders and employee groups represent new demands to which managers must respond. Management has traditionally been concerned with demands from new technologies, suppliers, customers, governmental regulations, and economic conditions and has had to figure out ways to manage the organization to satisfy these demands and to survive. In other words, pressures from many different sources lead to adjustments on the part of the organization. But how do organizations adjust and respond? How can an organization and its management make sense of an environment full of continuously changing demands?

In this chapter, we provide insight into the complexities of environmental demands. We do it in two ways. First, we examine the environment within which organizations operate and discuss various perspectives from which management can deal with it. Second, we consider the technology of the organization—the ways in which an organization transforms its inputs into

---

[1] "The Battle for Corporate Control," *Business Week,* May 18, 1987, pp. 102–109.
[2] " 'Not Going to Sit Around and Allow Management to Louse Things Up,' " *Business Week,* May 18, 1987, p. 107.

outputs. We focus on these factors again in Chapter 15, which describes how they influence the design of the organizational structure.

ORGANIZATIONAL ENVIRONMENTS

The **organizational environment** includes all elements—people, other organizations, economic factors, and objects—that are outside the boundaries of the organization. People in the organizational environment include customers, donors, regulators, inspectors, and shareholders. Among the other organizations are competitors, legislatures, and regulatory agencies. Economic factors include interest rates, the trade deficit, and the growth rate of the gross national product. Objects include such things as buildings, vehicles, and trees. Events that may affect organizations involve occurrences of weather, elections, or war.

It is necessary to determine the boundaries of the organization in order to understand where the environment begins. These boundaries may be somewhat elusive, or at least changeable, and thus difficult to define. But for the most part we can say that certain people, groups, or buildings are either in the organization or in the environment. For example, a college student shopping for a personal computer is part of the environment of Apple Computer, Inc., Compaq, IBM, and other computer manufacturers. However, if the student works for one of these computer manufacturers, he or she is not part of that company's environment but is within the boundaries of the organization.

This definition emphasizes the expanse of the general environment within which the organization operates. It may, indeed, give managers the false impression that the environment is outside their control and interest. But because the environment completely encloses the organization, managers must be constantly concerned about it. As Jeffrey Pfeffer and Gerald R. Salancik have said, "Organizations are inescapably bound up with the conditions of their environment."[3]

The manager, then, faces an enormous, vaguely specified environment that somehow affects the organization. To try to manage the organization within such an environment may seem overwhelming. The alternatives for the manager are (1) to ignore the environment because of its complexity and focus on managing the internal operations of the company, (2) to exert maximum energy in gathering information on every part of the environment and trying to react to every environmental factor, and (3) to pay attention to some aspects of the environment, responding only to those that most clearly affect the organization.

To ignore environmental factors entirely and focus on internal operations leaves the company in danger of missing major environmental shifts, such as

---

[3] Jeffrey Pfeffer and Gerald R. Salancik, *The External Control of Organizations: A Resource Dependence Perspective* (New York: Harper & Row, 1978), p. 1.

changes in customer preferences, technological breakthroughs, and new regulations. To expend inordinate amounts of energy, time, and money exploring each and every facet of the environment may take more out of the organization than it returns.

The third alternative represents the most prudent course of action: to carefully analyze those segments of the environment that most affect the organization and to respond accordingly. The issue, then, is to determine which parts of the environment are appropriate for the attention of the manager. In the remainder of this section, we present three perspectives on the organizational environment: the analysis of environmental components, environmental turbulence, and environmental uncertainty.

Environmental Components

The first task is to identify the environmental components that are important to the organization. The general environment can be divided into nine components: human resources, competitors, shareholders, economy, market, physical resources, socio-cultural factors, government, and financial resources, as shown in Figure 14.1.

HUMAN RESOURCES   The human resources component is made up of the general labor market, including the people who work or look for work (potential employees) and the suppliers of talent, such as employment agencies, colleges and universities, and trade schools. Note that, although employees are part of the internal operations of the organization, the general labor market is external and so is part of the environment. The human resources component also includes the labor unions that serve as the dominant suppliers and representatives of labor for the organization.

COMPETITORS   Competitors include all those people and organizations that compete in the same market with the same or similar products or services or for the same customers. The competitive environment can change a great deal over time. For example, for years the major U.S. automobile manufacturers understood that they were competing only with each other for the U.S. car buyer. In the 1950s and 1960s, they found that they were also in competition with Sears, Roebuck, other automobile repair facilities, and auto parts manufacturers, because customers had a choice between fixing their old cars and buying new ones. Japanese manufacturers became a major competitive force in the 1970s. Today, Honda Motor Co., Ltd., the Japanese manufacturer, is building cars in Ohio so fast that it is closing in on Chrysler Corp. as the third largest U.S. maker of cars.[4]

SHAREHOLDERS   Shareholders, as we noted earlier, are flexing new muscle, in part because pension fund managers and corporate raiders have convinced

---

[4] "The Americanization of Honda," *Business Week*, April 25, 1988, pp. 90–96.

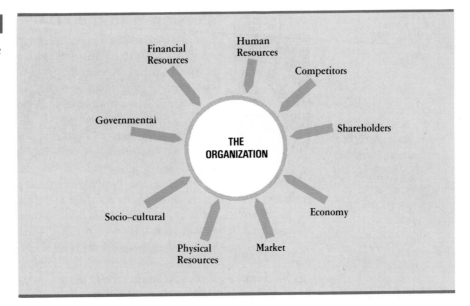

Figure 14.1

An Organization and the Components of Its Environment

even small investors that they have the right to make demands of the company's management.[5] There may be some confusion regarding whether shareholders are internal or external to the organization. In some organizations, the majority of shareholders are employees, directors, and managers of the company. In such cases, the shareholders are part of the company and not part of the environment. But in many organizations, most shareholders are not employees, managers, officers, or directors. The majority of owners of stock in some corporations are large pension funds and other institutional investors.

ECONOMY   The economic component of the environment includes the basic factors of the national and global economy that reflect buying and spending patterns, such as interest rates, trade deficits, housing starts, new factory orders, unemployment rates, and economic growth. The unemployment rate is obviously related to the general labor market, included earlier under the heading Human Resources, but is also referred to as an indicator of economic conditions.

MARKET   The market component of the environment comprises customers, clients, and all potential consumers of the organization's product or service. Customers indicate whether the product or service is acceptable by their willingness to pay for it. Changes in customers' preferences directly affect the company, its sales performance, its manufacturing schedules, and its inventories. Peters and Waterman have emphasized that one of the characteristics of an excellent company is staying close to the customer.[6]

---

[5] "The Battle for Corporate Control."

[6] Thomas J. Peters and Robert H. Waterman, Jr., *In Search of Excellence: Lessons from America's Best-Run Companies* (New York: Harper & Row, 1982).

Working With the FDA

Many drug companies, and some patients waiting for new drugs, view the Food and Drug Administration (FDA) as the enemy. The FDA's regulatory procedures take months, sometimes years. Its approval is never certain, and even when it does allow a company to market a drug, sometimes the slow process means the company loses out to a competitor. Dealing with the FDA gives some drug company executives nightmares.

Merck & Co. takes a very different view. "We want to make [the FDA] part of the development process,"* says the company's vice-president for regulatory affairs. His approach is likely to become more common in the industry, because Merck is envied as one of the 1980s' biggest success stories. After having floundered in the mid-1970s, Merck recently topped the list of *Fortune* magazine's most admired companies. Its financial progress has been astonishing; in less than two years, its stock price quadrupled, and its market value jumped from twenty-third in the country to seventh, ahead of companies like Ford and GM, which have much higher revenues. In the pharmaceutical industry, Merck is the one to watch.

Such success is not, of course, simply a product of getting along well with government regulators. Merck's approach to its business is unusual in many ways. Unlike many companies that use available cash to diversify, Merck has sold its non-drug businesses. Ninety percent of its revenues come from drugs, and its one major recent acquisition was Banyu Pharmaceutical Co. of Tokyo, which it bought to gain a foothold in the $25 billion Japanese drug market. Even moving that far from the company's own strengths may have been a mistake. No one faults Merck's desire to move closer to the Japanese drug market, the second biggest in the world after the United States'. But no American company

PHYSICAL RESOURCES   Physical resources include all of the physical raw materials used as inputs into the organization's transformation process. Examples include parts, such as plastic, steel, and windows, as well as buildings, warehouses, tools, and equipment. Shortages in raw materials caused by supplier problems, such as strikes, can create serious problems for the organization.

SOCIO-CULTURAL FACTORS   The socio-cultural component includes all of the personal and social factors that affect people in and around the organization—the workforce, customers, suppliers, and competitors. Such factors have many effects on management decisions. Cultural factors, for example, may determine what holidays are paid for as part of the company benefit plan. It may be necessary to make adjustments for differences in values among employees in different parts of the world or even in different groups within the U.S. population. Motivational and disciplinary programs, the design of jobs, the use of autonomous work groups, and the degree to which work groups participate in decision making may need to be built around the socio-cultural features of specific population segments.

had ever acquired such a large Japanese company, and Merck learned only after the purchase how badly Banyu had been mismanaged.

Merck's focus on doing one thing well includes spending almost half a million dollars a year on research and development, a figure that represents 10 percent of the pharmaceutical research budget in the United States.

All of its research could be wasted, however, if the company did not know how to deal with the FDA. Merck's latest and potentially most important triumph was obtaining approval for Mevacor, a drug that interferes in the process that creates cholesterol in human blood. Merck's scientists worked on the project for three decades, and its regulatory affairs group got involved nine years before Merck asked for FDA approval. This group knows FDA procedures and processes intimately. Unlike other companies that jealously guard their secrets from the government until they apply for approval, Merck keeps the FDA informed of all its problems and tests. The regulatory vice-president explains, "If they are ever surprised, they will be more skeptical."**

With such preparation, the FDA was not skeptical when it received the company's 41,000 pages of documentation on its new drug in November 1986. It granted Merck a public hearing on Mevacor after only three months. To make the presentation, the company sent fifty people who had been training for the hearing for months. The FDA was impressed with what it heard, and in August, less than ten months after the process began, it gave Merck approval for a drug that will be a leader in a market that may soon be worth billions of dollars.

* John A. Byrne, "The Miracle Company," *Business Week,* October 19, 1987, p. 88.
** Ibid.

Sources: John A. Byrne, "The Miracle Company," *Business Week,* October 19, 1987, 84–90; Stuart Gannes, "Merck Has Made Biotech Work," *Fortune,* January 19, 1987, 58–64; Lee Smith, "Merck Has an Ache in Japan," *Fortune,* March 18, 1985, 42–48.

GOVERNMENT   All organizations must comply with laws and regulations of local, state, and federal governments. Typical regulations deal with environmental impact, hiring, taxes, competitive practices, and labor relations and collective bargaining. The impact of governmental regulations can be great. When Honda established its Marysville, Ohio, plant, for example, it hired employees from a limited area to build local community relations. By doing so it excluded the minority population forty miles away in Columbus. It settled with the Equal Employment Opportunity Commission by paying $6 million and promising to boost minority hiring.[7] The effect of governmental regulations on another company, Merck & Co., Inc., is described in *Management in Action*.

FINANCIAL RESOURCES   Financial resources include all sources of money available to the organization. For publicly held corporations, these include stocks and bonds as well as borrowed money from a variety of sources. Privately held organizations may seek funds from lenders and sometimes from venture

---

[7] "The Americanization of Honda."

capitalists. For not-for-profit organizations, funding sources may include charitable contributions, legislative acts, and fee-for-service arrangements. Without an adequate source of capital, most organizations cannot survive.

In summary, these nine components cover the major environmental factors that affect organizations. In most situations, only a subset of these components affect an organization significantly.

Environmental Turbulence

Dividing the environment into separate and distinct segments is useful for analysis and understanding of each of the components; however, it can lead to a rather disjointed perspective. Another way of looking at the environment takes a more integrated view. This perspective, made popular by Emery and Trist,[8] is based on the notion of open systems theory and the causal nature of environments.[9] It emphasizes the interrelatedness of environmental parts and the interchanges the organization has with these interrelated parts.

Emery and Trist defined four types of environments: placid randomized, placid clustered, disturbed reactive, and turbulent fields. Table 14.1 shows these four types, their characteristics, and some examples of each.

In the **placid randomized environment,** goals and problems are relatively simple and unchanging. Environmental components tend not to be related to each other, so the organization can deal with them individually and in a simple, adaptive mode with relatively small organizational units. There are few good examples of this most simple and static environment.

The **placid clustered environment** is also relatively unchanging, but environmental components are interrelated in clusters. Organizations in this type of environment tend to grow to be large, centralized, controlled, and coordinated.

In the **disturbed reactive environment,** the components form interrelated clusters but change more rapidly. Heavy competition exists between organizations that are similar in nature. Companies in this environment tend to use large-scale bureaucratic structures to provide the necessary redundancies to be competitive.

The fourth type of environment represents the primary contribution of the environmental turbulence approach. The **turbulent field,** the most complex and dynamic environment, is characterized by rapid change that arises from the complexities and multiple interconnections among environmental compo-

---

[8] F. E. Emery and E. L. Trist, "The Causal Texture of Organizational Environments," *Human Relations,* February 1965, pp. 21–32.

[9] L. von Bertalanffy, "The Theory of Open Systems in Physics and Biology," *Science,* Vol. 111, 1950, pp. 23–29; E. C. Tolman and E. Brunswik, "The Organism and the Causal Texture of the Environment," *Psychological Review,* Vol. 42, 1935, pp. 43–77; and S. C. Pepper, "The Conceptual Framework of Tolman's Purposive Behaviorism," *Psychological Review,* Vol. 41, 1934, pp. 108–133.

Table 14.1	Type of Environment	Characteristics of Type	Examples
Environmental Classifications of Emery and Trist	Placid randomized	Slow change, if any	Few in modern economy
		Few interrelationships between environmental components	Small job shop or family-operated business in an isolated area
		Few new threats or opportunities	
		Changes are random and unpredictable.	
	Placid clustered	Slow change	Container industry
		Environmental components are interrelated.	Some mass production manufacturing
		Change is relatively predictable.	
		Some planning is possible.	
	Disturbed reactive	Moderate change	Automobile industry
		Few large firms dominate.	Steel industry
		Heavy competition	Soft drink industry
		Organizations are interrelated within an industry.	
		Competitive actions produce reactions.	
	Turbulent fields	Very rapid change	Computer hardware and software industry
		Change is unpredictable.	Communications industry
		Change may come from technological breakthrough, government regulation, or customer preferences.	
		Increasingly prevalent	

nents. Organizations have difficulty dealing with the environment individually and may seek relationships with others in the same turbulent field. The turbulent field characterizes such rapidly changing industries as the information processing and information transmission industries.

Environmental Uncertainty

Another view of the environment focuses on the uncertainty of the environment and the impact that different environments have on different organizations. Not all forces in the general environment affect all organizations in the same way. Hospital Corporation of America, for example, is very much influenced by government regulations and medical and scientific developments. McDonald's Corp., on the other hand, is affected by quite different environmental forces—consumer demand, disposable income, cost of meat and bread, and gasoline prices. Thus, the **task environment**—the specific set of environmental forces that affect the operations of an organization—varies among organizations.

But the environmental characteristic that seems to have the most influence on the structure of the organization is uncertainty. **Environmental uncertainty** exists when managers have little information about environmental events and their impact on the organization.[10] Uncertainty has been described as resulting from complexity and dynamism in the environment. **Environmental complexity** is the number of environmental components that impinge on organizational decision making, and **environmental dynamism** is the degree to which these components change.[11] With these two dimensions, we can determine the degree of environmental uncertainty, as illustrated in Figure 14.2.

In cell 1, a low-uncertainty environment, there are few important components, and they change infrequently. A company in the cardboard container industry might have a highly certain environment when demand is steady, manufacturing processes are stable, and government regulations have remained largely unchanged.

In cell 4, in contrast, many important components are involved in decision making, and they change often. Thus, cell 4 represents a high-uncertainty environment. The banking environment is now highly uncertain. With deregulation and the advent of interstate operations, banks must now compete with insurance companies, brokerage firms, real estate firms, and even department stores. The toy industry is also in a highly uncertain environment. As they develop new toys, toy companies must stay in tune with movies, television shows, and cartoons as well as public sentiment. In the period 1983 to 1988, the Saturday morning cartoons were little more than animated stories about children's toys. Recently, however, due to disappointing sales of many toys

---

[10] Richard L. Daft, *Organization Theory and Design*, 2nd ed. (St. Paul, Minn.: West, 1986), p. 55.

[11] Robert B. Duncan, "Characteristics of Organizational Environments and Perceived Uncertainty," *Administrative Science Quarterly*, September 1972, pp. 313–327.

| Figure 14.2 | Classification of Environmental Uncertainty |

ENVIRONMENTAL COMPLEXITY

Simple   *Complex*

RATE OF ENVIRONMENTAL CHANGE

Static

Cell 1:
Low Perceived Uncertainty

1. Small Number of Factors and Components in the Environment
2. Factors and Components Are Somewhat Similar to One Another
3. Factors and Components Remain Basically the Same

Example: *Cardboard Container Industry*

Cell 2:
Moderately Low Perceived Uncertainty

1. Large Number of Factors and Components in the Environment
2. Factors and Components Are Not Similar to One Another
3. Factors and Components Remain Basically the Same

Example: *State Universities*

Dynamic

Cell 3:
Moderately High Perceived Uncertainty

1. Small Number of Factors and Components in the Environment
2. Factors and Components Are Somewhat Similar to One Another
3. Factors and Components of the Environment Continually Change

Example: *Fashion Industry*

Cell 4:
High Perceived Uncertainty

1. Large Number of Factors and Components in the Environment
2. Factors and Components Are Not Similar to One Another
3. Factors and Components of Environment Continually Change

Example: *Banking Industry*

Source: Reprinted from "Characteristics of Organizational Environments and Perceived Uncertainty" by Robert B. Duncan, published in *Administrative Science Quarterly,* Vol. 17, No. 3, by permission of *Administrative Science Quarterly.*

presented in cartoons designed to promote them, most toy companies have left the toy-based cartoon business.[12]

Environmental characteristics and uncertainty have been important factors in explaining organizational structure, strategy, and performance. For example, the characteristics of the environment affect how managers perceive the environment, which in turn affects how they adapt the structure of the organization to meet environmental demands.[13] This relationship is shown in Figure 14.3a. The environment has also been shown to affect the degree to

[12] Joseph Pereira, "Toy Makers Lose Interest In Tie-Ins with Cartoons," *The Wall Street Journal,* April 28, 1988, p. 29.

[13] Masoud Yasai-Ardekani, "Structural Adaptations to Environments," *Academy of Management Review,* January 1986, pp. 9–21.

Gorbachev's Book Heralds Changes in the Soviet Business Environment

In his speeches and his recent book, Soviet leader Mikhail S. Gorbachev has called for *perestroika,* or restructuring of the economy and society, and *glasnost,* or openness. American business executives might find that they approve of many of Gorbachev's changes, and even the way his book came into being. An American associated with publisher Harper & Row told Soviet authorities that Americans would like tc learn directly from Gorbachev what *perestroika* means. Gorbachev liked the idea and completed the book in 1987 so that Harper & Row could publish it in time for the seventieth anniversary of the Russian Revolution. Western observers are watching eagerly to see how these new policies will affect the ways the Soviet people do business.

Gorbachev's changes fall into three general categories: ending the abuses of the past, allowing more dialogue about the problems and possibilities of the present, and encouraging capitalistic and democratic incentives to make people work harder in the future. All three types of changes are limited by communist ideological boundaries, yet they are having an effect.

Not surprisingly, some of the most visible and radical results of Gorbachev's policies have involved the ouster of political leaders. While most purges of the past have been for political and ideological reasons, many of the present attacks on the powerful are aimed, at least ostensibly, at eliminating corruption. In 1986 Soviet Deputy Trade Minister Vladimir N. Sushkov and his wife Valentina, of the State Committee for Science and Technology, were arrested after they returned from one of their many foreign trade trips. The pair received long jail terms after being convicted of accepting $2.3 million worth of goods in foreign bribes, including 1,565 pieces of gold jewelry.

which a firm's strategy enhances its performance.[14] (See Figure 14.3b.) That is, a certain strategy will enhance organizational performance to the extent that it is appropriate for the environment the organization operates in. Finally, the environment is directly related to organizational performance, as shown in Figure 14.3c.[15] The environment and the organization's response to it are clearly crucial to the organization's success. The Soviet leader Mikhail S. Gorbachev is initiating many significant changes in the economy and the rules within which businesses operate in the U.S.S.R. *International Perspective* gives more detail on these changes and the uncertainty they have created for managers.

---

[14] John E. Prescott, "Environments as Moderators of the Relationship Between Strategy and Performance," *Academy of Management Journal,* June 1986, pp. 329–346.

[15] Timothy M. Stearns, Alan N. Hoffman, and Jan B. Heide, "Performance of Commercial Television Stations As an Outcome of Interorganizational Linkages and Environmental Conditions," *Academy of Management Journal,* March 1987, pp. 71–90.

Some key players in the largest Soviet agricultural scandal to date did not get off so easily. Soviet police accused officials in the Republic of Uzbekistan of padding cotton production figures by 4.5 million tons over five years. The local Communist Party boss committed suicide when confronted with the evidence, and at least two other officials have been sentenced to death.

While Gorbachev may hope to scare officials and business leaders out of participating in corrupt practices, he is also trying to encourage all workers to increase their productivity by using some of the incentives of free enterprise. The government now allows people to engage in small private businesses and to cultivate their own land and sell the produce for profit. Earnings are being tied more directly to hard, productive work, and producers are being urged to think more in terms of market demand and profit. As Gorbachev himself puts it, "Our people have missed the proprietary role."*

Glasnost, the new openness in Soviet life, has roused the most interest in the West. Soviet leaders and newspaper editors have become much more candid and critical about the country's failings, past and present. Whether this openness will extend to the kind of free communication of ideas that underlies the American economy and society remains to be seen.

One aspect of Gorbachev's presentation may be symbolic of the limits of the Soviet changes. While Americans were eagerly purchasing Gorbachev's new book, so few copies were printed in the USSR that almost no Russians could read it.

Sources: Peter Galuszka, "Sending a Message Loud and Clear: No More Graft," *Business Week,* July 6, 1987, 44–45; John Pearson, "Reading Between the Lines of Gorbachev's 'Long Letter,'" *Business Week,* February 8, 1988, 12; Henry Trewhitt, "Gorbachev's Revolution," *U.S. News & World Report,* November 9, 1987, 68–69.

* John Pearson, "Reading Between the Lines of Gorbachev's 'Long Letter,'" *Business Week,* February 8, 1988, 12.

ORGANIZATIONAL RESPONSES

An organization's response to its environment can take many forms. In this section, we describe three particular ways that this response or adaptation can take place: through the structural contingency, resource dependence, or population ecology perspectives.

Structural Contingency Perspective

One of the most popular approaches to the study of the organization and its environment is the **structural contingency perspective,** which suggests that the best structure for an organization is dependent, or contingent, on the environment in which it operates. This approach will be discussed in more detail in Chapter 15; here, we briefly discuss the concept to emphasize the importance of the environment's effect on organizations.

Figure 14.3

Three Important
Perspectives on the
Environment-
Organization
Relationship

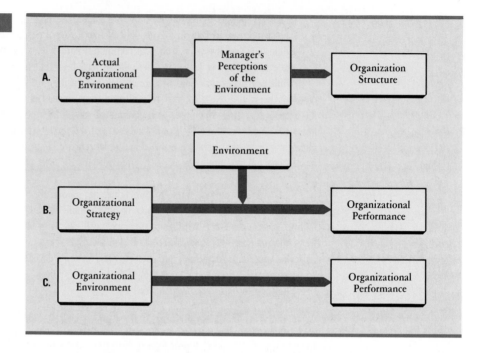

One of the earliest structural contingency approaches is the framework presented by Paul R. Lawrence and Jay W. Lorsch, who examined companies in three different industries and their environments.[16] They categorized the environment of the plastics industry as diverse, dynamic, and uncertain; the environment of the container industry as stable and certain; and the environment of the food industry as midway between the other two.

The effective firms in the plastics industry were found to be highly *differentiated* and have similar features that enabled them to prosper in the uncertain environment characteristic of that industry—tasks were divided among departments and employees' primary orientation was toward the goals of their departments. When departments were highly differentiated, Lawrence and Lorsch found a high potential for conflict among the functional specialists because of their vastly different orientations. Yet the uncertain environment demanded that the groups collaborate for the overall benefit of the organization. The authors used the term *integration* to refer to the process of collaboration to resolve conflict. In plastics firms, they found, integration was often accomplished by individuals, groups, or departments whose primary role was to resolve conflict.

---

[16] Paul R. Lawrence and Jay W. Lorsch, *Organizations and Environment: Managing Differentiation and Integration* (Homewood, Ill.: Irwin, 1969; first published by the Division of Research, Graduate School of Business Administration, Harvard University, 1967).

The container companies, in contrast, were in a more certain environment and were less differentiated in structure and orientation, experienced less conflict, and thus had less need for formal integrating groups or individuals. Most conflicts were resolved by a person in a top management position.

Environmental uncertainty was a major factor in understanding why firms in these two industries were either successful or unsuccessful. The successful firms' structures were appropriate to meet the needs of the environment. As noted, the next chapter gives more detail on organizational structure.

Resource Dependence Perspective

Another view of the relationship between the organization and the environment emphasizes the importance of resources. Recall from Figure 14.1 that three of the environmental components are resources—human, financial, and physical. Organizations need resources to operate. For example, a bank could not function without the money that customers deposit and that other customers withdraw in the form of loans. The bank must also have people to be tellers, loan officers, customer service personnel, and managers.

The more important and scarce the resource, the more the organization depends on the environment—specifically, on the environmental component that provides the resource. Naturally, the organization is vulnerable to problems if the supply of the scarce input is threatened, reduced or cut off. For example, if the supply of an essential raw material is stopped, as with a strike by a supplier's employees, the company may have to shut down its operation. Prior to the development of a non-strike agreement between the labor unions and the steel companies in the 1970s, as labor contract renewal time neared for workers in the steel industry, automobile companies used to stockpile steel for months in case of a strike by steelworkers. The steel companies, in turn, considered the car companies valuable to their existence, since a strike by auto workers could affect the demand for steel.

Organizations must maintain **resource exchanges** with their environments in order to survive.[17] They can accomplish such exchanges in two primary ways: by developing interorganizational linkages and by changing the environment,[18] as shown in Figure 14.4. Developing interorganizational linkages involves identifying organizations that control vital resources and then developing relationships with those organizations to try to assure a constant flow of raw materials. Interorganizational linkages can take the form of (1) joint ventures, (2) contractual relationships, (3) mergers, (4) acquisitions, or (5) cooptation of outsiders, such as the appointment of leaders of other organizations to the company's board of directors.

---

[17] Ephraim Yuchtman and Stanley Seashore, "A System Resource Approach to Organizational Effectiveness," *American Sociological Review*, December 1967, pp. 891–903.

[18] Daft, *Organization Theory and Design*, pp. 70–76.

Figure 14.4

The Resource
Dependence Perspective

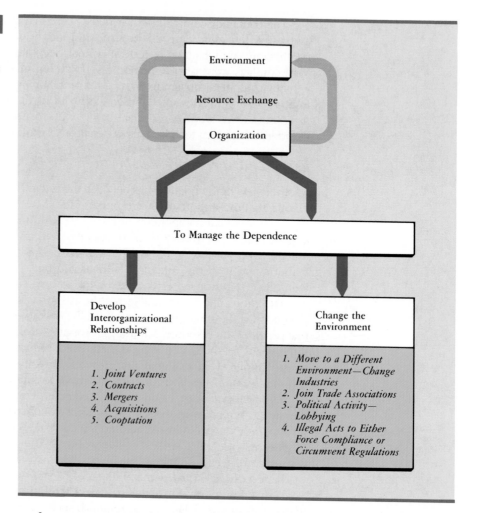

It may sometimes be easier to change the environment so that the organization's current structure will be appropriate than to make major structural adjustments. To change the environment, the organization can do several things: (1) change the organization to operate in a different set of environmental conditions, as the tobacco companies have done during the last decade by buying companies in recreation, leisure, clothing, and food industries to reduce their dependence on tobacco products, (2) join trade associations to further the cause of the entire industry, (3) engage in political activities such as lobbying in attempts to alter regulations affecting the organization, and (4) engage in behaviors—perhaps even illegal activities—in order to affect other organizations in the environment. An example of this last type is the insider stock trading schemes in which individuals engage in illegal practices by twisting the rules to make a more favorable environment for trading.

CHAPTER 14   Environment and Technology

The more the organization depends on other organizations for scarce resources, the more likely the organization will be to either develop interorganizational relationships or seek to change the environment. If, on the other hand, the organization depends very little on other organizations for its resources, it may remain free to do as it pleases with few threats from the environment. However, such freedom is rare in the current complex business environment.

Population Ecology Perspective

The population ecology perspective of organizations proposes that organizations survive on the basis of fit between their structural attributes and environmental characteristics.[19] It is similar to the biological theory of natural selection in its emphasis on survival of the fittest. When there is an overabundance of a species—more than the environment can support—survival of the fittest determines which individuals last and which die. Environments and organizations may function in much the same way. When the environment cannot support all of the organizations that exist, those that maintain the best fit with the environment will survive.

The personal computer market may be experiencing this phenomenon. Soon after Apple showed that a market existed for these machines, personal computer manufacturers seemed to spring up overnight. However, after several years of technological development and expansion of products and related services, the number of companies in the industry began to decrease. We no longer hear of Osborne Computer Corp. or Victor Technologies Inc., for example. The primary players in the personal computer market are IBM, Apple, Compaq, Tandy/Radio Shack, and a few others who specialize in certain applications, such as networking. It can be argued that these companies have survived through a process of natural selection.

The population approach provides a fascinating means for comparing industries over the years. It can help explain what happens as entire industries change. However, it has several limitations.[20] It is not specific in many areas. For example, although it stresses the total capacity of the environment to support a certain number of organizations, it has done little, as yet, to help explain why some organizations survive and others do not. Therefore, it cannot provide prescriptions for managers to use to adapt a specific organization for survival.

The three approaches to organizational response, or adaptation, to the environment described in this section—the structural contingency, resource dependence, and population ecology perspectives—provide somewhat different

[19] Howard E. Aldrich and Jeffrey Pfeffer, "Environments of Organizations," *Annual Review of Sociology,* 1976, pp. 80–83.

[20] Arthur G. Bedeian, *Organizations: Theory and Analysis,* 2nd ed. (Chicago: Dryden, 1984), pp. 187–189.

Table 14.2

Comparison of Three
Approaches to
Environmental-
Organizational Response
and Adaptation

	Approach		
Feature	*Structural Contingency*	*Resource Dependence*	*Population Ecology*
Optimal fit	Yes	No	Yes
Resources	No	Yes	No
Managerial prescriptions	Yes	Yes	No

views of the relationship between an organization and its environment. Although they differ in some respects, there are areas of congruence as well. These similarities and differences are summarized in Table 14.2. The structural contingency and the population ecology approaches assume that there is an optimal fit between the organization and the environment. The resource dependence view, on the other hand, focuses on the resource exchange between the organization and various environmental components. The structural contingency and the resource dependence approaches assume that managers can make decisions to adapt the organization to its environment. The population ecology perspective does not deal with managerial involvement in determining the optimal fit.[21] All three perspectives emphasize the importance of the environment-organization relationship.

TECHNOLOGY FRAMEWORKS

Organizational technology, like environmental pressures, continues to be a source of concern for managers. In systems theory, **technology** refers to the mechanical and intellectual processes that transform inputs into outputs. For example, the primary technology employed by Mobil Corporation transforms crude oil (input) into gasoline, motor oil, heating oil, and other petroleum-based products (outputs). Prudential Insurance Company uses actuarial tables and information processing technologies to produce its insurance services. Of course, most organizations use multiple technologies: Mobil Oil, for example, uses research and information processing technologies in its laboratories where new petroleum products and processes are generated.

Although there is general agreement with the systems view of technology, the means by which this technology has been evaluated and measured have varied widely. Five approaches to examining the technology of the organization are shown in Table 14.3 and discussed in the remainder of this chapter. For

---

[21] Aldrich and Pfeffer, "Environments of Organizations."

Table 14.3	Approach	Classification of Technology
Summary of Several Approaches to Technology	Woodward (1958 and 1965)	Unit or small batch Large batch and mass production Continuous process
	Burns and Stalker (1961)	Rate of technological change
	Perrow (1967)	Routine Nonroutine
	Thompson (1967)	Long-linked Mediating Intensive
	Aston Studies: Hickson, Pugh, and Pheysey (1969)	Work flow integration; operations, materials, and knowledge technologies

convenience, we have classified these approaches according to the names of their proponents.

Woodward

In an early study of the relationship between technology and organizational structure, Joan Woodward categorized manufacturing technologies by their complexity. Her research was based on the practices of a hundred British manufacturing companies, primarily electronics, chemical, and engineering firms.

Woodward identified the simplest technological classification as unit or small batch production. This type of production is used, for example, in the manufacture of custom products, in which customized parts are made one at a time or in small batches. Large batch or mass production, as used in automobile assembly lines, is more complicated and involves manufacturing standardized parts in very large batches. The most complex technologies are those of continuous-process production, in which a continuous stream of material is run through a process, such as through pipes and heating, cooling, and separation tanks. Chemical plants and petroleum refineries use continuous-process production.

Woodward found that the span of control and the number of levels in the hierarchy were very similar for the successful firms within a technological classification. Supervisory span of control decreased and executive span of control and number of levels of management increased as technological complexity increased from unit to large batch to continuous-process.[22]

---

[22] Joan Woodward, *Management and Technology: Problems of Progress in Industry*, no. 3 (London: Her Majesty's Stationery Office, 1958) and *Industrial Organizations: Theory and Practice* (London: Oxford University Press, 1965).

Although Woodward developed her classification scheme in the late 1950s, her categories are still useful for analyzing manufacturing organizations. Some critics have argued that her classifications are simplistic and may represent smoothness of the production system rather than technological complexity.[23] Nevertheless, Woodward's work has made a significant contribution toward better understanding of organizations and technology.

Burns and Stalker

At about the same time as Woodward was publishing her work, several other researchers were considering the fit between technology and structure. Tom Burns and George M. Stalker examined twenty manufacturing firms in England and Scotland—fifteen electronics firms, four research organizations, and a major manufacturing organization.[24] Based on their study, they proposed that the rate of change in the technology determines the best method of structuring the organization. For example, if the rate of change is slow, the most effective design is bureaucratic—or, to use Burns and Stalker's term, *mechanistic*. But if the technology is changing rapidly, the organization needs a structure that allows more flexibility and quicker decision making so that it can react quickly to change. This design is called *organic*. These organizational designs are discussed in more detail in Chapter 15.

Perrow

Another view of the technology-structure fit was developed by Charles Perrow.[25] On the basis of his research with juvenile correction facilities, hospitals, and numerous manufacturing firms, Perrow developed a technological continuum, with routine technologies at one end and nonroutine technologies at the other. Whereas Woodward and Burns and Stalker dealt primarily with manufacturing firms, Perrow claimed that all organizations could be classified on his routine-to-nonroutine continuum.

The degree of routineness of a technology is defined by the number of exceptions to routine encountered in the work and the type of search processes used in deciding on a response to the exceptions. Where there are few exceptions and the search processes are based on logical, rational analysis, the technology is routine. A manufacturer of standardized products, such as Procter & Gamble or General Foods Corp., is likely to use routine technology, as well as such organizational features as low interdependence between groups, coordination by planning, and a highly formalized and centralized structure.

---

[23] Bedeian, *Organizations: Theory and Analysis*.

[24] Tom Burns and George M. Stalker, *The Management of Innovation* (London: Tavistock, 1961).

[25] Charles B. Perrow, "A Framework for the Comparative Analysis of Organizations," *American Sociological Review*, April 1967, pp. 194–208.

Where many exceptions are encountered and no well-established ways to solve the problems exist, the technology is nonroutine. High-tech research and development firms such as Hewlett-Packard Co. and Tandem Computers Inc., for example, tend to use nonroutine technology and to have high interdependence between groups, coordination through feedback and mutual adjustment, and a flexible structure.[26]

Thompson

Another approach to the technology of organizations was proposed by James D. Thompson.[27] His technological categories, which he argued could be used to classify all organizations, are long-linked, mediating, and intensive.

Long-linked technologies are serially linked operations, whose relationships are much like the sequential interdependence discussed in Chapter 10. Operation A feeds to operation B, which feeds to operation C, and so on through the entire process. The assembly line is the best example of the long-linked technology.

Mediating technology links otherwise independent units of the organization or different types of customers. Examples include banks, employment agencies, schools, and telephone companies. In banks, for example, some customers are depositors of money and some are borrowers. The bank serves the role of bringing these types of customers together. Each customer's needs are first categorized according to type; then their transaction is handled in a standard manner. Thus, the technology consists of linking units' uniform operating practices, rules, and controls.

Intensive technologies use skills, crafts, or services in an appropriate and often unique way to accomplish a task. A typical user of intensive technology is the general hospital. Despite increasing standardization in hospitals, each patient still must be handled individually. Skills and resources are applied to each case in a unique combination that depends on the patient's condition and response to treatment.

Thompson suggested that organizations arrange themselves to protect the dominant technology, smooth out problems, and minimize coordination costs. Structural components such as inventory, warehousing, and shipping help buffer the technological transformation subsystem from environmental disturbances. For example, inventories and warehousing help manufacturing systems function as if the environment accepted output at a steady rate. In fact, though, demand for products is usually cyclical or seasonal and is subject to many disturbances. The warehouse inventory makes it possible to produce at a constant rate,

---

[26] Charles B. Perrow, *Organizational Analysis: A Sociological View* (London: Tavistock, 1970).

[27] James D. Thompson, *Organizations In Action* (New York: McGraw-Hill, 1967).

maximizing technological efficiency and thus the organization's ability to respond to the fluctuating demands of the market.

Aston Studies

A group of English researchers at the University of Aston, including David J. Hickson, Derek S. Pugh, and Diana C. Pheysey, examined the relationship between technology and structure for fifty-two firms near Birmingham, England.[28] They focused their attention on the transformation of inputs into outputs and the flow of work (work flow integration). These researchers broke technology down into three categories: operations, materials, and knowledge. Operations technology includes the techniques used in the transformation process. Materials technology deals with the specific characteristics of the materials—for example, hardness, availability, ease of machining, and ease of transportation. Knowledge technology refers to the level of technological sophistication and the complexity and specificity of knowledge required to do the job.

The Aston studies continued over several years as the researchers examined many aspects of organizational structure, size, and type and compared their results with those of Woodward and others. They concluded that operations technology is associated with organizational structure in those areas of the organization affected by the work flow. They also showed that when technology differs from one part of the organization to another, the organizational structure of the parts differs as well.

These perspectives on technology are somewhat similar in that all (except the Aston typology) reflect the adaptability of the technological system to change, as shown in Figure 14.5. Large batch or mass production, routine, and long-linked technologies are not very adaptable to change. At the opposite end of the continuum, continuous process, nonroutine, and intensive technologies are readily adaptable to change.

TECHNOLOGY AND TODAY'S ORGANIZATION

Several myths exist concerning the impact of technology on the organization. First, it is often assumed that this impact is limited to the production function. In fact, the effects of technology are much more far-reaching. One such effect is found in hospitals and health care facilities. As *A Look At Research* demonstrates, the introduction of new diagnostic equipment means much more than moving

---

[28] David J. Hickson, Derek S. Pugh, and Diana C. Pheysey, "Operations Technology and Organization Structure: An Empirical Reappraisal," *Administrative Science Quarterly,* September 1969, pp. 378–397.

Figure 14.5

Technology Continuum

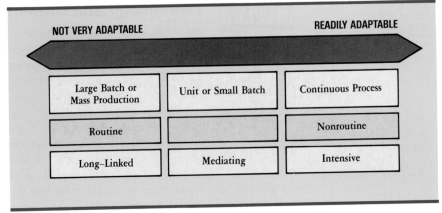

Source: Adapted table, "Summary of the Thompson, Woodward, and Perrow Technological Typologies" from *Organizations: Theory and Analysis,* Second Edition, by Arthur G. Bedeian, copyright © 1984 by Holt, Rinehart and Winston, Inc., reprinted by permission of the publisher.

in a piece of apparatus. New office technologies are also being examined for their impact on the structure of the office.[29]

A second myth is the assumption that relatively simple technologies are old, boring, and therefore incapable of being useful in the modern age of high technology. There are numerous examples of unit or small batch production systems that can benefit from advances in manufacturing technology. Computer-integrated manufacturing has proved valuable in the aerospace industry and to many makers of custom-made products, for example.[30] In these situations, a new technology producing a computerized flow of information about the production process is added to the basic unit or small batch technology.

A third myth is the assumption that expenditures of large sums of money on new technology will allow an organization to reduce the skill level of employees and thus reduce overall payroll and training costs. This "de-skilling" does occur in some situations, such as when complex procedures and decision parameters can be programmed into a computer routine. However, more training is often required for employees to be able to run more complex machinery, monitor automatic equipment, and install or repair sophisticated systems. The difficult task for management is to determine the requirements of

[29] John Storey, "The Management of New Office Technology: Choice, Control, and Social Structure in the Insurance Industry," *Journal of Management Studies,* January 1987, pp. 43–62.

[30] Cynthia A. Lengnick-Hall, "Technology Advances in Batch Production and Improved Competitive Position," *Journal of Management,* Spring 1986, pp. 75–90.

A LOOK AT RESEARCH

Technology and Organizational Change

How exactly does a technological change affect an organization? Some people talk about "technological imperative," believing that the introduction of new technology necessarily leads to certain changes within the organization. However, a recent report on the effects of new technology in hospital radiology departments showed that the same situation can produce very different reactions.

The researcher, Stephen R. Barley, studied the radiology departments at two hospitals before and after the hospitals began using new computed tomography (CT) scanners to scan patients' entire bodies. Traditionally in a radiology department, technologists run the machines and radiologists interpret the x-ray images. Radiologists have had a professional monopoly on interpretation, and they have also routinely taken over control of the machines, since they had been trained to know the equipment. The radiologists have clearly been in command of the whole process.

The two hospitals bought the same machine and the work groups underwent changes in both departments, but the effects of those changes were radically different. They demonstrated that the institutions' planning and personnel decisions made a great difference in how the two groups of workers interacted within themselves.

Each hospital had to hire and reassign personnel to operate the new scanner. One hospital, Suburban, hired one radiologist and two technologists who had experience with the scanners. The radiologist acknowledged the technologists' expertise in a variety of ways, often praising them for their knowledge. When the hospital shifted new, inexperienced radiologists onto the scanner, the technologists had to teach the radiologists how to use the machines. The radiologists grew uncomfortable with this change in expertise from themselves to the technologists (as this reversed the normal order of things) and a rift began developing between the two groups. Gradually the technologists took over running the machines and the radiologists withdrew to their offices.

To run its new machine, Urban Hospital hired one outside radiologist and reassigned one of its veterans who was well informed about the CT field. These radiologists were the only experts in the department, and they dominated operations more than did their counterparts at Suburban. The Urban technologists did not learn how to run the scanner as quickly as did the technologists at Suburban. They relied on the radiologists, who came to view them as incompetent. However, when Urban rotated new, inexperienced radiologists to the CT scanner, they worked together with the experienced technologists in a process that Barley called "mutual execution."

Besides showing that no two organizations will react in the same way to a technological change, Barley demonstrated that a new machine can have positive effects on the relations between personnel who use it. His work also seems to show that groups with mutual respect who work together to learn something may tend to form the best relationships.

Source: Stephen R. Barley, "Technology as an Occasion for Structuring: Evidence From Observations of CT Scanners and the Social Order of Radiology Departments," *Administrative Science Quarterly,* 31 (1986): 78–108.

the new technology.[31] Managers must identify the level of skills required, the number of personnel needed, and the points in the process where the need for people will be either larger or smaller.

Organizational structure bears the major impact of technology. The relationship between an organization and its technologies turns out to be much more complex than anyone, including Joan Woodward, first assumed in the 1950s. In the next chapter, we address the relationship of the organization to environment and technology in more detail.

SUMMARY OF KEY POINTS

Environment and technology summarize the major sets of pressures or demands on the organization. The environment includes all elements outside the organization's boundaries. It can be viewed in terms of its components, its causal nature, and its uncertainty. The components include human resources, competitors, shareholders, the economy, the market, physical resources, sociocultural factors, government, and financial resources.

Focusing on the causal nature of the environment emphasizes the relationship among the environmental components and the degree to which they change. Four types of environments emerge: placid randomized, placid clustered, disturbed reactive, and turbulent fields.

Environmental uncertainty exists when managers have little information about environmental events and their impact on the organization. Two factors contribute to environmental uncertainty: complexity and dynamism. A complex and dynamic environment is the most uncertain.

Three approaches to organizational response, or adaptation, to the environment are the structural contingency, resource dependence, and population ecology perspectives. The structural contingency perspective suggests that the structure of the organization depends on the environment in which it operates. The resource dependence perspective focuses on the exchanges between the organization and the various environmental components. As the organization seeks to manage its relationships with environmental components, it may either develop interorganizational relationships or try to change the environment. According to the population ecology perspective, organizations survive on the basis of the fit between their structural attributes and environmental characteristics.

The technology of the organization includes all the processes an organization uses to transform inputs into outputs. The impact of technology on organizations has been frequently studied. Woodward classified technologies as unit or small batch, large batch or mass production, and continuous process. Burns and

---

[31] Paul Adler, "New Technologies, New Skills," *California Management Review,* Fall 1986, pp. 9–27.

Stalker described the impact of technology on organizations in terms of the rate of technological change. Perrow focused on the routine or nonroutine nature of the work. Thompson described technology as long-linked, mediating, or intensive. Finally, the Aston studies described work flow integration and the operations, materials, and knowledge technologies.

DISCUSSION QUESTIONS

1. Define *organizational environment* and *organizational technology.* In what ways do these concepts overlap?

2. Describe the environment of your college or university by giving examples of each of the nine environmental components and discussing the complexity and dynamism of the environment.

3. Under what conditions would it be possible for a person to be part of an organization and part of the organization's environment?

4. Are you, or is anyone you know, a shareholder in a company? In what ways is a shareholder part of the environment as well as part of the organization? Discuss what conflicts could arise from a shareholder's being part of both the environment and the organization.

5. In the early 1980s, Chrysler Corp. was on the verge of bankruptcy. Discuss how the near-failure of Chrysler could have been a result of its failure to maintain a proper resource exchange with its environment and how its recovery could have been due to its ability to reestablish an appropriate resource exchange.

6. According to the population ecological perspective, what is the most important factor in determining organizational success? What can managers do to help their organizations survive? What is the role of chance in organizational success?

7. How would you describe the technology of management? Does managing people in organizations use a technology similar to those described by Thompson and Perrow or those described by Woodward and the Aston studies? Explain.

8. Is the technology of management different for lower-level managers (supervisors) than for upper-level managers (the CEO and vice presidents)?

9. How would you describe the technology of the college or university you attend? To what extent does this technology affect the way the organization operates (structure, decision making, and so on)?

10. If someone asked why you are studying environment and technology in a course on organizational behavior, how would you respond?

Case 14.1   AT&T: Picking Up the Pieces

In 1984, as the result of a long and expensive lawsuit, the federal government broke American Telephone & Telegraph Company into pieces. AT&T had enjoyed a "regulated monopoly" in the American telephone business for most of this century. It employed more people than any other private company, owned four out of five telephones in America, had more stockholders than any other company in the world, and earned consistent, healthy profits.

But the government decided that AT&T was too large and powerful, and in 1974 the Justice Department sued the company for antitrust violations, claiming its monopoly was illegal. As a result of the suit, AT&T had to rid itself of three-quarters of its $150 billion in assets. Many of those assets became companies in themselves, collectively known as "Baby Bells." The court placed numerous restrictions on the activities in which the parent company and the Baby Bells could engage, and left a smaller, weaker AT&T to fend for itself in a suddenly much more competitive communications industry.

At first, the former giant floundered badly. It had matured as a utility regulated by the government, not as a competitive company. Since government regulators consider a utility's costs in making rate decisions, the old AT&T had few incentives to cut costs. The company did much of its business with its own divisions, and had little experience with competitive efficiency. Some of the provisions of the divestiture made the situation even worse; the company was forced to separate its long-distance business from its office-systems business, creating duplicate bureaucracies. Such duplication only added to the historical redundancy of systems like accounting and data processing within the old AT&T divisions.

These were the kinds of problems that the company's chairman, James E. Olson, wanted to solve when he called two dozen of his top executives together on Labor Day 1986. Assembling these executives from often competitive divisions was a symbolic way of trying to glue back in place the pieces of the shattered company. Olson elicited a pledge of support for mutual goals from each person, and then they all set about turning the ailing company around.

The turnaround involved a lot of consolidation. Different financial systems, payroll procedures, and phone and data networks were merged into one. The company reversed a long-standing policy of developing its own products and began to buy from outsiders when possible, rather than duplicate other companies' research work. Costs began diminishing, and the company's situation began to improve. In effect, it was learning to use its traditional strengths in new ways, while getting rid of some of the corporate fat it had accumulated as a monopoly.

Nowhere were these trends more evident than in the company's computer business. At its worst point, the company was losing almost $1 billion a year on its computers. AT&T had gotten into computers because its other businesses were mature and it foresaw that sending computer transmissions over telephone lines was going to become very profitable. The breakup agreement gave it the right to mix computers and telephones, but it ran into formidable competition from IBM, and it left the job of selling computers to people who were selling the company's other products and were not familiar with computers.

To cut the tremendous losses, the computer division trimmed expenses, began buying outsiders' products rather than creating all of its own, and established closer ties to other AT&T divisions. Most importantly, the division relied on an old strength to pull it through difficult times. The old AT&T Bell Laboratories, some of the most respected labs in the world, had created the Unix operating system for computers in the 1970s. Because regulations prohibited the company from selling the system, AT&T licensed Unix to universities and computer makers. Over the years, the system gained wide support among programmers, in part because AT&T did not keep close control over it and programmers were therefore able to adapt it for their own purposes. Now, with the rights to sell the system, AT&T has developed a new version, making rivals in the computer world nervous.

Having developed as a regulated company, and after struggling to survive the trust-busters, the company now has a chance to prove that it can win in a more openly competitive environment, whether it is selling telephone service or computer networks.

Case Questions:

1. The old AT&T was America's leading "cradle-to-grave" employer, a very comfortable place to work. What changes has the breakup brought to the AT&T work environment?

2. In what ways has AT&T responded to government intervention in its businesses?

Case Sources:

Richard Brandt, "Unix: The Soul of a Lot of New Machines," *Business Week*, March 14, 1988, 94–96; John J. Keller, "AT&T: The Making of a Comeback," *Business Week*, January 18, 1988, 56–62; Milton Moskowitz, Michael Katz, and Robert Levering, *Everybody's Business* (San Francisco: Harper & Row, 1980), 420–426.

| Case 14.2 | # Technological Shake-Up at Smith, Burns, & Graulik |

The law firm of Smith, Burns, & Graulik handled most of the legal work for a small midwestern town. The firm employed three secretaries—Pam Henry, Melvin Tarn, and Judi Maylocks. The three got along well; in fact the office was known as the best place in town to work—that is, until the technology in the office began to change.

When Pam Henry, the oldest of the secretaries, joined the firm in 1955, her work day consisted of responding to the call, "Take a letter please, Mrs. Henry," hurrying into one of the big offices, scribbling shorthand on a pad while the boss dictated, then typing out the letter and submitting it for the boss's approval. Quick and accurate at each step in the process, she became the most important person in the office.

In the 1970s, the firm hired Tarn and Maylocks and introduced a new machine into the office—the dictaphone. The three secretaries spent most of their days hooked up to an earphone, typing out the dictation that one of the lawyers had recorded the day before. Tarn, who could not imagine himself jotting squiggles on a yellow pad, liked the system. Maylocks, who had been an English major, complained about the lawyers' grammar and the long pauses on the tape. Mrs. Henry hated the whole system. Her tape player never seemed to be functioning right, the volume was always too loud or too soft, and the contraption made her so nervous that her formerly perfect typing began to suffer. She still ran the office and made more money than the others, but she felt like a bumbling newcomer.

Then, in 1984, the company purchased a personal computer. Mrs. Henry would not go near it. Tarn tolerated it and learned how to type his letters on it. Judi Maylocks, in contrast, was fascinated by it. She created stock paragraphs—the kinds of paragraphs she had typed so often she knew them by heart—and saved them on disks so that she could construct certain kinds of letters or court documents almost instantly. She took the computer manuals home to read and learned to use the accounting software that came with the machine.

Gradually the office became a very tense place. The three secretaries had always worked as a pool, each taking the next piece of work when she or he got done with the last one. Now the lawyers began asking Maylocks to do specific documents because they knew she could turn them out in half the time it took the other two. They began to realize the value of all the material she had stored on disk, and they consulted her often, asking for copies of documents they had sent out months ago. They also began to appreciate the value of having all their accounts on the computer, available at any time, and of being able to save money by having their accountant check the books less often.

All of this attention was not lost on Melvin Tarn and Pam Henry, who began to resent Judi Maylocks and her machine. Mrs. Henry began to spend more of her time in the waiting room, drinking coffee and smoking cigarettes, and Tarn sabotaged Maylocks' work on a couple of occasions so she would not seem so perky and efficient. Maylocks saw what was happening, and she tried to familiarize the other two with the machine so she could spread the work out, but they perceived her attempts as trying to impress them with her superiority, and they did not respond.

Finally, the lawyers caught on to the problem and had a meeting with the three secretaries, during which all the animosity was expressed. One of the older lawyers who was new to the firm was surprised and delighted to hear that Mrs. Henry preferred old-fashioned dictation and asked her if she would mind dusting off her shorthand notebook. That suggestion led to a reorganization of the entire office to be more consistent with each person's skills and preferences. Judi Maylocks took official charge of the work she was already doing, and because that work amounted to minor legal research and accounting, she was given a raise and the title of administrative assistant. Melvin Tarn and Pam Henry divided up the other office responsibilities; there were still plenty of letters that had to be dictated, and enough filing and other jobs to keep everyone busy.

At first Judi Maylocks feared that her co-workers would resent her title and raise, but in fact both agreed that she deserved them. They just had not liked the feeling that she, as an equal, was making them look bad, and they had worried that they should be matching her efforts. But once they all had more clearly defined responsibilities and were doing work they felt comfortable with, the office was a much more pleasant place.

Case Questions:

1. Could the lawyers have made the office more efficient if they had insisted that all three secretaries learn all the functions of the computer?

2. In what ways did technology sharpen or blur the distinctions between jobs in the law firm?

Experiential Exercise

Purpose: This exercise will help you develop better understanding of the environmental components that affect several different types of organizations.

Format: Working in small groups in class, you will analyze the environment of an organization in terms of its components, the turbulence of the environment, the relative importance of the environmental components to the organization, and the uncertainty of the environment.

Procedure: Your instructor will place you in groups of four to six people. Each group will analyze the environment of an organization by answering the following questions. The instructor may provide each group with an organization to analyze or may provide a list of organizations from which each group can select an organization. Although you may not have all the information you need to do a complete analysis, your knowledge of the general environment should be enough to illustrate its importance to the organization.

1. What are the environmental components of the organization that your group is to study?
2. Which components are most important to the organization? Which are least important?
3. How would you characterize the environment in terms of its turbulence? (How much are the components changing? How much are they related to each other?)
4. How would you characterize the uncertainty of the environmental components? (Are there many important components? At what rate do they change?)
5. What types of organizational responses or adaptations has the organization implemented in the recent past?

6. What types of organizational responses or adaptations do you think the organization will need to implement in the near future?

Each group should make notes of the answers to the questions and be prepared to discuss them in class. You will be able to compare your analysis with the analyses done by other groups.

Variations: The instructor may use several variations in this exercise. As noted, each group may be assigned an organization, or a list may be provided from which each group may choose an organization. One interesting possibility is to assign all groups the same organization and compare their different points of view. Or one organization may be assigned to half of the groups and a very different organization to the other half. The two organizations are compared in class discussion.

Follow-up Questions

1. What kinds of differences did you observe in the environmental analyses of the different organizations and groups?

2. Which part of the analysis was the most difficult to do? Was it difficult for most groups? Why was that part difficult for your group?

3. Were the groups' recommendations for future organizational response or adaptation similar, or were they very different? What accounts for the similarities or differences?

C H A P T E R

15

Organization Design

Chapter Objectives

After reading this chapter, you should be able to

▶ summarize and discuss three major universal organization design approaches.

▶ describe three contingency approaches to organization design.

▶ summarize Mintzberg's classification of five structural forms.

▶ define *matrix organization design* and summarize its advantages and disadvantages.

▶ discuss contemporary approaches to organization design.

rom 1982 to 1986 Kemper Corporation increased its sales of high-yielding insurance from $3.9 million to $327 million, and operating earnings were up by 190 percent during the first half of 1986. Kemper was able to do this while expanding its businesses in mutual funds, stock brokerage, property-casualty insurance, and other investment services.[1]

The financial service industry has changed for insurance companies, banks, and brokerage firms owing to deregulation of many services and increased competition among many formerly unrelated firms. Ten years ago no industry was more stable and unchanging than the insurance industry. Most companies were highly centralized with many rules and procedures that prescribed how employees were to sell insurance, prepare paperwork, and process claims. Currently, however, insurance companies are in competition with banks and brokerage firms in an increasingly complex industry.

As a conglomerate in the financial services industry, Kemper has recorded phenomenal growth by managing its various businesses in a very decentralized manner. It allows the different arms of the organization to run independently. The many brokerage firms it has bought share the parent company's products and services but remain independent, maintaining their local names and regional identifications. Allowing the businesses to retain their autonomy provides them with the ability to react more quickly to changing market conditions.

Kemper has designed its organization to coordinate its many businesses and the people who work in them so as to produce strong sales and earnings in a rapidly changing environment. Other organizations in the financial services industry, such as several banks that have failed, have not been as successful.

*W*hy is it that some financial institutions are successful in the new environmental conditions and others are not? One of the determining reasons is the organization's design. Within the organization, design coordinates the efforts of the people, work groups, and departments. Designing a system of task, reporting, and authority relationships that leads to the efficient accomplishment of organizational goals is a challenge managers must be prepared to face. In Chapters 13 and 14, we discuss the tools with which managers design a system that will enable an organization to be effective. In this chapter we integrate these basic elements of structure, environment, and technology by presenting several perspectives on organization design.

Organization designs vary from rigid bureaucracies to flexible matrix systems. Most theories of organization design represent either a universal or a contingency approach. A **universal approach** is one whose prescriptions or propositions are designed to work in any situation or circumstance. Thus a universal design prescribes the "one best way" to structure the jobs, authority, and reporting relationships of any organization, regardless of such factors as

---

[1] "The Loose-Reins Approach Pays Off for Kemper," *Business Week,* September 8, 1986, pp. 78–79.

the organization's external environment, the industry, and the type of work to be done. A **contingency approach**, on the other hand, suggests that the desired outcome of organizational efficiency can be achieved in several ways. In a contingency design, specific conditions such as the environment, technology, and the organization's work force determine the structure. The distinction between the universal and contingency approaches is shown in Figure 15.1. This distinction is similar to the one between universal and contingency approaches to motivation (Chapter 5), job design (Chapter 8), and leadership (Chapter 11). Although no one particular form of organization is generally accepted, the contingency approach to organization design most represents current thinking.

In this chapter, we discuss organization designs based on the universal approach and the contingency approach. We later examine the Mintzberg framework for classifying organization structures. The chapter concludes with an examination of the matrix design and a discussion of contemporary organization design.

UNIVERSAL APPROACHES TO ORGANIZATION DESIGN

Three of the most popular and influential universal approaches to organization design are the ideal bureaucracy of Max Weber, the classic principles of Henri Fayol, and the human organization of Rensis Likert. Although all are universal approaches, their concerns and structural prescriptions are quite different.

The Ideal Bureaucracy

The term *bureaucracy* has come to be associated with rigid rules and procedures, red tape, passing the buck, sluggishness, and inefficiency. However, the first theorist of bureaucracy, Max Weber, writing at the turn of the century, conceived of a bureaucracy as a powerful and efficient form of administration. Weber's *ideal bureaucracy* is an organizational system characterized by a hierarchy of authority and a system of rules and procedures that, if followed, would create a most effective system for large organizations.

Weber was trained in Germany as a lawyer and had wide-ranging intellectual interests. He published books and articles on history, law, political science, and religion, but he is best known for his contributions to sociology and particularly for his theory of bureaucracy.[2] Weber claimed the bureaucratic form of administration was superior to other forms of management with respect to stability, control, and predictability of outcomes.[3]

---

[2] John B. Miner, *Theories of Organizational Structure and Process* (Chicago: Dryden, 1982), p. 386.

[3] Max Weber, *The Theory of Social and Economic Organization,* A. M. Henderson and Talcott Parsons, trans. (New York: Oxford University Press, 1947).

Figure 15.1   Universal and Contingency Approaches to Organization Design

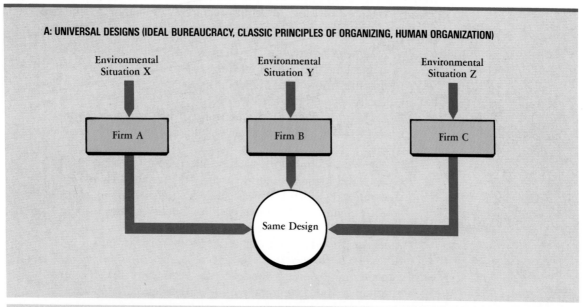

A: UNIVERSAL DESIGNS (IDEAL BUREAUCRACY, CLASSIC PRINCIPLES OF ORGANIZING, HUMAN ORGANIZATION)

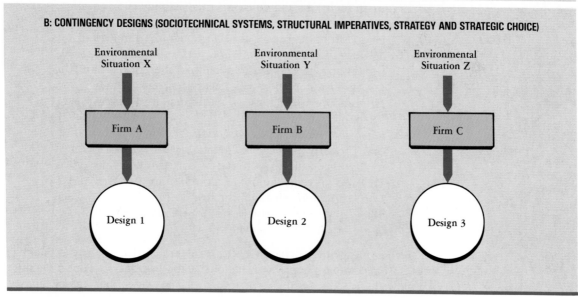

B: CONTINGENCY DESIGNS (SOCIOTECHNICAL SYSTEMS, STRUCTURAL IMPERATIVES, STRATEGY AND STRATEGIC CHOICE)

Weber's ideal bureaucracy has seven essential characteristics. (Three of these characteristics have been previously discussed as key aspects of organization structure—division of labor, hierarchy of authority, and rules and procedures.)

1. *Rules and procedures.* A system of rules and procedures defines the duties of employees and is strictly enforced so that the actions of all members of the organization are controlled and predictable.

2. *Division of labor.* Tasks are clearly divided among employees who have the competence and authority to carry them out.

3. *Hierarchy of authority.* Each position reports to a position one level higher in the hierarchy. This creates a chain of command (which later was called a *scalar chain*) in which each member of the organization is supervised by a single higher-ranking individual, except the top position, which usually reports to a board of directors or the owners.

4. *Technical competence.* The selection and promotion of organization members are based on technical competence and training. This dictum ensures that individuals are qualified to do their jobs and enhances predictability and control. Favoritism, nepotism, and friendship are specifically excluded from the process of selection and promotion.

5. *Separation of ownership.* Employees, especially managers, should not share in the ownership of the organization. This assures that employees will make decisions in the best interests of the organization rather than for their own personal interests.

6. *Rights and property of the position.* The rights and control over property associated with an office or position belong to the organization, not to the person who holds the office. This also prevents the use of a position for personal ends.

7. *Documentation.* All administrative decisions, rules, and actions are detailed in writing to provide a continuous record of the organization's activities.[4]

Weber meant these characteristics to assure order and predictability in relationships among people and the jobs in the bureaucracy. But it is easy to see how these same features can lead to sluggishness, inefficiency, and red

---

[4] This summary of the elements of bureaucracy is based on the Henderson and Parsons translation of Weber's *Theory of Social and Economic Organization* and on the discussion of bureaucracy in Arthur G. Bedeian, *Organizations: Theory and Analysis,* 2nd ed. (Chicago: Dryden, 1984) and in Richard L. Daft, *Organization Theory and Design,* 2nd ed. (St. Paul, Minn.: West, 1986).

tape. If any of the characteristics are carried to an extreme, or are violated, the administrative system can easily break down. For example, if never-ending rules and procedures bog employees down with finding the precise rule to follow every time they do something, responses to routine client or customer requests may slow to a crawl. Moreover, subsequent theorists have said Weber's view of authority is too rigid and have suggested that the bureaucratic organization may impede creativity and innovation and result in a lack of compassion for the individual in the organization.[5] In other words, the impersonality that is supposed to foster objectivity in a bureaucracy may result in serious difficulties for both employees and the organization. However, some organizations retain some characteristics of a bureaucratic structure while remaining innovative and productive. For more on the new bureaucracy, see *Management in Action*.

The Classic Principles of Organizing

A second universal design was presented at the turn of the century by Henri Fayol, a French engineer and chief executive officer of a mining company. Drawing on his experience as a manager, Fayol was the first to classify the essential elements of management—now usually called *management functions*—as planning, organizing, command, coordination, and control.[6] In addition, he presented fourteen principles of organizing that he considered an indispensable code for managers. These principles are shown in Table 15.1.

Fayol's principles have proved extraordinarily influential; they have served as the basis for the development of generally accepted means of organizing. For example, Fayol's unity of command means that employees should receive directions from only one person, and unity of direction means that tasks with the same objective should have a common supervisor. Combining these two principles with division of labor and authority and responsibility results in a system of tasks and reporting and authority relationships that is the very essence of organizing. Fayol's principles thus provided the framework for the organization chart and the coordination of work.

The classic principles have been criticized on several counts. They ignore such factors as individual motivation, leadership, and informal groups—the human element in organizations. This line of criticism asserts that the classic principles result in a mechanical organization into which people must fit, regardless of their interests, abilities, or motivations. The principles have also been criticized for their lack of operational specificity, in that Fayol described the principles as universal truths but did not specify the means of applying

---

[5] For more discussion of these alternative views, see Miner, *Theories of Organizational Structure and Process*.

[6] This summary of the classic principles of organizing is based on Henri Fayol, *General and Industrial Management*, Constance Storrs, trans. (London: Pittman, 1949); and the discussions in Bedeian, *Organizations: Theory and Analysis*, pp. 58–59 and Miner, *Theories of Organizational Structure and Process*, pp. 358–381.

Restructuring Chrysler's Production

"I look for eager beavers who do more than they're expected," * says Chrysler chief Lee Iacocca. He found such an eager beaver in ex-fullback Richard E. Dauch, who made a name for himself by overhauling Volkswagen's assembly plant in Westmoreland, Pennsylvania. Ever since Iacocca lured Dauch to Chrysler in 1980, the two of them have implemented changes at all levels, helping Chrysler to jump from last to first among American automakers in returns on sales and productivity. Such a dramatic turnaround has been achieved through some seemingly drastic steps. These included laying off half Chrysler's workers (both blue- and white-collar), reducing the number of layers of management, and changing spending and research plans.

Such moves at the top would not have succeeded without the major restructuring on the factory floor for which Dauch has been responsible. In the early 1980s Chrysler's product was poor and its costs high. But by 1986, thanks in part to Dauch's work, Chrysler was making over $200 more per vehicle than Ford and $900 more than General Motors. Yet these changes cost Chrysler relatively little by industry standards.

Iacocca preaches "being honest," communicating in "plain language," "laying the facts on the table," and encouraging "equality of sacrifice." ** Using such approaches and his talents as a salesman, Iacocca has persuaded Chrysler employees to take pay cuts and the government to back a huge loan to Chrysler, and has convinced customers to buy different variations on the K-car for years.

Dauch has taken his cue from Iacocca, and enthusiastically promotes Chrysler's new approach to its work and its workers. He stresses worker education by giving some workers (even those with

many of them. Finally, Fayol's classic principles have been discounted because they were not supported by scientific evidence—Fayol presented them as universal principles, backed by no evidence other than his experience.[7]

The Human Organization

Rensis Likert called his approach to organization design the *human organization*.[8] Because Likert and others had criticized Fayol's classic principles for overlooking human factors, it is not surprising that his approach centered on the principles of supportive relationships, employee participation, and overlapping work groups. The term *supportive relationships* suggests that in all organizational activities, individuals should be treated in such a way that they experience feelings of support, self-worth, and importance. *Participation* means

---

[7] Miner, *Theories of Organizational Structure and Process*, pp. 358–381.

[8] See Rensis Likert, *New Patterns of Management* (New York: McGraw-Hill, 1961), and *The Human Organization: Its Management and Value* (New York: McGraw-Hill, 1967) for a complete discussion of the human organization.

experience) at a new plant over 100 hours of training and by drastically increasing the percentage of factory personnel with college degrees. His cheerleading slogans dot factory walls and he makes scores of joint appearances with Marc Stepp, United Auto Workers Vice President. Absenteeism and work stoppages have greatly diminished. Workers have more control over vacations and overtime. The number of job classifications has been cut sharply—from ninety-three to ten in one assembly plant—because the company expects its workers to be more flexible.

One of Dauch's first steps in changing Chrysler's production was to improve quality in ways customers would notice. In five years, the number of robots and the computers that control them quadrupled, with a resulting drop in squeaks, rattles, and customer complaints. The production process no longer tolerates mistakes on the assembly line, and the lines themselves have been rebuilt to bring the cars to the workers. To cut costs and increase quality, Chrysler has reduced the number of its suppliers and demands high quality; to increase inventory turnover, it demands just-in-time-delivery.

These changes have brought Chrysler to the top. With other automakers now taking lessons from Chrysler as well as the Japanese, the changes at Chrysler may have effects throughout the industry.

Sources: "Price of Power: What It's Like on the Inside," *U.S. News & World Report,* May 20, 1985, 68; Alex Taylor III, "Lee Iacocca's Production Whiz," *Fortune,* June 22, 1987, 36–44; William J. Hampton, "Why Chrysler Can't Afford To Go Off Its Diet," *Business Week,* October 5, 1987, 84.

* Price of Power: What It's Like on the Inside," *U.S. News & World Report*, May 20, 1985, 68.
** Ibid.

that the work group needs to be involved in decisions that affect it, thereby enhancing the sense of supportiveness and self-worth.

The principle of *overlapping work groups* means work groups are linked as shown in Figure 15.2, with managers serving as linking pins between groups. Each manager (except the highest ranking) is a member of two groups: a work group that he or she supervises and a management group composed of the manager's peers and their supervisor. Coordination and communication grow stronger when the managers perform the linking function by sharing problems, decisions, and information both upward and downward in the groups to which they belong. The human organization concept rests on the assumption that people work best in highly cohesive groups oriented toward organizational goals. Management's function is to make sure the work groups are linked together for effective coordination and communication.

Likert described four systems of organizing, the characteristics of which are summarized in Table 15.2. System 1 is called Exploitive Authoritative and can be characterized as the classic bureaucracy, while System 4, the Participative Group, is the organization design Likert favored. System 2, the Benevolent

Table 15.1	Principle	Fayol's Comments
Fayol's Classic Principles of Organizing	1. Division of work	Individuals and managers work on the same part or task.
	2. Authority and Responsibility	Authority—right to give orders; power to exact obedience; goes with Responsibility for reward and punishment
	3. Discipline	Obedience, application, energy, behavior Agreement between firm and individual
	4. Unity of command	Employee receives orders from one superior
	5. Unity of direction	One head and one plan for activities with the same objective
	6. Subordination of individual interest to general interest	Objectives of the organization come before objectives of the individual
	7. Remuneration of personnel	Pay should be fair to the organization and the individual; discussed various forms
	8. Centralization	Proportion of discretion held by the manager compared to that allowed to subordinates
	9. Scalar chain	Line of authority from lowest to top
	10. Order	A place for everyone and everyone in their place
	11. Equity	Combination of kindness and justice; Equality of treatment
	12. Stability of tenure of personnel	Stability of managerial personnel; time to get used to work
	13. Initiative	Power of thinking out and executing a plan
	14. Esprit de corps	Harmony and union among personnel is strength

Source: From *General and Industrial Management* by Henri Fayol. Copyright © 1987 by David S. Lake Publishers, Belmont, CA 94002. Used by permission.

Authoritative system, and System 3, the Consultative system, are less extreme than either System 1 or System 4.

Likert described all four systems in terms of eight organizational variables: leadership processes, motivational forces, communication processes, interaction-influence processes, decision-making processes, goal-setting processes, control processes, and performance goals and training. Let us run through the characteristics of System 4:

1. Leaders show complete trust and confidence in employees. Employees feel free to discuss their jobs with their supervisor, who solicits and uses their ideas and opinions.

2. The organization recognizes and uses the full range of employee motives; attitudes are favorable to and supportive of organizational goals.

3. Communication flows freely and in all directions (upward,

Figure 15.2   Likert's Overlapping Work Groups (The Linking Pin Organization)

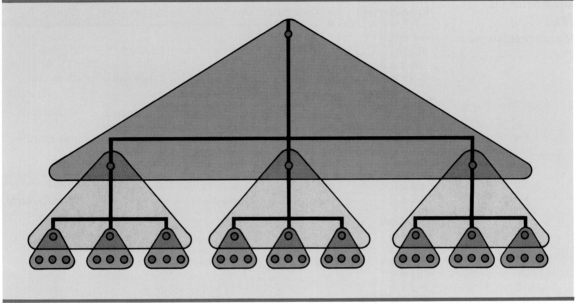

Source: Rensis Likert, *New Patterns of Management* (New York: McGraw-Hill, 1961), p. 105. Reprinted by permission.

downward, and horizontally), is initiated at all levels, and promotes a closeness between subordinate and supervisor.

4. Interaction-influence processes between employees are extensive and friendly, with much confidence, trust, and teamwork. Employees can influence the goals, methods, and activities in their work groups.

5. Decisions are made throughout the organization at the level where the information is most adequate. Decision making is integrated by the system of overlapping groups.

6. Goal setting is a group activity; the goals are fully accepted by all involved.

7. Control processes are the concern of people throughout the organization; there are strong pressures to obtain complete and accurate information for self-guidance and coordinated problem solving.

8. Top management sets high performance goals for the organization, and employees receive a great deal of management training.[9]

[9] Adapted from Likert, *Human Organization,* pp. 197–211.

Table 15.2

Characteristics of Likert's Four Management Systems

Characteristic	System 1: Exploitive Authoritative	System 2: Benevolent Authoritative	System 3: Consultative	System 4: Participative Group
Leadership				
• Trust in subordinates	None	None	Substantial	Complete
• Subordinates' ideas	Seldom used	Sometimes used	Usually used	Always used
Motivational forces				
• Motives tapped	Security, status	Economic, ego	Economic, ego, and others	All motives
• Level of satisfaction	Overall dissatisfaction	Some moderate satisfaction	Moderate satisfaction	High satisfaction
Communication				
• Amount	Very little	Little	Moderate	Much
• Direction	Downward	Mostly downward	Down, up	Down, up, lateral
Interaction–influence				
• Amount	Very little	Little	Moderate	Much
• Cooperative teamwork	None	Virtually none	Moderate	Substantial
Decision making				
• Locus	Top	Policy decided at top	Broad policy decided at top	All levels
• Subordinates involved	Not at all	Sometimes consulted	Usually consulted	Fully involved
Goal setting				
• Manner	Orders	Orders with comments	Set after discussion	Group participation
• Acceptance	Covertly resisted	Frequently resisted	Sometimes resisted	Fully accepted
Control processes				
• Level	Top	All levels	Some below top	All levels
• Information	Incomplete, inaccurate	Often incomplete, inaccurate	Moderately complete, accurate	Complete, accurate
Performance	Mediocre	Fair to good	Good	Excellent

Source: Adapted from Rensis Likert, *New Patterns of Management* (New York: McGraw-Hill, 1961), pp. 223–233; and Rensis Likert, *The Human Organization* (New York: McGraw-Hill, 1967), pp. 197, 198, 201, 203, 207, 210, and 211. Reprinted by permission.

Likert believed that work groups should be able to overlap horizontally as well as vertically where necessary to accomplish tasks. This feature is directly contrary to the classic principle that advocates unity of command. In addition, Likert favored the linking-pin concept of overlapping work groups for making decisions and resolving conflicts, rather than the hierarchical chain of command.

Research support for Likert's human organization emanates primarily from his and his associates' work at the Institute for Social Research at the University of Michigan. Although their research has upheld the basic propositions of the approach, it is not entirely convincing. One review of the evidence has suggested that although research has shown characteristics of System 4 to be associated with positive worker attitudes and, in some cases, increased productivity, it is not clear that the characteristics of the human organization "caused" the positive results.[10] It may have been that positive attitudes and high productivity allowed the organization structure to be participative and provided the atmosphere for the development of supportive relationships. Likert's design has also been criticized for focusing almost exclusively on individuals and groups and not dealing extensively with structural issues.[11] Overall, the most compelling support for this approach is at the individual and work group levels. Support for System 4 as a universally applicable organizational system is not strong.

CONTINGENCY APPROACHES TO ORGANIZATION DESIGN

Weber, Fayol, and Likert each proposed an organization design that is independent of the nature of the organization and its environment. Although each of these approaches contributed to an understanding of the organizing process and the practice of management, none has proved universally applicable. In this section we turn to several contingency designs, which attempt to specify the conditions, or contingency factors, under which they are likely to be most effective. The contingency approach to organization structure has been criticized as being unrealistic in that managers are expected to observe a change in one of the contingency factors and to make a rational structural alteration. On the other hand, Donaldson has argued that it is reasonable to expect that organizations respond to lower organizational performance that may result from a lack of response to some significant change in one or several contingency factors.[12] Research continues into the contingencies of organization structure, an example of which is shown in *A Look at Research.*

---

[10] Miner, *Theories of Organizational Structure and Process*, pp. 17–53.

[11] Daniel Katz and Robert L. Kahn, *The Social Psychology of Organizations*, 2nd ed. (New York: Wiley, 1978), pp. 278–282.

[12] Lex Donaldson, "Strategy and Structural Adjustment To Regain Fit and Performance: In Defense of Contingency Theory," *Journal Of Management Studies*, January 1987, pp. 1–24.

A LOOK AT

RESEARCH

Refining Contingency Theory

A recent study of the outcomes of surgery and the procedures followed in hospital operating rooms has helped to refine contingency theories. Led by Claudia Bird Schoonhoven, the researchers looked at the outcomes of fifteen surgical procedures on 8,593 patients operated on in seventeen different hospitals. By relating variables of organization structure and task uncertainty to the success of the operations, the researchers showed that traditional contingency theories may have oversimplified the relationships between the two variables.

Schoonhoven makes a number of criticisms regarding shortcomings of traditional contingency theories. She finds that most of the theories suffer from a lack of clarity, using terms like "appropriate for" and "consistent with" to describe the relationship between an organization's structure and other factors. These vague terms blur the actual nature of the interactions being studied and make it difficult for researchers to test the theories empirically.

Schoonhoven's most specific criticism focuses on the monotonic nature of a typical contingency hypothesis such as "the greater the technological uncertainty, the greater the positive impact of destandardization on effectiveness." She hypothesized that this kind of relationship would be more complex, and that at certain levels of technological uncertainty, increased destandardization would actually decrease effectiveness.

The results confirmed Schoonhoven's hypotheses. She found that increases in destandardization, decentralization, and professionalization improved overall efficiency when there was a high level of uncertainty in the operating room, that is, when the flow of patients and types of operations in the operating room varied significantly. Below a certain level of uncertainty, however, increases in each of these variables actually led to decreases in efficiency.

These results indicate that a change in organization structure that increases effectiveness in one operating room may decrease effectiveness in another. They suggest that an organization contemplating these types of changes should carefully assess the level of uncertainty within the particular organizational unit. The organization needs to establish the level of uncertainty at which a particular change—more or less standardization, for instance—may lead to greater efficiency.

Perhaps the most surprising results concerned the effects of professionalization. Most people would probably assume that increasing the level of professional training of employees could only improve an organization's effectiveness. Contrary to this assumption, the results showed that increased professionalization actually had negative effects on the operations' outcomes when the degree of task uncertainty was relatively low.

This study supports the general theory that the results of organizational change depend on a number of factors. But it also cautions contingency theorists that these results may be more complex than traditional theory would indicate, and it demonstrates a clear need for more empirical testing of the theories.

Source: Claudia Bird Schoonhoven, "Problems With Contingency Theory: Testing Assumptions Hidden Within the Language of Contingency 'Theory,'" *Administrative Science Quarterly*, 26 (1981), 349–377.

Sociotechnical Systems Theory

The foundation of the sociotechnical systems approach to organizing is systems theory, discussed in Chapter 1. There we defined a *system* as an interrelated set of elements functioning as a whole. A system has numerous subsystems, each of which, like the overall system, includes inputs, transformation processes, outputs, and feedback. We also defined an *open system* as one that interacts with its environment. Figure 15.3 shows how the environment and subsystems interact in a system. Note that a complex system is made up of numerous subsystems in which the outputs of some are the inputs to others. A sociotechnical systems approach views the organization as an open system structured to integrate the two important subsystems: the technical (task) subsystem and the social subsystem.

The *technical (task) subsystem* is the means by which inputs are transformed into outputs. The transformation processes may be the way that steel is formed, cut, drilled, chemically treated, and painted; or the ways that information is processed in an insurance company or financial institution. Quite often, significant scientific and engineering expertise is applied to these transformation processes to get the highest productivity and the lowest costs. For example, Fireplace Manufacturers Inc. of Santa Ana, California, a manufacturer of prefabricated metal fireplaces, implemented new *just-in-time (JIT)* manufacturing and inventory systems to improve the productivity of its plant.[13] JIT is a system in which component parts arrive just in time to be used in the manufacturing process; thereby reducing the costs of storing them in a warehouse until they are needed. It, in effect, redesigns the transformation process, from the introduction of raw materials to the shipping of the finished product. In three years Fireplace Manufacturers' inventory costs dropped from $1.1 million to $750,000, while sales doubled over the same period. The transformation process is usually regarded as technologically and economically driven; that is, whatever process is most productive and costs the least is generally the most desirable.

The *social subsystem* includes the interpersonal relationships that develop among people in organizations. Employees learn each other's work habits, strengths, weaknesses, and preferences, while developing a sense of mutual trust in each other. The social relationships may be manifested in personal friendships and interest groups. Communication, both about work and about employees' common interests, may be enhanced by friendship or hampered by antagonistic relationships. The Hawthorne studies (discussed in Chapter 1) were the first serious studies of the social subsystems in organizations.[14]

---

[13] Steven P. Galante, "Small Manufacturers Shifting to 'Just-In-Time' Techniques," *The Wall Street Journal,* December 21, 1987, p. 25.

[14] Elton Mayo, *The Human Problems of an Industrial Civilization* (New York: MacMillan, 1933); and F. J. Roethlisberger and W. J. Dickson, *Management and the Worker* (Cambridge: Harvard University Press, 1939).

| Figure 15.3 | Interaction of the Environment and Subsystems |

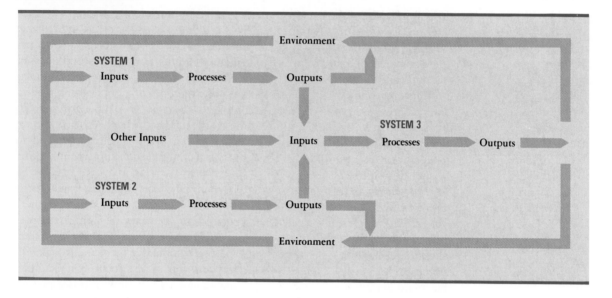

The sociotechnical systems approach was developed by members of the Tavistock Institute in England as an outgrowth of a study of coal mining. The study concerned new mining techniques that were introduced to increase productivity but failed because they entailed splitting up well-established work groups.[15] The Tavistock researchers concluded that the social subsystem had been sacrificed to the technical subsystem. Thus improvements in the technical subsystem were not realized because of problems in the social subsystem. Recently, a company that implemented JIT systems, Lifeline Systems, Inc., a manufacturer of electronic medical equipment, recognized the potential problems of employee acceptance and emphasized the role of management in getting employees to go along with the changes.[16]

The Tavistock group proposed that an organization's technical and social subsystems could be integrated through *autonomous work groups* (discussed in Chapter 8). Autonomous work groups are related to task design, and particularly job enrichment, but also bring in concepts of group interaction, supervision, and other characteristics of organization design. The aim of autonomous work groups is to make technical and social subsystems work together for the benefit of the larger system. Accordingly, to structure the task, authority, and reporting relationships around work groups, organizations should

---

[15] Eric L. Trist and K. W. Bamforth, "Some Social and Psychological Consequences of the Longwall Method of Coal-Getting," *Human Relations*, February 1951, pp. 3–38.

[16] Steven P. Galante, "Small Manufacturers Shifting To 'Just-In-Time' Techniques."

Figure 15.4   Socio-Technical Systems—Integration of Social and Technical Subsystems

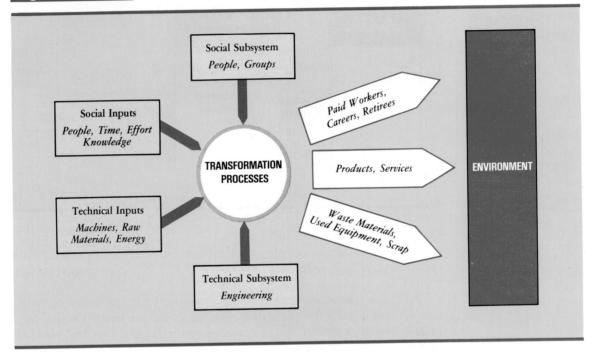

delegate decisions regarding job assignments, training, inspection, rewards, and punishments to the work groups. Management has the responsibility of coordinating the groups according to the demands of the work and task environment. Figure 15.4 shows how the relationships among the environment and the technical and social subsystems should be integrated according to the sociotechnical systems approach.

As we note in Chapter 14, the sociotechnical approach isolates four types of environments: placid randomized, placid clustered, disturbed reactive, and turbulent fields.[17] Organizations in turbulent environments tend to have autonomous work groups and to rely less on hierarchy and more on the autonomous work groups coordinating their work with each other. Sociotechnical systems theory asserts that the role of management is twofold: to monitor the environmental factors that impinge on the internal operations of the organization, and to coordinate the social and technical subsystems.

Two major criticisms have been leveled against the sociotechnical systems approach. First, little research has been done on how the environmental types

---

[17] Fred E. Emery and Eric L. Trist, "The Causal Texture of Organizational Environments," *Human Relations,* February 1965, pp. 21–32.

Figure 15.5

Structural Imperatives
Approach

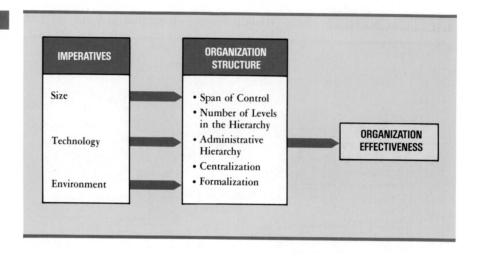

affect the characteristics of the work groups. Second, the approach fails to clearly predict how individual differences might affect participation in work groups.[18]

Although the sociotechnical systems approach has not been thoroughly tested, the approach has been tried with some success in the General foods plant in Topeka, Kansas, the Saab-Scania project in Sweden, and the Volvo plant in Kalmar, Sweden[19] (the latter discussed in Chapter 8). The development of the sociotechnical systems approach is significant in its departure from the universal approaches to organization design and in its emphasis on jointly harnessing the technical and human subsystems. It is also notable for its classification of the environment into four types, each with distinct characteristics that affect organizational functioning.

Structural Imperatives

The structural imperatives approach to organization design has probably been the most discussed and researched contingency approach of the last thirty years. The perspective was not formulated by a single theorist or researcher, and it has not evolved from a systematic and cohesive research effort. Rather, it has gradually emerged from a vast number of studies that have sought to address the question, "What are the compelling factors that determine how the organization must be structured to be effective?" As shown in Figure 15.5, the

---

[18] Miner, *Theories of Organizational Structure and Process*, pp. 85–116.

[19] Richard E. Walton, "How to Counter Alienation in the Plant," *Harvard Business Review*, November–December 1972, pp. 70–81; Richard E. Walton, "Work Innovations at Topeka: After Six Years," *Journal of Applied Behavioral Science*, July–August–September 1977, pp. 422–433; and Pehr G. Gyllenhammar, "How Volvo Adapts Work to People," *Harvard Business Review*, July–August 1977, pp. 102–113.

Figure 15.6   Impact of Large Size on Organization Structure

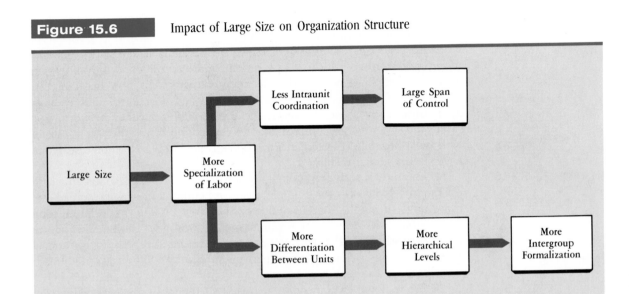

three factors that have been identified as **structural imperatives** are environ-ment, technology, and size. Environment and technology were discussed in Chapter 14 in terms of the many different ways they are classified and studied. In this section we add size to environment and technology as an important factor to be considered in designing organizations.

THE SIZE IMPERATIVE   The size of an organization can be gauged in many ways; we usually measure it in terms of total number of employees, value of the organization's assets, total sales in the previous year (or the number of clients served), or physical capacity. The method of measurement is a very im-portant consideration, although the different measures are usually correlated.[20]

It is generally assumed that larger organizations have a more complex structure than smaller ones. Research on the relationship between size and structure supports that view. Peter Blau and his associates concluded that large size is associated with more specialization of labor, a larger span of control, more hierarchical levels, and more formalization.[21] These multiple effects are shown in Figure 15.6. Increasing size leads to more specialization of labor within a work unit, which increases the amount of differentiation between work units and the number of levels in the hierarchy and consequently the need for

[20] John R. Kimberly, "Organizational Size and the Structuralist Perspective: A Review, Critique, and Proposal," *Administrative Science Quarterly,* December 1976, pp. 571–597.

[21] Peter M. Blau and Richard A. Schoenherr, *The Structure of Organizations* (New York: Basic Books, 1971).

more intergroup formalization. With more specialization within the unit, there is less need for coordination between groups; thus the span of control can be larger. Larger spans of control mean fewer first-line managers, but the need for more intergroup coordination may require more second- and third-line managers and staff personnel to coordinate them. Large organizations may therefore be more efficient because of their large spans of control and reduced administrative overhead; however, the greater differentiation between units makes the system more complex. Studies carried out by researchers associated with the University of Aston in Birmingham, England, and other researchers have shown similar results.[22]

Economies of scale are another advantage of large organizations. In a large operation, fixed costs—for example, plant and equipment—can be spread over more units of output, thereby reducing the cost per unit. In addition, some administrative activities, such as purchasing, clerical work, and marketing, can be accomplished for a large number of units at the same cost as for a small number of units. Their cost can then be spread over the larger number of units, again reducing unit cost.

Recently, however, companies such as AT&T Technologies, General Electric's Aircraft Engine Products Group, and S. C. Johnson & Son, Inc., have gone against the conventional wisdom that larger is always better in manufacturing plants. They cite the smaller investment required for smaller plants, the reduced need to produce a variety of products, and the desire to decrease organizational complexity (that is, reduce the number of hierarchical levels and shorten lines of communication) as the main reasons. In a number of instances, the smaller plant has resulted in increased feelings of team spirit, improved productivity, and higher profits.[23]

Traditionally, as organizations have grown, several layers of advisory staff have been added to help coordinate the complexities inherent in any large organization. In contrast, a current trend is to cut staff throughout the organization. Known as *organizational downsizing,* this popular trend is aimed primarily at reducing the size of corporate staff. Companies such as Mobil, AT&T, and Burlington Northern have recently cut back headquarters and corporate staff significantly.[24] The results have been mixed, with some observers noting that indiscriminate across-the-board cuts may leave the organization weak in certain key areas. However, positive results often include quicker decision making since fewer layers of management must approve every decision.

---

[22] The results of these studies are summarized very well in Richard H. Hall, *Organizations: Structure and Process,* 3rd. ed. (Englewood Cliffs, N.J.: Prentice-Hall, 1982), pp. 89–94. For a recent study in this area, see John H. Cullen and Kenneth S. Anderson, "Blau's Theory of Structural Differentiation Revisited: A Theory of Structural Change or Scale?" *Academy of Management Journal,* June 1986, pp. 203–229.

[23] "Small Is Beautiful Now in Manufacturing," *Business Week,* October 22, 1984, pp. 152–156.

[24] Thomas Moore "Goodbye, Corporate Staff," *Fortune,* December 21, 1987, pp. 65–76.

Table 15.3	Characteristic	Mechanistic	Organic
	Structure	Hierarchical	Network based on interests
Mechanistic and Organic Structures	Interactions, communication	Primarily vertical	Lateral throughout
	Work directions, instructions	From supervisor	Through advice, information
	Knowledge, information	Concentrated at top	Throughout
	Membership, relationship with organization	Requires loyalty, obedience	Commitment to task, progress, expansion

Other studies have found that the relationship between size and structural complexity is not as clear as was indicated by the Blau results. Instead, these studies suggest that size must be examined in relation to the technology of the organization.[25]

THE TECHNOLOGY IMPERATIVE   As discussed in Chapter 14, the technology employed by an organization to transform inputs into outputs is a major factor to be considered in designing its structure. In that chapter we reviewed the different approaches to technology of Woodward, Burns and Stalker, Perrow, Thompson, and the researchers at the University of Aston.[26] Burns and Stalker also categorized organization structures as either mechanistic or organic. As summarized in Table 15.3, a **mechanistic structure** is primarily hierarchical in nature, interactions and communications are primarily vertical, instructions come from the boss, knowledge is concentrated at the top, and continued membership requires loyalty and obedience. In contrast, the **organic structure** is structured like a network, interactions and communications are more lateral and horizontal, knowledge resides wherever it is most useful to the organization,

---

[25] Richard H. Hall, J. Eugene Haas, and Norman Johnson, "Organizational Size, Complexity, and Formalization," *American Sociological Review,* December 1967, pp. 903–912.

[26] Joan Woodward, *Industrial Organizations: Theory and Practice* (London: Oxford University Press, 1965), and *Management and Technology: Problems of Progress in Industry,* no. 3 (London: Her Majesty's Stationery Office, 1958); Tom Burns and G. M. Stalker, *The Management of Innovation* (London: Tavistock Publications, 1961); Charles B. Perrow, "A Framework for the Comparative Analysis of Organizations," *American Sociological Review,* April 1967, pp. 194–208; Charles B. Perrow, *Organizational Analysis: A Sociological View* (Belmont, Calif.: Brooks/Cole; London: Tavistock Publications, 1970); James D. Thompson, *Organizations in Action* (New York: McGraw-Hill, 1967); and David J. Hickson, Derek S. Pugh, and Diana C. Pheysey, "Operations Technology and Organization Structure: An Empirical Reappraisal," *Administrative Science Quarterly,* September 1969, pp. 378–397.

and membership requires a commitment to the tasks of the organization. Burns and Stalker noted that if the rate of technological change is slow, the most effective design is a mechanistic structure. But if the technology is changing rapidly, the organization will need a structure that provides more flexibility and quicker decision making to react quickly to change: an organic structure.

One of the major contributions of the study of organizational technology is the revelation that organizations have more than one important "technology" that enable them to accomplish their tasks. Recall that the Aston studies noted that organizations have operations, materials, and knowledge technology. Instead of examining technology in isolation, the Aston group also recognized that size and technology are related in determining organization structure.[27] And in smaller organizations, they found that technology had more direct effects on the structure. In large organizations, though, they found, like Blau, that structure depended less on the operations technology and more on size considerations such as the number of employees. In other words, in small organizations the structure depended primarily on the technology, whereas in large organizations the need to coordinate complicated activities was the most important factor. Thus, both organizational size and technology are important considerations in organization design.

ENVIRONMENTAL CONSIDERATIONS   In Chapter 14 we discussed several perspectives on the organizational environment: the concept of environmental uncertainty, the resource dependence view, and the population perspective. These varying viewpoints provide the organization designer with different frameworks for understanding how environmental factors influence the organization.

An organization attempts to continue as a viable entity in a dynamic environment. The environment completely encloses the organization, and managers must be constantly concerned about it. The organization as a whole, as well as departments and divisions within it, is created to deal with different challenges, problems, and uncertainties. James D. Thompson suggested that organizations design a structure to protect the dominant technology of importance to the organization, smooth out any problems, and keep down coordination costs.[28] Thus, organization structures are designed to coordinate relevant technologies and protect them from outside disturbances. Structural components such as inventory, warehousing, and shipping help buffer the technology used to transform inputs into outputs. For instance, demand for products is usually cyclical or seasonal and is subject to many disturbances, but the warehouse inventory helps the manufacturing system function as if the environment accepted output at a steady rate, maximizing technological efficiency and helping the organization respond to fluctuating demands of the market.

---

[27] Hickson, Pugh, and Pheysey, "Operations Technology and Organization Structure."

[28] Thompson, *Organizations In Action,* pp. 51–82.

Strategy and Strategic Choice

The final contingency approach to organization design considered here is based on the strategic orientation of the organization. *Strategy* is defined in Chapter 13 as the design of a game plan to achieve organizational goals.[29] Kellogg, for example, has pursued a strategy that combines product differentiation and market segmentation in attempting to be the leader in the ready-to-eat cereal industry. Over the years Kellogg has successfully introduced new cereals from different grains, in different shapes, sizes, colors, and flavors, to provide any type of cereal the consumer might want.[30]

After studying the history of seventy companies, Alfred Chandler drew certain conclusions about the relationship between an organization's structure and its business strategy.[31] Chandler observed that a growth strategy to expand into a new product line is usually matched with some type of decentralization— a decentralized structure being necessary to deal with the problems of the new product line.

Chandler's "structure follows strategy" concept seems like common sense. Yet it is contradicted by the structural imperatives approach, which recommends that design decisions be based on size, technology, and environment, not strategy. This apparent clash has been resolved by refining the strategy concept to include the role of the top-management decision maker in determining the organization's structure.[32] In effect, this view inserts the manager-decision maker between the structural imperatives and the structural features of the organization. This distinction can be understood by comparing Figure 15.7 with Figure 15.5.

Figure 15.7 shows the structural imperatives as contextual factors within which the organization must operate and that affect the purposes and goals of the organization. The manager's choices for organization structure are affected by the organization's purposes and goals, the imperatives, and the manager's personality, value system, and experience.[33] Organizational effectiveness depends on the fit among the imperatives, the strategies, and the structure.

Another perspective on strategy—structure linkage—is that the relationship may be a reciprocal one. That is, structure may be set up to carry out, or

---

[29] See Arthur A. Thompson, Jr., and A. J. Strickland, III, *Strategic Management,* 3rd ed. (Plano, Tex.: Business Publications, 1984), pp. 19–27.

[30] Thompson and Strickland, *Strategic Management,* pp. 56–57.

[31] Alfred D. Chandler, *Strategy and Structure: Chapters in the History of the American Industrial Enterprise* (Cambridge: MIT Press, 1962).

[32] For more information on managerial choice, see John R. Montanari, "Managerial Discretion: An Expanded Model of Organizational Choice," *Academy of Management Review,* April 1978, pp. 231–241; and John Child, "Organizational Structure, Environment, and Performance: The Role of Strategic Choice," *Sociology,* Vol. 6, 1972, pp. 1–22.

[33] H. Randolph Bobbitt and Jeffrey D. Ford, "Decision Maker Choice as a Determinant of Organizational Structure," *Academy of Management Review,* January 1980, pp. 13–23.

Figure 15.7   Strategic Choice Approach to Organization Design

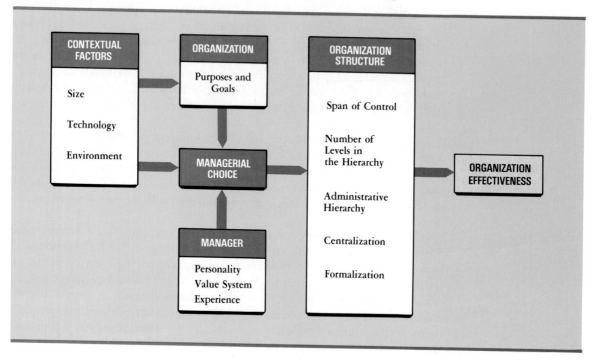

implement, the strategy, but it may also affect the strategic decision-making process via the centralization, or decentralization, of decision making and formalization of rules and procedures.[34] Thus, strategy determines structure, which, in turn, affects strategic decision making.

The role of strategic choice in determining organization structure actually goes a step beyond the view that structure follows strategy. However, it has received less research attention than have structural imperatives. And of course, some might simply view strategy as another imperative along with size, technology, and environment. Strategy does, though, seem to differ from the imperatives because it is a product of the analysis of the imperatives and an articulation of the organization's direction, purpose, and plans for the future. For an example of this strategy—structural linkage in an international setting—see *International Perspective*.

---

[34] James W. Fredrickson, "The Strategic Decision Process and Organization Structure," *Academy of Management Review*, April 1986, pp. 280–297.

International Perspective

Preparing to Go Private

Renault, the French automotive giant, is a *régie*, a company owned and financed by the French government. Gradually, however, it is becoming responsible for its own finances and one day will become "privatized," and sell shares to individuals. To prepare for the shift, Renault's last two leaders have had to speed the company through a crash course of reorganization, following many of the patterns familiar to managers in independent companies who respond to their markets and shareholders.

Renault's financial figures for the first half of the 1980s reveal the need for change. In 1987, the company owed almost $9 billion. Between 1982 and 1985, Renault's market share dropped from 40 percent to 30 percent in France and from 14.5 percent to 10.7 percent in Europe as a whole. While other auto manufacturers' productivity was increasing rapidly, Renault's output-per-worker actually fell between 1981 and 1985.

To solve Renault's problems, the French Socialist government of François Mitterand turned to two men who had been instrumental in revitalizing other ailing companies. Georges Besse, former president of a uranium company and an aluminum-and-chemicals group, took over in 1985; after his assassination in 1986, he was succeeded by Raymond Levy, who had been running a Belgian steel company.

Under Besse, the company radically changed its goals. It had been focusing on providing its workers with jobs and benefits, on helping French industry, and on expanding into other markets. Now the focus was on profit. And to make a profit, the company had to attack its own weaknesses on a number of fronts.

Although observers argue about the exact cause of Renault's difficulties, they agree on a number of structural problems at Renault. The company's tight hierarchy and functional organization led to a lack of lateral communication and made impossible the kind of matrix structure that has succeeded so well for many Japanese automakers. Matters became worse when a previous chairman tried suddenly to fragment the traditional centralized hierarchy. The decentralization of the company led to duplication of efforts and to the creation of countless managerial levels. Communication became even worse and decision making even slower.

Besse and Levy began their reorganization by simplifying the hierarchy, eliminating layers of management, laying off thousands of workers, and rewarding Renault's management for merit rather than seniority. Executives' pay now depends on their ability to reach goals, and over 400 young executives are enrolled in a career development program.

These restructuring strategies, as well as a series of cost-cutting measures, allowed Renault to turn a profit in 1987 for the first time in the decade. With labor unions strongly opposed to privatization but both profits and market share rising, the French government and the company's managers continue to face a difficult choice about what the company's goals should be and which structure would best promote those goals.

Sources: Linda Bernier, "Levy's New Designs For Renault," *International Management*, October 1987, 79–84; Jean-Jacques Renaux, "The Man Who Would Rebuild Renault," *Automotive News*, August 5, 1985, 37, 39.

THE MINTZBERG FRAMEWORK

Although we have examined universal and contingency approaches to organization design, we have not yet considered specific designs. In the remainder of this chapter, we describe concrete organizational designs. The universe of possible designs is large, but fortunately it is possible to identify a few basic forms that designs take.

Henry Mintzberg proposed a range of coordinating mechanisms that are found in operating organizations.[35] In his view, organization structure corresponds to the way tasks are first divided and then coordinated. Mintzberg described five major ways in which tasks are coordinated: by mutual adjustment, by direct supervision, and by standardization of worker (or input) skills, work processes, or outputs. These five methods can exist side by side within an organization. They are illustrated in Figure 15.8.

Coordination by mutual adjustment simply means that workers use informal communication to coordinate with each other, whereas *coordination by direct supervision* means that a manager or supervisor coordinates the actions of workers. As noted, *standardization* may be used as a coordination mechanism in three different ways: we can standardize the *worker skills* that are inputs to the work process; the *processes* themselves, that is, the methods workers use to transform inputs into outputs; or the *outputs,* that is, the products or services or the performance levels expected of workers. Standardization is usually developed by staff analysts and enforced by management such that skills, processes, and output meet predetermined standards.

Mintzberg further suggested that the five coordinating mechanisms roughly correspond to stages of organizational development and complexity. In the very small organization, individuals working together communicate informally, achieving coordination by mutual adjustment. As more people join the organization, coordination needs become more complex, and direct supervision is added. For example, two or three people working in a small fast-food business can coordinate the work simply by talking to each other about the incoming orders for hamburgers, fries, and drinks. However, in a larger restaurant with more complex cooking and warming equipment and several shifts of workers, direct supervision becomes necessary.

In large organizations, standardization is added to mutual adjustment and direct supervision to coordinate the work. What type of standardization depends on the nature of the work situation—that is, the organization's technology and environment. When the organization's tasks are fairly routine, standardization of work processes may achieve the necessary coordination. Thus, the larger fast-food outlet may standardize the making of hamburger patties: the meat is weighed, put into a hamburger press, and squashed into a patty. McDonald's is well known for this type of standardized process.

---

[35] Henry Mintzberg, *The Structuring of Organizations: A Synthesis of the Research* (Englewood Cliffs, N.J.: Prentice-Hall, 1979).

Figure 15.8

Mintzberg's Five
Coordinating
Mechanisms

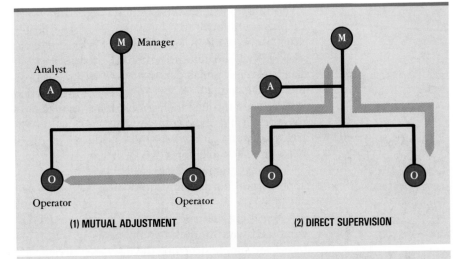

(1) MUTUAL ADJUSTMENT

(2) DIRECT SUPERVISION

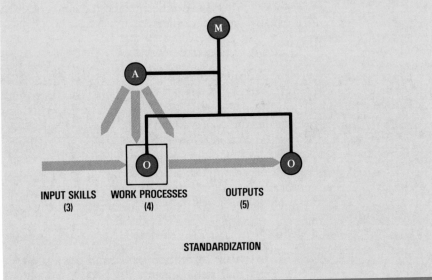

INPUT SKILLS (3)   WORK PROCESSES (4)   OUTPUTS (5)

STANDARDIZATION

Source: Henry Mintzberg, *The Structuring of Organizations: A Synthesis of the Research.* © 1979, p. 4. Reprinted by permission of Prentice-Hall, Inc., Englewood Cliffs, N.J.

In other complex situations, standardization of the output may allow the workers to do the work in any appropriate manner as long as the output meets specifications. Thus, the cook may not care how the hamburger is pressed, only that the right amount of meat is used and the patty is the correct diameter and thickness. The worker may use any process as long as the output is a standard burger.

A third possibility, most often adopted in situations where processes and outputs are difficult to standardize, is to coordinate work by standardizing the skills of the workers. In a hospital, for example, each patient must be treated as a special situation; the hospital process and output can therefore not be standardized. Similar diagnostic and treatment procedures may be used with more than one patient, but the skills of the physicians and nurses, which are standardized through their professional training, are relied upon to coordinate the work. In the most complex of work situations, however, organizations may have to depend on workers' mutual adjustment to coordinate their own actions; here, the salient elements of coordination are the workers' professional training and their communication skills. In effect, mutual adjustment can be an appropriate coordinating mechanism in both the simple and most complex situations.

Mintzberg pointed out that the five methods of coordination can be combined with the basic components of structure to develop five structural forms: the simple structure, the machine bureaucracy, the professional bureaucracy, the divisionalized form, and the adhocracy. These Mintzberg called *pure* or *ideal* types of designs.

Simple Structure

The **simple structure** characterizes relatively small, usually young organizations in a simple, dynamic environment. The organization has little specialization and formalization, and its overall structure is organic. Power and decision making are concentrated in the chief executive, often the owner-manager, and the flow of authority is from the top down. Direct supervision is the primary coordinating mechanism. Given its dynamic and often hostile environment, the organization must adapt quickly to survive. Most small businesses—a car dealership, a locally owned retail clothing store, or a candy manufacturer with only regional distribution—have a simple structure.

Machine Bureaucracy

The **machine bureaucracy** is typical of a large, well-established company in a simple and stable environment. Work is highly specialized and formalized, and decision making is usually concentrated at the top. Standardization of work processes is the primary coordination mechanism. Because the environment is both simple and stable, this highly bureaucratic structure does not have to adapt quickly to changes. Examples include large mass production firms, such as Container Corporation, some automobile companies, and providers of services to mass markets, such as insurance companies.

Professional Bureaucracy

Usually found in a complex and stable environment, the **professional bureaucracy** relies on standardization of skills as the primary means of coordination. There is much horizontal specialization by professional area of expertise but little formalization. Decision making is decentralized and takes place where the expertise is. The only means of coordination available to the organization is standardization of skills—the professionally trained employees. Although it lacks centralization, the professional bureaucracy stabilizes and controls its tasks with rules and procedures developed in the relevant profession. Hospitals, universities, and consulting firms are typical examples.

Divisionalized Form

The **divisionalized form** characterizes old and very large firms operating in a relatively simple, stable environment with several diverse markets. It resembles the machine bureaucracy except that it is divided according to the different markets it serves. There is some horizontal and vertical specialization between the divisions (each defined by a market) and headquarters. Decision making is clearly split between headquarters and the divisions, and standardization of outputs is the primary means of coordination. The mechanism of control required by headquarters encourages the development of machine bureaucracies in the divisions. The classic example of the divisionalized form is General Motors, which in a reorganization in the 1920s adopted a design that created divisions for each major car model.[36] Although the divisions have been reorganized and the cars changed several times, the concept of the divisionalized organization is still very evident at GM.[37] General Electric, as another example, uses a two-tiered divisionalized structure, dividing its numerous businesses into strategic business units, which are further divided into sectors.[38]

Adhocracy

The **adhocracy** is typically found in young organizations engaged in highly technical fields where the environment is complex and dynamic. Decision making is spread throughout the organization, and power is in the hands of experts. There is horizontal and vertical specialization but little formalization, resulting in a very organic structure. Coordination is by mutual adjustment through frequent personal communication and liaison devices. Specialists are not grouped together in functional units, but are deployed into specialized market-oriented project teams.

The typical adhocracy is usually established to foster innovation, something to which the other four types of structures are not particularly well suited. Numerous U.S. organizations—Johnson & Johnson, Procter & Gamble, Monsanto,

---

[36] See Harold C. Livesay, *American Made: Men Who Shaped the American Economy* (Boston: Little, Brown, 1979), pp. 215–239, for a good discussion of Alfred Sloan and the development of the divisionalized structure at General Motors.

[37] Anne B. Fisher, "GM Is Tougher Than You Think," *Fortune,* November 10, 1986, pp. 56–64.

[38] Thompson and Strickland, *Strategic Management,* p. 212.

and 3M, for example—are known for their innovation and constant stream of new products.[39] These organizations are either structured totally as an adhocracy or have large divisions set up as an adhocracy. Johnson & Johnson, for example, established a new-products division over thirty years ago to encourage continued innovation, creativity, and risk-taking. The division continues to succeed as more than 200 new products have been introduced by Johnson & Johnson in the United States in the past five years.

Mintzberg believed that the most important consideration in designing an organization was the fit between parts. Not only must there be a fit between the structure, the structural imperatives (technology, size, and environment), and organizational strategy, but the components of structure (rules and procedures, decision making, specialization) must also fit together and be appropriate for the situation. Mintzberg suggested that when these characteristics were not put together properly, an organization would not function effectively.[40]

MATRIX ORGANIZATION DESIGN

One other organizational form deserves attention here: the matrix organization design. Matrix design is consistent with the contingency approach, because it is only useful in certain situations. One of the earliest implementations of the matrix design was at TRW Systems Group in 1959.[41] Following TRW's lead, other firms in aerospace and high-technology fields created similar matrix structures.

The **matrix design** attempts to combine two different designs to gain the benefits of each. The most common matrix form superimposes product or project departmentalization on a functional structure (see Figure 15.9). Each department and project has a manager; each employee, however, is a member of both a functional department and a project team. The dual role means that the employee has two supervisors, the department manager and the project leader.

A matrix structure is appropriate when three conditions exist:

1. There is external pressure for a dual focus, meaning that factors in the environment require the organization to focus its efforts equally on responding to multiple external factors and on emphasizing internal operations.

---

[39] Kenneth Labich, "The Innovators," *Fortune*, June 6, 1988, pp. 51–64.

[40] Henry Mintzberg, "Organization Design: Fashion or Fit," *Harvard Business Review*, January–February 1981, pp. 103–116.

[41] Harvey F. Kolodny, "Managing in a Matrix," *Business Horizons*, March–April 1981, pp. 17–24.

Figure 15.9   A Matrix Design

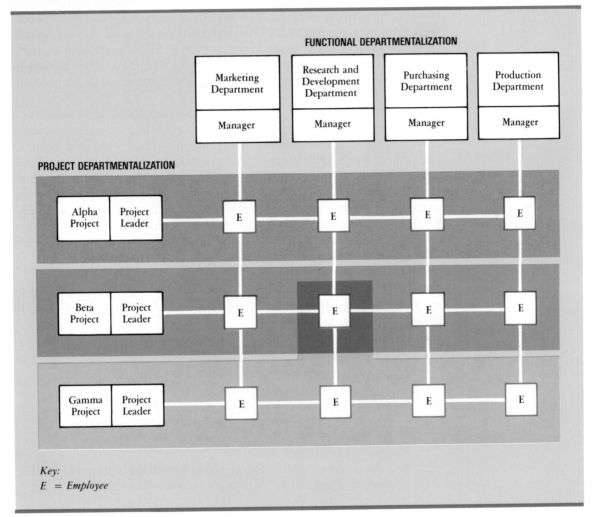

FUNCTIONAL DEPARTMENTALIZATION

Marketing Department	Research and Development Department	Purchasing Department	Production Department
Manager	Manager	Manager	Manager

PROJECT DEPARTMENTALIZATION

Alpha Project / Project Leader — E — E — E — E

Beta Project / Project Leader — E — E — E — E

Gamma Project / Project Leader — E — E — E — E

Key:
E = Employee

2. There are pressures for a high information-processing capacity.

3. There are pressures for shared resources.[42]

In the aerospace industry in the early 1960s, these conditions were all present. Private companies had a dual focus: their customers, primarily the federal government, and the complex engineering and technical fields in which they

[42] Stanley M. Davis and Paul R. Lawrence, *Matrix* (Reading, Mass.: Addison-Wesley, 1977), pp. 11–36.

were engaged. Moreover, the environment of these companies was changing very rapidly. Technological sophistication and competition were on the increase, resulting in growing environmental uncertainty and, consequently, an added need for information processing. The final condition stemmed from the pressure on the companies to excel in a very competitive environment despite limited resources. The companies concluded that it was inefficient to assign their highly professional—and highly compensated—scientific and engineering personnel to just one project at a time.

Built into the matrix structure is a flexible and coordinated response to internal and external pressures. Members can be reassigned from one project to another as demands for their skills change. They may work for a month on one project, be assigned to the functional home department for two weeks, and then be reassigned to another project for the next six months. The matrix form improves project coordination by assigning project responsibility to a single leader rather than dividing it among several functional department heads. Furthermore, communication is improved, since employees can communicate about the project with the members of the project team as well as with members of the functional unit to which they belong. In this way, solutions to project problems may emerge from either group.

The matrix organizational form thus provides several benefits for the organization. It is not, however, trouble free. Typical problems include the following:

1. The dual reporting system may cause role conflict among employees.
2. Power struggles may occur over who has authority on which issues.
3. Matrix organization is often misinterpreted to mean that all decisions must be made by a group; as a result, group decision-making techniques may be used when they are not appropriate.
4. If the design involves several matrices, each laid on top of another, there may be no way to trace accountability and authority.[43]

Only under the three conditions listed earlier is the matrix design likely to work. In any case, it is a complex organizational system that must be carefully coordinated and managed to be effective.

CONTEMPORARY ORGANIZATION DESIGN

The current proliferation of design theories and alternative forms of organization provide the practicing manager with a dizzying array of choices. The task of

---

[43] Davis and Lawrence, *Matrix*, pp. 129–154.

the organization manager-designer is to examine the firm within its situation and to design a form of organization that meets its needs. The three dominant themes of current design strategies are the effects of technological (or environmental) change, the importance of people, and the necessity of staying in touch with the customer.

Technological change is most evident in the information processing that has been revolutionized by microelectronics.[44] The effects on organizational communication have been significant, as discussed in Chapter 18. Because modern information processing is so fast, enhances coordination among work groups, and provides almost instantaneous feedback on performance, allowing better control of operations, its impact is felt in the structural form itself. Contemporary structural designs must be capable of handling this type of information technology.

Current design strategies also reflect a strong concern for people. In their best-selling book on effective companies, *In Search of Excellence,* Thomas J. Peters and Robert H. Waterman, Jr., stress the theme of productivity through people.[45] Well-run organizations treat their employees as adults who need to be developed and nurtured as valued resources. The organization structure and processes are the primary vehicles for accomplishing that task. The performance appraisal, reward, and communication systems must be integrated into the overall structure of the organization to provide relevant information regarding the firm and the employees' roles in it and appropriate feedback on the results of employees' efforts. The structure must provide people with jobs that are appropriate for their skills, coordinated with others, consistent with the purpose of the organization, and capable of providing a sense of belongingness and contribution to the organization.

The final design factor has an external focus—staying in touch with the customer, client, or constituent. Peters and Nancy K. Austin have followed up on the Peters-Waterman theme by stressing the importance of an external orientation.[46] They emphasize paying attention to the end users of the firm's product or service. Organization designers need to develop systems for encouraging and rewarding employee behaviors that keep them in touch with such groups. The systems must also allow employees to act on what they learn, correcting deficiencies, and making adjustments to current offerings and developing new products or services to meet new demands.

These three dominant factors argue for a contingency design perspective. Unfortunately, there is no "one best way." The designer must consider the

---

[44] John Child, *Organizations: A Guide to Problems and Practice* (New York: Harper & Row, 1984), p. 246.

[45] Thomas J. Peters and Robert H. Waterman, Jr., *In Search of Excellence: Lessons from America's Best-Run Companies* (New York: Harper & Row, 1982), pp. 235–278.

[46] Thomas J. Peters and Nancy K. Austin, "A Passion for Excellence," *Fortune,* May 13, 1985, pp. 20–32.

impact of multiple factors—sociotechnical systems factors, the structural imperatives, strategy, changing information technology, people, and a concern for end users—on his or her particular organization.

SUMMARY OF KEY POINTS

A universal approach to organization design suggests that its prescriptions will work in any situation or circumstance. A contingency approach, on the other hand, suggests that there are several ways to achieve an outcome, the best way depending on one or several factors.

Weber's ideal bureaucracy, Fayol's classic principles of organizing, and Likert's human organization are important universal design approaches. Weber's bureaucratic form of administration was intended to assure stability, control, and predictable outcomes. The ideal bureaucracy is characterized by rules and procedures, division of labor, hierarchy of authority, technical competence, separation of ownership, rights and property differentiation, and documentation.

Fayol presented a fourteen-point code for managers. His classic principles, which included departmentalization, unity of command, and unity of direction, became generally accepted means of organizing. Taken together, the fourteen principles provided the basis for the modern organization chart and the coordination of work.

Likert's human organization was based on the principles of supportive relationships, employee participation, and overlapping work groups. He described the human organization in terms of eight variables based on the assumption that people work best in highly supportive and cohesive work groups oriented toward organization goals.

Important contingency approaches to organization design center on sociotechnical systems, structural imperatives, and organizational strategy. The sociotechnical systems approach viewed the organization as an open system structured to integrate two important subsystems: the technical (task) subsystem and the social subsystem. According to this approach, organizations should structure the task, authority, and reporting relationships around the work group by delegating to it decisions regarding job assignments, training, inspection, rewards, and punishments. The task of management is to monitor the environment and coordinate the structures, rules, and procedures.

The structural imperatives are size, technology, and environment. In general, large organizations have more complex structures and usually more than one technology. The structure of small organizations, on the other hand, may be dominated by one core operations technology. The structure of the organization is also established to fit with the environmental demands and buffer the core operating technology from environmental changes and uncertainties.

Initially, strategy was seen as the determinant of structure—the structure of the organization was designed to implement its purpose, goals, and strategies. The concept of managerial choice in determining organization structure represents a modification of this view. The manager designs the structure to accomplish organizational goals, guided by an analysis of the contextual factors, the strategies of the organization, and personal preferences.

Mintzberg's ideal types of organization design were derived from a framework of coordinating mechanisms. The five types are simple structure, machine bureaucracy, professional bureaucracy, divisionalized form, and adhocracy. Most organizations have some characteristics of each type, but one is likely to predominate. Mintzberg believed that the most important consideration in designing an organization is the fit between parts of the organization.

The matrix design combines two types of structure (usually, functional and project departmentalization) to gain the benefits of each. It usually results in a multiple command and authority system. Benefits of the matrix form are increased flexibility, cooperation, communication, and use of skilled personnel. Its problems are usually associated with the dual reporting system and the complex management system needed to coordinate work.

Contemporary organization design is contingency oriented. Three factors influencing design decisions are the changing information and technological environment, concern for people as a valued resource, and the need to keep in touch with customers.

DISCUSSION QUESTIONS

1. Why is it important to distinguish between organization structure and organization design?

2. Explain why the ideal bureaucracy is usually not considered an ideal anymore.

3. Why do bureaucracies tend to be characterized by slow decision making?

4. Discuss how the federal government continues to observe the bureaucratic principles of separation of ownership and of rights and property in making appointments to high-level government positions.

5. Do you feel that the classic principles of organizing and the human organization are opposites? Why or why not?

6. What might be the advantages and disadvantages of structuring the faculty members at your college or university as an autonomous work group?

7. What do you think are the purpose, goals, and strategies of your college or university? How are they reflected in its structure?

8. Which of Mintzberg's pure forms is best illustrated by a major national political party (Democratic or Republican)? Religious organizations? A football team? The U.S. Olympic Committee?

9. In a matrix organization would you rather be a project leader, a functional department head, or a highly trained technical specialist? Why?

10. Discuss what you think the important design considerations will be for organization designers in the year 2000.

Case 15.1

The Japanese Succeed Where the British Failed

In 1984, Japan's Sumitomo Rubber Industries Ltd. (SRI) bought Dunlop Tire Corporation, a venerable British tire-making company founded by John Dunlop, inventor of the pneumatic tire. In less than three years, SRI managers pulled Dunlop back from the brink of collapse, making it an efficient and healthy world competitor. The takeover provides insights into the success of Japanese management techniques not only on the factory floor, but for empire building as well.

The Japanese company's takeover of Dunlop's holdings in France, Germany, and Britain parallels in some ways Dunlop's own growth. By the First World War, Dunlop had established a network of overseas factories, including one built in Japan in 1909 that was a major manufacturer until the 1960s. Dunlop was one of a number of British companies that became multinationals in the early part of this century; SRI, somewhat similarly, is part of the currently growing wave of multinationals based in Japan.

Dunlop's empire, however, reflected the management problems that led many multinationals to falter. British companies often built foreign plants without thorough investigation of the local business environment, and sometimes merely as a result of a top executive's whims. This lax attitude often extended to the choice of people to run the foreign plants. The British did not like to give locals a strong voice in management, but they also preferred not to send their best managers abroad, which resulted in poorly managed, unprofitable subsidiaries. In addition, British companies often resisted management changes and were very slow to relinquish outdated ideas. They have been among the last Western companies to try to expand markets to the Orient.

When SRI bought Dunlop, by contrast, the parent company's interest in its new plants was obvious. SRI invested heavily in new production technology and sent top management officials to advise local executives. The company has successfully maintained the delicate balance between allowing local managers to run the operations of the plants and ensuring, through its advisers, that the plants follow the best production methods and aspire to Japanese-level quality.

SRI has been particularly successful in improving labor relations at its new factories, despite often drastic cutbacks in the labor force. The company uses an open style of management, informing the workers about the company's performance and plans, and being more responsive to workers' ideas. SRI reduced union objections to worker cutbacks by promising that investment in new equipment would improve working conditions. By getting workers involved in decision making and by breaking down barriers between workers and management, SRI has created an attitude best expressed by the competitiveness that workers display in their attempts to outproduce workers at the company's other European plants. The company posts the monthly production goals and results of each factory.

With this new attitude, a new emphasis on communications, training, management development, and modernized production techniques, SRI has made the old Dunlop plants more flexible and responsive. One concrete result is that making a new tire mold now takes ten weeks instead of twenty-five. The world will continue to watch the Japanese tactic of exporting management to see if Japanese multinationals can escape the fate of the British companies that they are now swallowing.

Case Questions:

1. What are the advantages and disadvantages of giving local managers control over the operations of a foreign subsidiary's plants?

2. What kind of management approaches and organizational structure would most likely encourage local workers to develop loyalty to a foreign owner?

Case Sources:

Jules Arbose, "What's Behind The Rebirth of Dunlop In Europe? The Japanese," *International Management*, July/August 1987, 65–68; Geoffrey Jones, "Foundations of Foreign Success," *Management Today*, June 1987, 86–130.

Case 15.2

A Structural Straightjacket at Wild Wear

Wild Wear, Inc., makes clothes, raingear, and sleeping bags for hikers and other outdoor enthusiasts. The company began when Myrtle Kelly began sewing pile jackets that her husband Ray sold on college campuses. It now employs almost 500 people organized into traditional divisions such as marketing, manufacturing, and research and development.

Not so long ago, it became apparent that although Wild Wear's balance sheet appeared healthy, the company was stagnant. Everyone seemed to work hard, and the company's products seldom flopped, yet Wild Wear seemed to have developed a "me too" posture, bringing new products to market a season or a full year after competitors.

The Kellys, who still run the company, pored over performance appraisals looking for the weak points that might be holding the company back. But it seemed that the personnel department had been doing its work. R & D was coming up with a respectable number of new products, the manufacturing facility was modern and efficient, and the marketing tactics often won praise from customers.

Baffled, the Kellys called a meeting of middle-level managers, hoping they could provide some answers that they had missed. They were shocked when they noticed that the managers were introducing themselves as they came in and sat down. People who had been working in the same company for years had never even met! The meeting began with this observation, and for ninety minutes the Kellys sat back and listened to the problems their managers raised.

It became clear that, in the attempt to grow from a family operation into a company, the Kellys had assumed that the two needed to be very different. When they started out, the two of them handled all aspects of the business. Ray would hear from a customer that backpackers really needed a certain product, would pass the idea on to Myrtle and order the materials she needed, and within a few weeks would offer the product to the same—now delighted— customer. As the company grew, the Kellys began to worry about their lack of formal business training and hired professionals to run each division and set up appropriate rules and procedures.

What they had created, the middle managers informed them, was a number of very efficient, productive divisions that might as well have been separate companies. The R & D people might come up with a new breathable fabric for raingear only to find that production had just begun making a new rainwear line out of the old fabric and that marketing was turning all its attention to selling the big inventory of sleeping bags. Each division did the best it could with the information it had, but that information was very incomplete. Products progressed linearly from one division to the next, but it always seemed as though an idea that had been ahead of its time did not yield a product until the time had passed.

To remedy the problem, the Kellys decided to call in a management consultant to create more of a matrix structure for Wild Wear. While they were waiting for the consultant's solutions, they began holding weekly "Horizon" meetings. The group of middle managers would get together every Monday and discuss what they saw on their horizon. After less than a month of such meetings, the excitement generated seemed to promise better things for Wild Wear, as the managers stretched to expand their own horizons and to help others bring their ideas to light.

Case Questions:

1. What would be the ideal organizational design for a company like Wild Wear?

2. What does Wild Wear's experience say about the need for periodic corporate restructuring?

**Experiential
Exercise**

Purpose: This exercise will help you understand the factors that determine the design of organizations.

Format: You will interview employees of a small- to medium-sized organization and analyze the reasons for its design. (You may want to coordinate this exercise with the one in Chapter 13.)

Procedure: Your first task is to find a local organization with between fifty and five hundred employees. (It should not be part of your college or university.) If you did the exercise for Chapter 13, you might want to use the same company for this exercise. The organization should have more than two hierarchical levels, but it should not be too complex to understand in a short period of study. You may want to check with your professor before contacting the company. Your initial contact should be with the highest-ranking manager you can reach. You should be sure that top management is aware of your project and gives its approval.

Using the material in this chapter, you will interview employees to obtain the following information on the structure of the organization:

1. What is the organization in business to do? What are its goals and its strategies for achieving them?
2. How large is the company? What is the total number of employees? How many work full time? How many work part time?
3. What are the most important components of the organization's environment?
4. Is the number of important environmental components large or small?
5. To what degree do these components change, that is, how fast or slowly do they change?
6. Would you characterize the organization's environment as certain, uncertain, or somewhere in between? If in between, describe in more detail approximately how certain or uncertain.
7. What is the organization's dominant technology—how does it transform inputs into outputs?
8. How rigid is the company in its application of rules and procedures? Is it flexible enough to respond to environmental changes?
9. How involved are employees in the daily decision making related to their jobs?
10. What methods are used to ensure control over the actions of employees?

Interview at least three employees of the company at different levels and in different departments. One should hold a top-level position. Be sure to ask the questions in a way that the employees will understand; they may not be familiar with some of the terminology used in this chapter.

The result of the exercise should be a report describing the technology, environment, and structure of the company. You should discuss the extent to which the structure is appropriate for the organization's strategy, size, technology, and environment. If it does not seem appropriate, you should explain the reasons. If you have also used this company for the exercise in Chapter 13, you can comment further on the organization chart and its appropriateness for the company. You may want to send a copy of your report to the cooperating company.

Follow-up Questions

1. Which aspects of strategy, size, environment, and technology were the most difficult to obtain information on? Why?

2. If there were differences in the responses of the employees you interviewed, how do you account for them?

3. If you were the president of the organization you analyzed, would you structure it in the same way? Why or why not? If not, how would you structure it differently?

4. How did your answers to questions 2 and 3 differ from your answers in the exercise following Chapter 13?

CHAPTER 16

Organizational Culture

Chapter Objectives

After reading this chapter, you should be able to

▶ define *organizational culture* and explain how it affects employee behavior.

▶ summarize the historical development of the concept of organizational culture.

▶ describe three views of culture in organizations.

▶ discuss the key elements of managing the organizational culture.

*T*he employees of Tenant Co. are gathering for a magic show and other live entertainment to celebrate Zero Defect Day—a day they observe every eighteen months. All around them, the factory walls are covered with murals of game birds and game fish. The employees are proud of their work environment and the quality of their work. Near the end of the day, they renew their pledge to "make it right the first time." An employee group awards stuffed teddy bears to employees who have taken significant roles in solving problems and meeting quality goals.[1]

Tenant Co. has changed from a company with nearly fatal quality problems in 1979 to a world leader in the manufacture of floor maintenance equipment in 1988. The company started its turnaround with textbook-quality improvement programs, but these standardized approaches eventually developed into values deeply held by Tenant employees. A culture that includes symbolic teddy bears and ritualistic all-day celebrations of quality keeps morale, quality, and productivity high.

*T*enant's organizational culture is not unique in its importance to the company; many successful firms have credited strong culture with tremendous contributions to their achievements. But what is organizational culture? Where does it come from and how does a company get one? This chapter discusses organizational culture, its origins, and its management.

THE NATURE OF ORGANIZATIONAL CULTURE

In the early 1980s, organizational culture became a central concern in the study of organizational behavior. Hundreds of researchers began to work in this area. Numerous books were published, important academic journals dedicated entire issues to the discussion of culture, and—almost overnight—organizational behavior textbooks that omitted culture as a topic of study became obsolete.

Interest in organizational culture was not limited to the ivory towers of academia. Businesses expressed an interest in culture that was far more intense than their interest in other aspects of organizational behavior. *Business Week*, *Fortune*, and other business periodicals published stories that touted culture as the key to an organization's success and suggested that managers who could manage through their organization's culture would almost certainly rise to the top.[2]

Although the enthusiasm of the early 1980s has waned somewhat, the study of organizational culture remains important. Many researchers have begun to

---

[1] "Making It Right The First Time," *Fortune*, March 28, 1988, p. 48.
[2] See "Corporate Culture: The Hard to Change Values That Spell Success or Failure," *Business Week*, October 27, 1980, pp. 148–160; and Charles G. Burck, "Working Smarter," *Fortune*, June 15, 1981, pp. 68–73.

weave the important aspects of organizational culture into their research in the more traditional topics. There are now relatively few headline stories in the popular business press about culture and culture management, but organizational culture has become a common topic in discussing current management. The enormous amount of study of culture that was completed in the early 1980s has fundamentally shifted the way both academics and managers look at organizations. Some of the concepts developed in the analysis of organizational culture have become basic parts of the business vocabulary, and the analysis of organizational culture is one of the most important specialties in the field of organizational behavior.

What Is Organizational Culture?

A surprising aspect of the recent rise in interest in organizational culture is that the concept, unlike virtually any other concept in the field of organizational behavior, has no single widely accepted definition. Indeed, it often appears that authors feel compelled to develop their own definitions, which range from very broad to highly specific. For example, Deal and Kennedy define a firm's culture as "the way we do things around here."[3] This very broad definition presumably could include the way a firm manufactures its products, pays its bills, treats it employees, and performs any other organizational operation. More specific definitions include those of Schein, "the pattern of basic assumptions that a given group has invented, discovered, or developed in learning to cope with its problems of external adaptation and internal integration,"[4] and Peters and Waterman, "a dominant and coherent set of shared values conveyed by such symbolic means as stories, myths, legends, slogans, anecdotes, and fairy tales."[5] Table 16.1 lists several important definitions of organizational culture.

Despite the apparent diversity of these definitions, a few common attributes emerge. First, virtually all the definitions refer to some set of values held by individuals in a firm. These values define what is good or acceptable behavior and what is bad or unacceptable behavior. In some organizations, for example, it is unacceptable to blame customers when there are problems or difficulties. Here, the value "the customer is always right" tells managers what actions are acceptable (not blaming the customer) and what actions are not acceptable (blaming the customer). In another organization, the dominant values might support blaming customers for problems, or penalizing employees that make mistakes, or treating employees as the firm's most valuable assets. In each case,

---

[3] T. E. Deal and A. A. Kennedy, *Corporate Cultures: The Rites and Rituals of Corporate Life* (Reading, Mass.: Addison-Wesley, 1982), p. 4.

[4] E. H. Schein, "The Role of the Founder in Creating Organizational Culture," *Organizational Dynamics,* Summer 1983, p. 14.

[5] Thomas J. Peters and Robert H. Waterman, *In Search of Excellence: Lessons from America's Best-Run Companies* (New York: Harper & Row, 1982), p. 103.

Table 16.1	Definition	Source
Definitions of Organizational Culture	"a belief system shared by an organization's members"	J. C. Spender, "Myths, Recipes, and Knowledge-Bases in Organizational Analysis" (Unpublished manuscript, Graduate School of Management, University of California at Los Angeles, 1983), p. 2.
	"strong, widely-shared core values"	C. O'Reilly, "Corporations, Cults, and Organizational Culture: Lessons from Silicon Valley Firms" (Paper presented at the Annual Meeting of the Academy of Management, Dallas, Texas, 1983), p. 1.
	"the way we do things around here"	T. E. Deal and A. A. Kennedy, *Corporate Cultures* (Reading, Mass. Addison-Wesley, 1982), p. 4.
	"the collective programming of the mind"	G. Hofstede, *Culture's Consequences: International Differences in Work-related Values* (Beverly Hills, Calif.: Sage, 1980), p. 25.
	"collective understandings"	J. Van Maanen and S. R. Barley, "Cultural Organization: Fragments of a Theory" (Paper presented at the Annual Meeting of the Academy of Management, Dallas, Texas, 1983), p. 7.
	"a set of shared, enduring beliefs communicated through a variety of symbolic media, creating meaning in people's work lives"	J. M. Kouzes, D. F. Caldwell, and B. Z. Posner, "Organizational Culture: How It Is Created, Maintained, and Changed" (Presentation at OD Network National Conference, Los Angeles, October 9, 1983).
	"a set of symbols, ceremonies, and myths that communicate the underlying values and beliefs of that organization to its employees"	W. G. Ouchi, *Theory Z* (Reading, Mass.: Addison-Wesley, 1981), p. 41.
	"a dominant and coherent set of shared values conveyed by such symbolic means as stories, myths, legends, slogans, anecdotes, and fairy tales"	T. Peters and R. H. Waterman, *In Search of Excellence* (New York: Harper & Row, 1982), p. 103.
	"the pattern of basic assumptions that a given group has invented, discovered, or developed in learning to cope with its problems of external adaptation and internal integration"	E. H. Schein, "The Role of the Founder in Creating Organizational Culture," *Organizational Dynamics*, Summer 1985, p. 14.

Table 16.2	NCR's Mission: Create Value for Our Stakeholders
NCR's Basic Values	NCR is a successful growing company dedicated to achieving superior results by assuring that its actions are aligned with stakeholder expectations. Stakeholders are all constituencies with a stake in the fortunes of the company. NCR's primary mission is to create value for our stakeholders.
	We believe in conducting our business activities with integrity and respect while building mutually beneficial and enduring relationships with all of our stakeholders.
	We take customer satisfaction personally: we are committed to providing superior value in our products and services on a continuing basis.
	We respect the individuality of each employee and foster an environment in which employees' creativity and productivity are encouraged, recognized, valued and rewarded.
	We think of our suppliers as partners who share our goal of achieving the highest quality standards and the most consistent level of service.
	We are committed to being caring and supportive corporate citizens within the worldwide communities in which we operate.
	We are dedicated to creating value for our shareholders and financial communities by performing in a manner that will enhance returns on investments.

Source: Courtesy of National Cash Register Corporation.

values help members of an organization to understand how they should act in that organization.

A second attribute common to many of the definitions in Table 16.1 is that the values that make up an organization's culture are often taken for granted. That is, rather than being written down in a book or made explicit in a training program, they are basic assumptions made by employees of the firm. It may be as difficult for an organization to articulate these basic assumptions as it is for people to articulate their personal beliefs and values. Several authors have argued that organizational culture is a powerful influence on individuals in firms precisely because it is not explicit but rather becomes an implicit part of employees' values and beliefs.[6]

Some organizations have been able to articulate the key values in their cultures. Some have even written down these values and made them part of formal training procedures. For example, at Hewlett-Packard Co., a brief summary of "The HP Way" is given to all new employees. This pamphlet describes the basic values of the culture at Hewlett-Packard.[7] Another company, NCR, has

[6] See M. Polanyi, *Personal Knowledge*, (Chicago: University of Chicago Press, 1958); E. Goffman, *The Presentation of Self in Every Day Life* (New York: Doubleday, 1959); and P. L. Berger and T. Luckman, *The Social Construction of Reality* (Garden City, N.Y.: Anchor, 1967).

[7] W. G. Ouchi, *Theory Z: How American Business Can Meet the Japanese Challenge* (Reading, Mass.: Addison-Wesley, 1981).

recently begun a national advertising campaign featuring its statement of organizational values. This statement is shown in Table 16.2.[8]

Even when firms are able to articulate and describe the basic values that make up their cultures, though, the values most affect actions when people in the organization take them for granted. An organization's culture is not likely to powerfully influence behavior when employees must constantly refer to a handbook to remember what that culture is. When the culture becomes part of them—when they can ignore what is written in the book because they have already embraced the values it describes—then the culture can have an important impact on actions in the organization.

The final attribute shared by many of the definitions in Table 16.1 is an emphasis on the symbolic means through which the values in an organization's culture are communicated. Although, as noted, companies can sometimes directly describe these values, their meaning is perhaps best communicated to employees through the use of stories, examples, and even what some authors call myths or fairy tales. Stories typically symbolize important implications of values in a firm's culture. Often, they develop a life of their own. As they are told and retold, shaped and reshaped, their relationship to what actually occurred becomes increasingly tenuous. Yet these stories communicate the meaning of organizational values much more powerfully than a listing of values in a booklet.

Some organizational stories have become very famous. Two examples from Hewlett-Packard demonstrate how stories help communicate and reinforce important organizational values. One of the key values listed in "The HP Way" is that Hewlett-Packard avoids bank debt. A story is told of a senior manager in the finance area who was given free rein to develop a financing plan for a new investment. As she applied all the best finance theory, it became clear to her that part of the financial package should include bank debt. When her proposal reached Mr. Hewlett and Mr. Packard, however, it was rejected—not because the financial reasoning was not sound but because at Hewlett-Packard "we avoid bank debt."[9] This story shows that avoiding bank debt is more than a slogan at Hewlett-Packard—it is a fact.

Another value at Hewlett-Packard is that "employees are our most important asset." A story that helps communicate the reality of this value tells what happened when the company was struggling through some difficult financial times. While virtually all the other firms in the industry were laying people off (the story goes), HP asked all its employees to take one day of unpaid vacation every two weeks. By working nine days and then taking one day off, the firm was able to avoid layoffs. All employees were hurt, because all received a

---

[8] See the NCR advertisement in *Fortune,* February 29, 1988, pp. 62–63.

[9] A. Wilkins, "Organizational Stories as Symbols Which Control the Organization," in Louis R. Pondy, Peter J. Frost, Gareth Morgan, and Thomas C. Dandridge, eds., *Organizational Symbolism* (Greenwich, Conn.: JAI Press, 1983), pp. 81–82.

Table 16.3	Contributor	Areas of Study	Methods of Study
Social Science Contributions to Organizational Culture Analysis	Anthropology	• Human cultures • Values and beliefs of society	• Thick description • Interviews and observations
	Sociology	• Categorization of social system structures	• Systematic interviews • Questionnaires • Statistics
	Social Psychology	• Creation and manipulation of symbols • Use of stories	• Surveys • Observations • Statistics
	Economics	• Economic conditions of a company in a society	• Statistics • Mathematical modeling

reduction in pay, but no employees had to bear the total cost of the firm's reduced performance.[10] The message communicated by this story is a strong one: Hewlett-Packard will go to great lengths to avoid layoffs, to keep its employment team intact.

We can use the three common attributes of definitions of culture just discussed to develop a definition with which most authors could probably agree: **Organizational culture** is the set of values, often taken for granted, that help people in an organization understand which actions are considered acceptable and which are considered unacceptable. Often, these values are communicated through stories and other symbolic means.[11]

The Historical Foundations of the Study of Organizational Culture

Although research on organizational culture exploded onto the scene in the early 1980s, the antecedents of this research can be traced to the origins of social science. Understanding the contributions of other social science disciplines is particularly important in the case of organizational culture, for many of the dilemmas and debates that continue in this area reflect differences in historical research traditions. Table 16.3 summarizes various approaches.

ANTHROPOLOGICAL CONTRIBUTIONS   Of all the social science disciplines, anthropology is most closely related to the study of culture and cultural phenomena. Indeed, anthropology can be defined as the study of human

---

[10] Wilkins, "Organizational Stories."

[11] This definition is very similar to the definition of culture proposed in M. R. Lewis, "Culture Yes, Organization No" (Paper presented at the Annual Meeting of the Academy of Management, Dallas, Texas, 1983).

cultures.[12] Anthropologists seek to understand how the values and beliefs that make up a society's culture affect the structure and functioning of that society. Many anthropologists believe that to understand the relationship between culture and society it is necessary to look at a culture from the point of view of the people in a society—from the "native's point of view."[13] To reach this level of understanding, these anthropologists immerse themselves in the values, symbols, and stories that people in a society use to bring order and meaning to their lives.

People who study organizations in the anthropological tradition try to immerse themselves in the cultures they are studying. Although these cultures are located in large modern corporations rather than among primitive tribes in New Guinea or the Philippines, the questions asked are the same: How do people in this culture know what kinds of behavior are acceptable and what kinds of behavior are unacceptable? How is this knowledge understood? How is this knowledge communicated to new members?

Practitioners of this anthropological approach usually use **thick description methods,** which involve attempting to describe the totality of day-to-day life through in-depth questioning and observation.[14] Such methods are quite different from those used in other areas of organizational behavior research—experiments and questionnaire-based surveys, for example. Through this intense descriptive effort, the values and beliefs that underlie actions in an organization become clear. These values can only be fully understood in the context of the organization in which they developed, however. In other words, a description of the values and beliefs of one organization is not transferable to those of other organizations.

SOCIOLOGICAL CONTRIBUTIONS   Sociologists have also had a long-term interest in studying the causes and consequences of culture. Many sociological methods and theories have found expression in the analysis of organizational cultures.

In studying culture, sociologists have most often focused on informal social structure. Emile Durkheim, an important early sociologist, argued that the study of myth and ritual is an essential complement to the study of structure and rational behavior in societies.[15] By studying rituals, Durkheim argued, we can understand the most basic values and beliefs of a group of people. This same argument was developed by another sociologist, Max Weber, in his now-famous description of the relationship between the Protestant ethic and the development

[12] A. L. Kroeber and C. Kluckhohn, "Culture: A Critical Review of Concepts and Definitions," in *Papers of the Peabody Museum of American Archaeology and Ethnology,* Vol. 47, No. 1 (Cambridge, Mass.: Harvard University Press, 1952).

[13] C. Geertz, *The Interpretation of Cultures* (New York: Basic Books, 1973).

[14] Geertz, *The Interpretation of Cultures,* pp. 5–6.

[15] E. Durkheim, *The Elementary Forms of Religious Life,* trans. J. Swain (New York: Collier, 1961), p. 220.

of capitalism in Western Europe.[16] Weber argued that the religious values and beliefs of individuals in Western Europe supported the accumulation of material goods. The effort to accumulate material goods, in turn, was an important prerequisite for the development of capitalist economies.

This sociological approach to the study of culture is perhaps most evident in the methods used to study organizational culture. Sociologists use systematic interviews, questionnaires, and other quantitative research methods rather than the thick description methods of anthropologists. Whereas anthropologists usually produce a book-length description of values, attitudes, and beliefs that underlie the behaviors of people in one or two organizations,[17] practitioners using the sociological approach usually produce a fairly simple typology of cultural attributes and then show how the cultures of a relatively large number of firms can be analyzed with this typology.[18]

Although both the anthropological and sociological approaches to studying organizational culture are important, the recent emergence of organizational culture as a major field of research primarily reflects work done in the sociological tradition. The major pieces of research on organizational culture that later spawned widespread business interest—including Ouchi's *Theory Z,* Deal and Kennedy's *Organizational Cultures,* and Peters and Waterman's *In Search of Excellence*[19]—used sociological methods. Later in this chapter, we review some of this work in more detail.

SOCIAL PSYCHOLOGICAL CONTRIBUTIONS   Most research on organizational culture has used anthropological or sociological methods and theories. However, some has borrowed heavily from social psychology. Social psychological theory, with its emphasis on the creation and manipulation of symbols, provides a natural setting within which to analyze organizational culture.

For example, research in social psychology suggests that people tend to use stories or information about a single event more than they use multiple observations to make judgments.[20] Thus, the fact that your neighbor had trouble with a certain brand of automobile means that you will probably conclude that the brand is bad, even though the car company can generate reams of statistical data to prove that your neighbor's car was a rarity.

The impact of stories on decision making suggests an important reason why organizational culture has such a powerful influence on the people in an

---

[16] H. H. Gerth and C. Wright Mills, *From Max Weber* (New York: Oxford University Press, 1976), pp. 267–362.

[17] See, for example, B. Clark, *The Distinctive College* (Chicago: Adline, 1970).

[18] See Ouchi, *Theory Z,* and Peters and Waterman, *In Search of Excellence.*

[19] See Ouchi, *Theory Z,* Deal and Kennedy, *Corporate Cultures*, and Peters and Waterman, *In Search of Excellence.*

[20] E. Borgida and R. E. Nisbett, "The Differential Impact of Abstract vs. Concrete Information on Decisions," *Journal of Applied Social Psychology,* July–September 1977, pp. 258–271.

organization. Unlike other organizational phenomena, culture is best communicated through stories and examples, and these become the basis on which individuals in the organization make judgments. If a story says that blaming customers is a bad thing to do, then blaming customers is a bad thing to do. This value is communicated much more effectively through the cultural story than through some statistical analysis of customer satisfaction.[21]

CONTRIBUTIONS OF ECONOMICS   The influence of economics on the study of organizational culture, although it has not been as significant as the influence of anthropology and sociology, is significant enough to warrant attention. Economic analysis treats organizational culture as one of a variety of tools that managers can use to give some economic advantage to the organization.

When sociological and anthropological research on culture moves beyond simply describing the cultures of companies, it usually focuses on linking the cultural attributes of firms with their performance. Ouchi, in *Theory Z,* for example, does not just say that Type Z companies are different from other kinds of companies, he asserts that Type Z firms will outperform other firms.[22] When Peters and Waterman say they are *In Search of Excellence,* they define excellence, in part, as consistently high financial performance.[23] These authors are seeking cultural explanations of financial success.

Researchers disagree about the degree to which culture affects organizational performance. The conditions under which organizational culture is linked with superior financial performance have been investigated by several authors.[24] This research suggests that, under some relatively narrow conditions, this culture-performance link may exist. However, simply because a firm has a culture does not mean that it will perform well. A variety of cultural traits can actually hurt performance.

Consider, for example, a firm whose culture includes values like "customers are too ignorant to be of much help," "employees cannot be trusted," "innovation is not important," and "quality is too expensive." This firm has a strong culture, but its financial success is far from assured. Clearly, the relationship between culture and performance depends, to some extent at least, on the content of the values that exist in an organization's culture.

---

[21] J. Martin and M. Power, "Truth or Corporate Propaganda: The Value of a Good War Story," in Louis R. Pondy, Peter J. Frost, Gareth Morgan, and Thomas C. Dandridge, eds., *Organizational Symbolism* (Greenwich, Conn.: JAI Press, 1983), pp. 93–108.

[22] A. Wilkins and W. G. Ouchi, "Efficient Cultures: Exploring the Relationship Between Culture and Organizational Performance," *Administrative Science Quarterly,* September 1983, pp. 468–481; and W. G. Ouchi, "Markets, Bureaucracies, and Clans," *Administrative Science Quarterly,* March 1980, pp. 129–141.

[23] Peters and Waterman, *In Search of Excellence.*

[24] J. B. Barney, "Organizational Culture: Can It Be a Source of Sustained Competitive Advantage?" *Academy of Management Review,* July 1986, pp. 656–665.

THREE BASIC APPROACHES TO DESCRIBING ORGANIZATIONAL CULTURE

No single framework has emerged for describing the values in organizational cultures; however, several frameworks have been suggested. Taken together, these models provide insights into the dimensions along which organizational cultures vary.

The Parsons AGIL Model

One framework for analyzing the content of cultural values comes from the American sociologist Talcott Parsons.[25] Parsons was a general sociological theorist whose work was dominant during the period from the 1940s through the 1960s but came to be seen as too abstract and obscure to inform more recent sociological work. Interest in Parsons began to wane during the late 1960s, and his work is usually studied now only in classes on the history of sociological thought.[26]

Yet embedded in Parsons' work is perhaps the first attempt to develop a framework for understanding the content of values in cultural systems, including organizational culture systems. Parsons developed the **AGIL model** to specify certain functions that any social system—whether a society, an economy, or an organization—must meet to survive and prosper. These functions are represented by the letters AGIL: A for adaptation, G for goal attainment, I for integration, and L for legitimacy. A social system, to survive and prosper, must be able to adapt, attain its goals, integrate its parts, and be considered legitimate to people and other organizations external to itself. Table 16.4 describes these functions further.

Adaptation and **goal attainment** are relatively clear concepts. To adapt successfully, a social system must be aware of its environment, understand how that environment is changing, and make the appropriate adjustments. To attain its goals, a social system must have processes that specify those goals, as well as specific strategies for reaching them.

Parsons' concepts of integration and legitimacy are perhaps somewhat less clear. **Integration** refers to the need that every social system has to keep its constituent parts together. The parts of a social system must be brought in contact with one another, interdependencies understood and organized, and the need for coordinated action resolved. **Legitimacy** refers to the need that every social system has to be granted the right to survive by elements in its

[25] T. Parsons, *The Structure of Social Action* (New York: McGraw-Hill, 1937); T. Parsons and E. Shills, eds., *Toward a General Theory of Action* (Cambridge, Mass.: Harvard University Press, 1951).

[26] See, for example, W. Buckley, *Sociology and Modern Systems* (Englewood Cliffs, N.J.: Prentice-Hall, 1967).

Table 16.4 Parsons' AGIL Model	

Adaptation: the ability to adapt to changing circumstances	*Goal Attainment:* the ability to articulate and reach system objectives
Integration: the ability to integrate different parts of a system	*Legitimacy:* the right to survive and be accepted

environment. A social system is said to be legitimate, in this sense, when society as a whole agrees that it is appropriate for that system to continue.

Clearly, Parsons' AGIL model is abstract. How does it help describe the dimensions along which values in an organizational culture may vary? The answer to this question is found in the recognition that an organization's cultural values are some of the most important tools that it can use to accomplish the AGIL functions. Thus, Parsons would expect to see that some of an organization's cultural values have to do with how it adapts to changes in its environment. Other cultural values should address how the firm defines and reaches its goals. Still others should affect how the firm integrates and unites its parts to make a coherent whole. And finally, some of the organization's cultural values should help maintain its legitimacy in the environment.

We can find examples of values that fulfill all these functions in real organizations. When a company's managers say that they value technological change (as is asserted at 3M), they are stating a value that has to do with adaptation.[27] When a firm enshrines the value of "adding economic wealth to shareholders" at the center of its culture (as Hewlett-Packard does), it is partially meeting criteria for goal attainment.[28] When a firm says that its most important assets are its people (as many firms, including Westinghouse, do), it is addressing the need to integrate the diverse parts of its organization.[29] Finally, when a company says that its goal is to meet the needs of all its external constituent groups, including society at large (as NCR has suggested), it is addressing the question of legitimacy.[30]

Parsons' AGIL model is a relatively abstract approach to describing the dimensions along which the values in organizational cultures can vary. Its abstract nature reflects an attempt to develop a general framework for analysis—a framework that can be applied in the analysis of any organizational culture.

[27] Peters and Waterman, *In Search of Excellence.*
[28] Peters and Waterman, *In Search of Excellence.*
[29] J. Main, "Westinghouse's Cultural Revolution," *Fortune,* June 15, 1981, p. 74.
[30] See the NCR advertisement in *Fortune,* February 29, 1988, pp. 62–63.

Table 16.5	Cultural Value	Expression in Japanese Companies	Expression in Type Z American Companies	Expression in Typical U.S. Companies
The Ouchi Framework	*Commitment to employees*	Lifetime employment	Long-term employment	Short-term employment
	Evaluation	Slow and qualitative	Slow and qualitative	Fast and quantitative
	Careers	Very broad	Moderately broad	Narrow
	Control	Implicit and informal	Implicit and informal	Explicit and formal
	Decision making	Group and consensus	Group and consensus	Individual
	Responsibility	Group	Individual	Individual
	Concern for people	Wholistic	Wholistic	Narrow

The Ouchi Framework

In contrast to this very general framework, a series of authors have attempted to develop models for analyzing the cultural systems of specific groups of organizations. One of the first researchers to focus explicitly on analyzing the cultures of a limited group of firms was William G. Ouchi. Ouchi analyzed the organizational cultures of three groups of firms, which he characterized as typical American firms, typical Japanese firms, and **Type Z** American firms.[31]

Through his analysis, Ouchi developed a list of seven points on which these three types of firms can be compared. Ouchi argued that the cultures of typical Japanese firms and American Type Z firms are very different from the cultures of typical American firms and that these differences explain the success of many Japanese firms and many American Type Z firms, at the expense of typical American firms. The seven points of comparison developed by Ouchi are presented in Table 16.5.

COMMITMENT TO EMPLOYEES   According to Ouchi, typical Japanese and Type Z American firms share the cultural value of trying to keep employees. Thus, both these types of firms lay off employees only as a last resort. In Japan, the value to "keep employees on" often takes the form of lifetime employment. A person who begins working at some Japanese firms has a virtual guarantee that she or he will never be fired. In the United States, at Type Z companies, this cultural value is manifest in a commitment to what Ouchi called "long-term employment." Under Japanese lifetime employment, employees usually

---

[31] Ouchi, *Theory Z*.

cannot be fired. Under U.S. long-term employment, workers and managers can be fired, but only if they are not performing acceptably.

Ouchi suggested that typical U.S. firms do not have the same cultural commitment to employees as Japanese firms and U.S. Type Z firms. For this reason, typical U.S. firms have an expectation of short-term employment for their workers and managers. In reality, U.S. workers and managers spend their entire careers in a relatively small number of companies. Still, the cultural expectation exists that if there were a serious downturn in a firm's fortunes, workers and maybe even managers would be let go. [32]

EVALUATION   Ouchi observed that in Japan and in American Type Z companies, appropriate evaluation of workers and managers is thought to take a very long time—up to ten years—and requires the use of qualitative, as well as quantitative, information about performance. For this reason, promotion in these firms is relatively slow, and promotion decisions are made only after interviews with many people who have had contact with the person being evaluated.

In typical American firms, on the other hand, the cultural value around evaluation suggests that evaluation can be, and should be, done rapidly and should emphasize quantitative measures of performance. This value tends to encourage short-term thinking among workers and managers.

CAREERS   Ouchi next observed that the careers most valued in Japanese and Type Z American firms span multiple functions. In Japan, this value has led to very broad career paths, which may lead to experience in six or seven distinct business functions. The career paths in Type Z U.S. firms are somewhat less broad.

However, the career path valued in typical U.S. firms is considerably narrower. Ouchi's research indicated that most U.S. managers perform only one or two different business functions in their careers. This narrow career path reflects, according to Ouchi, the values of specialization that are part of so many U.S. firms.

CONTROL   All organizations must exert some level of control. (In terms of Parsons' model, they must integrate their parts.) Without control, it is impossible to achieve coordinated action. Thus, it is not surprising that firms in the United States and Japan have developed cultural values related to organizational control and how to manage it.

Most Japanese and Type Z American firms assume that control will be exercised through informal, implicit mechanisms. One of the most powerful of these mechanisms is the organization's culture. Managers expect to obtain guidance in what actions to take from the culture of their firm. Stories, for

---

[32] W. J. Hampton, "The Next Act at Chrysler," *Business Week*, November 3, 1986, pp. 66–69.

example, communicate important information about what upper-level managers expect lower-level managers to do.

In contrast, typical U.S. firms expect that guidance will come not from informal and implicit cultural values but rather through explicit directions taking the form of job descriptions, delineation of authority, and various rules and procedures. Stories about control may exist in these firms, but the stories typically communicate the message that to stay out of trouble, it is best to follow explicit, written guidelines.

DECISION MAKING   Japanese and Type Z firms hold the strong cultural expectation that decision making will occur in groups and that it will be based on principles of full information sharing and consensus. In most typical U.S. firms, individual decision making is considered appropriate. Managers and workers given the responsibility of making decisions are not expected—and certainly not required—to obtain information or suggestions from others in the firm.

RESPONSIBILITY   Closely linked with Ouchi's discussion of group versus individual decision making is his discussion of responsibility. Here, however, the parallels between Japanese firms and Type Z American firms break down. Ouchi showed that in Japan strong cultural norms support collective responsibility—that is, the group as a whole, rather than a single person, is held responsible for decisions made by the group. In both Type Z American firms and typical American firms, individuals expect to take responsibility for decisions.

Linking individual responsibility with individual decision making—as typical American firms do—seems logically consistent. After all, if individuals are expected to make decisions, then it seems to make sense that they should be held responsible for the decisions they make. Similarly, group decision making and group responsibility—the situation in Japanese firms—seem to go together. But how do Type Z American firms combine the cultural values of group decision making and individual responsibility?

Ouchi suggested that the answer to this question depends on a cultural value we have already discussed: slow and qualitative evaluation. The first time a manager uses a group to make a decision, it is not possible to tell whether the outcomes associated with that decision result from the manager's influence or the quality of the group. However, if a manager works with many different groups over time, and if these groups consistently generate positive results for the organization, then it is likely that the manager is skilled at getting the most out of groups. This manager can be held responsible for the outcomes of group decision-making processes. Similarly, managers that consistently fail to work effectively with the groups assigned to them can be held responsible for the lack of results from the group decision-making process.

Ouchi suggested that the value of individual responsibility in U.S. Type Z firms reflects very strong cultural norms of individuality and individual responsibility in American society as a whole. As suggested by Parsons' notion of legitimacy, organizational cultures do not exist in isolation from broader cultural influences. Societal expectations and values can strongly influence the values in an organization's culture.

CONCERN FOR PEOPLE   The last cultural value examined by Ouchi deals with a concern for people. Not surprisingly, in Japanese firms and Type Z firms, the cultural value that dominates is a wholistic concern for workers and managers. Wholistic concern extends beyond concern for a person simply as a worker or manager to concern with that person's home life, hobbies, personal beliefs, hopes, fears, and aspirations. In typical American firms, the concern for people is a narrow one that focuses on the workplace.

THEORY Z AND PERFORMANCE   Ouchi argued that the cultures of Japanese and Type Z firms help them outperform typical American firms. Toyota is now trying to import the management style and culture that has been successful in Japan into its new manufacturing facilities in North America. For more on Toyota's effort, see *International Perspective*. The reasons for Toyota's success have often been attributed to the ability of Japanese and Type Z firms to systematically invest in their employees and in their operations over long periods of time and thus to obtain steady and significant improvements in long-term performance.

The Peters and Waterman Approach

Tom Peters and Robert Waterman, in their best seller *In Search of Excellence,* focused even more explicitly than Ouchi on the relationship between organizational culture and performance. Peters and Waterman chose a sample of highly successful U.S. firms and sought to describe the management practices that led these firms to be successful.[33] Their analysis rapidly turned to the cultural values that led to successful management practices. These "excellent" values are listed in Table 16.6.

BIAS FOR ACTION   According to Peters and Waterman, successful firms have a bias for action. Managers in these firms are expected to make decisions even if all the "facts aren't in." Peters and Waterman argued that for many important decisions, all the facts will never "be in." Delaying decision making in these situations is the same as never making a decision. Meanwhile, other firms will probably have captured whatever business initiative existed. On average, according to Peters and Waterman, organizations with cultural values that include a bias for action outperform firms without such values.

STAY CLOSE TO THE CUSTOMER   Peters and Waterman believe that firms whose organizational cultures value customers over everything else will outperform firms without this value. According to these authors, the customer

---

[33] Peters and Waterman, *In Search of Excellence.*

International Perspective

Toyota City Comes to the U.S.

Detroit is no longer the car capital of the world. The true "motor city" is in Japan, three hours by train from Tokyo, and it is called Toyota City. There, with eight major factories (and two others nearby), Toyota Motor Corp., the number one automaker in Japan and number three in the world, produces twice as many cars as American manufacturers build in Detroit. And now that Toyota is producing cars on American soil, it has exported the culture developed in Toyota City to such unlikely places as Georgetown, Kentucky, and Fremont, California.

Understanding Toyota's culture requires some knowledge of the Toyota family, which runs the Toyota group. Sakichi Toyoda, grandfather of the company's current president, was the son of a poor carpenter. He founded the family business by inventing machines for making textiles, and the company eventually changed its product to cars. Because it supplied military equipment to the government during World War II, it was not allowed to build cars after the war, and in the early 1950s the business nearly went bankrupt. The Toyoda family seems to remember its poor origins and difficult times, for popular stories have arisen concerning the family's legendary frugality, and one of the major ingredients in Toyota's success has been its ability to cut costs.

Its management techniques are another important ingredient. Some analysts say that Toyota pulled away from its archrival, Nissan Motor Company, by concentrating on management while Nissan was putting money into computers and robots. According to one Toyota slogan, "Every employee is a brother;" workers have taken on many of the close-knit, secretive habits of the Toyoda family. While pressing employees to cut costs (often by using some of the ten million suggestions employees have made in the past thirty-five years), Toyota also fosters company loyalty and worker commitment. In Toyota City, the company organizes recreational programs and clubs, provides low-cost housing loans and company stores, and charters a cruise ship for a company trip every year.

Many of the techniques that Toyota has brought to its joint venture with General Motors in Fremont, California, are typical of Japanese management approaches. Barriers between ranks are downplayed, and everyone participates in four minutes of calisthenics to begin the day. Employees work in teams, rotating jobs rather than doing the same thing every day for years. No one has reported workers running back to their jobs after breaks, as they sometimes do in Japan, but Toyota has transformed the Fremont plant from one of the worst to one of the most efficient in the industry.

The long-term success of Toyota's ability to export its culture will depend on whether it can continue to push its employees without creating revolts. Toyota has not had to worry about Japanese unions since the 1950s, when it ended strikes by firing thousands of workers. But American employees are already complaining about the pressures to speed up and work ever more efficiently. Japanese social scientists say that such pressures, and the intense competition they foster, take their toll on employees' physical and mental health. It remains to be seen how much Toyota is willing to modify its corporate culture—and perhaps lower its profit expectations—to be successful with American workers.

Sources: Larry Armstrong, "Toyota's Fast Lane," *Business Week*, November 4, 1985, 42–46; Joel Dreyfuss, "Toyota Takes Off the Gloves," *Fortune*, December 22, 1986, 77–84; George Raine, "Build Cars Japan's Way," *Newsweek*, March 31, 1986, 43.

Table 16.6

The Peters and
Waterman Framework

Attributes of an Excellent Firm
1. Bias for action
2. Stay close to the customer
3. Encourage autonomy and entrepreneurship
4. Encourage productivity through people
5. Hands-on management
6. Stick to the knitting
7. Simple form, lean staff
8. Simultaneously loosely and tightly organized

provides a source of information about current products, a source of ideas about future products, the ultimate source of a firm's current financial perform-ance, and the source of future performance as well. Focusing on the customer, meeting the customer's needs, pampering the customer when necessary—these are actions that lead to superior performance.

Peters and Waterman also suggest that firms that are good at keeping close to the customer do so not because the sales manager or the marketing handbook says that it is a good idea. For true customer-satisfying companies, customer satisfaction lies at the core of organizational culture.

AUTONOMY AND ENTREPRENEURSHIP   Peters and Waterman maintained that successful firms fight the lack of innovativeness and the bureaucracy that are usually associated with large size. They do this by breaking the company into small, more manageable pieces and then encouraging independent, creative, even risk-taking activity within these smaller business segments. Stories are often told in these organizations of the junior engineer who, by taking a risk, is able to influence major product decisions or of the junior manager, dissatisfied with the slow pace of a product's development, who implements a new and highly successful marketing plan. These kinds of actions are not just encouraged, then, but are the "stuff of organizational legends."

PRODUCTIVITY THROUGH PEOPLE   Like Ouchi, Peters and Waterman believe that successful firms recognize that their most important assets are their people—both workers and managers—and that the organization's purpose is to let its people flourish. Again, this commitment to people is not simply written on plaques or announced in company magazines. Rather, it is a basic value of the organizational cultures—a belief that treating people with respect and dignity is not only appropriate, but essential to success.

HANDS-ON MANAGEMENT   Peters and Waterman noted the tendency, in many large companies, for senior managers to lose touch with the basic businesses they are in. Presidents of large electronics firms end up knowing less about electronics than they do about office politics, for example, and presidents of large automobile companies end up knowing less about cars than about finance.

To counter this tendency, Peters and Waterman noted that the firms they studied insisted that their senior managers stay in touch with the firms' essential business. It is an expectation, reflecting a deeply embedded cultural norm in these firms, that managers should manage not from behind the closed doors of their offices, but by "wandering around" the plant, the design facility, the research and development department, and so on.

STICK TO THE KNITTING   Another cultural value characteristic of the firms identified by Peters and Waterman as excellent is their reluctance to engage in business outside their expertise. These firms reject the concept of diversification—the practice of buying and operating businesses in unrelated industries. If managers in one of these companies suggest that the company begin operations in an unrelated business, the response to their efforts is not likely to be "where are the figures that justify this business move?" Rather, others in the firm are likely to simply shake their heads and say "That's not the way we do business around here."

SIMPLE FORM, LEAN STAFF   According to Peters and Waterman, successful firms tend to have few administrative layers and relatively small corporate staff groups. In many organizations, managers measure their status, prestige, and importance by the number of people that report to them. In excellently managed companies, according to Peters and Waterman, importance is not measured by the number of people that report to a manager but by the manager's impact on the organization's performance. The cultural values in these firms tell managers that their staffs' performance is important, not their size.

SIMULTANEOUSLY LOOSELY AND TIGHTLY ORGANIZED   The final attribute of organizational culture identified by Peters and Waterman seems to make no sense. How can a firm be simultaneously loosely organized and tightly organized? The resolution of this apparent paradox is found in the firms' values. The firms are tightly organized because all their members understand and believe in the firms' values. This common cultural bond makes a strong glue that holds the firms together.

At the same time, however, the firms are loosely organized, since they tend to have less administrative overhead, fewer staff members, fewer rules and regulations. All this, Peters and Waterman believe, encourages innovativeness and risk taking.

This loose structure is only possible because of the common values held by people in the firm. When these people must make decisions, they can evaluate their options in terms of the organization's underlying values—whether the options are consistent with a bias for action, service to the customer, and so on. By referring to commonly held values, individuals in firms can often

Figure 16.1

Three Elements of
Managing Organizational
Culture

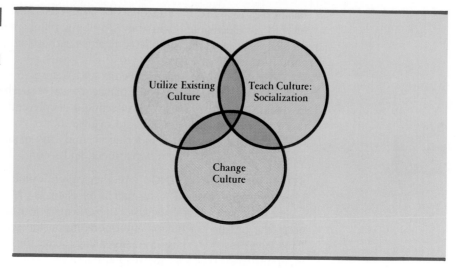

make their own decisions about what actions to take. In this sense, the tight
structure of common cultural values makes the loose structure of fewer
administrative controls possible.

MANAGING ORGANIZATIONAL CULTURE

The work of Ouchi, Peters and Waterman, and many others demonstrates two
important facts. First, organizational cultures differ among firms, and second,
these different organizational cultures can affect a firm's performance. Based
on these observations, managers in the early 1980s began to be concerned
about how they could best manage the cultures of their organizations. Three
elements of managing organizational culture—taking advantage of the existing
culture, teaching organizational culture, and changing organizational culture—
are shown in Figure 16.1.

Taking Advantage of the Culture That Already Exists

Most managers are not in a position to create an organizational culture. Rather,
they work in an organization that already has cultural values. For these managers,
the central issue in managing through culture is how best to utilize the cultural
system that already exists in the firm.

To take full advantage of an existing cultural system, managers must first
be fully aware of what values the culture includes and what behaviors or actions
those values support. Becoming fully aware of an organization's values is not
usually easy, however. It involves more than reading a pamphlet about what

the company believes in. It requires that managers develop a deep understanding of how organizational values operate in the firm—an understanding that usually comes only through experience.

Understanding, once developed, can be used to evaluate the performance of others in the firm. Articulating organizational values can be useful in managing the behavior of others. For example, suppose a subordinate in a firm with a strong cultural value of "sticking to its knitting" develops a business strategy that involves moving into a new industry. Rather than attempting to argue that this business strategy is economically flawed or conceptually weak, the manager that understands the corporate culture can point to an organizational value: "In this firm, we believe in sticking to our knitting."

Senior managers that understand their organization's culture can communicate that understanding to lower-level individuals in the firm. Over time, as these lower-level managers begin to understand and accept the firm's culture, they will require less direct supervision. Their understanding of corporate values will guide their decision making.

Teaching the Organizational Culture: Socialization

Socialization is the process through which individuals become social beings.[34] As studied by psychologists, it is the process through which children learn to be adults in a society—the way they learn what is acceptable and polite behavior and what is not acceptable, the way they learn to communicate, the way they learn to interact with others, and so on. In complex societies, the socialization process may take many years.

Organizational socialization is the process through which employees learn about a firm's culture and pass their knowledge and understanding on to others. Just as people are socialized into societies, they are also socialized into organizations. That is, they come to know, over time, what is acceptable in an organization, what is not, how to communicate their feelings, how to interact with others. They learn through observation and through efforts by managers to communicate this information to them. See A *Look at Research* for more insight into socialization in organizations.

A variety of organizational mechanisms have been shown to affect the socialization of workers in organizations.[35] Most important are the examples that people new to a firm see in the behavior of experienced people. Through example, new employees develop a repertoire of stories that they can use to guide their actions. When a decision needs to be made, people new in the firm can ask, "What would my boss do in this situation?"

---

[34] Socialization has also been defined as "the process by which culture is transmitted from one generation to the next." J. W. M. Whiting, "Socialization: Anthropological Aspects," in D. Sils, ed., *International Encyclopedia of the Social Sciences,* Vol. 14 (New York: Free Press, 1968), p. 545.

[35] Barney, "Organizational Culture."

A LOOK AT

RESEARCH

Corporate Socialization

What happens when a new employee first becomes exposed to an organization's culture? Does the employee modify previously held values to conform to those of the organization? A British study of graduate trainees at two different companies sheds light on these questions, and on the usefulness of the work of Roger Harrison in understanding and assessing an organization's culture.

Harrison classifies corporate "character" into four different kinds of cultures, based on power, role, task, and the person. According to him, a power culture is characterized by internal competitiveness and a desire to dominate external opposition. In a role culture, typical of most large bureaucracies, rules and procedures dominate, and hierarchy and status are always important. A task culture focuses on getting the job done in the most efficient way, even if that means upsetting roles and hierarchies. Organizations with person orientations care more about the personal growth and needs of the organization's personnel than about roles or tasks.

In the British study, the researchers, led by J. E. Hebden, tested and interviewed the trainees as they were given a taste of each of their company's different divisions. A questionnaire developed by Roger Harrison was used as part of the testing. Based on Harrison's classification system, the questionnaire asks subjects to respond to sixty statements such as "Competition is for personal power and advantages." The respondents indicate how they feel about each statement and how they think their organization views it. The questionnaire yields results that show how individuals feel about power, role, task, and person orientations and also which orientations they perceive their organization to value.

Some of the results of the study were striking. Even at the first interview, most of the trainees saw a discrepancy between their own values and those of their organizations. Whereas the trainees were oriented toward the task and interested in fulfilling roles and in personal growth, they saw their organizations as being more interested in power and uninterested in personal aspects. The greatest difference between the two sets of values that emerged concerned the task orientation. In the beginning, most trainees saw both themselves and their organizations as being dedicated to the task. However, the trainees at both companies gradually realized that their organizations were not as interested as they were in getting the job done.

The results of the questionnaire and of the interviews showed that the trainees' socialization included becoming aware of the differences between their own preferences and those of their organizations. Hebden concluded that in most cases, socialization does not mean that employees change their values to match those of the organization. Instead, employees grow to understand the differences between values and to discover ways to cope with those differences.

Source: J. E. Hebden, "Adopting an Organization's Culture: The Socialization of Graduate Trainees," *Organizational Dynamics,* Summer 1986, 54–72.

This is not to suggest that formal training, corporate pamphlets, and corporate statements about organizational culture are unimportant in the socialization process. However, these factors tend to support the socialization process based on people closely observing the actions of others.

In some organizations, the culture written down in pamphlets and presented in formal training sessions conflicts with the values of the organization as they are expressed in the actions of people in the firm. For example, a firm may say that employees are its most important asset but may treat employees badly. In this setting, new employees quickly learn that the rhetoric of the pamphlets and formal training sessions has little to do with the reality of the organizational culture. Employees that are socialized into this system usually come to accept the actual cultural values, not those that are formally espoused.

Changing Organizational Culture

Much of the discussion to this point has assumed that an organization's culture enhances its performance. When this is the case, learning what an organization's cultural values are and using these values to help socialize new workers and managers is very important, for such actions help the organization to succeed. However, as Ouchi's and Peters and Waterman's research indicates, not all firms have cultural values that are consistent with high performance. Ouchi found that Japanese firms and American Type Z companies have performance-enhancing values, whereas typical American firms have performance-reducing values. In their study, Peters and Waterman identified performance-enhancing values associated with successful companies. By implication, some firms not included in Peters and Waterman's study must have had performance-reducing values. What should a manager do that works in a company that has performance-reducing values?

The answer to this question is, of course, that top managers in such firms should try to change their organizations' cultures. However, this is a very difficult thing to do. [36] For all the reasons that culture is a powerful influence on behavior—the fact that it embodies the basic values in the firm, the fact that it is often taken for granted, and the fact that it is typically communicated most effectively through stories or other symbols—it resists change. When managers attempt to change a culture, they are attempting to change people's basic assumptions about what is and what is not appropriate behavior in an organization.

Despite these difficulties, some organizations have changed their cultures from performance-reducing to performance-enhancing.[37] This change process will be described in more detail in Chapter 22, which discusses organizational change and development. Here, several elements of the cultural change process are briefly summarized.

---

[36] Barney, "Organizational Culture."

[37] Main, "Westinghouse's Cultural Revolution"; "Corporate Culture," *Business Week*.

MANAGING SYMBOLS   Research has suggested that organizational culture is understood and communicated through the use of stories and other symbolic media. If this is correct, then managers interested in changing cultures should attempt to substitute stories and myths that support new cultural values for stories and myths that support old ones. They can do so by creating situations that give rise to new stories.

Suppose an organization has traditionally held the value "employee opinions are not important." When management meets in this company, the ideas and opinions of lower-level people—when they are discussed at all—are normally rejected as foolish and irrelevant. The stories that support this cultural value tell about managers who tried to make a constructive point, only to have that point lost in personal attacks from superiors.

An upper-level manager interested in creating a new story, one that shows lower-level managers that their ideas are important and valuable, might ask a subordinate to prepare to lead a discussion in a meeting and follow through by asking the subordinate to take the lead when the topic arises. The subordinate's success in the meeting will become a new story—a story that may displace some of the many stories that suggest that the opinions of lower-level managers do not matter.

THE DIFFICULTY OF CHANGE   Changing a firm's culture is a long and difficult process, much more easily derailed than kept moving toward the desired end. A primary problem is that upper-level managers, no matter how dedicated they might be to implementing some new cultural value, may sometimes make mistakes and revert to old patterns of behavior. This happens, for example, when a manager dedicated to implementing the value that lower-level employees' ideas are important vehemently attacks a subordinate's ideas.

This mistake generates a story that supports old values and beliefs. After such an incident, lower-level managers believe, deep in their souls, that the boss may say that she or he wants their input and ideas but that nothing could be further from the truth. No matter what the boss says, no matter how consistent his or her behavior, some credibility has been lost, and culture change has been made more difficult. The difficulties of imposing a culture on an organization are further illustrated in *Management in Action*.

THE STABILITY OF CHANGE   The process of changing a firm's culture starts with a need for change and moves through a transition period wherein efforts are made to adopt new values and beliefs. In the long run, a firm that successfully changes its culture will find that the new values and the new beliefs are just as stable and just as influential as the old values. Value systems tend to be self-reinforcing. Once they are in place, changing them requires an enormous amount of effort.[38] Thus, if a firm can change its culture from performance-reducing to performance-enhancing, it is likely that new values will remain in place for a long time.

---

[38] Barney, "Organizational Culture."

Abusing "Corporate Culture"

Because the concept of corporate culture has taken such strong hold in American business, some companies try to change their fortunes by changing their culture, or even use an official culture to hide a very different reality. Anthropologist Peter C. Reynolds became an inside witness to such abuses when he spent fifteen months working as a software trainer in a computer company that quintupled in size and then collapsed in less than three years. Reynolds's observations provide interesting commentary on the attempt to manipulate an organizational aspect that is among the most difficult to change.

Executives at the company—Reynolds calls it "Falcon"—created a document called "Falcon Values," which was supposed to embody the company's culture and values. Ironically, although one of the document's goals was to preserve the loose, open feel of a start-up company, it was written in secret by top executives working with a hired consultant. Then, following strict hierarchical procedures, the document was passed down to middle managers for their approval. "Falcon Values" advocated open communication, yet by the time most of the company's employees saw it, it was already the accepted summary of company standards. Perhaps most disturbing, even while executives were writing that "Attention to detail is our trademark; our goal is to do it right the first time," they were knowingly selling defective computers.

Some Falcon employees felt that "Falcon Values" was created precisely to quiet criticism about company problems. Instead of eliminating those problems, however, the document compounded them. Employees who read it saw its hypocrisy, and many lost faith in the company's other decisions and products. According to Reynolds, employees recognized that "hierarchy, secrecy, and expediency" topped the list of Falcon's real values. The discrepancy between reality and the official company line struck employees as hypocritical and made many of them cynical about the company.

Whether management was using "Falcon Values" to cover up shoddy work or whether it simply wanted to state the ideals toward which the company could strive, Falcon's failure shows the difficulty of imposing a particular set of values on a group of people. Reynolds also concluded from his experience that trying to create a homogeneous culture within an organization can be both impossible and counterproductive. He argues that corporate culture consists of many small subcultures made up of programmers or maintenance people or everyone on the bowling team—people who share values and interests. Rather than eliminate this kind of cultural diversity, Reynolds says, corporations should determine whether it is in the best interests of the company. A company like Falcon that attempts to impose culture may find itself in the same position as a music teacher trying to press Mozart on a Springsteen fan.

Sources: Peter C. Reynolds, "Imposing a Corporate Culture," *Psychology Today,* March 1987, 33–38; Peter C. Reynolds, "Corporate Culture on the Rocks," *Across the Board,* October 1986, 51–56; Address given by Peter C. Reynolds at the May 1986 meeting of the American Association for the Advancement of Science.

SUMMARY OF KEY POINTS

Organizational culture has become one of the most important, most talked about subjects in the field of organizational behavior since it burst on the scene in the 1980s with books by Ouchi, Peters and Waterman, and others. Interest has not been restricted to academics. Practicing managers are also interested in organizational culture, especially as it relates to performance.

Despite this interest, there is relatively little agreement about how to define organizational culture. A comparison of several important definitions suggests that most have three things in common: They define culture in terms of the values that individuals in organizations use to prescribe appropriate behavior; they assume that these values are usually taken for granted; and they emphasize the stories and other symbolic means through which the values are usually communicated.

Current research on organizational culture reflects various research traditions. The most important contributions have come from anthropology and sociology. Anthropologists have tended to focus on the organizational cultures of one or two firms and have used thick description to help outsiders understand organizational culture from the "natives' point of view." Sociologists have usually used survey methods to study the organizational cultures of larger numbers of firms.

Two other influences on current work in organizational culture are social psychology, with its emphasis on the manipulation of symbols in organizations, and economics. The economics approach sees culture both as a tool used to manage and as a determinant of performance.

Although no single framework for describing organizational culture has emerged, several have been suggested. One of the earliest, and most abstract, is Parsons' AGIL model. More recent efforts in this area have been Ouchi's comparison of U.S. and Japanese firms and Peters and Waterman's description of successful firms in the United States.

Ouchi and Peters and Waterman suggested several important dimensions along which organizational values vary, including treatment of employees, definitions of appropriate means for decision making, and assignment of responsibility for the results of decision making.

Managing the corporate culture requires attention to three factors. First, managers can take advantage of cultural values that already exist in an organization and use their knowledge of them to help subordinates understand the values. Second, employees need to be properly socialized, or trained, in the cultural values of the organization, either through formal training or by experiencing and observing actions of higher-level managers. Third, managers can change the culture of the organization through managing the symbols, dealing with the extreme difficulties of such a change, and relying on the permanence of the new organizational culture once the change has been made.

In summary, organizational culture is a powerful and pervasive influence in organizations. It is more abstract than many other organizational characteristics (and therefore more difficult to manage) in that it is best understood in its symbolic representations.

DISCUSSION QUESTIONS

1. A sociologist or an anthropologist might suggest that the culture in U.S. firms simply reflects the dominant culture in the society as a whole. Therefore, to change the organizational culture of a company, one must first deal with the inherent values and beliefs of the society. How would you respond to this claim?

2. Psychology has been defined as the study of individual behavior. More specifically, organizational psychology is the study of individual behavior in organizations. Many of the theories described in the early chapters of this book are based in organizational psychology. Why was this field not identified as a contributor to the study of organizational culture, along with anthropology, sociology, social psychology, and economics?

3. Describe the culture of an organization you are familiar with. It might be one in which you currently work, one in which you have worked, or one in which a friend or family member works. What values, beliefs, stories, and symbols are significant to employees of the organization?

4. Discuss the similarities and differences among the organizational culture approaches of Parsons, Ouchi, and Peters and Waterman.

5. Describe how symbols and stories are used in organizations to communicate values and beliefs. Give some examples of how symbols and stories have been used in organizations with which you are familiar.

6. Leadership is discussed in Chapter 11. What is the role of leadership in developing, maintaining, and changing organizational culture?

7. Review the characteristics of organizational structure described in preceding chapters and compare them with the elements of culture described by Ouchi and Peters and Waterman. Describe the similarities and differences and explain how some of the characteristics of one may be related to characteristics of the other.

8. Discuss the role of organizational rewards in developing, maintaining, and changing the organizational culture.

Case 16.1   Tandem's Most Successful Export—Its Culture

California-based Tandem Computers Inc. is a favorite of both Wall Street investors and management experts. Chief Executive Jimmy Treybig founded the company in 1974 after realizing that his former employer, Hewlett-Packard Co., was unresponsive to customer demand for a computer that would not break down. Tandem made its reputation by building NonStop computer systems, which contain identical processors working in parallel, so that if one breaks down, another will take over its functions. Tandem claims that none of its machines have ever been returned, and its computers handle some of the busiest, most important data-processing jobs in the world. The NonStop system that links the New York and American stock exchanges, for instance, handles up to 450 million transactions a day, and even during the stock market crash of October 1987 it did not break down. Based on such successes, Tandem's recent financial growth has been impressive: 1987 was its first billion-dollar year, with net income two-thirds higher than in 1986.

Equally famous is Tandem's corporate culture, which has been described as "Californiaesque." In the company's early years, Treybig avoided making organizational charts and holding committee meetings. The company had no punch clocks, and Treybig tried to maintain a personal relationship with all his employees. Tandem's Friday afternoon beer blasts became legendary. A major slump in the mid-1980s forced some changes in the company's culture, however; Treybig had to become, in his words, a manager, not a cheerleader. Yet Tandem has preserved most of what was unique and effective about its corporate culture, and it has been exporting that culture far from Silicon Valley.

Europe is now the fastest-growing computer market, and foreign customers increasingly demand that computer companies provide worldwide support and manufacturing. Tandem now gets over 40 percent of its revenues from abroad, and some industry analysts are surprised to find that its employees elsewhere in the world develop the same loyalty to the company as their American counterparts do.

In part to introduce Tandem's foreign employees to its corporate culture, the company produced an employee handbook known simply as "The Book," noting in the preface that putting the Tandem culture into print "fills most of us with horror." The culture outlined in "The Book," including the beer blasts, seems as popular in London as in Cupertino. Perhaps more important, the philosophy that the Friday parties are designed to encourage—open communication across all boundaries of rank—continues to be crucial to Tandem's operations.

At home, Treybig makes his appointment calendar available to all employees. Around the world, virtually all Tandem workers have electronic mail terminals that give them instant access to anyone in the company. A secretary who is upset about pay increases can send an angry message directly to Treybig, as happened in 1985 when the company was in financial trouble. The company also uses the electronic mail system to conduct employee opinion surveys every six months. Company branches use satellite dishes to pick up televised material broadcast from Tandem's own facilities, and teleconferencing brings company leaders virtually face-to-face with employees in Europe. This emphasis on open communication has allowed the company to integrate its worldwide operations to a remarkable degree.

A sense that the boss is listening, even though he is thousands of miles away, combined with an employee stock ownership plan and constant after-hours gatherings and volunteer work, creates unusually good employee morale. Even in the company's bad years, employee turnover was lower than the industry average, and in good years it is close to half that average. Tandem's story demonstrates that a company really can live up to the employee-centered goals to which many businesses give lip service.

Case Questions

1. How do you think Peters and Waterman would assess the corporate culture at Tandem?

2. What are the disadvantages of having such open corporate communication?

Case Sources

Leigh Bruce, "Exporting Tandem's Californiaesque Corporate Culture," *International Management,* July/August 1987, 34–36; Jagannath Dubashi, "Instant Gratification," *Financial World,* January 26, 1988, 42–43; Anne Ferguson, "Tandem on Target," *Management Today,* June 1987, 81; Brian O'Reilly, "How Jimmy Treybig Turned Tough," *Fortune,* May 25, 1987, 102–104.

* Leigh Bruce, "Exporting Tandem's Californiaesque Corporate Culture," *International Management,* July/August 1987, 35.

Case 16.2   Surviving Plant World's Hard Times

In ten years, Plant World had grown from a one-person venture to the largest nursery and landscaping business in its area. Its founder, Myta Ong, combined a lifelong interest in plants with a botany degree to provide a service that her customers appreciated. Just as important to Ong, she had managed the company's growth so that even with twenty full-time employees working in six to eight crews, the atmosphere—the organizational culture—of the company was still as open, friendly, and personal as it had been when her only "employees" were friends who would volunteer to help her move a heavy tree.

To maintain that atmosphere, Ong involved herself more with personnel and less with plants as the company grew. With hundreds of customers and scores of jobs at any one time, she could no longer say without hesitation whether she had a dozen arborvitae bushes in stock or when Mrs. Carnack's estate would need a new load of bark mulch. But she knew when Rose had been up all night with her baby, when Gary was likely to be late because he had driven to see his sick father over the weekend, and how to deal with Ellen when she was depressed because of her boyfriend's behavior. She kept track of the birthdays of every employee and even of their children. She was up every morning by 5:30, arranging schedules so that John could get his son out of day care at 4:00 or so Martina could be back in town for her afternoon equivalency classes.

All this attention to employees may have led Ong to make a single bad business decision that almost destroyed the company. She provided extensive landscaping to a new mall on credit, and when the mall never opened and its owners went bankrupt, Plant World found itself in deep trouble. The company had virtually no cash and had to pay off the bills for the mall plants, most of which were not even salvageable.

One Friday Ong called a meeting and leveled with her employees: either they would not get paid for a month, or Plant World would fold. The news hit the employees hard. None of them was rich, and many waited for the Friday paycheck before buying groceries for the week. The local unemployment rate was low, and they knew they could find other jobs.

But as they looked around, they wondered whether they could ever find this kind of job. Sure, the pay was not the greatest, but the tears in the eyes of some were not because of pay or personal hardship—they were for Ong, her dream, and her difficulties. They never thought of her as the boss, or called her anything but Myta. And leaving the group would not be just a matter of saying goodbye to fellow employees. If Bernice left, the company softball team would lose its best pitcher, and the Sunday game was the height of everyone's week. Where else would they find people who spent much of the weekend working on the best puns with which to assail each other on Monday morning? At how many offices would everyone show up twenty minutes before starting time just to catch up with friends on other crews? What other boss would really understand when you simply said, "I don't have a doctor's appointment, I just need the afternoon off"?

Ong gave her employees the weekend to think over their decision: whether to take their pay and look for another job or to dig into their savings and go on working. Knowing it would be hard for them to quit, she told them they did not have to face her on Monday—if they did not show up, she would send them their checks. But when she arrived at 7:40 Monday morning, she found the entire group already there, ready to work even harder to pull the company through. They were even trying to top each other with puns about being "mall-contents."

Case Questions

1. How would you describe the corporate climate at Plant World?

2. How large can such a company get before it needs to change its culture and structure?

Experiential Exercise

Purpose: This exercise will help you discover some of the fascination as well as the difficulty of examining culture in organizations.

Format: The class will be divided into groups of four to six people. Each group will analyze the organizational culture of a college class. Students in most classes that use this book will have taken many courses at the college they attend and should therefore have several classes in common.

Procedures: The class is divided into groups of four to six people on the basis of classes the students have had in common.

1. Each group should first decide which class it will analyze. Each person in the group must have attended the class.

2. Next, each group should list the cultural factors to be discussed. Items to be covered should include:

— stories about the professor.

— stories about the exams.

— stories about the grading.

— stories about other students.

— the use of symbols that indicate the values of the students.

— the use of symbols that indicate the values of the professor.

— other characteristics of the class as suggested by the frameworks of Ouchi and Peters and Waterman.

3. Students should carefully analyze the stories and symbols to try to understand their underlying meanings. As analysts of the culture, students should seek stories from other members of the group to be sure that all aspects of the class are covered.

4. Students should take notes as these items are discussed.

5. After twenty to thirty minutes of work in groups, the instructor will reconvene the entire class and ask each group to share its analysis with the rest of the class.

Follow-up Questions

1. What was the most difficult part of this exercise? Did other groups experience the same difficulty?

2. How did your group overcome this difficulty? How did other groups overcome it?

3. Do you believe that your group's analysis accurately describes the culture of the class you selected? Could other students who analyzed the culture of the same class come up with a very different result? How could that happen?

4. If the professor wanted to try to change the culture in the class that you analyzed, what steps would you recommend that he or she take?

Organizational
Processes

P A R T V

Part Contents

C H A P T E R

17

Decision Making and Creativity

Chapter Objectives

After reading this chapter, you should be able to

- ▶ define *decision making*, identify its basic elements, and discuss its importance in organizations.
- ▶ summarize the differences between the rational and behavioral models of decision making.
- ▶ discuss the differences between individual and group decision making.

- ▶ identify the key factors that affect group decision making.
- ▶ explain three techniques for group problem solving.
- ▶ summarize the elements of the creative process.

*I*magine yourself as one of fifty-three passengers sitting in a Boeing 737 waiting for the scheduled 7:50 A.M. takeoff of your flight from Phoenix to Los Angeles. An announcement comes over the intercom: the flight has been canceled because of equipment problems. You and your fellow passengers deplane and wait patiently in the boarding area. But suddenly, you notice that luggage is still being put on the airplane. A stream of other passengers walks by you and boards the plane you just left! You watch in amazement as the plane taxis and takes off. Most of your fellow passengers are eventually seated on the next flight to Los Angeles at 10:10 A.M, but business meetings and connections have already been missed. Some passengers are outraged; others are more philosophical about the strange occurrence.

Passengers on a Southwest Airlines flight faced this situation at Phoenix Sky Harbor Airport on March 11, 1988.[1] A Southwest spokesperson eventually explained that a gear problem had forced out of service the plane that was originally scheduled for a flight from Phoenix to San Diego. Because connections for the flight to San Diego were more complex and extensive than connections for the Los Angeles flight, the jet that had been scheduled to fly to Los Angeles was sent to San Diego. The Los Angeles–bound passengers, it was decided, could easily catch a later flight. The switching of equipment from one flight to another is not that uncommon— especially for carriers, such as Southwest, that have no extra planes available for such emergencies.

*H*ave you ever wondered how a company or an individual could possibly have made a decision that seemed to you to be ridiculous? Certainly, there were questions that morning about the decisions and the decision makers of Southwest Airlines. But from the company's perspective, the decision may have been appropriate.

Decisions are made regarding all of the resources a company has available as it endeavors to reach its goals. These decisions determine what organizational goals will be and how they will be accomplished. Decision making is thus the mechanism that involves all organizational activities and affects virtually all members of the organization, both as individuals and as members of groups.

Without a decision-making mechanism, an organization would collapse into a collection of individuals, each pursuing a different goal. For example, suppose a football quarterback made no decision regarding the next play but simply said to his teammates, "OK, let's run a play." The eleven players might take any position, start at any time, and run in any direction.

Now consider what actually happens on a football field. Before each play, the quarterback considers information from several sources—the game plan worked out by the coaching staff, the other team's tendencies, his own team's strengths and weaknesses, and the current situation (down, field position, and

---

[1] Ken Western, "Bumped Passengers Watch "Faulty" Jet Fly Off," *The Arizona Republic,* March 12, 1988, pp. B1, B8.

the like). He then decides which play to run and which formation and snap count to use and communicates the decision to the team members. Because of their training, the other players know what to do and when to do it. Alternatively, the decision may be made by a group; some football coaches call all offensive plays after consulting with the assistant coaches on the sidelines and in the pressbox.

The football example illustrates three important characteristics of decision making: (1) a decision can be made by an individual or a group, (2) even a brief decision-making process can be both logical and complex, and (3) information is an indispensable element of the decision-making process. A decision integrates the actions of individuals and makes their efforts pay off in terms of group or organizational effectiveness. Of course, success depends on the individuals' training, their willingness to perform their duties, and their motivation to work hard. But the decision initiates the action. As the starting point, it is of vital importance to the understanding of organizational processes.

DEFINITION AND CLASSIFICATION OF DECISIONS

Decision making is choosing one alternative from several. In the football example, the quarterback can run any of perhaps a hundred plays. With the goal of scoring a touchdown always in mind, he chooses the play that seems to promise the best outcome. His choice is based on his understanding of the game situation, the likelihood of various outcomes, and his preference for each outcome.

The basic elements of decision making are shown in Figure 17.1. A decision maker's actions are guided by a goal. Each of several alternative courses of action is linked with various outcomes. Information is available regarding the alternatives, the likelihood that each outcome will occur, and the value of each outcome relative to the goal. On the basis of his or her evaluation of the information, the decision maker chooses one alternative.

Decisions made in organizations can be classified according to frequency and information conditions. In a decision-making context, *frequency* describes how often a particular decision recurs, and *information conditions* describe how much information about the predictability of various outcomes is available.

Programmed and Nonprogrammed Decisions

The frequency of recurrence determines whether a decision is programmed or nonprogrammed. A **programmed decision** recurs often enough for a decision rule to be developed. A **decision rule** tells the decision maker which alternative to choose once he or she has information about the decision situation. Whenever the situation is encountered, the appropriate decision rule is used. Programmed decisions are usually highly structured; that is, the goals

Figure 17.1   Elements of Decision Making

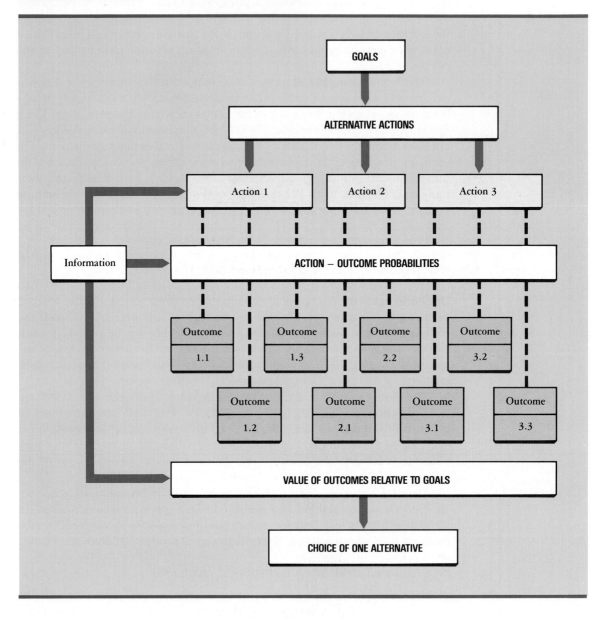

are clear and well known, the decision-making procedure is already established, and the sources and channels of information are well defined.[2]

An example of a programmed decision is the determination of the number of parts to order to replenish production inventory. The quantity to order is given by a formula called the economic order quantity (EOQ):

$$EOQ = \sqrt{\frac{2RS}{C}}$$

R = yearly parts requirement
S = cost of ordering the parts
C = cost of keeping the parts in inventory

A manager facing the recurring decision of how many units to order simply feeds current information into the formula to determine the order quantity.

However, when a problem or decision situation has not been encountered before, the decision maker cannot rely on a previously established decision rule. Such a decision is said to be a **nonprogrammed decision,** and it requires problem solving. **Problem solving** is a special kind of decision making in which the issue is unique; it requires development and evaluation of alternatives without the aid of a programmed decision rule. Nonprogrammed decisions are poorly structured, because information is ambiguous, there is no clear procedure for making the decision, and the goals are often vague.[3]

A nonprogrammed decision was required of General Motors in 1986 when it faced a significant drop in operating income and sagging market share. In November of 1986, General Motors announced plans to shut down eleven plants over an eighteen month period, with more cuts to be announced later. It expected to reduce its salaried work force by 25 percent and cut capacity by 11 percent. The cuts were to eliminate more than 29,000 jobs in four states.[4] Although the auto industry seems to face difficulty every few years, each situation is different, requiring a nonprogrammed decision or set of decisions to be made.

The characteristics of programmed and nonprogrammed decisions are summarized in Table 17.1. Note that programmed decisions are more common at the lower levels of the organization, whereas a primary responsibility of top management is to make the difficult, nonprogrammed decisions that determine the long-term effectiveness of the organization. By definition, the strategy decisions for which top management is responsible are poorly structured and nonroutine and have far-reaching consequences.

---

[2] Herbert Simon, *The New Science of Management Decision* (New York: Harper & Row, 1960), p. 1.

[3] Simon, *The New Science of Management Decision.*

[4] "Reality Has Hit General Motors—Hard," *Business Week,* November 24, 1986, p. 37.

Table 17.1

Characteristics of
Programmed and
Nonprogrammed
Decisions

Characteristics	Programmed Decisions	Nonprogrammed Decisions
Type of decision	Well structured	Poorly structured
Frequency	Repetitive and routine	New and unusual
Goals	Clear, specific	Vague
Information	Readily available	Not available, unclear channels
Consequences	Minor	Major
Organizational level	Lower levels	Upper levels
Time for solution	Short	Relatively long
Basis for solution	Decision rules, set procedures	Judgment and creativity

Programmed decisions, then, can be made according to previously tested rules and procedures. Nonprogrammed decisions generally require the decision maker to exercise judgment and creativity.[5] All problems require a decision, in other words, but not all decisions require problem solving.

Information Conditions

Decisions are made to bring about desired outcomes, but the information about those outcomes varies. The range of available information can be represented as a continuum, shown in Figure 17.2, whose endpoints represent complete certainty and complete uncertainty. At points between the two extremes, the decision maker has some information about the possible outcomes and may be able to estimate the probability of their occurrence.

Different information conditions present different challenges to the decision maker.[6] For example, say that the marketing manager of a toy company is trying to determine whether to launch an expensive promotional effort for a new video game. For simplicity, assume there are only two alternatives—to promote the game or not to promote it. Figure 17.3 shows that under conditions of *certainty,* the manager knows the outcomes of each alternative. If the new game is promoted heavily, the company will realize $1 million profit. Without a large promotional program, the company will realize only $200,000 profit. Here the decision is simple: promote the game.

---

[5] See Bernard M. Bass *Organizational Decision Making* (Homewood, Ill.: Irwin, 1983), pp. 13–15, for a discussion of poorly structured and well-structured problems.

[6] See George P. Huber, *Managerial Decision Making* (Glenview, Ill.: Scott, Foresman, 1980), pp. 90–115, for a discussion of decision making under conditions of certainty, risk, and uncertainty.

Figure 17.2

Information Conditions
and Decision Making

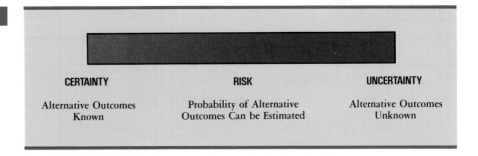

CERTAINTY	**RISK**	**UNCERTAINTY**
Alternative Outcomes Known	Probability of Alternative Outcomes Can be Estimated	Alternative Outcomes Unknown

In a *risk* situation, the decision maker cannot know with certainty what the outcome of a given action will be but has enough information to estimate the probabilities of occurrence of various outcomes. Thus, working from information gathered by the market research department, the marketing manager in our example can estimate the likelihood of each outcome in a risk situation. In this case, the alternatives are defined by the size of the market. As Figure 17.3 shows, the probability for a large video game market is 0.6, and the probability for a small market is 0.4. The manager can calculate the expected value of the promotional effort based on these probabilities and the expected profits associated with each. To find the expected value of an alternative, the manager multiplies each outcome's value by the probability of its occurrence: the sum of these calculations for all possible outcomes represents that alternative's expected value. In this case, the expected value of alternative 1—to promote the new game—is as follows:

$$
\begin{array}{r}
0.6 \times \$1{,}000{,}000 = \$600{,}000 \\
+\ 0.4 \times \$\ \ \ 200{,}000 = \$\ \ 80{,}000 \\
\hline
\text{Expected value of alternative 1} = \$680{,}000
\end{array}
$$

The expected value of alternative 2 (in section B of Figure 17.3) is $140,000. The marketing manager should choose the first alternative, because its expected value is higher. A caution is in order, however: although the numbers look convincing, they are based on incomplete information and only estimates of probability.

The decision maker who does not have enough information to estimate the probability of outcomes (or perhaps even to identify the outcomes at all) faces complete *uncertainty*.[7] In the toy company example, this might be the case if the sales of video games had recently collapsed and it was not clear whether the precipitous drop was temporary or permanent or when information

---

[7] See Bass, *Organizational Decision Making,* pp. 83–89, for a discussion of uncertainty.

Figure 17.3   Alternative Outcomes under Different Information Conditions

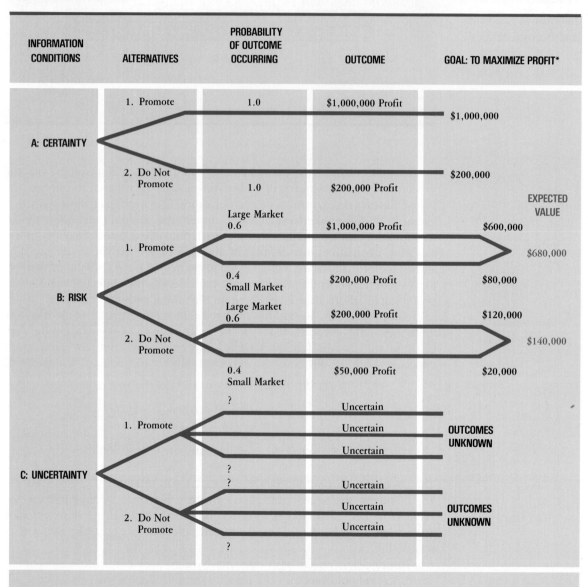

INFORMATION CONDITIONS	ALTERNATIVES	PROBABILITY OF OUTCOME OCCURRING	OUTCOME	GOAL: TO MAXIMIZE PROFIT*
A: CERTAINTY	1. Promote	1.0	$1,000,000 Profit	$1,000,000
	2. Do Not Promote	1.0	$200,000 Profit	$200,000

EXPECTED VALUE

B: RISK	1. Promote	Large Market 0.6	$1,000,000 Profit	$600,000
		0.4 Small Market	$200,000 Profit	$80,000
	2. Do Not Promote	Large Market 0.6	$200,000 Profit	$120,000
		0.4 Small Market	$50,000 Profit	$20,000

$680,000

$140,000

C: UNCERTAINTY	1. Promote	?	Uncertain	OUTCOMES UNKNOWN
			Uncertain	
			Uncertain	
	2. Do Not Promote	? ?	Uncertain	OUTCOMES UNKNOWN
			Uncertain	
		?	Uncertain	

Profit includes income less all costs of promotion and production.

to clarify the situation would be available. Under such circumstances, the decision maker may wait for more information to reduce uncertainty or rely on judgment, experience, and intuition to make the decision.

MODELS OF THE DECISION-MAKING PROCESS

Several models of decision making offer insights into the process. The rational model is appealing because of its logic and economy. Yet these very qualities raise questions about the model, since actual decision making is often not a wholly rational process. The behavioral model is an attempt to account for the limits on rationality in decision making. Features of both these models are combined in the practical model, and the conflict model focuses on the decision-making processes individuals use in difficult situations.

The Rational Model

The **rational decision-making model** outlines a systematic, step-by-step process. The model assumes that the organization is economically based and managed by decision makers who are entirely objective and have complete information.[8] Figure 17.4 identifies the steps of the model, starting with a statement of a goal and running neatly through the process until the best decision is made, implemented, and controlled. Organizations around the world use rational decision-making processes to solve difficult problems, as discussed in *International Perspective*.

STATEMENT OF SITUATIONAL GOAL   The rational decision-making process begins with the statement of the situational goal, or desired end state. The goal of a marketing department, for example, may be to obtain a certain market share by the end of the year.

Some models of the decision-making process do not include the goal as part of the process. We include it because it is the standard used to determine whether there is a decision to be made.

IDENTIFICATION OF THE PROBLEM   The purpose of problem identification is to gather information bearing on the goal. If there is a discrepancy between the goal and the actual state, action may be needed to rectify the situation. In the marketing example, the group may gather information about the company's actual market share and compare it with the desired market share. A difference between the two represents a problem that necessitates a decision. Reliable information is very important in this step. Inaccurate information can lead to a decision that does not need to be made or, worse, no

---

[8] See Bass, *Organizational Decision Making,* pp. 27–31, on the economic theory of the firm.

Figure 17.4

Rational Model of the
Decision-Making
Process

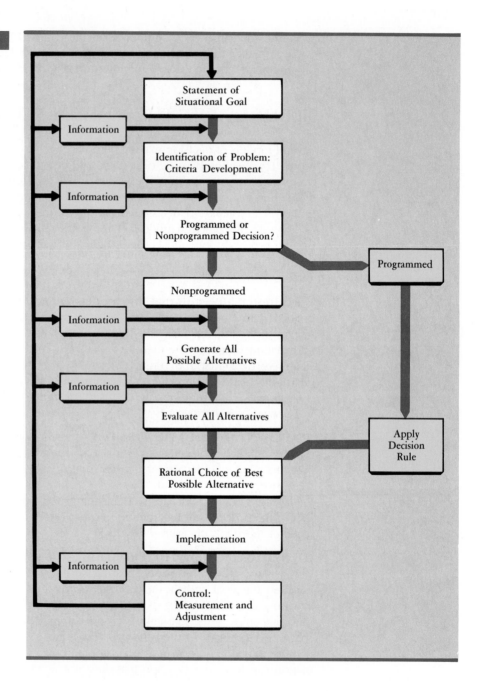

decision when one is required. For example, if market research information indicates that market share goals have almost been reached and that sales will increase next quarter, the decision makers may see no need to change the marketing program. If the market share information is wrong, however, a future decision to change the promotional effort may come too late.

DETERMINATION OF DECISION TYPE   Next, the decision makers must determine if the problem calls for a programmed or a nonprogrammed decision. If a programmed decision is needed, the appropriate decision rule is invoked, and the process moves on to the choice among alternatives. A programmed marketing decision may be called for if analysis reveals that competitors are outspending the company on print advertising. Because creating and buying space for print advertising is a well-developed function of the marketing group, it requires only a programmed decision.

Although it may seem simple to diagnose a situation as programmed, apply a decision rule, and arrive at a solution, mistakes can occur. Choosing the wrong decision rule or assuming the problem calls for a programmed decision when a nonprogrammed decision is actually required can result in unacceptable decisions.

The same caution applies to the determination that a nonprogrammed decision is called for. If the situation is wrongly diagnosed, the decision maker wastes time and resources seeking a new solution to an old problem, or "reinventing the wheel." Nevertheless, this apparent inefficiency may occasionally be justified. It may be prudent to work through the problem-solving process if the consequences of the decision are so great that failure must be avoided at almost any cost.

GENERATION OF ALTERNATIVES   The next step in making a nonprogrammed decision is to generate alternatives. The rational model assumes that decision makers will generate all possible alternative solutions to the problem. Because even simple business problems can have scores of possible solutions, this assumption is unrealistic.

Decision makers may rely on education and experience as well as knowledge of the situation to generate alternatives.[9] In addition, they may seek information from other people, such as peers, subordinates, and supervisors. Decision makers may analyze the symptoms of the problem for clues or fall back on intuition or judgment to develop alternative solutions. If the marketing department in our example determines that a nonprogrammed decision is required, it will need to generate alternatives for increasing market share.

Although the generation of alternatives is treated here as a stage of the decision-making process, it can have a broader application. In some models of strategic management, environmental scanning, a concept similar to generation

---

[9] Richard L. Daft, *Organizational Theory and Design*, 2nd ed. (St. Paul, Minn.: West, 1986)

International
Perspective

Decision-Making Strategies for a Not-For-Profit Organization

World Wildlife Fund Inc. is the largest private conservation organization in the world. Established in 1961, it now has affiliates in 23 countries, and it has put over $130 million into five thousand projects in 130 countries. It focused initially on saving individual species, such as the Bengal tiger of India. More recently the Fund has expanded its efforts to include entire ecosystems. Recognizing the inherent value of the world's tropical forests and the fact that they will disappear in a few decades if cutting continues at the present rate, the Fund has embarked on some unique strategies to preserve forested areas around the world. Thomas Lovejoy, a Fund member, came up with a concept that is now helping to protect wild areas in Third World countries that have large foreign debts: three-way swaps in which conservation organizations pay off a portion of a country's debt at a discount, and in return the country sets aside parks and reserves.

Like most not-for-profit organizations, the Fund has two sides, which sometimes seem at odds with each other. On the one hand, it is a business that tries to raise money, and on the other hand it is a charity that tries to slow the destruction of the world by profit-making organizations. Largely because of this divided organizational purpose, the Fund's British operation remained relatively stagnant in the 1970s until G. J. Medley became its director and set about reorganizing the Fund and its decision making, as he had done for the subsidiary of a large multinational corporation.

First, Medley looked at personnel and separated conservationists from businesspeople. While reorganizing the company and instituting management by objectives, Medley wanted to make sure that those people working in fund-raising had a professional, businesslike approach; conservationists could work in other departments. This rearrangement foreshadowed a key decision by the management team charged with strategic planning: the Fund always considered itself a conservation organization, but the team decided that it was in fact a fund-raising business.

This redefinition helped the team in its next series of decisions, defining key areas of the Fund's operations. It started with sixty such areas, which eventually boiled down to nine—most of them, such as "marketing" and "net funds," very similar to the key areas that a profit-making company would identify. Next the management team examined each area in terms of its strengths, weaknesses, opportunities, and threats.

After these processes had clarified the Fund's position and future possibilities, the team moved on to create general strategies, action plans to implement those strategies, and budgets to meet its objectives.

The result of bringing business decision-making techniques to the Fund was dramatic: net funds increased fivefold and productivity per employee increased sixfold in less than a decade. By becoming more businesslike, the Fund was able to increase its charity.

Sources: Jeff B. Copeland, "Buying Debt, Saving Nature," *Newsweek*, August 31, 1987, 46; Lis Harris, "Brother Sun, Sister Moon," *The New Yorker*, April 27, 1987, 80–99; G. J. Medley, "Strategic Planning for the World Wildlife Fund," *Long Range Planning*, Vol. 21, No. 1, 1988, 46–54.

of alternatives, plays an important role.[10] **Environmental scanning** is the process of constantly searching the business environment for new opportunities and threats to the business. The generation of alternatives may be more realistically understood, then, as an ongoing process of environmental scanning useful in problem detection and diagnosis as well as in the alternative generation and evaluation phases of decision making.

EVALUATION OF ALTERNATIVES   Evaluation involves the assessment of all possible alternatives against predetermined decision criteria. The ultimate decision criterion is, "Will this alternative bring us nearer to the goal?" In each case, the decision maker must examine an alternative for evidence that it will reduce the discrepancy between the desired state and the actual state. The evaluation process usually includes (1) complete description of the anticipated outcomes (benefits) of each alternative, (2) evaluation of the anticipated costs of each alternative, and (3) estimation of the uncertainties and risks associated with each alternative.[11]

In most decision situations, the decision maker does not have perfect information regarding the outcomes of all alternatives. At one extreme, as shown in Figure 17.2, outcomes may be known with certainty; at the other, the decision maker has no information whatsoever, so that the outcomes are entirely uncertain. But risk is the most common situation.

Management science has developed various techniques to help the decision maker evaluate alternatives. Linear programming, for instance, is a mathematical method that enables a decision maker to determine how limited resources can be shared by several activities in order to maximize productivity.[12] A classic example of a linear programming application is the caterer's problem—whether to launder soiled napkins and reuse them or purchase new ones. Linear programming can provide the information needed to determine the best combination of new purchases and laundering. Although quantitative methods can provide decision makers with more information about the likely outcomes of alternatives, the decision makers remain responsible for using the information and making the decision.

CHOICE OF AN ALTERNATIVE   The choice of an alternative is the crucial step in the decision-making process. Choice consists of selecting the alternative with the highest possible payoff, based on the benefits, costs, risks, and

---

[10] John R. Montanari, "Some Tips on Clinical Policy Formulation," *Medical Group Management Journal*, Vol. 23, 1976, pp. 24–27.

[11] Milan Zeleny, "Descriptive Decision Making and Its Applications," *Applications of Management Science*, Vol. 1, 1981, pp. 327–388; and Henry Mintzberg, Duru Raisinghani, and Andre Thoret, "The Structure of 'Unstructured' Decision Processes," *Administrative Science Quarterly*, June 1976, pp. 246–275.

[12] See Hamdy A. Taha, "Linear Programming," in Joseph J. Moder and Salah E. Elmaghraby, eds., *Handbook of Operations Research* (New York: Van Nostrand Reinhold, 1978), pp. 85–119, for a discussion of linear programming.

uncertainties of all alternatives. In the video game promotion example, the decision maker evaluated the two alternatives by calculating their expected values. Following the rational model, he or she would choose the one with the largest expected value.

Even in the rational model, however, difficulties can arise in choosing an alternative. First, when two or more alternatives have equally high payoffs, the decision maker must obtain more information or use some other criterion to make the choice. Second, when no single alternative will accomplish the objective, some combination of two or three alternatives may have to be implemented. Finally, if no alternative or combination of alternatives will solve the problem, the decision maker must obtain more information, generate more alternatives, or change the situational goals.[13]

An important part of the choice phase is the consideration of **contingency plans**—alternative actions that can be taken if the primary course of action is unexpectedly disrupted or rendered inappropriate.[14] Planning for contingencies is part of the transition between choosing the preferred alternative and implementing it. In developing contingency plans, the decision maker usually asks questions such as, "What if something unexpected happens during the implementation of this alternative?" "If the economy goes into a recession, will the choice of this alternative ruin the company?" "How can we alter this plan if the economy suddenly rebounds and begins to grow?"

IMPLEMENTATION   Implementation puts the decision into action. It uses the commitment and motivation of those who participated in the decision-making process (and may actually bolster individual commitment and motivation). To be successful, implementation requires the proper use of resources and good management skills. Following the decision to promote the new video game heavily, for example, the marketing manager must implement the decision by assigning the project to a work group or task force. The success of this team depends on the leadership, the reward structure, the communications system, and the group dynamics.

Sometimes the decision maker begins to doubt a choice already made. This doubt is called *post decision dissonance* or *cognitive dissonance*.[15] (Cognitive dissonance is discussed in Chapter 3 as it relates to attitude-behavior consistency.) To reduce the tension created by the dissonance, the decision maker may seek to rationalize the decision further with new information.

---

[13] See E. Frank Harrison, *The Managerial Decision-Making Process,* 2nd ed. (Boston: Houghton Mifflin, 1981), pp. 41–43, for more on choice processes.

[14] Donald C. Hambrick, and David Lei, "Toward an Empirical Prioritization of Contingency Variables for Business Strategy, *Academy of Management Journal,* December 1985, pp. 763–788; and Ari Ginsberg and N. Ventrakaman, "Contingency Perspectives of Organizational Strategy: A Critical Review of the Empirical Research," *Academy of Management Review,* July 1985, pp. 412–434.

[15] Leon Festinger, *A Theory of Cognitive Dissonance* (Palo Alto, Calif.: Stanford University Press, 1957).

CONTROL—MEASUREMENT AND ADJUSTMENT   In the final step of the decision-making process, the outcomes of the decision are measured and compared with the desired goal. If a discrepancy remains, the decision maker may restart the decision-making process by setting a new goal (or reiterating the existing one). The decision maker, unsatisfied with the previous decision, may modify the subsequent decision-making process to avoid another mistake. Changes can be made to any part of the process, as illustrated in Figure 17.4 by the arrows leading from the control step to each of the other steps. Decision making is therefore a dynamic, self-correcting, and never-ending process in organizations.

Suppose the marketing department mentioned earlier implements a new print advertising campaign. After implementation, it will constantly monitor market research data and compare its new market share to the desired market share. If the advertising has the desired effect, no changes will be made in the promotion campaign. If, however, the data indicate no change in the market share, additional decisions and implementation of a contingency plan may be necessary.

The Coca-Cola Company faced the need to change after it introduced the new Coke. The product was based on four-and-a-half years of testing and market research, but after only three months on the market, with declining market share and complaints from bottlers, Coca Cola announced the return of the old formula under the name Coca-Cola Classic.[16]

STRENGTHS AND WEAKNESSES OF THE RATIONAL MODEL   The rational model has several strengths as an approach to decision making. It forces the decision maker to consider a decision in a logical, sequential manner, and the in-depth analysis of alternatives enables the decision maker to choose on the basis of information rather than emotion or social pressure.

The rigid assumptions of the rational model are often unrealistic, however.[17] The amount of information available to managers is usually limited by either time or cost constraints, and most decision makers have limited ability to process information about the alternatives. In addition, not all alternatives lend themselves to quantification in terms that will allow for easy comparison. Finally, because they cannot predict the future, it is unlikely that decision makers will know all possible outcomes of each alternative.

The Behavioral Model

The crucial assumption of the behavioral model is that decision makers operate with **bounded rationality** rather than the perfect rationality assumed by the

---

[16] John Koten and Scott Kilman, "How Coke's Decision to Offer 2 Colas Undid 4½ Years of Planning," *The Wall Street Journal*, July 15, 1985, pp. 1, 8.

[17] See Harrison, *The Managerial Decision-Making Practices*, pp. 53–57, for more on the advantages and disadvantages of the rational model.

rational model. The assumption rests on the argument that although individuals may seek the best solution to a problem, the demands of processing all information bearing on the problem, generating all possible solutions, and choosing the single best solution are beyond the capabilities of most decision makers. Thus, individuals will accept less than ideal solutions based on a process that is neither exhaustive nor entirely rational. Decision makers operating with bounded rationality limit the inputs to the decision-making process and base decisions on judgment and personal biases as well as logic.[18]

The **behavioral model** is characterized by (1) the use of procedures and rules of thumb, (2) suboptimizing, and (3) satisficing. Uncertainty in decision making can be initially reduced by reliance on procedures and rules of thumb. If, for example, increasing print advertising has increased a company's market share in the past, the linkage may be used by company employees as a rule of thumb in decision making. When the previous month's market share drops below a certain level, the company might increase its print advertising expenditures by 25 percent during the following month.

Suboptimizing, the second feature of the behavioral model, is knowingly accepting less than the best possible outcome. It is frequently not feasible to optimize a particular decision in a real-world situation, given organizational constraints. To avoid unintended negative effects on other departments, product lines, or decisions, the decision maker must often suboptimize.[19] An automobile manufacturer, for example, can cut costs dramatically and increase efficiency if it schedules the production of one model at a time. Thus, the production group's optimal decision is single-model scheduling. But the marketing group, seeking to optimize its sales goals by offering a wide variety of models, may demand the opposite production schedule: short runs of entirely different models. The groups in the middle, design and scheduling, may suboptimize the benefits the production and marketing groups are seeking by planning long runs of slightly different models. This is the practice of the large auto manufacturers, such as General Motors, which make several body styles in several different models on the same production line.

The final feature of the behavioral model is **satisficing**—examining alternatives only until a solution that meets minimal requirements is found and then ceasing to look for a better one.[20] The search for alternatives is usually a sequential process guided by procedures and rules of thumb based on previous experiences with similar problems. Often, when the first minimally acceptable choice is encountered, the search ends. The resulting choice may narrow the discrepancy between the desired and the actual states, but it is not likely to be

---

[18] See James G. March and Herbert A. Simon, *Organizations* (New York: Wiley, 1958), for more on the concept of bounded rationality.

[19] Herbert A. Simon, *Administrative Behavior: A Study of Decision Making Processes in Administrative Organization,* 3rd ed. (New York: Free Press, 1976).

[20] Richard M. Cyert and James G. March, *A Behavioral Theory of the Firm* (Englewood Cliffs, N.J.: Prentice-Hall, 1963), p. 113; and Simon, *Administrative Behavior.*

the optimal solution. As the process is repeated, incremental improvements will slowly reduce the discrepancy between the actual and desired states.

A Practical Model

Because of the unrealistic demands of the rational model and the limited, short-run orientation of the behavioral model, neither approach is entirely satisfactory. However, the worthwhile features of each can be combined in a practical model of decision making, shown in Figure 17.5. The steps in the process are the same as in the rational model; however, the conditions recognized by the behavioral model are added to provide a more realistic approach. For example, rather than generate all alternatives, the practical model suggests that the decision maker should try to go beyond rules of thumb and satisficing limitations and generate as many alternatives as time, money, and other practicalities of the situation allow. In this synthesis of the two approaches, the rational model provides an analytical framework for making decisions, while the behavioral model provides a moderating influence.

The Conflict Model

Although the models just described have provided significant insight into decision making, they do not fully explain the processes people engage in when they are nervous, worried, and agitated over making a decision that has major implications for them, their organization, or their family. One attempt to provide a more realistic view of individual decision making is the model presented by Irving L. Janis and Leon Mann.[21]

The Janis-Mann process, called the **conflict model,** is based on research in social psychology and individual decision processes. The model makes five assumptions. First, it deals only with important life decisions—marriage, schooling, career, major organizational decisions—that commit the individual or the organization to a certain course of action following the decision. Second, the model recognizes that procrastination and rationalization are mechanisms by which people avoid making difficult decisions. They are means of coping with the stress of the choice.

Third, the model explicitly acknowledges that some decisions are probably going to be wrong and that the fear of making a wrong decision can be a deterrent to making any decision at all. Janis and Mann suggest that since not all decisions can be correct, the decision maker should be concerned with the overall "batting average" of good versus bad decisions.

Fourth, the model provides for **self-reactions**—comparisons of alternatives with internalized moral standards. Internalized moral standards guide decision making as much as economic and social outcomes. A proposed course of action

---

[21] Irving L. Janis and Leon Mann, *Decision Making: A Psychological Analysis of Conflict, Choice, and Commitment* (New York: Free Press, 1977).

Figure 17.5   Practical Model of Decision Making

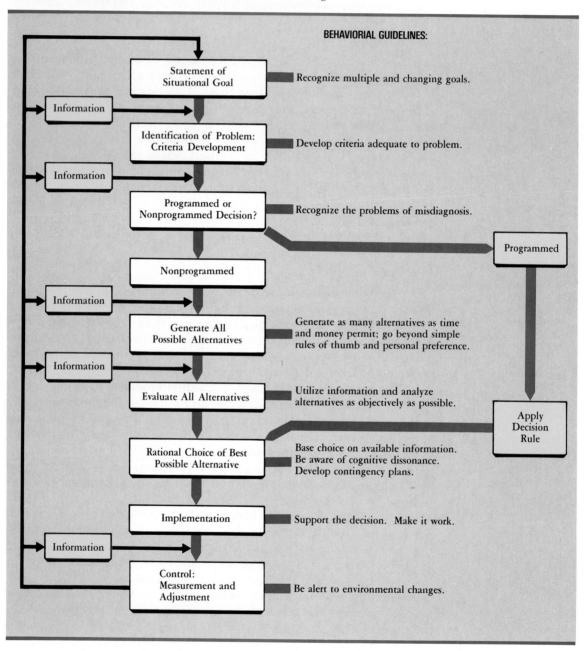

may offer many economic and social rewards, but if it violates the decision maker's moral convictions, it is unlikely that it will be chosen.

Finally, the model recognizes that at times the decision maker is ambivalent about alternative courses of action; in such circumstances, it is very difficult to make a wholehearted commitment to a single choice. Major life decisions seldom allow compromise, however, they are usually either/or decisions that require total commitment to one course of action.

The Janis-Mann conflict model of decision making is shown in Figure 17.6. A concrete example will help to explain each step. Our hypothetical individual is Richard, a thirty-year-old engineer, with a working wife and two young children. Richard has been employed at a large manufacturing company for eight years. He keeps abreast of his career situation through visits with peers at work and in other companies, feedback from his manager and others regarding his work and future with the company, the alumni magazine from his university, and other sources.

At work one morning, Richard learns that he has been passed over for a promotion for the second time in a year. He investigates the information, which can be considered negative feedback, and confirms it. As a result, he seeks out other information regarding his career at the company, the prospect of changing companies, and the possibility of going back to graduate school to get an MBA. At the same time, he asks himself, "Are the risks serious if I do not make a change?" If the answer is no, Richard will continue his present activities. In the model's terms, this option is called **unconflicted adherence.** If the answer is yes or maybe, Richard will move to the next question in the model.

The second step asks, "Are the risks serious if I do change?" If Richard goes on to this step, he will gather information about potential losses from making a change. He may, for example, find out whether he would lose health insurance and pension benefits if he changed jobs or went back to graduate school. If he believes that changing presents no serious risks, Richard will make the change, called an **unconflicted change.** Otherwise, he will move on to the next step.

Suppose Richard has determined that the risks are serious whether he makes a change or not. Now he is in a bind. He believes he must make a change because he will not be promoted further in his present company. Yet serious risks are associated with making a change—perhaps loss of benefits, uncertain promotion opportunities in another company, lost income from going to graduate school for two years. In the third step Richard wonders, "Is it realistic to hope to find a better solution?" He continues to look for information that can help him make the decision. If the answer to this third question is negative, Richard may give up the hope of finding anything better and opt for what Janis and Mann call **defensive avoidance;** that is, he will make no change and avoid any further contact with the issue. But a positive response will move Richard to the next step.

Figure 17.6   Janis-Mann Conflict Model of Decision Making

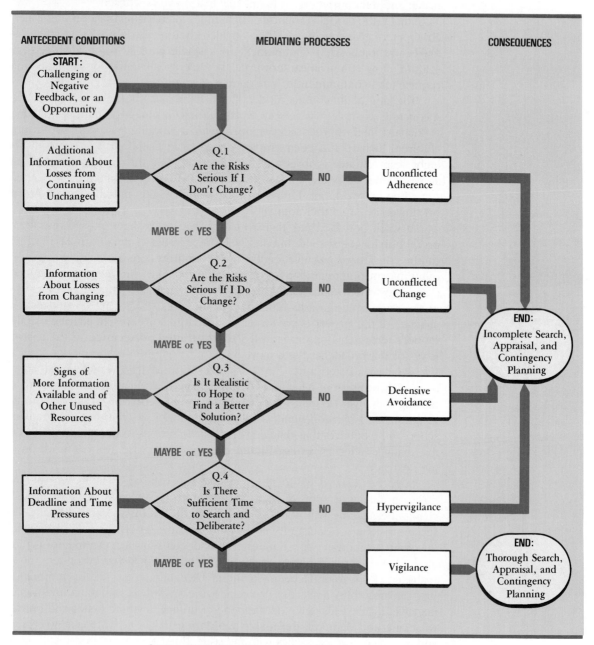

Source: Reprinted with permission of The Free Press, a division of Macmillan, Inc. from *Decision Making: A Psychological Analysis of Conflict, Choice, and Commitment* by Irving L. Janis and Leon Mann.

Here, the decision maker, who now recognizes the serious risks involved and yet expects to find a solution, asks, "Is there sufficient time to search and deliberate?" Richard now asks himself how quickly he needs to make a change. If he believes he does not have time to deliberate much longer, perhaps because of his age, he will enter what Janis and Mann call **hypervigilance.** In this state he may experience severe psychological stress and engage in frantic, superficial pursuit of some satisficing strategy. (This might also be called panic!) If, on the other hand, Richard feels that he has two to three years to consider various alternatives, he will undertake **vigilant information processing,** in which he will thoroughly investigate all possible alternatives, weigh their costs and benefits before making a choice, and develop contingency plans.

In the actual situation from which this example was drawn, Richard did in fact engage in vigilant information processing. He subsequently entered the MBA program at the local university and completed his degree by attending classes in the evening while retaining his job. Soon after graduation, he accepted a better job at another manufacturing company.

Negative answers to the questions in the conflict model lead to responses of unconflicted adherence, unconflicted change, defensive avoidance, and hypervigilance. All are coping strategies that result in incomplete search, appraisal, and contingency planning. A decision maker who gives the same answer to all the questions will always engage in the same coping strategy. However, if the answers change as the situation changes, the individual's coping strategies may change as well.

The decision maker who answers positively to each of the four questions is led to vigilant information processing, a process similar to that outlined in the rational decision-making model. The decision maker objectively analyzes the problem and all alternatives, thoroughly searches for information, carefully evaluates the consequences of all alternatives, and diligently plans for implementation and contingencies.

ESCALATION OF COMMITMENT

Sometimes people continue to try to implement a decision in spite of clear and convincing evidence that substantial problems exist. **Escalation of commitment** refers to the tendency to persist in an ineffective course of action when evidence indicates that the project is doomed to failure. A recent example is the decision by the government of British Columbia to hold EXPO '86 in Vancouver. Originally, the organizers expected the project to break even financially, so that the province would not have to increase taxes to pay for it. As work progressed, it became clear that expenses were far greater than had been projected. But organizers considered it too late to call off the event, in spite of the huge losses that were obviously going to occur. Eventually, the province conducted a $300 million lottery to try to cover the costs.[22] Similar examples abound in stock market investment, in political and military situations, and in organizations developing any type of new project.

Staw has suggested several possible reasons for escalation of commitment.[23] Some projects require much front-end investment and little return until the end, so that the investor must stay in until the end to get any payoff. These "all or nothing" projects require unflagging commitment. Furthermore, investors or project leaders often become so ego-involved with their project that their self-identity is totally wrapped up in it.[24] Failure or cancellation seems to threaten their reason for existence. Therefore, they continue to push the project as potentially successful in spite of strong evidence to the contrary. Other times, the social structure, group norms, and group cohesiveness all support a project so strongly that cancellation is impossible. Organizational inertia may also force an organization to maintain a failing project. Thus, escalation of commitment is a phenomenon that has a strong foundation. For an example of the research basis of this phenomenon, see *A Look at Research*.

How can an individual or organization recognize that a project needs to be stopped before it results in "throwing good money after bad?" Several suggestions have been made; some are easy to put to use, and others are more difficult. Having good information about a project is always a first step to prevention of the escalation problem. It is usually possible to schedule regular sessions to discuss the project, its progress, the assumptions on which it was originally based, the current validity of these assumptions, and any problems with the project. An objective review is necessary to maintain control.

Some organizations have begun to make separate teams responsible for the development and the implementation of a project in order to reduce ego-involvement. The people who initiate a project are often those who know the most about it, however, and their expertise can be valuable in the implementation process. Staw suggests that a general strategy for avoiding the escalation problem is to try to create an "experimenting organization" in which every program and project is reviewed regularly and managers are evaluated on their contribution to the total organization rather than to specific projects.[25]

Although several suggestions have been made on how to prevent the escalation problem, much more research on its causes and prevention is needed.

---

[22] Jerry Ross and Barry M. Staw, "Expo 86: An Escalation Prototype," *Administrative Science Quarterly*, June 1986, pp. 274–297.

[23] Barry M. Staw, "Escalation of Commitment to a Course of Action," *Academy of Management Review*, October 1981, pp. 577–587.

[24] Joel Brockner, Robert Houser, Gregg Birnbaum, Kathy Lloyd, Janet Deitcher, Sinaia Nathanson, and Jeffrey Z. Rubin, "Escalation of Commitment to an Ineffective Course of Action: The Effect of Feedback Having Negative Implications for Self-Identity," *Administrative Science Quarterly*, March 1986, pp. 109–126.

[25] Barry M. Staw and Jerry Ross, "Good Money After Bad," *Psychology Today*, February 1988, pp. 30–33.

A LOOK AT

RESEARCH

Throwing Good Money After Bad

Countless observers of organizational behavior in the past decade have stressed the importance of the ability to change and adapt to new conditions. Although our society values perseverance, the business world increasingly seems to need leaders who know when to change tack, when to cut their losses and try something different. Therefore, a number of researchers are investigating the factors that influence an individual's commitment to a failing course of action, in an effort to discover the elements that lead a manager to continue investing resources in a project that seems doomed to failure.

One group of researchers, led by Joel Brockner, performed experiments using Tufts University undergraduates as subjects. The subjects performed a perceptual task: guessing the relative amounts of black and white space on a card decorated with geometrical designs. After the first two cards, subjects had to pay increasing amounts to make each guess, using $3.50 given to them by the experimenters, then using their own money if the $3.50 ran out. The experimenters provided the students with feedback purporting to show how well they were doing; they rewarded each guess with a certain number of points. Subjects were told that anyone who gained enough points would win a jackpot, and they believed that they were winning points based on the accuracy of their guesses. In reality, the experimenters awarded points according to a programmed pattern that had nothing to do with how well the students guessed.

By varying the information they gave the subjects, the researchers could measure the effect of certain factors on the students' willingness to continue investing money. (They could stop at any point.) Subjects who were told that performance on the test positively correlated with intelligence, happiness, and success continued to invest longer than subjects who were told that the test said nothing about their personal skills. Both groups were getting feedback that should have told them they had no hope of winning the jackpot.

A second experiment refined the relationship between commitment to the task and personal identification with the results. One group was told that skill determined the experimental outcome, and another group was told that luck was the main factor. The results showed that those in the "luck" group were more likely to persist when the rewards for their guesses started out high and then dropped off. Those in the "skill" group kept investing longer when their rewards started low and then increased for a period.

In their simplest form, the results of these experiments show that people will persist in a failing endeavor if they see the success of that endeavor as a reflection of their own personal qualities. Only when initial success gives way to failure will people who personally identify with the outcome cut their losses as quickly as those who do not identify with the outcome. Future research will be needed to help organizational scientists determine how managers can achieve both a necessary degree of commitment to a project and enough separation from that project to allow them to know when it's time to call it quits.

Source: Joel Brockner, Robert Houser, Gregg Birnbaum, Kathy Lloyd, Janet Deitcher, Sinaia Nathanson, and Jeffrey Z. Rubin, "Escalation of Commitment to an Ineffective Course of Action: The Effect of Feedback Having Negative Implications for Self-Identity," *Administrative Science Quarterly*, 31 (1986), 109–126.

INDIVIDUAL VERSUS GROUP DECISION MAKING

Both individuals and groups make decisions in organizations. Individuals and groups are subject to different types of pressures as they make decisions. Considerable research has been done to compare the decision-making success of individuals and groups in various situations.[26] When is it better to have a group make a decision than an individual? Researchers have found that the answer depends on several factors: the type of decision, the knowledge and experience of the people involved, and the type of decision process involved.

In tasks that require an estimation, a prediction, or a judgment of accuracy—usually referred to as judgmental tasks—groups are usually superior to individuals, simply because more people contribute to the decsion-making process.[27] However, one especially capable individual may make a better judgment than a group.

In problem-solving tasks, groups generally produce more and better solutions than do individuals. But groups take far longer than individuals to develop solutions and make decisions. In addition, individual decision making avoids special problems of group decision making. If the problem to be solved is a fairly clear, straightforward one, it may be more appropriate to have a single capable individual concentrate on its solution. On the other hand, complex problems are more appropriate for groups. Such problems can be divided into parts and the parts assigned to individuals, who bring their results back to the group for discussion and decision making.

An additional advantage to group decision making is that it often creates greater interest in the task.[28] Heightened interest may increase the time and effort given to the task, resulting in more ideas, a more thorough search for solutions, better evaluation of alternatives, and improved decision quality. The characteristics of group and individual decision making are summarized in Table 17.2.

DECISION MAKING IN GROUPS

This section builds on the discussion of group dynamics in Chapter 9. As described there, people in organizations work in a variety of groups—formal and informal, permanent and temporary. Most of these groups make decisions that affect the welfare of the organization and the people in it. Here, we discuss factors and behaviors that affect group decision making.

---

[26] Marvin E. Shaw, *Group Dynamics: The Psychology of Small Group Behavior,* 3rd ed. (New York: McGraw-Hill, 1981), pp. 57–68.

[27] Shaw, *Group Dynamics.*

[28] Huber, *Managerial Decision Making,* pp. 140–148.

Table 17.2	Group	Individual
Characteristics of Group and Individual Decision Making	Slow process	Fast process
	More people to contribute ideas	For a judgmental task, a single expert may be preferable
	Complex tasks can be divided	Avoids special problems of group decision making, such as groupthink
	More thorough search for alternatives	
	More alternatives generated	
	Greater interest stimulated	

Basic Factors

The group factors discussed in Chapter 9—such as physical environment, size and composition, characteristics of members, and norms and cohesiveness—have a powerful impact on the effectiveness of group decision making. The physical environment, composition of the group, and the relative status of the members are particularly important.

The physical aspects of group meetings must be conducive to open discussion, with tables, chairs, and any necessary equipment available and in working order. In an inappropriate working environment, it can be significantly more difficult for group members to cooperate in the problem-solving process.

The composition of the group must be such that the similarities and differences of the members fit the demands of the problem. Recall that groups with a heterogeneous membership tend to produce a larger quantity of more diverse ideas than those whose membership is homogeneous. Heterogeneous groups are appropriate for tasks that require the generation and evaluation of many alternatives. However, it is often more difficult for a heterogeneous group to reach agreement; a homogeneous group is more appropriate when quick agreement is needed. The characteristics of individual members—personality, knowledge, expertise, experience, and so on—should also be compatible with the problem at hand.

The third important factor is the status or power relationships inherent in the group. Individuals with more status or power may have a particularly strong influence on the group's decision. Other members may believe these higher-status individuals have superior insight; or the higher-status members may influence reward allocation or may have some coercive power that can be wielded in the future. Depending on how they are managed, these and other sources of individual influence can assist or impede the group decision-making process.[29]

---

[29] Shaw, *Group Dynamics.*

Group Polarization

Members' attitudes and opinions with respect to an issue or a solution may change during the group discussion. Some studies of this tendency showed the change to be a fairly consistent movement toward a more risky solution, called **risky shift.**[30] Other studies and analyses have revealed that the group-induced shift is not always toward more risk; the group is just as likely to move toward a more conservative view.[31] Generally, the average of the group members' post-discussion attitudes tends to be more extreme than average pre-discussion attitudes.[32] This tendency, termed **group polarization,** is illustrated in Figure 17.7.

Several features of group discussion contribute to polarization.[33] When individuals discover in group discussion that their opinions are shared by others, they may feel more strongly about their opinions, resulting in a more extreme view. Persuasive arguments can also encourage polarization. If members who strongly support a particular position are able to express themselves cogently in the discussion, less avid supporters of the position may become convinced that it is correct. In addition, members may feel that because the group is deciding, they are not individually responsible for the decision or its outcomes. This diffusion of responsibility may enable them to accept and support a decision more radical than the ones they would make as individuals.

Polarization can profoundly affect group decision making. If group members are known to lean toward a particular decision before a discussion, it may be expected that their post-decision position will be even more extreme. Understanding this phenomenon may be useful for one who seeks to affect their decision.

Groupthink

Although highly cohesive groups are often very successful at accomplishing their goals, such groups have serious difficulties as well. One of them is groupthink. **Groupthink,** according to Irving L. Janis, is "a mode of thinking that people engage in when they are deeply involved in a cohesive in-group, when the members' strivings for unanimity override their motivation to

---

[30] James A. F. Stoner, "Risky and Cautious Shifts in Group Decisions: The Influence of Widely Held Values," *Journal of Experimental Social Psychology,* October 1968, pp. 442–459; and M. A. Wallach, N. Kogan, and D. J. Bem, "Group Influence on Individual Risk Taking," *Journal of Abnormal and Social Psychology,* August 1962, pp. 75–86.

[31] Dorwin Cartwright, "Risk Taking by Individuals and Groups: An Assessment of Research Employing Choice Dilemmas," *Journal of Personality and Social Psychology,* December 1971, pp. 361–378.

[32] S. Moscovici and M. Zavalloni, "The Group as a Polarizer of Attitudes," *Journal of Personality and Social Psychology,* June 1969, pp. 125–135.

[33] See Shaw, *Group Dynamics,* pp. 68–76, for more on group polarization.

Figure 17.7

Group Polarization

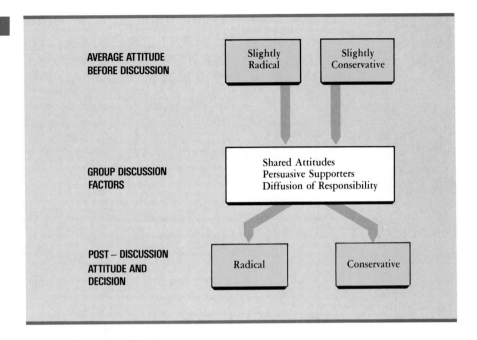

realistically appraise alternative courses of action."[34] When groupthink occurs, then, the group unknowingly makes unanimity, rather than the best decision, its goal. Groupthink can occur in decision making within organizations, as may have been the case in the E. F. Hutton checking scandal, illustrated in *Management in Action.*

GROUPTHINK SYMPTOMS   The groupthink process is outlined in Figure 17.8. The three primary conditions that foster the development of groupthink are cohesiveness, the leader's promotion of his or her preferred solution, and insulation of the group from expert opinions. A group in which groupthink has taken hold exhibits eight well-defined symptoms:

1. an illusion of invulnerability, shared by most or all members, that creates excessive optimism and encourages extreme risk taking.
2. collective efforts to rationalize in order to discount warnings that might lead members to reconsider assumptions before recommitting themselves to past policy decisions.
3. an unquestioned belief in the group's inherent morality, inclining the members to ignore the ethical and moral consequences of their decisions.

---

[34] Irving L. Janis *Groupthink,* 2nd ed. (Boston.: Houghton Mifflin, 1982), p. 9.

Management in ACTION

Groupthink at E. F. Hutton

In 1985 The E. F. Hutton Group Inc., one of the nation's largest brokerage firms, pleaded guilty to two thousand counts of wire and mail fraud, paid a fine of almost $3 million, and put over $9 million into funds to pay back defrauded banks and investors. The court case focused the nation's attention on banks' overdraft policies, but it also provided an example of how groupthink can cause trouble for even the mightiest institutions.

Hutton's crime involved a form of "check kiting." A money manager at a Hutton branch office would write a check on an account in bank A for more money than Hutton had in that account. Because of the time lag in the check-collection system, these overdrafts sometimes went undetected, and Hutton could deposit funds to cover the overdraft in bank A's account on the following day. Even if the bank noticed the overdraft, it was unlikely to complain, because Hutton was such an important customer and because certain kinds of overdrafts are fairly routine.

In any case, the Hutton manager would deposit the check from bank A into an account in bank B, where the money would start earning interest immediately. In effect, the scheme allowed Hutton to earn a day's interest on bank A's money without having to pay anything for it. A day's interest may not sound like much, but Hutton was getting as much as $250 million in free loans every day, and a day's interest on such a sum is substantial.

Everyone who has a checking account knows that bouncing checks is wrong, and you do not have to be a financial wizard to know that writing bad checks is illegal. So how could some of the country's most sophisticated money managers become involved in such unethical behavior?

The answer may well be groupthink. Hutton's employees were under a lot of pressure to make money, and the company no doubt paid more attention to profit figures than to how those figures were achieved. The practice may even have started accidentally, but once it got going, the money managers apparently wrote unnecessary checks solely to profit from the check kiting scheme as the money passed from bank to bank. Company employees evidently had the necessary company loyalty and commitment to enable groupthink to come into play. Most important, once it became clear that high-level executives were not going to stop the scheme, employees became very good at ignoring any information that might lead them to conclude that the practice was illegal. An internal Hutton memo recommended that "if an office is overdrafting their ledger balance consistently, it is probably best not to request an account analysis."* In other words, "let's all close our eyes to this problem."

The collective rationalization that characterizes groupthink was probably very easy to achieve in this case, since the line between legal and illegal overdrafting is fuzzy. Even after Hutton pleaded guilty, some in the industry contended that the company had done nothing illegal and would have won in court. But by ignoring the voices of caution and conscience and working just for short-term profit, Hutton's managers ended up severely damaging their company's reputation.

Sources: Daniel Goleman, "Following the Leader," *Science 85,* October 1985, 18; "A Violation of Business Ethics or Outright Fraud?" *ASA Banking Journal,* July 1987, 30–34; Harold Seneker, "Nice Timing," *Forbes,* January 27, 1986, 102.

* Daniel Goleman, "Following the Leader," *Science 85,* October 1985, 18.

Figure 17.8

Groupthink Process

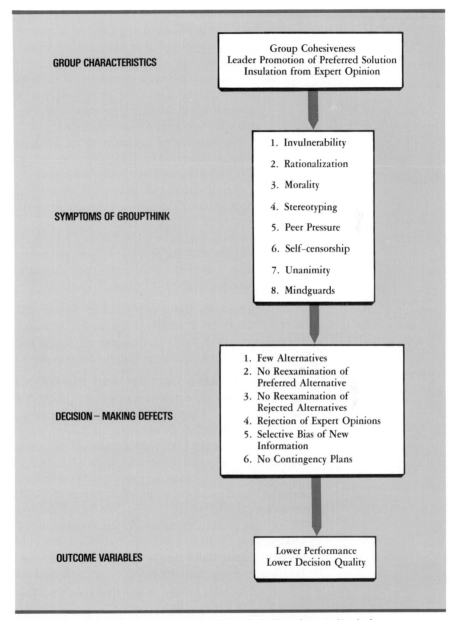

GROUP CHARACTERISTICS

Group Cohesiveness
Leader Promotion of Preferred Solution
Insulation from Expert Opinion

SYMPTOMS OF GROUPTHINK

1. Invulnerability
2. Rationalization
3. Morality
4. Stereotyping
5. Peer Pressure
6. Self–censorship
7. Unanimity
8. Mindguards

DECISION – MAKING DEFECTS

1. Few Alternatives
2. No Reexamination of Preferred Alternative
3. No Reexamination of Rejected Alternatives
4. Rejection of Expert Opinions
5. Selective Bias of New Information
6. No Contingency Plans

OUTCOME VARIABLES

Lower Performance
Lower Decision Quality

Source: Adapted from Gregory Moorhead, "Groupthink: Hypothesis in Need of Testing, " *Group & Organization Studies,* Vol. 7, No. 4 (December 1982), pp. 429–444. Copyright © 1982 by Sage Publications, Inc. Reprinted by permission of Sage Publications, Inc.

4. stereotyped views of "enemy" leaders as too evil to warrant genuine attempts to negotiate or as too weak or stupid to counter whatever risky attempts are made to defeat their purposes.

5. direct pressure on a member who expresses strong arguments against any of the group's stereotypes, illusions, or commitments, making clear that such dissent is contrary to what is expected of loyal members.

6. self-censorship of deviations from the apparent group consensus, reflecting each member's inclination to minimize the importance of his or her doubts and counterarguments.

7. a shared illusion of unanimity (partly resulting from self-censorship of deviations, augmented by the false assumption that silence means consent).

8. the emergence of self-appointed mindguards—members who protect the group from adverse information that might shatter their shared complacency about the effectiveness and morality of their decisions.[35]

Janis contends that the group involved in the Watergate cover-up, President Richard Nixon, H. R. Haldeman, John Ehrlichman, and John Dean, may have been a victim of groupthink. Evidence of most of the groupthink symptoms can be found in the unedited transcripts of the group's deliberations.[36]

DECISION-MAKING DEFECTS AND DECISION QUALITY   When groupthink dominates group deliberations, the likelihood that the decision-making defects shown in Figure 17.8 will occur increases. The group is less likely to survey a full range of alternatives and may focus on only a few (often one or two). In discussing a preferred alternative, the group may fail to examine it for non-obvious risks and drawbacks. Even when new information is obtained, the group may not re-examine previously rejected alternatives for non-obvious gains or some means of reducing apparent costs. The group may reject expert opinions that run counter to its own views and may choose to consider only information that supports its preferred solution. (The decision to launch the space shuttle Challenger in January 1986 may have been a product of groupthink, because negative information was ignored by the group that made the decision.[37]) Finally, the group may not consider any potential setbacks or countermoves by competing groups and, therefore, may not develop contingency plans. It should be noted that Janis contends that these six defects may arise from other common

---

[35] Janis, *Victims of Groupthink* (Boston: Houghton Mifflin, 1972), pp. 197–198.

[36] Janis, *Groupthink.*

[37] Richard J. Ference and Gregory Moorhead, "Group Decision Making Fiascoes Continue: Space Shuttle and Beyond," Working Paper, Arizona State University, 1988.

problems as well—fatigue, prejudice, inaccurate information, information overload, and ignorance.[38]

Defects in decision making do not always lead to bad outcomes or defeats. Even if its own decision-making processes are flawed, for example, one side can win a battle because of the poor decisions made by the other side's leaders. Nevertheless, decisions produced by defective processes have a lower probability of success.

RESEARCH BASIS OF GROUPTHINK The groupthink concept emerged from research on the decision-making procedures of several U.S. military and civilian groups responsible for decisions that contributed to a notable success or fiasco. The successes were the Cuban missile crisis of 1962 and the development of the Marshall Plan after World War II. The fiascoes included the Bay of Pigs invasion in 1961, the invasion of North Korea during the Korean War, the U.S. defense against the Japanese raid on Pearl Harbor in 1941, and the military escalation in Vietnam from 1964 to 1967. The research relied on news reports, memoirs, and, in some cases, interviews with participants.

Although the arguments for the existence of groupthink are convincing, the hypothesis has not been subjected to rigorous empirical examination. Research supports parts of the model but leaves some questions unanswered.[39]

PREVENTION OF GROUPTHINK Several suggestions have been offered to help the manager reduce the probability of groupthink in group decision making.[40] Summarized in Table 17.3, these prescriptions fall into four categories, depending on whether they apply to the leader, the organization, the individual, or the process. All are designed to facilitate the critical evaluation of alternatives and discourage the single-minded pursuit of unanimity.

Participation in Decision Making

A major issue in group decision making is the degree to which employees should participate in the process. Early management theories, such as those of the scientific management school, advocated a clear separation between the duties of managers and workers—management was to make the decisions, and employees were to implement them.[41] Other approaches have urged that

---

[38] Janis, *Groupthink,* pp. 193–197, and Gregory Moorhead, "Groupthink: Hypothesis in Need of Testing," *Group & Organization Studies,* December 1982, pp. 429–444.

[39] Gregory Moorhead and John R. Montanari, "Empirical Analysis of the Groupthink Phenomenon," *Human Relations,* May 1986, pp. 399–410; and Carrie Leana, "A Partial Test of Janis's Groupthink Model: The Effects of Group Cohesiveness and Leader Behavior on Decision Processes," *Journal of Management,* Spring 1985, pp. 5–18.

[40] Janis, *Groupthink.*

[41] Frederick W. Taylor, *The Principles of Scientific Management* (New York: Harper & Row, 1911).

Table 17.3

Prescriptions for
Prevention of
Groupthink

A. *Leader Prescriptions*
  1. Assign everyone the role of critical evaluator.
  2. Be impartial; do not state preferences.
  3. Assign the devil's advocate role to at least one group member.
  4. Use outside experts to challenge the group.

B. *Organizational Prescriptions*
  1. Set up several independent groups to study the same issue.
  2. Train managers and group leaders in groupthink prevention techniques.

C. *Individual Prescriptions*
  1. Be a critical thinker.
  2. Discuss the group deliberations with a trusted outsider and report back to the group.

D. *Process Prescriptions*
  1. Periodically break the group into subgroups to discuss the issues.
  2. Take time to study external factors.
  3. Hold second-chance meetings to rethink issues before making a commitment.

employees be allowed to participate in decisions in order to increase their ego-involvement, motivation, and satisfaction.[42] Numerous research studies have shown that whereas employees who seek responsibility and challenge on the job may find participation in the decision-making process both motivating and enriching, other employees may regard such participation as a waste of time and a management imposition.[43]

Whether employee participation in decision making is appropriate depends on the situation. The Vroom-Yetton-Jago model of leadership (discussed in Chapter 11) is one popular approach to determining the appropriate degree of employee participation.[44] The model includes decision styles that vary from autocratic (the leader makes the decision alone) to democratic (the group makes the decision with each member having an equal say). The choice of style rests on eight considerations, which are listed in Figure 11.5 and which concern the characteristics of the situation and the subordinates.

Participation in decision making is also related to organizational structure. For example, decentralization involves the delegation of some decision-making

---

[42] Rensis Likert, *New Patterns of Management* (New York: McGraw-Hill, 1961); and Chris Argyris, *Personality and Organization* (New York: Harper & Row, 1957).

[43] N. C. Morse and E. Reimer, "The Experimental Change of a Major Organizational Variable," *Journal of Abnormal and Social Psychology,* January 1956, pp. 120–129; and Lester Coch and John R. P. French, "Overcoming Resistance to Change," *Human Relations,* Vol. 1, 1948, pp. 512–532.

[44] Victor H. Vroom and Arthur G. Jago, *The New Leadership* (Englewood Cliffs, N.J.: Prentice-Hall, 1988).

authority throughout the organizational hierarchy. The more decentralized the organization, then, the more its employees tend to participate in decision making.

GROUP PROBLEM-SOLVING TECHNIQUES

A normally interacting group may have difficulty with any of several steps in the decision-making process. One common problem arises in the alternative generation phase: the search may be arbitrarily ended before all plausible alternatives have been identified. Several types of group interactions can have this effect. If members immediately express their reactions to the alternatives as they are first proposed, potential contributors may begin to censor their ideas to avoid embarrassing criticism from the group. Less confident group members, intimidated by members who have more experience, higher status, or more power, may also censor their ideas for fear of embarrassment or punishment. In addition, the leader of the group may limit idea generation by enforcing requirements having to do with time, appropriateness, cost, feasibility, and the like.

In order to improve the alternative generation process, managers may employ any of three techniques—brainstorming, the nominal group technique, or the Delphi technique—to stimulate the group's problem-solving capabilities.

Brainstorming

Brainstorming, a technique made popular in the 1950s, is most often used in the idea-generation phase of decision making and is intended to solve problems that are new to the organization and have major consequences. For example, suppose a bank faces the broad challenges of deregulation, changing economic conditions, and the possibility of interstate banking. Although it is currently the largest bank in the state, its major competitor is gaining ground. What can the bank do to stimulate deposits and to respond to the challenges it faces? Bank management might use brainstorming to approach these difficult decisions.

In brainstorming, the group convenes specifically to generate alternatives. The members present ideas and clarify them with brief explanations. Each idea is recorded in full view of all members, usually on a flip chart. To avoid self-censoring, no attempts to evaluate the ideas are allowed. Group members are encouraged to offer any ideas that occur to them, even those that seem too risky or impossible to implement. (The absence of such ideas, in fact, is evidence that the group members are engaging in self-censorship.) In a subsequent session, after the ideas have been recorded and distributed to members for review, the alternatives are evaluated.

The intent of brainstorming is to produce totally new ideas and solutions by stimulating the creativity of group members and encouraging them to build on the contributions of others. Brainstorming does not provide the resolution to the problem, an evaluation scheme, or the decision itself. Instead, it should produce a list of alternatives that is more innovative and comprehensive than one developed by the typically interacting group.

Nominal Group Technique

The **nominal group technique** (NGT) offers another means of improving group decision making. Whereas brainstorming is used primarily for alternative generation, NGT may be employed in other phases of decision making as well, such as identification of the problem and of appropriate criteria for evaluating alternatives. In NGT, a group of individuals is convened to address an issue. The issue is described to the group, and each individual writes a list of ideas; no discussion among the members is permitted. Following the five-to-ten-minute idea generation period, members take turns reporting their ideas, one at a time, to the group. The ideas are recorded on a flip chart, and members are encouraged to add to the list by building on the ideas of others. After all ideas have been presented, the members may discuss them and continue to build on them or proceed to the next phase. This part of the NGT process can also be carried out without a face-to-face meeting, for example, by mail, by telephone, or by computer. A meeting, however, helps members develop a group feeling and puts interpersonal pressure on the members to do their best in developing their lists.[45]

After the discussion, members privately vote on or rank the ideas or report their preferences in some other agreed-upon way. Reporting is private to reduce any feelings of intimidation that may exist within the group. After voting, the group may discuss the results and continue to generate and discuss ideas. The generation-discussion-vote cycle can continue until an appropriate decision is reached.

The nominal group technique has two principal advantages. It helps overcome the negative effects of power and status differences among group members, and it can be used in the problem exploration, alternative generation, and evaluation phases of decision making. Its primary disadvantage lies in its structured nature, which may limit creativity.

Delphi Technique

The **Delphi technique** was originally developed by the Rand Corporation as a method of systematically gathering the judgments of experts for use in developing forecasts. It is designed for groups that do not meet face to face. For instance, the product development manager of a major toy manufacturer

---

[45] See Bass, *Organizational Decision Making,* pp. 162–163, for more on nominal group technique.

might use the Delphi technique to probe the views of industry experts in order to forecast developments in the dynamic toy market.

The manager who desires the input of a group is the central figure in the process. After recruiting participants, the manager develops a questionnaire for them to complete. The questionnaire is relatively simple in that it contains straightforward questions dealing with the issue, trends in the area, new technological developments, and other factors the manager is interested in. The manager summarizes the responses and reports back to the experts with another questionnaire. This cycle may be repeated as many times as necessary to generate the information the manager needs.

The Delphi technique is useful when experts are physically dispersed, anonymity is desired, or the participants are known to have difficulty communicating with each other because of extreme differences of opinion.[46] This method also avoids the intimidation problems that may exist in decision-making groups. On the other hand, the technique eliminates the often fruitful results of direct interaction between group members.

CREATIVITY IN DECISION MAKING

A goal at 3M Company is to obtain 25 percent of sales from products that are less than five years old. To achieve this goal, 3M emloyees must constantly search for new ideas and breakthroughs that will keep the firm on the leading edge of its markets. Most companies consider this level of innovation impossible, but 3M frequently exceeds its goal through a combination of creativity and imagination.[47]

Creativity is an important dimension of individual behavior in organizations. Without creativity, organizations would never change, and their employees would stagnate. In this section, we define creativity and outline the creative process.

Definition of Creativity

Creativity is the process of developing original and imaginative views of situations. Creative behaviors include all of the following:

1. inventing a new product or service
2. inventing a new use for an existing product or service
3. solving a problem
4. resolving a dispute

---

[46] See Huber, *Managerial Decision Making,* pp. 205–212, for more on the Delphi technique.

[47] Stratford P. Sherman, "Eight Big Masters of Innovation," *Fortune,* October 15, 1984, pp. 66–84.

Unfortunately, creativity is not a mechanical process that can be turned on and off.[48] Some people are more creative than others, and no one is creative all the time.

The Creative Process

Despite its acknowledged importance, very little research has been done on creativity in organizational settings.[49] Nevertheless, a broad outline of the creative process, shown in Figure 17.9, has become generally accepted.[50]

PREPARATION The first step in the creative process is preparation. Preparation involves more than just sitting around waiting for something to happen; it is an active process that may require strenuous effort. Many writers, for example, travel extensively, seeking new experiences and talking to a variety of people. Education and training are also necessary for much creative work. An opera singer trains under a voice coach, a scientist spends long hours in a lab, and an actor takes drama classes, all preparing for creative activities. Creative decision makers study the issues surrounding a decision and participate extensively in group meetings where new ideas and alternative points of view abound, such as brainstorming meetings.

INCUBATION Incubation, the next step in the creative process, is a time for (often subconscious) reflection, thought, and consideration. During this time, a person shifts direct attention away from involvement in the problem—perhaps by literally "sleeping on it," or socializing with friends, or participating in some recreational activity such as hiking or mountain climbing. Ideas pertaining to the central issue are in the meantime maturing, and new ideas may be formulating in the person's mind. The desired outcome is something new—a novel idea, decision, or performance. Whatever form this burst of creativity takes, it is usually referred to as insight.

INSIGHT Insight is the breakthrough achieved as a result of preparation and incubation. Suppose a manager has been told by her boss that she must fire one of two key employees because of budget cuts. The manager wants to find a way to retain both employees. She prepares by analyzing all the budget information she can find and looking over the performance record of each employee. Then she goes to a movie with a friend to think things over. At some point—perhaps during intermission, over dessert after the movie, or while driving to work the next day—she suddenly recognizes a strategy for keeping both subordinates. This recognition is insight.

---

[48] Teresa M. Amabile, "The Social Psychology of Creativity: A Componential Conceptualization," *Journal of Personality and Social Psychology,* August 1983, pp. 357–376.

[49] Thomas Busse and Richard Mansfield, "Theories of the Creative Process: A Review and a Perspective," *Journal of Creative Behavior,* Vol. 4, 1980, pp. 91–103, 132.

[50] G. Wallas, *The Art of Thought* (New York: Harcourt Brace, 1926).

Figure 17.9

The Creative Process

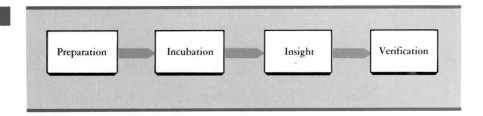

Preparation → Incubation → Insight → Verification

VERIFICATION   The last stage of the creative process is verification: determining whether an insight is valid. The manager just described, for example, may need to present her idea to her boss. If the boss approves the idea, and thus verifies it, it can be implemented. If the idea is not accepted, however, the manager may have to continue to search for new ideas and strategies. Similarly, scientists must test their breakthroughs in the laboratory, and authors must submit their work to editors for approval. Each of these checks represents a form of verification. Many verification systems have flaws, however. George Lucas took his script for *Star Wars* to several movie studios before he found one willing to produce the film.

SUMMARY OF KEY POINTS

Decision making is the process of choosing one alternative from several. The basic elements of decision making include a goal; alternative courses of action; potential outcomes of the alternatives, each with its own value relative to the goal; and a choice of one alternative based on evaluation of the outcomes. Information is available regarding the alternatives, outcomes, and values.

Programmed decisions are well-structured, recurring decisions made according to set decision rules. Nonprogrammed decisions involve nonroutine, poorly structured situations with unclear sources of information; they cannot be made according to existing decision rules.

Decision making may also be classified according to the information available. The classifications—certainty, risk and uncertainty—reflect the amount of information available regarding the outcomes of alternatives.

Decision making may be viewed as a completely rational process in which goals are established, a problem is identified, alternatives are generated and evaluated, a choice is made and implemented, and control is exercised. The behavioral model provides another view of the decision-making process. It is characterized by the use of procedures and rules of thumb, suboptimizing, and satisficing. The rational and behavioral views can be combined in a practical model. The Janis-Mann conflict model recognizes the personal anxiety individuals face when they make highly consequential decisions.

Escalation of commitment to an ineffective course of action occurs in many decision situations. It may be caused by psychological, social, ego, and organizational factors.

Both individuals and groups make decisions in organizations. An individual decision maker may be preferable when time is important, when the individual is especially capable, and when it is important to avoid the pitfalls of group decision making. Groups are appropriate for most problem-solving tasks, however, because groups generate more ideas and more interest.

Group decision making involves problems as well as benefits. One possible problem is group polarization, the shift of members' attitudes and opinions to a more extreme position following group discussion. Another difficulty is presented by groupthink, a mode of thinking in which the striving for unanimity overrides the critical appraisal of alternatives. Yet another concern involves employee participation in decision making. The appropriate degree of participation depends on the characteristics of the situation.

Brainstorming, the nominal group technique, and the Delphi technique are three methods for improving group decision making. These techniques reduce problems of poor communication, intimidation, and premature evaluation of ideas.

Creativity is the process of developing original and imaginative views of situations. The steps in the creative process are preparation, incubation, insight, and verification.

DISCUSSION QUESTIONS

1. Some people have argued that people, not organizations, make decisions and that the study of "organizational" decision making is therefore pointless. Do you agree with this argument? Why or why not?

2. What information did you use in deciding to enter the school that you are now attending?

3. When your alarm goes off each morning, you have a decision to make: whether to get up and go to school or work or stay in bed and sleep longer. Which type of decision is this: programmed or nonprogrammed? Why?

4. Describe a situation in which you experienced escalation of commitment to an ineffective course of action. What did you do about it? Do you wish you had handled it differently? Why or why not?

5. Describe at least three points in the decision-making process at which information plays an important role.

6. How does the role of information in the rational model of decision making differ from the role of information in the behavioral model?

7. Have you ever been a part of a group in which groupthink has occurred? Describe what happened in that group. How could you have prevented it from happening?

8. How are group polarization and groupthink similar? How are they different?

9. How do brainstorming, the nominal group technique, and the Delphi techniques differ?

10. Describe a recent decision situation in which you reached a state of hypervigilance. What could you have done to avoid the panic stage?

Gerald Ford, Chief Executive Officer

When Richard Nixon resigned on August 9, 1974, Gerald Ford, formerly Speaker of the House of Representatives, became president, taking on the nation's chief executive position in a difficult time. Many Americans had lost faith in the government as a result of the Watergate scandal, and they were suspicious of all political leaders. Some observers described Ford as a "eunuch,"* limited in popularity and power, haunted by his unpopular decision to pardon Nixon, without a real goal or agenda other than to try to bring the country back together.

Yet of all the presidents since Kennedy, Ford today may have the fewest virulent detractors. He did succeed in reuniting the country, at least to some extent, and many business leaders look to his time in office to learn how to handle an organization that must deal with a crisis in confidence or the resignation of top management. As the leader of the world's most powerful country and boss of about four million government employees, Gerald Ford did his job in the spotlight of public opinion, and people running much smaller organizations can learn from his decision-making processes.

Ford saw his own character as crucial to the reestablishment of faith in government leaders; his presidency depended on the public's belief that he was honest, strong, and a model of integrity. Of course, as an executive, Ford had to do much more than just set a good example. He told the *Harvard Business Review* that "I have spent my whole life trying to pull people together,"** and he used the team concept in running the country, as he had used it in sports and in the navy. Ford was not impressed with the popular notion that an executive's primary function is to provide a "vision" for the organization. He described himself as pragmatic: "My idea of vision is ensuring that we're making progress on a day-to-day basis."† He felt strongly that the chief executive must work with a trusted team and make decisions about who goes and who stays. Having picked the right people for the right jobs, however, the executive should delegate responsibility to those people and let them run their own operations.

---

* Fred Barnes, "The Ford Years," *The New Republic,* May 25, 1987, 8.
** "Gerald R. Ford: The Statesman as CEO," *Harvard Business Review,* September-October 1987, 78.
† Ibid, p. 78.

In practical terms, this meant that Ford gave great power to his cabinet officers and often became involved in their decisions only when the jurisdictions of two officials overlapped. He believed in making decisions quickly; "Indecision is often worse than wrong action,"†† he told interviewers. And he felt that presidential aides such as the White House chief of staff, should not try to act like the second-in-command or to speak for the president. Executives must provide a clear voice for their organization.

As a former congressman and a believer in delegating authority, Ford kept his door open to his staff at all times and encouraged debate. His chief of staff, Richard Cheney, recalls that the greatest weakness of this form of leadership appeared when someone brought up a "by the way" question that had not been thoroughly debated in Ford's office. When this happened, the president was liable to make quick decisions that sometimes left his staff groaning. In such cases, his advisers tried to blunt the effects of what they considered a bad decision by "staffing it out"—giving those working for the president time to investigate, argue, and if necessary modify the idea. If he was aware of this tactic, Ford probably approved of it, for it is a logical extension of a team philosophy and a delegation approach.

Case Questions

1. How was President Ford's open-door policy likely to affect his decisions?

2. Because Ford had not run for president, he had not made political promises to voters. Does his decision-making process seem to reflect a freedom from the responsibility that such promises entail?

Case Sources

"Hey, How About Sending Custer to the Little Bighorn?" *Across the Board,* January 1987, 29–33; "Gerald R. Ford: The Statesman as CEO," *Harvard Business Review,* September-October 1987, 77–81; Fred Barnes, "The Ford Years," *The New Republic,* May 25, 1987, 7–9.

<table>
<tr><td>Case 17.2</td><td></td></tr>
</table>

A Big Step for Peak Electronics

Lynda Murray, chief executive officer of Peak Electronics Corporation, faced a difficult decision. Her company was a leader in making parts for standard cassette and reel-to-reel tape recorders. Murray had watched with some misgivings as digital technology hit the market in the form of compact disc players, and she had to decide whether to lead Peak into the digital age. Even though digital tape players were encountering legal hurdles in the American

---

†† Ibid, p. 77.

market, they were starting to take hold in Japan and Europe. Was America—and Peak—ready for them?

Murray had plenty of help in making the decision. First she met with the company's marketing division. Everyone had an opinion. Some predicted that every audio component would be digital by the turn of the century, whereas others felt the popularity of even compact disc players was already waning. All agreed that they needed time to conduct surveys, gather data, and find out what the public really wanted and how much they would be willing to pay for it.

The people in research and development had a different approach. They seemed tired of making small improvements in a mature and perfected product. They had been reading technical material about digital tape, and they saw it as an exciting new technology that would give an innovative company a chance to make it big. Time was of the essence, they insisted. If Peak was to become an important supplier of parts for the new decks, it had to have the components ready. Delay would be fatal to the product.

A meeting of the vice presidents produced a scenario with which Murray was all too familiar. Years ago these executives had discovered that they could not out-argue each other in these meetings, but they had faith in their staffs' abilities to succeed where they had failed. Before Murray even walked into the room she knew what their recommendation would be—to create a committee of representatives from each division and let them thoroughly investigate all aspects of the decision. Such an approach had worked before, but Murray was not sure it was right this time.

Desperate to make the decision and get it out of her mind, Murray mentioned it to her fifteen-year-old son, who, it turned out, knew everything about digital tape. In fact, he told her, one of his friends—the richest one—had been holding off on buying a new tape deck in case he would be able to be on the cutting edge of digital recording. "It's gotta happen, Mom," her son said. "People want it."

Intellectually, Murray thought he was right. The past thirty years had shown that Americans had an insatiable appetitie for electronic gadgets and marvels. Quadraphonic sound and video discs were the only exceptions she could think of to the rule that if someone invented an improved way of reproducing images or sound, someone else would want to buy it.

But intuitively, Murray was not so sure. She had a bad feeling about the new technology. She felt that the record companies, who had lost the battle over normal taping, might get together with compact disc makers and audio equipment manufacturers to stop the digital technology from entering the American market. So far, no American company had invested substantially in the technology, so no one had an interest in funding the legal battle to remove the barriers to the new machines.

Exhausted, Murray went to bed. She hoped that somehow her subconscious mind would sort out all the important factors and she would wake up knowing the right decision.

Case Questions

1. What sources of information and opinion about the new technology seem most reliable? Which would you ignore?

2. If you were Murray, what would your next step be?

Purpose: This exercise will allow you to take part in a group decision and help you understand the difference between programmed and nonprogrammed decisions.

Format: You will be asked to perform a task individually and as a member of a group.

Procedure: *Part 1:* Listed below are ten typical organizational decisions. Your task is to determine whether they are programmed or nonprogrammed. Number your paper and write *P* for programmed or *N* for nonprogrammed next to each number.

Part II: Your instructor will divide the class into groups of four to seven people. All groups should have approximately the same number of members. Your task as a group is to make the determinations outlined in Part I. In arriving at your decisions, do not use such techniques as voting or negotiating ("OK, I'll give in on this one if you'll give in on that one.") The group should discuss the difference between programmed and nonprogrammed decisions and each decision situation until all members at least partially agree with the decision.

Decision List

1. Hiring a specialist for the research staff in a highly technical field.

2. Assigning workers to daily tasks.

3. Determining the size of the dividend to be paid to shareholders in the ninth consecutive year of strong earnings growth.

4. Deciding whether to approve an employee's absence for medical reasons as an officially excused absence.

5. Selecting the location for another branch of a 150-branch bank in a large city.

6. Approving the appointment of a new law school graduate to the corporate legal staff.

7. Making the annual assignment of graduate assistants to the faculty.

8. Approving the request of an employee to attend a local seminar in her special area of expertise.

9. Selecting the appropriate outlets for print advertisements for a new college textbook.
10. Determining the location for a new fast food restaurant in a small but growing town on the major interstate highway between two very large metropolitan areas.

Follow-up Questions

1. How much did group members disagree about which decisions were programmed and which were nonprogrammed?
2. What primary factors did the group discuss in making each decision?
3. Were there any differences between the members' individual lists and the group lists? Discuss the reasons for the similarities and differences.

C H A P T E R

18

Communication and Information Processing

Chapter Objectives

After reading this chapter, you should be able to

- ► define *communication* and discuss its purposes in organizations.
- ► summarize the basic processes and methods of communication.
- ► describe small group and organizational communication networks.

- ► identify and discuss several barriers to communication in organizations and how they can be overcome.
- ► discuss the impacts of computerized information processing and telecommunications in organizations.

ot so many years ago, a business person who needed to get a project report or a proposal across the country by Friday had to have it in the mail by Monday afternoon. Special delivery was about the only means available to speed delivery, and using it usually required special approval from a superior. As a rule, very little communication was considered important enough to receive that approval.

Then, along came the overnight express mail services. At first, people who received communications through these services must have thought the messages were very important for someone to have spent all that money to send them overnight. But before long, the cost began to seem insignificant compared with the importance of rapid delivery.

Now, yet another innovation—the fax machine—is revolutionizing communications. Why should a manager wait overnight to receive a memo from the Dallas office when she can have an exact copy of the original in her hands in Boston in a few minutes by using a fax machine? A fax machine uses telephone lines or high-speed digital lines to send a document electronically to a distant location, where it is reformed by another fax machine into an image on paper. Over 465,000 fax machines were sold in 1987, compared with less than half that number in 1986.[1] The cost can range from under $2,000 to over $12,000; however, the cost per piece of communication is said to be cheaper than that for overnight express mail service. Organizational communication has clearly taken another new turn.

This chapter focuses on the important processes of organizational communication and information processing. In Chapter 17, we pointed out the importance of information in the decision-making process. Here, we discuss why communication is important in organizations and how information is transferred and processed. We begin by explaining the elements that serve as a basis for the development of communication networks in organizations. Since communication is not always as efficient as it could be, we discuss several typical problems of organizational communication and methods by which communication can be improved. Finally, we discuss the potential effects of computerized information processing and telecommunications.

COMMUNICATION IN ORGANIZATIONS

Communication is the process by which two or more parties exchange information and share meaning.[2] It is an important process that has been studied from many perspectives. In this section, we provide an overview of the complex

---

[1] "It's a Fax, Fax, Fax, Fax World," *Business Week*, March 21, 1988, p. 136.

[2] Adapted from Charles A. O'Reilly, III, and Louis R. Pondy, "Organizational Communication," in Steven Kerr, Ed., *Organizational Behavior* (Columbus, Ohio: Grid, 1979), p. 121.

Table 18.1	Achieve coordinated action
Purposes of Organizational Communication	Share information — Organization goals — Task directions — Results of efforts (for example, performance appraisal) — Decision making Express feelings and emotions

and dynamic communication process by discussing what its purposes are and how the lack of information leads to uncertainty.

Purposes of Communication in Organizations

It is vital that communication occur between individuals and groups in all organizations. Some of the purposes of organizational communication are listed in Table 18.1. The primary purpose is to achieve coordinated action.[3] Just as the human nervous system responds to stimuli and coordinates responses by sending messages to the various parts of the body, communication coordinates the actions of the parts of an organization. Without communication, an organization would be merely a collection of individual workers attending to separate tasks. Organizational action would lack coordination and be oriented toward individual rather than organizational goals.

A second purpose of communication is information sharing. The most important information relates to organizational goals, which provide members with a sense of purpose and direction. Another information-sharing function of communication is the giving of specific task directions to individuals. Whereas information on organizational goals gives employees a sense of how their activities fit into the overall picture, task communication tells them what their job duties are and what they are not. Employees must also be provided information on the results of their efforts, as in performance appraisals.

Communication is essential to the decision-making process as well, as discussed in Chapter 17. Information, and thus information sharing, is needed to define problems, to generate and evaluate alternatives, to implement decisions, and to control and evaluate results.

Finally, communication expresses feelings and emotions. Organizational communication is far from a collection of facts and figures. People in organizations, like people anywhere else, often need to communicate such emotions as happiness, anger, displeasure, confidence, and fear.

Communication is an essential element of the manager's job. Managers must communicate with people at many different levels—those above, those

[3] Otis W. Baskin and Craig E. Aronoff, *Interpersonal Communication in Organizations* (Santa Monica, Calif.: Goodyear, 1980), p. 2.

A LOOK AT

RESEARCH

Communication, Job Satisfaction, and Job Performance

How do employees' reactions to the communication within their organization affect their work and their feelings about it? J. David Pincus investigated this question by analyzing questionnaires filled out by 327 nurses at an East Coast hospital. His results confirmed that organizational communication profoundly affects work performance and satisfaction, and identified a number of the most influential factors.

Pincus viewed satisfaction with organization communication in terms of nine dimensions: communication climate, supervisor communication, media quality (the clarity of written communication and the organization of meetings), horizontal communication, organizational integration (a measure of whether the information that employees receive is relevant to their jobs), personal feedback, organizational perspective, subordinate communication, and top management communication. As expected, he found that employees' perception of these dimensions affects both their feelings about their work and their job performance.

In general, the dimensions of communication satisfaction that involve relationships correlate positively with job satisfaction, whereas informational dimensions correlate more positively with job performance. Of the nine dimensions studied, three contributed most strongly to employee attitudes and performance: the communication climate, supervisor communication, and personal feedback. Pincus noted that all three involve both information transfer and personal interaction. The fact that these elements influence both satisfaction and performance indicates that a single communication strategy could improve both productivity and morale.

The study validated the common notion that employees' communication with their immediate supervisor affects their satisfaction and their performance, and it also revealed evidence that employees are affected by the way in which top management communicates with them. This suggests that top managers need to think about how their communication strategies might affect people with whom they seldom deal directly.

Pincus's research confirms what other studies have shown—that open, mutually trusting, two-way communication leads employees to be more satisfied with their jobs. It lends further support to the idea that business people need to be concerned not just with what they say, but with how, where, and when they say it.

Source: J. David Pincus, "Communication Satisfaction, Job Satisfaction, and Job Perform-ance," *Human Communication Research,* Spring 1986, 395–419.

below, and those at the same level in the hierarchy. A manager's communication with those who work for him or her may be the most important since all aspects of the work—training, task assignment, and performance appraisal—are delivered through communication. Managerial communication continues to be the focus of a great deal of research. One study is described in *A Look at Research.*

Communication is thus involved in many activities of the organization. Above all, it is the process through which individual and group activities and interactions are coordinated for the improvement of effectiveness.

Uncertainty and the Role of Information

As noted in Chapter 17, decisions must be made under uncertainty when little information is available on the outcomes of alternative actions. Uncertainty may also be defined in a more general sense as "the difference between the amount of information required to perform the task and the information already possessed by the organization."[4] The greater the uncertainty regarding the tasks of a work group, the more information the group needs to operate effectively and efficiently. In other words, when task uncertainty is high, the information processing of the individual or group responsible for the task must be correspondingly high to reduce the uncertainty.[5] If the uncertainty is not reduced, task performance will suffer.

Uncertainty occurs in organizations because of size, changes in the environment, and interdependencies between departments.[6] A large organization must coordinate a substantial number of people and tasks. This complexity inevitably creates uncertainty and thus requires more information processing. Changing customer demands, likes, and dislikes represent increasing uncertainty, to which the organization must respond with more innovative products and services. The need for a response or for more coordinated action among interdependent units requires managers to process more information, make decisions, and communicate them to other organization members.

THE BASIC COMMUNICATION PROCESS

Communication is a social process in which information is exchanged or a common understanding is established between two or more parties. The process is social because it involves two or more people. It is a two-way process and takes place over time rather than instantaneously. The communication process illustrated in Figure 18.1 is a loop between the source and the receiver.[7] Note

---

[4] Jay R. Galbraith, *Organization Design* (Reading, Mass.: Addison-Wesley, 1977), p. 36.

[5] See Joseph L. C. Cheng, "Paradigm Development and Communication in Scientific Settings: A Contingency Analysis," *Academy of Management Journal*, December 1984, pp. 870–877, for a study of task uncertainty and information processing in organizations.

[6] Richard L. Daft, *Organization Theory and Design*, 2nd ed. (St. Paul, Minn.: West, 1983), pp. 306–307.

[7] See Everett M. Rogers and Rekha Agarwala-Rogers, *Communication in Organizations* (New York: Free Press, 1976), for a brief review of the background and development of the source-message-channel-receiver model of communication.

Figure 18.1   Basic Communication Process

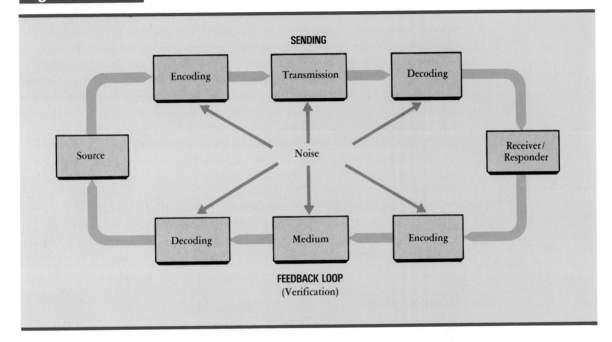

the importance of the feedback portion of the loop; upon receiving the message, the receiver responds with a message to the source to verify the communication. Each element of the basic communication process is important. If one part is faulty, the message may not be communicated as it was intended.

Source

The **source** is the individual, group, or organization interested in communicating something to another party. In group or organizational communication, an individual may send the message on behalf of the organization. The source is responsible for preparing the message, encoding it, and entering it into the transmission medium. In some cases, the receiver may choose the source of information,[8] as when a decision maker seeks information from trusted and knowledgeable individuals.

---

[8] Charles A. O'Reilly, III, "Variations in Decision Makers' Use of Information Sources: The Impact of Quality and Accessibility of Information," *Academy of Management Journal,* December 1982, pp. 756–771.

Encoding

Encoding is the process by which the message is translated from an idea or thought into symbols that can be transmitted. The symbols may be words and numbers, pictures, sounds, or physical gestures and movements. The source must encode the message in symbols that the receiver can decode properly— that is, the source and the receiver must attach the same meaning to the symbols. When we use the symbols of a common language, we assume that these symbols have the same meaning to everyone who uses them. Yet the inherent ambiguity of symbol systems can lead to decoding errors. In verbal communication, for example, some words have different meanings to different people.

Recently, travelers from New Mexico were looking for a parking place in upstate New York. These travelers found that the only available parking place was near a sign that said "no standing." The travelers assumed that the sign was intended for pedestrians and took the parking place. When they returned from shopping, they found a police officer putting a parking ticket on their car. To their dismay, they learned that in upstate New York "no standing" means "no parking." Sometimes, then, the use of a common language is not enough to avoid problems in communication.

Transmission

Transmission is the process through which the symbols that carry the message are sent to the receiver. The **medium** is the channel or path of transmission. The medium for face-to-face conversation is sound waves. The same conversation conducted over the telephone involves not only sound waves but also electrical impulses and the line that connects the two telephones. Communications media can range from an interpersonal medium, such as talking or touching, to a mass medium, such as a newspaper, a magazine, or a television broadcast. Different media have different capacities for carrying information—for example, a face-to-face conversation generally has more carrying capacity than a letter, since more than just words can be sent face-to-face.[9] In addition, the medium can help determine the effect the message has on the receiver. Calling a prospective client on the telephone to make a business proposal is a more personal approach than sending a letter, for example, and is likely to elicit a different response.

Decoding

Decoding is the process by which the receiver of the message interprets its meaning. The receiver uses knowledge and experience to interpret the symbols

---

[9] See Richard L. Daft and Robert H. Lengel, "Information Richness: A New Approach to Managerial Behavior and Organization Design," in Barry M. Staw and L. L. Cummings, Eds., *Research in Organizational Behavior* (Greenwich, Conn.: JAI Press, Vol. 6, 1984), pp. 191–233, for more on media and information richness.

of the message, and in some situations may consult an authority, such as a dictionary or a codebook. The meaning the receiver attaches to the symbols may be the same as or different from the meaning intended by the source. If the meanings are different, of course, communication breaks down, and a misunderstanding is likely to occur.

Receiver/Responder

The **receiver** of the message may be an individual, a group, or an individual acting as the representative of a group. Until the decoding step, the source has been active and the receiver passive. However, it is the receiver who decides whether to decode the message, to make an effort to understand it, and to respond. Moreover, the intended receiver may not get the message at all, whereas an unintended receiver may—depending on the medium and symbols used by the source and the attention level of potential receivers.

Feedback

The receiver's response to the message constitutes the feedback loop of the communication process. **Feedback** verifies the message: it tells the source whether the message has been received and understood. The feedback may be as simple as a phone call from the prospective client expressing interest in the business proposal or as complex as a written brief on a complicated point of law sent from an attorney to a judge.

Noise

Noise is any disturbance in the communication process that interferes with or distorts communication. Noise can be introduced at virtually any point in the process. The principal type, called **channel noise,** is associated with the medium.[10] Radio static and television "ghosts" are good examples of channel noise. When noise interferes in the encoding and decoding processes, poor encoding and decoding can result.

COMMUNICATION NETWORKS

Communication links individuals and groups in a social system. Initially, task-related communication links develop in an organization so that employees can get the information they need to do their jobs and coordinate their work with that of others in the system. Over a long period, these communication relationships become a sophisticated social system composed of both small group communication networks and a larger organizational network. These

---

[10] See Jerry C. Wofford, Edwin A. Gerloff, and Robert C. Cummins, *Organizational Communication* (New York: McGraw-Hill, 1977), for a discussion of channel noise.

networks serve to structure both the flow and the content of communication and to support the organizational structure.[11] The pattern and content of communication also support the culture, beliefs, and value systems that enable the organization to operate.[12]

Small Group Networks

To examine interpersonal communication in a small group, we can observe the patterns that emerge as the work of the group proceeds and information flows from some people in the group to others.[13] Four such patterns are shown in Figure 18.2; the lines identify the communication links most frequently used in the groups.

The **wheel network** describes a pattern in which information flows between the person at the end of each spoke and the person in the middle. Those on the ends of the spokes do not directly communicate with each other. The wheel network is a feature of the typical work group, where the primary communication occurs between the members and the group manager. In the **chain network,** each member communicates with the person above and below, except for the individuals on each end, who communicate with only one person. The chain network is typical of communication in a vertical hierarchy, in which most communication travels up and down the chain of command. Each person in the **circle network** communicates with the people on both sides but not with anyone else. The circle pattern is often found in task forces and committees. Finally, all the members of an **all-channel network** communicate with all the other members. The all-channel network is often found in informal groups that have no formal structure, leader, or task to accomplish.

In each of these types of small group networks, communication can be described in terms of four characteristics:

1. The *density* of the communication—the quantity of communication between members;
2. The *distance* between members—how far the message must travel through the network to reach the receiver.
3. The *relative freedom* of a member *to use different paths to communicate* with others—the ease with which members communicate with each other.

---

[11] See Daniel Katz and Robert L. Kahn, *The Social Psychology of Organizations*, 2nd ed. (New York: John Wiley, 1978), for more about the role of organizational communication networks.

[12] Maryan S. Schall, "A Communication-Rules Approach to Organizational Culture," *Administrative Science Quarterly*, December 1983, pp. 557–586.

[13] See Wofford, Gerloff, and Cummins, *Organizational Communication*, and Marvin E. Shaw, *Group Dynamics: The Psychology of Small Group Behavior*, 3rd ed. (New York: McGraw-Hill, 1981), pp. 150–161, for good discussions of small group communication networks and research on this subject.

Figure 18.2

Small Group
Communication
Networks

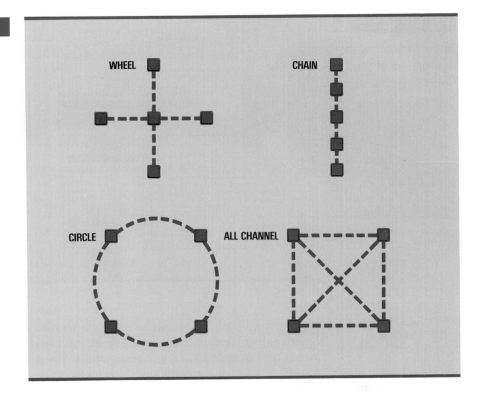

4. The *centrality of the positions* of members—how central or peripheral a member is to the group. Those members with central positions are usually more committed to the work of the group than those in less central positions.[14]

In a high-density situation or a situation in which communication must travel a great distance, there is a greater chance that the communication will be distorted by noise. Improvements in electronic communication technology (such as computer mail systems) are reducing this effect, however.

Position in the group refers to the place of one person in the communication network relative to the others in the network. A relatively central position provides an opportunity for the person to communicate with all of the other members. Thus, a member in a relatively central position can control information flow and may become a leader of the group. This leadership position is separate and distinct from the formal group structure, although a central person in a group may also emerge as a formal group leader over a long period of time.

---

[14] Peter R. Monge, Jane A. Edwards, and Kenneth K. Kirste, "Determinants of Communication Network Involvement: Connectedness and Integration," *Group & Organization Studies*, March 1983, pp. 83–112.

Figure 18.3

Factors Influencing the
Development of Small
Group Communication
Networks

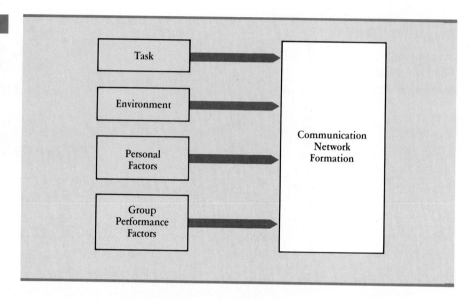

Communication networks form spontaneously and naturally as the interactions among workers continue. They are rarely permanent, since they change as the tasks, interactions, and memberships change. The patterns and characteristics of small group communication networks are determined by the factors summarized in Figure 18.3. The task is crucial in determining the pattern of the network. If the group's primary task is decision making, an all-channel network may develop to provide the information needed to evaluate all possible alternatives. If, however, the group's task mainly involves the sequential execution of individual tasks, a chain or wheel network is more likely, since communication among members may not be important to the completion of the tasks.

The environment (the type of room in which a group works or meets, the seating arrangement, the placement of chairs and tables, the geographical dispersion, and other aspects of the group's setting) can affect the frequency and types of interactions among members. For example, if most members work on the same floor of an office building, the members who work three floors down may be considered outsiders and may develop weaker communication ties to the group. They may even develop a separate communication network.

Personal factors also influence the development of the communication network. These include technical expertise, openness, speaking ability, and the degree to which members are acquainted with each other. For example, in a group concerned mainly with highly technical problems, the person with the most expertise may dominate the communication flow during a meeting.

The group performance factors that influence the communication network include composition, size, norms, and cohesiveness. For example, group norms in one organization may encourage open communication across different levels and functional units, whereas the norms in another organization may discourage such lateral and diagonal communication. These performance factors are discussed in Chapter 9.

Since the outcome of the group's efforts depends on the coordinated action of its members, the communication network strongly influences group effectiveness. Thus, to develop effective working relationships in the organization, managers need to make special efforts to manage the flow of information and the development of communication networks. The manager can, for example, arrange offices and work spaces to foster communication among certain employees. Managers may also attempt to involve members who typically contribute little during discussions by asking them direct questions, such as "What do you think, Tom?" or "Maria, please tell us how this problem is handled in your district." Methods such as the nominal group technique, discussed in Chapter 17, can also encourage participation.

Organizational Communication Networks

An organization chart shows reporting relationships from the line worker up to the chief executive officer of the firm. The lines of an organization chart also represent channels of communication through which information flows; yet communication may also follow paths that cross traditional reporting lines. Information moves not only from the top down—that is, from the chief executive officer to group members—but also upward from group members to the CEO.[15] In fact, a good flow of information to the CEO is an important determinant of success for the organization.[16]

Jimmy Treybig, founder and president of Tandem Computers, recently discovered the hard way that information needs to flow in both directions. Several years ago Tandem was very successful, and much of its success was attributed to its open and unstructured communications—communications exemplified by the Friday afternoon beer parties held on company grounds. At these Friday sessions, Treybig gave motivational speeches to rally employees around company goals and visited with employees on a very casual basis. Communication was casual and friendly, but the information flow about the company was usually top-down. Few other forms of communication were employed, and no organizational charts or signs of formal structure were allowed. Eventually, though, the company's revenues began to fall, and Treybig discovered that he also needed to hold regular business meetings with managers and department heads to get more job- and task-related information flowing

---

[15] Michael J. Glauser, "Upward Information Flow in Organizations: Review and Conceptual Analysis," *Human Relations*, August 1984, pp. 613–644.

[16] Irving S. Shapiro, "Managerial Communication: The View from the Inside," *California Management Review*, Fall 1984, pp. 157–172.

from the bottom up. After some tough decisions were made during regular staff meetings, the company seemed to get back on track.[17]

Downward communication generally provides directions, whereas upward communication provides feedback to top management. Co mmunication that flows horizontally or crosses traditional reporting lines is usually related to task performance and often travels faster than vertical communication, since it need not follow organizational protocols and procedures.

Organizational communication networks may diverge from reporting relationships as employees seek better information with which to do their jobs. Employees often find that the easiest way to get their jobs done or to obtain the necessary information is to go directly to employees in other departments rather than through the formal channels shown on the organization chart. Figure 18.4 shows a simple organization chart and the organization's real communication network. The communication network links the individuals who most frequently communicate with one another; the firm's CEO, for example, communicates most often with employee 5. (This does not mean that individuals not linked in the communication network never communicate—only that their communications are relatively infrequent.) Perhaps the CEO and the employee interact frequently through other activitites, such as church, outside organizations, or sporting events. Such interactions may lead to close friendships that carry over into business relationships. The figure also shows that the group managers do not have important roles in the communication network, contrary to common-sense expectations.

The roles that people play in organizational communication networks can be analyzed in terms of their contribution to the functioning of the network.[18] The most important roles are labeled in Figure 18.4, part B. A *gatekeeper* (employee 5) has a strategic position in the network that allows him or her to control information moving in either direction through a channel. A *liaison* (employee 15) serves as a bridge between groups, tying groups together and facilitating the communication flow needed to integrate group activities. Employee 13 performs the interesting function of *cosmopolite*, an employee who links the organization to the external environment by, for instance, attending conventions and trade shows, keeping up with outside technological innovations, and having more frequent contact with sources outside the organization. This person may also be an *opinion leader* in the group. Finally, the *isolate* (employee 3) and the *isolated dyad* (employees 2 and 9) tend to do their work alone and to interact and communicate little with others.

Each of these roles and functions plays an important part in the overall functioning of the communication network and in the organization as a whole.

---

[17] Brian O'Reilly, "How Jimmy Treybig Turned Tough," *Fortune*, May 25, 1987, pp. 102–104.

[18] See R. Wayne Pace, *Organizational Communication: Foundations for Human Resource Development* (Englewood Cliffs, N.J.: Prentice Hall, 1983), for more on the development of communication networks.

Figure 18.4   Comparison of an Organization Chart and the Organization's Communication Network

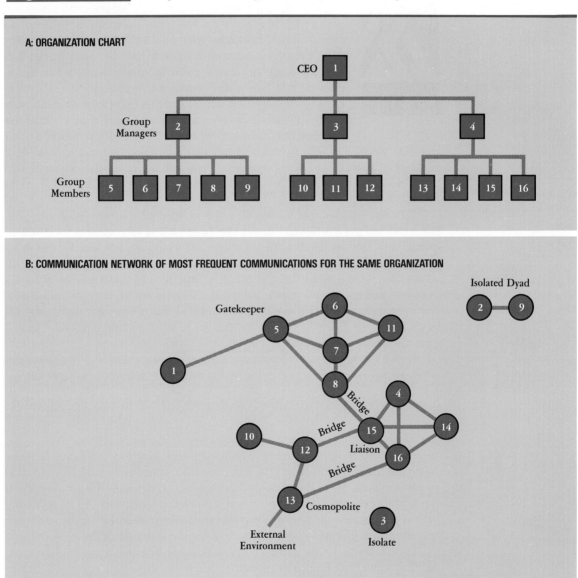

A: ORGANIZATION CHART

CEO

Group Managers

Group Members

B: COMMUNICATION NETWORK OF MOST FREQUENT COMMUNICATIONS FOR THE SAME ORGANIZATION

Isolated Dyad

Gatekeeper

Bridge

Bridge

Liaison

Bridge

Cosmopolite

External Environment

Isolate

Can Communication Revive GM?

General Motors Corp. is one of the world's largest and best-known corporations, with over 800,000 employees and $100 billion in annual sales. Yet recently the automaking giant has watched sales slump and has been attacked for being too big and too slow to compete in worldwide "car wars." Some observers, both inside and outside the company, believe that communication is both the root of and the most likely solution to many of GM's problems.

A typical complaint is that GM executives do not listen—that they invest in technology without asking the people who are going to use it whether they have suggestions about how best to use it. A United Auto Workers executive says, "I'm pleased with GM's investment in technology, but perhaps it hasn't made an equal investment in people."* An executive who does business with GM echoes these sentiments when talking about GM's much-heralded Saturn project: "GM overemphasizes technology and forgets the workers."**

GM's most outspoken critic has been H. Ross Perot, who built Electronic Data Systems Corp. from scratch and sold it to General Motors in 1984 for $2.5 billion. Perot refuses to blame what the company itself calls "the frozen middle" (managers and supervisors), and instead blames its top managers, who, he says, refuse to listen and refuse to change. He agrees with other critics that GM will not recover from its slump until it starts making better use of its human resources by listening to workers, treating them with respect, and ending the friction between labor and management. Perot's parting from GM may provide the perfect symbol of what is wrong with the company: GM bought him out for $750 million on the condition that he would not criticize publically. Again, it seems, GM did not want to listen.

Some at GM recognize the communication problems and have embarked on an extensive plan to increase two-way communication throughout the company, to keep employees better informed

Understanding these roles can help both managers and group members facilitate communication. For instance, the manager who wants to be sure that the CEO receives certain information is well advised to go through the gatekeeper. If the employee who has the technical knowledge necessary for a particular project is an isolate, the manager can take special steps to integrate the employee into the communication network, at least for the duration of the project.

Recent research has indicated some possible negative impacts of communication networks. Employee turnover has been shown to occur in clusters related to employee communication networks.[19] That is, employees who communicate regularly in a network may share feelings about the organization,

---

[19] David Krackhardt and Lyman W. Porter, "The Snowball Effect: Turnover Embedded in Communication Networks," *Journal of Applied Psychology*, February 1986, pp. 50–55.

about management decisions and the reasons for them, and to go as far as possible toward open communication. The job is tremendous, since General Motors already has a least 350 publications in its North American operations alone, and recent reorganization has given more autonomy to local units.

Besides sending all employees the publications produced by corporate headquarters, GM has been promoting workshops for public speaking and advanced communication, providing videotapes of confidential management meetings, and giving all units satellite links to company headquarters to try to establish two-way televised discussions between corporate executives and managers in the field. A new publication, *GM Management Journal* is, according to its director, "a means of bringing our total 60,000 managers into a more informed relationship with corporate thinking and strategy."† It deals with tough issues such as plant closings and executive bonuses, which were previously off-limits for middle managers.

GM's future success may well hinge on such efforts more than on increased plant automation or stylish new models. Although the new measures seem certain to improve the company's effectiveness at broadcasting its message, GM's critics will be watching to see whether the changes also lead people at the top to do more listening.

Sources: Eric Gelman, "GM Boots Perot," *Newsweek,* December 15, 1986, 56–62; Bruce H. Goodsite, "General Motors Attacks Its Frozen Middle," *IABC Communication World,* October 1987, 20–23; Brian S. Moskal, "Is GM Getting a Bum Rap?" *Industry Week,* January 12, 1987, 41–44.

* Brian S. Moskal, "Is GM Getting a Bum Rap?" *Industry Week*, January 12, 1987, 42.
** Ibid.
† Bruce H. Goodsite, "General Motors Attacks Its Frozen Middle," *IABC Communication World,* October 1987, 23.

and thus influence each others' intentions to stay or quit. Communication networks, therefore, may have both positive and negative consequences.

As is discussed in earlier chapters, a primary function of organizational structure is to coordinate the activities of many people doing specialized tasks. Communication networks in organizations provide this much-needed integration.[20] In fact, in some ways, communication patterns influence the way an organization is structured.[21] Some companies are finding that the need for better communication forces them to create smaller divisions. The fewer managerial levels and improved team spirit of these divisions tend to enhance

---

[20] Monge, Edwards, and Kirste, "Determinants of Communication Network Involvement."

[21] Karl E. Weick and Larry D. Browning, "Argument and Narration in Organizational Communication," *Journal of Management,* Summer 1986, pp. 243–259.

communication flows.[22] Whatever the size of organizations, however, organizational performance is affected most by the quality of communication within work groups.[23] General Motors has recently initiated a major effort to improve communications throughout the organization. See *Management in Action*.

METHODS OF COMMUNICATION

The three primary methods of communicating in organizations are written, oral, and nonverbal communication. Quite often, the methods are combined. Considerations that affect the choice of method include the audience (whether it is physically present), the nature of the message (its urgency or secrecy), and the costs of transmission. Table 18.2 lists various forms each method can take.

Written Communication

Typical organizations produce a great deal of written communication of many kinds. A *letter* is a formal means of communicating with an individual, generally someone outside the organization. Probably the most common form of written communication in organizations is the *office memorandum,* or *memo.* Memos are usually addressed to a person or group inside the organization.[24] They tend to deal with a single topic and are more impersonal (as they are often destined to more than one person) but less formal than a letter.

Other common forms of written communication include reports, manuals, and forms. *Reports* generally summarize the progress or results of a project and often provide information to be used in decision making. *Manuals* have various functions in organizations. Instruction manuals tell employees how to operate machines; policy and procedures manuals inform them of organizational rules; and operations manuals describe how to perform tasks and respond to work-related problems. *Forms* are standardized documents on which to report information. As such, they represent attempts to make communication more efficient and information more accessible. A performance appraisal form is an example.

Oral Communication

The most prevalent form of organizational communication is oral. Oral communication takes place everywhere—in informal conversations, in the process of doing work, in meetings of groups and task forces, and in formal speeches

---

[22] "Small Is Beautiful Now in Manufacturing," *Business Week*, October 22, 1984, pp. 152–156.

[23] Robert A. Snyder and James H. Morris, "Organizational Communication and Performance," *Journal of Applied Psychology*, August 1984, pp. 461–465.

[24] William J. Seiler, E. Scott Baudhuin, and L. David Shuelke, *Communication in Business and Professional Organizations* (Reading, Mass.: Addison-Wesley, 1982).

Methods	Examples
Written	Letters, memos, reports, manuals, forms
Oral	Informal conversations, group discussions, task-related exchanges, formal speeches
Nonverbal	Human elements; facial expression, body language Environmental elements: office design, building architecture

Table 18.2

Methods of
Communication in
Organizations

and presentations. This form of communication is particularly powerful because it includes not only speakers' words but also their changes in tone, pitch, speed, and volume. As listeners, people use all of these cues to understand oral messages. Moreover, receivers interpret oral messages in the context of previous communications and, perhaps, the reactions of other receivers.

Nonverbal Communication

Nonverbal communication includes all the elements associated with human communication that are not expressed orally or in writing. Sometimes, it conveys more meaning than words. Human elements include facial expressions and physical movements, both conscious and unconscious. Facial expressions have been categorized as (1) interest-excitement, (2) enjoyment-joy, (3) surprise-startle, (4) distress-anguish, (5) fear-terror, (6) shame-humiliation, (7) contempt-disgust, and (8) anger-rage.[25] The eyes are the most expressive component of the face.

Physical movements and "body language" are also highly expressive human elements. Body language includes both actual movement and body positions during communication. The handshake is a common form of body language. Other examples include making eye contact that expresses a willingness to communicate; sitting on the edge of a chair, which may indicate nervousness or anxiety; and sitting back with the arms folded, which may mean an unwillingness to continue the discussion.

Environmental elements, such as buildings, office space, and furniture, can also convey messages. A large office, expensive draperies, plush carpeting, and elegant furniture can combine to remind employees or visitors that they are in the office of the president and chief executive officer of the firm. On the other hand, the small metal desk set in the middle of the shop floor accurately communicates the organizational rank of a first-line supervisor. Thus, office arrangements convey status, power, and prestige and create an atmosphere for doing business. The physical setting can also be instrumental in the development

[25] Silvan S. Tompkins and Robert McCarter, "What and Where Are the Primary Affects? Some Evidence for a Theory," *Perceptual and Motor Skills*, February 1964, pp. 119–158.

of communication networks, because a centrally located person can more easily control the flow of task-related information.[26]

MANAGING ORGANIZATIONAL COMMUNICATION

As simple as the process of communication may seem, messages are not always understood. The degree of correspondence between the message intended by the source and the message understood by the receiver is called **communication fidelity**.[27] Fidelity can be diminished anywhere in the communication process, from the source to the feedback. Moreover, organizations may have characteristics that impede the flow of information. Figure 18.5 summarizes the most common types of breakdowns and barriers in organizational communication. Note how the problems relate to the parts of the basic communication process.

Improving the Communication Process

An understanding of potential problems is essential to the improvement of organizational communication. Using the basic communication process, we can identify several ways to overcome typical problems.

SOURCE   The source may intentionally withhold or filter information on the assumption that the receiver does not need it to understand the communication. Withholding information, however, may render the message meaningless or cause an erroneous interpretation. For example, during a performance appraisal interview a manager may not tell the employee all of the sources of information used to make the evaluation, thinking that the employee does not need to know. If the employee were to know, however, he or she might be able to explain certain behaviors or otherwise alter the manager's perspective of the evaluation, and thereby make it more accurate. Selective filtering may cause a breakdown in communication that cannot be repaired, even with good follow-up communication.[28]

To avoid filtering, the communicator needs to understand why it occurs. Filtering can result from lack of understanding of the receiver's position, a need on the sender's part to protect his or her own power by limiting the receiver's access to information, or doubts about what the receiver might do with the information. The sender's primary concern, however, should be the message. In essence, the sender must determine exactly what message she or

---

[26] Robert T. Keller and Winfred E. Holland, "Communicators and Innovators in Research and Development Organizations," *Academy of Management Journal*, December 1983, pp. 742–749.

[27] Pace, *Organizational Communication*.

[28] Losana E. Boyd, "Why 'Talking It Out' Almost Never Works Out," *Nation's Business*, November 1984, pp. 53–54.

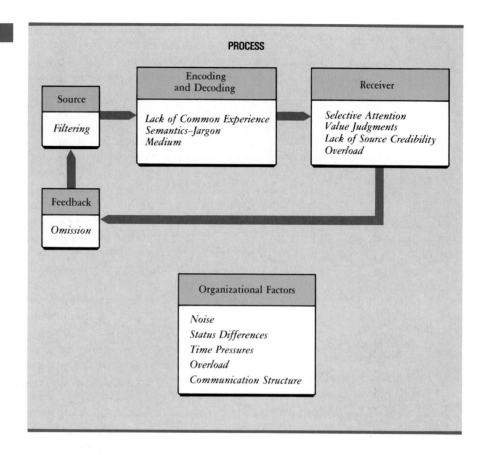

Figure 18.5

Communication Problems in Organizations

PROCESS

Source

Filtering

Encoding and Decoding

Lack of Common Experience
Semantics–Jargon
Medium

Receiver

Selective Attention
Value Judgments
Lack of Source Credibility
Overload

Feedback

Omission

Organizational Factors

Noise
Status Differences
Time Pressures
Overload
Communication Structure

he wants the receiver to understand, send the receiver enough information to understand the message but not enough to create an overload, and trust the receiver to use the information properly.

ENCODING AND DECODING   Encoding and decoding problems occur as the message is translated into or from the symbols used in transmission. Such problems can relate to the meaning of the symbols or to the transmission itself. As shown in Figure 18.5, encoding and decoding problems include lack of common experience between source and receiver, problems related to semantics and the use of jargon, and difficulties with the medium.

Clearly, the source and the receiver must share a common experience with the symbols that express the message if they are to encode and decode them in exactly the same way. People who speak different languages experience problems in this category. But even people who speak the same language can misunderstand each other, as previously stated.

Semantics is the study of language forms, and semantic problems occur when people attribute different meanings to the same words or language forms.

For example, when discussing a problem employee, the division head may tell her assistant, "We need to get rid of this problem." The division head may have meant that the employee should be scheduled for more training or transferred to another division. However, the assistant may interpret the statement differently and fire the problem employee.

The specialized or technical language of a trade, field, profession, or social group is called *jargon*. Jargon may be a hybrid of standard language and the specialized language of a group. The use of jargon makes communication within a close group of colleagues more efficient and meaningful, but outside the group, it has the opposite effect. Sometimes a source who is comfortable with jargon uses it unknowingly to communicate with receivers who do not understand it, thus causing a communication breakdown. In other cases, the source may use jargon intentionally to obscure meaning or to show outsiders that he or she belongs to the group that uses the language.

The use of jargon is acceptable if the receiver is familiar with it. Otherwise, it should be avoided. Repeating a message that contains jargon in clearer terms should help the receiver to understand the message. In general, the source and the receiver should clarify the set of symbols to be used before they communicate. The receiver can also ask frequent questions and, if necessary, ask the source to repeat all or part of the message.

The source must send the message through a medium appropriate to the message itself and the intended receiver. For example, a commercial run on an AM radio station will not have its intended effect if the people in the desired market segment listen only to FM radio. The source can change the medium of transmission, use multiple media, or increase the volume (loudness) to increase the likelihood that the message will be received. The receiver can monitor several media regularly to maximize her or his receiving capacity.

RECEIVER   Several communication problems originate in the receiver, including problems with **selective attention, value judgments, source credibility,** and **overload.** Selective attention exists when the receiver attends to only selected parts of a message—a frequent occurrence with oral communication. For example, in a college class some students may hear only part of the professor's lecture as their minds wander to other topics. To focus receivers' attention on the message, senders often engage in attention-getting behaviors, such as varying the volume, repeating the message, and offering rewards.

Value judgments involve the degree to which a message reinforces or challenges the receiver's basic personal beliefs. If a message reinforces the receiver's beliefs, he or she may pay close attention and believe it completely, without examination. On the other hand, if the message challenges those beliefs, the receiver may entirely discount it. Thus, if a firm's sales manager had predicted that the demand for new baby-care products will increase substantially over the next two years, he may ignore reports that the birth rate is declining.

The receiver may also judge the credibility of the source of the message. If the source is perceived to be an expert in the field, the listener may pay close attention to the message and believe it. Conversely, if the receiver has little respect for the source, she or he may disregard the message. The receiver considers both the message and the source in making value judgments and determining credibility. An expert in nuclear physics may be viewed as a credible source in building a nuclear power plant and yet be disregarded, perhaps rightly, on evaluating the birth rate. This is one reason that a trial lawyer asks an expert witness about his or her education and experience at the beginning of testimony—to establish credibility.

A receiver experiencing communication overload is receiving more information than she or he can process. In organizations, this can happen very easily—a receiver can be bombarded with computer-generated reports and messages from superiors, peers, and sources outside the organization. Unable to take in all the messages, decode them, understand them, and act on them, the receiver may use selective attention and value judgments to focus on the messages that seem most important. Although this type of selective attention is necessary for survival in an information-glutted environment, it may mean that vital information is lost or overlooked.

FEEDBACK   The purpose of feedback is **verification;** the receiver sends a message to the source indicating receipt of the message and the degree to which it was understood. The lack of feedback can cause at least two problems. First, the source may need to send another message that depends on the response to the first; if no feedback is received, the source may not send the second message or may be forced to send the original message again. Second, the receiver may act on the unverified message. If the message was misunderstood, the resulting act may be inappropriate.

Because feedback is so important, the source must actively seek it, and the receiver must supply it. Often it is appropriate for the receiver to repeat the original message as an introduction to the response, although the medium or symbols used may be different. Nonverbal cues can provide instantaneous feedback. These include body language and facial expressions, such as anger or disbelief.[29]

The source needs to be concerned with the message, the symbols, the medium, and the feedback from the receiver. Of course, the receiver is concerned with these things, too, but from a different point of view. In general, the receiver needs to be source-oriented, just as the source needs to be receiver-oriented. Table 18.3 gives specific suggestions for improving the communication process.

---

[29] Snyder and Morris, "Organizational Communication and Performance."

Table 18.3	*Focus*	Source		Receiver	
		Question	*Corrective Action*	*Question*	*Corrective Action*
Improving the Communication Process	Message	What idea or thought are you trying to get across?	Give more information. Give less information. Give entire message.	What idea or thought does the sender want you to understand?	Listen carefully to the entire message, not just part of it.
	Symbols	Does the receiver use the same symbols, words, jargon?	Say it another way. Employ repetition. Use receiver's language or jargon. Before sending, clarify symbols to be used.	What symbols are being used—for example, foreign language, technical jargon?	Clarify symbols before communication begins. Ask questions. Ask sender to repeat message.
	Medium	Is this a channel that the receiver monitors regularly? Sometimes? Never?	Use multiple media. Change medium. Increase volume (loudness).	What medium or media is the sender using?	Monitor several media.
	Feedback	What is the receiver's reaction to your message?	Pay attention to the feedback, especially nonverbal cues. Ask questions.	Did you correctly interpret the message?	Verify receipt of message. Repeat message.

Improving Organizational Factors in Communication

Organizational factors that can create communication breakdowns or barriers include noise, status differences, time pressures, and overload. As previously stated, disturbances anywhere in the organization can distort or interrupt meaningful communication. Thus, the noise created by a rumored takeover can disrupt the orderly flow of task-related information. Status differences between source and receiver can cause some of the communication problems just discussed. For example, a firm's chief executive officer may pay little attention to communications from employees far lower in the organization chart, and employees may pay little attention to communications from the CEO. Both are instances of selective attention prompted by the organization's status system.

Time pressures and communication overload are also detrimental to communication. When the receiver is not allowed enough time to understand incoming messages, or when there are too many messages, he or she may misunderstand or ignore some of them.

Effective organizational communication provides the right information to the right person at the right time and in the right form. Table 18.4 summarizes how this goal can be achieved.

REDUCE NOISE   Noise is a primary barrier to effective organizational communication. A common form of noise is the rumor grapevine, an informal

Table 18.4

Guidelines for
Improving
Organizational Factors
in Communication

Organizational Goal: Provide the right information to the right person at the right time
and in the right form

- Reduce noise.
  Use and monitor the grapevine.

- Foster informal communication.
  Develop mutual trust.

- Create a balanced information system.

system of communication that coexists with the formal system.[30] The grapevine usually transmits information faster than official channels. Because the accuracy of this information is often quite poor, however, the grapevine can distort organizational communication. Management can reduce the effects of the distortion by using the grapevine as an additional channel for the dissemination of information and by constantly monitoring it for accuracy.

FOSTER INFORMAL COMMUNICATION   Thomas J. Peters and Robert H. Waterman have described communication in excellent companies as "a vast network of informal, open communications."[31] Informal communication fosters mutual trust, which minimizes the effects of status differences. It also allows information to be communicated when needed rather than when the formal information system allows it to emerge. Peters and Waterman further describe communication in effective companies as chaotic and intense, supported by the reward structure and the physical arrangement of the facilities. This means that the performance appraisal and reward system, offices, meeting rooms, and work areas are designed to encourage frequent, unscheduled, and unstructured communication throughout the organization.

DEVELOP A BALANCED INFORMATION SYSTEM   Many large organizations have developed elaborate formal information systems to cope with the potential problems of information overload and time pressures. In many cases, however, the systems have created problems rather than solving them. Often, they produce more information than managers and decision makers can comprehend and use in their jobs. They also often use only formal communication channels; various informal lines of communication are ignored. Furthermore, the systems frequently provide whatever information the computer is set up to provide—information that may not apply to the most pressing problem at hand. The result of all these drawbacks is a loss of communication effectiveness.

---

[30] Keith Davis and John W. Newstrom, *Human Behavior at Work: Organizational Behavior*, 7th ed. (New York: McGraw-Hill, 1985), pp. 314–323.

[31] Thomas J. Peters and Robert H. Waterman, Jr., *In Search of Excellence: Lessons from America's Best-Run Companies* (New York: Harper & Row, 1982), p. 121.

International Perspective

Communicating Overseas

The importance of dealing with businesspeople outside the United States increases every year, as more American companies expand their sales and operations overseas. Successful communication with their foreign counterparts is obviously crucial for employees of such companies, yet a history of communicating well with other Americans does not guarantee that an American businessperson will be well received in another country. Besides the obvious language and cultural differences, Americans must cope with subtle differences in the ways in which people from other countries do business.

To increase the chances that an interaction with foreign businesspeople will be successful, international communication experts recommend

— preparing. Americans have a reputation for thinking that what works in Peoria will work anywhere. Businesspeople who are going abroad need to study the customs, history, and culture of their host country thoroughly so they do not become victims of such thinking.

— avoiding stereotyping. Assuming that all Germans are punctual and efficient or that all French people are arrogant will not make an American popular.

—understanding differences and emphasizing similarities. An American will get nowhere by constantly pointing out that "we don't do it that way in Philadelphia."

— being patient. Bureaucracies can be even more frustrating than usual to someone unfamiliar with the language and the culture.

Organizations need to balance information load and information-processing capabilities.[32] In other words, they must take care not to generate more information than people can handle. It is useless to produce sophisticated statistical reports that managers have no time to read. Furthermore, the new technologies that are making more information available to managers and decision makers must be unified to produce usable information.[33] Information production, storage, and processing capabilities must be compatible with each other and, just as important, with the needs of the organization. Official communication with organizations in Europe can also be improved by many of the same factors. For more specific examples, see *International Perspective*.

Some companies—for example, General Electric Co., McDonnell Douglas Corp., Anheuser-Busch Inc., and McDonald's—have recently formalized an

---

[32] Charles A. O'Reilly, "Individual and Information Overload in Organizations: Is More Necessarily Better?" *Academy of Management Journal*, December 1980, pp. 684–696.

[33] James L. McKenney and F. Warren McFarlan, "The Information Archipelago—Maps and Bridges," *Harvard Business Review*, September–October 1982, pp. 109–119.

— keeping a sense of humor. An American working abroad for the first time will make mistakes and encounter situations that seem absurd. Laughter is a healthier response to such situations than anger or irritation.

— being sensitive to differences in time and space perceptions. People around the world differ vastly in their sense of punctuality and in their feeling for the appropriate distance between participants in a conversation.

— recognizing rank and status. In China the decision maker may seem to be just another member of the group, whereas in Japan seating around a table can tell an informed viewer a lot about individuals' relative status.

— adjusting to differences in body language. An American may interpret a Japanese nod to mean yes, when actually it means no.

— avoiding condescension. Businesspeople may feel that they have been sent to "the boonies," but if they give that impression to their hosts, meetings will not go well.

— understanding names. Chu Heshu should be addressed as Madame Chu; Jorge Rojas Neto should not be addressed as Mr. Neto, because *Neto* means "the third."

— learning status symbols. People communicate with things as well as with words. Americans need to recognize, and in some cases imitate, the use of symbols in their host country.

Sources: Clive Bashleigh, "Confessions of a Far-Flung Communicator," *IABC Communication World*, October 1986, 14–15; Roger Haywood, "You Can't Just Shout Louder to Be Heard in Europe," *IABC Communication World*, January 1987, 29–35; Sondra Snowdon, "How to Gain the Global Edge," *IABC Communication World*, August 1986, 28–30.

upward communication system that uses a corporate "ombudsman."[34] This position is usually held by a highly placed executive that is available outside the formal chain of command to hear employees' complaints. The system provides an opportunity for disgruntled employees to complain without fear of losing their jobs and may help some companies achieve a balanced communication system.

ELECTRONIC INFORMATION PROCESSING AND TELECOMMUNICATIONS

Changes in the workplace are occurring at an astonishing rate. Many are based on new technologies—computerized information-processing systems, new types of telecommunication systems, and combinations of these. Managers can now

---

[34] Michael Brody, "Listen to Your Whistleblower," *Fortune*, November 24, 1986, pp. 77–78.

send and receive memos and other types of communication on their computer terminals. In addition, a whole new industry is developing in the long-distance transmission of data between computers.[35]

At one large university a computer system connects the president with all the vice presidents and deans. Each can enter a note, memo, or letter into the system and send it to any or all of the others. The president reports that the system has resulted in faster communication and much shorter memos. A teleconferencing system enables the president to conduct conference calls with the presidents and staffs of other universities across the country. Besides saving days of travel and thousands of dollars in expenses, the teleconference can accomplish more than a face-to-face meeting because the participants have access to all their information resources during the meeting. Computer conferencing is now being used in many business applications, including market and opinion research studies.[36]

These types of systems are becoming commonplace in organizations. The "office of the future" is already here. The fax systems discussed earlier are typical of the advance of electronic communication systems in use today. More than $600 million were spent on office fax systems in 1987.[37] Technological advances and their widespread adoption have created the so-called electronic office—that is, an integrated communication-information office system.[38] The electronic office links managers, clerical workers, professional workers, and sales personnel in a communication network that uses a combination of computerized data, storage, retrieval, and transmission systems.

One such system is the totally computerized Human Resource Information System (HRIS) recently put into use by the Rorer Group, the world's twenty-sixth largest manufacturer of pharmaceuticals.[39] This system manages information on all of the company's 8,000 employees, including name, position, education, employment history, and pay. Through a network of personal computers, every properly authorized office in the company can gain access to the information on the system. That means HRIS data are available any time they are needed—not only to computer experts who know the system but to authorized managers throughout the company. Such systems make information available to aid decision making on a daily basis.

The effects of automated office systems on the communication system and the management of the organization are only now being studied. Research

---

[35] "Ma Blue: IBM's Move into Communications," *Fortune*, October 15, 1984, p. 52.

[36] Starr Roxanne Hiltz, "Computerized Conferencing for Opinion Research," *Public Opinion Quarterly*, Winter 1979, pp. 562–571.

[37] "It's A Fax, Fax, Fax, Fax World."

[38] D. W. Conrath, C. A. Higgins, C. S. Tachenkarg, and W. M. Wright, "The Electronic Office and Organizational Behavior—Measuring Office Activities," *Computer Networks*, December 1981, pp. 401–410.

[39] Tony Pompili, "Rapid Expansion Smoothed with LAN Personnel System," *PC Week*, August 25, 1987, pp. C1, C9.

conducted among office workers using a new electronic office system indicated that attitudes toward the system were generally favorable. The users reported improvements in "communications, information access, preparation of written material, and worker collaboration."[40] On the other hand, reduction of face-to-face meetings may depersonalize the office. Some individuals are also concerned that companies are installing electronic systems with little concern for the social structures of the office.[41] As departments adopt computerized information systems, activities of work groups throughout the organization are likely to become more interdependent, which may alter power relationships among the groups.[42] Most employees quickly learn the system of power, politics, authority, and responsibility in an office. A radical change in work and personal relationships caused by new office technology may disrupt normal ways of accomplishing tasks, thereby reducing productivity. Other potential problems include information overload, the loss of records in a "paperless" office, and the dehumanizing effects of electronic equipment.

In effect, new information-processing and transmission technologies mean new media, symbols, message transmission methods, and networks for organizational communication. These technologies must be more fully integrated with each other before their benefits can be fully realized.[43] It is clear that these will affect the daily activities of individual workers as well as the communication networks and social systems within organizations, but the extent of their effects is not yet apparent. New information-processing technologies that provide more—though not necessarily better—information may place even more responsibility on the manager who must use the information properly.[44]

SUMMARY OF KEY POINTS

Communication and information are involved in all activities of the organization. Communication is the process by which two parties exchange information and share meaning. The difference between the amount of information required to perform a task and the information already possessed by the organization is known as uncertainty. The greater the uncertainty regarding the tasks of the

---

[40] Don Tapscott, "Investigating the Electronic Office," *Datamation*, March 1982, pp. 130–138.

[41] Marty Gruhn, "Trends and Analysis in Word Processing," *Office Administration and Automation*, November 1983, pp. 100–101.

[42] Carol S. Saunders, "Management Information Systems, Communications, and Department Power: An Integrative Model," *Academy of Management Review*, July 1981, pp. 431–442.

[43] Paula Lippin, "Telecommunications: Where It Is and Where It's Going," *Administrative Management*, September 1980, pp. 34–38, 87.

[44] Irving M. Klempner, "Information Technology and Personal Responsibility," *Special Libraries*, April 1981, pp. 157–162.

organization, the more information the organization needs to operate effectively and efficiently.

Communication between individuals, groups, or organizations is a process in which a source sends a message and a receiver responds. The source encodes a message into symbols and transmits it through a medium to the receiver, who decodes the symbols. The receiver then responds with feedback, an attempt to verify the meaning of the original message. Noise—anything that distorts or interrupts communication—may interfere in virtually any stage of the process.

Communication networks are systems of information exchange within organizations. Patterns of communication emerge as information flows from person to person in a group. Typical small group communication networks include the wheel, chain, circle, and all-channel networks. They can be described in terms of the density of communication, the distance between members, the relative freedom of a member to use different paths to communicate with others, and the positions of members.

The organizational communication network, which describes the real communication links in an organization, is usually different from the arrangement on an organization chart. Roles that people play in organizational communication networks include the gatekeeper, liaison, cosmopolite, and isolate.

People in organizations communicate through written, oral, and nonverbal means. Written communications include letters, memos, reports, and the like. Oral communication is the type most commonly used. Personal elements, such as facial expressions and body language, and environmental elements, such as office design, communicate nonverbally.

Managing communication in organizations involves understanding the several types of problems that can interfere with effective communication. Problems relate to the communication process itself and to organizational factors, such as status differences.

The fully integrated communication-information office system—the electronic office—links personnel in a communication network through a combination of computers and electronic transmission systems. The effects of such systems have not yet been fully realized.

DISCUSSION QUESTIONS

1. How is communication in organizations an individual process as well as an organizational process?

2. In situations of high task uncertainty, why is it necessary that there be more communication?

3. Describe a situation in which you found yourself trying to carry on a conversation when no one was listening. Were any messages sent during the "conversation"?

4. The typical college classroom provides an example of attempts at communication—the professor tries to communicate the subject to the students. Describe classroom communication in terms of the basic communication process described in the chapter.

5. Is there a communication network (other than professor-to-student) in the class in which you are using this book? If so, identify any specific roles that people play in the network. If not, why has no network developed? What would be the benefits of having a communication network in this class?

6. Why might educators typically focus most communication training on the written and oral methods and pay little attention to the nonverbal methods? Do you think that more training emphasis should be placed on nonverbal communication? Why?

7. Is the typical classroom form of transferring information from professor to student an effective form of communication? Where does it break down? What are the communication problems in the college classroom?

8. Whose responsibility is it to solve classroom communication problems: the students', the professor's, or the administration's?

9. Have you ever worked in an organization in which communication was a problem? If so, what were some of the causes of the problem?

10. What methods were used, or should have been used, to improve communication in the situation you described in question 9?

11. Would the use of advanced computer information processing or telecommunications have helped solve the communications problem you described in question 9?

12. What types of communication problems will new telecommunications methods most likely be able to solve? Why?

Case 18.1

Communicating Benefits

Employee benefit plans have been undergoing radical changes recently. Flexible benefit packages and new forms of health maintenance organizations have greatly increased the kinds of benefits, the number of choices available, and the complexity of the material that explains the benefits to employees. Now companies that have spent years developing the most attractive, useful benefit programs are turning their attention to perfecting the ways in which they communicate information about those programs. No one benefits from options that employees do not know about or cannot understand.

A recent survey of personnel administrators' benefit priorities found that most ranked "improved employee communications" second only to managing health care costs. However, even when communications have become a high priority, trying to explain benefits effectively is not an easy job. People read benefit plans selectively; many do not want to read anything about death or injury, and they may give up entirely if they are confused by the language or the presentation of a plan.

Jane Voisard, the manager of a newly formed Texas-based bank holding company, MCorp, faced such problems when she needed to find a way to explain the new flexible benefit package to employees. Her approach by-passed many of the expensive high-tech communication options, instead following common-sense principles of identifying her audience and their needs and addressing those needs as clearly and simply as possible.

First Voisard commissioned a survey that told her who her audience was—mostly women in their twenties—and what they needed to know. Most employees reacted favorably to the benefit package but felt they did not understand it, and very few understood or appreciated the complex savings and pension plan options. As a result of this survey, Voisard saw her job as producing a magazine that explained in clear, simple terms the positive aspects of the plan's more complicated benefits. She tried to make the plan sound less intimidating by keeping the publication's tone friendly and positive.

Most people, she felt, are put off by the endless numbers and complexity of many benefit packages. So she used down-to-earth explanations and found that fewer employees enrolled in plans that they really did not want. To keep the tone humorous and informal, Voisard used pictures of employees to demonstrate various options; for instance, an employee stands among three children and a dog, all of whose casts and neck braces indicate that they have made full use of medical benefits. She also used employees' signed testimonials about various benefits, thus increasing the authenticity of the publication's personal flavor.

Rather than cram the magazine with fine print, Voisard favored bright colors, white space, and easy-to-read type to make it look uncluttered and to encourage people to read it. The success of her efforts were demonstrated by an increase in benefit enrollment following the first edition of her magazine. That success has helped spur other forms of communication about benefits: newsletters, reports in other company publications, and individual computer summaries of each employee's benefits. Because employees now have a much better sense of what the company's benefit plans offer, the $65,000 that MCorp invested in the magazine may have done more to make employees happy than ten times that much spent on increasing benefit options.

Case Questions

1. What special problems does a company face in trying to communicate about benefits?

2. How might Marshall McLuhan's famous statement "the medium is the message" apply to this case?

Case Sources:

Bob Martin, "Razor Sharp Clarity with the Edge," *Personnel Journal,* November 1986, 66–67; Deborah A. Watters, "New Technologies for Benefits Communication," *Personnel Administrator,* November 1986, 100–114.

Case 18.2   Heading Off a Permanent Misunderstanding

Mindy Martin was no longer speaking to Al Sharp. She had been wary of him since her first day at Alton Products; he had always seemed distant and aloof. She thought at first that he resented her MBA degree, her fast rise in the company, or her sense of purpose and ambition. But she was determined to get along with everyone in the office, so she had taken him out to lunch, praised his work whenever she could, and even kept track of his son's little league feats.

But all that ended with the appointment of the new Midwest marketing director. Martin had her sights on the job and thought her chances were good. She was competing with three other managers on her level. Al was not in the running because he did not have a graduate degree, but his voice was thought to carry a lot of weight with the top brass. Martin had less seniority than any of her competitors, but her division had become the leader in the company, and upper management had praised her lavishly. With a good recommendation from Al, she felt, she would get the job.

Instead, Walt Murdoch received the promotion and moved to Topeka. Martin was devastated. It was bad enough that she did not get the promotion, but she could not stand the fact that Murdoch had been chosen. She and Al Sharp had taken to calling Murdoch "Mr. Intolerable," since neither of them could stand his pompous arrogance. She felt that his being chosen was an insult to her; it made her rethink her entire career. When the grapevine confirmed her suspicion that Al Sharp had strongly influenced the decision, she determined to reduce her interaction with Sharp to a bare minimum.

Relations in the office were very chilly for almost a month. Sharp soon gave up trying to get back in Martin's favor, and they began communicating only in short, unsigned memos. Finally William Attridge, their immediate boss, could tolerate the hostility no longer and called the two in for a meeting. "We're going to sit here until you two become friends again," he said, "or at least until I find out what's bugging you."

Martin resisted for a few minutes, denying that anything had changed in their relationship, but when she saw that Attridge was serious, she finally said, "Al seems more interested in dealing with Walter Murdoch." Sharp's jaw dropped; he sputtered, but could not say anything. Attridge came to the rescue.

"Walter's been safely kicked upstairs, thanks in part to Al, and neither of you will have to deal with him in the future. But if you're upset about that promotion, you should know that Al had nothing but praise for you and kept pointing out how this division would suffer if we buried you in Topeka. With your bonuses, you're still making as much as Murdoch. If your work here continues to be outstanding, you'll be headed for a much better place than Topeka."

Martin, feeling somewhat ashamed, looked up at Al Sharp, who shrugged and said, "You want to go get some coffee?"

Over coffee, Mindy told Al what she had been thinking for the past month and apologized for treating him unfairly. Al explained that what she saw as aloofness was actually respect and something akin to fear: he viewed Mindy as brilliant and efficient. Consequently he was very cautious, trying not to offend her.

The next day the office was almost back to normal. But a new ritual had been established—Mindy and Al took a coffee break together every day at ten. Soon their teasing and friendly competition loosened up everyone with whom they worked.

Case Questions

1. What might have happened if William Attridge had not intervened?

2. Are the sources of the misunderstanding between Martin and Sharp common or unusual?

Experiential Exercise

Purpose: This exercise demonstrates the importance of feedback in oral communication.

Format: You will be an observer or play the role of either a manager or an assistant manager trying to tell a coworker the location at which a package of important materials is to be picked up. The observer's role is to make sure the other two participants follow the rules and to observe and record any interesting occurrences.

Procedure: The instructor will divide the class into groups of three people each. (Any extra members can be roving observers.) The three people in each group will take the roles of manager, assistant manager, and observer. In the second trial, the manager and the assistant manager will switch roles.

Trial 1: The manager and the assistant manager should turn their backs to each other so that neither can see the other. Here is the situation: the manager is in another city that he or she is not familiar with but that the assistant manager knows quite well. The manager needs to find the small office of a supplier to pick up drawings of a critical component of the company's main product. The supplier will be closing for the day in a few minutes; the drawings must be picked up before closing time. The manager has called the assistant manager to get directions to the office. However, the connection is faulty—the manager can hear the assistant manager but the assistant manager can only hear enough to know the manager is on the line. The manager has redialed once, but there was no improvement in the connection. Now there is no time to lose. The manager has decided to get the directions from the assistant without asking questions.

Just before the exercise begins, the instrutor will give the assistant manager a detailed map of the city that shows the locations of the supplier's office and the manager. The map will include a number of turns, stops, stoplights, intersections, and shopping centers between these locations. The assistant manager can study it for no longer than a minute or two. When the instructor gives the direction to start, the assistant manager decribes to the manager how to get from his or her present location to the supplier's office. As the assistant manager gives the directions, the manager draws the map on a piece of paper.

The observer makes sure that no questions are asked and records the beginning and ending times, as well as the way in which the assistant manager tries to communicate particularly difficult points (including points about which the manager obviously wants to ask questions) and any other noteworthy occurrences.

After all pairs have finished, each observer "grades" the quality of the manager's map by comparing it with the original and counting the number of obvious mistakes. The instructor will ask a few managers who believe they have drawn very good maps to tell the rest of the class how to get to the supplier's office.

Trial 2: In trial 2, the manager and the assistant manager switch roles, and a second map is passed out to the new assistant managers. The situation is the same as in the first trial, except that the telephones are working properly and the manager can ask questions of the assistant manager. The observer's role is the same as in trial 1—recording the beginning and ending times, the methods of communication, and any other noteworthy occurrences.

After all pairs have finished, the observers grade the maps, just as in the first trial. The instructor will then ask a few selected managers to tell the rest of the class how to get to the supplier's office. The subsequent class discussion should center on the experiences of the class members and the follow-up questions.

Follow-up Questions

1. Which trial resulted in more accurate maps? Why?
2. Which trial took longer? Why?
3. How did you feel when a question needed to be asked but it could not be in trial 1? Was your confidence in the final result affected differently in the two trials?

CHAPTER 19

Performance Appraisal

Chapter Objectives

After reading this chapter, you should be able to

- ▶ define *performance appraisal* and discuss the purposes of appraisal.
- ▶ describe the elements of performance appraisal.
- ▶ describe the major performance appraisal techniques and their strengths and weaknesses.
- ▶ identify and discuss the uses of performance appraisal information.

estinghouse Electric Corporation recently designed and implemented a new performance appraisal system to go with a new compensation system for its office workers at its Pittsburgh headquarters. The project was initiated by the human resource department and utilized an outside consultant. A comprehensive analysis of each job description was completed and used to develop performance standards for each position. Other features included training for both the raters and the ratees, protection against the major flaws of most performance appraisal systems, provisions for one appraisal session for each employee to take place in the spring of each year, and a new form that includes the job description and performance standards for the position. In keeping with its emphasis on participative management, all of this was accomplished via a task force made up of twenty-five employees and twenty managers. The task force meetings took place in company offices and on company time. The system is now in use, and the reaction of everyone involved is quite positive.[1]

*N*ot every performance appraisal system is as comprehensive or receives such glowing reviews. In fact most managers and employees have very few positive things to say about performance appraisal in their organization.

"Let's be frank: most managers hate conducting performance appraisals."[2] Managers use many different excuses to avoid formally appraising the performance of employees who work for them. The most common excuses are:

"It takes too much time."

"The form we use is bad."

"I am not qualified to judge others."

"No one does it to me."

"It is so painful."

To some employees, performance appraisal is an annual ordeal in which "the boss tries to explain to me why I'm not getting a raise." Other employees look forward to their performance appraisals as opportunities to examine their work and their career prospects. At the management level, some line managers dread the performance appraisal system forced on them by the human resources department because of the paperwork required. Top management, in contrast, may view performance appraisal as the most important part of human resource management.

What is this nearly universal organizational event that is so important to some and so loathsome to others? How can this one aspect of organizational

---

[1] David B. Cowfer and Joanne Sujansky, "Appraisal Development at Westinghouse," *Training and Development Journal*, July 1987, pp. 40–43.

[2] Walter Kiechel, III, "How to Appraise Performance," *Fortune*, October 12, 1987, pp. 239–240.

life provoke such disparate feelings and reactions? After defining the relevant terms and relationships of performance appraisal, this chapter discusses important performance appraisal processes and issues.

PERFORMANCE APPRAISAL IN ORGANIZATIONS

Performance appraisal, or performance evaluation, is the process by which a manager (1) evaluates an employee's work behaviors by measurement and comparison with previously established standards, (2) records the results, and (3) communicates them to the employee. A **performance appraisal system** (PAS) comprises the organizational processes and activities involved in performance appraisals, as shown in Figure 19.1. Performance appraisal is an activity that involves a manager and an employee, whereas the PAS includes the organizational policies, procedures, and resources that support the activity. The timing and frequency of evaluations, determination of who appraises whom, measurement procedures, methods of recording the evaluations, and storage and distribution of information are all aspects of the performance appraisal system.

Although most organizations have standardized control systems for managing other types of resources and monitoring their use, the system for managing human resources has typically been neither a standardized nor a generally accepted part of organizational life. This is a residue of large-scale economic shifts. When the U.S. economy was primarily based in manufacturing, the evaluation of performance was very simple. A manager could evaluate a worker by counting the number of units produced. In a service economy, however, output is not so easily measured and counted, and the evaluation of performance is a much more subjective and less clearly defined process. Often, then, there is serious conflict not only over how evaluation should be conducted but also over whether it should be conducted at all.

The modern human resource system may be divided into four parts: acquisition of human resources (recruitment and selection), training and development, motivation, and compensation. Performance appraisal is involved in all four parts and serves to tie them together by providing feedback information for all of the other parts.[3] Indeed, performance appraisal has been called one of the most powerful and important tools for managing human resources in an organization.[4]

---

[3] Gary P. Latham and Kenneth N. Wexley, *Increasing Productivity Through Performance Appraisal* (Reading, Mass.: Addison-Wesley, 1981).

[4] Charles J. Fombrun and Robert L. Laud, "Strategic Issues in Performance Appraisal: Theory and Practice," *Personnel*, November–December 1983, pp. 23–31.

Figure 19.1

Performance Appraisal and the Performance Appraisal System

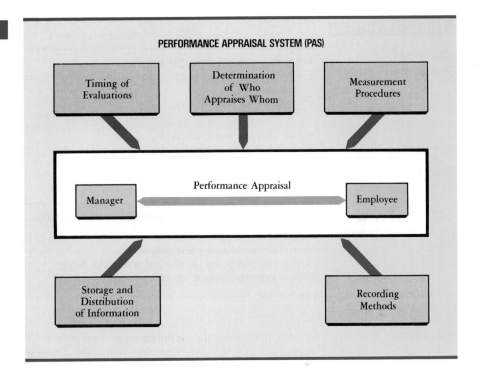

Purposes of Performance Appraisal

Performance appraisal may serve as many as twenty different purposes,[5] but the most basic is to provide information about work behaviors. Other purposes of performance appraisal can be grouped into two broad categories: judgmental and developmental, as shown in Table 19.1.

Performance appraisals with a judgmental orientation focus on past performance; they are concerned mainly with the measurement and comparison of performance and also with the uses of the information that is generated.[6] Judgmental performance appraisals are often used in part to control employee behaviors. The organization rewards desired behaviors with wage raises, promotions, and entrance into high-potential employee development programs and punishes undesirable behaviors with transfers and layoffs, denial of wage increases, and demotions. Performance appraisal can provide the necessary

---

[5] H. John Bernardin and Richard W. Beatty, *Performance Appraisal: Assessing Human Behavior at Work* (Boston: Kent, 1984).

[6] L. Cummings and Donald P. Schwab, *Performance in Organizations: Determinants and Appraisal* (Glenview, Ill.: Scott, Foresman, 1973).

Table 19.1 Purposes of Performance Appraisal	**Basic Purpose:**

Basic Purpose:
To provide information about work performance
Other Purposes:
Judgmental Orientation
Provide a basis for reward allocation Provide a basis for promotions, transfers, layoffs, and so on Identify high-potential employees Validate selection procedures Evaluate previous training programs
Developmental Orientation
Foster work improvement Identify training and development opportunities Develop ways to overcome obstacles and performance barriers Establish supervisor-employee agreement on expectations

documentation for the termination of employees. (See *Management in Action.*) Performance appraisals with a judgmental orientation also provide valuable feedback on how effective the organization's selection procedures and training programs have been.

Performance appraisals with a developmental orientation focus on future performance and use information resulting from evaluations for performance improvement. If improved future performance is the intent of the appraisal process, the manager may focus on goals or targets for the employee, the elimination of obstacles or problems that hinder performance, and future training needs.

ELEMENTS OF PERFORMANCE APPRAISAL

The performance appraisal systems used by organizations vary greatly in their methods and in their effectiveness. Some are successful, and some are not; some are constantly being changed in a search for improvements. There is no one way to perfect a PAS, but three factors are crucial to success: commitment to objectives, job analysis, and measurement.

Commitment to Objectives

A successful performance appraisal system is based on a strong commitment from the entire organization, especially top management. This commitment is made manifest in the objectives of the performance appraisal system. Top

Preparing for Termination

Until recently, a company was able to fire an employee whenever it wanted. Employment was considered to be "at will," and an employer did not have to justify letting an employee go. Even today, only about half of the three million employees discharged every year are covered by specific contracts and labor agreements that limit a company's discretion in firing. However, courts and state legislatures have been defining and expanding situations in which a company may not fire an employee at will. As businesses attempt to cope with these legal changes, properly executed performance appraisals become even more important.

Courts have ruled that a company may not fire an employee at will if it has given the employee an implied contract, if the firing relates to the employee's public policy activity, or if the company has not acted fairly and in good faith. An implied contract means that the firm has given the employee reason to think that he or she can look forward to extended employment. Such an implication can take the form of oral statements from company officials, such as, "You've got a bright future with us." Public policy activity includes jury duty, reporting illegal conduct by an employer, and refusing to perform illegal or unethical tasks for one's company. Although more than half the states currently protect an employee from being fired for such activities, only a handful hold that in the absence of a contract, an employer must treat an employee fairly and in good faith, or the employee will have grounds for a lawsuit.

Recent legal challenges to a company's right to dismiss employees have led to changes in hiring policies and human resource management in general, and to reassessments of performance appraisals in particular. At a minimum, many firms are looking at the language in their personnel documents to make sure that it does not imply contractual obligations. Employers who want to protect themselves from lawsuits are paying much more attention to performance appraisals, since written evaluations can constitute important evidence in defending the company against a wrongful-termination lawsuit. Inaccurate, overly optimistic appraisals can haunt an employer in court, so managers are being advised to be honest, specific, and direct, even when it is difficult to criticize someone they work with and like. If a company fires an employee because of a history of poor work, that history must be documented in the appraisals; mediocre appraisals are grounds for withholding promotion, but not for dismissal.

Most companies also need to upgrade the performance appraisal process so that the object and the standards of evaluation are clear, consistent, explicit, and unbiased. As courts are increasingly asked to make judgments about companies' employment decisions, personnel policies will come under ever greater scrutiny. A firm's violation of its own written personnel policies is one of the most common reasons for a court to rule in favor of a fired employee, whereas a detailed record of performance appraisals that justifies a company's action is the best defense.

Sources: Kenneth R. Gilberg, "Employee Terminations: Risky Business," *Personnel Administrator*, March 1987, 40–46; William H. Holley, Jr., and Roger S. Wolters, "An Employment-At-Will Vulnerability Audit," *Personnel Journal*, April 1987, 130–138; Jim Hubble, "Survey: Good Faith and Fair Dealing: An Analysis of Recent Cases," *Montana Law Review*, May 1987, pp. 193–211.

management must know what they want the PAS to accomplish and communicate their objectives to those responsible for developing and managing the system, as well as to all employees covered by the system. Clear objectives and strong organizational commitment give supervisors confidence that the time and effort they devote to performance evaluation is worthwhile and give employees more interest in using the evaluations to change behaviors and improve performance. Clearly stated objectives also allow managers to monitor the program, evaluate it periodically, and make any necessary adjustments.[7]

Job Analysis

The second element of an effective PAS is a sound job analysis system that provides comprehensive and accurate descriptions of all jobs in the organization.[8] **Job analysis** is the process of systematically gathering information about specific jobs for use in developing a performance appraisal system, in writing job or position descriptions, and in developing equitable pay systems. If an employee's job performance is to be evaluated fairly, the job must be precisely and clearly defined.[9]

In undertaking job analysis, an organization must consider the factors summarized in Figure 19.2. Job analysis information may be gathered in various ways and by various people, from the job incumbent, to a specialist in the human resources department, to an outside consultant. It is of utmost importance to know the purpose of gathering the information, because particular performance evaluation methods require specific types of information from the job analysis. Therefore, the job analysis method must match the uses for the information. Some methods of job analysis can be very time consuming and expensive; others can be simple and inexpensive. The organization must be certain that the information gained from the analysis will be important enough and will be used enough to justify the expense.

There are several job analysis methods. The best method for a given organization is the one that provides information appropriate for the PAS and is the most practical for the situation. Since the job analysis method is a major determinant of the structure of the pay system that results,[10] managers must be careful in selecting the proper job analysis technique. Job analysis methods

---

[7] See Marshall Whitmire, "Program Evaluation of a Medical Center Performance Appraisal System" (unpublished doctoral dissertation, Arizona State University, 1985), for a discussion of the importance of setting objectives for the PAS.

[8] See Richard I. Henderson, *Performance Appraisal* (Reston, Va.: Reston, 1984); and Bernardin and Beatty, *Performance Appraisal*, for more detailed discussions of job analysis.

[9] Ronald G. Wells, "Guidelines for Effective and Defensible Performance Appraisal Systems," *Personnel Journal*, October 1982, pp. 776–782.

[10] Robert M. Madigan and David J. Hoover, "Effects of Alternative Job Evaluation Methods on Decisions Involving Pay Equity," *Academy of Management Journal*, March 1986, pp. 84–100.

Figure 19.2

Job Analysis Process

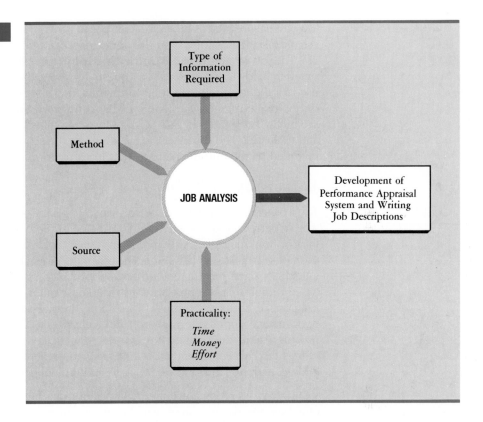

include the critical incident technique, the functional job analysis technique, and the job inventory technique.

The **critical incident technique** involves interviewing individuals who are familiar with the target job (the job-holder and his or her peers, clients, supervisor, and subordinates). Each is asked to describe specific incidents of effective and ineffective behaviors in the job.[11] The job analyst uses these "critical incidents" to write behavioral statements of job expectations and to develop a performance appraisal system based on the expectations.

The **functional job analysis technique** identifies specific tasks that make up a job and examines how much each task involves data, people, and things. Each task's complexity in each of these respects is rated on a ten-point scale. Tasks can be further rated with respect to instructions, reasoning, mathematics, and language.[12] The evaluator can compare tasks within a given job or between

---

[11] See Latham and Wexley, *Increasing Productivity Through Performance Appraisal*, for a more detailed discussion of the critical incident method of job analysis.

[12] H. C. Olson, S. A. Fine, D. C. Myers, and M. C. Jennings, "The Use of Functional Job Analysis in Establishing Performance Standards for Heavy Equipment Operators," *Personnel Psychology*, Vol. 34, 1981, pp. 351–364.

jobs to ensure that ratings are consistent across job classifications and can establish standards for use in the performance appraisal system.

The **job or position inventory technique** involves asking the incumbent or other knowledgeable persons questions about the job. The questionnaire used for the inventory may focus primarily on worker-oriented issues or strictly on job-related issues. Designers of these instruments usually claim that they are highly reliable and valid; so the scores for different jobs can be compared and evaluated. The organization can then use the scores and other information provided by the questionnaire to develop a performance appraisal system.

Measurement of Performance

The cornerstone of a good performance appraisal system is the method by which performance is measured. The measurement method provides the information managers use in making such decisions as salary adjustment, promotion, transfer, and training. The courts and Equal Employment Opportunity guidelines have recommended that performance appraisal measurements be based on job-related criteria rather than some other criteria, such as age, sex, religion, or national origin.[13] In addition, the measurement systems used in performance appraisals must be valid, reliable, and free of bias in order to provide useful information for the decision maker. They must not produce ratings that are consistently too lenient or too severe or that bunch up in the middle, and they must be free of halo and timing errors.

VALIDITY   Fred N. Kerlinger has written that when we question the validity of a measure, we are asking whether it measures what we think it measures.[14] The **validity** of a performance evaluation method is the extent to which it reflects actual employee performance. For example, if Mary is the highest performer in a work group but performance evaluations indicate that Felipe is highest and Mary is near the bottom, we have reason to question the validity of the PAS.

Several types of validity are relevant to performance appraisal. **Content validity** is the extent to which the measurement adequately assesses all important aspects of job performance. For example, consider Mary and Felipe. If the method by which they are evaluated measures only the performance factors in which Felipe excels and none of those in which Mary is outstanding, the system is not measuring the full content of job performance and cannot be considered valid.

Convergent validity is the extent to which different measures agree in their evaluations of the same performance. Felipe may be rated higher than

---

[13] Leonard Berger, "Promise of Criterion-Referenced Performance Appraisal (CRPA)," *Review of Public Personnel Administration*, Vol. 3, 1983, pp. 21–32.

[14] Fred N. Kerlinger, *Foundations of Behavioral Research*, 2nd ed. (New York: Holt, Rinehart, and Winston, 1973).

Mary by method 1 but lower than Mary by method 2. When ratings of performance do not agree, we must question the convergent validity of the measures. **Discriminant validity** is the extent to which ratings of the same type of performance agree more than ratings of different types of performance. For example, ratings have discriminant validity if raters 1 and 2 both rate Mary high on performance quality and low on performance quantity.

RELIABILITY   A measurement system's **reliability** is the extent to which its results are consistent. (This quality is also called *stability, consistency, dependability*, and *repeatability*.) If the same performance is measured several times in the same way and the results are very similar, the measurement may be called reliable. If, on the other hand, the results are very different, we may question the reliability of the method. For example, if we use a computerized system to count the number of pieces in a box twenty times and always obtain the same result, we can call the instrument and the method reliable. But if we count the pieces manually twenty times and obtain a different number each time, we may conclude that the manual method of counting pieces is unreliable.

Another important aspect of reliability is the extent to which ratings by more than one rater agree. If two raters evaluate the same performance very differently, we can question the **interrater reliability** of the method. In the case of Mary and Felipe, suppose several different people rated Felipe's performance—his peers, his subordinates, and his immediate supervisor. If these ratings differ, the interrater reliability is low. On the other hand, if the ratings are fairly consistent, the interrater reliability is high. Several techniques exist for establishing the interrater reliability of multiple raters.[15]

FREEDOM FROM BIAS   A third condition of performance evaluation measurements is that they be free of bias. **Bias** is a personal preference or inclination that undermines impartial judgment, as in a prejudice for or against some person or group of people based on race, age, sex, seniority, or the like. In performance appraisal, a biased rater might consistently evaluate members of a certain group either higher or lower because of their membership in that group. Bias in ratings can also result from applying different criteria to different groups.[16] Bias in ratings makes the information provided less meaningful and compromises the objectives of the appraisal system.

RESTRICTION OF RANGE   Leniency, severity, and central tendency problems in performance evaluation are special cases of the tendency of some raters to restrict the range of ratings they use. Figure 19.3 illustrates three problems

---

[15] Neal Schmitt, Raymond A. Noe, and Rand Gottschalk, "Using the Lens Model to Magnify Raters' Consistency, Matching, and Shared Bias," *Academy of Management Journal*, March 1986, pp. 130–139.

[16] Taylor Cox, Jr., and Stella M. Nkomo, "Differential Performance Appraisal Criteria: A Field Study of Black and White Managers," *Group & Organization Studies*, March–June 1986, pp. 101–119.

Figure 19.3

Three Types of
Restriction of Range
Problems in
Performance Evaluations

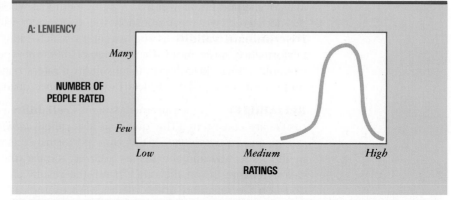

A: LENIENCY

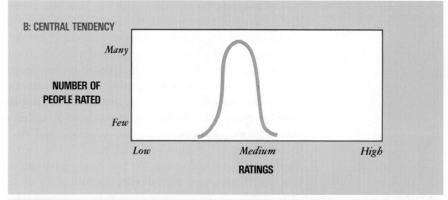

B: CENTRAL TENDENCY

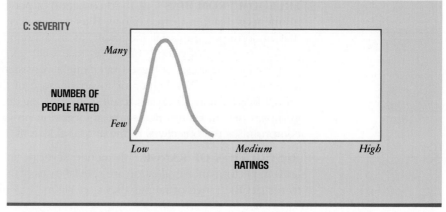

C: SEVERITY

that result from restriction of range. As part A shows, when a rater's evaluations of performance are consistently high (that is, when the standard deviation is very small and the mean is skewed toward the higher end of the scale), the rater is said to be too **lenient**. When the rater assigns all performance a moderate rating, with few if any high or low ratings, the restriction of range problem is called **central tendency**; the standard deviation is low and the mean is centered in the middle of the scale (see Figure 19.3, part B). Part C illustrates the problem of **severity**; here, the rater assigns a low value to most or all performance, resulting in a small standard deviation and a mean that is skewed toward the low end of the scale.

In each of these situations, the rater is unable to distinguish between different performance levels. Recent research has indicated that the tendency to be lenient rather than accurate depends to some extent on other factors, such as the purpose of the appraisal, especially for self-ratings. For example, employees rating themselves tend to be more lenient if the rating is to be used in evaluating them for rewards or sanctions. They tend to be more accurate, though, if they know the rating will be validated by someone else.[17]

HALO ERROR   **Halo error** occurs when a rater consistently assigns the same rating to all aspects of a person's performance, regardless of the actual performance level, because of the rater's impression of the person. Several factors, such as personal feelings and prior expectations, can result in halo errors in ratings.[18]

For Felipe and Mary, assume that the PAS requires the evaluation of several aspects of individual performance and that Felipe's and Mary's actual performance levels are those shown in Figure 19.4, part A. If the rater evaluates their performance as shown in part B, we have two examples of halo error. Actual performance levels differed substantially across the five factors, yet the ratings were very similar, Mary's being consistently low and Felipe's consistently high. Halo error distorts PAS information and, like other problems of measurement, may compromise the objectives of the performance evaluation system.

TIMING ERRORS   Timing can have a major impact on performance appraisal. In general, evaluations made immediately following the performance are more accurate.[19] A delay of several weeks or months between performance and rating

---

[17] Jiing-Lih Farh and James D. Werbel, "Effects of Purpose of the Appraisal and Expectations of Validation on Self-Appraisal Leniency," *Journal of Applied Psychology*, August 1986, pp. 527–529.

[18] Anne S. Tsui and Bruce Barry, "Interpersonal Affect and Rating Errors," *Academy of Management Journal*, September 1986, pp. 586–599; and Eileen A. Hogan, "Effects of Prior Expectations on Performance Ratings: A Longitudinal Study," *Academy of Management Journal*, June 1987, pp. 354–368.

[19] Kevin P. Murphy, Barbara A. Gannett, Barbara M. Herr, and Judy A. Chen, "Effects of Subsequent Performance on Evaluations of Previous Performance," *Journal of Applied Psychology*, August 1986, pp. 427–431; Kevin R. Murphy and William K. Balzer, "Systematic Distortions in Memory-Based Behavior Ratings and Performance

Figure 19.4

Examples of Halo Error
in Performance
Evaluation

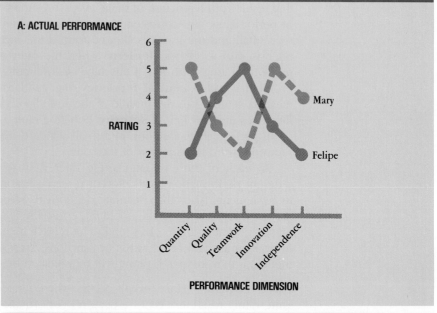

A: ACTUAL PERFORMANCE

RATING

Quantity Quality Teamwork Innovation Independence

Mary

Felipe

PERFORMANCE DIMENSION

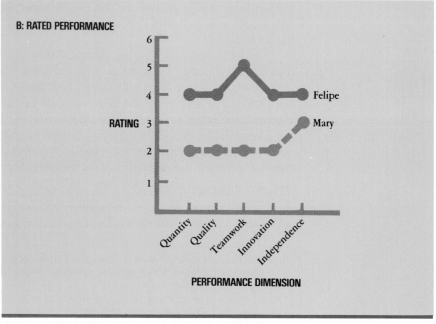

B: RATED PERFORMANCE

RATING

Quantity Quality Teamwork Innovation Independence

Felipe

Mary

PERFORMANCE DIMENSION

can result in significant rating errors. A related timing problem, **recency error**, occurs when a rater remembers only the most recent behaviors in evaluating an employee. Most employees are careful to perform very well as the time for performance evaluation approaches. If the rater considers only this behavior in the evaluation, strong bias in the rating can result. Since accuracy is higher when the rating is based on several observations of performance over a period of time, the rater can reduce timing errors by using numerous observations and recording evaluations very soon after the behavior has occurred.

When the conditions of validity, reliability, or freedom from bias are not met, or when restriction of range, halo error, or timing errors are present, the effectiveness of the measurement system may be reduced. Moreover, PAS measurement errors are likely to have a ripple effect in the organization. For example, suppose the division manager of the plant where Felipe and Mary work must promote one of them to a new staff position. He will undoubtedly consult performance appraisal records as a source of information about the two candidates. If an underlying measurement problem has consistently distorted the ratings, he may unwittingly promote the person less qualified or less appropriate for the position.

PERFORMANCE APPRAISAL TECHNIQUES

Organizations employ many different appraisal techniques, most of them derived from one or more of the methods described in this section. The techniques are grouped here according to whether they evaluate employees individually or in comparison with others.

Individual Evaluation

Individual performance appraisal methods vary greatly. Of course, each method has advantages and disadvantages. The major problems common to all methods are restriction of range and the inability to discriminate variable levels of performance.

GRAPHIC RATING SCALES   One of the simplest methods of rating individual performance is the graphic rating scale, illustrated in Figure 19.5. A graphic rating scale may use one global measure of performance, as shown in part A, or multiple measures of performance, as shown in part B. The rater simply checks or circles the point on the scale that best represents the performance level of the employee.

[19] (*cont.*) Evaluations: Consequences for Rating Accuracy," *Journal of Applied Psychology*, February 1986, pp. 39–44; and Robert L. Heneman and Kenneth N. Wexley, "The Effects of Time Delay in Rating and Amount of Information Observed on Performance Rating Accuracy," *Academy of Management Journal*, December 1983, pp. 677–686.

Figure 19.5

Graphic Rating Scales

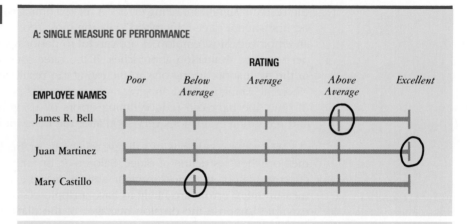

A: SINGLE MEASURE OF PERFORMANCE

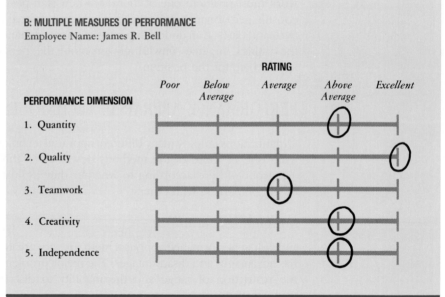

B: MULTIPLE MEASURES OF PERFORMANCE
Employee Name: James R. Bell

Graphic rating scales suffer from virtually all of the measurement problems previously discussed. For example, having a scale with an odd number of points encourages the central tendency problem. Graphic rating scales may also help produce halo error. Since the focus of the evaluation is on only one person at a time, there is no comparison made between employees. Therefore, the rater may focus on one trait of the ratee, resulting in halo error. Another weakness is that graphic rating scales provide little information that can be used for employee development and performance improvement.

On the other hand, graphic rating scales are easy to use and require little time and effort to develop. They have been around for so long that they remain popular in organizations, especially for the evaluation of hourly and nonexempt personnel.[20] (Nonexempt personnel are those who, as stipulated by the Fair Labor Standards Act and the Walsh-Healy Act,[21] must receive overtime pay for work over eight hours per day or over forty hours per week.) Indeed, graphic rating scales are the most widely used performance appraisal technique; a recent study showed that over 65% of the reporting companies used graphic rating scales for hourly personnel and over 50% used them for nonexempt personnel.[22]

CHECKLISTS   The checklist rating method provides a list of work behaviors and requires the rater to check those that best describe the employee. In some cases, the items are weighted according to the importance of the behaviors. The list of behaviors and the weights assigned to them are usually generated by a group of people familiar with the job in question, such as employees, supervisors, and personnel specialists.

Checklists, unfortunately, are prone to the same problems as graphic rating scales. Since both systems yield numerical ratings, though, the results are easy to use for comparisons of employees and lend themselves to computer application.

ESSAYS   A third type of individual rating method requires the rater to write narrative essays describing employee behaviors. These essays may be based on the memory of the rater or on a diary of critical incidents that the rater keeps during the period covered by the evaluation. Essays often give a much richer picture of the employee's performance than rating scales or checklists do. They may also be more accurate, especially if based on a regularly kept diary of critical incidents. Short essays or notes from a diary can often be used in conjunction with quantitative methods to provide an example or justification for a numerical rating.

Essays not based on a well-kept diary, however, may be susceptible to the same halo errors as other evaluation techniques that rely on the memory of the evaluator.[23] In addition, essays may not allow comparisons between employees, because there may be no comparable points in narratives on different workers. Another problem with essays is that they often describe an employee's personality traits rather than incidents of good or poor work behaviors. Thus, it may be necessary to train raters using this technique to focus on work behavior. The essay approach is not as easy to develop or use

---

[20] Fombrun and Laud, "Strategic Issues in Performance Appraisal."

[21] Wendell L. French, *The Personnel Management Process*, 5th ed. (Boston: Houghton Mifflin, 1982), p. 420.

[22] George T. Milkovich and John W. Boudreau, *Personnel/Human Resource Management: A Diagnostic Approach*, 5th ed. (Plano, Texas: Business Publications, 1988).

[23] Richard I. Henderson, *Compensation Management: Rewarding Performance* (Reston, Va.: Reston, 1979).

as quantitative methods, nor does it lend itself to numerical or computer analysis.[24]

BEHAVIORALLY ANCHORED RATING SCALES   One of the newer performance evaluation methods uses behaviorally anchored rating scales (BARS). Developed in 1963 by Patricia C. Smith and Lorne M. Kendall,[25] this method combines graphic rating scales with statements of employee behaviors that characterize, or "anchor," various points on the scales. Usually, several different scales are used to evaluate an employee's performance—one for each important aspect of behavior. An example of such a scale is shown in Figure 19.6. To develop BARS, experts (individuals familiar with the job) write behavioral statements, verify that the statements are clearly written and accurately reflect actual behaviors of employees on the job, develop scales that correlate the behavioral statements with numerical values, and verify the association between the statement and the position on the scale.

Raters find it relatively easy to use BARS; they need only read each anchor on a particular scale and rate the employee somewhere on the continuum. Advantages of the method include good interrater reliability, a reduction of some of the common measurement errors, such as restriction of range and halo error, a focus on job-related behaviors rather than employee characteristics, and usefulness in training and development.

The use of BARS involves several potential disadvantages, however. Development may take a considerable amount of time, and scales may need fairly constant updating as jobs change with new technology. Therefore, the system can be very expensive to develop and maintain. In addition, raters sometimes have difficulty rating an employee's behavior when the anchors do not exactly represent the behaviors the rater has observed.

Two other types of scales similar to BARS have been developed: behavioral expectation scales (BES) and behavioral observation scales (BOS). Behavioral expectation scales use statements of expected behaviors as anchors; behavioral observation scales use a five-point scale for each behavioral statement and require the rater to indicate how frequently the employee engages in the behavior. A behavioral observation scale is shown in Figure 19.7. Like BARS, BES and BOS focus on job behaviors rather than employee characteristics. None of these methods, however, is necessarily superior to more traditional individual methods. Despite the development work and research that have gone into them, behaviorally anchored rating scales have not solved the measurement problems of performance evaluation.[26]

---

[24] Bernardin and Beatty, *Performance Appraisal*.

[25] Patricia C. Smith and Lorne M. Kendall, "Retranslation of Expectations: An Approach to the Construction of Unambiguous Anchors for Rating Scales," *Journal of Applied Psychology*, Vol. 47, 1963, pp. 149–155.

[26] Milkovich and Boudreau, *Personnel/Human Resource Management: A Diagnostic Approach*, pp. 201–202.

Figure 19.6

A Behaviorally Anchored
Rating Scale (BARS)

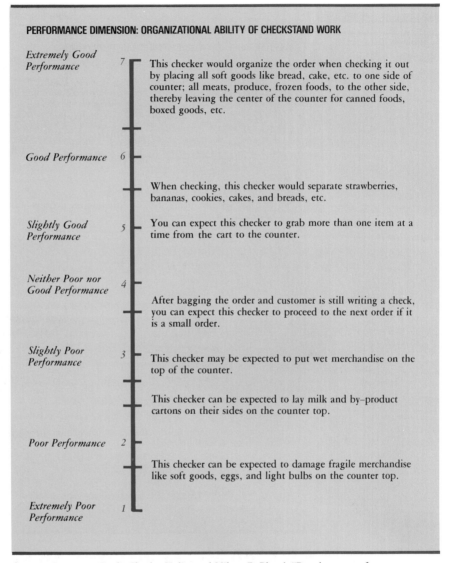

PERFORMANCE DIMENSION: ORGANIZATIONAL ABILITY OF CHECKSTAND WORK

Extremely Good Performance	7	This checker would organize the order when checking it out by placing all soft goods like bread, cake, etc. to one side of counter; all meats, produce, frozen foods, to the other side, thereby leaving the center of the counter for canned foods, boxed goods, etc.
Good Performance	6	
		When checking, this checker would separate strawberries, bananas, cookies, cakes, and breads, etc.
Slightly Good Performance	5	You can expect this checker to grab more than one item at a time from the cart to the counter.
Neither Poor nor Good Performance	4	
		After bagging the order and customer is still writing a check, you can expect this checker to proceed to the next order if it is a small order.
Slightly Poor Performance	3	This checker may be expected to put wet merchandise on the top of the counter.
		This checker can be expected to lay milk and by-product cartons on their sides on the counter top.
Poor Performance	2	
		This checker can be expected to damage fragile merchandise like soft goods, eggs, and light bulbs on the counter top.
Extremely Poor Performance	1	

Source: Lawrence Fogli, Charles Hulin, and Milton R. Blood, "Development of First-Level Behavioral Job Criteria," *Journal of Applied Psychology*, February 1971, p. 7. Copyright 1971 by the American Psychological Association. Reprinted by permission of the author.

Figure 19.7

A Behavioral
Observation Scale
(BOS)

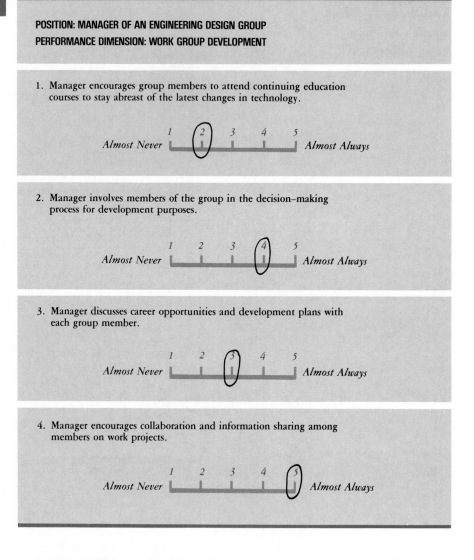

POSITION: MANAGER OF AN ENGINEERING DESIGN GROUP
PERFORMANCE DIMENSION: WORK GROUP DEVELOPMENT

1. Manager encourages group members to attend continuing education courses to stay abreast of the latest changes in technology.

Almost Never   1 2 3 4 5   Almost Always

2. Manager involves members of the group in the decision–making process for development purposes.

Almost Never   1 2 3 4 5   Almost Always

3. Manager discusses career opportunities and development plans with each group member.

Almost Never   1 2 3 4 5   Almost Always

4. Manager encourages collaboration and information sharing among members on work projects.

Almost Never   1 2 3 4 5   Almost Always

FORCED CHOICE   The forced choice method is based on a list of behavioral statements solicited from people knowledgeable about the job. These statements are screened and grouped on the rating form so that they appear to be equally desirable. The rater must choose the one item from each group that best describes the performance of the employee. Sometimes raters are also asked to check the item that is least descriptive of the employee's behavior. This method has an unusual feature: the rater does not know the weighted values of the behavior statements when the employee is being evaluated. After the evaluation has been completed, the values of the items chosen by the rater are summed (usually by the Personnel Department staff), yielding an overall index of the employee's performance.

The forced choice system is less vulnerable than some to halo error and central tendency measurement problems, but the system is time consuming to develop and maintain. In addition, raters may lack confidence in the system, because they do not know the values of their ratings.[27] Finally, the forced choice system has not been as useful as other methods for performance development and improvement because the result of the evaluation is an overall index of performance rather than a set of behavioral statements that can be discussed with the employee.

MANAGEMENT BY OBJECTIVES   The final individual method of evaluation, management by objectives, or MBO, measures task outcomes rather than behaviors. Chapter 6 discussed MBO in detail as a motivational tool; this section reviews its positive and negative aspects as a performance appraisal system. If the goals set out for employees are specific and measurable, the MBO system avoids the validity, reliability, and halo error problems of other appraisal methods. Moreover, an MBO system can provide useful feedback for employee development and performance improvement. Because performance goals are different for each employee, however, results cannot easily be compared. In addition, the mechanics of the MBO system—the cycle of goal setting, discussion, reporting, and review—demand a considerable amount of time and paperwork.

The effectiveness of MBO as an appraisal technique has been questioned on other grounds as well. In emphasizing results, the system may fail to consider the legal, ethical, or social ramifications of job behaviors.[28] For example, the system may institutionalize pressure to reach a goal, thus suggesting that the end justifies the means. Such a message may invite inappropriate behavior— for instance, illegal campaign contributions, attempted bribery, or other illegal acts. Thus, the MBO system's focus on outcomes can inadvertently foster conduct harmful to the long-term interests of the organization. All things considered, however, there is no evidence to suggest that behavior-oriented methods of appraisal such as those previously discussed are better than the MBO outcome-oriented method. Both types of approaches have weaknesses that the manager must be aware of.

Comparative Evaluation

The appraisal methods discussed so far evaluate employees one at a time. Other methods require the comparative evaluation of two or more employees. In general, these methods were developed to eliminate the central tendency problem and to provide information useful for reward allocation decisions.

---

[27] Bernardin and Beatty, *Performance Appraisal.*

[28] See Latham and Wexley, *Increasing Productivity Through Performance Appraisal,* for a more detailed discussion of this controversy.

RANKING   Ranking involves arranging all employees in the same job classification in order of their performance. Most such systems use only one global criterion of performance. The rater reflects on the performance of the employees and assigns them rankings. Since most raters find it easy to identify the best and worst performers, it may be easier to rank the top and bottom performers first and then work toward the middle.

Ranking provides information regarding the relative performance of employees (a notable weakness of most individual methods) and by definition eliminates the central tendency measurement problem. But ranking does have drawbacks. Rankings based on a single global performance criterion tend to reduce a very complex set of behaviors to a single number, making the method particularly vulnerable to halo error bias. It is also difficult to use a ranking procedure for a large number of employees.

Rankings cannot reveal the degrees of difference in performance levels. Assume, for instance, that three employees are ranked as follows: Martina first, John second, and Camilla third. From this information, we cannot determine how much better Martina is than John or how much worse Camilla is than John. Martina may be only slightly better than John, and Camilla may be totally incompetent. On the other hand, Martina may be far superior to the other two, who are about even. When human resource decisions on transfers, layoffs, or raises must be made, the decision maker must supplement rankings with additional information. Otherwise, he or she will be forced to base tough decisions on inadequate information. For similar reasons, the ranking method also provides very little information for use in performance improvement or development.

FORCED DISTRIBUTION   The forced distribution method requires the evaluator to assign employees to categories on the basis of their performance but limits the percentage of employees that can be placed in any one category. The organization using this system determines how many categories to use and what percentage of employees to place in each category. For example, as shown in Figure 19.8, part A, the system may require that employees be placed in five categories ranging from excellent to poor. The percentages are set up to approximate a bell curve, much like the grading scales in some college classes. A second system, illustrated in Figure 19.8, part B, allows only three equal categories.

The forced distribution method involves some of the same advantages and disadvantages as the ranking method. The central tendency problem is avoided, but halo error problems may still exist. The forced distribution system avoids at least one difficulty of the ranking method by not requiring the evaluator to assign a discrete number to each individual, even when the performance of two or more individuals is essentially the same. On the other hand, because it places all employees into only a few groups, the forced distribution method provides even less information than the straight ranking system.

Figure 19.8

Two Examples of
Forced Distribution
Ranking Systems

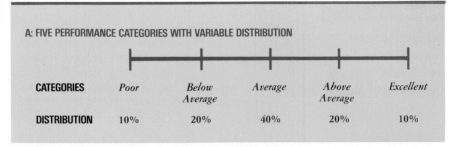

A: FIVE PERFORMANCE CATEGORIES WITH VARIABLE DISTRIBUTION

CATEGORIES	Poor	Below Average	Average	Above Average	Excellent
DISTRIBUTION	10%	20%	40%	20%	10%

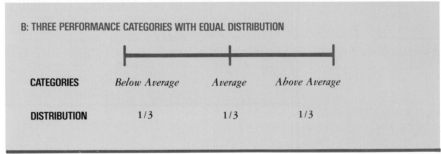

B: THREE PERFORMANCE CATEGORIES WITH EQUAL DISTRIBUTION

CATEGORIES	Below Average	Average	Above Average
DISTRIBUTION	1/3	1/3	1/3

PAIRED COMPARISON   The third comparative technique, the paired comparison method, calls for the comparison of all employees two at a time.[29] Generally, one evaluator compares his or her ratees two at a time on one global performance criterion. By identifying the better performer in each pair, the evaluator can develop a list similar to the results of the straight ranking method. The advantage of the paired comparison method is that the evaluator is not overwhelmed and possibly confused by having to rank many employees at one time. However, if there are many employees, this method may be cumbersome to use. Halo error problems and limited feedback information are additional disadvantages.

As a whole, the comparative methods incorporate safeguards against the measurement problems of the individual rating systems, such as the restriction of range. However, they may yield even less information for decision makers than the individual methods.

Multiple-Rater Comparative Evaluation

Recent years have seen the development of new techniques that combine several different evaluation methods. To avoid the problems of halo error and restriction of range, as well as certain validity problems, the systems generally use more than one rater. They may also use a comparison procedure to reflect

---

[29] See Henderson, *Performance Appraisal*, for a more detailed discussion of several paired comparison techniques.

Figure 19.9

Examples of Scaled Comparisons Used in the Objective Judgment Quotient (OJQ) Method

1. CRITERION: PROBLEM SOLVING

a. John Smith	*Much Better*	*Slightly Better*	*Equal*	*Slightly Better*	*Much Better*	Mary Barnes
b. Excellent	*Much Better*	*Slightly Better*	*Equal*	*Slightly Better*	*Much Better*	John Smith
c. Jerry Wood	*Much Better*	*Slightly Better*	*Equal*	*Slightly Better*	*Much Better*	Average
d. Above Average	*Much Better*	*Slightly Better*	*Equal*	*Slightly Better*	*Much Better*	Mary Barnes

performance differences among employees. One such system is the **objective judgment quotient,** or **OJQ, method.**[30]

Employees participate in the development of job-related criteria for the OJQ evaluation, then select several people (generally five to eight), including their supervisor, to evaluate them. The rating form contains several scaled comparison items, examples of which are shown in Figure 19.9. Each rater scores several people on numerous job criteria. The scales for each job dimension compare one person with another and also with descriptive adjectives ranging from excellent to poor. From these comparisons, a performance profile for each employee can be calculated. The performance profile shows the employee how he or she stands on all performance criteria in comparison with all other rated employees.

The OJQ method provides good safeguards against most of the measurement problems discussed earlier. Since the system requires the manipulation of many rating scores, evaluating numerous employees requires a computer. The system's major problems include the expense of development and maintenance and the reluctance of employees to accept a complex procedure. In particular, supervisors may view the method as a threat to their power, since they are no longer the sole evaluators. Finally, this and other new appraisal methods have not been extensively used or tested.

Another evaluation technique that uses multiple raters and usually compares more than one employee involves an assessment center. Many companies use assessment centers for evaluation and development. See *International Perspec-*

[30] Mark R. Edwards, "OJQ Offers Alternative to Assessment Center," *Public Personnel Management Journal*, Vol. 12, 1983, pp. 146–155.

International Perspective

Development Centers at British Telecom

For more than thirty years, companies have been using assessment centers to help them choose people to hire and promote. Typically, a successful assessment center relies on careful analysis of the job in question, the creation of work simulations that parallel as closely as possible actual on-the-job situations, and the training of people (usually managers who supervise the job being filled) as role-players and assessors. Recently British Telecom joined a small number of other companies in taking the assessment center a step further by creating a development center.

British Telecom is in many ways the British equivalent of the American Telephone and Telegraph Company before diversification; it has been plagued with problems of late, and in 1985 some of its divisions underwent major structural changes. To deal with these changes, some British Telecom units wanted to train suitable employees to be the managers of the next decade. They used many techniques associated with traditional assessment centers, but instead of using the information they gathered to make hiring decisions, the company used it to create individual development programs for employees.

To create a development center, British Telecom and its consultants first agreed on the objective: to help future senior managers develop broad-based managerial skills. Then, using questionnaires and interviews with people currently in the targeted positions, the company defined the dimensions of managerial effectiveness, coming up with a list of thirteen priorities. Next it designed the center itself. Using ideas from company managers, consultants came up with ways to simulate typical situations that the new managers would face—negotiating with union representatives, for instance, or handling a meeting with a big customer who has a major service problem.

When the program was announced, the company was careful to make it clear that employees were to be the beneficiaries of the center. Participants nominated themselves and went through two days of tests, exercises, and job simulations, during which they were assessed by managers specially trained for the purpose. At the end of the process, the company came up with a unique development path for each participant.

It is too early to evaluate the results of British Telecom's center, but similar assessment programs at other companies have proved their cost-effectiveness. A study at Coca-Cola USA, for instance, looked at the costs of hiring new employees with and without an assessment center. The study found that those hired without the help of an assessment center were more than three times as likely to be fired as those hired with such help. Although the initial cost of hiring in the latter case was about 6 percent higher than normal, the lower rate of employee turnover meant that the company saved about $700,000 over the time of the study. If companies such as British Telecom can show that development centers yield equivalent savings, such centers are likely to become much more widespread in the near future.

Sources: Fredric D. Frank, David W. Bracken, Michael R. Struth, "Beyond Assessment Centers," *Training and Development Journal*, March 1988, 65–67; David Rodger and Christopher Mabey, "BT's Leap Forward from Assessment Centres," *Personnel Management*, July 1987, 32–35; Lynn Slavenski, "Matching People to the Job," *Training and Development Journal*, August 1986, 54–57.

tive for more on assessment centers and an example of a company that uses a similar resource: a development center.

PERFORMANCE APPRAISAL ISSUES

At least two questions are relevant to all methods of performance evaluation. The first—"Who does the appraisal?"—deals with the beginning of the process. The second—"How is the appraisal information used?"—is concerned with the results.

Who Does the Appraisal?

In most appraisal methods, the employee's primary evaluator is the supervisor,[31] but many other people who observe or are affected by the employee can contribute to the process. Some of these individuals are shown in Figure 19.10.

Appraisal problems often arise if the supervisor has less than full knowledge of the employee's performance. For example, the supervisor may have little first-hand knowledge of the performance of an employee who works alone outside the company premises, such as a salesperson who makes solo calls on clients or a maintenance person who handles equipment problems in the field. Similar problems may arise when the supervisor has a limited understanding of the technical knowledge involved in an employee's job.

One solution to these problems is a multiple-rater system that incorporates the ratings of several people who have experience with the performance of the employee being rated. Another possible solution is to use the employee as an evaluator. Although they may not actually do so, most employees can evaluate themselves in an unbiased manner.[32] Self-appraisals may be appropriate for evaluating and comparing a given employee's performance in different categories, such as performance quality, interpersonal skills, and team leadership, and they can be quite useful for development and performance improvement. Self-appraisals have little value for comparisons of the performance of different individuals, however.[33]

Whoever performs the evaluation must be properly trained. Training is usually designed to reduce rating errors by increasing the rater's observation and categorization skills.[34] In training sessions, raters are typically given examples of different performance levels and methods of recording observations, such as diary keeping. Employees usually perceive performance appraisals to be fair

---

[31] Henderson, *Performance Appraisal.*

[32] P. A. Mabe and S. G. West, "Validity of Self-Evaluation of Ability: A Review and Meta Analysis," *Journal of Applied Psychology,* June 1982, pp. 280–296.

[33] Clive Fletcher, "What's New in Performance Appraisal," *Personnel Management,* February 1984, pp. 20–22.

[34] Bernardin and Beatty, *Performance Appraisal.*

Figure 19.10

Potential Raters of
Employee Performance

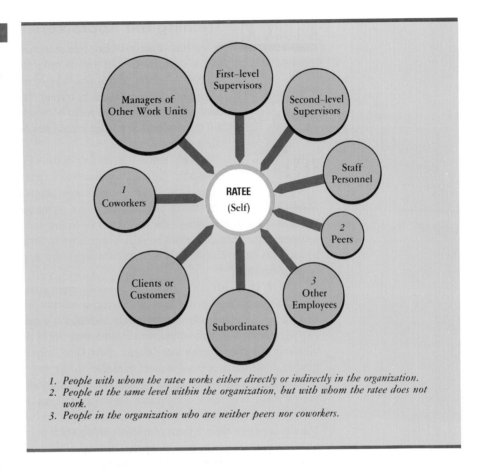

1. *People with whom the ratee works either directly or indirectly in the organization.*
2. *People at the same level within the organization, but with whom the ratee does not work.*
3. *People in the organization who are neither peers nor coworkers.*

if raters are trained and utilize some form of diary to record actual events.[35] See *A Look at Research* for more on training for performance appraisers.

How Is the Appraisal Information Used?

The end product of performance appraisal is information. This information can be used as a basis for feedback, reward allocation, training and development, and personnel planning. All these uses can benefit both the employee and the organization if the appraisal system is functioning properly.

Feedback tells the employee where she or he stands in the eyes of the department managers. Appraisal results, of course, are also used to decide and justify reward allocations. Performance evaluations may be used as a starting

---

[35] Jerald Greenberg, "Determinants of Perceived Fairness of Performance Evaluations," *Journal of Applied Psychology*, May 1986, pp. 340–342.

A LOOK AT

RESEARCH

Training the Appraisers

As performance appraisals have become increasingly important, researchers have tried to determine the best ways to make sure that appraisals are valid and accurate. A number of programs have been designed to improve individual raters' performance appraisals by training the raters in the appraisal process. David E. Smith surveyed the results of research on such programs and found that the most popular training method may be the least effective in improving rating accuracy.

Smith reviewed twenty-four studies, categorizing them by method of presentation (lecture, group discussion, or practice and feedback) and by content (Rater Error Training, Performance Dimension Training, and Performance Standards Training). The training programs were judged on the basis of how well they reduced the two most common rater errors—the tendency to be lenient and the tendency to allow a global judgment to taint ratings of particular skills (the halo error). Some programs were also judged on how well they taught raters to make accurate evaluations—that is, evaluations similar to those made by rating experts.

One of Smith's primary conclusions came as no surprise to educators: getting the raters actively involved in the training process improves their rating accuracy. Techniques involving practice and feedback were found to be the most consistently successful at increasing rating accuracy.

All three types of training programs reduced rating errors. However, reducing errors did not necessarily help raters improve their accuracy. Rater Error Training, the most widely used training program, is effective in reducing mistakes, particularly halo errors. But both Performance Dimension Training and Performance Standards Training were much more effective at teaching raters to make more accurate evaluations. Performance Dimension Training identifies the relevant limits of performance, which helps raters make evaluations free of global effects. Performance Standards Training helps give raters a frame of reference within which to evaluate performance; by learning how their appraisals match those of experts, raters can adjust their standards and their evaluations. In addition, this method seems to be most effective at combating the most common kinds of error.

To increase accuracy in ratings, Smith recommends a combination of Performance Dimension Training and Performance Standards Training. His conclusion is equally applicable to many other areas of training and education: teaching people to recognize errors helps them to avoid making mistakes, but to do a good job, they need to understand the dimensions and standards of performance of the job they are evaluating.

Source: David E. Smith, "Training Programs for Performance Appraisal: A Review," *Academy of Management Review*, January 1986, 22–40.

point for discussions on training, development, and improvement. And finally, the data produced by the performance appraisal system can be used to prepare personnel needs forecasts and management succession plans and to guide human resource activities such as recruiting, training, and development programs. Performance appraisal information can indicate that an employee is ready for promotion or that he or she needs additional training to gain experience in another area of company operations. It may also show that an individual does not have the skills for a certain job and that another person should be recruited to fill that particular role.

Job performance feedback is the primary use of appraisal information. Norman Maier has described three approaches to appraisal feedback: (1) tell and sell, (2) tell and listen, and (3) problem solving.[36] In the *tell and sell* approach, the manager gives the appraisal information and reward decision to the employee. In the *tell and listen* approach the manager also listens to the employee's responses, but the comments are not used to adjust the performance appraisal or to begin a discussion of long-term concerns such as training. *Problem solving* adds to the tell and listen approach an opportunity for the manager and employee to discuss differences of opinion and explore opportunities for the employee's development and improvement. At the same time, the organization can benefit from the information employees share with their managers—for instance, their future plans and their career aspirations.

SUMMARY OF KEY POINTS

Performance appraisal is the process by which work behaviors are measured and compared with established standards and the results recorded and communicated. Its purposes are to evaluate employees' work performance and to provide information for such organizational uses as compensation, personnel planning, and training and development.

The elements of performance appraisal are commitment to objectives, job analysis, and measurement. Clear objectives and strong organizational commitment make appraisal systems meaningful to supervisors and employees. Job analysis provides job-based information to be used in developing a performance appraisal system, as well as in writing job or position descriptions. Measurement issues include validity, reliability, bias, restriction of range, halo error, and timing problems.

Performance can be appraised through individual assessment methods (graphic rating scales, checklists, essays, behaviorally anchored rating scales, forced choice, and management by objectives); comparative techniques (ranking, forced distribution, and paired comparison); and new approaches that use multiple raters and comparative methods. Each method has advantages and disadvantages.

---

[36] Norman R. F. Maier, *The Appraisal Interview* (New York: John Wiley, 1958).

Primary disadvantages center on measurement problems such as validity, reliability, personal bias, restriction of range, and halo and timing errors.

Two basic issues of performance evaluation are who does the appraisal and how the appraisal information is used. More and more organizations are involving several people familiar with an employee's performance in his or her evaluation. Appraisal information is used in giving feedback to the employee, making decisions regarding reward allocation, planning training and development programs, and planning for future personnel needs.

DISCUSSION QUESTIONS

1. Why are employees not simply left alone to do their jobs instead of being evaluated at regular intervals?

2. In what ways is your performance as a student evaluated?

3. If you have had a performance evaluation in a full-time or part-time job, answer the following questions: What performance appraisal method was used? Was it an appropriate method? If your performance in a job has never been evaluated, discuss some of the reasons why not.

4. If you were the manager of a work group, which type of performance appraisal method do you think you would use? Why?

5. Suppose you are president of the college or school you attend. What type of performance appraisal system would you use for your employees? How would the evaluation procedure differ for the football coach, the dean of the College of Business, and the head of custodial services?

6. As a middle manager, would you want your subordinates or your peers to participate in evaluating your performance? Why or why not?

7. As a student in this class, would you want your classmates or other students in the school to evaluate your performance? Why or why not?

Case 19.1   ## Comparable Worth and Job Evaluation

A court case in the state of Washington that ended without a clear victory may nonetheless have far-reaching effects on the ways jobs are evaluated and compensated. The case has helped to create a national debate about the term "comparable worth," and it has increased the pressure on employers to develop formal job evaluations.

The state to some degree brought the lawsuit on, by commissioning a study of the pay of state employees in 1974. The study found that workers in jobs predominantly held by women were paid about 20 percent less than workers in jobs held largely by men, even though the skills, responsibilities, requirements, and conditions of the jobs were similar. Responding to its study, the state passed a law requiring that the pay inequities be phased out over a ten-year period, but that was too slow for some state employees, who filed a lawsuit in 1982 to force the state to do something about the inequities immediately. The plaintiffs won the first round in district court in 1983, but lost the appeal when the circuit court ruled that the state was not obliged "to eliminate an economic inequality which it did not create."* The state finally settled out of court, granting pay raises that will amount to almost half a billion dollars by the time they are fully implemented in 1992.

The case, and others like it, was based on the Equal Pay Act of 1963 and Title VII of the Civil Rights Act of 1964, which state unequivocally that women and men must be paid the same amount for doing the same job. The concept of comparable worth stretches that relatively simple law; its proponents argue that two people doing work of comparable value to their employer or to society should be paid the same amount. Although this idea might seem to be simple common sense, it is not current policy for most American employers. Women still earn less than two-thirds what men earn for comparable work, and the National Academy of Science has concluded, "Not only do women do different work than men but also the work women do is paid less, and the more an occupation is dominated by women, the less it pays."**

Although the original Washington lawsuit has been settled, others are reaching the courts, and several states and cities have passed laws based on comparable worth. In 1985, for instance, Los Angeles instituted a comparable worth system which, among other things, will bring the pay of typists up to that of drivers and warehouse workers, who were traditionally paid about 15 percent more.

Although the concept of comparable worth continues to be controversial, all American employers must now pay attention to it, if only to protect themselves against future lawsuits. Both companies trying to pay their employees equitably and those trying to fend off litigation have found formal job evaluations to be a key tool. Job evaluations enable an employer to compare the worth of very different jobs.

Systematic evaluations look at factors such as education and training, knowledge and experience, specialized skills, responsibility, interaction with the public, and job complexity. Typically, an employer weights each of these factors by assigning it a number, comes up with another number that indicates how much a particular job requires each factor, and multiplies the two figures. For instance, the employer might feel that communication responsibilities are particularly important, earning a .9 rating on a 0-to-1 scale. A managerial position with average communication responsibilities might get 50 points on a 1-to-100 scale for that factor. Multiplying the two numbers yields a total score for that

---

* Janet Conant and George Raine, "A Loss for Comparable Worth," *Newsweek*, September 16, 1985, p. 36.
** Marsha Katz, Helen Lavan, and Maura Sendelback Malloy, "Comparable Worth: Analysis of Cases and Implications for HR Management," *Compensation and Benefits Review*, May–June 1986, p. 26.

factor, in this case 45 points. By adding those points to the points in every other category for a particular job, the employer comes up with that job's total point value. The company can then assign a dollar value to each point and pay its employees accordingly.

There are problems with such job evaluation systems—how to factor in unusual skills or special tasks, for instance. But they do hold promise, and not just as a defensive maneuver taken by companies that are trying to protect themselves from lawsuits. They may gradually reduce the amount of favoritism and subjectivity, and therefore the amount of bad feeling, associated with compensation decisions.

Case Questions

1. Most opponents of comparable worth argue that the free market should determine pay scales. Which position makes more sense to you?

2. What advantages and disadvantages lie in setting up a formal, clearly defined job evaluation system?

Case Sources

John W. Johnson, "Working With Comparable Worth," *Association Management*, December 1985, 68–71; John E. Kasper, "The Point Plan," *Association Management*, December 1985, 73–75; Marsha Katz, Helen Lavan, and Maura Sendelbach Malloy, "Comparable Worth: Analysis of Cases and Implications for HR Management," *Compensation and Benefits Review*, May–June 1986, 26–38; "Typist-Driver," *Time*, May 20, 1985, 23; Janet Conant and George Raine, "A Loss for Comparable Worth," *Newsweek*, September 16, 1985, p. 36.

Case 19.2   The Principal's Dilemma

Marion Stanworth had been principal of Chester High School for less than a year, and she was more than a little anxious as she sat down to do her first appraisal of the teachers working under her. The anxiety turned to outright dread when Stanworth began to look at the forms she was expected to fill out. She could not remember exactly what kinds of forms her former school had used. Then, it had not mattered much, because she knew all the teachers and their supervisors, what their biases were, and how students related to them, and she felt confident that she could make a fair and accurate appraisal no matter what questions the form asked. Now, although she knew all the names and faces that she was evaluating, she felt less confident about her overall judgment and had to rely more on the reports that the department heads turned in and on the questions on the form—which probably had not been changed, she thought, since the school was built.

She almost gave up and went home when she saw that the first three questions all related to the teacher's appearance: Was the teacher dressed appropriately? Was the teacher neatly groomed? Did the teacher present the proper model of appearance for Chester students to emulate? Stanworth recalled her mental image of Ken Briar, the teacher in question. Was a handlebar mustache the right kind of model for students? Did the fact that he never wore a coat and tie mean that he should get a lower rating than Dick Krebbs, the biology teacher, who wore a bow tie and a white shirt that he could not keep tucked in? And what difference did it make anyway in a high school that had recently passed what she thought of as a minimalist dress code?

Mentally resolving not to let her own values be subverted by those represented by the form, she circled "excellent" for the first three questions and went on, wondering how she came to be doing a multiple-choice test in the first place. The next questions wanted to know about teaching methods, or rather "method;" Stanworth quickly noted that the form assumed that all teachers lectured all the time. Did the lectures reach an appropriate conclusion before the bell rang? Did they cover as much material as those of the other teachers of the subject? How was Mr. Briar's enunciation?

Stanworth had been to some of Ken Briar's classes and had been impressed that he had elicited comments from almost every student about the Spanish-American War, but she could not for the life of her remember anything about his enunciation. She remembered that students still had their hands raised when the bell rang; clearly the discussion was not finished. Was she supposed to hold that against him?

Hoping to find a question that would allow her to comment on the students' enthusiasm for Briar's class, she scanned the rest of the form. There were a number of questions on discipline. Was the noise level too loud? Did he often send unruly students to her office? When she thought she had seen all the questions about appearance, she found two more about the condition in which Briar kept his homeroom.

Finally, near the end of the form, Stanworth found a question about how the teacher related to students: Does the teacher violate the bounds between teacher and student and appear to pick favorites? After spending some time trying to decide whether "yes" or "no" was more damaging or more honest, she moved on to the last question, which asked for the department chair's rating of the teacher, on a one-to-five scale, and left a half-inch space for "principal's or department chair's comments."

Trying to calm her anger and frustration, Stanworth thought of everything that could be said in favor of the form. It was consistent; she could probably go back forty years and find how the American history teacher in those days had been rated on appearance. It was quick; she could have filled it out in five minutes if she had not gotten so upset about it. And it yielded a numerical score, which was important for merit pay purposes.

Unable to face the task any longer, Stanworth threw the form into the trash and called the superintendent of schools to make an appointment to talk about instituting a new evaluation system. She was sure that whatever they came up with would take more time to fill out than the present form, but she knew that even if she spent two hours evaluating Ken Briar, she would feel better about it than if she just circled twenty-five answers and moved on.

Case Questions

1. How valid and reliable is the instrument Stanworth is trying to fill out? What are the sources of problems?

2. What would be the basis for a better evaluation form in a high school?

**Experiential
Exercise**

Purpose: This exercise asks you to apply the concepts of job analysis discussed in the chapter to a job with which you are familiar.

Format: You will form small groups to analyze a job. The results will be presented in class and the findings compared.

Procedure: Each group should choose a job found on or near campus. The following is a list of typical jobs that might be interesting to analyze:

College dean	Bartender
Computer operator	Professor
Graduate teaching assistant	Secretary
Pizza delivery person	Librarian
Professional athlete	Coach
Newspaper editor	Waiter

Be sure to choose a job about which you can easily gather good information. You can obtain information by interviewing job holders and others who are familiar with the job, by using a position analysis questionnaire, by observation, or by other methods. Use all available resources and be creative in your thinking.

There are many ways to organize the information you gather. One way is to categorize job activities into tasks that deal with people, data, and things, as is done in Functional Job Analysis (FJA). FJA attempts to identify exactly what the worker does in the job as well as the results of the worker's behavior—what gets done. In addition, FJA examines why the job is done and what tools, equipment and instructions are available. Finally, it analyzes the job according to how much it involves interacting with people, being familiar with data, and manipulating things.

You can analyze the job you have chosen by answering the questions on the Functional Job Analysis Worksheet that follows. The final section on the worksheet lists activities that deal with data, people, and things. Describe the task of the job you have chosen by using words and numbers from each list. Within each category of worker functions, describe the task according to degree of difficulty. Information on the average amount of time the worker spends on each task may be helpful. By categorizing job activities in this way, you will be able to compare the information you have gathered with that developed by other teams. Remember, you are analyzing a job, not the person doing the job. (More information on FJA is available in the library, if you need it.)

In class, groups will present their findings on the board or on charts. Each group should list the job and the activities and tasks it involves. The group may comment on the difficulty of each task and the job's overall difficulty, and may compare job similarities and differences. Groups should share with the class the procedures they used to gather data and comment on the usefulness of each method in generating meaningful information.

Functional Job Analysis Worksheet

Job title

Primary job duties

Performs what action?

To whom or what?

To produce or achieve what?

Using what tools or instructions?

Worker Functions

Data	*People*	*Things*
0 Synthesize	0 Act as mentor	0 Set up
1 Coordinate	1 Negotiate	1 Perform precision work
2 Analyze	2 Instruct	2 Operate, control
3 Compile	3 Supervise	3 Drive, operate
4 Compute	4 Divert	4 Manipulate
5 Copy	5 Persuade	5 Tend
6 Compare	6 Speak-signal	6 Feed
	7 Serve	7 Handle
	8 Take instruction	

Follow-up Questions

1. Were you surprised by the level of difficulty of any of the jobs? Why or why not?

2. Did descriptions of the same job differ depending on the source of the information?

3. Which methods of gathering data seemed to yield the best results?

CHAPTER 20

Careers in Organizations

Chapter Objectives

After reading this chapter, you should be able to

- ▶ describe individual and organizational perspectives on careers.
- ▶ identify three elements of career choices.
- ▶ summarize a model of individual career choice decision making.
- ▶ identify the typical career stages and discuss their importance to individuals and organizations.
- ▶ discuss organizational career planning and career management.

fter earning a graduate business school degree in 1962, Henry B. Schacht began his career as a financial analyst for an investment firm. Just two years later, with help from contacts he had developed on that job, he moved to Cummins Engine Company, Inc., as vice president of finance. And by 1969, backed by Cummins's largest stockholder, he had become president of the company. Schacht's rise at Cummins culminated in 1977, when he became chairman.[1]

Douglas I. Flaherty also graduated from a graduate business program in 1962. He has worked in finance, at times as a financial executive, for numerous companies. At his previous position he engineered an agreement to merge with another company and then lost his job because of the takeover. He eventually caught on as a financial vice president at another company. If he had it to do over again, he said that he would go to medical school.[2]

Douglas I. Flaherty is not the only person who has not rapidly risen to the top in his or her chosen field. In fact, many people feel that they are in the wrong occupation. In a recent study initiated by Robert Half International, vice presidents and personnel directors from 100 of the nation's top 1,000 corporations estimated that 24.3 percent of employees (that is, almost one out of four workers) are unhappy and/or unsuccessful because they are in the wrong occupation or profession.[3] This means that nearly 30 million people are unhappy in their jobs. The impact on organizational productivity is immense. Clearly, if this problem is to be solved, both individuals and organizations need to know more about careers, career choices, and career management.

Why are so many people dissatisfied with their jobs and careers? How can organizations help employees pursue the careers that offer the greatest benefit to both the employees and the organization? Why do many people change not only their jobs but also the type of work they do several times during their work lives? How can organizations assure that when employees leave the organization, either by quitting or retiring, they will be quickly and efficiently replaced by highly qualified people?

The issues reflected in these questions have led organizations to invest large amounts of money, time, and effort in developing career management programs. In addition, researchers have begun to systematically study careers. This chapter examines both individual and organizational perspectives on careers by describing several aspects of career choices (such as the choice of occupation and the choice of organization), presenting information about career stages, and discussing organizational career planning.

---

[1] Earl C. Gottschalk, Jr., "Stars of 1962: How the Top Students at Harvard Business School Fare 20 Years Later," *The Wall Street Journal,* December 20, 1982, pp. 1, 12.

[2] Gottschalk, "Stars of 1962."

[3] *Banker's Digest,* June 22, 1987, p. 8.

INDIVIDUAL AND ORGANIZATIONAL PERSPECTIVES ON CAREERS

People often use the word *career* to refer to professional occupations of others and not to their own work or job. Indeed, many people do not even expect to have careers; they expect to have jobs.[4] A **career** is a "perceived sequence of attitudes and behaviors associated with work-related experiences and activities over the span of the person's life."[5] Whereas a job is what a person does at work to bring home a paycheck, a career is being engaged in a satisfying and productive activity.[6] Thus, a career involves a long-term view of a series of jobs and work experiences.

Individuals may have personal interests in careers—specifically, their own. As people evaluate job opportunities, those with a career perspective are usually concerned with factors such as those listed in Table 20.1. Note how these concerns have a long-term perspective—concerns for the future of technological change, economic conditions, and personal advancement. Many individuals see opportunities for advancement slowing as more people enter popular career fields. They see the rate of technical obsolescence accelerating with the advent of new and better computers and automated manufacturing processes. Individuals trying to establish their careers may have serious concerns when the rate of economic growth is declining. Individuals also perceive that new entrants are treated better than people already in the labor market—getting higher starting salaries, better opportunities, and the like. Further, companies are reorganizing and down-sizing, which increases uncertainty and decreases opportunities for advancement. Finally, aging is a concern—as people get older, they frequently see their career options narrowing and their opportunities shrinking.[7]

Organizations have a different perspective on careers.[8] They want to assure that managerial succession is orderly and efficient so that, when managers need to be replaced because of promotion, retirement, accident or illness, termination, or resignation, they can be replaced quickly and easily by highly qualified people. Organizations also want their employees to pursue careers in which they are interested and for which they have been properly trained. If individuals are unhappy with their career choices and opportunities, they may not perform well or may choose to leave the organization. Thus, organizations have an

---

[4] M. W. McCall and E. E. Lawler, III, "High School Students' Perceptions of Work," *Academy of Management Journal,* March 1976, pp. 17–24.

[5] D. T. Hall, *Careers in Organizations* (Santa Monica, Calif.: Goodyear Publishing, 1976), p. 4.

[6] M. Breidenbach, *Career Development: Taking Charge of Your Career* (Englewood Cliffs, N.J.: Prentice-Hall, Inc., 1988).

[7] C. Hymowitz, "Stable Cycles of Executive Careers Shattered by Upheaval in Business," *The Wall Street Journal,* May 26, 1987, p. 31.

[8] D. B. Miller, *Careers '79* (Saratoga, Calif.: Vitality Associates, 1979).

Table 20.1	
Individual Career Concerns	Opportunity for advancement slowing
	Technical obsolescence accelerating
	Rate of economic growth declining
	New entrants into the labor market receiving more favorable treatment
	Companies reorganizing
	Aging

Source: Adapted from C. Hymowitz, "Stable Cycles of Executive Careers Shattered by Upheavel in Business," *The Wall Street Journal.* May 26, 1987, p. 31. Reprinted by permission of *The Wall Street Journal.* ©Dow Jones & Company, Inc. (1987). All rights reserved.

interest in making sure that people are properly matched with good careers to achieve high levels of performance and lower levels of turnover.

Clearly, although their perspectives are not identical, individual employees and organizations can benefit from working together to improve career management. Career choices, however, remain in the hands of individuals.

CAREER CHOICES

Career choices occur more than once during a lifetime, since both people and career opportunities change. People need not be "locked in" to a particular career choice. Knowing that a change can be made should help individuals avoid becoming poor performers in their jobs as a result of career frustration.

Career choices are not something to take lightly, however; they are important in their own right and form the basis for future career decisions. As indicated in Figure 20.1, making a career choice involves six steps. First, an individual must become aware that a career choice is needed. This awareness may come about in a variety of ways. A recent high-school graduate may recognize the need to make a choice after being urged to find a job or declare a college major. A person already pursuing a career may consider choosing a new one after receiving a negative performance evaluation, being turned down for a big promotion, or being fired or laid off.

Second, the individual must obtain information about himself or herself and about available career options. Personal interests, skills, abilities, and desires can be identified by self-reflection as well as formal and informal consultation with others. In addition, information about the demands and rewards of various careers is available from numerous sources—career counselors, placement officers, friends, and family, for example.

The third step in the career choice process involves evaluating the information and looking for matches between the wants and needs of the

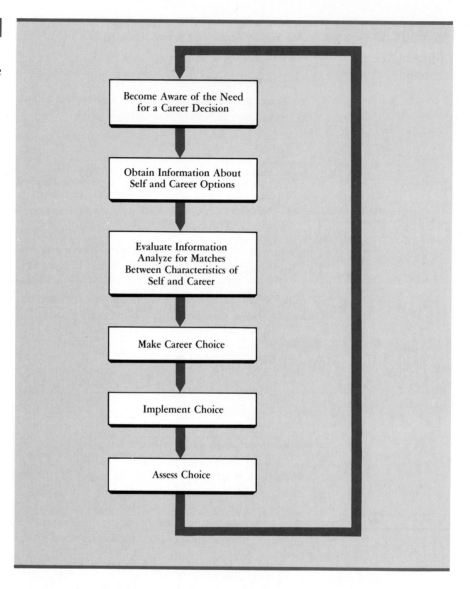

Figure 20.1

Simplified Model of
Individual Career Choice

individual and the characteristics of potential careers. This can be a frustrating and confusing time as the person finds that there are advantages as well as disadvantages to every career. Although the help of a good advisor or counselor is valuable, the next step—the decision—rests with the individual. In the fourth step, the individual must make a commitment to a career or a set of highly similar careers. Commitment means making the decision and initiating the next step, implementation.

Table 20.2		
Pressures in Individual Career Choice	Personal	Personal goals
		Personality
	Social	Family
		Friends
		Religion
	Work-related	Current position
		Organizational expectations

Implementing the decision involves actively pursuing the career—preparing through training, education, or internships; obtaining a position; and finally, working. After a time, the individual must assess the choice. As long as the result of the assessment is satisfactory, the individual continues to pursue the career; if the conclusion is not satisfactory, the individual becomes aware of the need for another career choice, and the process begins again.

In making career decisions, people are subjected to a number of pressures. As indicated in Table 20.2, these pressures may be personal, social, or work-related. An individual's personality and goals may be better suited to certain careers than to others, and a lack of agreement between the types of careers that seem to suit the person's personality and those appropriate to his or her personal goals can create internal, self-imposed conflicts. Social factors that create career pressure include urging from family or friends to quit a job or to take one job rather than another. Religious dictates can impose powerful career-related pressures on some individuals.

Work-related factors can also create career-related pressures. A person's current position in an organization, for example, may open certain career options; other options may simply be unavailable to one in that position. This is true of some state governmental jobs; if one wants to run for political office, one must resign any other government job first. In addition to formal requirements, informal expectations are associated with most positions in organizations. Certain job and career-related behaviors may be expected from a person in a particular position, which will usually put pressure on the jobholder to do the things expected. For example, coworkers may expect a colleague to seek managerial jobs in order to advance in the organization, when the person may enjoy her or his current position and may not wish to move into management.

Choice of Occupation

One major career choice confronting individuals is the choice of occupation. An **occupation,** or occupational field, is a group of jobs that are similar in terms of the type of tasks and training involved. They are usually found in many different organizations, as opposed to a job, which is organization-specific. The United States Bureau of the Census identifies hundreds, including such diverse occupations as accountants, auctioneers, bakers, carpenters, cashiers, dancers, embalmers, farmers, furriers, hucksters, loom fixers, newsboys, railroad conductors, receptionists, stockhandlers, waiters, weavers, and weighers.[9] Of course, these hundreds of occupations are not equally appealing to people.

Rankings of the desirability of occupations have often been made and seem to show a general stability. For instance, professions dominate the upper end of such evaluations. Physicians are nearly always among the occupations with the highest prestige, as are college and university professors, judges, and lawyers. The lowest-prestige occupations are more mixed. Bellhops, bootblacks, cleaners and janitorial workers, maids, teamsters, and ushers are among those consistently low in prestige.

Theories that explain how people choose among the many occupations available to them emphasize either content or process.[10] Content theories deal with factors—prestige, pay, and working conditions, for example—that influence career decisions. Process theories, on the other hand, deal with how people make these decisions.

Content theories focus on six major factors that influence what occupations people choose:

1. values and attitudes of the individual's family, especially parents[11]
2. interests and needs[12]
3. skills and abilities[13]
4. education
5. general economic conditions
6. political and social conditions

Process theories suggest that people make occupational choices in stages over time, seeking a match between their needs and occupational demands. According to this approach, although people begin thinking about occupations

---

[9] U.S. Bureau of the Census, *1980 Census of the Population: Alphabetical Index of Industries and Occupations* (Washington, D.C.: U.S. Government Printing Office, 1981).

[10] D. C. Feldman, *Managing Careers in Organizations* (Glenview, Ill.: Scott, Foresman and Company, 1988), pp. 189–192.

[11] P. M. Blau, J. W. Gustad, R. Jesson, H. S. Parnes, and R. C. Wilcox, "Occupational Choices: A Conceptual Framework," *Industrial and Labor Relations Review,* July 1956, pp. 531–543.

[12] Hall, *Careers in Organizations;* and J. L. Holland, *Making Vocational Choices* (Englewood Cliffs, N.J.: Prentice-Hall, 1973).

[13] D. C. Feldman and H. J. Arnold, "Personality Types and Career Patterns: Some Empirical Evidence on Holland's Model, *Canadian Journal of Administrative Science,* June 1985, pp. 192–210.

when they are very young, their thinking evolves and becomes more specific over time.[14]

One process model of occupational choice has been proposed by J. L. Holland. According to Holland, there are six basic personality types—realistic, investigative, artistic, social, enterprising, and conventional—each of which is characterized by a set of preferences, interests, and values. Occupations can also be grouped—working with things, working with observations and data, working with people, working in very ordered ways, exercising power, and using self-expression.[15] As people evaluate occupations over time, they attempt to match their occupational activities to their personality types. Table 20.3 shows Holland's proposed matching between personality types and various occupational activities.

Another process model is similar to the expectancy model of motivation introduced in Chapter 5. This framework assumes that people base their occupational choices on their probability of success.[16] Thus, in an expectancy approach, a person uses information on the anticipated outcomes of being employed in a given occupation and the probability of obtaining those outcomes to try to assess the attractiveness of the occupation.

This process may be used in comparing two occupations. For example, some people face a new occupational choice after several years in their chosen field. From an expectation point of view, the person may attempt to compare the costs and benefits of remaining in his or her current field against the advantages and disadvantages of a new occupation. The costs may be the loss of such things as seniority, pension benefits, and earning power if extensive retraining is involved. Benefits may include higher earnings long-term, different lifestyle, and daily activities which may seem inherently more enjoyable.

Choice of Organization

People must choose not only an occupation but also an organization in which to pursue that occupation. This is an important choice, since, for example, being an engineer for a municipal government may be far different from being an engineer for a private aerospace corporation. Indeed, some organizational differences—profit versus not-for-profit, large versus small, private versus governmental, and military versus nonmilitary, for instance—may be very

---

[14] E. Ginzberg, S. W. Ginzberg, W. Axelrod, and J. L. Herna, *Occupational Choice: An Approach to a General Theory* (New York: Columbia University, 1951), and Hall, *Careers in Organizations.*

[15] Holland, *Making Vocational Choices.*

[16] T. R. Mitchell and B. W. Knudsen, "Instrumentality Theory Predictions of Students' Attitudes Toward Business and Their Choice of Business as an Occupation," *Academy of Management Journal,* March 1973, pp. 41–52, and S. L. Rynes and J. Lawler, "A Policy-Capturing Investigation of the Role of Expectancies in Decisions to Pursue Job Alternatives," *Journal of Applied Psychology,* November 1983, pp. 620–631.

Table 20.3		
Holland Typology of Personality and Sample Occupations	**I. Realistic**	
	Personal Characteristics:	Shy, genuine, materialistic, persistent, stable.
	Sample Occupations:	Mechanical engineer, drill press operator, aircraft mechanic, dry cleaner, waitress.
	II. Investigative	
	Personal Characteristics:	Analytical, cautious, curious, independent, introverted.
	Sample Occupations:	Economist, physicist, actuary, surgeon, electrical engineer.
	III. Artistic	
	Personal Characteristics:	Disorderly, emotional, idealistic, imaginative, impulsive.
	Sample Occupations:	Journalist, drama teacher, advertising manager, interior decorator, architect.
	IV. Social	
	Personal Characteristics:	Cooperative, generous, helpful, sociable, understanding.
	Sample Occupations:	Interviewer, history teacher, counselor, social worker, clergyman.
	V. Enterprising	
	Personal Characteristics:	Adventurous, ambitious, energetic, domineering, self-confident.
	Sample Occupations:	Purchasing agent, real estate salesperson, market analyst, attorney, personnel manager.
	VI. Conventional	
	Personal Characteristics:	Efficient, obedient, practical, calm, conscientious.
	Sample Occupations:	File clerk, CPA, typist, keypunch operator, teller.

Source: Table, "Holland Typology of Personality and Occupations," from *Career Management* by Jeffrey H. Greenhaus, copyright © 1987 by The Dryden Press, a division of Holt, Rinehart and Winston, Inc. Reprinted by permission of the publisher.

important for the individual's ability to reach his or her goals and have a satisfying career.

Research suggests that in choosing an organization, individuals generally seek one that can provide some minimally acceptable level of economic return— a sort of "base pay." Beyond that, the most frequently sought-after features of an organization involve the opportunity it offers the individual to engage in interesting, challenging, or novel activities.[17] The type and size of the organization, its reputation, and its geographic location do not seem to be as important

---

[17] P. A. Renwick, E. E. Lawler, III, and staff, "What You Really Want From Your Job," *Psychology Today,* May 1978, pp. 53–65.

to people making career choices as the level of economic return and the nature of the activities in which they can expect to engage.[18]

Changing Careers

As people change, grow older, and mature, they may need to reevaluate their careers and make new choices. Someone who dropped out of school early in life, for example, may decide that the career options that have resulted from that choice are no longer acceptable and may return to school to open up new career opportunities. Life experiences may broaden a person's skills so that new career options become available. One increasingly popular career change option is to take one or more part-time jobs. Some interesting research suggests that the part-time option may benefit the employee as well as the organization. See *A Look at Research* for more about part-time job-holders.

Sometimes people find that as they have changed, their careers have changed. Although these people may not need to move from one occupation to another, some adaptation may be in order. Career adaptation may involve retraining to perform better on the job or to move to another job within the same career field. Adaptation may also mean changing organizations while pursuing the same career. The gradual changes that occur over time in careers are called **career stages**.

CAREER STAGES

Careers evolve through a series of stages—periods in which the individual's work life is characterized by distinctive needs, concerns, tasks, and activities. Career stages are closely associated with but not identical to the adult life stages identified by Erickson: adolescence, young adulthood, adulthood, and senescence.[19] As shown in Figure 20.2, there are generally five career stages—*entry, socialization, advancement, maintenance,* and *withdrawal.*

Entry

The entry stage is also known as the exploration stage. Exploration may be the more accurate label for the early part of the stage, in which self-examination, role tryouts, and occupational exploration occur. Individuals in this stage are usually, but not necessarily, young. This is the stage during which education and training are most commonly pursued. During the latter part of the stage, the individual enters a career, albeit tentatively, by trying out jobs associated with the career. This trial period may involve many different jobs as the

---

[18] D. C. Feldman and H. J. Arnold, "Position Choice: Comparing the Importance of Job and Organizational Factors," *Journal of Applied Psychology,* December 1978, pp. 706–710.

[19] E. H. Erikson, *Childhood and Society* (New York: Norton, 1963).

A LOOK AT

RESEARCH

Are Part-Timers Happier?

With changing demographics, more two-career couples, and the rise in consultants and people who work out of their homes, part-time workers have been gaining more attention. In 1967 13 percent of the labor force worked part-time; by 1984 that figure had risen to 18 percent. To investigate some of the effects of this trend, Ellen F. Jackofsky and Lawrence H. Peters studied almost 700 salespeople in a retail merchandising company. Their results give some indication of why more people are choosing to work part-time.

Of the salespeople studied, about 40 percent worked full-time, 23 percent worked part-time with regularly scheduled hours, and the remainder worked part-time with irregular hours, often during evenings, weekends, and holidays. All were paid salaries and treated in the same way by the company, except that the part-time workers did not receive standard benefits. The researchers administered a questionnaire to measure job satisfaction and attitudes about schedules and the possibility of quitting. Supervisors provided data about employee performance.

The performance of the three groups was essentially the same, which suggests that managers do not need to develop new policies to affect the performance of part-time workers. On the various measures of job satisfaction, however, the groups differed markedly. Full-time employees showed the least overall satisfaction with their jobs, whereas part-timers on irregular schedules were the most satisfied. The irregular part-timers also indicated that they were more satisfied than the other two groups with work, pay, and coworkers. Part-time workers with regular schedules experienced less conflict between their work and nonwork schedules than the other two groups did.

The researchers suggest that the structural flexibility of the company may have contributed to these somewhat surprising results. By giving part-time employees the option of working regular or irregular hours, the company may have avoided some conflicts between parenting and work. For instance, regular part-time working hours during the day might appeal to a parent who wants to be home while the other parent is working.

In effect, this research may say more about the full-time and part-time workers of the future than it says about employees in the past. More companies are allowing workers to create flexible schedules. If other research confirms the finding that people who work irregular part-time hours are satisfied and do good work, more companies may reexamine the way in which they devise work schedules, and more employees may challenge the advantages of a traditional full-time job.

Source: Ellen F. Jackofsky and Lawrence H. Peters, "Part-time Versus Full-time Employment Status Differences: A Replication and Extension," *Journal of Occupational Behaviour,* 8, 1987, 1–9.

Figure 20.2

A Model of Career Stages

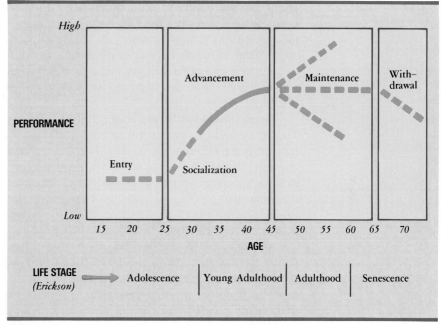

Source: From *Careers in Organizations* by Douglas T. Hall. Copyright © 1976 by Scott, Foresman and Company. Reprinted by permission.

individual explores a variety of organizations, occupations, and careers. Performance during this stage is represented in Figure 20.2 as a dashed line in order to indicate unpredictability.[20]

Socialization

The socialization stage has also been called the establishment stage. It usually begins with a trial period (shown in the figure by a dashed line) during which the individual continues to explore jobs, but much more narrowly than before. Then, as the individual becomes focused on a specific job, performance begins to improve. The individual is becoming established in the career. The sequence of getting established has been found to consist of three phases, which have been termed *getting in* (entry), *breaking in* (trial period), and *settling in* (establishment).[21]

During the socialization stage, people begin to form attachments and make commitments, both to others (new friends and coworkers) and to their

[20] Hall, *Careers in Organizations.*

[21] D. C. Feldman, "A Socialization Process That Helps New Recruits Succeed," *Personnel,* March–April 1980, pp. 11–23.

employing organizations. Employees begin to learn the organization's goals, norms, values and preferred ways of doing things; in other words, they learn the culture of the organization (see Chapter 16). In particular, they learn an appropriate set of role behaviors and develop work skills and abilities particular to their jobs and organizations; and they begin to demonstrate that, at least to some degree, they are learning to accept the values and norms of the organization.[22]

During the socialization stage, individuals must make many adjustments. They must learn to accept the fact that the organization and the people in it may be quite different from what they had anticipated. When they learn, for example, that other people do not appreciate their ideas, they must learn to deal with such resistances to change. Employees must also be prepared to face dilemmas that involve the making of on-the-job decisions. Dilemmas may pit loyalties to the job, to good performance, to the boss, and to the organization against each other. Career dilemmas may also involve ethical considerations.[23]

An organization can take actions to assure that the socialization stage is successful.[24] It can provide a relaxed orientation program for new personnel. It can see to it that the first job is challenging and that relevant training is provided. It can assure that timely and reliable feedback is provided to people in this early stage of their careers. Finally, it can place new personnel in groups with high standards to assure modeling of acceptable norms.

Advancement

The advancement stage is also known as the settling-down stage. Advancement begins to occur as the individual is recognized for the improved performance that comes with development and growth. The individual is learning his or her career and performing well in it. Soon he or she becomes less dependent on others, more independent.

As in the socialization stage, adjustments are often necessary within the advancement stage. Some individuals, of course, are less likely to make adjustments and learn than others. Those who are unsuccessful may change careers or may adapt in another way—by job hopping. **Job hopping** occurs when individuals make fewer adjustments within organizations but rather move to different organizations to advance their careers. This practice is becoming more characteristic of the advancement stage. It has gained acceptance and

---

[22] D. C. Feldman, "The Multiple Socialization of Organization Members," *Academy of Management Review*, April 1981, pp. 309–318.

[23] E. Schein, *Career Dynamics: Matching Individual and Organizational Needs* (Reading, Mass.: Addison-Wesley, 1978); and R. A. Webber, "Career Problems of Young Managers," *California Management Review*, Summer 1976, pp. 19–33.

[24] D. C. Feldman, "A Practical Program for Employee Socialization," *Organizational Dynamics*, Autumn 1976, pp. 64–80.

increased in recent years as more organizations have used outsiders to replace key managers to improve organizational performance.[25]

Vertical and horizontal, or lateral, movement also occurs frequently in the advancement stage. Vertical movement involves promotions, whereas lateral movement involves transfers. These kinds of movement teach people about several different jobs in the organization, a broadening experience that can benefit both the individuals and the organization. Organizations meet their staffing needs through such movement, and individuals satisfy their needs for achievement and recognition.

Job moves, whether to a new organization or within the same organization, can cause problems, however. Invariably, higher-level jobs bring increased demands for performance, and frequently there is less preparation for managers moving into these jobs. They are usually expected to step right into top executive positions and perform well, with little time for socialization into a new system. Further, moves often necessitate relocation to other parts of the country, placing stress on not only the job holder but also his or her family.

Organizations can take steps to manage promotions and transfers to reduce problems. Longer-term, careful career planning may reduce the need to relocate, since much of the broadening may be accomplished at one location. The timing and spacing of moves can be coordinated with, or at least adjusted to, the individual's family situation. More importantly, better training can be provided to enable the individual to make the move more readily and with substantially less stress.

Maintenance

In the maintenance stage, individuals develop a stronger attachment to their organizations and, hence, lose some career flexibility. Performance varies considerably in this stage. It may continue to grow, it may level off, or it may decline. If performance continues to grow, this stage continues as a direct extension of the advancement stage. If performance levels or drops, career changes may result.

If leveling off occurs, the individual is said to have reached a plateau in her or his career. Responses to plateauing can be effective or ineffective for the individual and the organization. Those who respond effectively to plateaus have been termed *solid citizens*; they have little chance for further advancement but continue to make valuable contributions to the organization. Those whose responses are ineffective are referred to as *deadwood*; they, too, have little chance for promotion, but they contribute little to the organization.[26]

---

[25] J. A. Bryne with A. L. Cowan, "Should Companies Groom New Leaders or Buy Them?" *Business Week,* September 22, 1986, pp. 94–96.

[26] T. P. Ference, J. A. F. Stoner, and E. K. Warren, "Managing the Career Plateau," *Academy of Management Review*, October 1977, pp. 602–612.

Mentoring

Mentoring has become a very popular concept—too popular, according to some. The idea is simple: an older, more experienced person helps a younger person grow and advance by providing advice, support, and encouragement. Good teachers, coaches, parents, and bosses all take on some mentoring functions, and in the past decade formal mentoring programs have been set up in schools as well as businesses.

The popularity of mentoring is based on relatively little research. Those who study the lives of successful people disagree about the importance of mentoring to successful careers, and the definition of the word has become stretched as its application has become more varied. Daniel J. Levinson, a Yale psychologist, concluded in his book *The Seasons of a Man's Life* that "the mentor relationship is one of the most complex and developmentally important a man can have in early adulthood."* Yet according to Levinson, true mentors help their protégés clarify and realize their dreams, whereas most business versions of mentoring are "a perversion."** A business mentor can help a young colleague realize his or her dreams only if those dreams happen to center on advancing in that particular company.

Despite such criticisms and qualifications, many businesses have recently implemented formal mentoring programs, and many others rely on more traditional informal networks. These companies believe that creating a bond between a senior and a junior employee helps both of the individuals involved and benefits the company as well. The mentor often gets in touch with the feelings and attitudes of a younger generation and can learn about new research and techniques from the protégé. The younger colleague can pick up practical skills from the mentor and also gain insights into the corporate culture and philosophy that could otherwise take years to discover. A strong, secure bond between the two can lead one or both to do more innovative, important work than they might do on their own.

Solid citizens become interested in establishing and guiding the next generation of organizational members. As a result, they frequently begin to act as mentors for younger people in the organization. As mentors, they show younger members the "ins and outs" of organizational politics and help them learn the values and norms of the organization. For more on mentoring, see *Management in Action*. These individuals also begin to reexamine their goals in life and rethink their long-term career plans. In some cases, this leads to new values (or the re-emergence of older ones) that cause the individuals to quit their jobs or pass up chances for promotions.[27] In other cases, individuals achieve new insights and begin to move upward again; such individuals are known as *late bloomers*.[28]

---

[27] D. LaBier, "Madness Stalks the Ladder Climbers," *Fortune*, September 1, 1986, pp. 79–84.

[28] F. Rice, "Lessons from Late Bloomers," *Fortune*, August 31, 1987, pp. 87–91.

For the company, this kind of bond can pay off in a number of ways. As the baby-boom generation ages, businesses have to try harder to find and keep good employees. An employee who feels secure in the company because of a good mentoring relationship is less likely to think about looking for another job. Mentors can be especially important for employees who might have trouble fitting into an organization. To move up in a company dominated by an old-boy network, for instance, women and minority employees often need contacts of their own in the company's higher ranks. Similarly, multinational corporations may find mentors useful in helping managers from other countries to fit into the culture of the corporation. Mentors can also help executives of merged companies adjust to the philosophies and expectations of their new employers.

To get the most out of mentoring programs, experts say, companies must do more than just put two people together and hope for the best. They need to determine what the goals of the program are—to teach specific skills, to help new people get along with other employees, or to introduce employees to corporate philosophies. Clarifying these goals should help the organization decide who will make the best mentors. Middle managers may be best at helping new people develop specific skills, whereas senior managers may be more effective at passing on the company's version. In any case, a key element in any mentoring program is matching the two individuals, for the protégé needs to feel that he or she is gaining a friend, not another boss.

Sources: "Guidelines for Successful Mentoring," *Training*, December 1984, 125; Dan Hurley, "The Mentor Mystique," *Psychology Today*, May 1988, 39–43; Michael G. Zey, "A Mentor For All Reasons," *Personnel Journal*, January 1988, 47–51.

  * Dan Hurley, "The Mentor Mystique," *Psychology Today*, May 1988, 42.
** Ibid, p. 43.

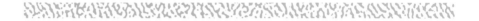

Individuals who have become deadwood are more difficult to deal with. However, their knowledge, loyalty, and understanding of plateauing represent value to the organization which could be salvageable. Perhaps rewards other than advancement would keep these persons productive. Their jobs might be redesigned (see Chapter 8) to facilitate performance, or they might be reassigned within the organization. And, of course, career counseling programs (discussed later in this chapter) could help them to reach a better understanding of their situations and opportunities.[29]

If performance declines, the individual may be experiencing some type of midlife crisis, which is associated with such effects as awareness of physical aging and the nearness of death, a reduction in career performance, the recognition that life goals may not be met, and changes in family and work relationships. Individuals handle midlife crises differently. Some develop new

---

[29] R. C. Payne, "Mid-Career Block," *Personnel Journal*, April 1984, pp. 38–48.

patterns for coping with the pressures of careers. They may change careers or modify the way in which they are handling their current careers. Others have a more difficult time and may need professional assistance.

Changing jobs has become fairly common during the maintenance stage. Many such moves have proved to be highly beneficial to the person involved. Several "executive dropouts," for example, have become successful entrepreneurs, such as James L. Patterson, who left IBM to co-found Quantum Corporation.[30] Of course, not all job changes at this stage lead to success. Some job changers find, much to their dismay, that the grass is not greener in the new job, and they experience just as much frustration and disappointment as they did in the old job.[31]

Withdrawal

The final stage—the withdrawal, or decline, stage—frequently involves the end of full-time employment as the individual faces retirement and other end-of-career options. Some individuals begin new careers at this stage, and others level off, but the general pattern is one of decreasing performance. Again, individual adaptation may be positive—beginning a new career, helping others, or learning to accept retirement—or negative—becoming indifferent, giving up, or developing abnormally high dependence on family and friends.

Even though legislation may restrict an organization's power to force retirement at the age of sixty-five, many individuals nevertheless do quit full-time employment at about that age, and a number of organizations encourage even earlier retirement for many of their members. Problems may arise for people who are not prepared for the changes retirement brings. An individual who is not ready to retire or feels forced to do so may have an especially difficult time adapting to those changes. To help employees adjust, many organizations are initiating preretirement programs that include information on health, housing, financial planning, legal issues, time management, and social programs for maintaining involvement in the community.

Hall and Hall have argued that the use of the career growth cycle can help organizations manage careers, especially at this crucial stage.[32] The career growth cycle is shown in Figure 20.3. Initially, the organization assures that jobs offer challenging goals and supports employees' efforts to achieve those goals. If feedback is positive, the employees experience psychological success, which enhances their self-esteem and leads to greater involvement. Less positive feedback, however—which people often receive in the withdrawal stage—has

---

[30] J. Main, "Breaking Out of the Company," *Fortune*, May 25, 1987, pp. 81–88.

[31] L. Reibstein, "Crushed Hopes: When a New Job Proves to Be Something Different," *The Wall Street Journal*, June 10, 1987, p. 27.

[32] D. T. Hall and F. S. Hall, "What's New in Career Management," *Organizational Dynamics*, Summer 1976, pp. 17–33.

Figure 20.3   The Career Growth Cycle

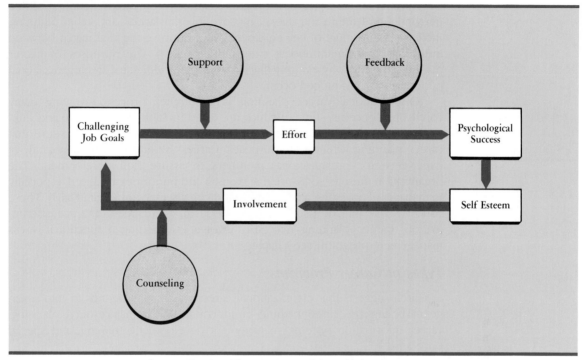

Source: Reprinted by permission of the publisher from "What's New in Career Management," by D. T. Hall and F. S. Hall, *Organizational Dynamics*, Summer 1976, pp. 31. © 1976 American Management Association, New York. All rights reserved.

the opposite effect. In this instance, the organization provides counseling to help the individual adapt to the changing circumstances.

ORGANIZATIONAL CAREER PLANNING

Career planning is the process of planning one's life work and involves evaluating abilities and interests, considering alternative career opportunities, establishing career goals, and planning practical development.[33] Organizations have a vested interest in the careers of their members, and career planning and development programs help them to enhance employees' job performance and thus the overall effectiveness of the organization.

[33] J. Walker, "Does Career Planning Rock the Boat?" *Human Resource Management*, Spring 1978, pp. 2–7.

Purposes of Career Planning

Organizational career planning programs can help companies identify qualified personnel and future managers, improve job satisfaction and other attitudes, increase involvement of key employees, and improve the vital match between individual and organizational wants and needs.[34] The purposes of career planning, then, involve assuring that such enhanced individual and organizational performance does indeed occur.

Organizational career planning is a complex process involving many conflicting concerns, some of which are listed in Table 20.4. Reliable and valid personnel decision techniques must be used in organizations to assure that career planning achieves its purposes. Careers should provide a breadth of experience for organizational members to assure skill development. The organization must act to assure that women and minorities are hired, especially in managerial positions, and that these individuals are compensated fairly. These concerns also include issues such as nepotism, dual careers, and age discrimination. Career planning may also involve establishing a functional stress management program (see Chapter 7).

Types of Career Programs

Research suggests that organizational career planning programs fit into seven general categories: career pathing, career counseling, human resource planning, career information systems, management development, training, and special programs.[35]

CAREER PATHING   Career pathing is the identification of career tracks, or sequences of jobs, that represent a coherent progression vertically and laterally through the organization. Figure 20.4 illustrates two such paths—one for an engineering/technical career and one for a sales/marketing career. Paths like these may be clearly specified in some organizations, whereas other organizations may allow far more flexibility. Most organizations do not adhere too strictly to specific career paths, since that might limit the full utilization of individual potential, and there are always many exceptions to specified paths.[36] Such organizations provide opportunities for both horizontal and vertical movement to enable individuals to develop their skills and breadth of experience. Some career paths may include assignments overseas to help prospective top managers gain an understanding of its international operations. See *Interna-*

[34] C. S. Granrose and J. D. Portwood, "Matching Individual Career Plans and Organizational Career Management," *Academy of Management Journal*, December 1987, pp. 699–720.

[35] M. A. Morgan, D. T. Hall, and A. Martier, "Career Development Strategies in Industry—Where Are We and Where Should We Be?" *Personnel*, March–April 1979, pp. 13–30.

[36] T. A. DiPrete, "Horizontal and Vertical Mobility in Organizations," *Administrative Science Quarterly*, December 1987, pp. 422–444.

Table 20.4	
Organizational Career Planning Concerns	Reliable and valid personnel decision techniques
	Breadth of experience provided
	Hiring of women
	Dual careers
	Nepotism
	Employee benefits
	Vocational rehabilitation
	Stress management
	Equal pay
	Affirmative action
	Hiring of minorities
	Age discrimination
	Skill development

tional Perspective for more on succeeding as an expatriate manager. Career paths usually have a time frame (frequently five to ten years), may be updated periodically, and may be developed to assure that the work experiences are relevant to a particular target (that is, higher-level) position in the organization.

CAREER COUNSELING   Organizations use both informal and formal approaches to career counseling.[37] Counseling occurs informally as part of the day-to-day supervisor-subordinate relationship and often during employment interviews and performance evaluation sessions as well (see Chapter 19). More formally, career counseling is often provided by the personnel department and is available to all personnel, especially those who are being moved up, down, or out of the organization.[38]

HUMAN RESOURCE PLANNING   Human resource planning involves forecasting an organization's human resource needs, developing replacement charts (charts showing planned succession of personnel) for all levels of the organization, and preparing inventories of the skills and abilities needed by individuals to move within the organization. As shown in Figure 20.5, human resource planning and development systems can be quite complex and involve both

[37] N. C. Hill, "Career Counseling: What Employees Should Do—and Expect," *Personnel,* August 1985, pp. 41–46.

[38] W. Kiechel, III, "Passed Over," *Fortune,* October 13, 1986, pp. 189–191; and J. C. Latack and J. B. Dozier, "After the Ax Falls: Job Loss as a Career Transition," *Academy of Management Review,* April 1986, pp. 375–392.

Figure 20.4

Examples of Possible
Career Paths

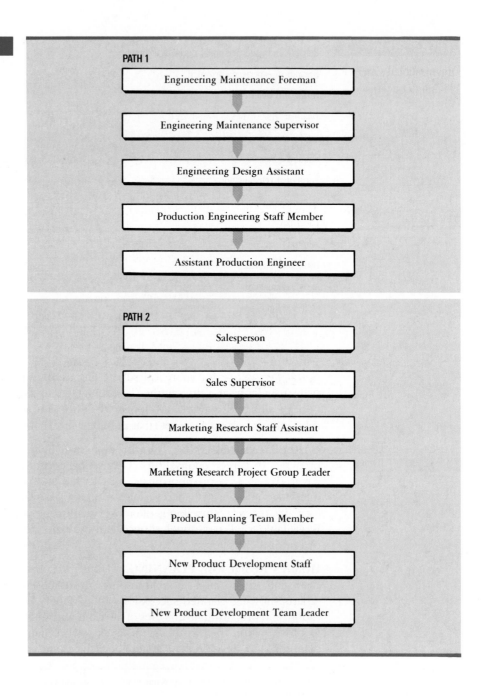

PATH 1

Engineering Maintenance Foreman

Engineering Maintenance Supervisor

Engineering Design Assistant

Production Engineering Staff Member

Assistant Production Engineer

PATH 2

Salesperson

Sales Supervisor

Marketing Research Staff Assistant

Marketing Research Project Group Leader

Product Planning Team Member

New Product Development Staff

New Product Development Team Leader

individual and organizational activities. Basically, though, such systems involve developing plans, matching organization and individuals, assessing needs, and implementing the plans. It is the specific applications that lead to the complexity of the system.

CAREER INFORMATION SYSTEMS   When internal job markets are combined with formal career counseling to establish a career information center for organizational members, the result is a career information system. Internal job markets exist when job openings within the organization are announced first to organization members. News about openings may appear on bulletin boards, in newsletters, and in memoranda. A career information center keeps up-to-date information about such openings, as well as information about employees who are seeking other jobs or careers within the organization. Career information systems, then, can serve not only to develop the organization's resources but also to provide information that may increase the motivation of organization members to perform.

MANAGEMENT DEVELOPMENT   Management development programs vary considerably. They may consist simply of policies that hold managers directly responsible for the development of their successors, or they may set out elaborate formal educational programs. Management development is receiving increasing attention in all types of organizations. On average, managers are participating in from twenty to forty hours per year of education and development activities[39] dealing with such topics as time management, problem solving and decision making, strategic planning, and leadership. Developmental programs in smaller organizations (those with less than 1,000 employees) tend to focus on management and supervisory skills, communication, and behavioral skills. In larger organizations, developmental activities typically concentrate on executive development, new management techniques, and computer literacy.[40] Management development is discussed in more detail in Chapter 23.

TRAINING   More specialized efforts to improve skills are usually termed **training**. These activities include on-the-job training, formalized job rotation programs, in-house training sessions for the development of specific technical job skills, programs on legal and political changes that affect specific jobs, tuition reimbursement programs, and student intern programs. The emphasis is usually on specific job skills, with immediate performance being of greater concern than long-term career development. Of course, continued improvement in job performance carries implications about evolving career opportunities.

SPECIAL PROGRAMS   Training and development programs may be designed for and offered to special groups within an organization. Preretirement programs

---

[39] E. H. Burack, *Creative Human Resource Planning and Applications: A Strategic Approach* (Englewood Cliffs, N.J.: Prentice-Hall, 1988).

[40] Burack, *Creative Human Resource Planning and Applications.*

International Perspective

Succeeding Overseas

What does it take to succeed in an overseas assignment? How can someone tell whether he or she should make a career of working in a foreign country? Research and the experiences of Americans working for multinational corporations provide some answers.

Many companies have sent the wrong people overseas because they have tried to use the same criteria for foreign appointments as they use for domestic promotions. Certainly technical competence is important abroad as well as at home, but those who have worked overseas rank it as less important than such "unbusinesslike" matters as the feelings of the candidate's spouse about moving abroad. To succeed in a foreign country, a businessperson may need very different skills from those that help the average American executive get to the top.

A good expatriate manager should be flexible, open-minded, and well rounded; some consultants on international management list "breadth" as the most important single characteristic. Placed suddenly into a new environment, expatriate managers must be flexible enough to use very different resources and methods, but they also cannot be seen as pushovers. In their personal lives, they need to be emotionally stable enough to keep an even keel even when they have no control over or understanding of what is going on around them. They also must be able to find substitutes in their new surroundings for those activities that bring them pleasure and reduce stress at home. Someone who can easily substitute sushi for steak and meditation for Monday night football will do well overseas.

Besides these personal qualities, good overseas managers need to have particular skills for working with people. They should be self-motivated and self-reliant, but they cannot be loners. They almost certainly will need the cooperation of those around them, and to get it they must be good listeners who are able to respect and appreciate attitudes and ideas that differ radically from their own. Although knowing the host language is obviously important, research has shown that it is even more important for Americans working abroad to be willing to use the language, to make mistakes, to laugh at their errors, and to pick up jokes, anecdotes, and slang in the host language. These skills are not simply tools to get business transacted but ways to improve interactions and understand the new culture.

Such understanding is part of another subtle but very important factor: perceptual openness. Good expatriate managers must not only tolerate the foreign culture but appreciate and value it on its own terms. They should be curious, not judgmental, about the new culture. As much as possible, they need to see the world through their hosts' eyes.

Sources: Lennie Copeland and Lewis Griggs, "The Internationable Employee," *Management Review,* April 1988, 52–53; Allen L. Hixon, "Why Corporations Make Haphazard Overseas Staffing Decisions," *Personnel Administrator,* March 1986, 91–94; Mark Mendenhall and Gary Oddou, "The Dimensions of Expatriate Acculturation: A Review," *Academy of Management Review,* 10:1, 1985, 39–47.

Figure 20.5   A Human Resource Planning and Development System

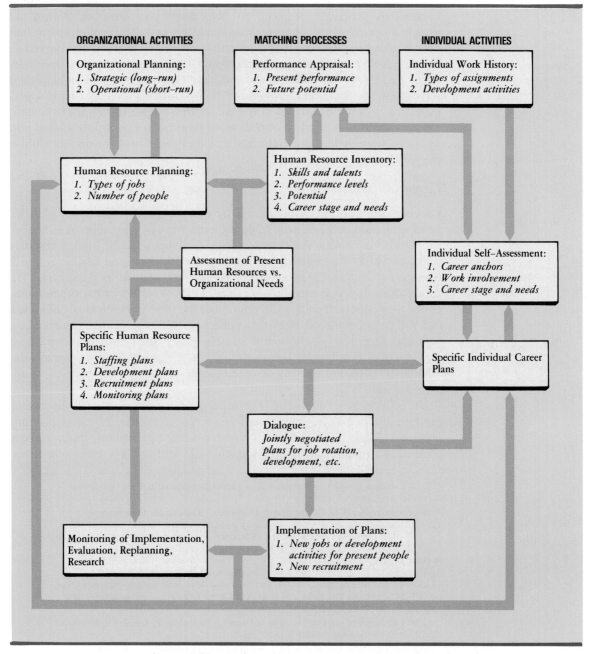

Source: Edgar H. Schein, *Career Dynamics: Matching Individual and Organizational Needs*, copyright © 1978, Addison-Wesley Publishing Company Incorporated, Reading, MA, p. 4, Figure 1.2. Reprinted with permission.

offer one example, as do programs designed to help members of the organization cope with midlife career crises. Many organizations now offer outplacement counseling—programs designed to help employees who are leaving the organization, either voluntarily or involuntarily.[41] Outplacement programs help people preserve their dignity and self-worth when they are fired and can reduce negative feelings toward the organization. Other special programs have been developed for women, minorities, and handicapped personnel to help them solve their special career problems.[42] Some organizations also have special programs to assist personnel in the career move from technical positions to managerial ones. Still other organizations have begun programs to deal with smokers, since it has become clear that they pose health risks not only to themselves but also to others.[43]

Career Management

Career management is the process by which organizational career planning is implemented. As shown in Table 20.5, top management support is needed to establish a climate that fosters career development. All human resource activities within the organization must be coordinated, and human resource managers from various areas should be involved at least as consultants. The career planning programs must be open to all members of the organization, and so they must be flexible to accommodate the variety of individual differences that will be encountered. Realistic feedback should be provided to participants with the focus on psychological success rather than simply advancement. Implementation of new programs should begin with small pilot programs that emphasize periodic assessment of employee skills and experiences of the program itself.[44]

It is extremely important that supervisors be involved and be trained carefully lest they neglect or mishandle their role and negate the career planning programs. Their role includes communicating information about careers; counseling to help subordinates identify skills and options; evaluating subor-

---

[41] T. M. Camden, "Using Outplacement as a Career Development Tool," *Personnel Administrator,* January 1982, pp. 35–44.

[42] See, for example, D. D. Bowen and R. D. Hisrich, "The Female Entrepreneur: A Career Development Perspective," *Academy of Management Review,* April 1986, pp. 393–407; "Male vs. Female: What a Difference It Makes in Business Careers," *The Wall Street Journal,* December 9, 1986, p. 1; M. Sullivan, "In Dad's Footsteps: More Women Find a Niche in the Family Business," *The Wall Street Journal,* May 28, 1987, p. 29; D. D. Van Fleet and J. Saurage, "Recent Research on Women in Leadership and Management," *Akron Business and Economic Review,* Summer 1984, pp. 15–24; and E. M. Van Fleet and D. D. Van Fleet, "Entrepreneurship and Black Capitalism," *American Journal of Small Business,* Fall 1985, pp. 31–40.

[43] A. M. Freedman, "Cigarette Smoking Is Growing Hazardous to Careers in Business," *The Wall Street Journal,* April 23, 1987, pp. 1, 19.

[44] Adapted from Feldman, *Managing Careers in Organizations,* pp. 189–192. See also K. B. McRae, "Career-Management Planning: A Boon to Managers and Employees," *Personnel,* May 1985, pp. 56–61.

Table 20.5	Coordination with other human resource activities
Key Ingredients for Career Management	Involvement of supervisors
	Use of human resource managers as consultants
	Periodic skill assessment
	Realistic feedback about career progress
	Top management support
	Equal access and open enrollment
	Focus on psychological success rather than advancement
	Flexibility for individual needs
	Climate setting for career development
	Small pilot programs
	Periodic program assessment

Source: From *Managing Careers in Organizations* by Daniel C. Feldman. Copyright © 1988 by Scott, Foresman and Company. Reprinted by permission.

dinates' performance, strengths, and weaknesses; coaching or teaching skills and behaviors; advising about the realities of the organization; serving as a mentor or role model for subordinates; brokering, or bringing together subordinates and those who might have positions better suited to them; and referring subordinates to opportunities.[45]

Results of Career Planning

Organizational career planning has many important results.[46] Ideally, the most significant ones are its benefits. Employees develop more realistic expectations of what is expected of them on the job and what their future with the organization will entail. Supervisory roles in career counseling are clarified, personal career planning ability is increased through knowledge and education, and personnel systems within the organization are more effectively utilized. All of these effects serve to strengthen career commitment as individuals develop plans to take charge of their careers. Ultimately, then, the organization is able to better use the talent of its members, turnover is reduced, and individual and corporate performance is increased.

[45] Z. B. Leibowitz and N. K. Schlossberg, "Training Managers for Their Role in a Career Development System," *Training and Development Journal,* July 1981, pp. 72–79.

[46] Walker, "Does Career Planning Rock the Boat?"

These benefits are not, however, guaranteed. If the existence of an organizational career planning program raises individual expectations unrealistically, dysfunctional consequences may result. Anxiety may increase, supervisors may find that they spend too much time counseling their subordinates, and personnel systems may become overloaded. These effects lead to frustration, disappointment, and reduced commitment. In the end, talent is not well used, turnover increases, and individual and organizational performance suffers. The key to not raising employee expectations unrealistically is for all supervisors and managers to be trained to be careful to only provide realistic information about jobs and the true prospects for an employee. Clearly, organizations must use career planning programs carefully to ensure that their results are positive.

SUMMARY OF KEY POINTS

Individuals' concerns about careers are related to their perceived opportunities for success. Organizations, on the other hand, want to assure smooth managerial succession and high levels of individual and organizational performance. These two different perspectives are compatible, since individuals achieving their career goals are likely to be high performers. Thus, organizations can achieve their objectives by helping individuals achieve theirs.

Career choice occurs whenever an individual makes a conscious decision about beginning or continuing a career. It involves six steps: becoming aware of the need for a career choice, getting information about oneself and career options, evaluating the information, making a career choice, implementing that choice, and assessing the choice.

In addition to a basic career choice, people make two associated types of decisions—a choice of occupation and a choice of organization. Content and process theories of occupational choice recognize both the complexity of the process by which such choices are made and the variety of forces that influence the choices. Organizational choice generally involves selecting an organization that will provide some minimally acceptable level of economic benefit, as well as the opportunity to engage in interesting, challenging, or novel activities.

Research suggests that careers evolve through a series of general stages. Although career stages are closely associated with adult life stages, they are not the same. The career stages are entry, socialization, advancement, maintenance, and withdrawal.

Organizations engage in career planning to achieve a variety of purposes of value to both the organizations and the individuals in them. Seven general categories of career planning programs exist: career pathing, career counseling, human resource planning, career information systems, management development, training, and special programs.

Career management is the process by which organizational career planning is implemented. It requires top management support, the widespread use of human resource personnel, and a favorable climate for utilizing the organization's human resources to the fullest. Especially important is the involvement and cooperation of supervisors.

The results of organizational career planning may be beneficial or dysfunctional. Careful monitoring of the program should assure that benefits are obtained. Such benefits include the development of realistic expectations on the parts of all involved with a resultant full utilization of human resources to increase both individual and organizational performance.

DISCUSSION QUESTIONS

1. Have you known anyone who seemed to be in the wrong occupation? What evidence made it seem that way?

2. Are individual and organizational perspectives on careers always compatible? Why or why not?

3. What career choices might exist for someone with an undergraduate business degree? A graduate business degree?

4. Differentiate the terms *jobs, occupations,* and *careers* from one another.

5. Discuss the five career stages and discuss what options might exist for an individual who changes careers during one of the latter stages.

6. What happens when a relatively young worker—say someone in his or her mid-forties—moves into the career stage of maintenance or withdrawal? Is this positive for the organization or the individual? What can the organization do about it?

7. Briefly discuss each of the seven general categories of career planning programs. How might each of these apply to people at different career stages?

8. What is meant by the statement that careers are managed? Who does the managing of careers?

9. Is the concept of organizational career planning realistic in the rapidly changing environment of today's business? Why or why not?

10. Changing occupations in mid-career can be a traumatic event. What is the role of the organization in helping employees to change jobs in the middle of their careers?

Case 20.1   The Case of the Glass Ceiling

More and more women are entering the business world and working their way up through the management ranks. In the mid-1970s, fewer than one-quarter of all American corporate managers were women; a decade later, that figure had grown to about 37 percent. More women are also getting MBAs, the traditional first step to the executive suite. In 1967 women earned only 2 percent of the country's MBAs. A decade later, that figure was up to 12 percent, and by 1987 it had risen to over 33 percent. The faces of women vice presidents smile from the pages of business magazines, heralding the changes in corporate America.

Nevertheless, very few of these women make it to the top of their organizations. Women executives seem to bump their heads against a "glass ceiling" in their rise to the top. Women are promoted less quickly than equally qualified men, become stalled much more often in middle-management ranks, and earn less money despite equal performance appraisals—as much as 42 percent less, according to one study.

Business leaders faced with such facts have traditionally offered a variety of reasons for the shortage of women in top executive positions: women choose family over career, or they drop out of the work force, or they do not have the same drive, motivation, and toughness as their successful male peers. Yet research shows that none of these arguments holds up. Women who become executives are much more likely than men to have sacrificed a marriage or a family, and men are just as likely as women to refuse a promotion that would give them less time with their family. Studies of the character traits of male and female executives find many more similarities than differences.

Women have problems reaching the top, current researchers find, because of various forms of subtle, ingrained bias among those responsible for making promotions. Women are held to higher standards than men are, and they are often caught in difficult binds. Like all good leaders, executive women are expected to take risks, yet they are often given less room to fail than men are. Companies want executive women to be tough, to avoid the stereotype of the emotional, easily flustered female, yet male managers often criticize women for being too "masculine." Companies want women to be ambitious, yet women who demand equal pay and equal treatment for their work are seen as "pushy" and are passed over for promotions. Very often women who are high on the corporate ladder say that they did not push for equality and were blind to issues of gender during their rise.

One study showed that women's success is attributed more often to luck than to ability; logically enough, companies more often reward ability. Other studies have demonstrated that simply increasing the number of women in a given company or division does not solve the problem. Resistance to women working in a given area drops as more women enter the field, but then rises again when about 15 percent of the people in that area are female. This resistance may be caused in part by the observation that areas in which women dominate tend to be viewed as less important; men who see an influx of women into their area justifiably fear that their own work may be devalued.

Although the glass ceiling has not disappeared nearly as quickly as many observers had predicted, there is hope. Unlike the older white males who now head most corporations, many of tomorrow's male CEOs have grown up competing and cooperating with women in school and work and thus may lack some of their predecessors' perceptual biases. Ironically, some of the qualities traditionally viewed as "feminine" have increased the demand for women in some areas, especially in human resource and service sector work, where what some see as women's greater intuition and personnel abilities are especially valued. Eventually, demographic changes may force American companies to promote more women; the white male with a supportive, stay-at-home wife is becoming very rare.

Case Questions:

1. What problems and opportunities does the rise of women in executive ranks pose for American companies?

2. In your experience, have you seen any particular barriers that women have to overcome to be successful?

Case Sources:

Laurie Baum, "Corporate Women," *Business Week,* June 22, 1987, 72–78; Mary Anne Devanna, "Women in Management: Progress and Promise," *Human Resource Management*, Winter 1987, 469–481; Ann M. Morrison, Randall P. White, and Ellen Van Velsor, "Executive Women: Substance Plus Style," *Psychology Today*, August 1987, 18–26.

| Case 20.2 | ## Tom Wayland's Choice |

Tom Wayland was a superb engineer. Rather than graduate with a mechanical engineering degree and go right to work, he spent an extra three semesters in college to finish a second major in electrical engineering. He took a job at Precision Products and soon distinguished himself, coming up with a new design for a temperature-sensitive switch that the company sold to all three American automakers to use in air-conditioning systems. By the age of thirty-three, Wayland had been promoted to chief of engineering at Precision, a position that had always been held by people with doctorates. But after enjoying two years at the top of his area, Wayland wondered, "What next?"

Wayland had always strived to keep all his options open, yet as he evaluated his situation and tried to plan for the future, he found the number of possibilities overwhelming. Back in college, his goal had been to reach something like the position he now held. Precision paid him well, and company engineers and executives uniformly respected him. His wife, Tenny Barton, was working her way up in the management of a nearby computer company, and their two children were in elementary school and did not demand quite as much of their parents' time as they had. Most people who had reached his position, Wayland thought, would breathe a sigh of relief, relax, and enjoy family life and a stable job.

But the prospect of spending the rest of his career in the same position depressed Wayland. Although his rise at Precision had been fast, the company president had made it clear that technical expertise alone would not get Wayland out of engineering and into an executive suite. Wayland had considered going back to school and getting an MBA, but the time he would have to take off from the job would mean lost income for his family. Besides, he was not sure that he wanted to deal with finances, marketing, and personnel; he liked being an engineer and saw executive positions as stressful and uncreative.

Sometimes Wayland thought that his growing dissatisfaction was a sign that he missed the challenge of proving himself to people who were not yet convinced of his abilities. He was sure that he could land a job at a larger company and work his way up to a position with more pay, power, and prestige. But a skeptical voice in his head told him that to be chief of engineering anywhere else he would need a Ph.D., and he doubted that a larger corporation would have the same friendly atmosphere as Precision.

A number of Wayland's colleagues at Precision had gone out on their own, and their success encouraged Wayland to consider that option. The life of a consultant would give him a lot of freedom and could lead to some interesting challenges, though Wayland feared that he would miss working with others. He also considered starting his own business, building something that he could call his own, perhaps making a fortune or creating a product that would make him famous. But that was a big, risky step, and Wayland was not sure he had the drive to be an entrepreneur.

Finally Wayland thought about teaching. He had enjoyed college immensely, and he liked working with younger engineers. He was confident that with a Ph.D. he could get a college teaching job, but he would be forty before he could complete the degree, and he knew he would never make a salary that equalled what Precision was paying him. Teaching math or science in a local high school would be intriguing, he thought, but he feared he would go stale after a short time.

Tenny discussed all the options with her husband and said she would support whatever decision he made. He appreciated her confidence in him, but it did not make the decision any easier. So, after months of debating with himself, Wayland decided to get some advice from his mentor, Rudolph Bailey, who had been chief of engineering when Wayland joined the company and was now vice president for research and development. Bailey had watched a lot of engineers move up and out of the company, and Wayland hoped that the older man could at least help him narrow his choices.

Case Questions

1. What seems to be Wayland's best choice? Why?

2. Besides talking to his wife and his mentor, what else might Wayland do to help make his important career decision?

Experiential Exercise

What career are you planning to pursue? Why? Have you carefully assessed the match between your skills, abilities, and wants and those appropriate for success in that career?

Purpose: This exercise will give you an opportunity to evaluate your career plans and the career options you face.

Format: You will need to work alone to complete a worksheet that helps you analyze your thoughts and plans about your career. After you have filled out the worksheet as best you can, you and another member of the class will review each others' worksheets.

Procedure: Use the worksheet (Figure 20.6) to analyze your chosen career. Some of you may already have begun your careers and may therefore have a good idea of how to answer the questions. On the other hand, some of you may not be too clear about what career you want to pursue after you leave school. If this is the case, choose the career you think you want, and do your best to answer the questions.

Start in the left-hand column, Column 1, and list four to six major tasks or activities required in the job you wish to hold three to five years from now. Then move to Column 2 and list the skills that will be required to do each of those tasks. Finally, moving to the several parts of Column 3, evaluate the degree to which your present qualities fulfill the skill requirements listed in Column 2.

The questions in columns 4–6 refer to the tasks and activities described in Column 1. In Column 4, you are to indicate the extent to which the task or activity will change in the next five years. In Column 5, indicate the importance of the task to the overall job five years from now. Finally, in Column 6, indicate what things you are doing to become better qualified for the job five years from now.

Finally, pair up with another person in the class and compare worksheets. Working together, make suggestions for improving each other's worksheets by filling in blank spots on both worksheets, making better estimates of future tasks, and explaining the rationale for your answers on the worksheet.

Follow-up Questions

1. As a result of this exercise, do you have a better picture of what your career might be? Explain your answer.

2. Do you now know some specific steps you can take to be ready for possible career changes in the next five years? What are some of those steps?

Figure 20.6   Career Assessment Worksheet

COLUMN 1	COLUMN 2	COLUMN 3			COLUMN 4	COLUMN 5	COLUMN 6
Task or Activity	Skill Required	Education Very Little Very Much 1 2 3 4 5	Experience Very Little Very Much 1 2 3 4 5	Personal Characteristics Bad Fit Good Fit 1 2 3 4 5	Change in the Task in 5 Years Very Little Very Much 1 2 3 4 5	Importance of the Task in 5 Years Not Important Very Important 1 2 3 4 5	Your Preparation for this Task in 5 Years Not Ready Very Ready 1 2 3 4 5
1.							
2.							
3.							
4.							
5.							
6.							

CHAPTER

21

International Aspects of Organizations

Chapter Objectives

After reading this chapter, you should be able to

▶ describe the emergence of international management.

▶ describe individual behavior in an international context.

▶ discuss the individual-organization interface in an international context.

▶ identify and discuss organizational characteristics in an international context.

▶ describe organizational processes in an international context.

▶ summarize organizational change in an international context.

M anagers at Lionel Train Company thought they were on the right track in moving their operations to Tijuana, Mexico. After all, wages were only 55 cents an hour, so how could they lose? Thus, they closed their plant in Michigan, gave all the workers termination notices, and packed up.

Unfortunately, things didn't work out as planned. First, the company forced just-fired workers to load their trucks. As a result, the packing was done poorly. Next, the trucks were stalled at the border because of communications problems with customs agents. Then the company found it couldn't hire managerial talent locally and had to send down more U.S. managers than originally planned. Finally, the workers that were available were not motivated enough to do a high-quality job. The company saw its market share drop by 10 percent and annoyed customers by failing to fill orders.

So, Lionel packed up again and moved back home. It leased the plant it had earlier sold and rehired many of its former workers. Things are almost the same as before, but not quite—many of the rehired workers are still angry at the company for moving in the first place.[1]

*L*ionel's experiences provides many insights into international business and its relation to organizational behavior. The company moved in the first place to take advantage of cheaper labor. Communications problems disrupted the move, as did a lack of managerial talent. Local labor conditions led to motivational problems. Finally, even though U.S. workers have been rehired, they still hold negative attitudes toward the company and no doubt have a low level of organizational commitment.

This chapter is about organizational behavior in an international context. We first trace the emergence of international management. Subsequent discussions parallel the overall organization of the book by relating international issues to individual behavior, the individual-organization interface, organizational characteristics, organizational processes, and organizational change and development.

THE EMERGENCE OF INTERNATIONAL MANAGEMENT

In many ways, international management is nothing new. Centuries ago, for example, the Roman army was forced to develop a management system to deal with its widespread empire.[2] From a business standpoint, however, international management is relatively new, at least to the United States.

---

[1] "Some Firms Resume Manufacturing in U.S. After Foreign Fiascoes," *The Wall Street Journal*, October 14, 1986, pp. 1, 27.

[2] M. J. Gent, "Theory X in Antiquity, or the Bureaucratization of the Roman Army," *Business Horizons*, January–February 1984, pp. 53–54.

The Growth of International Business

The volume of international trade in 1980, in current dollars, was fifteen times greater than the amount in 1960. And the figures have escalated even more rapidly since then. What has led to this dramatic increase? As shown in Figure 21.1, three major factors account for much of its momentum.

First, communication and transportation have changed dramatically over the past few decades. Telephone service has improved, communication networks span the globe and can interact via satellite, and access to remote areas has been vastly improved. Thus, it's simply easier to conduct international business today.

Second, businesses have expanded internationally to increase their markets. Companies in smaller countries (like Nestle Company Inc. in Switzerland, for example) recognized long ago that their domestic markets were too small to sustain much growth and therefore moved into international activities. Many American firms, on the other hand, had all the business they could handle until recently, so they are just beginning to consider international opportunities.

Finally, more and more firms are moving into the international realm as a way to control costs. Our opening vignette noted that Lionel moved to lower its labor costs. Although things didn't work out as planned, many other firms are successfully using inexpensive labor in the Far East and Mexico.[3]

Trends in International Business

The most striking trend in international business is obvious—growth. More and more businesses are entering the international marketplace, including many smaller firms. We read a great deal about the threat of foreign companies. For example, successful Japanese automobile firms like Toyota and Nissan produce higher-quality cars for lower prices than do American firms. What we often overlook, though, is the success of American firms abroad. Ford, for example, has long had a successful business in Europe and today employs less than half its total workforce on U.S. soil. And there are literally dozens of products that American firms make better than anyone else in the world.[4]

Business transactions are becoming increasingly blurred across national boundaries. Ford owns 25 percent of Mazda, General Motors and Toyota have a joint venture in California, Ford and Volkswagen have one in Argentina, and Honda and British Sterling have one worldwide.

And beyond business, other organizational forms have increased their international involvement as well. Universities offer study programs abroad, health care and research programs span national boundaries, international

---

[3] Henry W. Lane and Joseph J. DiStefano, *International Management Behavior* (Ontario, Canada: Nelson, 1988).

[4] Christopher Knowlton, "What America Makes Best," *Fortune*, March 28, 1988, pp. 40–54.

Figure 21.1

Forces That Have
Increased International
Business

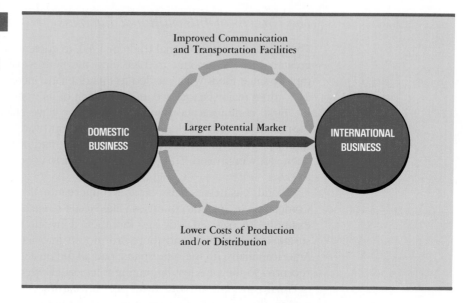

postal systems are working more closely together, and sports programs are increasingly being transplanted to different cultures.

In many ways, then, we are becoming a truly global economy. No longer will a firm be able to insulate itself from foreign competitors (or opportunities). Thus, it is absolutely imperative that every manager develop and maintain at least a rudimentary understanding of the dynamics of international management.[5]

Cross-Cultural Differences and Similarities

Since the primary concern of this discussion is human behavior in organizational settings, our focus will be on differences and similarities in behavior across cultures. Unfortunately, research in this area is still in its infancy.[6] Thus, many of the research findings we can draw on are preliminary, at best.

Still, a few basic ideas about differences and similarities can be noted at a general level. First, it should be recognized that cultures and national boundaries do not necessarily coincide. For example, some areas of Switzerland are very much like Italy, other parts like France, and still other parts like Germany. Similarly, within the U.S., there are profound cultural differences between, say, Southern California, Texas, and the East Coast.[7]

---

[5] Richard M. Steers and Edwin L. Miller, "Management in the 1990s: The International Challenge," *Academy of Management Executive*, February 1988, pp. 21–22.

[6] Nancy J. Adler, Robert Doktor, and S. Gordon Redding, "From the Atlantic to the Pacific Century: Cross-Cultural Management Reviewed," *Journal of Management*, Summer 1986, pp. 295–318.

[7] Simcha Ronen and Oded Shenkar, "Clustering Countries on Attitudinal Dimensions: A Review and Synthesis," *Academy of Management Review*, July 1985, pp. 435–454.

Given this basic assumption, one recent review of the literature on international management reached five basic conclusions.[8] First, behavior in organizational settings does indeed vary across cultures. Thus, employees in companies based in Japan, the United States, and West Germany are likely to have different attitudes and patterns of behavior.

Second, culture itself is one major cause of this variation. That is, the behavioral differences noted above may be caused in part by different standards of living, different geographical conditions, and so forth; yet culture itself is also a major factor apart from other considerations.

Third, although behavior within organizational settings (e.g., motivation and attitudes) remains quite diverse across cultures, organizations themselves (e.g., organizational design and technology) appear to be increasingly similar. Hence, managerial practices at a general level may be more and more alike, but the people who work within organizations are still quite different.

Fourth, the same manager behaves differently in different cultural settings. For example, Japanese executives who come to work in America slowly begin to act more like American managers and less like Japanese managers. This is a source of concern for them when they are transferred back home to Japan.[9]

Finally, cultural diversity can be an important source of synergy in enhancing organizational effectiveness. Organizations that adopt a multinational strategy can become more than a sum of their parts. Operations in each culture can benefit from operations in other cultures through an enhanced understanding of how the world works.[10]

INDIVIDUAL BEHAVIOR IN AN INTERNATIONAL CONTEXT

The first two conclusions just noted clearly suggest that individual behavior varies across cultures. These variations can be viewed in terms of individual differences, managerial behavior, motivation, and rewards across cultures.

Individual Differences Across Cultures

Figure 21.2 highlights some of the more important dimensions along which behavior varies. These dimensions were identified in a large-scale study of 160,000 people working in sixty countries.[11]

---

[8] Adler, Doktor, and Redding, "From the Atlantic to the Pacific Century."

[9] Brian O'Reilly, "Japan's Uneasy U.S. Managers," *Fortune*, April 25, 1988, pp. 245–264.

[10] Tamotsu Yamaguchi, "The Challenge of Internationalization," *Academy of Management Executive*, February 1988, pp. 33–36.

[11] Geert Hofstede, *Culture's Consequences: International Differences in Work Related Values* (Beverly Hills, Calif.: Sage Publications, 1980).

Figure 21.2

Differences Across
Cultures In Individual
Behavior

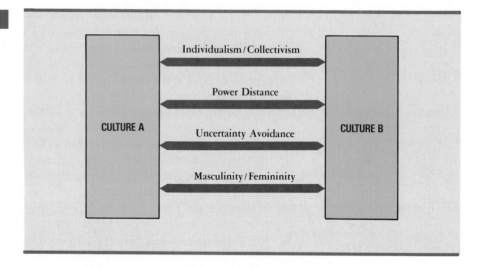

INDIVIDUALISM/COLLECTIVISM **Individualism** is a state in which people view themselves first as individuals and believe their own interests and values take priority. **Collectivism,** on the other hand, is a feeling that the good of the group or society should come first.

People in a culture characterized by individualism tend to put their careers before their organizations and usually assess situations in terms of how decisions and alternative courses of action will affect them personally. People in a culture dominated by collectivism often put the needs of the organization before their own needs and view decisions and alternatives in terms of their impact on the organization.

The United States, Australia, Great Britain, the Netherlands, Canada, and New Zealand are among the most individualistic cultures. Colombia, Pakistan, Taiwan, Peru, Singapore, Japan, Mexico, Greece, and Hong Kong are among the countries in which collectivism is strongest.

POWER DISTANCE **Power distance** reflects the extent to which employees accept the idea that people in an organization rightfully have different levels of power. In a high-distance culture, for example, a boss makes decisions simply because he is the boss—others do not question it but simply follow instructions. In a low-power-difference culture, however, employees recognize few power differences and follow the boss's lead only when they believe the boss is right or when they feel explicitly threatened.

The United States, Israel, Austria, Denmark, Ireland, Norway, Germany, and New Zealand represent cultures with a low power distance. Spain, France, Japan, Singapore, Mexico, Brazil, and Indonesia are examples of cultures with a high power distance.

UNCERTAINTY AVOIDANCE   **Uncertainty avoidance** is the extent to which people in a culture accept or avoid feelings of uncertainty. Employees in Denmark, the United States, Canada, Norway, Singapore, Hong Kong, and Australia are among those that can tolerate high levels of uncertainty. On the other hand, workers in Israel, Austria, Japan, Italy, Argentina, Peru, France, and Belgium are more highly motivated to avoid uncertainty in their work lives.

MASCULINITY/FEMININITY   The degree of masculinity or femininity is seen as the extent to which cultures value things like assertiveness and materialism, on the one hand, or people and the quality of life, on the other. Masculine societies define male-female roles more rigidly than do feminine societies. Japan and Austria are highly masculine; the United States slightly masculine; and Norway, Sweden, Denmark, and Finland highly feminine.

Managerial Behavior Across Cultures

Individual differences across cultures can obviously shape managerial behavior as well as employee behavior. Beyond those differences, however, there are other differences specific to managerial behavior.[12]

In general, these differences relate to managerial beliefs about the role of authority and power in the organization. For example, managers in Indonesia, Italy, and Japan tend to believe that the purpose of an organizational structure is to let everyone know who his or her boss is. Managers in the United States, Germany, and Great Britain, in contrast, think the organizational structure is intended to coordinate group behavior and effort. On another dimension, Italian and German managers think it is all right to bypass one's boss in order to get things done, whereas managers in Sweden and Great Britain hold the strongest beliefs against bypassing one's superior.

Figure 21.3 illustrates findings on another interesting point. As shown, managers in Japan strongly believe that a manager should be able to answer any question he or she is asked. Thus, they place a premium on expertise and experience. In contrast, Swedish managers have the lowest concern for knowing all the answers. They view themselves as problem solvers and facilitators who make no claim to omnipotence.

Some recent evidence also suggests that managerial behavior is rapidly changing, at least among European managers. In general, they are becoming more career-oriented, better educated, more willing to work cooperatively with labor, more willing to delegate, and more cosmopolitan.[13]

---

[12] André Laurent, "The Cultural Diversity of Western Conceptions of Management," *International Studies of Management and Organization*, Spring–Summer 1983, pp. 75–96.

[13] Richard I. Kirkland, Jr., "Europe's New Managers," *Fortune*, September 29, 1986, pp. 56–60.

Figure 21.3   Differences Across Cultures in Managers' Beliefs About Answering Questions from Subordinates

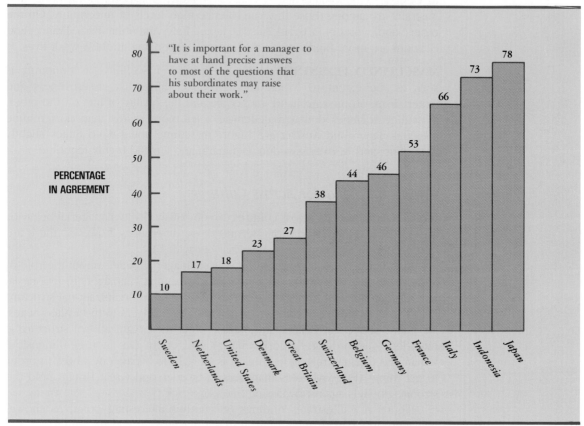

"It is important for a manager to have at hand precise answers to most of the questions that his subordinates may raise about their work."

PERCENTAGE IN AGREEMENT

Sweden 10, Netherlands 17, United States 18, Denmark 23, Great Britain 27, Switzerland 38, Belgium 44, Germany 46, France 53, Italy 66, Indonesia 73, Japan 78

Source: Reprinted from *International Studies of Management and Organization*, Vol. XIII, No. 1–2, Spring–Summer 1983, by permission of M. E. Sharpe, Inc., Armonk, N. Y. 10504.

Motivation Across Cultures

Some specific implications can also be drawn regarding motivation across cultures. Maslow's hierarchy of needs, for example, has been shown to vary across some cultures and remain stable across others. In some countries, such as Japan and Greece, security needs are most important, whereas social needs tend to dominate in Sweden and Norway.[14] On the other hand, the hierarchy seems to be fairly stable in Peru, India, Mexico, the Middle East, and parts of Canada.[15]

---

[14] Adler, Doktor, and Redding, "From the Atlantic to the Pacific Century."

[15] Nancy J. Adler, *International Dimensions of Organizational Behavior* (Boston: Kent, 1986).

Research has also found that the need for achievement, Herzberg's two-factor theory, and the expectancy theory of motivation all vary across cultures. For example, many American managers expect that their hard work will lead to high performance. In contrast, Moslem managers believe that their success is determined solely by God.[16] *International Perspective* provides insights into the motivational patterns of would-be entrepreneurs in Europe.

Rewards Across Cultures

To date, no one has systematically studied reward systems across cultures. However, given that motivational processes vary across cultures, it follows logically that the rewards people want also vary.

For example, job security will clearly be more valued in some cultures than in others. Similarly, employees in some cultures—the United States, for instance—will put greater emphasis on individual rewards such as recognition, promotion, and merit salary increases. In other cultures, such as Japan, employees may place a higher value on group rewards and recognition.

Whatever the situation, the manager must be prepared to thoroughly assess what employees want before presuming to know. Adler provides two examples wherein American managers overgeneralized from their own experiences and failed to anticipate problems. In one, salaries were increased for a group of Mexican workers. Unexpectedly, they started working fewer hours. Why? Because their higher salaries allowed them a better life style and they wanted to enjoy it. In the other case, a Japanese employee was promoted by an American manager as a reward for high performance. This made him feel less a part of the group and led to a performance decline.[17]

THE INDIVIDUAL-ORGANIZATION INTERFACE IN AN INTERNATIONAL CONTEXT

Just as individual behavior varies from culture to culture, so does the interface between people and organizations. As Figure 21.4 illustrates, four key areas of variation are job design, group dynamics, leadership, and power and conflict.

Job Design Across Cultures

Job design clearly varies across cultures.[18] Many such differences have already been noted in Chapter 8 and will only be summarized here. Scandanavian companies, especially Volvo in Sweden, have been pioneers in the use of work teams as a basis for job design. Workers in West Germany have also enjoyed

---

[16] Adler, *International Dimensions of Organizational Behavior.*

[17] Adler, *International Dimensions of Organizational Behavior*, pp. 132–133.

[18] Ricky W. Griffin, *Task Design* (Glenview, Ill.: Scott, Foresman, 1982).

International Perspective

Starting Up In Europe

Although the word *entrepreneur* is French, to many Europeans the concept seems American. In fact, until recently, many on the other side of the Atlantic viewed business startups with distaste, associating them with Americans who get rich too quickly, flaunt their money, and belong on America's soap operas. Almost one-third of those responding to a 1986 poll in Great Britain regarded people who started their own companies as having the lowest status in the country.

Yet for a number of reasons, that attitude, and the actual number of European entrepreneurs, is rapidly changing. Unemployment has been stuck at around 11 percent in Europe for most of the decade, and Europeans are starting to realize that new companies provide more jobs more quickly than esablished ones. There's also an upsurge of fresh blood in the European business community as a result of the maturing of Europe's baby boom generation, which is about a decade behind that of the United States.

Perhaps more important is a new attitude of European governments and banks towards entrepreneurs and venture capital. In Britain, Prime Minister Margaret Thatcher has been trying to encourage "an enterprise culture" in order to cut down on an unemployment rate that has tripled since she took office. Her government has slashed the top income tax rate from 98 percent to 60 percent and gives tax credits to start-ups.

Similar changes spell better days for entrepreneurs on the Continent. Italy has a new law permitting banks to get into the venture capital business, and new consulting firms, over-the-counter markets, and stock option plans are changing the face of European business from Spain to Sweden. Many of the people entering business are young, well-educated, and more interested in marketing and strategy than those in the more research-oriented traditional companies. They are being joined by a growing number of people who have tired of their successes in big companies, people like Jean-Luc Grand-Clement who left an executive position with Motorola, started his own company in the early 1970s, went back to Motorola when his first start-up failed, and now heads European Silicon Structures, funded by $46 million from a Boston-based venture capital group.

Some of Europe's most visible entrepreneurial successes—chief among them Richard Branson—must get credit for influencing attitudes about starting a business. Branson got his start selling ads for a student magazine from a phone booth; he is now the third-most-admired person in Britain, after Prince Charles and the Pope. His empire has expanded from records and recording contracts to include Virgin Atlantic Airways, a fast-growing, successful airline. Branson captures the imagination of Europe's youth by setting transatlantic speedboat and balloon records. As long as he and other European entrepreneurs keep flying high, Europe seems almost assured of a new generation of business people as motivated to start their own businesses as their American cousins.

Source: Based on "Europe's New Entrepreneurs" by Richard I. Kirkland, Jr., *Fortune*, April 27, 1987. © 1987 Time Inc. All rights reserved.

Figure 21.4

Differences Across
Cultures in Individual-
Organization Interface

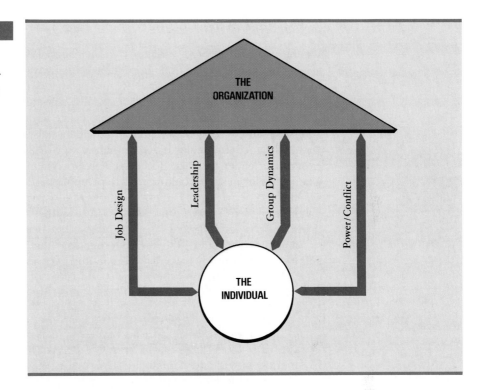

innovative and progressive approaches to the design of their jobs. And in many
ways, the participative management systems and quality circle programs so
widespread in Japan represent aspects of job design. Beyond simple case
analyses, however, job design has not been systematically studied across cultural
boundaries.

Group Dynamics Across Cultures

As already noted, cultures differ in the importance they place on group
membership. Attention has also been focused on how to deal with groups made
up of people from different cultures.[19]

In general, a manager in charge of a culturally diverse group can expect
several things. First, there is a high probability that distrust will exist among
group members. Stereotyping will also present a problem. Finally, communication problems will almost certainly arise. Thus, the manager needs to recognize
that such groups will seldom function smoothly, at least at first. Therefore, he
or she may need to spend additional time helping the group through the rough
spots as it matures and should allow a longer-than-normal time before expecting
it to carry out its assigned charge.

---

[19] Adler, *International Dimensions of Organizational Behavior.*

Leadership Across Cultures

We have already noted variations in managerial behavior across cultures. Leadership per se is also quite important. In many ways, the issue of leadership in an international context parallels our earlier discussions of leadership as a situational process in Chapter 11. Specifically, cultural factors comprise another important set of situational elements that dictate appropriate leadership style.

For example, one highly important situational factor already discussed is power distance. In a culture with a high power distance, employees routinely expect the leader to make decisions, solve problems, and assign tasks. Thus, when a leader in such a culture tries to promote participation, his or her efforts are likely to be rebuked. Under conditions of low power distance, on the other hand, employees expect a greater say in how they do their jobs. Too much directive behavior and too few opportunities to participate may create problems.

Finally, we should note the different role that leaders play in different cultures. Only recently have managers in Europe, for example, recognized that their jobs extend beyond the formal boundaries of managerial roles. And as shown clearly in *Management in Action*, leaders in Japan can pay a high price for their failures.

Power and Conflict Across Cultures

In America, power and conflict are a normal part of work life. When we see people striving to increase their power or two people arguing, we really think nothing of it. In general, we accept that these things, as long as they don't become too dysfunctional, are just a part of doing business.

In some other countries—Great Britain, for example—power and conflict are even more pronounced. This stems in part from the generally hostile nature of labor-management relations in that country. Bitter strikes, among other things, make conflict commonplace.

The Japanese are at the other extreme. Attempts to increase one's power are frowned upon, and instigating or promoting conflict is considered unseemly.

ORGANIZATIONAL CHARACTERISTICS IN AN INTERNATIONAL CONTEXT

At a still higher level of analysis, we can examine cultural influences on environment, technology, organizational structure, and organizational design.

Environment and Technology Across Cultures

Variation in environment across cultures can be assessed at several different levels. As described in Chapter 14, environments can be viewed in terms of

Management in ACTION

"The Highest Form of Apology"

In 1985 when a Japan Air Lines jet crashed killing 500 people, its president, Yasumoto Takagi, made arrangements for burying the dead, called victims' families, and then promptly resigned. So did the president of Kikkoman Corporation after his company was hit by a scandal about tainted wine. And in 1987, when a subsidiary of Toshiba sold sensitive military technology to the Soviet Union, both CEO Sugiichiro Watari and Chairman Shoichi Saba also gave up their posts.

These executive actions, which Toshiba calls "the highest form of apology," may seem bizarre to Americans. After all, no one at Boeing resigned after the JAL crash, which may have been caused by a faulty Boeing repair. No Union Carbide executives quit after the company's plant in Bhopal, India was the site of this era's worst industrial accident. "Golden parachutes" that ease executives out of their positions are more common in America than public apologies.

The difference between the two business cultures centers around different definitions of delegation. While American executives give both responsibility and authority to their employees, Japanese executives delegate only authority—the responsibility is still theirs. Although Toshiba made it clear that the subsidiary that had sold the sensitive technology to the Soviets had its own management, the Toshiba top executives said they "must take personal responsibility for not creating an atmosphere throughout the Toshiba group that would make such activity unthinkable, even in an independently run subsidiary."*

Such acceptance of community responsibility is not unique to businesses in Japan. School principals in Japan have resigned when their students committed major crimes after hours. Even if they don't quit, Japanese executives will often accept primary responsibility in other ways, such as taking the first pay cut when a company gets into financial trouble. Such personal sacrifices, even if they are largely symbolic, help to create the sense of community and employee loyalty that is crucial to the Japanese way of doing business.

Harvard Business School professor George Lodge calls the ritual acceptance of blame "almost a feudal way of purging the community of dishonor," and to some Americans, such resignations look cowardly. However, in an era in which both business and governmental leaders seem particularly adept at passing the buck, many Americans would probably welcome an infusion of the Japanese sense of responsibility. If, for instance, American automobile company executives offered to reduce their own salaries before they asked their workers to take pay cuts, negotiations would probably take on a very different character.

Source: Christopher J. Chipello, "Matter of Honor: Japanese Top Managers Quick to Resign When Trouble Hits Firm," *The Wall Street Journal,* July 10, 1987. 19. Reprinted by permission of *The Wall Street Journal.* © Dow Jones & Company, Inc. (1987). All rights reserved.

* Christopher J. Chipello, "Matter of Honor: Japanese Top Managers Quick to Resign When Trouble Hits Firm," *The Wall Street Journal,* July 10, 1987, 19.

their complexity and their dynamism. Figure 21.5 shows that within any culture, the environment may be more or less complex and more or less dynamic.

ENVIRONMENTAL COMPLEXITY AND DYNAMISM   Many cultures have relatively stable environments. For example, the economies of Sweden, Japan, and the United States are fairly stable. Although competitive forces within them vary, they generally remain strong, free-market economies. In contrast, the environments of some countries are much more dynamic. For example, France's policies on socialism versus private enterprise seem to change dramatically with each election. At present, far-reaching changes in the economic and management philosophies of most Western European countries make their environments much more dynamic.

Environments also vary widely in terms of their complexity. The Japanese culture, which is fairly stable, is also quite complex. Japanese managers are subject to an array of cultural norms and values that are far more encompassing and resistant to change than those faced by American managers. India, too, has an extremely complex environment still influenced by its old caste system.

TECHNOLOGY   Technological variations come in two forms: variations in available technology and in attitudes toward technology. Available technology affects how organizations can do business. Many underdeveloped countries, for example, lack electric power sources, telephones, and trucking equipment, much less computers and robots. A manager working in such a country must be prepared to deal with many frustrations. For example, a few years ago some Brazilian officials convinced an American company to build a high-tech plant in their country. Midway through construction, however, the government of Brazil decided that it would not allow the company to import some accurate measuring instruments it needed to produce its products. The new plant was abandoned before it ever opened.[20]

Attitudes toward technology also vary across cultures. Surprisingly, Japan has only recently begun to support basic research. For many years, the government of that country encouraged its companies to take basic research findings discovered elsewhere (often in the United States) and figure out how to apply them to consumer products (applied research). Now, however, the government has changed its stance and has started to encourage basic research as well.[21] Most of the Western nations have a generally favorable posture toward technology, whereas China and other Asian countries (with the exception of Japan) do not.

---

[20] Andrew Kupfer, "How to Be a Global Manager," *Fortune*, March 14, 1988, pp. 52–58.

[21] "Going Crazy in Japan—In a Break from Tradition, Tokyo Begins Funding a Program for Basic Research," *The Wall Street Journal*, November 10, 1986, p. 20D.

Figure 21.5

International
Environments

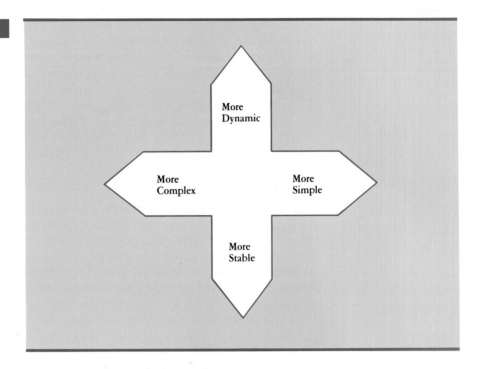

Organization Structure and Design Across Cultures

Cross-cultural considerations related to organizational structure and design include not only similarities and differences between firms in different cultures but also structural features of multinational organizations.

BETWEEN-CULTURE ISSUES   By between-culture issues, we mean comparisons of the organizational structure and design of companies operating in different cultures. As might be expected, there are both differences and similarities. For example, one recent study compared the structures of fifty-five American and fifty-one Japanese manufacturing plants. Results suggested that the Japanese plants had less specialization, more "formal" centralization (but less "real" centralization), and taller hierarchies than their American counterparts. The Japanese structures were also less affected by their technology than were the U.S. plants.[22]

Many cultures still take a traditional view of organizational structure not unlike the approaches used in this country during the days of classical

---

[22] James R. Lincoln, Mitsuyo Hanada, and Kerry McBride, "Organizational Structures in Japanese and U.S. Manufacturing," *Administrative Science Quarterly*, September 1986, pp. 338–364.

organizational theory. For example, Tom Peters, a leading American management consultant and co-author of *In Search of Excellence*, recently spent some time lecturing to managers in China. They were not interested in his ideas about decentralization and worker participation, however. Instead, the question most often asked involved how a manager determined the optimal span of control.[23]

In contrast, many European companies are patterning themselves more and more after successful American firms. This stems in part from corporate raiders in Europe emulating their American counterparts and partly from a more highly educated managerial work force. Taken together, these two forces have caused many European firms to become more decentralized and to adopt divisional structures by moving from functional to product departmentalization.[24]

MULTINATIONAL ORGANIZATION   More and more firms have entered the international arena and have found it necessary to adapt their design to better cope with different cultures.[25] After a company has achieved a moderate level of international activity, for example, it often establishes an international division such as the one shown in Figure 21.6. Levi Strauss uses this organizational design. One division, Levi Strauss International, is responsible for the company's business activities in Europe, Canada, Latin America, and Asia.

For an organization that has become more deeply involved in its international activities, a logical form of organizational design is the international matrix, illustrated in Figure 21.7. This type of matrix arrays product managers across the top. Project teams headed by foreign market managers cut across the product departments. A company with three basic product lines, for example, might establish three product departments. (Of course, it contains domestic advertising, finance, and operations departments as well.) Foreign market managers can be designated for, say, Canada, Japan, Europe, Latin America, and Australia. Each foreign market manager is responsible for all three of the company's products in his or her market.[26]

Finally, at the most advanced level of multinational activity, a firm might become an international conglomerate. Nestle and Unilever N.V. fit this typology. Each has an international headquarters (Nestle in Vevey, Switzerland, and Unilever in Rotterdam, Netherlands) that coordinates the activities of businesses scattered around the globe. Nestle, for example, has over three hundred factories in fifty countries and markets its products in literally every country in the world. Over 96 percent of its business is done outside of Switzerland, and only 7,000 of its 160,000 employees reside in its home country.

---

[23] "The Inscrutable West," *Newsweek*, April 18, 1988, p. 52.

[24] Kirkland, "Europe's New Managers"; Shawn Tully, "Europe's Takeover Kings," *Fortune*, July 20, 1987, pp. 95–98.

[25] Lane and DiStefano, *International Management Behavior*.

[26] William H. Davison and Philippe Haspeslagh, "Shaping a Global Product Organization," *Harvard Business Review*, July–August 1982, pp. 125–132.

Figure 21.6

International Division
Approach to
Organizational Design

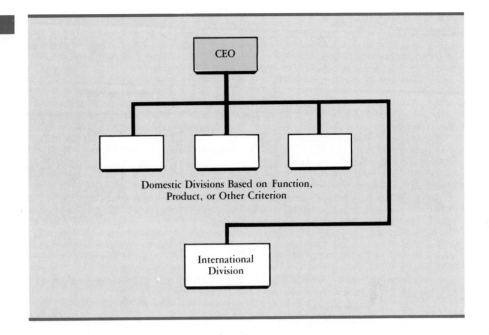

ORGANIZATIONAL PROCESSES IN AN INTERNATIONAL
CONTEXT

Basic organizational processes—in particular, decision making, communication, performance appraisal, and processes related to careers—can also be influenced by international forces.

Decision Making Across Cultures

Chapter 17 describes the steps involved in making decisions. Nancy Adler recently explained how these steps, in a slightly modified form, can vary across cultures.[27] The steps she identified and the range of variation are shown in Table 21.1.

First, managers in different cultures are likely to recognize problems and decision situations differently. Americans, for example, see problems as situations that require change. In contrast, managers in cultures like Indonesia's and Thailand's argue that one should accept the situation as it is instead of trying to change it.

Second, managers in some cultures see information as fact and make decisions accordingly. Others see information in terms of its possibilities and

---

[27] Adler, *International Dimensions of Organizational Behavior.*

Figure 21.7   An International Matrix

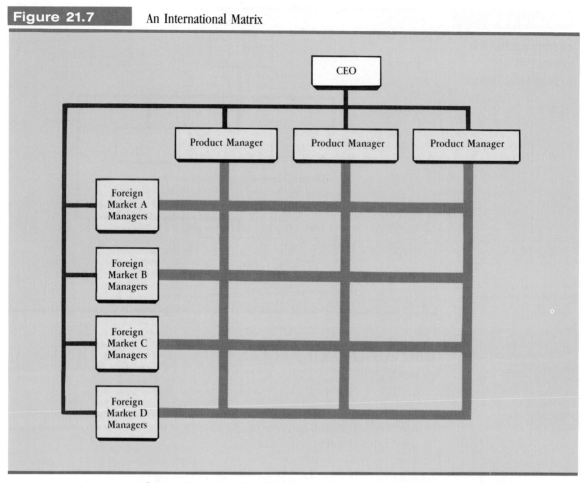

Source: From Ricky W. Griffin, *Management,* 2nd ed. (Boston: Houghton Mifflin, 1987), p. 739. Used by permission.

use it as a means of generating alternatives. For example, managers in some countries might see the citizens of an underdeveloped nation as being too poor to buy the products their companies make and might therefore choose not to introduce the products there. Other managers might see the same reality but figure out how to lower the products' cost to make them more affordable.

Third, people in different cultures see different alternative solutions to problems. Managers in some cultures, such as the United States, tend to see future-oriented alternatives, for example, whereas other managers, such as those in Great Britain, focus more on the past. Thus, Americans might be more inclined to figure out a new technology for doing something, and the British might concentrate on modifying an existing technology to do the same thing.

Table 21.1	Steps in Decision Making	Cultural Variations	
Cultural Variations in Decision Making	1. Problem Recognition	*Problem Solving* Situation should be changed	*Situation Accepting* Some situations should be accepted, not changed
	2. Information Search	*Gather "facts"*	*Gather ideas and possibilities*
	3. Constructing Alternatives	*New, future-oriented alternatives* People can learn and change	*Focus includes past, present, and future alternatives* Adults cannot change substantially
	4. Choice	*Individuals make decisions* Decision making responsibility delegated Decisions made quickly Decision rule: Is it true or false?	*Groups make decisions* Only senior management makes decisions Decisions made slowly Decision rule: Is it good or bad?
	5. Implementation	*Fast* Managed from the top Responsibility of one person	*Slow* Involves the participation of all levels Responsibility of the group

Source: From Nancy J. Adler, *International Dimensions of Organizational Behavior* (Boston: Kent Publishing Co., 1985), p. 136. © by Wadsworth, Inc. Reprinted by permission of PWS-KENT Publishing Co., a division of Wadsworth, Inc.

Next, there are variations in people's perceptions about making choices. The notion of power distance, discussed earlier, has clear implications as to who is expected to make the choices. Time urgency also varies. For example, Americans make decisions very rapidly, whereas managers in some other cultures, as in the Middle East, are more deliberate and dislike having to make snap decisions.

Finally, cultures differ in how chosen alternatives are implemented. In the United States, for example, managers tend to think the implementation of decisions should be managed from the top and be the responsibility of one person. In contrast, Japanese managers think that participation is needed at all levels and that responsibility should be shared.

Communication Across Cultures

Communication is one of the organizational processes most obviously affected by the international environment, partially because of language issues and partially because of coordination issues.

LANGUAGE   Differences in language are compounded by the fact that the same word can mean different things in different cultures. For example, Chevrolet's Nova didn't fare well in Italy until managers there changed its name—it seems that in Italian, *no va* means "doesn't go." Table 21.2 lists some interesting examples of communication foibles across cultures.

	Source of Problem	Examples
Table 21.2 Examples of International Communication Problems	Language	One firm, trying to find a name for a new soap powder, tested the chosen name in 50 languages. In English, it meant "dainty." Translations into other languages meant "song" (Gaelic), "aloof" (Flemish), "horse" (African), "hazy or dimwitted" (Persian), "crazy" (Korean); and the name was obscene in several Slavic languages.
		Chevy's "Nova" was *no va* in Italian, which means "doesn't go."
		Coca-Cola in Chinese became "Bite the head of a dead tadpole."
		Idioms cannot be translated literally: "to murder the King's English" becomes "to speak French like a Spanish cow" in French.
	Nonverbal signs	Shaking your head up and down in Greece means no, and swinging it from side to side means yes.
		In most European countries, it is considered impolite not to have both hands on the table.
		The American sign for OK is an obscenity in Spain.
	Colors	Green: Popular in Moslem countries Suggests disease in jungle-covered countries Suggests cosmetics in France, Sweden, Netherlands
		Red: Blasphemous in African countries Stands for wealth and masculinity in Great Britain
	Product	Campbell Soup Company was unsuccessful in Britain until the firm added water to its condensed soup so the cans would be the same size as the cans of soup the British were used to purchasing.
		Long-life packaging, which is used commonly for milk in Europe, allows milk to be stored for months at room temperature if it is unopened. Americans are still wary of it.
		Coke had to alter the taste of its soft drink in China when the Chinese described it as "tasting like medicine."

Sources: Adapted from: David A. Ricks, *Big Business Blunders: Mistakes in Multinational Marketing* (Homewood, Ill.: Dow Jones–Irwin, 1983); Nancy Bragganti and Elizabeth Devine, *The Traveler's Guide to European Customs and Manners* (St. Paul, Minn.: Meadowbrook Books, 1984); several *Wall Street Journal* articles.

Note in the table that elements of nonverbal communication also vary across cultures. For example, colors and body language can convey quite a different message in one culture than in another. Thus, managers should be forewarned that they can take nothing for granted in dealing with people from another culture—they must take the time necessary to become as fully acquainted as possible with the verbal and nonverbal languages of that culture.

COORDINATION   International communication is closely related to issues of coordination. For example, an American manager who wants to talk with his or her counterpart in Hong Kong or Singapore must contend not only with differences in language but also with a time difference of several hours. When the American manager needs to talk on the telephone, the Hong Kong executive may be home in bed asleep. Organizations are having to find increasingly innovative methods for coordinating their activities in scattered parts of the globe. Merrill Lynch & Co., Inc., for example, has developed its own satellite-based telephone network to monitor and participate in the worldwide money and financial markets.[28]

Performance Evaluation Across Cultures

Cross-cultural variation in performance evaluation includes two points of particular interest: what constitutes performance and how people respond to evaluation.

MEASURES OF PERFORMANCE   Unfortunately, little has been written about what constitutes performance in various cultures. Some insights, however, can be inferred from our earlier discussion of motivation. Recall, for example, the case of the Mexican workers who worked fewer hours after getting pay increases. Perhaps they saw their performance in terms of how much time they gave to the organization. Workers in a highly group-focused culture, such as Japan's might shy away from performance measures that assess the individual's contributions. Instead, they may see their performance in terms of what they contribute to the group.

REACTIONS TO EVALUATION   Similar differences characterize responses to actual evaluations of performance. People in some cultures accept critical evaluation, and negative feedback about performance may be appreciated and may result in improved performance. In other cultures, however, people may take criticism much more seriously. Indeed, a recipient of criticism may be embarrassed enough to withdraw from the organization. The manager dealing with a new culture should develop a clear understanding of the role of performance feedback and its likely effects before undertaking any form of performance evaluation.

---

[28] "How Merrill Lynch Moves Its Stock Deals All Around the World," *The Wall Street Journal*, November 9, 1987, pp. 1, 8.

Careers Across Cultures

An understanding of careers, described in Chapter 20, is becoming increasingly important for managers. It should come as no surprise that there are international implications to be drawn from career-related concerns. Some of these center on career paths in different cultures, and others involve career concerns for managers in international businesses.

CULTURAL VARIATIONS IN CAREERS   Perhaps the most important career-related issue for the manager to understand is that different cultures have different norms and standards relevant to career paths. The U.S. culture, for example, generally approves of people who are ambitious, who want to succeed, and who strive for advancement. In other cultures, personal ambition is less acceptable. The Japanese, for example, are expected to put organizational concerns and priorities above personal ones. Working to better one's own position in the organization is considered unseemly.

Widespread sex discrimination exists in many parts of the world. In Japan and Finland, for example, women are quite restricted in their opportunities for advancement. Japanese women are expected to become wives and mothers. Even those who graduate from college usually take jobs as clerks and seldom move up the corporate ladder. (Fortunately, this is beginning to change a bit, although the changes are still hard to see in most organizations.[29]) And in Finland, even though women have a strong heritage of working outside the home, they lag behind men in both income and opportunities for advancement.[30]

INTERNATIONAL CAREER PATHS   As businesses become more and more international, they must devote more attention to how this change affects the careers of their managers. For example, a manager who is transferred from New York to Dallas to Seattle obviously experiences a certain amount of trauma, but this pales by comparison to what happens to the manager transferred from New York to Tokyo to Bangkok. Thus, the firm must consider carefully both the advantages and disadvantages of international assignments.[31] *A Look at Research* provides additional insights into how international transfers affect people.

---

[29] "Look Whose Sun Is Rising Now: Career Women," *Business Week*, August 25, 1986, p. 50.

[30] Kaisa Kauppinen-Toropainen, Irja Kandolin, and Elina Haavio-Mannila, "Sex Segregation of Work in Finland and the Quality of Women's Work," *Journal of Organizational Behavior*, Vol. 9, 1988, pp. 15–27.

[31] Mark Mendenhall and Gary Oddou, "The Dimensions of Expatriate Acculturation: A Review," *Academy of Management Review*, January 1985, pp. 39–47.

A LOOK AT
RESEARCH

Learning to Succeed Abroad

A recent series of surveys of American, European, and Japanese multinational corporations has revealed that American employees sent abroad are much less successful than their European and Japanese peers at adapting productively to their new surroundings. More than half of the American companies surveyed had to fire or recall 10 to 20 percent of the employees sent overseas; only about 3 percent of European companies and 14 percent of Japanese companies had equivalent failure rates.

A number of factors contribute to the failure of American managers to adapt to overseas work. Both the manager and the manager's spouse typically have difficulty adjusting to the new environment, and American companies seldom provide them with adequate preparation for dealing with the new culture. Most American companies choose employees for foreign assignments based on their technical skill rather than on their abilities to adapt and relate to other people; the latter may be comparatively more important for success abroad. Overseas assignments also tend to be relatively short, giving employees little time to adjust as well as the impression that these assignments are relatively unimportant. American employees sent overseas worry, with some justification, that they will lose chances for promotion while they're abroad.

European and Japanese managers sent abroad tend to adapt more successfully than their American counterparts partly because of their different corporate cultures, and partly because of differences in training and emphasis. Within Japanese and European corporate cultures, executives are much less likely than American executives to leave their companies for other jobs, and therefore foreign companies are more ready to invest time and money in training employees for new positions and to give them time to adapt. Whereas most American overseas assignments are measured in months, European and Japanese companies typically send their employees abroad for five years; many Japanese multinationals do not expect their employees to be fully productive until their third year.

European and Japanese companies also tend to value overseas jobs more highly. These companies depend on exports to a greater extent than do most American multinationals, so they send their best people and give them extensive training in language and culture. Rather than seeing their overseas assignments as a detour from the fast track, the employees of foreign multinationals see their work abroad as a valuable part of their career development. European and Japanese multinationals also make a much greater effort than their American counterparts to supply institutional support for their employees abroad, often setting up mentoring systems in which someone in corporate headquarters is always watching out for the overseas employee.

In short, the paths to expatriate success are clearly marked. It remains for American corporations to determine whether they are interested enough in such success to make the necessary changes in their corporate priorities.

Source: Based on Rosalie L. Tung, "Expatriate Assignments: Enhancing Success and Minimizing Failure," *Academy of Management EXECUTIVE,* Vol. 1, No. 2, 1987, pp. 117–126.

ORGANIZATION CHANGE IN AN INTERNATIONAL CONTEXT

Finally, we should note the international implications of organization change. Organization change and development are discussed in the next two chapters, so the discussion at this point will, of necessity, be brief.

One factor to consider is how international environments can dictate organizational change. As we will see later, the environment can be a significant factor in bringing about organizational change. Given the additional environmental complexities faced by multinational organizations, it follows logically that organizational change may be even more critical to them than to purely domestic organizations.

A second point to remember is that acceptance of change varies widely around the globe. In some cultures, as noted earlier, change is a normal and accepted part of organizational life. In other cultures, change causes many more problems. The manager in an international setting should remember that techniques to manage change that worked routinely back home may not work at all and may even trigger negative responses if used indiscriminately in foreign cultures.[32]

SUMMARY OF KEY POINTS

International business has rapidly become an important part of almost every manager's life. This trend is likely to become even more important in the future. Thus, the manager should recognize that there are both similarities and differences across cultures.

One important concern is individual behavior. The manager must recognize that patterns of individual differences, managerial behavior, motivation, and rewards vary across cultures.

The individual-organization interface also varies across cultures. Particularly important are concerns related to job design, group dynamics, leadership, and power and conflict.

International management also involves an understanding of how organizational characteristics vary in an international context. Environment, technology, and organizational structure and design are especially important characteristics to understand.

---

[32] Alfred M. Jaeger, "Organization Development and National Culture: Where's the Fit?" *Academy of Management Review*, January 1986, pp. 178–190.

Also important to understand are a variety of organizational processes, such as decision making, communication, performance evaluation, and processes related to careers. Forces for and techniques of organizational change also vary systematically from culture to culture.

DISCUSSION QUESTIONS

1. Identify ways in which international business affects local businesses in your community.

2. All things considered, do you think people from diverse cultures are more alike or more different? Why do you feel this way?

3. What stereotypes exist about the motivational patterns of workers from other cultures?

4. What can American managers learn about individual behavior from other cultures? What can managers in other cultures learn about individual behavior from American managers?

5. Which dimension of the individual-organization interface is most likely to vary across cultures? Which is least likely to vary?

6. If you had just been appointed leader of a group of employees from another culture, what things would you do first to be more effective?

7. At present, the United States limits the exportation of high-tech equipment such as computers to Russia. Do you agree or disagree with this policy? Why?

8. If you worked for a company and were offered a temporary assignment abroad, would you be inclined to take it? Why or why not?

9. Suppose you worked for a firm that recently transferred in a manager from another country. The transfer represents this manager's first international exposure. What might you do to help his or her adjustment?

10. What are the advantages and disadvantages of transferring managers across a variety of locations scattered around the world?

Case 21.1   Exporting Corporate Culture

In the face of a mature U.S. fast foods market growing at only 1 percent a year, McDonald's is exporting the golden arches at an ever-increasing rate. About 40 percent of the new restaurants it opens each year are not on American soil. McDonald's restaurants in forty-six foreign countries account for about 20 percent of its $11 billion yearly sales, and the company is negotiating with Hungary and Yugoslavia, trying to be among the first food companies to break into Eastern Europe. Clearly McDonald's is having no trouble exporting its products, but can it also export its unique corporate culture?

In America, McDonald's is not just an enormously successful business; it has an effect on our national culture that many compare to that of the Disney empire. At least within the company itself, founder Ray Kroc is now treated with the reverence usually reserved for cult leaders. Mr. Kroc, who died in 1984, still appears on training videotapes, and new employees still hear his pronouncements on business and people, aphorisms like "If you've got time to lean, you've got time to clean." But how do you translate that into French or Japanese?

The secret to McDonald's overseas success, it seems, is the company's insistence that every store retain the core of Mr. Kroc's corporate culture while allowing each individual owner to adapt some elements to suit the local populace. When the McDonald's in Paris did not meet the company's cleanliness standards, the company was so displeased that it fought for four years in French courts to deny its name to the American businessman who was developing the restaurants. On the other hand, if you visit the golden arches in Thailand, you can get a milk shake flavored with durian, a Southeast Asian fruit thought to be an aphrodisiac.

Such balancing between what is quintessentially McDonald's and what can be changed to suit the local market is a tricky act for McDonald's top brass. The company has learned a lot from its franchisers—including ideas for some of its most popular products, like McD.L.T. and Egg McMuffin—so it tries to stay open to innovations from around the world. When Den Fujita wanted to open the first Japanese McDonald's in downtown Tokyo, McDonald's head-quarters argued vehemently that he should follow standard practice and go into business in the suburbs. Fujita won the argument, his Tokyo store soon set company sales records, and the company began a worldwide trend into inner cities.

As McDonald's moves around the world, what does not vary are the company's approach to finding new store owners and the way the stores themselves do business. Rather than MBAs or restaurateurs, the company seeks out entrepreneurs who show a solid faith in the company's values. It interviews such people and puts them through rigorous screening before it will let them open a McDonald's. A McDonald's franchiser in Perth, Australia sold his house, worked in a McDonald's for five days, and then put in twenty weeks of unpaid service, doing the lowliest of McDonald's chores, to prove he had the right attitude.

The McDonald's standards of quality are the same worldwide. The company supplies local owners with an operating manual the size of a phone book containing rigid rules about how often the bathrooms must be cleaned, how hot the grease must be, and how long a burger can sit under the heat lamps. These rules assure McDonald's customers that a Big Mac in New York will taste the same as a "biggu makku" at "Makudonarudo" in Tokyo. And that assurance reaps handsome profits.

Case Questions:

1. What lessons can other franchises learn from McDonald's experience exporting its products and corporate culture?

2. Harvard professor Arthur Kleinman says, "Their ads act as if all cultures should be the same as ours or they're missing something. That's a bad message." Do you agree?

Case Sources:

Kathleen Deveny, "McWorld?," *Business Week*, October 13, 1986, 78–86; Robert Johnson, "McDonald's Combines a Dead Man's Advice with Lively Strategy," *The Wall Street Journal*, December 18, 1987, 1; Frederick Hiroshi Katayama, "Japan's Big Mac," *Fortune*, September 15, 1986, 114–120; Madlyn Resener, Cheryl Debes, Graham Lloyd, and Rik Turner, "From Singapore to Sao Paulo, A Network of True Believers," *Business Week*, October 13, 1986, 80–81.

Case 21.2   Culture Shock

Warren Oats was a highly successful executive for American Auto Suppliers, a Chicago-based company that makes original equipment specialty parts for Ford, GM, and Chrysler. Rather than retreat before the onslaught of Japanese automakers, AAS decided to counterattack and use its reputation for quality and dependability to win over customers in Japan. Oats had started in the company as an engineer and worked his way up to be one of a handful of senior managers who had a shot at the next open vice presidential position. He knew he needed to distinguish himself somehow, so when he was given a chance to lead the AAS attack on the Japanese market, he jumped at it.

Oats knew he did not have time to learn Japanese, but he had heard that many Japanese executives speak English, and the company would hire a translator anyway. The toughest part about leaving the United States was persuading his wife Carol to take an eighteen-month leave from her career as an attorney with a prestigious Chicago law firm. She finally persuaded herself that she did not want to miss an opportunity to learn a new culture, so with all the information they could gather about Japan from their local library, they headed for Tokyo.

Known as an energetic, aggressive salesperson back home, Warren Oats wasted little time getting settled. As soon as his office had a telephone—and well before all his files had arrived from the States—Oats made an appointment to meet with executives of one of Japan's leading automakers. Oats reasoned that if he was going to overcome the famous Japanese resistance to foreign companies, he should get started as soon as possible.

Oats felt very uncomfortable at that first meeting. He got the feeling that the Japanese executives were waiting for something, or that everyone but him was in slow motion. The Japanese did not speak English very well and seemed grateful for the presence of the interpreter, but even the interpreter seemed slow, as if trying to figure out the translation of each phrase. Frustrated by this seeming lethargy, and beginning to be skeptical about the famous Japanese efficiency, Oats got right to the point. He made an oral presentation of his proposal, waiting patiently for the translation of each sentence, then handed the leader of the Japanese delegation a packet with the specifics of his proposal, got up, and took his leave, the translator trailing behind as if wanting to drag out the process even further.

By the end of their first week, both Warren and Carol were frustrated. Warren's office phone had not rung once, which did not make him optimistic about his meeting with another top company the following week. Carol could scarcely contain her irritation with what she had perceived of the Japanese way of life. She had been sure that a well-respected American lawyer would have little trouble securing a job within a Japanese multi-national corporation, but had met with several executives who seemed to feel insulted that she was asking them for a job. And the way they treated their secretaries! After only a week in Japan, both Carol and Warren Oats were ready to go home.

A month later, their perspective had changed radically. They both looked back on those first meetings with embarrassment. Within that month, they had both learned a lot about the Japanese sense of protocol and attitudes towards women. Warren Oats felt he was beginning to get the knack of doing business with the Japanese in their manner: establishing a relationship slowly, almost ritualistically, waiting through a number of meetings before bringing up the real business at hand, and then doing so circumspectly. It was difficult for Warren to slow down his pace, and it made him nervous to be so indirect, but he was beginning to see some value in the sometimes embarrassing learning process he was going through. Perhaps, he thought, he could become a consultant for other executives who needed to learn the lessons he was beginning to understand.

Case Questions:

1. What specific errors did Warren and Carol Oats make during their first week in Japan?

2. If you were talking to a foreign businessperson making a first contact with an American company, what advice would you give?

Experiential Exercise

Purpose: This exercise will help you develop a better understanding of the complexities involved in international management.

Format: The instructor will divide the class into small groups of three to four people each. Assume you are a task force for a medium-size manufacturing company. Top management has just decided to open a new facility in a foreign location. (Your instructor will specify the location for your group.) Your assignment is to learn as much about the culture of that location as possible and report back to top management about the advantages and disadvantages of the location. Try to identify three major advantages and three major concerns that need to be addressed. Report your findings to the class.

Follow-Up Questions

1. In a situation like this, can you ever learn all you need to know about a foreign culture and how it will affect a business?
2. How easy or difficult is it to learn about other cultures?

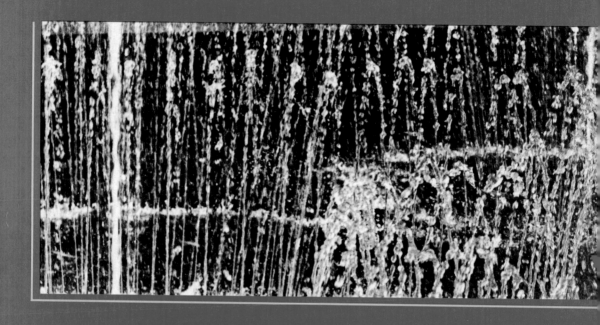

Organization
Change
and
Development

PART VI

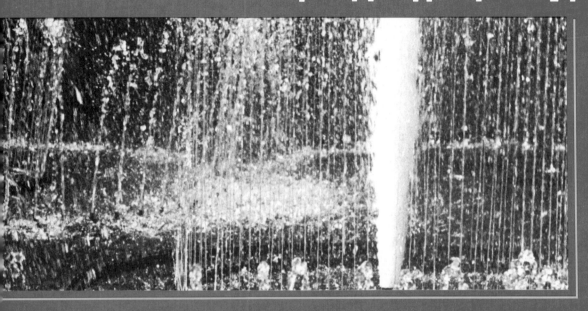

CHAPTER 22

Organization Change

Chapter Objectives

After reading this chapter, you should be able to

- ▶ summarize the dominant forces for change in organizations.

- ▶ discuss the ten major social trends in the United States.

- ▶ explain resistance to change from organizational and individual sources.

- ▶ describe the process of planned organization change.

*"I*magine a clock face with 60 minutes on it. Let the clock stand for the time men have had access to writing systems. Our clock would thus represent something like 3,000 years, and a minute on our clock 50 years. On this scale, there were no significant media changes until about nine minutes ago. At that time, the printing press came into use in Western culture. About three minutes ago, the telegraph, photograph, and locomotive arrived. Two minutes ago: the telephone, rotary press, motion pictures, automobile, airplane, and radio. One minute ago, the talking picture. Television appeared in the last ten seconds, the computer in the last five, and communications satellites in the last second. The laser beam—perhaps the most potent medium of communication of all—appeared only a fraction of a second ago.

"It would be possible to place almost any area of life on our clock face and get roughly the same measurements. For example, in medicine, you would have almost no significant changes until about one minute ago. In fact, until one minute ago, as Jerome Frank has said, almost the whole history of medicine is the history of the placebo effect. About a minute ago, antibiotics arrived. About ten seconds ago, open-heart surgery. In fact, within the past ten seconds there probably have been more changes in medicine than is represented by all the rest of the time on our clock. This is what some people call the 'knowledge explosion.' It is happening in every field of knowledge susceptible to scientific inquiry.

"The standard reply to any comment about change (for example, from many educators) is that change isn't new and that it is easy to exaggerate its meaning. To such replies, Norbert Wiener had a useful answer: the difference between a fatal and a therapeutic dose of strychnine is 'only a matter of degree.' In other words, change isn't new; what's new is the degree of change. As our clock-face metaphor was intended to suggest, about three minutes ago there developed a qualitative difference in the character of change. Change changed."[1]

CHANGE IN ORGANIZATIONS

News Item 1. People aged twenty-seven through forty-three, a group known as the "baby boomers," are becoming extremely influential in terms of political power, buying power, and demands on business, education, health care, and government institutions. The group's power derives from sheer numbers, high levels of education and income, and a distinct generational value system.[2]

News Item 2. Scientific breakthroughs with respect to superconductors suggest that by 1990, an inexhaustible supply of cheap energy will

---

[1] Neil Postman and Charles Weingartner, *Teaching as a Subversive Activity* (New York: Delacorte Press, 1969), pp. 10–11.

[2] Kenneth Labich, "The Arrival of the Baby-Boomer Boss," *Fortune*, August 15, 1988, pp. 58–63; "Baby Boomers Push For Power," *Business Week*, July 2, 1984, pp. 52–56; and Geoffrey Colvin, "What the Baby Boomers Will Buy Next," *Fortune*, October 15, 1984, pp. 28–34.

produce desk-top computers as powerful as today's bigger number-crunchers and trains that will fly above their rails at jet airplane speeds.[3]

News Item 3. General Motors no longer just makes cars. In 1984 GM began moving into other businesses by investing in data processing, electronics, and artificial intelligence. In 1985 the company bought a major aerospace firm. These investments are partly a preparation for the automobile industry of the future and partly a diversification strategy. In either case, the once slumbering giant of automobile manufacturing has signaled its commitment to radical change.[4]

These news items are typical of items appearing in major business publications every day. Each phenomenon is both a cause and an effect of the massive changes under way in society. Even as the baby boomers are creating changes in marketing, politics, and management, they must react to many changes in work rules, organizational cultures, and technology. Superconductors and new forms of energy transmission may dramatically reshape many kinds of information processing and transportation, but they are also a product of the increasing value placed on technological innovation. General Motors feels compelled to react to its changing environment through diversification; yet the synergy between its acquisitions and its automotive divisions may result in the creation of entirely new concepts in transportation, thereby substantially changing the environment.

The common denominator of these news items is change—change within, by, and often in spite of organizations. Such change can emanate from people (baby boomers), from technology (superconductors), or from organizations themselves (General Motors). Change can also be forced as when a new law mandates changes in the way a class of firms does business. Most CEOs agree that there are so many forces for change constantly bombarding organizations that it is hard to make long-range plans.[5] John A. Georges, CEO of International Paper, noted: "Changes have always existed. But now they're more intense and occur in more rapid sequence than in the past."[6] Thus, all organizations are in a constant state of flux, whether they recognize it and manage it, resist it, or ignore it.

Throughout this book we present organizational behavior as the study of four subject areas: the individual, the individual-organization interface, the organization, and organizational processes. Although we have divided the areas for discussion purposes, we note in the opening chapter that they are integrally

---

[3] John H. Wilson, "The New World of Superconductivity," *Business Week*, April 6, 1987, pp. 98–100.

[4] "GM Moves Into a New Area," *Business Week*, July 16, 1984, pp. 48–54.

[5] Carrie Gottlieb, "And You Thought You Had It Tough," *Fortune*, April 25, 1988, pp. 83–84.

[6] Gottlieb, "And You Thought You Had It Tough," p. 84.

related and overlap to a large extent. In this chapter, we turn our attention to a topic that draws on all four areas—the basic concepts and processes of organizational change. Chapter 23 discusses specific applications and techniques of change, with special emphasis on organizational development.

FORCES FOR CHANGE

An organization is subject to many pressures for change from a variety of sources—far too many to discuss here. Moreover, because the complexity of events and the rapidity of change are increasing, as demonstrated earlier by our clock face analogy, it is difficult to predict what type of pressure for change will be most significant in the next decade. It is possible, however—and important—to discuss the broad categories of pressures that will probably have major effects on organizations. The four areas in which the pressures for change seem most powerful involve people, technology, information processing and communication, and competition. These four categories and examples of each are shown in Table 22.1.

People

Approximately 56 million people were born between 1945 and 1960. These baby boomers are significantly different from previous generations with respect to education, expectations, and value systems.[7] As this group has aged, the median age of the U.S. population has gradually increased; it recently passed thirty-two years of age for the first time.[8] The special characteristics of baby boomers show up in distinct purchasing patterns that affect product and service innovation, technological change, and marketing and promotional activities.[9] Employment practices, compensation systems, promotion and managerial succession systems, and the entire concept of human resource management are also affected.

Other population-related pressures for change involve the generations that sandwich the baby boomers: the increasing numbers of senior citizens and those born after 1960. The parents of the baby boomers are living longer, healthier lives than previous generations, and they expect now to live the "good life" that they missed when they were raising their children. The impact of the large numbers of senior citizens is already evident in part-time employment practices, in the marketing of everything from hamburgers to packaged tours of Asia, and in the service areas, such as health care, recreation, and financial services.[10] The post-1960 generations that will be entering the job market over

---

[7] "Baby Boomers Push For Power."

[8] "Americans' Median Age Passes 32," *The Arizona Republic*, April 6, 1988, pp. A1, A5.

[9] Colvin, "What the Baby Boomers Will Buy Next."

[10] Alan L. Otten, "The New Old," *The Wall Street Journal*, May 11, 1987, pp. 1, 15.

Category	Examples
People	Baby boomers Senior citizens Coming generations
Technology	Manufacturing in space Robotics
Information processing and communication	Artificial intelligence Computer, satellite communications Videoconferencing
Competition	World-wide markets Emerging nations

Table 22.1

Pressures for
Organization Change

the next ten to fifteen years will be different from the baby boomers—but how? Will they be more or less liberal? More or less job- or career-oriented? More or less materialistic? More or less internationally aware? The answers to these questions and others will need to be asked—and answered—as these generations make their presence felt in organizations.

Technology

Not only is technology changing but the rate of technological change is itself increasing. In 1970, for example, all engineering students owned slide rules and used them in almost every class. By 1976, slide rules had given way to portable electronic calculators. In the mid-1980s some universities began issuing microcomputers to entering students or assuming that students already owned them. This is just one instance of increasingly rapid change.

Interestingly, change as it affects organizations is self-perpetuating. Advances in information technology have meant that more information is generated within organizations and it circulates more quickly. Employees are consequently able to respond more quickly to problems, which enables the organization to respond faster to demands from other organizations, customers, and competitors.[11] New technology will affect organizations in ways we cannot yet predict. Artificial intelligence—computers and software programs that think and learn in much the same way as human beings do—is already assisting in geological exploration.[12] Several companies are developing systems to manufacture chemicals and exotic electronic components in space. Robotics is developing so rapidly that annual U.S. sales of robots are expected to exceed $7 billion by

[11] Peter Nulty, "How Personal Computers Change Managers' Lives," *Fortune*, September 3, 1984, pp. 38–48.

[12] "Artificial Language Is Here," *Business Week*, July 9, 1984, pp. 54–62.

1990.[13] Robot sales in other countries, most notably Japan, are expected to increase even faster. Thus, as organizations respond more quickly to changes, change occurs more rapidly, which in turn necessitates even more rapid response.

Information Processing and Communication

Advances in information processing and communication have paralleled each other. A new generation of computers, which will mark another major increase in processing power, is being designed. Satellite systems for data transmission are already in use. People today can carry telephones in their briefcases next to their personal computers and pocket-sized televisions.

In the future, people may not need offices as they work with computers and communicate through new data transmission devices. Work stations, whether or not they are in offices, will be more electronic than paper-and-pencil. And videoconferencing has already become available at competitive prices.[14]

Competition

Although competition is not a new force for change, competition today has some significant new twists. First, most markets will soon be international because of decreasing transportation and communication costs and the increasing export orientation of business. And in the future, competition from the industrialized countries, such as Japan and Germany, will take a back seat to competition from the booming industries of developing nations. An example close to home is the maturing economy of Mexico. Developing nations may soon offer different, newer, cheaper, or higher-quality products, while enjoying the benefits of low labor costs, abundant supplies of raw materials, expertise in certain areas of production, and financial protection from their governments that may not be available in the older industrialized states. Organizations that are not ready for these new sources of competition in the next decade may not exist by the year 2000.

Ten Social Trends

In conjunction with the pressures for change, it is worthwhile to examine ten social trends discussed by John Naisbitt.[15] Naisbitt has asserted that these trends, summarized in Table 22.2, are transforming U.S. society. Some of the trends are related to new technology—for example, the development of an information

---

[13] Robert U. Ayres and Steven M. Miller, *Robotics: Applications and Social Implications* (Cambridge, Mass.: Ballinger, 1983).

[14] "Videoconferencing: No Longer Just a Sideshow," *Business Week*, November 12, 1984, pp. 116–120.

[15] John Naisbitt, *Megatrends: Ten New Directions Transforming Our Lives* (New York: Warner Books, 1982).

Table 22.2	From	To
Ten Trends of Social Transformation	Industrial society	Information society
	Forced technology	High tech/High touch
	National economy	World economy
	Short term	Long term
	Centralization	Decentralization
	Institutional help	Self-help
	Representative democracy	Participatory democracy
	Hierarchies	Networking
	North	South
	Either/or	Multiple option

Source: Based on John Naisbitt, *Megatrends: Ten New Directions Transforming Our Lives* (New York: Warner Books, 1982).

society and the trend toward high tech/high touch. **High tech/high touch** refers to Naisbitt's contention that the more new technology is forced on people, the more need there is for the human touch. Other trends are related to demographic change, such as shifts in the U.S. population from the North to the South, toward better education, and toward an emphasis on participatory democracy. Naisbitt has claimed that the United States is in a "time of parenthesis," an interval between eras. It is moving from an industrial to an information society in which brain power will be more important than physical power. This change will require new organizational forms, increased mobility and substantial retraining of workers, more participation of workers in managing organizations, and a long-term orientation toward planning, management results, and compensation.

The pressures for change are interdependent and affect organizations in many ways. For example, competition is influenced by communication and information processing as well as by population dynamics, but it also serves as a stimulus to technological development. In addition, these environmental factors affect the management of people within organizations. They create new challenges and shorten the period in which organizations must respond if they are to avoid major problems. All organizations must change to survive.[16] The decision is not whether to change, but how. Tom Peters has identified the traits of American companies showing superior performance, and has recommended

---

[16] Stephen R. Michael, "Organizational Change Techniques: Their Present, Their Future," *Organizational Dynamics*, Summer 1982, pp. 67–80.

a three-point plan for American companies that wish to be in the forefront of growth and change in an international environment. (See *A Look at Research*.)

RESISTANCE TO CHANGE

Just as change is inevitable, so is resistance to change. Paradoxically, organizations both promote and resist change. As an agent for change, the organization asks prospective customers or clients to change their current purchasing habits by switching to the company's product or service and asks current customers to change by increasing their purchases. At the same time, the organization resists change in that its structure and control systems protect the daily tasks of producing a product or service from uncertainties in the environment. Since an organization is constantly buffeted by the forces of change, it must have some elements of permanence to avoid mirroring the instability of the environment. Yet it also must react to external shifts with internal change to maintain currency and relevance in the marketplace.

A commonly held view is that all resistance to change needs to be overcome, but that is not always the case. Resistance to change can be compared to the property of materials that restricts the passage of electrical current and causes the material to give off heat, a property also known as resistance. The heating coils in a toaster, waffle iron, and hair dryer all use this principle. If the resistance is complete, however, no current flows, and no heat is given off. Thus, resistance to the passage of current is useful as long as some current can flow through the material.

Similarly, organizational resistance to change need not be eliminated entirely but can be used and controlled for the benefit of the organization. By revealing a legitimate concern that a proposed change may not be good for the organization, resistance may alert the organization to investigate and re-examine the change.[17] For example, an organization may be considering the acquisition of a company in a completely different industry. Resistance to such a proposal may cause the organization to examine more carefully the advantages and disadvantages of the move. Without resistance, the decision might be made before the pros and cons have been sufficiently explored.

Resistance may come from the organization, the individual, or both. It is often difficult to determine the ultimate source, however, since organizations are composed of individuals. Various types of organizational and individual sources of resistance are summarized in Table 22.3.

---

[17] Paul R. Lawrence, "How to Deal with Resistance to Change," *Harvard Business Review*, May–June, 1954, reprinted in Gene W. Dalton, Paul R. Lawrence, and Larry E. Greiner, eds., *Organizational Change and Development* (Homewood, Ill.: Irwin, 1970), pp. 181–197.

A LOOK AT

RESEARCH

The Superior Performers

Despite the increase in the intensity of international competition and despite the growing international trade deficit, there are some bright stars in the American economy. There is emerging a new managerial elite in the United States with the skills to compete very well in the international arena. The traits of these superior performers have been found to be as follows:

1. First and foremost, the new elite produces quality goods and services.
2. The second trait is "somewhat smaller is much more beautiful."* The flatter the organization, the fewer supervisors, the better the performance.
3. Today's world-class competitor is more innovative, more flexible, more adaptable to change, more "fleet of foot."
4. The new leaders are closer to their customers, are more concerned with customer needs, and are more focused on customer service.
5. The final trait of the new U.S. business champion is superior international business skills.

In order to further improve the effectiveness of corporate America, we need to turn up the heat—to renew our energies to transform U.S. firms into dynamic advocates of these elite traits. Thus, to be international champions, companies must first be the champions of growth, transformation, and change. To accomplish this end, a three-point plan is suggested.

1. Increase investment in innovation, R&D, and modernization.
2. Fight attempts at protectionism, which only decreases competition to the point that firms no longer stay lean and tough. Protectionism destroys industrial productivity.
3. As our economy is transformed to meet the new international competition, we must support programs that will retrain and relocate displaced workers.

Source: Tom Peters, "Competition and Compassion," *California Management Review*, Summer 1986, pp. 11–27.

* Tom Peters, "Competition and Compassion," *California Management Review*, Summer 1986, p. 16.

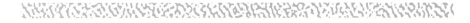

Organizational Sources of Resistance

Daniel Katz and Robert L. Kahn have identified six major organizational sources of resistance.[18] Of course, not every organization or every change situation displays all six sources.

---

[18] Daniel Katz and Robert L. Kahn, *The Social Psychology of Organizations*, 2nd ed. (New York: John Wiley, 1978), 36–68.

Table 22.3		
Organizational and Individual Sources of Resistance	**Organizational Sources**	**Examples**
	Overdetermination	Employment system, job descriptions, evaluation and reward system
	Narrow focus of change	Structure changed with no concern given to other issues, e.g., jobs, people
	Group inertia	Group norms
	Threatened expertise	People move out of area of expertise
	Threatened power	Decentralized decision making
	Resource allocation	Increased use of part-time help
	Individual Sources	**Examples**
	Habit	Altered tasks
	Security	Altered tasks or reporting relationships
	Economic factors	Changed pay and benefits
	Fear of the unknown	New job, new boss
	Lack of awareness	Isolated groups not heeding notices
	Social factors	Group norms

OVERDETERMINATION   Organizations have several systems designed to maintain stability. For example, consider how organizations control employees' performance. To make sure that as employees they will do the job the organization desires, job candidates must meet specific requirements before being hired. As soon as a person is hired, he or she is given a job description, and the supervisor trains, coaches, and counsels the employee in job tasks. The new employee usually serves some type of probationary period that culminates in a performance review; thereafter, the employee's performance is regularly evaluated. Finally, rewards, punishment, and discipline are administered depending on the level of performance. The system is overdetermined in that the same effect on employee performance could probably be achieved with fewer procedures and safeguards.

Overdetermination has also been called structural inertia.[19] That is, the structure of the organization provides resistance to change because it was designed to maintain stability.

---

[19] See Michael T. Hannah and John Freeman, "Structural Inertia and Organizational Change," *American Sociological Review*, April 1984, pp. 149–164, for an in-depth discussion of structural inertia.

NARROW FOCUS OF CHANGE   Many efforts to create change in organizations adopt too narrow a focus. Any effort to force change in the tasks of individuals or a group must take into account the interdependencies among organizational elements, such as people, structure, tasks, and the information system. For example, some attempts at redesigning jobs are not successful because the organizational structure within which jobs must function is inappropriate for the redesigned jobs.[20]

GROUP INERTIA   When an employee attempts to change his or her work behavior, the group may resist by refusing to change other behaviors that are necessary complements to the individual's changed behavior. That is, group norms may act as a brake on individual attempts at behavior change.

THREATENED EXPERTISE   A change in the organization may threaten the specialized expertise that individuals and groups have developed over the years. A job redesign or a structural change may transfer the responsibility for a specialized task from the current expert to someone else, thus threatening the specialist's expertise and building his or her resistance to the change.

THREATENED POWER   Any redistribution of decision-making authority may threaten an individual's power relationships with others. If an organization is decentralizing its decision making, managers who wielded their decision-making powers in return for special favors from others may resist the change because they do not want to lose their power base.

RESOURCE ALLOCATION   Groups happy with current resource allocation methods may resist any change that they feel may threaten their future allocations. Resources in this context can mean anything from monetary rewards and equipment to additional seasonal help to more computer time.

These six sources explain most types of organization-based resistance to change. All except the second (the narrow focus of change) are based on people and social relationships. Furthermore, many of these sources of resistance can be traced to groups or individuals afraid of losing something—resources, power, or comfort in a routine.

Individual Sources of Resistance

Individual sources of resistance to change are rooted in basic human characteristics, such as needs and perceptions. Researchers have identified six reasons for individual resistance to change.[21]

---

[20] Gregory Moorhead, "Organizational Analysis: An Integration of the Macro and Micro Approaches," *Journal of Management Studies*, April 1981, pp. 191–218.

[21] David A. Nadler, "Concepts for the Management of Organizational Change," in J. Richard Hackman, Edward E. Lawler, III, and Lyman W. Porter, eds., *Perspectives on Behavior in Organizations*, 2nd ed. (New York: McGraw-Hill, 1983), pp. 551–561; and G. Zaltman and R. Duncan, *Strategies for Planned Change* (New York: John Wiley, 1977).

HABIT   It is easier to do a job the same way every day. If the steps in the job are repeated over and over, the job becomes easier and easier. But learning an entirely new set of steps makes the job more difficult. For the same amount of return (pay), most people prefer to do easier work rather than harder work.

SECURITY   Some employees like the comfort and security of doing things in the same old way. They gain a feeling of constancy and safety in knowing that some things stay the same, despite all the change going on around them. Thus, people who feel that their security is threatened by a change are likely to resist the change. For instance, the many changes that occurred in jobs, departments, and divisions at General Motors when the company reorganized several years ago evoked some resistance because they threatened employees' security.[22]

ECONOMIC FACTORS   Change may also threaten employees' steady paychecks. They may fear that change will make their jobs obsolete.

FEAR OF THE UNKNOWN   Some people fear anything unfamiliar. Changes in reporting relationships and job duties create anxiety for such employees. Employees become familiar with their boss, their job, and relationships with others within the organization, such as contact people for certain situations. These relationships and contacts are useful in facilitating their work. Any disruption of familiar patterns may create fear because it can cause delays and the feeling that nothing is getting accomplished. The previously mentioned changes at GM created a situation described as "quicksand"—there were so many transfers of people between divisions that it became difficult to find phone numbers for coworkers.[23]

LACK OF AWARENESS   Because of perceptual limitations, such as lack of attention or selective attention, a person may not recognize a change in a rule or procedure and thus may not alter behavior. People may pay attention only to those things that support their point of view. As an example, employees in an isolated regional sales office may not notice—or may ignore—directives from headquarters regarding a change in reporting procedures for expense accounts. They may therefore continue the current practice as long as possible.

SOCIAL FACTORS   People may resist change for fear of what others may think. As we have mentioned before, the group can be a powerful motivator of behavior. Employees may feel that change will hurt their image, result in ostracism from the group, or simply make them "different." For example, an employee who agrees to conform to work rules established by management may be ridiculed by others who openly disobey the rules. The Japanese may

---

[22] Melinda Grenier Guiles, "GM's Smith Presses for Sweeping Changes but Questions Arise," *The Wall Street Journal*, March 14, 1985, pp. 1, 18.

[23] Guiles, "GM's Smith Presses for Sweeping Changes."

International Perspective

Is Japan Really a Superstar?

Most foreigners see Japan as an economic superstar, second only to the United States in the free world and destined to be first by the turn of the century. Yet few Japanese share that opinion. Despite Japan's amazing economic growth since the end of World War II, most Japanese see their country as a small island nation with very few natural resources. They realize that they must import 70 percent of their food and 99 percent of their oil and essential minerals. Thus, they see their economy as especially vulnerable to international forces beyond their control.

This vision of vulnerability is a national mind-set among the Japanese. They also believe that increases in their personal wealth (Japanese incomes are now comparable to those in the United States) have been far less than perceived by the rest of the free world. The average Japanese perceives himself or herself as living in a cramped, expensive apartment, limited to poor recreational facilities, and paying high prices for consumer goods. Thus, the Japanese feel that they are not as affluent as Americans and are convinced that their nation's wealth does not really exist.

Another element of the Japanese scenario is its historic tendency toward isolation. Japan is slowly emerging onto the world scene, but its emergence is stirring nationalistic sentiments in other nations, especially in the United States, where many people resent the fact that Japanese are buying U.S. companies, running U.S. plants, and dominating U.S. markets.

Above all, Japan must recognize that it is an international economic force—it is for real—and it must assume the responsibilities that this role demands. The Japanese must stop focusing on what makes them different from others and begin focusing on those factors that make them an integral part of the international arena.

Sources: Barbara Buell, "Japan Just Can't Believe It's a Superstar," *Business Week*, July 13, 1987, p. 64; Frank Gibney, *Japan: The Fragile Super Power* (New York: W. W. Norton & Company, 1979); G. Packard, "Japan: A Valued U.S. Partner Peers at the Future," *Context*, Vol. 13, No. 2, 1984, pp. 1–7.

be facing a similar resistance to change by not recognizing their role in the international marketplace. (See *International Perspective.*)

Managing Resistance

Managing resistance to change is much like managing organizational conflict, a topic discussed in Chapter 12. Rather than think of resistance as something to be avoided or overcome, managers should recognize it as a cue to re-examine the merits of a proposed change. Resistance can be constructive if it prompts managers to communicate more with employees, re-evaluate the decision to make a change, and perhaps search for new ways to reach the desired goals. A new method may be better than the one originally proposed.

It may, for example, accomplish the desired goals with less resistance and thus less expense. Moreover, re-evaluating the proposed change in response to employee resistance may be a symbolic act that tells employees management listens to and cares about them.[24] Table 22.4 lists examples of six methods for dealing with resistance to change.[25]

EDUCATION AND COMMUNICATION   If resistance is based on inaccurate or inadequate information, a program of communication about the change may be appropriate. Communication can help dissipate some fears of unknown elements, such as a new job or a supervisor change. Such an effort is likely to work best when it is undertaken before the change is implemented, the reasons for the change are fully explained, and communication is two-way.

PARTICIPATION AND INVOLVEMENT   Resistance may be reduced when those affected by the change are involved in designing it. This strategy is especially useful when employee commitment is essential to successful implementation. It is important to note, however, that involving employees in the change can be quite time consuming and must be managed properly. This approach can be useful in overcoming resistance caused by a narrow focus of change and by lack of awareness.

FACILITATION AND SUPPORT   Facilitation and support are effective in combating problems arising from desires for security and fear of the unknown. When employees are having difficulty in adjusting to new arrangements and new ways of doing things, a manager may need to arrange for additional training or provide extra emotional support while employees become accustomed to the new system. Such facilitation may take time and effort. When employees are struggling with a new machine or technique, it is very easy for a supervisor to stop by their work area and encourage them to work harder, but it takes more time to sit down with them over a cup of coffee and listen to their problems. Although a discussion over coffee may not solve these problems, it leaves a message that the supervisor (and maybe top management) cares, which may encourage the employees to work harder to solve the problem.

NEGOTIATION AND AGREEMENT   If people or groups are losing something significant in the change and if they have enough power to resist strongly (as a union might), a manager may use a negotiation strategy. Negotiation before implementation can make the change go much more smoothly. Should problems arise later, the conflicting parties can be referred to the negotiated agreement. This is a useful technique when resistance is due to threatened power relationships and group factors.

---

[24] Jeffrey Pfeffer, "Management as Symbolic Action: The Creation and Maintenance of Organizational Paradigms," in L. L. Cummings and B. M. Staw, eds., *Research in Organizational Behavior*, Vol. 3 (Greenwich, Conn.: JAI Press, 1981), pp. 1–52.

[25] John P. Kotter and Leonard S. Schlesinger, "Choosing Strategies for Change," *Harvard Business Review*, March–April 1979, pp. 106–114.

Table 22.4	**Method**	**Examples**
Methods for Managing Resistance to Change	Education and communication	Open communication Training programs to increase awareness
	Participation and involvement	Collaborative design of changes
	Facilitation and support	Emotional support and attentiveness Specific problem-related training
	Negotiation and agreement	Labor contract Mutual goal-setting sessions
	Manipulation and cooptation	Appointment of a member of an opposing group, such as a member of the union, to company board of directors
	Coercion	Threats of punishment or dismissal for noncompliance

MANIPULATION AND COOPTATION   In situations in which other methods are not working or are not available, a manager may resort to the manipulation of information, resources, and favors to overcome resistance. Cooptation may involve including representatives of groups likely to offer resistance in the design and implementation of the change, whether or not the manager is really interested in their ideas. The manager hopes that inclusion in a planning group will cause the resisters to support the change when it is introduced into the organization. When Chrysler was in difficulty, for example, it tried to forestall labor union resistance to change by electing the union president to the corporate board of directors. The technique is often used when resistance is due to resource allocations, economic factors, habit, and group factors.

COERCION   Managers may resort to coercion to overcome resistance if all other methods fail or for some reason are inappropriate. Compliance can be coerced by threats of pay reduction, loss of job, or demotion or transfer. Although force may be a quick method of overcoming resistance, it can seriously affect employee attitudes and result in adverse consequences in the long run.

PROCESSES FOR PLANNED ORGANIZATION CHANGE

External elements may force change on an organization. Ideally, however, the organization will not only respond to change but anticipate it, prepare for it through planning, and incorporate it in the organizational strategy.

Process Models

Planned organization change requires a systematic process of moving from one condition to another. Three approaches to change that emphasize the change process are discussed in this section: Lewin's three-step change process, an expanded process model, and action research.

Figure 22.1

Lewin's Process of
Organization Change

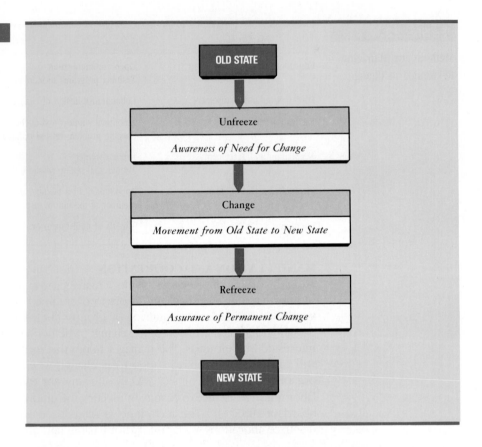

LEWIN'S THREE-STEP CHANGE PROCESS   Kurt Lewin has suggested that efforts to bring about planned change in organizations should approach change as a multistage process.[26] His model of planned change is made up of three steps: "unfreezing," change, and "refreezing," as shown in Figure 22.1.

Unfreezing is the process by which people become aware of the need for change. Satisfaction with current practices and procedures may result in little or no interest in making changes. The key factor in unfreezing is making employees knowledgeable about the importance of a change and how their jobs will be affected by it. The employees who will be most affected by the change must be made aware of the need for it, in effect making them dissatisfied enough with current operations to be motivated toward change.

Change is the movement from an old state to a new one—in Naisbitt's terms, the time of parenthesis or transformation.[27] Change may mean the

---

[26] Kurt Lewin, *Field Theory in Social Science* (New York: Harper & Row. 1951).

[27] Naisbitt, *Megatrends.*

installation of new equipment, the restructuring of the organization, the implementation of a new performance appraisal system—anything that alters existing relationships or activities.

Refreezing makes new behaviors relatively permanent and resistant to further change. Examples of refreezing include repeating newly learned skills in a training session and role playing to teach how the new skill can be used in a real-life work situation. Refreezing is necessary because, without it, the old ways of doing things might soon reassert themselves while the new ways were forgotten. For example, many employees who attend special training sessions apply themselves diligently and resolve to change things in their organizations. But when they return to the workplace, they find it easier to conform to the old ways than to make waves. There are usually few if any rewards for trying to change the organizational status quo. In fact, the personal sanctions against doing so may be difficult to tolerate. Learning theory and reinforcement theory (Chapter 2) can play important roles in the refreezing phase.

EXPANDED PROCESS MODEL   Perhaps because Lewin's model is very simple and straightforward, virtually all models of organizational change use his approach. However, it does not deal with several important issues. A more complex, and more helpful, approach is illustrated in Figure 22.2. This approach looks at planned change from the perspective of top management. The model incorporates Lewin's concept as part of the implementation phase.

In this approach, top management perceives that certain forces or trends call for change, and the issue is subjected to the organization's usual problem-solving and decision-making processes (see Chapter 17). Usually, top management defines its goals in terms of what the organization or certain processes or outputs will be like after the change. Alternatives for change are generated and evaluated, and an acceptable one is selected.

Early in the process the organization may seek the assistance of a **change agent**—a person who will be responsible for managing the change effort. The change agent may also help management recognize and define the problem or the need for the change and may be involved in generating and evaluating potential plans of action The change agent may be a member of the organization or an outsider, such as a consultant. An internal change agent is likely to know the organization's people, tasks, and political situations, which may be very helpful in interpreting data and understanding the system; but an insider may also be too close to the situation to view it objectively. (In addition, a regular employee would have to be removed from his or her regular duties to concentrate on the transition.) An outsider, then, is often received better by all parties because of her or his assumed impartiality.

Unless the change agent is a member of top management, his or her power to bring about change must emanate from some source other than hierarchical position and legitimate authority within the organization. Although the support

Figure 22.2

An Expanded Model of the Organization Change Process

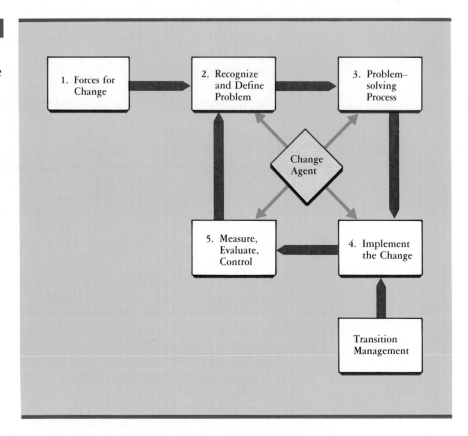

of top management is essential, it is not enough. Michael Beer describes five sources of power for the change agent:

1. High status given by members of the client organization, based on their perception that the change agent is similar to them in behaviors, language, values, and even dress.
2. Trust in the change agent based on his or her consistent handling of information and maintaining a proper role in the organization.
3. Expertise in the practice of organizational change.
4. Established credibility based on experiences with previous clients or previous projects with the client organization.
5. Dissatisfied constituencies inside the organization who see the change agent as the best opportunity to change the organization to meet their needs.[28]

---

[28] Michael Beer, *Organization Change and Development: A Systems View* (Santa Monica, Calif.: Goodyear, 1980), p. 78.

Under the direction and management of the change agent, the organization implements the change through Lewin's unfreeze, change, and refreeze process. (In Chapter 23 we will discuss several specific methods of organizational change.) In the final step, evaluation and control, the change agent and the top management group assess the degree to which the change is having the desired effect. That is, progress toward the goals of the change is measured. If necessary, appropriate changes are made.

The more the change agent is involved in the steps of the change process, the less distinct they become. As the change agent becomes immersed in defining and solving the problem with members of the organization, she or he becomes a "collaborator" or "helper" to the organization. When this happens, the change agent may be working with many different individuals, groups, and departments within the organization on different phases of the change process. Because of the total involvement of the change agent in every phase of the project, it may not be readily observable when the change process is moving along from one stage to another. Throughout the process, however, the change agent brings in new ideas and viewpoints that help members look at old problems in new ways. Change often comes from the conflict that results when the change agent challenges the organization's assumptions and generally accepted patterns of operation.

ACTION RESEARCH   Another view of the organization change process is **action research**, which is usually referred to as an organization change process that is based on a research model; specifically one that contributes toward the betterment of the sponsoring organization and contributes to advancement of knowledge of organizations in general.[29] In action research, the researcher, or change agent, is usually an outside person who is involved in the total change process, from diagnosis to evaluation. This person usually contracts with the sponsoring organization to engage in organizational research, whereas the typical change agent is called in to make a specific change.

The research process is usually composed of in-depth searching, asking questions, interviewing employees, and evaluating records, all of which lead to analysis and synthesis of information. The researcher's questioning of employees and searching leads to the development of suggested actions for the organization. The action researcher works with the employees of the organization to develop action plans that best meet the needs of all concerned.

The researcher uses the initial data gathered in the early stages as points of comparison for data gathered during and after any subsequent change that may be made in the organization. In this manner the researcher can evaluate the effects on the organization of the changes. The evaluation of the organization and any changes taken to improve it over a period of change can provide valuable information to both the organization and the researcher.

---

[29] Peter A. Clark, *Action Research and Organizational Change* (New York: Harper & Row, 1972).

Transition Management

Organizational change does not happen overnight or over a weekend. It takes time for employees to absorb even simple changes. For example, suppose a change involves the creation of a new position—a coordinator between two departments. It will take some time for employees in the departments to become accustomed to going through the coordinator with certain types of requests and seeking a decision or approval from that person. Much more time and effort may be required for employees to adapt to complex changes. Such changes need to be managed, not merely implemented. The results of major changes within organizations may take years to fully realize. For example, K mart has been changing its stores and expanding into new areas since 1985. (See *Management in Action.*)

Transition management is the process of systematically planning, organizing, and implementing change, from the disassembly of the current state to the realization of a fully functional future state within an organization.[30] Once change begins, the organization is in neither the old state nor the new state. Yet business must continue. Transition management ensures that business continues while the change is occurring, and thus it must begin before the change occurs. The members of the regular management team must take on the role of transition managers and coordinate organizational activities with the change agent. An interim management structure or interim positions may be created to ensure continuity and control of the business during the transition. Communication of the changes to all involved, from employees to customers and suppliers, plays a key role in transitional management.[31]

An Integrated Process of Organization Change

Successful organizational change projects integrate all or most of the elements of change discussed so far in this chapter. The integrative framework, illustrated in Figure 22.3, shows how the organization is relatively stable at time 1; unfreezes, changes, and refreezes in time 2; and becomes a new, stable system in time 3. Throughout the process, transition management keeps the organization functioning.

Recent changes at Keithley Instruments, Inc., (KII) illustrate the management of a major change.[32] KII, a manufacturer of industrial and scientific equipment, suffered in 1979 from a cluttered shop floor, inventory uncertainty, frequent

---

[30] Linda S. Ackerman, "Transition Management: An In-Depth Look at Managing Complex Change," *Organizational Dynamics,* Summer 1982, pp. 46–66; and David A. Nadler, "Managing Transitions to Uncertain Future States," *Organizational Dynamics,* Summer 1982, pp. 37–45.

[31] Noel M. Tichy and David O. Ulrich, "The Leadership Challenge—A Call for the Transformational Leader," *Sloan Management Review,* Fall 1984, pp. 59–68.

[32] Perry Pascarella, "Change Champion Builds Teamwork," *Industry Week,* March 19, 1984, pp. 61, 64.

K mart is Looking For a Little Respect

When Joseph E. Antonini took over as CEO at K mart in 1987, he announced, "My goal is to make K mart the most respected dominant retailer in America." That's quite a goal for the retailing company that emerged from S. S. Kresge Co. and expanded across the nation as a low-cost, no-nonsense retailer with 2,200 stores offering blue-light specials to blue-collar buyers.

Antonini's objective is simple: expand the store's customer base to include a more affluent and a more fashion-conscious consumer. He plans to achieve this goal through two major marketing strategies: (1) upgrading the stores and the merchandise and (2) adding a wide variety of specialty stores.

The K mart stores have already been upgraded in appearance and customer conveniences. Further, the company's own private-label merchandise is being upgraded. A big step in this direction was the firm's first celebrity line—the Jaclyn Smith Signature Collection of women's sportswear. The line was an instant success; 75 percent of the first order was sold out in only eleven weeks. With the backing of hostess Martha Stewart, K mart is introducing another celebrity line in its "Kitchen Korner" home fashion department. Stewart, a professional caterer, columnist, and author, was introduced during the 1987 Christmas season through television advertising and full-page advertisements in six magazines.

A successful expansion into specialty stores began with the acquisition of Walden Books Co. Inc. a 955-bookstore chain. The Pay Less drugstore chain was next, followed by Home Centers Inc., a chain of do-it-yourself warehouse stores renamed Builders Square. Together, the specialty stores accounted for 10.5 percent of K mart's 1986 sales. By 1991, K mart expects the specialty stores to bring in 20 percent of its sales. K mart has even joined Sears and J. C. Penney in the business of home retailing by television (home video shopping) by entering into an agreement with Consumer Discount Network (CDN) to supply nonelectric merchandise. Any way you look at it, K mart should finally get a little respect.

Sources: "K mart Boss Wants Chain to Become Most Respected in U.S.," *The Arizona Republic*, October 4, 1987, pp. E1, E9; "Attention, K mart Shoppers!" *Direct Marketing*, May 1987, p. 8; and "K mart to Santa: Ho, Ho, Ho-Hum," *Business Week*, December 7, 1987, pp. 60–61.

production errors, and worker discontent. The company had grown very quickly from a relatively small, well-organized operation based on engineering expertise to a large, poorly structured one in which production bottlenecks occurred regularly. As one person put it, the organization was limiting the people.

Hired as director of human resources, Mark Frohman acted as an internal change agent. In fact, though, because he had been with the company only a short time, he was an outsider in many ways. Before holding meetings with employees throughout the organization, Frohman convinced top management to write down the company's purpose and goals, which he used as guidelines for change. The change strategy included training, redesign of jobs and work

Figure 22.3

Integrated Process of
Organization Change

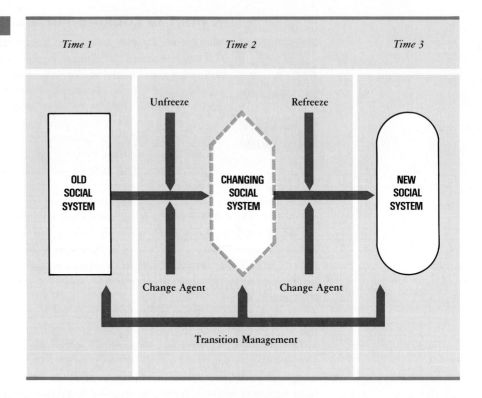

flow, and development of better communications. The key element of the
change was the establishment of production teams, the first of which was
formed in October 1979. Top manufacturing managers held one- and two-day
meetings to plan the change and the make-up of the production teams.
Supervisors received training that included case studies, lectures, discussion,
and role-playing on participative team management. Team members attended
one-day meetings on the company itself, its products, and basic economics.

Although the first team was initially uncertain about its role, it was a success.
Other teams were formed, and by the end of 1982, all production in the
company was being accomplished by twelve production teams. Each group
meets twice a month to review performance, discuss problems, and set goals
for the next period. The ratio of raw materials to finished goods has decreased,
the rate of in-warranty repairs has decreased, and the labor relations atmosphere
has improved. KII reported that in the five-year period ending in 1983, sales
nearly doubled to $35 million, and profits increased to $2 million despite a
recessionary economy. As the change agent, Frohman was involved in the entire
process, from problem diagnosis to implementation. He used an integrated
change process to effect major changes in the organization.

SUMMARY OF KEY POINTS

Change may be forced on an organization, or an organization may change in response to the environment or an internal need. The forces for change are interdependent and influence organizations in many ways. Currently, the areas in which the pressures for change seem most powerful involve people, technology, information and communication, competition, and social trends.

Resistance to change may arise from one or several individual and organizational sources. Resistance may indicate a legitimate concern that the change is not good for the organization and may warrant a re-examination of plans. Resistance to change can be managed through communicating and educating employees more effectively and involving employees in the change as much as possible.

Planned organizational change involves anticipating change and preparing for it. Lewin described organizational change in terms of unfreezing, change, and refreezing. In the expanded model of planned change, top management recognizes forces that call for change, engages in a problem-solving process to design the change, and implements and evaluates the change. Some organizations may use a change agent, either a member of the organization or an outsider, to manage the change process. The change agent may help define and solve the problem and may fully collaborate in the change, evaluation, and control phases of the process.

Once change begins, the organization is in a transition stage—neither the old state nor the new state—but the business of the organization must continue. So that the organization will function during this period, it is helpful to plan, organize, and implement organizational change systematically, from disassembly of the current state to creation of a fully functional new state. This process of transition management begins before the actual change occurs with proper planning and organizing.

DISCUSSION QUESTIONS

1. Which of the four subject areas of organizational behavior is most important to the study of organizational change? Why?

2. Is most organizational change forced on the organization by external factors or created from inside? Explain.

3. Can you think of a broad category of pressures for organizational change other than the five discussed in the chapter? If so, briefly describe it.

4. Describe a trend that John Naisbitt's book *Megatrends* may have missed or that has developed since it was published. How might it affect organizations?

5. Which sources of resistance to change present the most problems for an internal change agent? For an external change agent?

6. Who is more responsible for managing resistance to change—the change agent or the transition management team?

7. Would you expect resistance to change to occur frequently or infrequently? Why?

8. Which stage of the Lewin model of change do you think is the most often overlooked? Why?

9. What are the advantages and disadvantages of having an internal change agent rather than an external change agent?

10. Why do you think the task of transition management could be difficult?

Case 22.1

Amax Changes Its Ways

Clarence Allen Born, the grandson of a weathered and dynamite-deafened mining man, obtained his geology degree from the University of Texas at El Paso. One of his first jobs was at Amax Inc.'s big Climax molybdenum mine in 1967. Two decades later, he came back to Amax as chief executive officer to try to save the nation's largest mining firm. Amax had lost $1.7 billion over four straight losing years. Competition from low-cost mining operations in developing countries and highly cyclical demand for the thirty-two minerals that the company mined were identified as the major problems.

Molybdenum presented the major product problem. The mineral was scarce in the late 1970s and brought soaring prices that led to large Amax profits. However, a 50-percent increase in the world supply of "moly" sent prices tumbling and turned Amax profits into huge losses.

Born knew what had to be done, declaring, "If you can't fix it, sell it. If you can't sell it, shoot it." Born quickly applied all three cures and narrowed the firm's focus from thirty-two minerals to just three—aluminum, coal, and gold. Dispatched from the firm were a number of top executives who had failed to recognize and deal with the many changes facing the industry. Born has made Amax much leaner and more focused than it was five years ago.

Born also acquired Alumax, an aluminum company, from two Japanese firms—Mitsui & Co. Ltd. and Nippon Steel Corporation. Since the acquisition, aluminum ingot prices have shot up by 60 percent, and Alumax's finished metal products have helped smooth Amax's cyclic problems.

Amax has also become the nation's biggest low-sulfur coal producer. It has made profitable expansions into the gold market; higher gold prices helped boost its gold unit's 1987 profits to more than twice their 1986 levels. Harold Brown, former U.S. Secretary of Defense and a current Amax director, says of Born, "He's decisive. He lays out a few goals and goes after them."

Case Questions

1. What were some of the forces of change that damaged Amax's business?

2. Why do you think key Amax executives had failed to respond appropriately to the changes in the mining and industrial environment?

3. What do Born's actions at Amax suggest to you about his personal characteristics?

Case Sources

James R. Norman, "Amax Finds a Way out of the Abyss," *Business Week,* October 26, 1987, pp. 82–83; Bruce W. Fraser, "Allen Born, AMAX," *Financial World,* April 21, 1987, p. 56; Justine Gerety, "AMAX," *American Metal Market,* February 9, 1988, pp. 2, 6.

Case 22.2

Spooked by Computers

The New England Arts Project had its headquarters above an Italian restaurant in Portsmouth, New Hampshire. The project had five full-time employees, and during busy times of the year, particularly during the month before Christmas, it hired as many as six part-time workers to type, address envelopes, and send out mailings. Although each of the five full-timers had a title and a formal job description, an observer would have had trouble telling their positions apart. Suzanne Clammer, for instance, was the executive director—the head of the office—but she could be found typing or licking envelopes just as often as Martin Welk, who had been working for less than a year as office coordinator, lowest in the project's hierarchy.

Despite a constant sense of being a month behind, the office ran relatively smoothly. No outsider would have had a prayer of finding a mailing list or a budget in the office, but project employees knew where almost everything was, and after a quiet fall they did not mind having their small space packed with workers in November. But a number of the federal funding agencies on which the project relied began to grumble about the cost of the part-time workers, the amount of time the project spent on handling routine paperwork, and the chaotic condition of its financial records. The pressure was on to make a radical change, and finally one day Martin Welk said it: "Maybe we should get a computer."

To Welk, fresh out of college, where he had written his papers on a word processor, computers were just another tool to make a job easier. But his feeling was not shared by the others in the office, the youngest of whom had fifteen years' more seniority than he did. A computer would eat the project's mailing list, they said, destroying any chance of raising funds for the year. It would send the wrong things to the wrong people, insulting them and convincing them that the project had become another faceless organization that did not care. They swapped horror stories about computers that had charged them thousands of dollars for purchases they had never made or that had assigned the same airplane seat to five different people.

"We'll lose all control," Suzanne Clammer complained. She saw some kind of office automation as inevitable, yet she kept thinking that she would probably quit before it came about. She liked hand-addressing mailings to arts patrons whom she had met, and she felt sure that the recipients contributed more because they recognized her neat blue printing. She remembered the agonies of typing class in high school, and felt too old to take on something new which was bound to be much more confusing. Two of the other employees, with whom she had worked for a decade, called her after work to ask in ashamed voices if the prospect of a computer in the office meant that they should be looking for other jobs. "I have enough trouble with English grammar," one of them wailed. "I'll never be able to learn Pascal or Lotus or whatever these new languages are."

One morning Martin Welk was surprised when Clammer called him into her office, shut the door, and asked him if he could recommend any computer consultants. She had read an article that explained how a company could waste thousands of dollars by adopting integrated office automation in the wrong way, and she figured the project would have to hire somebody for at least six months to get the new machines working and to teach the staff how to use them. Welk was pleased because it seemed that Clammer had accepted the idea of a computer in the office, but he realized that as the resident authority about computers, he had a lot of work to do before they went shopping for machines.

Case Questions

1. What kinds of resistance to change have the employees of the project displayed?

2. How should Martin Welk work to overcome the resistance?

Experiential Exercise

Purpose: This exercise will help you understand the complexities of change in organizations.

Format: Your task in this exercise is to plan the implementation of a major change in an organization.

Procedure: The class will be divided into five groups of approximately equal size. Your instructor will assign each group one of the following changes:

1. A change from the semester system to the quarter system (or the opposite, depending on the school's current system).
2. A requirement that all work—homework, examinations, term papers, problem sets—be done on computers.
3. A requirement that all students live on campus.
4. A requirement that all students have reading, writing, and speaking fluency in at least three languages, including English and Japanese, to graduate.
5. A requirement that all students room with someone in the same major.

First decide what individuals and groups must be involved in the change process. Then decide how the change will be implemented, using Lewin's Process of Organizational Change (Figure 22.1) as a framework. Consider how to deal with resistance to change, using Tables 22.3 and 22.4 as guides. Decide whether a change agent should be used (internal or external). Develop a realistic timetable for full implementation of the change. Is transition management appropriate?

After all groups have developed plans, they will present them to the class.

Follow-Up Questions

1. How similar were the implementation steps for each change?

2. Were the plans for managing resistance to change realistic?

3. Do you think any of the changes could be successfully implemented at your school? Why or why not?

C H A P T E R

23

Organization Development

Chapter Objectives

After reading this chapter, you should be able to

- ▶ define *organization development*.
- ▶ discuss system-wide organization development.
- ▶ discuss task-technological change.
- ▶ discuss group and individual change techniques.

- ▶ identify and discuss the major problems facing organization development efforts.
- ▶ identify and discuss five keys to successful organization development.

*I*nternational Flavors & Fragrances, Inc. (IFF) is the world's largest manufacturer of flavors and fragrances for cosmetic, household, and industrial products. Goods ranging from McDonald's salad dressing to detergents made by Unilever and Procter & Gamble contain flavors or fragrances made by IFF. Approximately 20 percent of its business is in the perfume industry; it recently developed the new "Eternity" fragrance for Calvin Klein. In spite of its apparently strong position, however, the company experienced sluggish growth and disappointing performance in the three years ending in 1986. Then, by the end of 1987, its earnings and growth had shot up 20 percent.[1] How did IFF accomplish this extraordinary turnaround in such a short time?

The key to the company's turnaround was a reorganization of its domestic and international divisions, a revitalizing of its creative staff, and an aggressive pursuit of European sales. On taking over in August 1985 as chief executive officer, Eugene P. Grisanti reduced the number of management levels and pushed decision making down to lower levels in the organization. In addition, he managed to get product development groups in New York and Paris to cooperate with each other. As a result, the company is returning to its former levels of growth and profitability.

*T*he change at IFF is an example of how a company can turn itself around. Throughout this book, we illustrate organizational behavior with examples from many organizations. In addition to exemplifying topics such as motivation, organizational behavior modification, leadership, and decision making, many of the examples also illustrate organizational change and development. Indeed, many of the concepts discussed in other contexts, such as learning and job design, are mobilized as techniques of organization development. One of the few universal imperatives of organizational behavior is that organizations must adapt to changing times or be left behind. This chapter reviews the specific techniques that organizations commonly use to change themselves.

We begin with a discussion of organization development as a special area of study, practice, and expertise. We then discuss the primary methods of organizational change, beginning with system-wide organization development practices and task-technological change and concluding with group and individual approaches. The chapter's last section addresses the problems and principles of managing organization development.

OVERVIEW OF ORGANIZATION DEVELOPMENT

On one level, organization development is simply the way organizations change and evolve. Organizational change can involve personnel, technology, competition, and other areas. Employee learning and formal training, transfers,

---

[1] "International Flavors Smells Like Money Again," *Business Week,* April 18, 1988, p. 70.

promotions, terminations, and retirements are all examples of personnel-related changes. Thus, in the broadest sense, the term *organization development* means organizational change.[2] However, the term as used here means something more specific. Over the past twenty years, organization development (OD) has emerged as a distinct field of study and practice. There is now substantial agreement as to what OD is in general, though arguments about details continue.[3] Our definition of organization development is an attempt to describe a very complex process in a simple manner. It is also an attempt to capture the best points of several definitions offered by writers in the field.

Definition of Organization Development

Organization development is the process of planned change and improvement of organizations through the application of knowledge of the behavioral sciences. Three points in this definition make it simple to remember and use. First, OD involves attempts to plan organizational changes, thus excluding spontaneous, haphazard initiatives. Second, the specific intention of OD is to improve organizations. This point excludes changes that merely imitate those of another organization, are forced on an organization by external pressures, or are undertaken merely for the sake of changing. Third, the planned improvement must be based on knowledge of the behavioral sciences, such as psychology, sociology, cultural anthropology, and related fields of study, rather than on financial or technological considerations. Under our definition, the replacement of manual personnel records with a computerized system would not be considered an instance of organization development. Although the change has behavioral effects, it is a technology-driven reform rather than a behavioral one. Likewise, alterations in record keeping necessary to support new government-mandated reporting requirements are not a part of organization development, because the change is obligatory and the result of an external force.

Although many experts accept a basic definition similar to ours, they vary in the emphasis they place on its elements. Michael Beer has stressed the process of OD by adding that organizational improvement comes about through system-wide data collection, diagnosis, action planning, implementation, and evaluation.[4] The process he has discussed is much the same as the change process presented in Chapter 22. Wendell L. French and Cecil H. Bell have accented changing the organizational culture in their approach to OD.[5] They

---

[2] W. Warner Burke, *Organization Development: Principles and Practices* (Boston: Little, Brown, 1982).

[3] Burke, *Organization Development;* and Michael Beer, *Organization Change and Development: A Systems View* (Santa Monica, Calif.: Goodyear, 1980).

[4] Beer, *Organization Change and Development.*

[5] Wendell L. French and Cecil H. Bell, *Organization Development: Behavioral Science Interventions for Organization Improvement,* 2nd ed. (Englewood Cliffs, N.J.: Prentice-Hall, 1978).

say the aim of OD is to improve the collaborative management of the organization's culture—that is, the joint management by employees and managers of the organization's prevailing patterns of activities, interactions, norms, feelings, beliefs, attitudes, and values. The importance of culture has also been underscored by W. Warner Burke, who has suggested that a change cannot be considered organization development unless it modifies the culture of the organization.[6] These viewpoints are valuable supplements to our definition.

Scope of Organization Development

Change can be introduced into the organization in any number of places. Viewing the organization as a social system of interrelated parts, however, emphasizes that a change in any one element has impacts throughout the organization.

Suppose, for instance, that an organization wishes to change its performance appraisal system (discussed in Chapter 19). A new performance appraisal system can affect supervisor-subordinate relationships, the reward system, peer relationships, and many other systems. If the new system significantly changes how highly valued behaviors and activities are measured or observed, employee relationships may be drastically altered, both socially and professionally. The changed relationships may, in turn, affect attitudes, commitment to the organization, willingness to work, and productivity.

With this clarification of our definition of OD, we are ready to examine some popular organization development techniques currently used in organizations. The three types of techniques—system-wide, task-technological, and group and individual—are illustrated in Figure 23.1.

SYSTEM-WIDE ORGANIZATION DEVELOPMENT

System-wide approaches to organization development may be placed in four basic categories: (1) reorganization, or structural change; (2) goal-setting programs; (3) quality-of-work-life programs; and (4) collateral organizations. *International Perspective* describes a system-wide change—the reorganization of the entire structure of Midland Bank in the United Kingdom.

Reorganization or Structural Change

The most comprehensive type of organizational change involves a major reorganization, usually referred to as a structural change—a system-wide rearrangement of task division and authority and reporting relationships. A structural change affects performance appraisal and rewards, decision making, and communication and information processing systems.

---

[6] Burke, *Organization Development.*

Figure 23.1   Methods of Organization Development

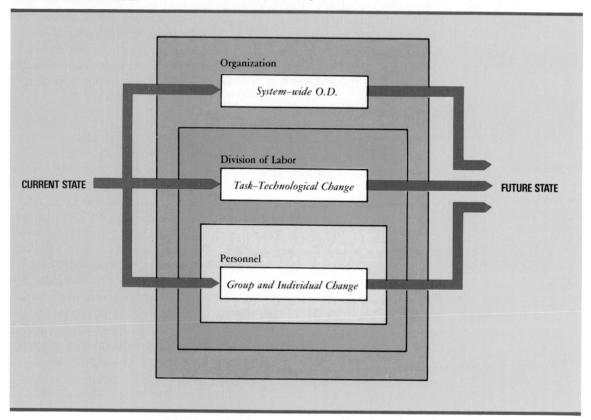

An organization may change the way it divides tasks into jobs, the way it groups jobs into departments and divisions, and the way it arranges authority and reporting relationships among positions. It may move from functional departmentalization to a system based on products or geography, for example, or from a conventional linear design to a matrix design. Other changes may include dividing large groups into smaller ones or merging small groups into larger ones. In addition, the degree to which rules and procedures are written down and enforced, as well as the locus of decision-making authority, may be altered. If all these changes are made, the organization will have transformed both the configurational and operational aspects of its structure.

No system-wide structural change is simple.[7] A company president cannot just issue a memo notifying company personnel that on a certain date they will

---

[7] Danny Miller and Peter H. Friesen, "Structural Change and Performance: Quantum Versus Piecemeal-Incremental Approaches," *Academy of Management Journal,* December 1982, pp. 867–892.

International
Perspective

Organizational Change: A British Banker's Recommendations

Midland Bank is Britain's fourth largest bank. Like most other large banks, it invested heavily around the world in the late 1970s and early 1980s, buying banks in France, Germany, and the United States. But concentrating on investments did not pay off for Midland; it lost a lot of money during its ownership of Crocker National Corporation, a California bank, and it was slower than some of its competitors to respond to the sweeping reorganization of the British banking system in the mid-1980s.

Two executives, group chief executive Sir Christopher McMahon (appointed in 1986), and Midland Bank International's chief executive, Hervé de Carmoy, are looking to the future and making management decisions to turn the bank around. Well-managed change will be a key factor in the bank's recovery. Reacting to Midland's mistakes, and to its successes in reorganizing some of its banks, de Carmoy presented the World Banking Conference with his blueprint for successful change.

According to de Carmoy, the greatest challenge facing companies that want to undergo substantial change is to substitute a focus on people for most companies' fixation on financial and manufacturing concerns. He agrees with General Motors chairman Roger Smith, who concluded, after investing $40 billion in new technology with poor results, that what is wrong with American industry is not its technological backwardness but its approach to people. According to a survey, most of Midland's investors value financial skills much more highly than human resource skills in a bank officer. But, says de Carmoy, if the bank is to progress and grow, these values must change and the entire culture of the company must undergo a radical shift.

As examples of the kinds of change he is talking about, de Carmoy points to Midland's successes in reorganizing banks in France, Germany, and England. The French bank that Midland took over in 1979 was losing money rapidly and was plagued by bad loans and high costs. Midland's first move was to form a group of thirty officers from all levels and make them the "consultants of change." These consultants diagnosed the bank's strengths and weaknesses, identified four key areas, and assigned a task force drawn from the bank's staff to develop solutions to the problems in those areas. These solutions led to action—and eventually to a complete turnaround in the bank's financial situation—because they were developed by and had the commitment of a wide-ranging group of people.

The key to such successful reorganizations is a focus on people: customers, competitors, shareholders, and employees. Middle and senior managers must be given the opportunity to develop specific targets, encourage entrepreneurship, and perhaps create smaller, autonomous units within the organization. These units can be more flexible and respond more quickly to customers' needs, but the company must never become content with creating limited, isolated changes. The change needs to be integrated and global, and the number-one corporate policy must be the development and nurturance of people.

Source: Hervé de Carmoy, "How To Change Companies," *Management Today,* April 1987, 77–80; Marcia Berss, "A Misguided Investment," *Forbes,* May 5, 1986, 164; Janet Porter, "Midland Bank Chief Takes Helm at Crucial Time," *The Journal of Commerce,* September 4, 1986, 1A, 4A.

report to a different supervisor and be responsible for new tasks. Employees have months, years, and sometimes decades of experience in dealing with people and tasks in certain ways. When these patterns are disrupted, employees need time to learn the new tasks and to settle into the new relationships. Moreover, the change may be resisted for any or all of the reasons discussed in Chapter 22. Therefore, organizations must manage the change process. Transition management was discussed in Chapter 22, and the management of OD is reviewed in the last section of this chapter.

Goal Setting as Organization Development

Chapter 6 examined management by objectives (MBO) as a way to extend the individual goal-setting approach to motivation to the larger organization; and Chapter 19 presented MBO as a performance appraisal technique. Here we take a final look at MBO, this time as a system-wide approach to organizational change. Recall that MBO is a system in which manager and employee work out a mutually agreeable set of goals that will be targets for the employee to achieve during the next evaluation period. Since the goals are derived from the goals and strategy of the overall organization, management by objectives effectively ties together the strategic planning of the organization and the behaviors and task-related activities of individual employees.[8] Instituting MBO is a system-wide change, because MBO enables organizational strategy to permeate the whole organization, as shown in the model in Figure 6.4.

Another way to use goal setting as an agent of system-wide change is the team approach to MBO, called **collaborative management by objectives** (CMBO). Under this approach, the manager and subordinates set goals for the group.[9] Group goals are broken down into individual goals so that each member is accountable for performance. The method encourages widespread employee participation, may reduce some individuals' feelings of isolation, and lessens intragroup competition for goal accomplishment, since goals are shared. When individuals help set the group's goals, they usually feel more committed to them.

The introduction of collaborative management by objectives into an organization is a significant move toward increasing lower-level employees' participation in the management of the organization. Top management must be ready to accept and support increased teamwork, cooperation, and employee involvement if MBO or CMBO is to work as it should.

Quality-of-Work-Life Programs

Another system-wide change is the introduction of quality-of-work-life (QWL) programs. J. Lloyd Suttle has defined **quality of work life** as the "degree to

---

[8] Peter Drucker, *The Practice of Management* (New York: Harper & Row, 1954).

[9] Wendell L. French and Robert W. Holimann, "Management by Objectives: The Team Approach," *California Management Review,* Spring 1975, pp. 13–22.

which members of a work organization are able to satisfy important personal needs through their experiences in the organization."[10] QWL programs focus strongly on providing a work environment conducive to the satisfaction of individual needs. The emphasis on improving life at work developed during the 1970s, a period of increasing inflation and deepening recession. The development was rather surprising, since an expanding economy and substantially increased resources are the conditions that usually induce top management to begin people-oriented programs. Improving life at work was evidently viewed by top management as a means of improving productivity.[11]

Any movement with broad and ambiguous goals tends to spawn a diversity of programs, each claiming to be based on the movement's goals; and QWL is no exception. QWL programs differ substantially, though most espouse a goal of "humanizing the workplace."[12] Richard E. Walton has divided QWL programs into the eight categories shown in Figure 23.2.[13] Obviously, many different types of programs can be accommodated by the categories, from changing the pay system to establishing an employee bill of rights that guarantees workers the rights to privacy, free speech, due process, and fair and equitable treatment.

A ten-year effort at General Motors is one of the most comprehensive QWL programs yet instituted. Shop-floor employees have been involved in making improvements in jobs, work procedures, production and product design, and quality control.[14] QWL programs have also been successful at Xerox, IBM, and numerous smaller organizations. The benefits gained from the programs differ substantially, but they generally are of three types.[15] A more positive attitude toward the work and the organization, or increased job satisfaction, is perhaps the most direct benefit.[16] Another is increased productivity, although it is often difficult to measure and separate the effects of the QWL program from the effects of other organizational factors. A third benefit is increased effectiveness of the organization as measured by its profitability, goal accomplishment, shareholder wealth, or resource exchange. The third gain follows directly from the first two: if employees have more positive attitudes about the organization and their productivity increases, everything else being equal, the organization should be more effective.

---

[10] J. Lloyd Suttle, "Improving Life at Work—Problems and Prospects," in J. Richard Hackman and J. Lloyd Suttle, eds., *Improving Life at Work: Behavioral Science Approaches to Organizational Change* (Santa Monica, Calif.: Goodyear, 1977), p. 4.

[11] Suttle, "Improving Life at Work," pp. 5–6.

[12] Burke, *Organization Development.*

[13] Richard E. Walton, "Quality of Work Life: What Is It?" *Sloan Management Review,* Fall 1983, pp. 11–21.

[14] Burke, *Organization Development,* pp. 322–323.

[15] Suttle, "Improving Life at Work," pp. 9–14.

[16] Daniel A. Ondrack and Martin G. Evans, "Job Enrichment and Job Satisfaction in Greenfield and Redesign QWL Sites," *Group & Organization Studies,* March 1987, pp. 5–22.

Figure 23.2

Walton's Categorization of Quality-of-Work-Life (QWL) Programs

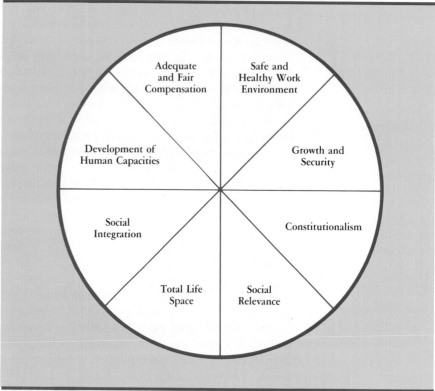

As useful as QWL programs can be, they do present several potential pitfalls.[17] First, management and labor must cooperate in the design and implementation of the program. Otherwise, each side may view the program as an opportunity to get something out of the other. Worker-management committees on work improvement can function effectively to increase cooperation. Second, the action plans that are developed must be followed through to completion. Plans can easily be lost and forgotten amidst the problems of the shop floor or office. Everyone—from top management to production employees—must remember to follow through on the plans. The third pitfall is the failure to support the often forgotten middle manager, who is pressured by both top management and line workers to implement the program.[18] Finally, the focus of QWL programs must be kept on the joint objectives of increasing

---

[17] Suttle, "Improving Life at Work," pp. 14–20.
[18] Leonard A. Schlesinger and Barry Oshry, "Quality of Work Life and the Manager: Muddle in the Middle," *Organizational Dynamics,* Summer 1984, pp. 4–19.

the quality of work life and maintaining organizational efficiency. There is no inherent incompatibility between the interests of the worker and the interests of the organization.[19]

Collateral Organizations

A **collateral organization** exists alongside—and thus is collateral to—the formal organization. It is set up by the formal organization, and its purpose is to solve problems the formal organization cannot handle.[20] A collateral organization is a planned structural adaptation of the formal organization that increases the latter's flexibility and responsiveness.[21] Most formal organizations have a prescribed hierarchy of authority and established rules and procedures. These can deal effectively with well-structured problems; this sort of problem solving is characterized by repetition, speed of handling, and efficiency. However, when problems such as an unexpected change in consumer preferences or a new technological development from an unusual source are encountered by an organization that does not regularly face them, the formal system may not be able to respond adequately. A collateral organization offers a means through which the organization can respond to such unusual situations and problems.

Table 23.1 compares the typical formal organization and the collateral organization. The collateral organization's all-channel communication network (a network in which everyone communicates with everyone else, regardless of status or position power) and its separateness from the formal organization permit information to cut across hierarchical lines. In general, a collateral organization is relatively permanent. It is not overlaid on the formal organization as in a matrix design, since it is distinct from the organization, nor is it an informal organization driven by the personal interests of the members. A collateral organization can best be described as a nonhierarchical problem-solving unit attached to a larger, formal organization.

A collateral organization can mitigate the rigidity and formalization of the parent organization. On routine matters, lower-level employees of the parent firm must go through formal channels to bring something to the attention of a top manager. However, on issues of concern to the collateral organization, such as new technological developments or a competitor's activities, employees of the lowest rank can often gain the attention of a top manager immediately to share information, make a decision, and possibly even begin implementation. Thus, the collateral organization serves as a permanent OD mechanism, constantly available to assist in communication of information and in problem

---

[19] David A. Nadler and Edward E. Lawler, III, "Quality of Work Life: Perspectives and Directions," *Organizational Dynamics,* Winter 1983, pp. 20–30.

[20] Dale E. Zand, "Collateral Organization: A New Change Strategy," *Journal of Applied Behavioral Science,* January–March 1974, pp. 63–89.

[21] David Rubinstein and Richard W. Woodman, "Spiderman and the Burma Raiders: Collateral Organization Theory in Action," *Journal of Applied Behavioral Science,* January–March 1984, pp. 1–21.

Table 23.1

Formal and Collateral
Organizations

Characteristic	Formal Organization (Bureaucratic Organization, Authority/Production Mode)	Collateral Organization (Parallel Organization, Knowledge/Problem Mode)
Primary purpose	Maximize output	Analyze or invent knowledge to solve problems
Task uncertainty	Routine operations, low uncertainty	Problem solving, high uncertainty
Levels of authority	Many	Few
Source of influence and power	Position in hierarchy	Ability to identify and solve problems
Use of rules	High	Low
Leadership	Function of level	Drawn from any level
Links to others in the organization	Few	Many
Division of labor	High	Low
Job assignments	Fixed	Rotational, flexible
Depiction (in charts)	Functionally specialized	Diagonal slices, mixed functions
Rewards	Pay and benefits	Learning, recognition, visibility, new contacts, bonus possibility

Source: David Rubinstein and Richard W. Woodman, "Spiderman and the Burma Raiders:
Collateral Organization Theory in Action," *The Journal of Applied Behavioral Science*, January–
February–March 1984, p. 4. Used by permission.

solving. However, the collateral organization does not guarantee adequate
solutions of ill-structured problems. Problem solving in the collateral organization is subject to the same problems that confront all problem-solving
groups—for instance, intolerance of dissent, groupthink tendencies, rigidity of
perceptions and beliefs, attention to unimportant issues, and inattention to
opinions of outsiders.[22]

TASK-TECHNOLOGICAL CHANGE

In this section we discuss organizational change affected through the direct or
indirect alteration of jobs—through task redesign or sociotechnical intervention.
Indirect change involves a shift in technology—the way in which inputs are

---

[22] Rubinstein and Woodman, "Spiderman and the Burma Raiders."

transformed into outputs. When technology is altered, so too are tasks.[23] The structural changes discussed in the preceding section are explicitly system-wide in scope, whereas the interventions in this section are more narrowly focused and may not seem to have the same far-reaching consequences. It is important to remember, though, that their impact is felt throughout the organization.

Task Redesign

The discussion of task design in Chapter 8 focused on job definition and motivation and gave little attention to implementing changes in jobs.[24] Here we examine task redesign as a mode of organizational change.

Suppose that, as the manager of the operations group in a medium-sized bank, you have noticed that absenteeism and turnover are increasing throughout the department. You have been concerned about the morale, attitude, and productivity of your subordinates. Having examined and rejected other possible plans, you believe the design of jobs throughout the department needs to be changed. Where do you go from there?

Several approaches to introducing job changes in organizations have been proposed—one by a co-author of this book, Ricky W. Griffin. This approach, presented here, is an integrative framework of nine steps that reflect the complexities of the interfaces between individual jobs and the total organization.[25] The process, shown in Table 23.2, includes the steps usually associated with change, such as recognition of the need for a change, selection of the appropriate intervention, and evaluation of the change. But Griffin's approach inserts four additional steps into the standard sequence: diagnosis of the overall work system and context, including examination of the jobs, technology, organization design, leadership, and group dynamics; evaluation of the costs and benefits of the change; formulation of a redesign strategy; and implementation of supplemental changes.

DIAGNOSIS   Diagnosis includes analysis of the total work environment within which the jobs exist. When job changes are being considered, it is important to evaluate the organizational structure, especially the work rules and decision-making authority within a department.[26] For example, if jobs are to be redesigned to give the employee more freedom in choosing work methods or scheduling work activities, diagnosis of the present system must determine

---

[23] Eric L. Trist and K. W. Bamforth. "Some Social and Psychological Consequences of the Longwall Method of Coal-Getting," *Human Relations,* Vol. 4, 1951, pp. 3–38.

[24] J. Richard Hackman and Greg Oldham, "Motivation Through the Design of Work: Test of a Theory," *Organizational Behavior and Human Performance,* August 1976, pp. 250–279; and J. Richard Hackman and Greg Oldham, *Work Redesign* (Reading: Mass.: Addison-Wesley, 1980).

[25] Ricky W. Griffin, *Task Design: An Integrative Approach* (Glenview, Ill.: Scott, Foresman, 1982).

[26] Gregory Moorhead, "Organizational Analysis: An Integration of the Macro and Micro Approaches," *Journal of Management Studies,* April 1981, pp. 191–218.

Table 23.2

Integrative Framework
for Implementation of
Task Redesign in
Organizations

Step 1: Recognition of a need for a change

Step 2: Selection of task redesign as a potential intervention

Step 3: Diagnosis of the work system and context
  a. Diagnosis of existing jobs
  b. Diagnosis of existing work force
  c. Diagnosis of technology
  d. Diagnosis of organization design
  e. Diagnosis of leader behaviors
  f. Diagnosis of group and social processes

Step 4: Cost/benefit analysis of proposed changes

Step 5: Go/no-go decision

Step 6: Formulation of the strategy for redesign

Step 7: Implementation of the task changes

Step 8: Implementation of any supplemental changes

Step 9: Evaluation of the task redesign effort

Source: Ricky W. Griffin, *Task Design: An Integrative Framework* (Glenview, Ill.: Scott, Foresman, 1982), p. 208.

if the rules will allow that to happen. Diagnosis must also include evaluation of the work group and intragroup dynamics (discussed in Chapter 9). Furthermore, it must determine if the workers have or can easily obtain the new skills to perform the redesigned task. Failure to do this has proven costly to GM and other companies. (See *Management in Action.*)

COST/BENEFIT ANALYSIS   It is extremely important to recognize the full range of potential costs and benefits associated with a job redesign effort. Some are direct and quantifiable; others are indirect and non-quantifiable. Redesign may involve unexpected costs or benefits; although these cannot be predicted with certainty, they can be weighed as possibilities. Table 23.3 lists possible costs and benefits of a task redesign intervention. Such things as short-term role ambiguity, role conflict, and role overload can be major stumbling blocks to a job redesign effort.

FORMULATION OF A STRATEGY   Implementing a redesign scheme takes careful planning, and developing a strategy for the intervention is the final planning step. Strategy formulation is a four-part process.[27] First, the organization must decide who will design the changes. Depending on the circumstances, the planning team may consist of only upper-level management, or it may include line workers and supervisors. Next, the team undertakes the actual

---

[27] Griffin, *Task Design.*

	Costs	Benefits
Table 23.3 List of Possible Costs and Benefits of Task Redesign Interventions	*Direct/Quantifiable*	*Direct/Quantifiable*
	1. Purchase of new technology 2. Down-time 3. Increased wages	1. Enhanced performance via improvements in the work system
	Indirect/Nonquantifiable	*Indirect/Nonquantifiable*
	1. Short-term role ambiguity, conflict, and/or overload following change 2. Alienation of some employees who oppose change	1. Improved employee satisfaction 2. Improved employee motivation 3. Improved quality of work life 4. Improved group performance norms
	Potential/Unexpected	*Potential/Unexpected*
	1. Unplanned snags and delays 2. Unplanned supplemental changes 3. Unplanned changes in organizational design 4. Unplanned morale problems with supervisors	1. Enhanced performance via improvements in employee effort 2. Improved employee commitment

Source: Ricky W. Griffin, *Task Design: An Integrative Framework* (Glenview, Ill.: Scott, Foresman, 1982), p. 208.

design of the changes based on job design theory and the needs, goals, and circumstances of the organization.

Third, the team decides the timing of the implementation, which may require a formal transition period during which equipment is purchased and installed, job training takes place, new physical layouts are arranged, and the "bugs" in the new system are worked out. (As noted in Management in Action, this is the step that GM mismanaged in its efforts to improve the robotic technology of its production systems.) Fourth, strategy planners must consider whether the job changes require adjustments and supplemental changes in other organizational components, such as reporting relationships and the compensation system.

IMPLEMENTATION OF SUPPLEMENTAL CHANGES   As mentioned, a major job redesign effort may dictate planned adjustments in other parts of the organization. For example, work rules established to support the previous arrangement of tasks may not be appropriate for the new jobs. The performance appraisal system should usually be changed to reflect the changes in task division and responsibility. The reward system, recruiting and selection criteria,

Management in ACTION

Adjusting to Robots

The new push for quality in American manufacturing has led many companies to turn to high-tech answers to their problems, particularly to computers and robots. Obviously, these companies have had to adjust their other technology to these changes. From the first mention of robots, many workers have feared (with some justification) that these "steel-collar workers" will eliminate jobs for humans. Now, however, more companies are focusing on what may be the most important and slowest adjustment to robots in the workplace—that undertaken by human personnel.

Quality became the most popular buzzword in American industry in the late 1970s, when it became clear that imports were beating out American products not just because they were cheaper but because they were better made and more reliable. Taking a close look at their manufacturing plants, American companies found that they were spending up to one-quarter of their operating budgets on finding and fixing mistakes in products that had not yet left the plant. Accustomed to solving their problems with technological improvements, many of these companies turned to robots to cut the defects from their manufacturing processes and slash the costly return rates.

Every year robots are becoming more versatile, lighter, and faster. They can be found throughout American industry, doing everything from building computers to stretching balloons to holding and positioning class rings for engravings. But the sudden shift to robots has created problems for many American organizations—particularly for American automakers, who purchased almost half of all robots sold in the United States in 1986.

For one thing, the automakers, especially General Motors Corp., tried to bring robots into their factories almost overnight. Japanese companies with long experience in using high-tech machines typically phase in new technology over a year or two; GM tried to do it, in some cases, in sixty to

physical layout, reporting relationships, and in-house training programs may also have to be adapted. Although it may be necessary to make some adjustments after the job changes have been implemented, careful advance planning can minimize potential problems.

Technological Implementation

As new technology is implemented, the tasks of and relationship among workers are also affected. The sociotechnical systems approach to organizational design views the organization as an open system structured to integrate two important subsystems—the technical (task) subsystem and the social subsystem. (The sociotechnical systems approach to organization design is discussed in more detail in Chapter 15.) Several attempts have been made to apply sociotechnical principles in the cause of organizational change, most notably at a Volvo plant

ninety days. American companies also found that to improve quality, they could not just buy better machines and continue with business as usual. Many discovered that quality improvements were impossible without major changes in management philosophy, starting from the top. Workers on the factory floor tended to be suspicious of new machines and new quality decrees unless they saw that management was serious about company-wide change. And middle managers were often most resistant, for in many instances they were being asked to become participants and coaches in a team effort rather than bosses who handed down rules.

Even with top-to-bottom commitment to technological changes, GM and other companies ran into difficulty introducing their new steel-collar workers to the factory floor. Robots replaced some workers, but those left behind often had to control or work with the new machines. This kind of work involved more complex skills than assembly-line exployees were used to. Workers who formerly tightened bolts all day now sometimes had to diagnose a robot problem and intervene before help could arrive. General Motors has found that preparing workers for such problems requires more than brief training sessions; only 8 percent of GM's workers have college degrees, and about 15 percent can neither read nor write, so a great deal of training is sometimes essential. Union rules, which sometimes mandate that workers close to retirement should be the last to receive training, can add to the problems.

No one is saying that the invasion of the robots will end, but it is slowing: GM, leading the trend, has cut back on its robot orders and slowed down the development of new production facilities. Having learned a lesson in quality and technology, American companies are now learning a lesson in organizational development.

Sources: Russell Mitchell, "Boldly Going Where No Robot Has Gone Before," *Business Week*, December 22, 1986, 45; Amal Kumar Naj, "The Human Factor," *The Wall Street Journal*, November 10, 1986, 36D–37D; Otis Port, "The Push for Quality," *Business Week*, June 8, 1987, 130–135.

in Kalmar, Sweden, and a General Foods Corp. plant in Topeka, Kansas.[28] Essentially, the sociotechnical approach to organizational change aims at enhancing organizational effectiveness by improving the fit among technology, structure, and social forces. In this it differs from other methods we have discussed, which focus on individual systems or system components. As the following examples show, sociotechnical changes involve much more than task redesign and have some potentially serious drawbacks.

At the Kalmar plant (as described in Chapter 8), autonomous work groups were created, each responsible for one complete step of the manufacturing

---

[28] Richard E. Walton, "From Hawthorne to Topeka and Kalmar," in E. L. Cass and Frederick G. Zimmer, eds., *Man and Work in Society* (New York: Van Nostrand Reinhold Co., 1975), reprinted in Wendell L. French, Cecil H. Bell, and Robert A. Zawacki, eds., *Organization Development: Theory, Practice, and Research,* Rev. ed. (Plano, Texas: Business Publications Inc., 1983), pp. 292–300.

process. The technology of automobile manufacturing was altered to incorporate the social factors embodied in the autonomous work groups. The groups made decisions regarding the assignment of employees to jobs, training, scheduling, and the speed of production to match the needs and abilities of the employees and the group. However, the Kalmar plant cost more to build and required more land than conventional plants and resulted in reduced production rates.[29]

At the General Foods Topeka facility, a new plant was designed to accommodate self-managing work teams. The company's usual management hierarchy was altered to include team leaders, who were to facilitate team development and decision making rather than plan, direct, and control activities of subordinates as supervisors in a conventional plant would. Following early success in the three years after startup in 1971, employees reported reduced commitment and enthusiasm.[30] Fewer team meetings were held, and production quality declined. However, these trends were turned around with renewed efforts to develop work teams and committees to deal with further evolution of the system, as well as the introduction in 1978 of a new dry dog food product.

GROUP AND INDIVIDUAL CHANGE

There are a vast number of ways to involve groups and individuals in organizational change. The retraining of a single employee can be considered an organizational change, if the training affects the way the employee does her or his job. Familiarizing managers with the Blake-Mouton grid or the Vroom-Yetton-Jago decision tree (Chapter 11) is an attempt at change. In the first case, the goal is to balance management concerns for production and people; in the second, it is to increase the participation of rank-and-file employees in the organization's decision making. In this section, we present an overview of four popular types of people-oriented change techniques: training, management development, team building, and survey-feedback.

Training

Training is generally designed to improve employees' job skills. Employees may be trained to run certain machines, taught new mathematical skills, or exposed to personal growth and development methods. Stress management programs are becoming popular to help employees, particularly executives,

---

[29] William F. Dowling, "Job Redesign on the Assembly Line: Farewell to the Blue-Collar Blues," *Organizational Dynamics*, Autumn 1973, pp. 51–67.

[30] Richard E. Walton, "The Topeka Work System: Optimistic Visions, Pessimistic Hypotheses, and Reality," in Robert Zager and Michael P. Rosow, eds., *The Innovative Organization* (Elmsford, N.Y.: Pergamon Press, 1982), pp. 260–287.

understand organizational stress and develop ways to cope with it.[31] Training may also be used in conjunction with other, more comprehensive organizational changes. For instance, if an organization is implementing an MBO program, training in establishing goals and reviewing goal-oriented performance is probably needed.

Among the many methods of training, the most common are lecture, discussion, a lecture-discussion combination, experiential methods, case studies, and films or video tapes. Training can take place in a standard classroom, either on company property or in a hotel, resort, or conference center. On-the-job training provides a different type of experience, in which the trainee learns from an experienced worker. Most training programs use a combination of methods determined by the topic, the trainees, the trainer, and the organization.

A major problem of training programs is transferring employee learning to the workplace. Quite often, an employee learns a new skill or a manager learns a new management technique but, upon returning to the normal work situation, finds it easier to go back to the old way of doing things. As discussed in Chapter 22, the process of refreezing is a vital part of the change process, and some way must be found to make the accomplishments of the training program permanent.

Management Development Programs

Management development programs, like employee training programs, attempt to foster certain skills, abilities, and perspectives. Often, when a highly qualified technical person is promoted to become the manager of a work group, he or she lacks training in how to manage or deal with people. In such cases, management development programs can be very important to organizations, both for the new manager and for his or her subordinates.

Typically, management development programs use the lecture-discussion method to some extent but rely most heavily on participative methods, such as case studies and role playing. Participative and experiential methods allow the manager to experience the problems of being a manager as well as the feelings of frustration, doubt, and success that are part of the job. The subject matter of this type of training program is problematic, however, in that management skills, including communication, problem diagnosis, problem solving, and performance appraisal, are not as easy to identify or to transfer from a classroom to the workplace as the skills required to run a machine. In addition, rapid changes in the external environment can make certain managerial skills obsolete in a very short time. As a result, some companies are approaching the development of their management team as an ongoing, career-long process and are requiring their managers to attend refresher courses periodically.

---

[31] James C. Quick and Jonathan D. Quick, *Organizational Stress and Preventive Management* (New York: McGraw-Hill, 1984).

One training approach involves managers in an intense exercise that simulates the daily operation of a real company.[32] Such simulations emphasize problem-solving behavior rather than competitive tactics and usually involve extensive debriefing, in which a manager's style is openly discussed and criticized by trained observers as the first step to improvement. IBM and AT&T have commissioned experts to create a simulation specifically for their managers. Although the cost of custom simulations is high, it is reportedly repaid in benefits from individual development.[33]

As corporate America invests hundreds of millions of dollars in management development, certain guiding principles are evolving: (1) management development is a multifaceted, complex, and long-term process for which there is no quick or simple solution; (2) organizations should pay close attention to the systematic identification of their unique developmental needs and evaluate their programs accordingly; (3) management development objectives must be compatible with organizational objectives; and (4) the utility and value of management development remains more an article of faith than a proven fact.[34]

Team Building

When interaction among group members is critical to group success and effectiveness, team development, or team building, may be useful. The term *team building* is used to emphasize the importance of members' working together in a spirit of cooperation.

Team building efforts generally have one or more of the following goals.

1. To set team goals and/or priorities.
2. To analyze or allocate the way work is performed.
3. To examine the way a group is working—that is, to examine processes such as norms, decision making, and communications.
4. To examine relationships among the people doing the work.[35]

One of these goals usually dominates the development effort. If no goal is dominant, considerable time and energy are wasted, because each member tends to engage in behaviors that will accomplish what he or she perceives to be the goal.[36] In a case in which the goals of the team-building effort are not clear, the process must start with the examination of the reasons for team

---

[32] Peter Petre, "Games That Teach You to Manage," *Fortune,* October 29, 1984, pp. 65–72.

[33] Petre, "Games That Teach You to Manage."

[34] Kenneth N. Wexley and Timothy T. Baldwin, "Management Development," *1986 Yearly Review of Management of the Journal of Management,* pp. 277–294.

[35] Richard Beckhard, "Optimizing Team-Building Efforts," *Journal of Contemporary Business,* Summer 1972, pp. 23–27, 30–32.

[36] Beckhard, "Optimizing Team-Building Efforts."

Figure 23.3

Team-Building Process

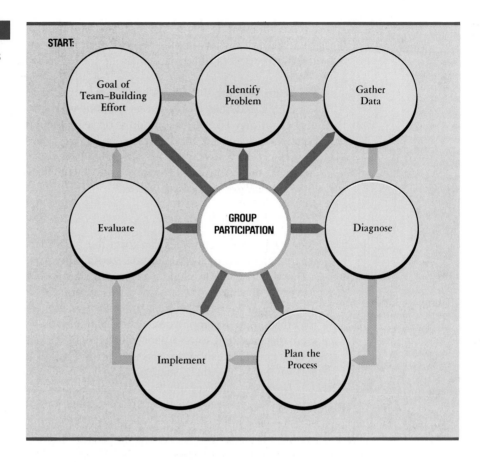

START:

Goal of Team–Building Effort

Identify Problem

Gather Data

Evaluate

GROUP PARTICIPATION

Diagnose

Implement

Plan the Process

building. The team-building effort then proceeds in much the same way as other change processes: identification of the problem, data gathering, diagnosis, planning, implementation, and evaluation,[37] as shown in Figure 23.3. Its distinctive feature is group participation at all points. The process is one in which the group is simultaneously the object of and a participant in the process. A change agent is usually needed at first but becomes increasingly less necessary as the group develops into a team. Occasionally—especially if the work situation or membership has changed—the mature, well-functioning team may need a consultant to observe and provide insight into its operation.[38]

Participation is especially important in the data gathering and evaluation phases of team development. In data gathering, the members share information

[37] William G. Dyer, "Basic Programs and Plans," in *Team Building: Issues and Alternatives* (Reading, Mass.: Addison-Wesley, 1977), pp. 41–50.

[38] Dianne McKinney Kellogg, "Contrasting Successful and Unsuccessful OD Consulting Relationships," *Group & Organization Studies,* June 1984, pp. 151–176.

on the functioning of the group. The opinions of the group are thus the foundation of the development process. In the evaluation phase, the members are the source of information about the effectiveness of the development effort.[39]

Team building should not be thought of as a one-time experience, perhaps something undertaken on a retreat from the workplace. Rather, it is a continuing process. It may take weeks, months, or years for a group to pull together and function as a team. Team development can be a way to train the group to solve its own problems in the future. Research on the effectiveness of team building as an OD intervention tool is mixed and inconclusive. For a brief summary of this research, see *A Look at Research*.

Survey-Feedback

Survey-feedback techniques can form the basis for a change process in which data are gathered, analyzed, summarized, and returned to those who participated in its generation for identification, discussion, and solution of problems. A survey-feedback process is often set in motion by either the organization's top management or a consultant hired to advise management. By providing information about employees' beliefs and attitudes, a survey can help management diagnose and solve organizational problems. A consultant or change agent usually coordinates the process and is responsible for data gathering, analysis, and summary. The three-stage process is shown in Figure 23.4.[40]

The use of survey-feedback techniques in an organization development process differs from their use in traditional attitude surveys. In an organization development process, data (1) are returned to employee groups at all levels in the organization and (2) are used as the basis for problem identification and solution by all employees working together in their normal work groups. In traditional attitude surveys, top management reviews the data and may or may not initiate a new program to solve problems the survey has identified.

DATA GATHERING   In the data gathering stage, the change agent interviews selected personnel from appropriate levels to determine the key issues to be examined. In a small study, these interviews may provide sufficient information to proceed to the next step. However, in more comprehensive studies in large organizations, the interviews serve as the basis for a survey questionnaire to be distributed to a large sample of employees.

The questionnaire may be a standardized instrument, an instrument developed specifically for the organization, or a combination of the two.

---

[39] William M. Vicars and Darrel D. Hartke, "Evaluating OD Evaluations: A Status Report," *Group & Organization Studies*, June 1984, pp. 177–188; and Bernard M. Bass, "Issues Involved in Relations Between Methodological Rigor and Reported Outcomes in Evaluations of Organizational Development," *Journal of Applied Psychology*, February 1983, pp. 197–201.

[40] Beer, *Organization Change and Development*.

A LOOK AT
RESEARCH

Research on Team Development

The concept of the organization as a team permeates popular American notions about how people work together. From cabinet officers reporting to the president of the United States to Cub Scouts, everyone is admonished to become a "team player," and our vocabulary is full of metaphors from sports and aphorisms from famous coaches such as Vince Lombardi. Americans take for granted that a dozen people working as a team will be more effective than the same people working independently.

Yet there is surprisingly little research to back up that assumption. In fact, a number of recent surveys of research studies on team development have concluded that the evidence is too ambiguous to allow organizational scientists to continue unequivocal advocation of team development. The studies do find fairly consistent improvements in the attitudes of people in groups that have undergone team development, but the effects of those attitudes on task performance are much less clear.

The surveys agree that the lack of good evidence for the positive effects of team development springs in part from methodological weaknesses of the studies. Team development is often used as just one element of an organizational development approach, which makes it difficult to isolate its effect. Typically, studies have not followed the groups in question for long enough, and often the change agent is also the project evaluator, which leads to substantial conflict of interest. Even more fundamental is the lack of a clear, consistent definition of team development. For example, one writer described four different models of team development: the goal-setting model, which works to set goals and plans to accomplish those goals; the interpersonal model, which focuses on developing relationships among team members; the role model, which attempts to help participants define their roles in the group; and the managerial grid model, which includes team development as a part of an overall organizational development strategy.

Paul F. Buller has suggested a different definition of team development, which he hopes will allow future researchers to avoid methodological problems and convincingly establish connections between team development and task performance. He advocates an approach in which a third-party facilitator leads a series of planned interventions with an intact work group, with the goal of increasing the group's ability to solve major problems. Such a concept should be effective, Buller feels, because a group that identifies, confronts, and solves its most debilitating problems should improve its performance.

People interested in organizational development need to keep close watch on the research being done by people such as Buller. It may turn out that research studies simply have not yet been refined enough to show the effect of team development, or it may be that what much of the country views as an organizational panacea is an illusion.

Sources: Paul F. Buller, "The Team Building–Task Performance Relation: Some Conceptual and Methodological Refinements," *Group & Organization Studies*, September 1986, 147–168; Kenneth P. De Meuse and S. Jay Liebowitz, "An Empirical Analysis of Team-Building Research," *Group & Organization Studies*, September 1981, 357–378; Richard W. Woodman and John J. Sherwood, "The Role of Team Development in Organizational Effectiveness: A Critical Review," *Psychological Bulletin*, Vol. 88, No. 8 (1980), 166–186.

Figure 23.4

Survey-Feedback
Process

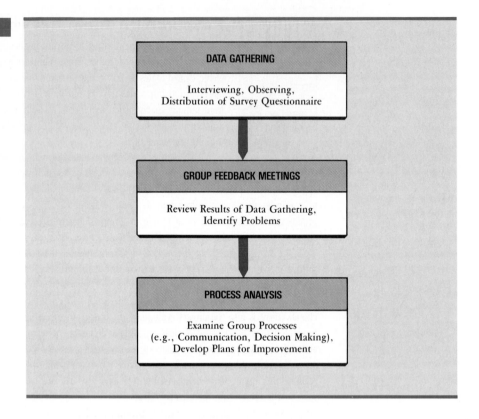

Standardized instruments are readily available, psychometrically sound, and thoroughly pretested; they may also offer comparison data from other organizations. Sometimes, however, they are not relevant to the organization under study and may confuse the situation more than they help it.

The questionnaire data are analyzed and aggregated by group or department to assure anonymity of individual respondents.[41] The change agent then prepares a summary of the results for the group feedback sessions. From this point on, the consultant is involved in the process as a resource person and expert.

FEEDBACK   The feedback meetings generally involve only two or three levels of management. These family groups, as they are called, are kept small to facilitate individual discussion and interaction. Meetings are usually held serially, beginning with a meeting of the top management group, which is followed by meetings of employees throughout the organization. Sessions are usually led by the group manager rather than the change agent in order to transfer "ownership" of the data from the change agent to the work group. The

---

[41] Jerome L. Franklin, "Improving the Effectiveness of Survey Feedback," *Personnel,* May–June 1978, pp. 11–17.

change agent helps the manager prepare for the meeting by reviewing the data and suggesting ways of stimulating discussion, problem identification, and problem solving. The feedback consists primarily of profiles of the groups' attitudes toward the organization, the work, the leadership, and other topics on the questionnaire. During the feedback sessions, members discuss reasons for the scores and the problems that the data reveal.

PROCESS ANALYSIS   In the process analysis stage, the group examines its process for making decisions, communicating, and accomplishing work, usually with the help of the consultant. Unfortunately, groups often overlook this stage as they become absorbed in the survey data and the problems revealed during the feedback sessions. Occasionally, group managers simply fail to hold feedback and process analysis sessions. Change agents should ensure that managers hold these sessions and that they are rewarded for doing so.[42] The process analysis stage is important because its purpose is to develop action plans for making improvements. Several sessions may be required to discuss the process issues fully and settle on a strategy for improvements. Groups often find it useful to document the plans as they are discussed and to appoint a member to follow up on implementation. Generally, the follow-up is concerned with whether communication and communication processes have actually been improved. A follow-up survey can be administered several months to a year later to assess how much these processes have changed since they were first reported.

The survey-feedback method is probably one of the most widely used organizational change and development interventions.[43] If any of its stages are compromised or omitted, however, the technique becomes less useful. A primary responsibility of the consultant or change agent, then, is to ensure that the method is fully and faithfully carried through.

MANAGING ORGANIZATION DEVELOPMENT

The management of change in organizations is one of the most difficult tasks of the modern manager. In this chapter and the preceding one, we emphasize that change is inevitable and that, for the well-being of the organization, it must be planned for and managed. Yet most organizational change and development efforts—including those that are well planned—encounter problems, some significant enough to threaten the entire change program. Typically, change efforts take longer than expected and incur higher costs than expected, and they may be only partially successful.[44]

---

[42] Franklin, "Improving the Effectiveness of Survey Feedback."

[43] Franklin, "Improving the Effectiveness of Survey Feedback."

[44] See John P. Kotter and Leonard A. Schlesinger, "Choosing Strategies for Change," *Harvard Business Review,* March–April 1979, pp. 106–114.

Given the difficulty of realizing organizational change, it is useful to discuss some criteria by which to judge the effectiveness of change efforts. A change effort can be considered effectively managed if:

1. The organization is moved from the current state to the planned future state.
2. The functioning of the organization in the future state meets expectations.
3. The transition is accomplished without undue cost to the organization and its individual members.[45]

In short, the desired system must be successfully established and must provide the expected benefits at minimal cost to the organization and its members. If the intended change is a new performance appraisal system, for instance, the change may be deemed a success when the new system is being used by managers to evaluate the performance of their employees, is providing the correct types of information in the right form to the right people at the appropriate time, and has been implemented without unreasonable cost to individual employees or to the organization as a whole. In practice, a manager or change agent would have to define the criteria for evaluating a change project more specifically. These broad criteria suggest the standards that a particular change ought to meet, however.

Major Problems in Organization Development Efforts

David A. Nadler has argued that the major problems of managing change can be organized into four categories: resistance, power, control, and task redefinition.[46] Figure 23.5 pairs these four problem categories with the four basic elements of the social system of the organization: people, structure, information system, and tasks. Note that the four basic elements of the social system are related to each other in such a way that what happens to one part affects all the others. Assuming that the current state has been properly diagnosed and the change to be implemented is appropriate, these four factors represent the major hurdles to effective organizational change.

RESISTANCE   We have already noted that resistance from employees is a key factor in any organizational change effort. A primary factor contributing to resistance is the organizational culture, which is usually the result of many years of getting things done in a certain way.

POWER   Power can become an important issue in the transition from the current state to the future state, especially when the change has a substantial impact on organizational structure and the people or groups that have the most

---

[45] David A. Nadler, "Concepts for the Management of Organizational Change," in J. Richard Hackman, Edward E. Lawler, III, and Lyman W. Porter, eds., *Perspectives on Organizational Behavior,* 2nd. ed. (New York: McGraw-Hill, 1983), pp. 551–561.

[46] Nadler, "Concepts for the Management of Organizational Change."

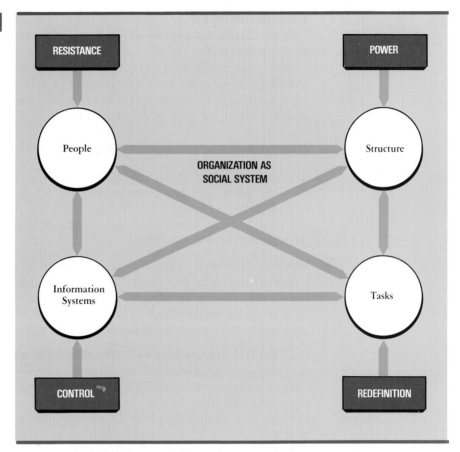

Figure 23.5

Four Major Problems in Change Management

power. The transition stage, during which the old structure is torn down and the new one is established, is fraught with uncertainty. People are naturally concerned about their place in the new order, and they may exercise power or engage in political activity to influence their future position. Typically, employees attempt to ensure that they will be in a better position in the new social order as they perceive it will be after the transition. These behaviors may or may not be appropriate for their current position or for the change as planned by management.

CONTROL   While the old system is being dismantled and the new one shaped, change and the associated uncertainties can make the existing means of processing information and maintaining control—such as the communication system, performance appraisal system, reward structures, and other organizational processes—irrelevant, inappropriate, and ineffective. Thus, it may be difficult to monitor and reward performance and take corrective action during the transition. The result is a loss of control.

TASK REDEFINITION   Because all parts of the system interact, individual jobs are affected by any change, even one intended to affect another part of the organization (for example, the performance appraisal system). Rather than let new tasks evolve in response to changes in other areas, the organization should specify what the employees' tasks are and how they relate to other new jobs. If attention is not given to redefining jobs, the change may not have its intended effects throughout the organization.

Keys to Successful Organization Development

In conclusion, we offer five keys to managing OD. They relate directly to the problems identified earlier and to our view of the organization as a social system. Each can influence the elements of the social system and may help the organization avoid some of the major problems in managing the change. The points and their potential impacts are listed in Table 23.4.

TAKE A HOLISTIC VIEW   Managers must take a holistic view of the organization and the OD project. Because the subsystems of the organization are interdependent, a limited view can endanger the change effort. A holistic view encompasses the culture and dominant coalition as well as the people, tasks, structure, and information subsystems.

SECURE TOP MANAGEMENT SUPPORT   The support of top management is essential to the success of any OD effort. As the organization's probable dominant coalition, it is a powerful element of the social system, and its support is necessary for dealing with control and power problems. For example, a manager who plans a change in the way tasks are assigned and responsibility is delegated in her department must notify top management and gain its support. Complications may arise if disgruntled employees complain to high-level managers who have not been notified of the change or do not support it. The employees' complaints may jeopardize the manager's plan—and perhaps her job.

ENCOURAGE PARTICIPATION   Problems related to resistance, control, and power can be overcome by broad participation in planning for OD. Giving people a voice in designing the change may give them a sense of power and control over their own destinies, which may help to win their support during implementation.

FOSTER OPEN COMMUNICATION   Open communication is an important factor in managing resistance to change and overcoming information and control problems during transition. Employees typically recognize the uncertainties and ambiguities that arise during a transition and seek information on the change and their place in the new system. In the absence of information, the gap may be filled with inappropriate or false information, which may endanger the change process. Rumors tend to spread through the grapevine faster than

Table 23.4

Keys to Successful
Change Management

Key	Impacts
Take a holistic view of the organization	Anticipate effects on social system and culture
Secure top management support	Get dominant coalition on the side of change; safeguard structural change; head off problems of power and control
Encourage participation by those affected by the change	Minimize transition problem of control, resistance, and task redefinition
Foster open communication	Minimize transition problems of resistance and information and control systems
Reward those who contribute to change	Minimize transition problems of resistance and control systems

accurate information can be disseminated through official channels. A manager should always be sensitive to the effects of uncertainty on employees, especially in a period of change; it seems that any news, even bad news, is better than no news.

REWARD CONTRIBUTORS   Although this last point is simple, it can easily be neglected. Employees who contribute to the change in any way need to be rewarded. Too often the only people who are acknowledged after a change effort are those who tried to stop it. Those who quickly grasp new work assignments, work harder to cover what otherwise might not get done in the transition, or help others adjust to changes deserve special credit—perhaps a mention in a news release or the internal company newspaper, special consideration in performance appraisal, a merit raise, or a promotion. From a behavioral perspective, individuals need to benefit in some way if they are to willingly help change something that eliminates the old, comfortable way of doing the job.

In the current dynamic environment, managers must anticipate the need for change and satisfy it with more responsive and competitive organizational systems. Since organizations must change or face elimination, these five keys to managing organizational change may also serve as general guidelines to managing organizational behavior.

SUMMARY OF KEY POINTS

Organization development is the process of planned change and improvement of organizations through the application of knowledge of the behavioral sciences. OD uses a systematic change process and focuses on managing the culture of the organization.

The most comprehensive change involves altering the structure of the organization through a reorganization of departments, reporting relationships, or authority systems. System-wide structural changes may also involve management by objectives, quality-of-work life projects, and the development of collateral organizations. Management by objectives is a system in which manager and employee work out a mutually agreeable set of goals for the employee to achieve during the next evaluation period. Quality-of-work-life programs focus on providing a work environment in which employees can satisfy individual needs. A collateral organization is a planned adaptation of the formal organization that exists alongside it and increases its flexibility, responsiveness, and problem-solving ability.

Task-technological changes alter the way the organization accomplishes its primary tasks. Task redesign includes, along with the steps usually associated with change, four additional steps: diagnosis, cost/benefit analysis, formulation of a redesign strategy, and implementation of supplemental changes. Socio-technical systems theory has been the basis for the redesign of the entire work system in several plants around the world. Changing tasks and the organization's technological base changes other elements of the social system as well.

Frequently used group and individual approaches to organizational change are training and management development programs, team building, and survey-feedback techniques. Training programs usually are designed to improve employees' job skills; help employees adapt to other organizational changes, such as an MBO program; or develop employees' awareness and understanding of problems such as workplace safety or stress. Management development programs attempt to foster in current or future managers the skills, abilities, and perspectives important to good management. Team-building programs are designed to help a work team (or group) develop into a mature, well-functioning team by helping it define its goals or priorities, analyze its tasks and the way they are performed, and examine relationships among the people doing the work. As used in the OD process, survey-feedback techniques involve gathering data, analyzing and summarizing it, and returning it to employees and groups for discussion and for identification and solution of problems.

The management of change in organizations requires careful diagnosis, planning, implementation, and control. Even then, change is likely to be slower than desired, more costly than expected, and less successful than planned. A change effort has been effectively managed if the desired change has taken place and expectations are being met without undue cost to the organization.

Major problems in achieving changes in organizations are resistance, power, control, and task redefinition. These problems are directly linked to the elements of the organization's social system. Five keys to successful management of change are taking a holistic view of the organization, obtaining the support of top management, encouraging participation in the design of change by all those affected by it, openly communicating throughout the process, and rewarding those who contribute to the change.

DISCUSSION QUESTIONS

1. How is organization development different from organizational change?

2. How and why would OD be different if the elements of the social system were not interdependent?

3. How does the view of structural reorganization as an OD technique extend the concepts of organization design presented in Chapter 15?

4. Do quality-of-work-life programs rely more on individual or organizational aspects of organizational behavior? Why?

5. Describe how the job of your professor could be redesigned. Include a discussion of other subsystems that would need to be changed.

6. How do you think the class in which you are using this book differs from a training program in an organization?

7. How do training and management development differ?

8. How might team building be compatible with the group development process discussed in Chapter 9?

9. How can a manager know that an OD effort has met the three criteria of effectiveness discussed in this chapter?

Case 23.1

Making the Postal Service Businesslike

The United States Postal Service is a huge business with two very different goals. On the one hand, it must please the Postal Service Board of Governors and Congress, both of which have been accused of meddling in the service's day-to-day business by second-guessing rate decisions and ordering the service to keep small, unprofitable post offices open. On the other hand, the Postal Service is like any other business: it must please its customers (the entire American populace), keep its 700,000 workers happy, and try to get its $33-billion-per-year operations to break even.

To deal with these potentially conflicting goals and with other problems, the Postal Service hired Preston Robert Tisch in 1986, signaling that it wanted to take a more businesslike approach than it had in the past. Tisch has a reputation for creating successful businesses. He and his brother Laurence started out by buying a New Jersey resort hotel in 1946 and now control an empire worth $16 billion, including the Loews Corporation and a 25-percent ownership of CBS, which Laurence now runs. Besides hotels, they have successfully invested in motels, theaters, insurance, tobacco, watches, and a defense contracting company. Surely someone with such a background could handle the mail.

When he was hired, Tisch admitted that he knew nothing about the postal business, but said that the service wanted him because he could manage well. He promised to change the service "from an operating mentality to a marketing mentality," so it would become more responsive to customers' needs. In Tisch's first months on the job, customers did see changes. He responded to business complaints by looking at alternatives to nine-digit Zip Codes and by having service employees meet with direct-mail companies and their clients to convince everyone that the Postal Service could handle big mailing jobs. In response to suggestions from postmasters, the service opened up stores that sell only stamps, changed local post office hours, and even occasionally delivered mail on Sunday.

But responding to customer's needs was not Tisch's only worry. When he was hired, he became the third postmaster general in three years, a turnover rate that some see as reflecting the political nature of the service. The first of the three, Paul Carlin, claimed that he was fired because he objected to a scheme to give equipment contracts to one company. Six months later, the board's vice chairman, Peter Voss, pleaded guilty to receiving kickbacks for helping a Dallas company win a $250 million Postal Service contract.

In fact, the country may be asking Robert Tisch to do the impossible by treating a political job like a business position. Some of Tisch's predecessors restructured the service and made it more efficient; it has even ended a number of recent years with surpluses. That is good news, but the next time Congress asks the Postal Service to tighten its belt another notch, the service may be in trouble. Federal Express, United Parcel Service, and a host of other companies continue to challenge its dominance in the business of moving paper and packages, and though its operations have become more efficient recently, the service has outraged many of its customers by cutting office window hours.

Tisch did score a major victory during his first year by negotiating a contract that reportedly kept pay increases down with two unions representing 579,000 workers. But he seemed uncertain of his new position. Although he gave up a $679,000 salary for the Postal Service's $86,200, he remained a director of Loews, which is a big mailer. The potential conflict of interest has kept him from getting involved in postal rate decisions, many of which would affect Loews. Tisch still spends much of his time in New York rather than Washington. Perhaps a veteran businessperson can never feel totally comfortable working under the constraints of being an arm of the government.

---

* Frances Seghers, "Bob Tisch Is Putting More Zip in the Post Office," *Business Week*, November 24, 1986, 72.

Case Questions

1. How do you think Robert Tisch should approach the Postal Service's problems?

2. What should the government do to make Tisch's job easier?

Case Sources

Howard Fields, "Preston Tisch Named Postmaster General," *Publishers Weekly,* August 22, 1986, 15; Barbara Love, "Tisch: What Stamp Will He Put on the USPS?" *Folio,* November 1986, 49–50; Frances Seghers, "Can Bob Tisch Get the Mail Moving?" *Business Week,* August 3, 1987, 29; Frances Seghers, "Bob Tisch Is Putting More Zip in the Post Office," *Business Week,* November 24, 1986, 72.

Case 23.2

The Trainees After Hours

The Managerial Process Group, one of many training classes at Southwest Mutual Insurance Company, ran from 2:00 to 5:00 on Friday afternoons. After the meeting, many of the group members met at Melody's Juice Bar for drinks and to discuss the class. Group rules prohibited them from conversing about the particular elements of the class discussions, but they felt free to talk about how the process group compared with other training classes.

On one particular Friday afternoon, Ralph Smith began the discussion. "I'm beginning to see what this group is all about," he said. "At first I thought it was about nothing at all—we just sit there and talk about ourselves and about how we felt when someone said something ten minutes ago. But now it seems to me that the frustrations I feel with the group are a lot like those I feel at work."

"Yes," agreed Janice Alberg. "When you said today that I was being sarcastic, I didn't think I was, and at first I got irritated. But then I started thinking about how often people think I'm being sarcastic when I'm not, and I started hoping that maybe if I could change in the group so that people don't view me as sarcastic, I could change outside the group as well, and get along better with everyone."

"And maybe it'll be Christmas tomorrow," Wendell Cort replied. "I prefer classes that give you something really solid to take away with you. When you get done with a time management class, you know how to revamp your schedule to get everything done. And after a writing class, you at least know how to fix a passive sentence. In the group I keep thinking, 'Yeah, I never thought of that,' but when I go to write it down later, it always seems so obvious. 'Don't be sarcastic,' or 'Be an active listener.' It's like they're trying to teach you how to be a human being."

"Is that so bad?" Janice asked.

"It's not the company's job, or any of their business," Wendell said.

"I don't know about that," Martin Snull put in. "Sure, when they teach you to write better or manage your time better or learn how to use the new computers, you can go out on the job the next day and use those things and maybe get more done for the company. I don't know about you—maybe I'm just hard to deal with—but I find that I spend an awful lot of my time trying to figure out how to deal with the people around me I don't get along with, or even people that I do get along with whom I have to approach in just the right way. Sometimes I wish everyone I worked with was in this group so they'd all understand more about the messages they give out and so they'd be more aware of how they can make their interactions more productive for everyone. Our fearless leader told us at the beginning that this wasn't a team development workshop, but in some ways I wish it were."

"Not me," said Wendell. "Then we'd all be polite and not want to barge into anyone else's territory. The thing I like about this group is that you can say what you feel, like 'Cut the crap.'"

"Yeah," said Janice, "but isn't part of the point of this group to help us say what we feel outside the class? I mean, isn't 'cut the crap' a pretty good company policy in general?"

"I don't know," Wally Day said, yawning, speaking up for the first time. "All this training stuff seems to me like a way in which the company can claim it's giving us benefits without ever contributing to our bank accounts. If they don't think I can get along with the people around me, they shouldn't have hired me. If I'm not going to get any work done after 2:00 on Friday afternoons, I wish they'd let me go play golf rather than sit around in room 3B with a bunch of other tired people. No offense."

"Well," Janice said after a pause, "I guess we know how you feel about training."

Case Questions:

1. What advantages and disadvantages do these group participants see in the training programs they have attended?

2. What can you conclude from this conversation about various types of training programs and the people who most benefit from them?

Experiential Exercise

Purpose: This exercise will help you understand the interrelationships among various methods of organization development.

Format: Your group will specify techniques to use in the implementation of the change you described in the experiential exercise for Chapter 22.

Procedure: The class will be divided into the same groups that worked together on the exercise in Chapter 22. Your task is to describe the techniques you would use to implement the change described in that exercise. You may use structural changes, task-technology methods, group and individual programs, or any combination of these. You may need to go to the library to gather more information on some techniques.

You should also discuss how you will deal with the common OD problems: resistance, power, control, and task redefinition. The five keys to successful change management discussed at the end of this chapter should play important roles in your plan.

Your instructor may make this exercise an in-class project, but it is also a good semester-ending project for groups to work on outside class. Either way, the exercise is most beneficial when the groups report their implementation programs to the entire class. Each group should report on which OD techniques are to be used, why they were selected, how they will be implemented, and how the typical OD problems will be avoided.

Follow-up Questions

1. Did different groups use the same technique in very different ways or to accomplish different goals?

2. Which techniques were used the most across the five change situations presented in the Experiential Exercise in Chapter 22? Why?

3. If you did outside research on OD techniques for your project, did you find any OD techniques that seemed more applicable than those in this chapter? If so, describe one of them.

APPENDIX

Theory and Research in Organizational Behavior

*T*hroughout the twenty-three chapters in this book, we have referred to theories and research findings as a basis for our discussions. In this brief appendix, we provide more information about how theories and research findings are developed.

First we highlight the role of theory and research. We then identify the purposes of research and describe the steps in the research process, types of research designs, and methods for gathering data. We conclude with a brief discussion of some related issues.

THE ROLE OF THEORY AND RESEARCH

Some managers and many students fail to see the need for research. They seem confused by what appears an endless litany of theories and by sets of contradictory research findings. They often ask, "Why bother?"

Indeed, few absolute truths have emerged from studies of organizational behavior. Management in general and organizational behavior in particular, however, are in many ways fields of study still in their infancy. Thus, it stands to reason that researchers in these fields have few theories that always work and that their research cannot always be generalized to settings other than the one in which it was originally conducted.

Still, theory and research play valuable roles.[1] Theories, for example, help investigators organize what they *do* know. They provide a guiding framework that managers can use to diagnose problems and implement changes. They also serve as road signs that can help managers solve many problems involving

---

[1] Jeffrey Pfeffer, "The Theory-Practice Gap: Myth or Reality?" *Academy of Management Executive*, February 1987, pp. 31–33.

people. Research also plays an important role. Each study conducted and published, for example, adds a little more to the storehouse of knowledge available to practicing managers. Questions are posed and answers discovered. Over time, researchers can become more and more confident about findings as they are repeated across different settings.[2]

PURPOSES OF RESEARCH

Researchers should try to approach problems and questions of organizational behavior scientifically. **Scientific research** is the systematic investigation of hypothesized propositions about the relationships among natural phenomena. The aims of science are to describe, explain, and predict phenomena.[3]

Research can be classified as basic or applied. **Basic research** is concerned with discovering new knowledge rather than solving particular problems. The knowledge discovered through basic research may not have much direct application to organizations, at least when it is first discovered.[4] Research scientists and university professors are the people who most often conduct basic research in organizational behavior.

Applied research, on the other hand, is research conducted to solve particular problems or answer specific questions. The findings of applied research are, by definition, immediately applicable to managers. Consultants, university professors, and managers themselves conduct much of the applied research performed in organizations.

THE RESEARCH PROCESS

To result in valid findings, research should be conducted according to the scientific process shown in Figure A.1. The starting point is a question or problem.[5] For example, a manager might want to design a new reward system to enhance employee motivation but might be unsure what types of rewards to offer or how to tie them to performance. This manager's questions are: "What kinds of rewards will motivate my employees?" and "How should those rewards be tied to performance?"

The next step is to review the literature to determine what is already known about the phenomenon. It is quite likely that something has been written about

[2] Eugene Stone, *Research Methods in Organizational Behavior* (Santa Monica, Calif.: Goodyear, 1978).

[3] Fred N. Kerlinger, *Foundations of Behavioral Research*, 3rd ed. (New York: Holt, Rinehart and Winston, 1987).

[4] Richard L. Daft, Ricky W. Griffin, and Valerie Yates, "Retrospective Accounts of Research Factors Associated with Significant and Not-So-Significant Research Outcomes," *Academy of Management Journal*, December 1987, pp. 763–785.

[5] Richard L. Daft, "Learning the Craft of Organizational Research," *Academy of Management Review*, October 1983, pp. 539–546.

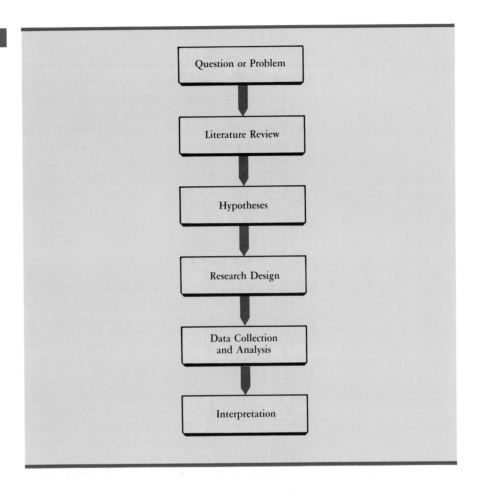

Figure A.1

The Research Process

most problems or questions faced by today's managers. Thus, the goal of the literature review is to avoid "reinventing the wheel" by finding out what others have already learned. Basic research is generally available in such journals as *Academy of Management Journal*, *Academy of Management Review*, *Administrative Science Quarterly*, *Journal of Applied Psychology*, *Organizational Behavior and Human Decision Processes*, and *Journal of Management*. Applied research findings are more likely to be found in sources such as *Harvard Business Review*, *Academy of Management Executive*, *Organizational Dynamics*, *Personnel Administrator*, and *Personnel Psychology*.

Based on the original question and the review of the literature, the researcher formulates hypotheses—statements of what he or she expects to find. The hypothesis is important in guiding the researcher's design of the study, because it provides a very clear and precise statement of what the researcher wants to test. That means the study can be specifically designed to test the hypothesis.

The research design is the plan for doing the research. We discuss the more common research designs later. As a part of the research design, the researcher must determine how variables will be measured. Thus, if satisfaction is one factor being considered, the researcher must decide how to measure it.

Common methods for gathering data are also discussed later. After data have been collected, they must be analyzed. Depending on the study design and hypotheses, data analysis may be relatively simple and straightforward or may require elaborate statistical procedures. Methods for analyzing data are beyond the scope of this discussion.

Finally, the results of the study are interpreted—that is, the researcher figures out what they mean. They may provide support for the hypothesis, may fail to support the hypothesis, or may suggest a relationship other than that proposed in the hypothesis. An important part of the interpretation process is recognizing the limitations imposed on the findings by weaknesses in the research design.

Some researchers go a step further and try to publish their findings. Several potential sources for publication are the journals mentioned in the discussion of literature review. Publication is important, because it helps educate other researchers and managers and also provides additional information for future literature reviews.[6]

TYPES OF RESEARCH DESIGNS

A **research design** is the set of procedures used to test the predicted relationships among natural phenomena. The design addresses such issues as how the relevant variables are to be defined, measured, and related to one another. Managers and researchers can draw on a variety of research designs, each with its own strengths and weaknesses. Four general types of research designs are often used in the study of organizational behavior. It should be noted that each type has several variations.[7] The four types are shown in Figure A.2.

Case Study

A **case study** is an in-depth analysis of one setting. This design is frequently used when little is known about the phenomena being studied and the researcher wants to look at relevant concepts intensively and thoroughly. A variety of methods are used to gather information, including interviews, questionnaires, and personal observations.[8]

---

[6] Larry L. Cummings and Peter Frost, *Publishing in Organizational Sciences* (Homewood, Ill.: Irwin, 1985).

[7] D. T. Campbell and J. C. Stanley, *Experimental and Quasi-Experimental Designs for Research* (Chicago: Rand McNally, 1963).

[8] R. Yin and K. Heald, "Using the Case Survey Method to Analyze Policy Studies," *Administrative Science Quarterly*, June 1975, pp. 371–381.

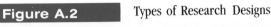

Figure A.2   Types of Research Designs

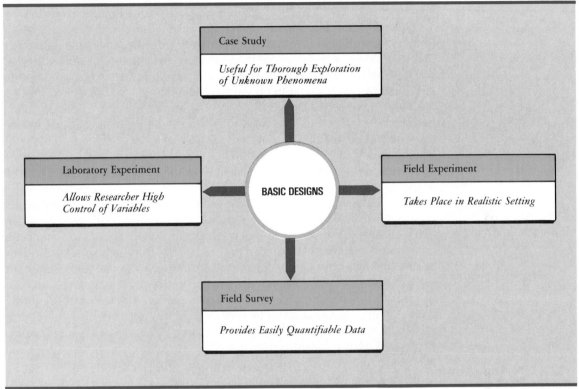

The case study research design offers several advantages. First, it allows the researcher to probe one situation in detail, yielding a wealth of descriptive and explanatory information. The case study also facilitates the discovery of unexpected relationships. Because the researcher observes virtually everything that happens in a given situation, she or he may learn issues beyond those originally chosen for study.

The case study design also has several disadvantages. It does not provide data that can be readily generalized to other situations, since the information is so closely tied to the situation studied. In addition, case study information may be biased by the closeness of the researcher to the situation. Case study research also tends to be very time consuming. Still, the case study can be an effective and useful research design, as long as the researcher understands its limitations and takes them into account when formulating conclusions.

Field Survey

A **field survey** usually relies on a questionnaire distributed to a sample of people chosen from a larger population. If a manager is conducting the study, the sample is often drawn from a group or department within her or his organization. If a researcher is conducting the study, the sample is usually negotiated with a host organization interested in the questions being addressed. The questionnaire is generally mailed or delivered by hand to participants at home or at work and may be returned by mail or picked up by the researcher. The respondents answer the questions and return the questionnaire as directed. The researcher analyzes the responses and tries to make inferences about the larger population from the representative sample.[9]

Field surveys can focus on a variety of topics relevant to organizational behavior, including employees' attitudes toward other people (such as leaders and coworkers), attitudes about the job (such as satisfaction with the job and commitment to the organization), and perceptions of organizational character-istics (such as the challenge inherent in the job and the degree of decentralization in the organization).

Field surveys provide information about a much larger segment of the population than do case studies. They also provide an abundance of data in easily quantifiable form, which facilitates statistical analysis and the compilation of normative data for comparative purposes. However, field surveys also have several disadvantages. First, survey information may reveal only superficial feelings and reactions to situations rather than deeply held feelings, attitudes, or emotions. Second, the design and development of field surveys require a great deal of expertise and can be very time consuming. Furthermore, relation-ships between variables tend to be accentuated in responses to questionnaires because of what is called common method variance. This means that people may tend to answer all the questions in the same way, creating false impression.

A final, very important disadvantage of field surveys is the researcher's lack of control. The researcher may not have control over who completes the questionnaire, when it is filled out, the mental or physical state of the person filling it out, and many other important conditions. Thus, the typical field survey has many inherent sources of potential error. Still, surveys can be a very useful means to gather large quantities of data and to assess general patterns of relationships between variables.

Laboratory Experiment

The researcher has the most control in a **laboratory experiment.** By creating an artificial setting similar to a real work situation, the researcher can control almost every possible factor in that setting. He or she can manipulate the variables in the study and examine their effects on other variables.[10]

As an example of how laboratory experiments work, consider the relation-

---

[9] Kerlinger, *Foundations of Behavioral Research.*

[10] Cynthia D. Fisher, "Laboratory Experiments," in Thomas S. Bateman and Gerald R. Ferris, eds., *Method and Analysis in Organizational Research* (Reston, Va.: Reston, 1984); Edwin Locke, ed., *Generalizing from Laboratory to Field Settings* (Lexington, Mass.: Lexington Books, 1986).

ship between how goals are developed for subordinates and the subordinates' subsequent level of satisfaction. To explore this relationship, the researcher might structure a situation in which some subjects (usually students but occasionally people hired or recruited from the community) are assigned goals while others determine their own goals. Both groups would then work on a hypothetical task relevant to the goals, and afterward all subjects would fill out a questionnaire designed to measure satisfaction. Differences in satisfaction could be attributed to the method used for goal setting.

Laboratory experiments avoid some of the problems of other types of research. Advantages include a high degree of control over variables and precise measurement of variables. A major disadvantage is the lack of realism; rarely does the laboratory setting exactly duplicate the real situation. A related problem is the difficulty in generalizing the findings to organizational settings. Finally, some organizational situations, such as plant closings or employee firings, cannot be simulated in a laboratory.

Field Experiment

A **field experiment** is similar to a laboratory experiment, but it is conducted in a real organization. In a field experiment, a researcher attempts to control certain variables and manipulate others in order to assess the effects of the manipulated variables on outcome variables. For example, an executive interested in the effects of flexible working hours on absenteeism and turnover might design a field experiment in which one plant adopted a flexible work schedule program while another plant, as similar as possible to the first, served as a control site. Attendance and turnover would be monitored at both plants. If attendance increased and turnover decreased in the experimental plant and there were no changes at the control site, the executive could probably conclude that the flexible work schedule program was successful.

The field experiment has certain advantages over the laboratory experiment. The organizational setting provides greater realism, making generalization to other organizational situations more valid. Disadvantages include the lack of control over other events that might occur in the organizational setting (such as other changes the firm might introduce), contamination of the results if the different groups discover their respective roles in the experiment and behave differently because of that knowledge, greater expense, and the risk that the experimental manipulations will contribute to problems within the company.

METHODS OF GATHERING DATA

The method of gathering data is a critical concern of the research design. Data-gathering methods may be grouped into four categories: questionnaires, interviews, observation, and nonreactive measures.[11]

---

[11] Stone, *Research Methods in Organizational Behavior.*

Questionnaires

A **questionnaire** is a collection of written questions about the respondents' attitudes, opinions, perceptions, and/or demographic characteristics. Usually the respondent fills out the questionnaire and returns it to the researcher. To facilitate scoring, researchers typically use multiple-choice questions. Some questionnaires have a few open-ended questions that allow respondents to elaborate on their answers. Designing a questionnaire that will provide the information desired by the researcher is a very complex task and one that has received considerable attention.

Interviews

An **interview** resembles a questionnaire, but the questions are presented to the respondent orally by an interviewer. The respondent is usually allowed to answer questions spontaneously rather than asked to choose among alternatives defined by the researcher. Interviews generally take much more time to administer than questionnaires, and they are more difficult to score. The benefit of interviews is the opportunity for the respondent to speak at length on a topic, thereby providing a richness and depth of information not normally yielded by questionnaires.

Observation

Observation, in its simplest form, is watching events and recording what is observed. Researchers use several types of observation. In structured observation, the observer is trained to look for and record certain activities or types of events. In participant observation, the trained observer actually participates in the organizational events as a member of the work team and records impressions and observations in a diary or daily log. In hidden observation, the trained observer is not visible to the subjects. A hidden camera or a specially designed observation room may be used.

Nonreactive Measures

When a situation is changed because of data gathering, we say the activity has caused a reaction in the situation. Nonreactive, or unobtrusive, measures have been developed for gathering data without disturbing the situation being studied. Nonreactive measures include examination of physical traces, use of archives, and simple observation. When questionnaires, interviews, and obtrusive observations may cause problems in the research situation, the use of nonreactive measures may be an appropriate substitute. At some universities, for example, sidewalks are not laid down around a new building until it has been in use for some time. Rather than ask students and faculty about their traffic patterns or try to anticipate them, the designers observe the building in use, see where the grass is most worn, and put sidewalks there.

RELATED ISSUES

Three other issues are of particular interest to researchers. These are causality, reliability and validity, and ethical concerns.[12]

Causality

Scientific research attempts to describe, explain, and predict phenomena. In many cases, the purpose of the research is to reveal **causality.** That is, researchers attempt to describe, explain, and predict the cause of a certain event. In everyday life, people commonly observe a series of events and infer causality about the relationship between them. For example, you might observe that a good friend of yours is skipping one of her classes regularly. You also know that she is failing that class. You might infer that she is failing the class because of her poor attendance. But the causal relation might be just the reverse. Your friend may have had a good attendance record until her poor performance on the first test destroyed her motivation and she stopped attending class. Given the complexities associated with human behavior in organizational settings, the issues of causality, causal inference, and causal relations are of considerable interest and importance to managers and researchers alike.

In the behavioral sciences, causality is difficult to determine because of the interrelationship among variables in a social system. Causality cannot always be empirically proved, but it may be possible to infer causality in certain circumstances. In general, two conditions must be met in order for causality to be attributed to an observed relationship among variables. The first is temporal order: if x causes y, then x must occur before y. Many studies, especially field surveys, describe the degree of association among variables with highly sophisticated mathematical techniques, but inferring a causal relationship is difficult, because the variables are measured at the same point in time. On the basis of such evidence, we cannot say whether one variable or event caused the other, whether they were both caused by another variable, or whether they are totally independent of each other.

The second condition is the elimination of spuriousness. If we want to infer that x caused y, we must eliminate all other possible causes of y. Quite often a seemingly causal relationship between two variables may be due to their joint association with a third variable, z. To say the relationship between x and y is causal, we must rule out z as a possible cause of y. In the behavioral sciences, so many variables might influence one another that tracing causal relationships is like walking in an endless maze. Yet despite the difficulties of the task, we must continue trying to describe, explain, and predict social phenomena in organizational settings if we are to advance our understanding of organizational behavior.[13]

---

[12] Philip M. Podaskoff and Dan R. Dalton, "Research Methodology in Organizational Studies," *Journal of Management*, Summer 1987, pp. 419–441.

[13] Stone, *Research Methods in Organizational Behavior*.

Reliability and Validity

The **reliability** of a measure is the extent to which it is consistent over time. For example, suppose a researcher measures a group's job satisfaction today with a questionnaire and then measures the same thing in two months. Assuming nothing has changed, individual responses should be very similar. If they are, the measure can be assessed as having a high level of reliability. Likewise, if question 2 and question 10 ask about the same thing, responses to these questions should be consistent. If measures lack reliability, little confidence can be placed in the results they provide.

Validity describes the extent to which research measures what it was intended to measure. Suppose, for example, a researcher is interested in employees' satisfaction with their jobs. To determine this, he asks them a series of questions about their pay, supervisors, and working conditions. He then averages their answers and uses the average to represent job satisfaction. We might argue that this is not a valid measure. Pay, supervision, and working conditions, for example, may be unrelated to the job itself. Thus, the researcher has obtained data that does not mean what he thinks it means—it is not valid. The researcher then must use measures that are valid as well as reliable.[14]

Ethical Concerns

Last, but certainly not least, the researcher must contend with ethical concerns. Two concerns, in particular, are important.[15] First, the researcher must provide adequate protection for participants in the study and not violate their privacy without their permission. For example, suppose a researcher is studying the behavior of a group of operating employees. A good way to increase people's willingness to participate is to promise that their identities will not be revealed. Having made such a guarantee, the researcher is obligated to keep it.

Likewise, participation should be voluntary. All prospective subjects in a study should have the right of not participating or of withdrawing their participation after the study has begun. Researchers should explain all procedures in advance to participants and should not subject them to any experimental conditions that could harm them either physically or psychologically. Many governmental agencies, universities, and professional associations have developed guidelines for researchers to use to guarantee protection of human subjects.

The other issue involves how the researcher reports the results. In particular, it is important that research procedures and methods be faithfully and candidly reported. This enables readers to assess for themselves the validity of the results reported. It also allows others to do a better job of replicating (repeating) the study, perhaps with a different sample, in order to learn more about how its findings generalize.

---

[14] Kerlinger, *Foundations of Behavioral Research*.

[15] Mary Ann Von Glinow, "Ethical Issues in Organizational Behavior," *Academy of Management Newsletter*, March 1985, pp. 1–3.

GLOSSARY

Absenteeism Failure to report to work. (5)

acceptance theory of authority Suggests that the authority of the manager depends on the subordinate's acceptance of the manager's right to give the directive and expect compliance. (13)

accommodation A type of intergroup interaction that occurs when the goals are compatible but not considered to be very important to goal attainment. (10)

action research The process used by a change agent consisting of (a) directing the organizational change and (b) documenting it to contribute to the empirical body of knowledge about organizations. (22)

adaptation In a social system, fitting into the environment by being aware of the environment, understanding how that environment is changing, and making the appropriate adjustments. (16)

adhocracy A form of organization design that has horizontal and vertical specialization but little formalization, resulting in a very organic structure. Decision making is spread throughout the organization. It is one of Mintzberg's structural forms and is typically found in young organizations engaged in highly technical fields where the environment is complex and dynamic. (15)

administrative hierarchy A system of reporting relationships in the organization, from the first level up through the president or CEO. (13)

AGIL model Developed by Parsons, this model specified certain functions that any social system must meet to survive and prosper: adaptation, goal attainment, integration, and legitimacy. (16)

all-channel network A small-group network in which all members communicate with all the other members. (18)

applied research Research conducted to solve particular problems or answer specific questions. (App.)

attribution The process by which we link an event to an environmental cause. (2)

attribution theory Suggests that we observe the behavior of others and then attribute causes to it. The theory is associated with Heider and Kelley. (2)

attributional view of employee motivation Employees observe their own behavior through the process of self-perception and then, based on these perceptions, decide whether their behavior is a response to external or internal causes and then are motivated by rewards that correspond to the causes of their behavior. (5)

authoritarianism The extent to which a person believes that there should be power and status differences within a social system such as an organization. The stronger the belief, the more the individual is said to be authoritarian. (3)

Note: The number in parentheses after each entry refers to the chapter in which the term is discussed.

authority Power that has been legitimized within a specific social context. (13)

autonomous work groups An innovation in task design whereby jobs are structured for groups rather than for individuals. The group itself is given considerable discretion in scheduling, individual work assignments, and other matters that have traditionally been management prerogatives. (8)

avoidance (negative reinforcement) A concept of reinforcement theory that occurs when the individual is engaging in desired behavior in order to avoid an unpleasant, or aversive, consequence. The effect of avoidance is to increase the frequency of a desired behavior. (2)

avoidance A type of intergroup interaction that occurs when the interaction is not considered to be important to either group's goal attainment and the goals are considered to be incompatible. (10)

*B***asic research** Research concerned with discovering new knowledge rather than solving particular problems. (App.)

behavior modification (OB Mod.) The application of reinforcement theory principles to individuals in organizational settings. It is usually aimed at increasing desired behaviors by employees through the use of positive reinforcement. (6)

behavioral approach (to leadership) Approach designed to determine the behaviors associated with effective leadership. These approaches to the study of leadership began in the late 1940s. (11)

behavioral model of decision making A decision-making model characterized by the use of procedures and rules of thumb, suboptimizing, and satisficing. (17)

behaviorally anchored rating scale (BARS) Essentially graphic rating scales with statements of employee behaviors that characterize, or "anchor," various points on the scale. It is a performance evaluation method developed by Smith and Kendall in 1963. (19)

bias A personal preference or inclination that undermines impartial judgment. (19)

bounded rationality A decision-making process whereby the decision maker limits the inputs to the decision-making process and makes decisions based on judgment and personal biases as well as logic. (17)

brainstorming A technique for stimulating imaginative and novel ideas. Participants in brainstorming are encouraged to suggest as many innovative and extreme ideas as possible as solutions to the identified problem.

Participants are forbidden to discourage the ideas of others and are encouraged to build on the ideas of others. (17)

bureaucracy A type of organizational structure proposed by Max Weber. The ideal bureacracy is characterized by Weber as having a hierarchy of authority, a system of rules and procedures, and division of labor. (15)

burnout The overall feeling of exhaustion a person feels when simultaneously experiencing too much pressure and too few sources of satisfaction. (7)

*C***areer** A perceived sequence of attitudes and behaviors associated with work-related experiences and activities over the span of the person's life. (20)

career management The process by which organizational career planning is implemented. (20)

career planning The process of planning one's life work; involves evaluating abilities and interests, considering alternative career opportunities, establishing career goals, and planning practical development. (20)

career stages The gradual changes that occur over time in careers. (20)

case study An in-depth analysis of one setting. This design is frequently used when little is known about the phenomena in question and the researcher wants to look at relevant concepts intensively and thoroughly. (App.)

causality The attempt by researchers to describe, explain, and predict the cause of a certain event. The purpose of scientific research is to reveal causality. (App.)

centralization Decision-making authority is concentrated at the top of the organizational hierarchy. (13)

central tendency In performance evaluation, the tendency of a rater to evaluate performance moderately, with few if any high or low ratings. (19)

chain network A small group network in which each member communicates with the person above and below, except the individuals on each end, who communicate with only one person. (18)

change agent A person who is responsible for managing the change effort in the organization. The change agent may be a member of the organization or an outsider. (22)

channel noise The principal type of noise in the communication process. (18)

charismatic leadership An approach to leadership that assumes charisma is an individual characteristic of the leader. Charisma is a form of interpersonal attraction that inspires support and acceptance. It is presumed that a supervisor who is very charismatic may be more successful in influencing subordinate behavior than one lacking charisma. (11)

circle network   A small group network in which each person communicates with the people on both sides but no one else. (18)

classic principles of organizing   Fourteen principles that provide the framework for the organization chart and the coordination of work. These principles were identified by Fayol and have been criticized for ignoring the human element in organizations. (15)

classical conditioning   An approach to learning stating that if a conditioned stimulus is repeatedly paired with an unconditioned stimulus, the conditioned stimulus will eventually become associated in the mind of the learner with the same response that is elicited by the unconditioned stimulus. This approach is associated with Pavlov and his experiments with dogs. (2)

classical organization theory   A branch of management that was concerned with structuring organizations effectively. (1)

coercive power   A base of power identified by French and Raven that exists when someone has the ability to punish or to inflict physical or psychological harm on someone else. (12)

cognitive dissonance   The anxiety a person experiences when two sets of knowledge or perceptions are contradictory or incongruent. It also occurs when a person behaves in a way inconsistent with her or his attitudes. (3)

cognitive process   A process that assumes people are conscious, active participants in how they learn. People draw on their experiences and use past learning as a basis for present behavior. People make choices about their behavior and then recognize the consequences of their choices. Finally, people evaluate those consequences and add them to prior learning, affecting future choices. (2)

cohesiveness   See **group cohesiveness.**

collaborative management by objectives (CMBO)   The team approach to management by objectives. The manager and subordinates set goals for the group; group goals are then broken down into individual goals so each member is accountable for performance. (23)

collaboration   A type of intergroup interaction that occurs when the interaction is important to goal attainment and the groups' goals are compatible. (10)

collateral organization   An organization that exists alongside the formal organization. Its purpose is to solve problems the formal organization cannot handle. (23)

collectivism   A feeling that the good of the group or society should come first. (21)

command group   A type of formal group that is relatively permanent. A command group is also referred to as a functional group. (9)

commitment   Individual's feelings of identification with and attachment to the organization. (3)

communication   A process in which information is exchanged or a common understanding is established between two or more parties. (18)

communication fidelity   The degree of correspondence between the message intended by the source and the message understood by the receiver. (18)

communication network   Links that develop so that employees can obtain the necessary information to do their jobs and coordinate their work with others in the system. It serves to structure both the flow and the content of communication and support the organization structure. (18)

competition   A type of intergroup interaction that occurs when the goals of the groups are incompatible and interactions are important to goal attainment of each group. (10)

compressed workweek   A work schedule in which an employee works a full forty-hour week in less than the traditional five days. Typically, an employee may work ten hours a day for four days, with an extra day off. (8)

compromise   A type of intergroup interaction that occurs when the interactions are of moderate importance to goal attainment and goals are neither completely compatible nor incompatible. (10)

configuration   The size and shape of an organization as depicted on an organization chart. (13)

conflict   A form of group interaction that occurs whenever one group perceives that its attempts to accomplish its goals have been frustrated by another group. (12)

conflict model   The Janis-Mann process of decision making based on research in social psychology and individual decision processes. The model makes five assumptions. (17)

content-process distinction   A differentiation of the need (content) and process theories of motivation. (5)

content validity In performance appraisal, the extent to which the measurement adequately assesses all important aspects of job performance. (19)

contingency approach to organization design The structure determined by specific conditions such as the environment, technology, and the organization's work force. (15)

contingency plans Alternative actions that can be taken if the primary course of action is unexpectedly disrupted or rendered inappropriate. (17)

contingency theory A theory that suggests that the relationship between any two variables is likely to be influenced by other variables. (1)

contingency theory of leadership A theory that contends that a leader's effectiveness depends upon a match between the leader's style and the favorableness of the situation. Situational favorability is determined by task structure, leader-member relations, and leader position power. The theory was advanced by Fiedler in 1967. (11)

controlling The process of monitoring and correcting the actions of the organization and people and activities within it so as to keep them headed toward their goal. (1)

convergent validity In performance appraisal, the extent to which different measures agree in the evaluations of the same performance. (19)

creativity The process of developing original and imaginative perspectives on situations. (17)

critical incident technique Involves interviewing individuals who are familiar with the target job; each person is asked to describe specific incidents of effective and ineffective behaviors in the job. (19)

*D*ecision making The process of choosing one alternative from several alternatives. (17)

decision rule A statement that tells the decision maker which alternative to choose once she or he has information about the decision situation. (17)

decision-making roles One of Mintzberg's three general categories of managerial roles including the entrepreneur, the disturbance handler, the resource allocator, and the negotiator roles. These roles closely relate to decision making. (1)

decoding The process by which the receiver of the message interprets its meaning. (18)

decoupling The functional separation in some way

of two groups whose tasks require that they interact. (10)

defensive avoidance In the conflict model of decision making, making no changes in present activities and avoiding any further contact with issues affecting the activities because there seems to be no hope of finding a better solution. (17)

Delphi technique A method of improving group decision making that involves systematically gathering the judgments of experts and developing forecasts. When using the Delphi technique, groups do not meet face to face. (17)

departmentalization The manner in which divided tasks are combined into work groups for coordination. The most common methods are by business function, process, product or service, customer, and geography. (13)

discipline An attempt to punish that is structured, official, and organizationally sanctioned. (2)

discriminant validity In performance appraisal, the extent to which ratings of the same type of performance agree more than ratings of different types of performance. (19)

dispositional view of attitudes A view that suggests that people respond in predictable ways depending on their affect, cognitions, and intentions. (3)

dissonance reduction An attempt by an individual to reduce the tension and discomfort that attitudes and behaviors not consistent with each other cause. Generally, the person tries to change the attitude, change the behavior, or perceptually distort the circumstances. (3)

distress A negative form of stress that can lead to dangerous side effects. (7)

disturbed reactive environment An environment in which the components form interrelated clusters but change more rapidly than in a placid reactive environment. There is heavy competition between organizations that are similar in nature. (14)

division of labor The extent to which the work of the organization is separated into different jobs to be done by different people. (13)

divisionalized form An organization design that resembles the machine bureaucracy except that it is divided according to the different markets it serves. Standardization of outputs is the primary means of coordination. It is one of Mintzberg's structural forms that characterizes old, very large firms operating in a relatively simple, stable environment with several diverse markets. (15)

*E***ffort-to-performance expectancy** The perceived probability that effort will lead to performance. The probability may range between 0 and 1.0. It is a major concept of expectancy theory. (5)

encoding The process by which the message is translated from an idea or thought into symbols that can be transmitted. (18)

environmental complexity The number of environmental components that impinge on organizational decision making. (14)

environmental dynamism The degree to which environmental components change. (14)

environmental scanning The process of constantly searching the business environment for new opportunities and threats to the business. (17)

environmental uncertainty A condition that exists when managers have little information about environmental events and their impact on the organization. It results from environmental complexity and environmental dynamism. (14)

equity theory A theory based on the premise that people want to be treated fairly and that they compare their own input-to-outcome ratio in the organization to the ratio of a comparison-other. If they feel that, in a relative sense, they are being treated inequitably, they take steps to reduce the inequity. The theory was articulated by Adams. (5)

ERG theory A theory that suggests that people may be motivated by more than one kind of need at the same time. The theory also includes a frustration-regression component and a satisfaction-progression component. Associated with Alderfer, this theory is an extension and refinement of Maslow's needs hierarchy. It identifies three basic need categories: existence, relatedness, and growth. (4)

escalation of commitment The tendency to persist in an ineffective course of action when evidence indicates the project is doomed to failure. (17)

eustress A positive form of stress that can motivate, stimulate, and, often, reward a person. (7)

expectancies The probabilities linking effort and performance and performance and rewards in the expectancy model. (5)

expectancy theory Assumes that motivation depends on how much we want something and how likely we think we are to get it. (5)

expert power A base of power identified by French and Raven that relates to control over expertise or, more precisely, over information. (12)

extinction A concept of reinforcement theory that decreases the frequency of undesired behavior, especially behavior that was previously rewarded. Extinction occurs when rewards are removed from behaviors that were previously reinforced. (2)

*F***eedback** Verification of a message sent from the receiver to the source. (18)

field experiment A type of research design similar to a laboratory experiment, but it is conducted in a real organization. The researcher is able to control certain variables and manipulate others in order to assess the effects of the manipulated variables on outcome variables. (App.)

field survey A type of research design that usually relies on a questionnaire distributed to a sample of people chosen from a larger population. The researcher analyzes the responses to the questionnaire and tries to make inferences about the larger population the sample was chosen to represent. (App.)

flexible reward system A compensation system that lets employees choose the combination of benefits that best suits their needs. (6)

flexible work schedules (flextime) A work schedule in which the work day is broken down into two categories: flexible time and core time. All employees must be at their work stations during core time, but they can choose their own schedules during flexible time. Flexible time enables employees to have some control over their working hours. (8)

flextime (flexible work schedules) See **flexible work schedules.**

forced choice method (in performance appraisal system) A method of evaluating individual performance whereby the rater must choose one item from among a group of behavioral statements which is most descriptive of the performance of the employee. (19)

forced distribution method (in performance appraisal system) A method of evaluating individual performance that forces the evaluator to assign employees to categories on the basis of their performance but limits the percentage of employees that can be placed in any one category. (19)

formal groups Groups established by the organization to do its work and usually identifiable on an organization chart. Include the command (functional) group, which is relatively permanent, and task (special projects) group, which is relatively temporary. (9)

formalization   The degree to which the jobs and activities of employees are codified by rules and procedures. (13)

friendship group   A type of informal group that is relatively permanent. The association among the members is due to friendly relationships and the pleasure that comes from being together. (9)

functional group   See **command group.**

functional job analysis technique   Identifies the specific tasks that make up a job and examines how much each task involves data, people, and things. Each task's complexity in each respect is rated from 1 to 10. (19)

*G*eneral adaptation syndrome (GAS)   Begins when a person first encounters a stressor. The basic threshold at which stress starts to affect individuals. The three stages of response to stress are alarm, resistance, and exhaustion. (6)

goal   A desirable objective individuals or organizations want to achieve. (6)

goal acceptance   The extent to which a person accepts a goal as his or her own. (6)

goal attainment   The reaching of goals in a social system. The system must have processes that specify those goals and specific strategies for reaching the goals. (16)

goal commitment   The extent to which an individual is personally interested in reaching a goal. (6)

goal difficulty   The extent to which a goal is challenging and requires effort. (6)

goal displacement   A process that occurs when groups overemphasize their own goals at the expense of the organization's. (10)

goal setting theory of motivation   This theory, developed by Locke, assumes that behavior is a result of conscious goals and intentions. Goal difficulty and goal specificity shape performance. (6)

goal specificity   Setting a goal in quantitative terms. It is consistently related to performance. (6)

graphic rating scale   One of the simplest methods of rating individual performance whereby the rater checks or circles the point on the scale that best represents the performance level of the employee. (19)

group   Two or more persons interacting with one another in such a manner that each person influences and is influenced by each other person. (9)

group cohesiveness   How strongly members of a

group feel about remaining in the group. Attraction to the group, resistance to leaving the group, and motivation to remain a member of the group are the forces that create cohesiveness. Group cohesiveness may be increased by competition or the presence of an external threat. (9)

group composition   The makeup of a group. It is often described in terms of the homogeneity or heterogeneity of the members. (9)

group development   The stages and activities groups progress through in order to become mature, effective groups. The four general stages are: mutual acceptance, communication and decision making, motivation and productivity, and control and organization. (9)

group performance factors   Factors that influence the formation and development of the group. They describe the way group members do their jobs and relate to each other. Primary factors are composition, size, norms, and cohesiveness. (9)

group polarization   The shift of member attitudes and opinions to a more extreme position following group discussion. It arises due to the expression of shared attitudes in the discussion, persuasive arguments by supporters of the extreme position, and the feeling that responsibility is diffused by the group process. (17)

group size   The number of members of a group. The size of a group can vary from two members to as many members as can interact and influence each other. (9)

groupthink   A mode of thinking that people engage in when they are deeply involved in a cohesive ingroup, when the members' strivings for unanimity override their motivation to realistically appraise alternative courses of action. (17)

*H*alo error   In performance appraisal, occurs when a rater consistently assigns the same rating to all aspects of a person's performance, regardless of the actual performance level, because of an overall favorable or unfavorable impression of the person. (19)

Hawthorne studies   A series of experiments that played a major role in developing the foundations of the field of organizational behavior. The studies were conducted at the Hawthorne Plant of Western Electric near Chicago between 1927 and 1932. The overall conclusion of the studies was that individual and social processes are too important to ignore. (1)

hedonism   A concept that dominated the earliest views on human motivation. Hedonism argues that

Glossary

people seek pleasure and comfort and try to avoid pain and discomfort. (4)

high tech/high touch   Refers to Naisbitt's contention that the more new technology is forced on people, the more need there is for the human touch. (22)

human organization   A system that centers on the principles of supportive relationships, employee participation, and overlapping work groups. The human organization is an approach to organization design presented by Likert. (15)

human relations movement   A movement that played a major role in developing the foundations of the field of organizational behavior. The basic premise of the movement was that people respond primarily to their social environment. McGregor's Theory X and Theory Y and Maslow's hierarchy of needs were predominant theories of this period. (1)

hypervigilance   In the conflict model of decision making, frantic and superficial pursuit of some satisficing strategy. (17)

*I*ndividual characteristics   One of five basic categories of organizational behavior concepts. Among such characteristics are learning, perception, attitudes, personalities, employee motivation, goal setting, rewards, and stress. (1)

individual differences   A set of factors that includes the ways we think, the ways we interpret our environment, and the ways we respond to that environment. (3)

individualism   A state in which people view themselves first as individuals and believe their own interest and values take priority. (21)

individual-organization interface   One of the five basic categories of organizational behavior concepts. It includes job design, role dynamics, group and intergroup dynamics, leadership, power, politics, and conflict. (1)

informal groups   Groups formed by members of an organization. They include the relatively permanent friendship group and the interest group, which may be less long-lived. (9)

informational roles   One of Mintzberg's three general categories of managerial roles including the monitor, the disseminator, and the spokesperson roles. These roles involve some aspect of information processing. (1)

inputs   An individual's contribution to the organization, such as experience, effort, and loyalty. (5)

integration   The need every social system has to keep its constituent parts together. The parts of the system must be brought in contact with one another, interdependences understood and organized, and the need for coordinated action resolved. (16)

interactionalism   A perspective that attempts to explain how people select, interpret, and change various situations. The individual and the situation are presumed to interact continuously; this interaction determines the individual's behavior. (1)

interest group   A type of informal group that is relatively temporary. An interest group is organized around a common interest of the members. (9)

intergroup behavior   The ways groups interact with each other. (10)

interpersonal demands   The demands from other people or groups confronting those in organizational settings, such as group pressures, leadership style, and personalities and behavior. (7)

interpersonal roles   One of Mintzberg's three general categories of managerial roles including figurehead, leader, and liaison roles. These roles are primarily social in nature. (1)

interrater reliability   The extent to which ratings by more than one rater agree. (19)

interview   A method of gathering data whereby questions are presented to the respondent by an interviewer. The respondent is usually allowed to answer questions spontaneously rather than asked to choose among alternatives defined by the researcher. (App.)

involvement   A person's willingness to go beyond the standard demands of his or her job as an organizational "citizen." (3)

*J*argon   The specialized or technical language of a trade, field, profession, or social group. (18)

job analysis   The process of systematically gathering information about specific jobs for use in developing a performance appraisal system and in writting job descriptions. (19)

job characteristics approach   Began with the work of Turner and Lawrence. They believed that workers would prefer complex, challenging tasks to monotonous, boring ones, and they predicted that job complexity would be associated with employee satisfaction and attendance. (8)

Job Characteristics Theory   A model of job enrichment that defines job enrichment as increasing the amounts of certain core dimensions—skill variety, task identity, task significance, autonomy, and feedback. The core dimensions lead to three psychological states that result in positive personal and work-related outcomes. (8)

job design　The specification of an employee's task-related activities, including both structural and inter-personal aspects of the job, as determined by both the organization's and the individual's needs and require-ments. (8)

job enlargement　Expansion of a worker's job to include tasks previously performed by other workers. Also called horizontal job loading, it is one alternative to job specialization. (8)

job enrichment　A technique based on Herzberg's two-factor theory of motivation. Employees could be motivated by positive job-related experiences through job loading (giving employees more control over those tasks added by horizontal loading). (8)

job hopping　Moving to different organizations rather than making adjustments within the present organiza-tion. (20)

job or position inventory approach　The incum-bent or other knowledgeable persons are asked ques-tions about a job; the questionnaire may focus primar-ily on worker-oriented issues or strictly job-related issues. (19)

job rotation　Systematically shifting workers from one job to another, with the goal of sustaining worker motivation and interest. It is one alternative to job specialization. (8)

job satisfaction or dissatisfaction　An individual's attitude toward his or her job. It is one of the most widely studied variables in the entire field of organiza-tional behavior. (3)

job sharing　An approach to work schedules whereby two part-time employees share one full-time job. For example, one person may perform the job from 8:00 A.M. until noon, and the other from 1:00 P.M. until 5:00 P.M. (8)

job specialization　An historical approach to the de-sign of jobs whereby jobs are scientifically studied, broken down into their smallest component parts, and then standardized across all workers doing those jobs. It is a rational, seemingly efficient way to organize jobs, but it can also cause problems due to the monotony of highly specialized, standardized tasks. (8)

*L*aboratory experiment　A type of research design whereby the researcher creates an artificial setting sim-ilar to a real work situation. The experimenter has a great deal of control and can manipulate the variables in the study and examine their effects on the other variables in the experiment. (App.)

leadership　Both a process and a property. As a proc-ess, leadership is the use of noncoercive influence to direct and coordinate the activities of group members toward goal accomplishment. As a property, leadership is the set of characteristics attributed to those who are perceived to employ such influence successfully. (11)

leadership substitutes　Individual, task, and organi-zational characteristics that tend to negate the leader's ability to affect subordinate satisfaction and perform-ance. (11)

leadership traits　Unique set of qualities or traits that early research leaders thought distinguished leaders from their peers. The traits were presumed to be rela-tively stable and enduring. (11)

leading　The process of getting members of the organization to work together in a fashion consistent with the goals of the organization. (1)

learning　A relatively permanent change in behavior or potential behavior that results from direct or indi-rect experience. (2)

legitimacy　The need every social system has to be granted the right to survive by elements in its environ-ment. (16)

legitimate power　A base of power identified by French and Raven that is granted by virtue of one's position in the organization. (12)

lenient　In performance evaluation, the tendency of a rater to evaluate performance consistently high. (19)

life change　Any meaningful change in a person's personal or work situation. (7)

life cycle theory　According to this theory, appropri-ate leader behavior depends on the maturity of the leader's followers. The maturity is how motivated, com-petent, experienced, and interested in accepting re-sponsibility the subordinates are. (11)

life trauma　Any single upheaval in an individual's life that disrupts his or her attitudes, emotions, or behaviors. (7)

linking role　A position for a person or a group that serves to coordinate the activities of two or more organizational groups. It is an organization-based strat-egy for managing intergroup interactions. (10)

locus of control　The extent to which a person be-lieves that his or her behavior has a direct impact on the consequences of that behavior. Individuals with an internal locus of control believe that if they work hard, they will be successful. People who have an external locus of control tend to think that what happens to them is a function of fate or luck. (3)

*M*achine bureaucracy   An organization design in which work is highly specialized and formalized, and decision making is usually concentrated at the top. It is one of Mintzberg's structural forms and is typical of a large, well-established company in a simple and stable environment. (15)

management by objectives (MBO)   A process in which managers and employees collaborate to set verifiable employee goals. Progress is periodically reviewed, and at the end of the process, employee performance is evaluated. (6)

management development   Attempts to foster certain skills, abilities, and perspectives important to good management. (23)

Managerial Grid   A framework for examining types of supervision developed by Blake and Mouton. Two dimensions are identified: concern for production and concern for people. It is suggested that a manager who has a high concern for people and production will be very effective. (11)

manifest needs theory   An abstract theory presented by Murray in 1938 and translated into a more concrete, operational framework by Atkinson. The theory assumes that people have a set of multiple needs that motivates behavior simultaneously rather than in a preset order. Each need has two components: direction and intensity. (4)

Maslow's hierarchy of needs   According to Maslow's theory, human needs are arranged in a five-tiered hierarchy of importance, from physiological needs at the bottom, to security needs, belongingness needs, esteem needs, and, at the top, self-actualization needs. (4)

matrix design   An attempt to combine two different designs to gain the benefits of each. In the most common form, product or project departmentalization is superimposed on a functional structure. (15)

mechanistic structure   A type of organization design that is primarily hierarchical in nature, interactions and communications are primarily vertical, instructions come from the boss, knowledge is concentrated at the top, and continued membership requires loyalty and obedience. Burns and Stalker state that this type of structure is appropriate if the rate of change in technology is slow. (15)

medium   The channel or path by which the encoded message travels from the source to the receiver. (18)

Michigan leadership studies   A program of research on leadership behavior conducted at the University of Michigan. Two basic forms of leader behavior were identified: job-centered and employee-centered leader behaviors. These styles are presumed to be at opposite ends of a single dimension. (11)

modeling   Learning through the experience of others. It is also referred to as vicarious learning. (2)

motivation   The set of factors that cause people to behave in certain ways. (4)

*N*eed for achievement   Reflects an individual's desire to accomplish a goal or task more effectively than in the past. High need achievers tend to set moderately difficult goals, assume personal responsibility for getting things done, want immediate feedback, and are preoccupied with the task. It is associated with the work of McClelland. (4)

need for affiliation   The need for human companionship. People with a high need for affiliation tend to want reassurance and approval from others, have a genuine concern for the feelings for others, and are likely to conform to the wishes of others, especially those with whom they strongly identify. (4)

need for power   The desire to control one's environment, including financial resources, material resources, information, and other people. (4)

need   A deficiency experienced by an individual (4)

negative reinforcement (avoidance)   A concept of reinforcement theory that occurs when the individual is engaging in desired behavior in order to avoid an unpleasant, or aversive, consequence. The effect of negative reinforcement is to increase the frequency of a desired behavior. (2)

noise   Any disturbance in the communication process that interferes with or distorts the intended communication. (18)

nominal group technique (NGT)   A method of improving group decision making whereby group members follow a generate-discussion-vote cycle until an appropriate decision is reached. (17)

nonprogrammed decision   A problem or decision situation that has not been encountered before such that the decision maker cannot rely on a previously established decision rule. A nonprogrammed decision is poorly structured because goals are vague, information is ambiguous, and there is no clear procedure for making the decision. (17)

norm The expected behavior or behavioral pattern in a certain situation. A norm is usually associated with a group and is established during the group development process. (9)

*O*bjective judgment quotient (OJQ) method A multiple-rater comparative system of evaluating employee performance differences. (19)

observation A method of gathering data that may include observing and recording events, structured observations, participant observation, and hidden observation. (App.)

occupation A group of jobs similar as to the type of tasks and training involved. (20)

Ohio State leadership studies A series of studies conducted by researchers at Ohio State University designed to assess subordinates' perceptions of their leaders' actual behavior. The studies identified two dimensions of leadership behavior: consideration and initiating structure. The two dimensions were presumed to be independent. (11)

operant conditioning (reinforcement theory) Suggests that behavior is a function of its consequences. It is generally associated with the work of Skinner. (2)

oral communication A form of communication in organizations. It is the most prevalent form of organizational communication. (18)

organic structure A type of organization design that is structured like a network, interactions are more lateral and horizontal, knowledge resides wherever it is most useful to the organization, and membership requires a commitment to the tasks of the organization. Burns and Stalker state that this type of structure is appropriate if the rate of change in technology is high. (15)

organization A group of people working together to achieve common goals. (13)

organization (and perception) The human tendency to view things in ordered, logical, and consistent systems of meaning. (3)

organization change and development One of the five basic categories of organizational behavior concepts. (1)

organization chart Shows all people, positions, reporting relationships, and lines of formal communication in the organization. (13)

organization development The process of planned change and improvement of organizations through the application of knowledge of the behavioral sciences, such as psychology, sociology, cultural anthropology, and other related fields of study. (23)

organization structure A system of task, reporting, and authority relationships within which the organization's work is done. (13)

organizational behavior (OB) The study of human behavior in organizational settings, the interface between human behavior and the organizational context, and the organization itself. (1)

organizational behavior modification (OB Mod) The application of reinforcement principles and concepts to people in organizational settings to achieve motivational improvements. (5)

organizational characteristics One of the five basic categories of organizational behavior concepts. Among such characteristics are organization structure, environment, technology, organization design, and organizational culture. (1)

organizational culture That set of values that help people in an organization understand which actions are considered acceptable and which are considered unacceptable. (16)

organizational environment The people, other organizations, economic factors, and objects that are outside the boundaries of the organization. (14)

organizational goals Objectives management seeks to achieve in pursuing the firm's purpose. (13)

organizational politics Activities carried out by people to acquire, enhance, and use power and other resources to obtain their preferred outcomes in a situation where there is uncertainty or disagreement. (12)

organizational processes One of the five basic categories of organizational behavior concepts. Includes decision making, creativity, communication, information processing, performance appraisal, careers, and international aspects of organizational behavior. (1)

organizational socialization The process through which employees learn about a firm's culture and pass their knowledge and understanding on to others. (16)

organizational stressors Factors in the workplace that can cause stress: task demands, physical demands, role demands, and interpersonal demands. (7)

organizing The process of designing jobs, grouping jobs into manageable units, and establishing patterns of authority among jobs and groups of jobs. (1)

outcomes Anything an individual receives from the organization as a result of performance such as pay, recognition, and intrinsic rewards, or anything that might possibly result from performance. (5)

overdetermination Also called structural inertia: The structure of the organization provides resistance to change because it was designed to maintain stability. (22)

overload More information than the receiver can process. (18)

P**aired comparison method** A method of evaluating individual performance that calls for the comparison of all employees two at a time. Generally, there is one evaluator who compares all employees two at a time on one global performance criterion. (19)

participative management A way of thinking about the human resources of an organization. Employees are viewed as valued human resources capable of making substantive and valuable contributions to organizational effectiveness. Employees are allowed the opportunity to participate in decisions. (5)

participative pay system The participation of employees in either the design of the compensation system or the administration of it, or both. (6)

path-goal theory of leadership A theory that focuses on appropriate leader behavior for various situations. The path–goal theory suggests that directive, participative, or achievement-oriented leader behavior may be appropriate, depending on the characteristics of the person and the environment. It was developed in the 1970s by Evans and House and is based on the expectancy theory of motivation. (11)

perception The set of processes by which the individual receives and interprets information about the environment. (2)

performance The total set of job-related behaviors engaged in by employees. (5)

performance appraisal (performance evaluation) The process of evaluating work behaviors by measurement and comparison to previously established standards, recording the results, and communicating them back to the employee. It is an activity between a manager and an employee. (19)

performance appraisal system (PAS) The organizational processes and activities involved in performance appraisals. It includes organizational policies, procedures, and resources that support the performance appraisal activity. (19)

performance-to-outcome expectancy A person's perception of the probability that performance will lead to certain other outcomes. The probability may range between 0 and 1.0. It is a major concept of expectancy theory. (5)

personal power Power that resides in the person, regardless of his or her position in the organization. (12)

personality The set of distinctive traits and characteristics that can be used to compare and contrast individuals. (3)

physical demands Demands relating to the setting of the job, such as temperature, office design, and poor lighting. (7)

placid clustered environment A relatively unchanging environment in which environmental components are interrelated in clusters. Organizations in this environment tend to be large, centralized, controlled, and coordinated. (14)

placid randomized environment A static environment in which goals and problems are relatively simple and unchanging and environmental components tend not to be related to each other. (14)

planning The process of determining the organization's desired future position and deciding how best to get there. (1)

Porter-Lawler model This model suggests that performance may lead to various intrinsic and extrinsic rewards. When an individual perceives the rewards as equitable, the rewards lead to satisfaction. (5)

position power Power that resides in the position, regardless of the person involved. (12)

positive reinforcement A concept of reinforcement theory in which positive reinforcement is a reward that follows desirable behavior. Its effect is to maintain or increase the frequency of a desired behavior. (2)

power The potential ability of a person or group to influence another person or group. (12)

power distance The extent to which employees accept the idea that people in an organization rightfully have different levels of power. (21)

problem solving A special kind of decision making in which the issue is unique. It requires development and evaluation of alternatives without the aid of a programmed decision rule. (17)

productivity How many goods and services an organization creates from its resources. (5)

professional bureaucracy An organization design in which standardization of skills is the primary means of coordination. Specialization is horizontal, and decision making is decentralized. It is one of Mintzberg's structural forms and is usually found in a complex, stable environment. It is a special type of bureaucracy. (15)

programmed decision A decision that recurs often enough for decision rules to be developed. A decision rule is a statement that tells the decision maker which alternative to choose once she or he has information about the decision situation, such as outcomes, action-outcome probabilities, and values of outcomes. (17)

projection Occurs when we see ourselves in others. (2)

punishment The presentation of unpleasant, or aversive, consequences as a result of undesirable behaviors. It is a concept of reinforcement theory that decreases the frequency of undesired behaviors. (2)

Quality circles (QCs) Small groups of volunteers who meet regularly to identify, analyze, and solve quality and related problems that pertain to their work. (5)

quality of work life The degree to which members of a work organization are able to satisfy important personal needs through their experiences in the organization. (23)

questionnaire A collection of written questions about the respondents' attitudes, opinions, perceptions, and/or demographic characteristics. (App.)

Rational decision-making model A systematic, step-by-step process that assumes the organization is economically based and managed by decision makers who are entirely objective and have complete information. The steps are: statement of goal, identification of the problem, determination of decision type, generation of alternatives, evaluation and choice of alternatives, implementation, and control. (17)

receiver An individual, a group, or an individual acting as the representative of a group that is the receiver of the message. (18)

recency error In performance evaluation, the rater remembers only the most recent behaviors in evaluating an employee. (19)

referent power A base of power identified by French and Raven that is basically power through identification. It usually manifests itself through emulation and imitation. (12)

refreezing The process of making new behaviors relatively permanent and resistant to further change. It is the third step of Lewin's model of planned change. (22)

reinforcement The consequences of behavior. The four basic kinds of reinforcement are positive, negative (avoidance), extinction, and punishment. (2)

reinforcement theory (operant conditioning) A theory that suggests that behavior is a function of its consequences. It is generally associated with the work of Skinner. (2)

reliability The extent to which a measurement system's results are consistent. (19, App.)

research design The set of procedures used to test the predicted relationships among natural phenomena. (App.)

resource exchanges The exchanges between the organization and the various environmental components. Accomplished by developing interorganizational linkages and changing the environment. (14)

responsibility The obligation to do something under the expectation that some act will be done or certain outputs achieved. (13)

restriction of range The tendency of some raters in performance evaluation to restrict the range of ratings that they assign to performance. The three types are leniency, severity, and central tendency problems. (19)

reward power A base of power identified by French and Raven that is the extent to which one person controls rewards that are valued by another. (12)

reward system All parts of the organization that are involved in the allocation of compensation and benefits to employees in exchange for their contributions to the organization. (6)

role The part an individual plays in the work group. (8)

role ambiguity A situation that occurs when it is unclear or uncertain what behavior is expected of a role occupant. (8)

role conflict A situation that arises when demands of or messages about roles are essentially clear but also contradict each other somewhat. The four types of role conflict are interrole, intrarole, intrasender, and person-role. (8)

role demands The demands of the expected set of behaviors (role) associated with a particular position in a group or organization. (7)

Glossary

*S*atisficing   A situation that occurs in decision making when the decision maker examines alternatives only until a solution that meets minimal requirements is found and then ceases to look for a better one. (17)

schedules of reinforcement   The various ways in which a manager may attempt to reinforce desired or undesired behavior. The five types of schedules include continuous reinforcement, fixed interval, variable interval, fixed ratio, and variable ratio. (2)

scientific management   An approach to designing jobs emphasizing efficiency. It served as the foundation for job specialization and mass production. Employees performed a small part of a complete task and were paid on a piece-rate system. Primarily associated with the work of Taylor, it was one of the first approaches to the study of management. (1)

scientific research   The systematic investigation of hypothesized propositions about the relationships among natural phenomena. (App.)

selection (and perception)   The process by which we pay attention to objects we are comfortable with and filter out those that cause us discomfort. (2)

selective attention   The receiver attends to only selected parts of a message. (18)

self-efficacy   An individual's belief that she or he can still accomplish goals, even if that person has failed in the past. (6)

self-monitoring   The extent to which people emulate the behavior of others. A high self-monitor tends to pay close attention to the behaviors of others and to model his or her own behavior after that of the individuals observed. A low self-monitor tends to react to situations without looking to others for behavioral cues. (3)

self-reactions   In the conflict model of decision making, comparisons of alternatives with internalized moral standards. (17)

semantics   The study of meaning in language forms. (18)

severity   In performance evaluation, the tendency of a rater to assign a low value to most or all performances. (19)

simple structure   An organization design that has little specialization and formalization, and its overall structure is organic. It is one of Mintzberg's structural forms and characterizes a relatively small, usually young organization in a simple, dynamic environment. (15)

situational view of attitudes   A view that argues that attitudes evolve from socially constructed realities. (3)

social information processing model   A perspective presented by Salancik and Pfeffer. The model suggests that through various processes, commitment, rationalization, and information saliency are defined. These attributional and enactment processes then combine with social reality construction processes to influence perceptions, attitudes, and behaviors. (8)

social learning   A specific type of vicarious learning. It is assumed that people learn behaviors and attitudes partly in response to what others expect of them. (2)

sociotechnical systems approach   An approach that views the organization as an open system structured to integrate the two important subsystems: the technical (task) subsystem and the social subsystem. The approach is based on systems theory. (15)

source   The individual, group, or organization interested in communicating something to another party. (18)

source credibility   The receiver considers both the message and the source in making value judgments and determining credibility. (18)

span of control   The number of people reporting to a manager. It defines the size of the organization's work groups. (13)

specialization   The number of distinct occupational titles or activities accomplished within the organization. (13)

stereotyping   The process of categorizing people into groups on the basis of certain characteristics or traits. (2)

stimulus discrimination   The ability of the individual to recognize differences between stimuli. (2)

stimulus generalization   The process by which people recognize the same or similar stimuli in different settings. (2)

strategic choice   A type of organization design whereby the manager is viewed as the decision maker. The manager's choices of how to structure the organization are affected by the purposes and goals, the imperatives, and her or his personality, value system, and experience. (15)

stress   A person's adaptive response to a stimulus that places excessive psychological or physical demands on that person. (7)

structural change   A type of organizational change that consists of a system-wide rearrangement of task division and authority and reporting relationships. (23)

structural contingency perspective A popular approach to the study of the organization and its environment. It suggests that the best structure for an organization is dependent, or contingent, on the environment it operates in. (14)

structural imperatives Factors that determine how the organization must be structured in order to be effective. The three factors that have been identified as structural imperatives are size, technology, and environment. (15)

suboptimizing Occurs in decision making when decision makers trade off the gains of some outcomes to avoid the potential negative aspects of those outcomes. Occurs when the less than best possible outcome is accepted. (17)

superordinate goal A solution to goal displacement, it is usually a goal of the overall organization and is more important than the more specific goals of interacting groups. (10)

survey-feedback A process of gathering, analyzing, and summarizing data and returning it to employees and groups for discussion, and identification and solution of problems. (23)

system An interrelated set of elements functioning as a whole. (1)

systems theory A theory popularized in the physical sciences and extended to the area of management. An organizational system receives various inputs from its environment, transforms these inputs into products or services, and creates various outputs of the system. The system receives feedback from the environment regarding those outputs. (1)

*T*ask demands Stressors associated with the specific job a person is performing, such as the job surgeons and coaches, for example, face. (7)

task environment The specific environmental forces that affect an organization's operations. (14)

task group A type of formal group that is relatively temporary. (9)

task interdependence The degree to which the activities of separate groups force them to depend on each other, thereby requiring more coordination to realize organizational goals. The three types of task interdependence are pooled, sequential, and reciprocal. (10)

task uncertainty A situation that arises whenever employees or work groups lack information about what

course of action to take or about future events that may affect them, the task, or the organization. (10)

team building Programs designed to assist a work team (group) in developing into a mature, well-functioning team by helping it define its goals or priorities, analyze its tasks and the way they are performed, and examine relationships among people doing the work. (23)

technology The mechanical and intellectual processes that transform inputs into outputs. (14)

tell and listen A method of providing performance evaluation feedback. The manager gives the employee the appraisal information and reward decision and also listens to the employee's responses, but the comments are not used to adjust the performance appraisal or to begin a discussion of long-term concerns. (19)

tell and sell A method of providing performance appraisal feedback. The manager gives the employee the appraisal information and reward decision. (19)

thick description methods Attempts to describe the totality of day-to-day life through in-depth questioning and observation. (16)

training Specialized efforts to improve specific employee job skills. Such activities include on-the-job training, formalized job rotation programs, and student intern programs. (20)

transition management The process of systematically planning, organizing, and implementing change, from the disassembly of the current state to the realization of a fully functional future state within an organization. (22)

transmission The process through which the symbols that carry the message are sent to the receiver. (18)

turbulent field In this most complex and dynamic environment, rapid change arises from the complexities and multiple interconnections among environmental components. (14)

turnover The permanent cessation of working for the organization. (5)

two-factor theory A theory that suggests that job satisfaction is a two-dimensional construct. One dimension ranges from satisfaction to no satisfaction and is affected by motivation factors. The other dimension ranges from dissatisfaction to no dissatisfaction and is affected by hygiene factors. It was developed by Herzberg in the late 1950s and early 1960s. (4)

Type A person A person who is extemely competitive, very devoted to work, has a strong sense of urgency, is aggressive, impatient, and very work oriented, has much drive, and wants to accomplish as much as possible as quickly as possible. (7)

Type B person   A person who, in comparison with the Type A person, is less competitive, less devoted to work, has a weaker sense of urgency, feels less conflict with people or time, has a more balanced and relaxed approach to life, has more confidence, and is able to work at a constant pace. (7)

Type Z (American firms)   One of the three types of firms analyzed by Ouchi. As compared to typical American and Japanese firms, Type Z American firms have a wholistic concern for workers and managers. The firms have a long-term employment commitment, evaluate employees slowly through both qualitative and quantitative information about performance, emphasize somewhat broad career paths, exercise control through informal, implicit mechanisms, have a strong cultural expectation that decision making will occur in groups and will be based on full information sharing and consensus, and expect individuals to take responsibility for decisions. (16)

*U*ncertainty avoidance   The extent to which people in a culture accept or avoid feelings of uncertainty. (21)

unconflicted adherence   In the conflict model of decision making, continuing with activities if doing so does not entail serious risks. (17)

unconflicted change   In the conflict model of decision making, making changes in present activities if doing so entails no serious risks. (17)

unfreezing   The process by which people become aware of the need for change. It is the first step of Lewin's model of planned change. (22)

universal approach   An approach whose prescriptions or propositions are designed to work in any situation or circumstance. This is the "one best way" to structure the jobs, authority, and reporting relationships of any organization, regardless of such factors as the organization's external environment, the industry, and the type of work to be done. (15)

*V*alences   The attractiveness or unattractiveness of any given outcome to any given person. It is a concept of expectancy theory. (5)

validity   The extent to which research measures what it is intended to measure. (App.)   The extent to which a performance evaluation method reflects actual employee performance. (19)

value judgments   The degree to which a message reinforces or challenges the receiver's basic personal beliefs. (18)

verification   The receiver indicates to the source that the receiver received the message and the degree to which it was understood. (18)

vertical-dyad linkage model   A model that stresses the importance of variable relationships between supervisors and each of their subordinates. Each superior-subordinate pair is referred to as a vertical dyad. Early in the history of the dyadic interaction, the supervisor initiates either an in-group or out-group relationship. The model was developed by Graen and Dansereau. (11)

vicarious learning   Learning through the experiences of others. It is also referred to as modeling. (2)

vigilant information processing   In the conflict model of decision making, thoroughly investigating all possible alternatives, weighing their costs and benefits before making a choice, and developing contingency plans. (17)

Vroom-Yetton-Jago model   First developed by Vroom and Yetton in 1973 and recently expanded by Vroom and Jago. Prescribes a leadership style appropriate to a given situation and presumes that one leader may display various leadership styles. The model is concerned with only one aspect of leader behavior: subordinate participation in decision making. The goals of the model are to protect the quality of the decision and ensure decision acceptance by subordinates. (11)

*W*heel network   A small group network pattern in which information flows between the person at the end of each spoke and the person in the middle. (18)

written communication   A form of communication in organizations. Common forms of written communication include letters, memos, reports, manuals, and forms. (18)

INDEX

Index

Index

Index

Index

Index

Index

Index

Index

Index